British Columbia Road Atlas

MW01622800

TABLE OF CONTENTS

Range & Twp Numbers Explanation .... Inside Front Cover
Road Map Legend .... Inside Front Cover
British Columbia Key Map 2-3
British Columbia Distance Chart 4
British Columbia Overview 4-5
Place Name Index 114-116
Road Name Index 117-127

Northern British Columbia Road Maps 6-23
Logging and Backroad Maps....................24-87
Airports 88
Skiing.................... 88
Parksville to Chemainus Area 88-89
Vancouver & Environs 90-91
Lower Fraser Valley....................92-93
BC Transit Info & BC Inland Ferry Info.................... 93
BC Ocean & Coastal Ferry Info 94
Duncan to Victoria....................94-95
Okanagan Valley 96-99
BC Wineries List 99
Victoria....................100-101
Nanaimo 102
Vancouver 103-105
Whistler.................... 106
Kamloops.................... 107
Kelowna.................... 108
Penticton 109
Prince George 109
Museums & Points of Interest List 110
BC Hydro Recreation Areas / Sites List.................... 110
Forest Recreation Sites List 110-112
Parks, Recreation Areas & Reserves List 112-113

How to Use this Atlas

Cover Photo: Lake O'Hara, Yoho National Park, British Columbia, Canada
Photo Credit: Pierre Leclerc

Published by:
GM Johnson & Associates Ltd.
604.299.7074
www.gmjohnsonmaps.com

DESTINATIONS - indicate the town or city the road or highway leads to.

NORTH ARROWS - indicate general direction pointing north.

GRID REFERENCES - are used to locate places, streets or roads in the index. See page 115 or 118 for further explanation.

PAGE ARROWS - indicate continued coverage of the map and page.

PAGE NUMBER

Key Map

100 0 100 200 kilometres
kilomètres
YUKON TERR.
ALASKA
Gulf of Alaska
Golfe d'Alaska
PACIFIC OCEAN
ALEXANDER ARCHIPELAGO
COAST MOUNTAINS
Yakutat
Skagway
Haines
Juneau
Sitka
Petersburg
Wrangell
Ketchikan
Carcross
Tagish
Johnsons Crossing
Teslin
Atlin
Watson Lake
Upper Liard
Good Hope Lake
Liard River
Dease Lake
Telegraph Creek
Glenora
Stewart
New Aiyansh
Hazelton
New Hazelton
Granisle
Terrace
Smithers
Houston
Burns Lake
François Lake
Kitimat
Kemano
Prince Rupert
Port Edward
Masset
Skidegate
Sandspit
Haida Gwaii
(Queen Charlotte Islands/ Iles de la Reine-Charlotte)
Ocean Falls
Bella Coola
Port Hardy
Port Alice
Port McNeill
Campbell River
Gold River
Courtenay
Tofino
Ucluelet
VANCOUVER ISLAND
ÎLE DE VANCOUVER
Dixon Entrance
Détroit de Dixon
Hecate Strait
Queen Charlotte Sound
Bassin de la Reine-Charlotte
6
7
8
9
10
12
13
14
16
17
20
21
22
23
28
29
30
31
32
33
34
40
41
49
50
51
61
62
63
74
75
86
1:1 000 000 scale road map pages
18
1:500 000 scale road map pages

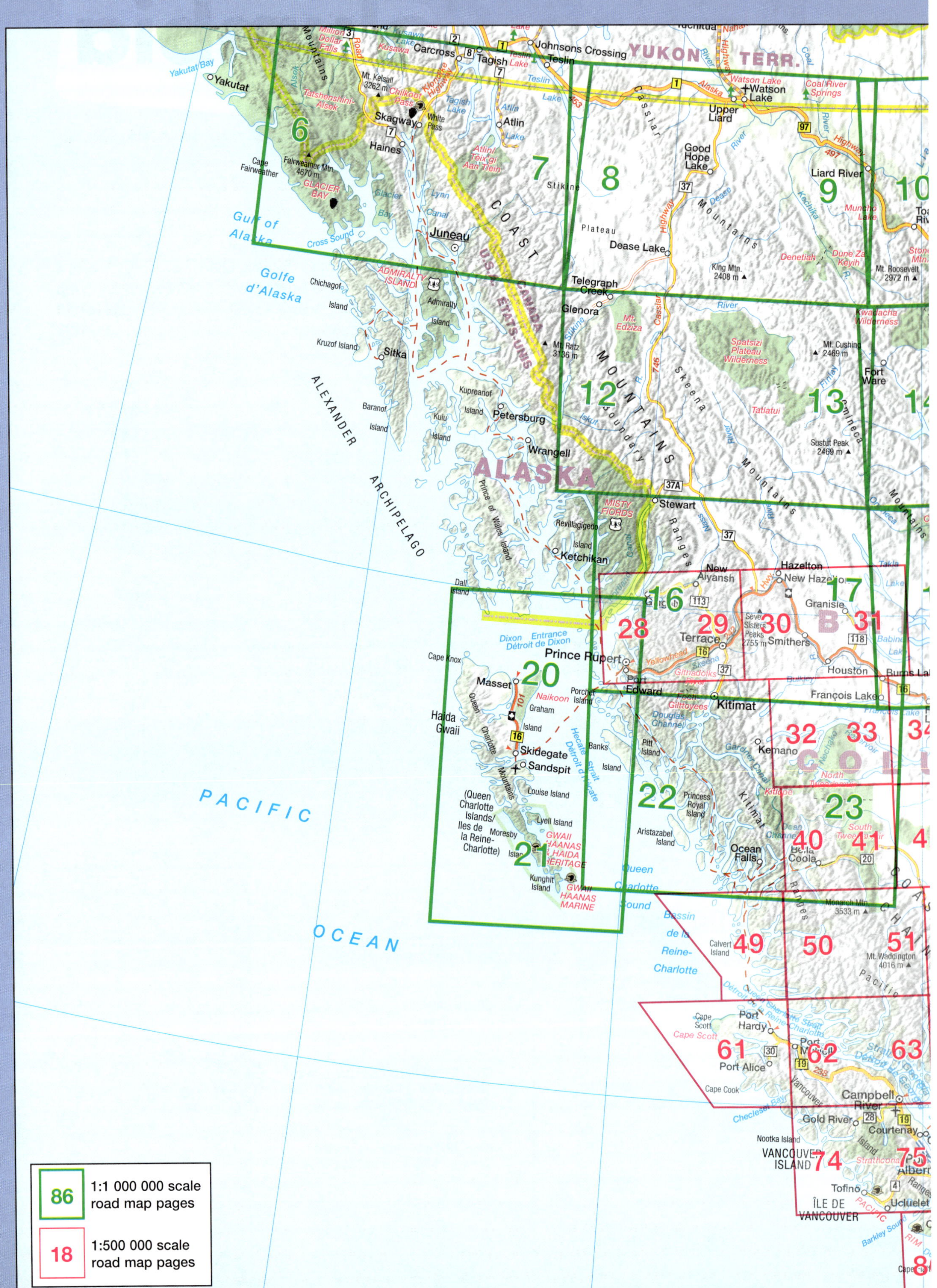

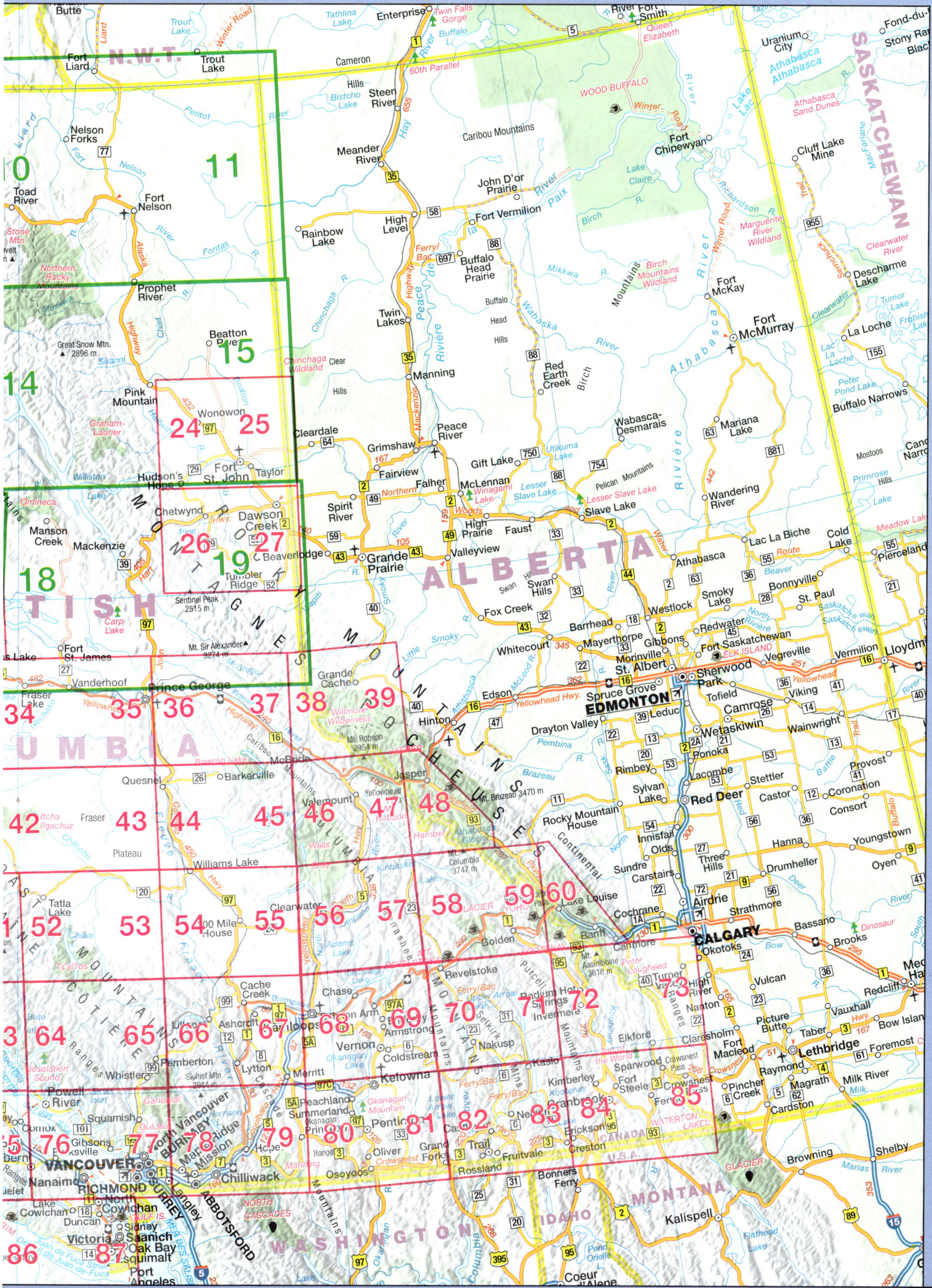

Scale 1:5 500 000 *Échelle*

100 0 100 200 kilometres *kilomètres*

British Columbia

Distance Chart

How to use:
The distance is indicated in kilometres where the two place names intersect. A • beside a distance means coastal ferry service is required.

Example

			Powell River
Port Hardy			•295
Penticton		•790	•525
Osoyoos	61	•791	•525
Nanaimo	403	•401	390	•113

	Bella Coola	Cache Creek	Campbell River	Cranbrook	Dawson Creek	Fort Nelson	Hope	Jasper, AB	Kamloops	Kelowna	Merritt	Nanaimo	Osoyoos	Penticton	Port Hardy	Powell River	Prince George	Prince Rupert	Princeton	Radium Hot Springs	Revelstoke	Tofino	Trail	Vancouver	Victoria	Watson Lake, YT	Whistler	Williams Lake
Whistler																												660
Watson Lake, YT																											2125	1464
Victoria																										•1492	•192	•583
Vancouver																									•69	2004	123	540
Trail																								626	•666	2215	750	750
Tofino																							•840	•227	321	•1500	•308	•757
Revelstoke																						•777	•270	565	•603	1964	685	497
Radium Hot Springs																					252	•1030	375	817	•856	1965	939	750
Princeton																				611	359	•495	345	282	•320	1869	403	405
Prince Rupert																			1365	1461	1460	•511	1711	1500	•504	988	1622	962
Prince George																		725	642	737	736	•995	988	777	•820	1228	899	238
Powell River																	•907	•1630	•411	•950	•695	•240	•757	•132	•202	•2135	•214	•670
Port Hardy																•295	•735	•10	•677	•1212	•960	512	•1020	•409	504	•999	•490	•942
Penticton															•790	•525	707	1429	111	513	260	•605	290	395	•433	1935	515	469
Osoyoos														61	•791	•525	754	1479	113	573	320	•606	232	395	•434	1984	516	517
Nanaimo													403	•401	390	•113	•790	•391	•291	•826	•572	208	•636	•23	112	•1380	•104	•552
Merritt												•280	202	154	•664	•400	552	1275	90	550	297	•481	432	270	•310	1781	390	315
Kelowna											132	•403	128	66	•790	•525	685	1410	166	445	190	•606	310	395	•433	1912	515	447
Kamloops										162	87	•363	285	230	•750	•485	525	1250	173	463	211	•565	471	355	•394	1753	475	285
Jasper, AB									439	601	525	•800	720	670	•1111	•925	375	1100	612	360	455	•1004	725	794	•831	1604	915	540
Hope								645	204	245	122	•163	243	245	•550	•280	635	1358	133	666	414	•367	476	150	•188	1864	270	394
Fort Nelson							1454	1137	1345	1505	1373	•1610	1575	1525	•1522	•1727	821	1513	1462	1496	1555	•1814	1805	1599	•1641	525	1717	1058
Dawson Creek						460	1040	676	930	1091	959	•1196	1160	1111	•1140	•1312	404	1130	1050	1038	1130	•1400	1393	1184	•1227	985	1305	644
Cranbrook					1181	1640	695	504	606	525	650	•853	450	510	•1240	•975	880	1604	560	142	395	•1057	231	845	•883	2108	965	890
Campbell River				•1001	•1345	•1751	•311	•951	•512	•552	•428	153	•555	•552	238	•57	•940	•238	•440	•975	•722	274	•785	•172	266	•1225	•253	•701
Cache Creek			•500	690	847	1260	193	523	84	244	111	•351	314	266	•737	•466	441	1164	200	547	295	•555	546	336	•380	1669	457	203
Bella Coola		659	•1158	1350	1100	1515	850	999	743	903	771	•1007	973	925	•1396	•1125	695	1418	860	1206	953	•1212	1205	995	•1039	1922	1114	455
Banff, AB	1236	575	•1003	276	962	1420	695	285	490	475	580	•855	604	542	•1242	•975	661	1385	642	132	282	•1060	506	850	•885	1887	967	779

N
N.W.T.
TERR.
ALBERTA
BRITISH
COLUMBIA
MONTAGNES ROCHEUSES
ROCKY MOUNTAINS
COAST MOUNTAINS
CHAÎNE CÔTIÈRE
WASHINGTON
IDAHO
MONTANA
CANADA
U.S.A.
60th Parallel
Watson Lake
Coal River Springs
Fort Liard
Trout Lake
Cameron Hills
Bistcho Lake
Steen River
WOOD BUFFALO
Fort Chipewyan
Lake Claire
Caribou Mountains
Meander River
John D'or Prairie
Fort Vermilion
Nelson Forks
Liard River
Toad River
Muncho Lake
Fort Nelson
Rainbow Lake
High Level
Buffalo Head Prairie
Buffalo Head Hills
Birch Mountains Wildland
Fort McKay
Denetiah
Dune Za Keyih
Stone Mtn.
Mt. Roosevelt 2972 m
Northern Rocky Mountains
Kwadacha Wilderness
Prophet River
Twin Lakes
Manning
Red Earth Creek
Mt. Cushing 2469 m
Fort Ware
Great Snow Mtn. 2896 m
Beatton River
Chinchaga Wildland
Clear Hills
Pink Mountain
Wonowon
Cleardale
Grimshaw
Peace River
Wabasca-Desmarais
Marian Lake
Sustut Peak 2469 m
Graham-Laurier
Hudson's Hope
Fort St. John
Taylor
Fairview
Falher
McLennan
Gift Lake
Lesser Slave Lake
Slave Lake
Wandering River
Chetwynd
Dawson Creek
Spirit River
High Prairie
Faust
Athabasca
Manson Creek
Mackenzie
Tumbler Ridge
Beaverlodge
Grande Prairie
Valleyview
Smoky Lake
Hazelton
New Hazelton
Granisle
Sentinel Peak 2515 m
Swan Hills
Westlock
Redwater
Fort Sask
Seven Sisters Peaks 2755 m
Smithers
Carp Lake
Fox Creek
Barrhead
Mayerthorpe
Gibbons
Morinville
St. Albert
Sherwood Park
Whitecourt
Mt. Sir Alexander 3274 m
Houston
Burns Lake
Fort St. James
Grande Cache
Spruce Grove
EDMONTON
Tofield
Kitimat
François Lake
Fraser Lake
Vanderhoof
Prince George
Edson
Leduc
Wetaskiwin
Hinton
Drayton Valley
Ponoka
Kemano
Willmore Wilderness
Mt. Robson 3954 m
JASPER
Rimbey
Lacombe
North Tweedsmuir
Bowron Lake
McBride
Jasper
Mt. Brazeau 3470 m
Sylvan Lake
Red Deer
Quesnel
Barkerville
Valemount
Rocky Mountain House
Innisfail
Olds
Three Hills
Itcha Ilgachuz
Fraser Plateau
Wells Gray
Mt. Columbia 3747 m
Sundre
Carstairs
Ocean Falls
Bella Coola
South Tweedsmuir
Williams Lake
Kicking Horse Pass
Lake Louise
BANFF
YOHO
Cochrane
Airdrie
CALGARY
Okotoks
Monarch Mtn. 3533 m
Tatla Lake
Clearwater
GLACIER
Golden
Canmore
Banff
Mt. Assiniboine 3618 m
100 Mile House
KOOTENAY
Turner Valley
High River
Nanton
Mt. Waddington 4016 m
Chilko Lake
Ts'yl-os
Revelstoke
Radium Hot Springs
Invermere
Peter Lougheed
Queen Charlotte Strait
Port Hardy
Cache Creek
Chase
Salmon Arm
Enderby
Armstrong
Port McNeill
Lillooet
Ashcroft
Kamloops
Vernon
Coldstream
Nakusp
Kaslo
Elkford
Claresholm
Port Alice
Pemberton
Lytton
Merritt
Kelowna
Sparwood
Fort Steele
Crowsnest Pass
Fernie
Kimberley
Cranbrook
Campbell River
Whistler
Desolation Sound
Powell River
Peachland
Summerland
Penticton
Okanagan Mountain
Nelson
Castlegar
Trail
Fruitvale
Erickson
Creston
WATERTON LAKES
Gold River
Courtenay
Comox
Squamish
North Vancouver
BURNABY
Maple Ridge
Mission
Princeton
Hope
Grand Forks
Rossland
Nootka Island
VANCOUVER ISLAND
ÎLE DE VANCOUVER
Port Alberni
Parksville
Gibsons
VANCOUVER
Chilliwack
Manning
Osoyoos
Oliver
Bonners Ferry
Tofino
Ucluelet
Nanaimo
RICHMOND
SURREY
Langley
ABBOTSFORD
NORTH CASCADES
Kalispell
Lake Cowichan
North Cowichan
Duncan
Sidney
Saanich
Victoria
Oak Bay
Esquimalt
Port Angeles
Cape Flattery
Juan de Fuca Strait
Détroit de Juan-de-Fuca
PACIFIC RIM
Barkley Sound
Strait of Georgia
Détroit de Georgia
Coeur d'Alene
SPOKANE
Everett

0 10 20 30 40 km
to Haines Junction, YK
Goatherd Mountain
Kluane Wildlife Sanctuary
Kusawa Lake
Mount Skukum 2382m
YUKON
Dalton Post
Shawshe (Dalton Post) Territorial Historic Site
Million Dollar Falls Territorial Campground
BRITISH COLUMBIA
ST. ELIAS MOUNTAINS
Tweedsmuir Glacier
Alsek River
Tatshenshini River
Haines Road
Kelsall
Chilkoot Pass National Historic Site
Mt. Foster 2173m
CANADA
U.S.A.
Chilkoot Pass
Fraser
White Pass
Chilkoot Trail
Chilkat Pass
ALSEK RANGES
Highway Subject to Periodic Winter Closings
Pacific Time Zone
Alaska Time Zone
Klondike Gold Rush National Historic Park
Mosquito Lake State Recreation Site
Alaska-Chilkat Bald Eagle Preserve
Dyea
Skagway
Tatshenshini-Alsek Provincial Wilderness Park
Pleasant Camp
Klukwan
"Eagle Council Grounds"
Chilkoot Lake State Recreation Site
Chilkoot Inlet
Haines
Grand Plateau Glacier
Grand Pacific Glacier
Portage Cove State Recreation Site
Chilkat Inlet
Chilkat State Park
Mt. Root 3920m
Chilkat Islands State Marine Park
Fairweather Mountain 4663m
Sullivan Island State Marine Park
Cape Fairweather
GLACIER BAY NATIONAL PARK
Brady Glacier
Glacier Bay
ALASKA
CHILKAT RANGE
Alaska Marine Highway
Lynn Canal
Lituya Bay
Habor Point
FAIRWEATHER RANGE
St. James Bay State Marine Park
Mt. La Perouse 10728 ft.
PACIFIC OCEAN
Visitor Center/ Glacier Bay Lodge
Bartlett Bay
Gustavus
Excursion Inlet
Shelter Island State Marine Park
Icy Point
Point Carolus
Pleasant I.
Lemesurier I.
Cape Spencer
Elfin Cove
Cross Sound
Icy Strait
Cape Bingham
Hoonah
CHICHAGOF
Yakobi Island
Pelican
3 4 5 6
A B

Scale 1:1 000 000 Échelle

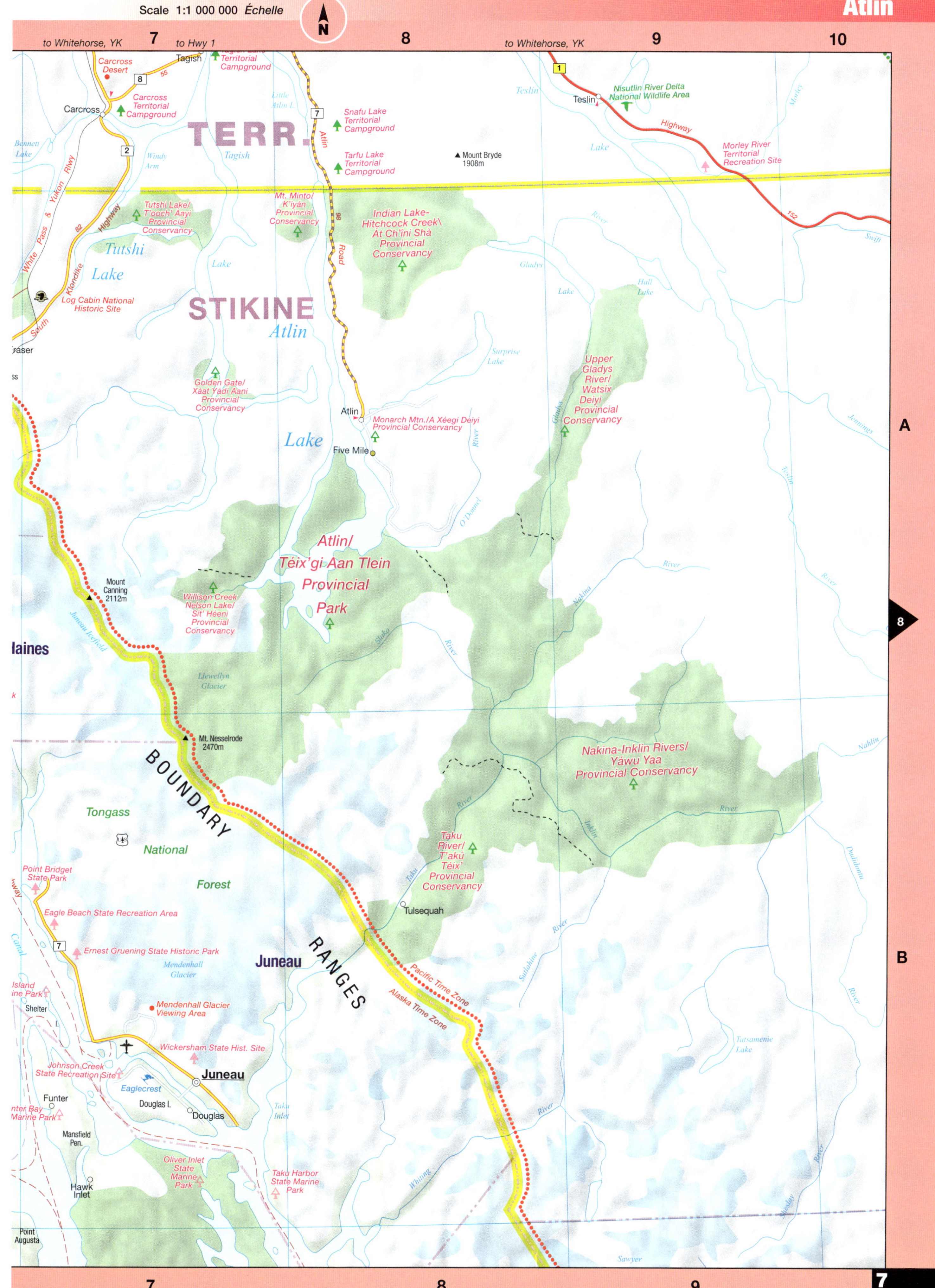

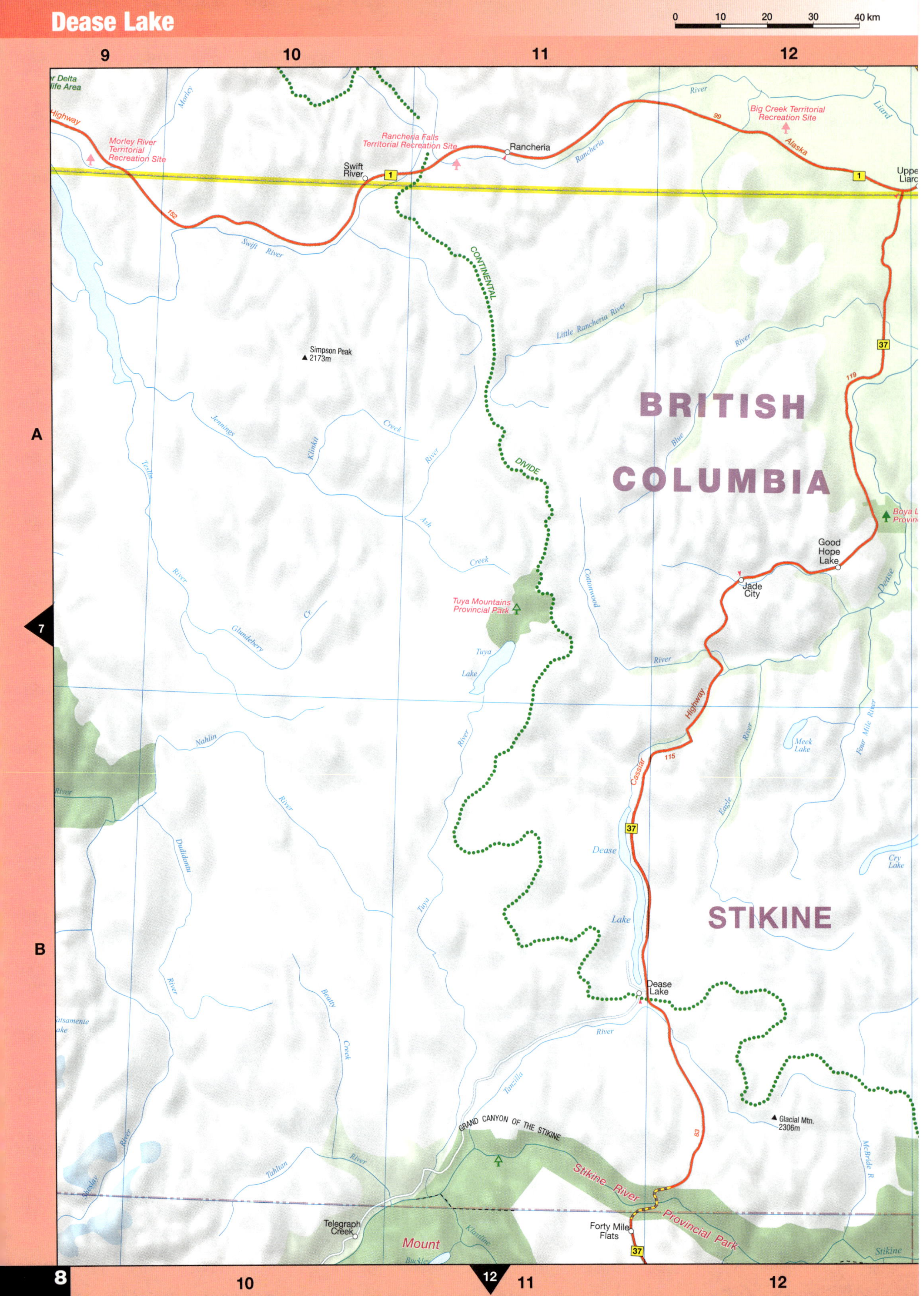

0 10 20 30 40 km
9
10
11
12
A
B
7
Morley River Territorial Recreation Site
Swift River
Rancheria Falls Territorial Recreation Site
Rancheria
Big Creek Territorial Recreation Site
Alaska Highway
Upper Liard
Swift River
Simpson Peak 2173m
Little Rancheria River
CONTINENTAL DIVIDE
BRITISH COLUMBIA
Jennings
Klinkit
Creek
Ash Creek
Blue
Teslin
River
Glundebery
Cottonwood
Good Hope Lake
Jade City
Tuya Mountains Provincial Park
Tuya Lake
Nahlin
Cassiar Highway
Meek Lake
Four Mile River
Eagle
Dudidontu
Dease Lake
Cry Lake
Tuya
STIKINE
Beatty Creek
Dease Lake
Tanzilla
Glacial Mtn. 2306m
GRAND CANYON OF THE STIKINE
Stikine River Provincial Park
McBride R.
Tahltan
Telegraph Creek
Forty Mile Flats
Mount
Klastline
Stikine

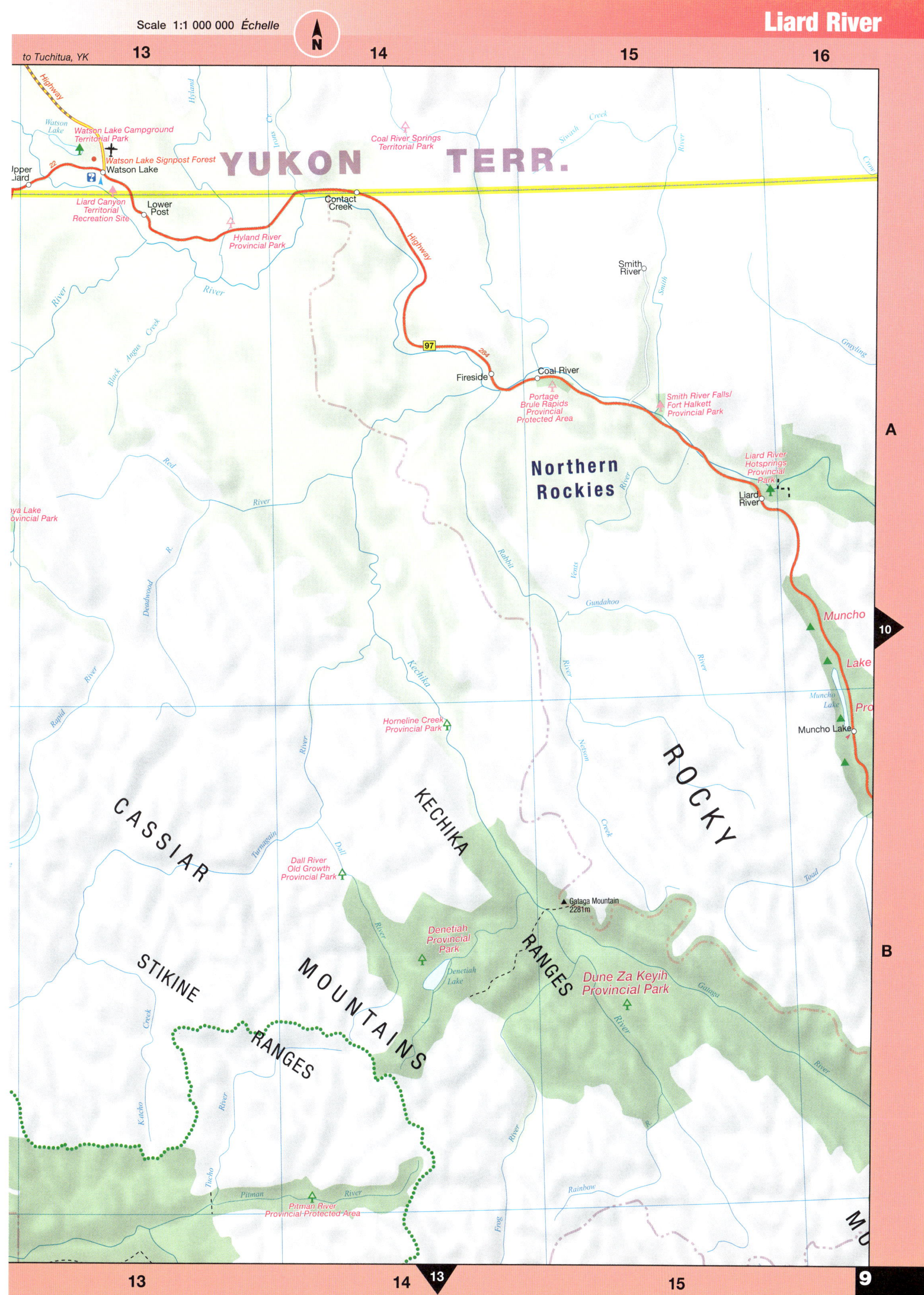
Scale 1:1 000 000 Échelle
N
to Tuchitua, YK
13
14
15
16
YUKON TERR.
Watson Lake Campground Territorial Park
Watson Lake Signpost Forest
Watson Lake
Upper Liard
Liard Canyon Territorial Recreation Site
Lower Post
Hyland River Provincial Park
Coal River Springs Territorial Park
Contact Creek
Highway
97
Fireside
Coal River
Portage Brule Rapids Provincial Protected Area
Smith River
Smith River Falls/ Fort Halkett Provincial Park
Liard River Hotsprings Provincial Park
Liard River
Northern Rockies
Muncho Lake
Muncho Park Lake
Muncho Lake
A
B
10
Horneline Creek Provincial Park
Dall River Old Growth Provincial Park
Denetiah Provincial Park
Denetiah Lake
Gataga Mountain 2281m
Dune Za Keyih Provincial Park
CASSIAR
STIKINE
RANGES
MOUNTAINS
KECHIKA
RANGES
ROCKY
Pitman River Provincial Protected Area
Kechika
Gundahoo
Rabbit
Turnagain
Rainbow
Frog
Gataga
Toad
Tucho
Kitcho
Deadwood
Black Angus Creek
Rapid
Red
Hyland
Irons Cr.
Siwash Creek
Grayling
Netson Creek
Dall
Pitman
13

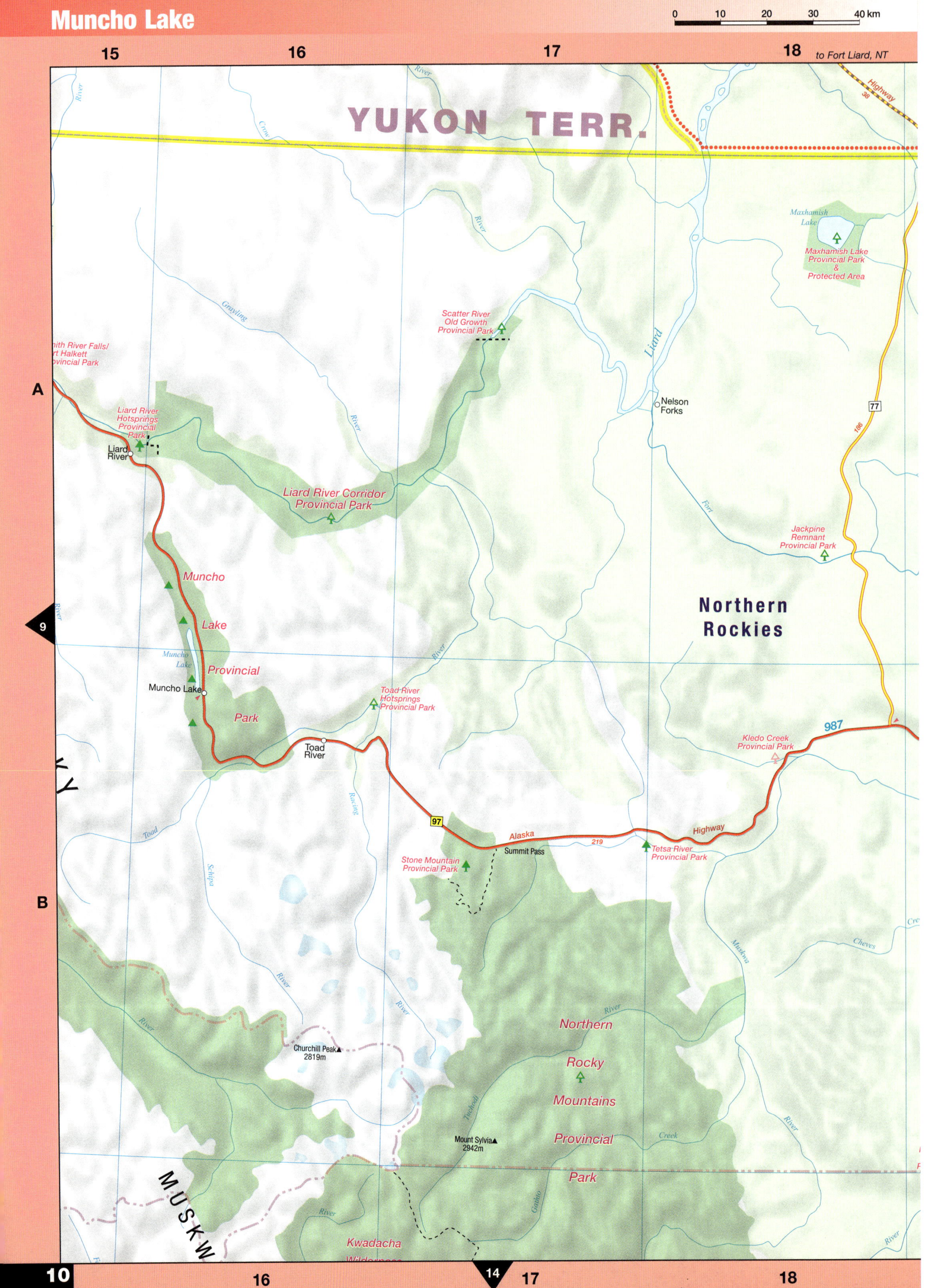
0 10 20 30 40 km
15
16
17
18
to Fort Liard, NT
YUKON TERR.
Highway 38
Maxhamish Lake
Maxhamish Lake Provincial Park & Protected Area
Scatter River Old Growth Provincial Park
Grayling
River
Liard
Nelson Forks
Smith River Falls/ Fort Halkett Provincial Park
A
Liard River Hotsprings Provincial Park
Liard River
Liard River Corridor Provincial Park
77
186
Fort
Jackpine Remnant Provincial Park
Northern Rockies
9
Muncho Lake Provincial Park
Muncho Lake
Toad River Hotsprings Provincial Park
Toad River
987
Kledo Creek Provincial Park
Racing
Toad
97
Alaska Highway
219
Summit Pass
Stone Mountain Provincial Park
Tetsa River Provincial Park
Schipa
B
Muskwa
Cheves
Churchill Peak 2819m
Northern Rocky Mountains Provincial Park
Tuchodi
Mount Sylvia 2942m
Creek
Gathto
MUSKW
Kwadacha Wilderness
16
14
17
18

Scale 1:1 000 000 Échelle

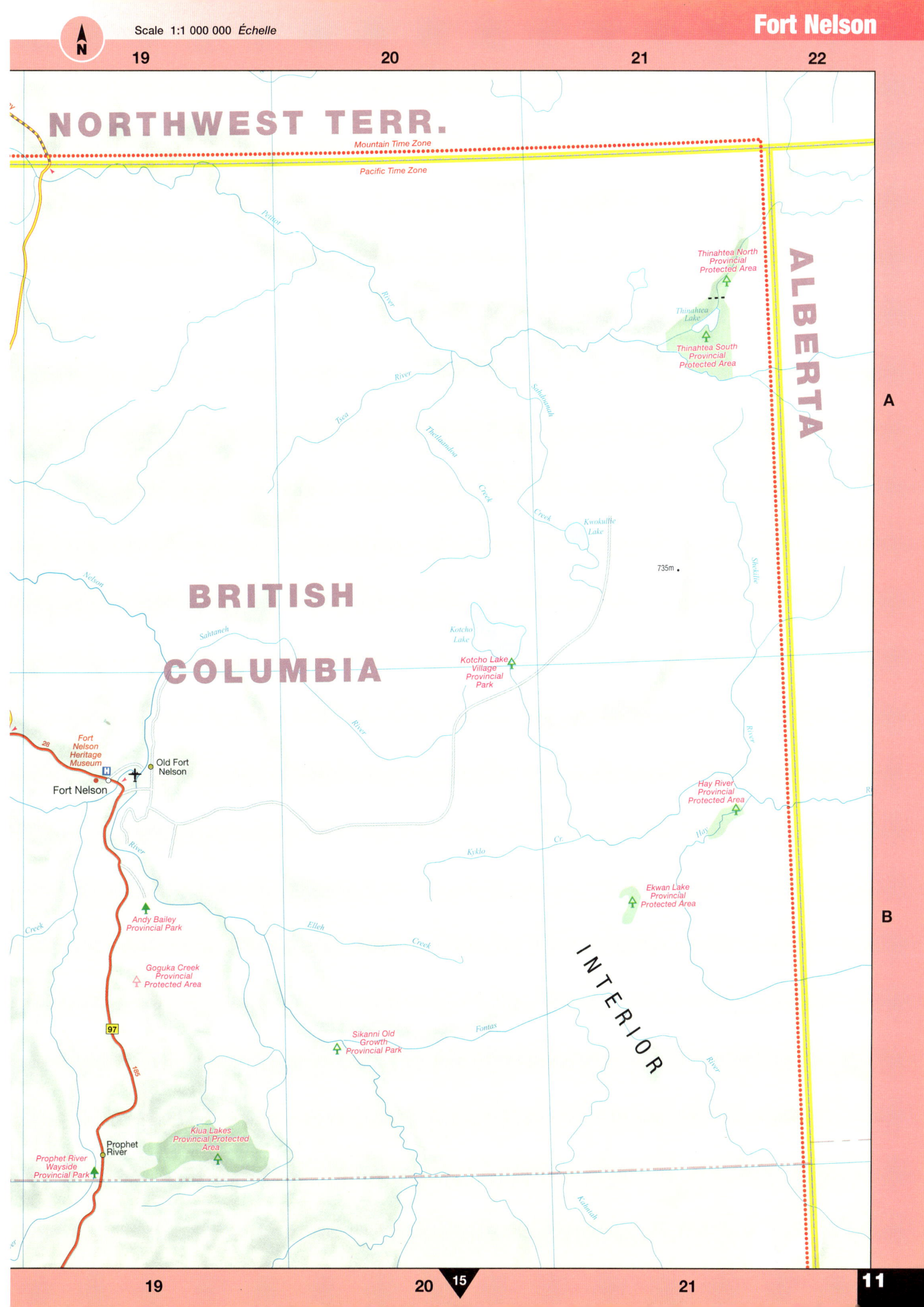

0 10 20 30 40 km
10
8
11
12
C
D
Stikine River Provincial Park
Forty Mile Flats
37
Iskut
Telegraph Creek
Glenora
Mount Edziza Provincial Park
Buckley Lake
Mt. Edziza 2787m
Nuttlude Lake
Mount Edziza Prov. Recreation Area
Kakiddi L.
Eddontenajon Lake
Tatogga
Mt. Cartmel 2175m
Kinaskan Lake
Todagin South Slope Provincial Park
Kinaskan Lake Provincial Park
Iskut River Hot Springs Provincial Park
Bob Quinn Lake
KITIMAT-STIKINE
Cassiar
Ninginsaw Provincial Park
Great Glacier Provincial Park
Choquette Hot Springs Provincial Park
Stikine
Bell II
Delta Peak 2298m
Highway
CANADA
U.S.A.
Craig Headwaters Provincial Protected Area
Lava Forks Provincial Park
ALASKA
Tongass National Forest
Mt. Lewis Cass 6864 ft.
Border Lake Provincial Park
Pacific Time Zone
Alaska Time Zone
Mt. Willibert 6779 ft.
Frank Mackie Glacier
Bowser Lake
Mt. Pattullo 2729m
Meziadin Junction
37A
Meziadin Lake Provincial Park
Bear Glacier Provincial Park
Ninemile
Stewart
Hyder
MISTY
Cambria Icefield
CLEVELAND PENINSULA
Yes Bay
Bell Island Hot Springs
Hassler Island
Deer Island
Burroughs Bay
Behm
Bradfield Canal
Fools Inlet

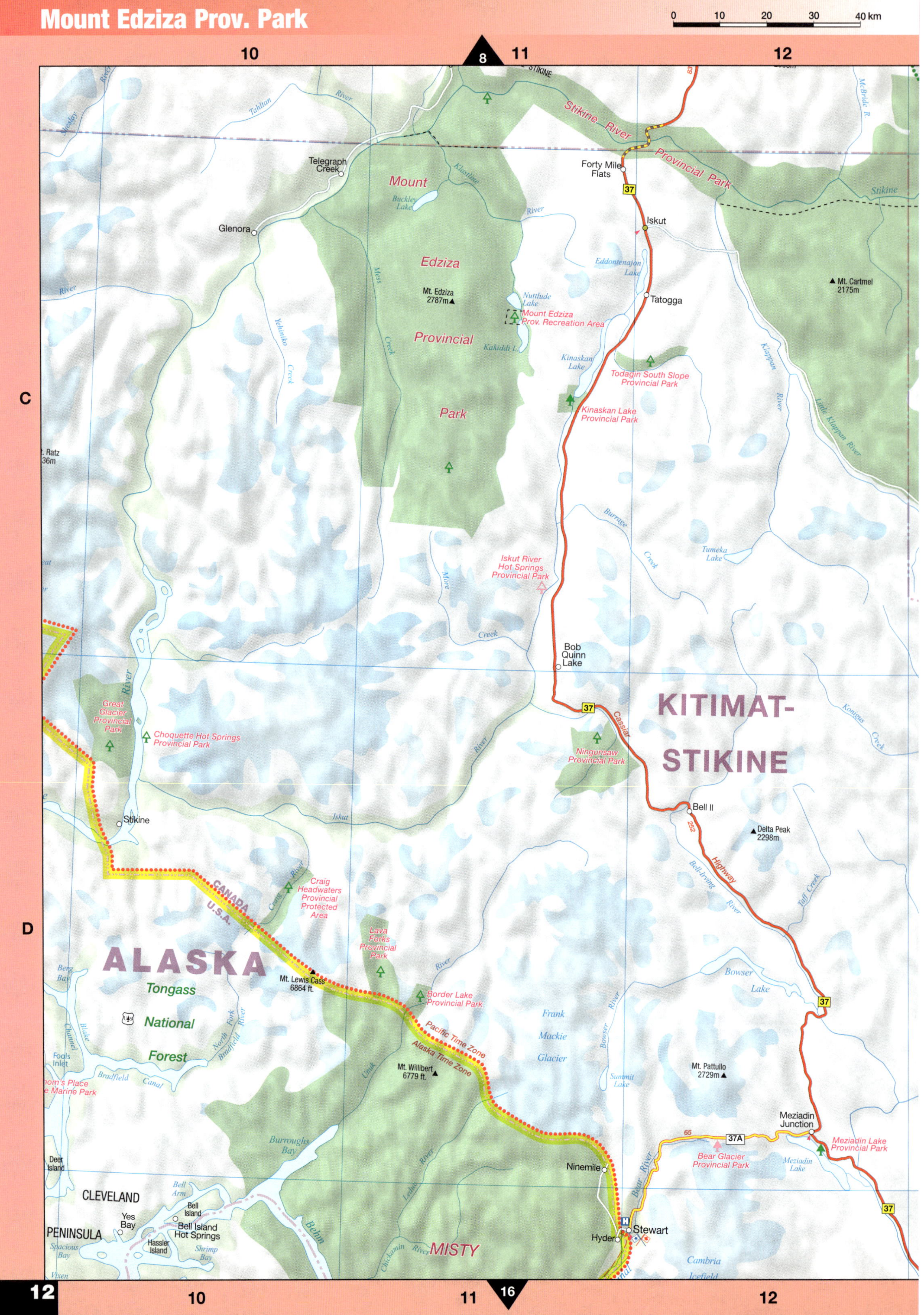

16

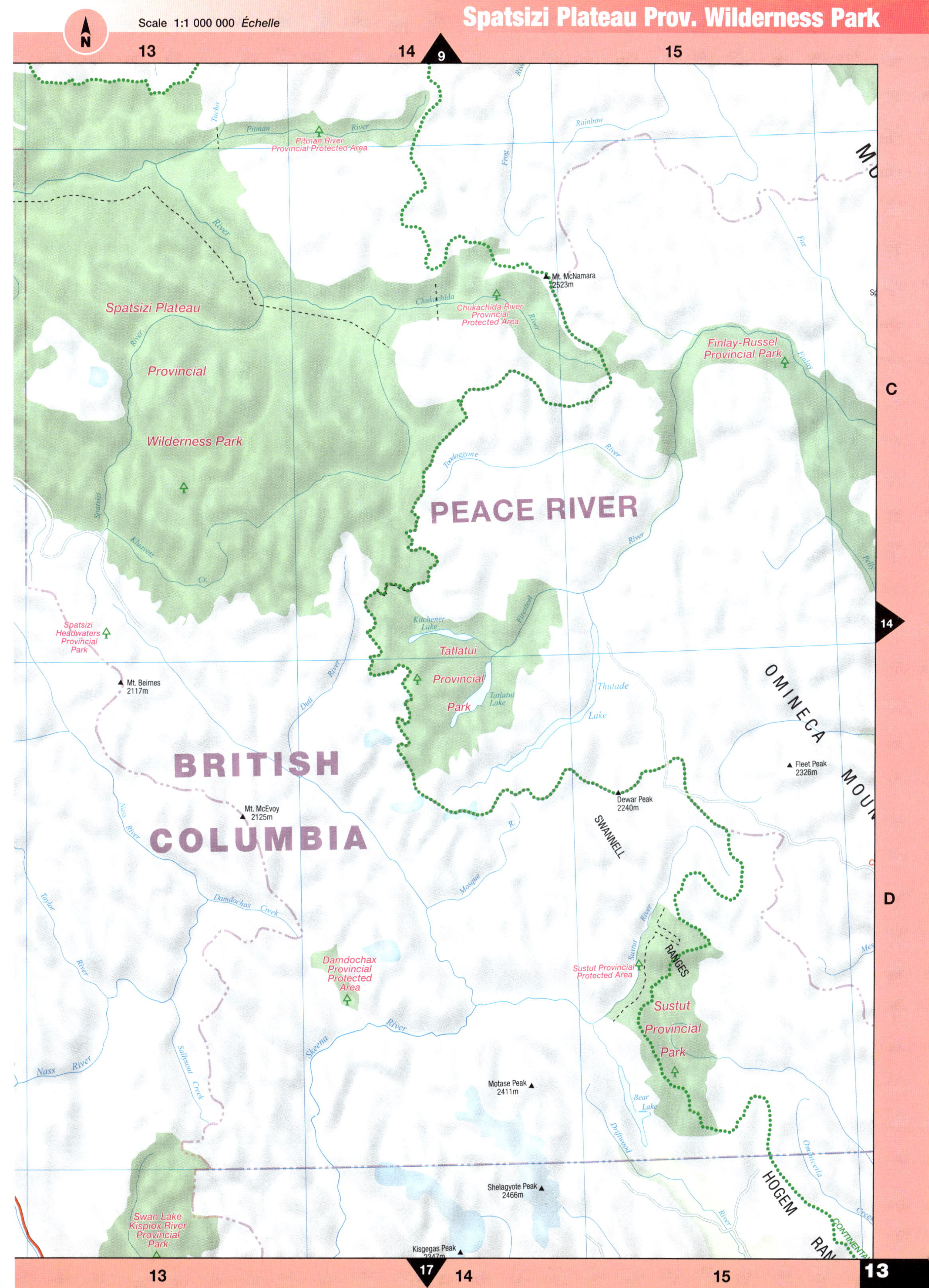
Scale 1:1 000 000 Échelle
Spatsizi Plateau Provincial Wilderness Park
Pitman River Provincial Protected Area
Chukachida River Provincial Protected Area
Mt. McNamara 2523m
Finlay-Russel Provincial Park
PEACE RIVER
Spatsizi Headwaters Provincial Park
Mt. Beirnes 2117m
Kitchener Lake
Tatlatui Provincial Park
Tatlatui Lake
Thutade Lake
OMINECA MOUN
Fleet Peak 2326m
Dewar Peak 2240m
SWANNELL RANGES
BRITISH COLUMBIA
Mt. McEvoy 2125m
Damdochax Creek
Damdochax Provincial Protected Area
Sustut Provincial Protected Area
Sustut Provincial Park
Skeena River
Nass River
Motase Peak 2411m
Bear Lake
Shelagyote Peak 2466m
HOGEM RAN
Swan Lake Kispiox River Provincial Park
Kisgegas Peak

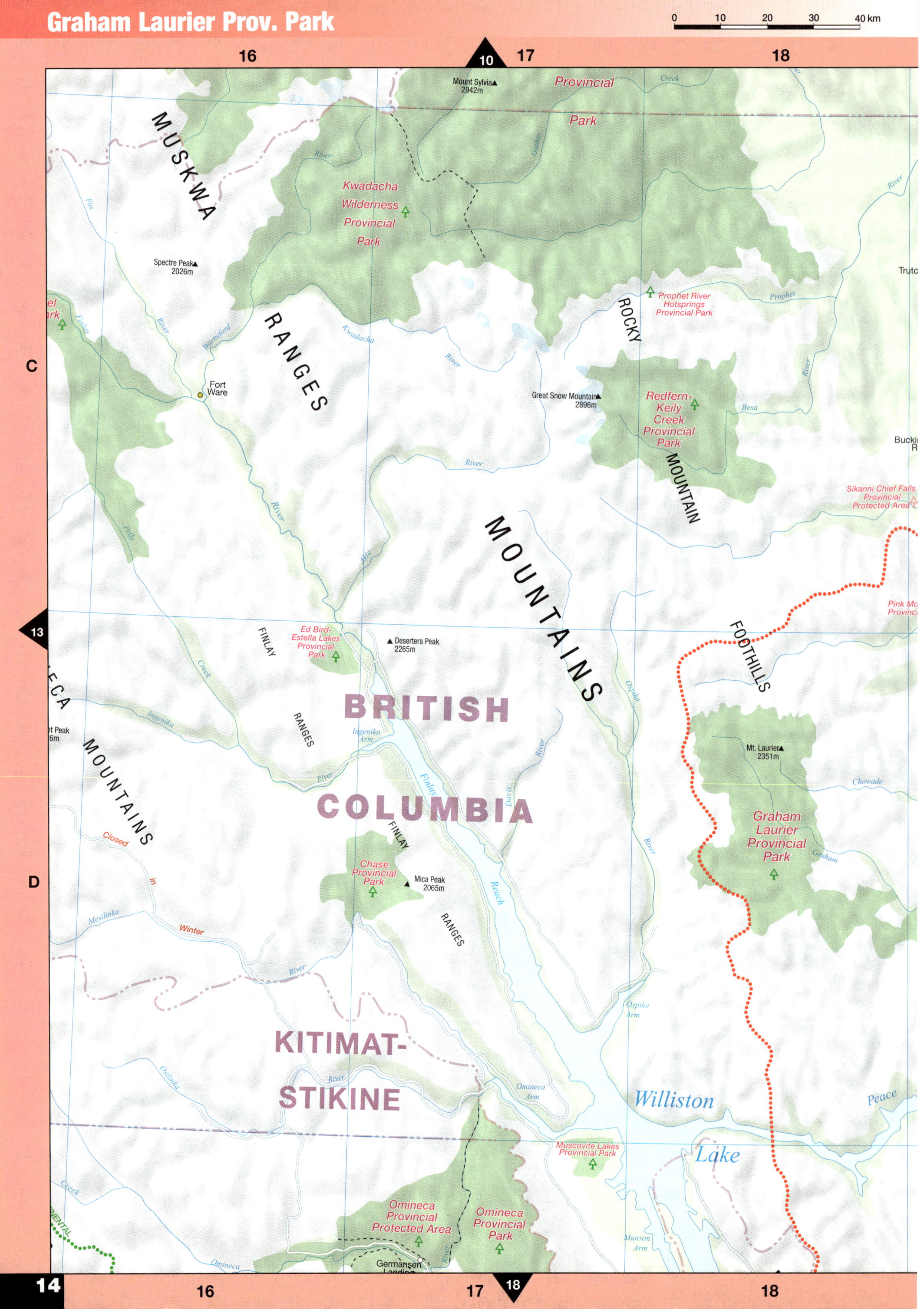
0 10 20 30 40 km
16
10
17
18
C
D
13
Mount Sylvia 2942m
Provincial Park
MUSKWA
Kwadacha Wilderness Provincial Park
Spectre Peak 2026m
RANGES
Fort Ware
Prophet River Hotsprings Provincial Park
ROCKY
Great Snow Mountain 2896m
Redfern-Keily Creek Provincial Park
MOUNTAIN
Sikanni Chief Falls Provincial Protected Area
MOUNTAINS
FOOTHILLS
FINLAY
Ed Bird-Estella Lakes Provincial Park
Deserters Peak 2265m
BRITISH
COLUMBIA
RANGES
Ingenika Arm
Mt. Laurier 2351m
Graham Laurier Provincial Park
MOUNTAINS
Closed
in
Winter
FINLAY
Chase Provincial Park
Mica Peak 2065m
RANGES
Finlay Reach
KITIMAT-
STIKINE
Omineca Arm
Ospika Arm
Williston
Lake
Peace
Muscovite Lakes Provincial Park
Omineca Provincial Protected Area
Omineca Provincial Park
Manson Arm
Germansen Landing
Trutch
18

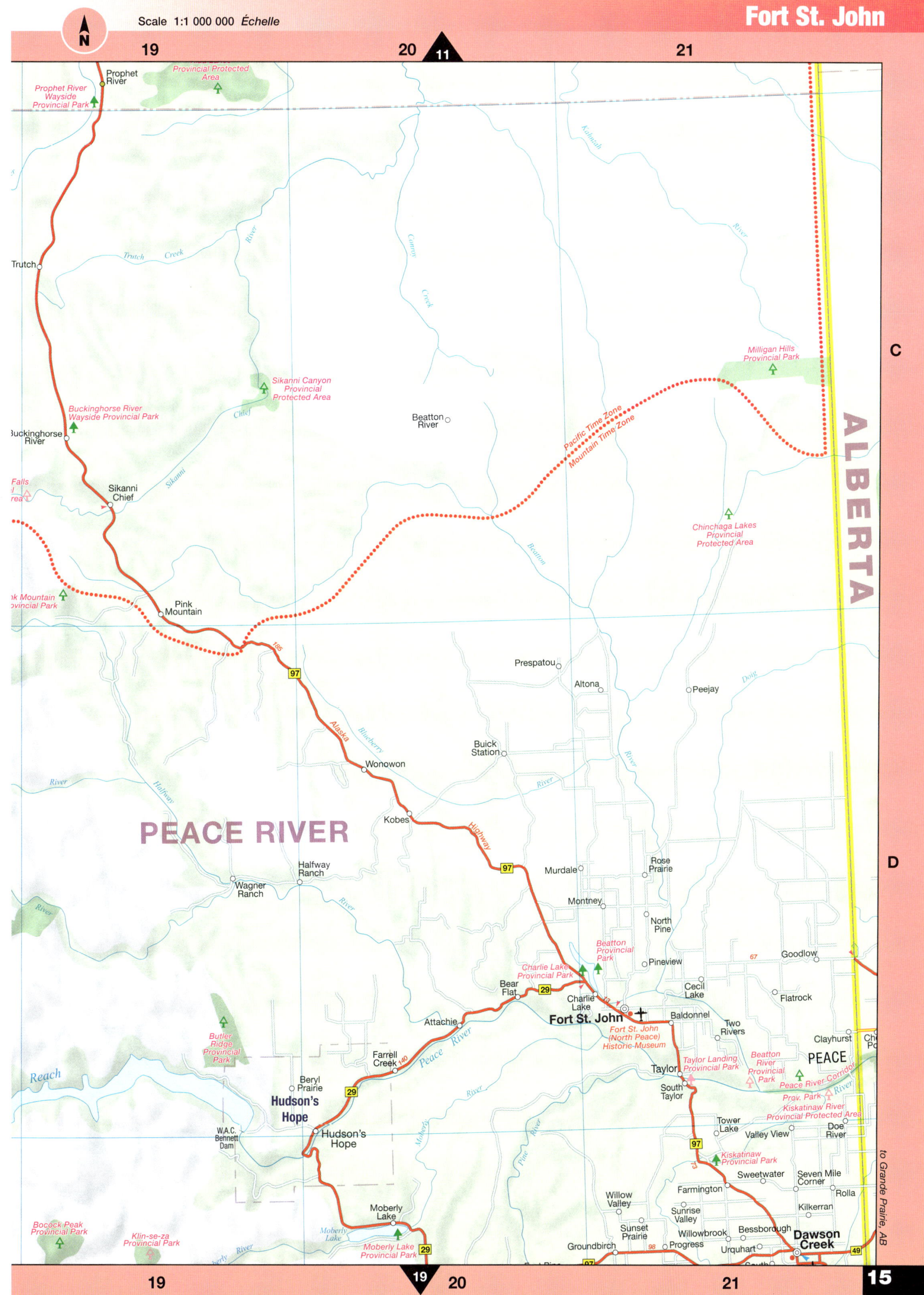
Scale 1:1 000 000 Échelle
19
20
11
21
C
D
ALBERTA
PEACE RIVER
Prophet River
Prophet River Wayside Provincial Park
Provincial Protected Area
Trutch
Trutch Creek
Sikanni Canyon Provincial Protected Area
Buckinghorse River Wayside Provincial Park
Buckinghorse River
Sikanni Chief
Pink Mountain
Beatton River
Pacific Time Zone
Mountain Time Zone
Milligan Hills Provincial Park
Chinchaga Lakes Provincial Protected Area
Prespatou
Altona
Peejay
Buick Station
Wonowon
Alaska Highway
Kobes
Halfway Ranch
Wagner Ranch
Murdale
Rose Prairie
Montney
North Pine
Pineview
Beatton Provincial Park
Charlie Lake Provincial Park
Goodlow
Cecil Lake
Flatrock
Bear Flat
Charlie Lake
Fort St. John
Fort St. John (North Peace) Historic Museum
Baldonnel
Two Rivers
Clayhurst
Attachie
Farrell Creek
Peace River
Butler Ridge Provincial Park
Beryl Prairie
Hudson's Hope
W.A.C. Bennett Dam
Taylor
Taylor Landing Provincial Park
Beatton River Provincial Park
PEACE
Peace River Corridor Prov. Park
Kiskatinaw River Provincial Protected Area
South Taylor
Tower Lake
Valley View
Doe River
Kiskatinaw Provincial Park
Sweetwater
Seven Mile Corner
Rolla
Farmington
Willow Valley
Sunrise Valley
Kilkerran
Moberly Lake
Moberly Lake Provincial Park
Sunset Prairie
Willowbrook
Bessborough
Dawson Creek
Groundbirch
Progress
Urquhart
Bocock Peak Provincial Park
Klin-se-za Provincial Park
Reach
to Grande Prairie, AB
97
29
185
140
67
73
98
49
19
20
21

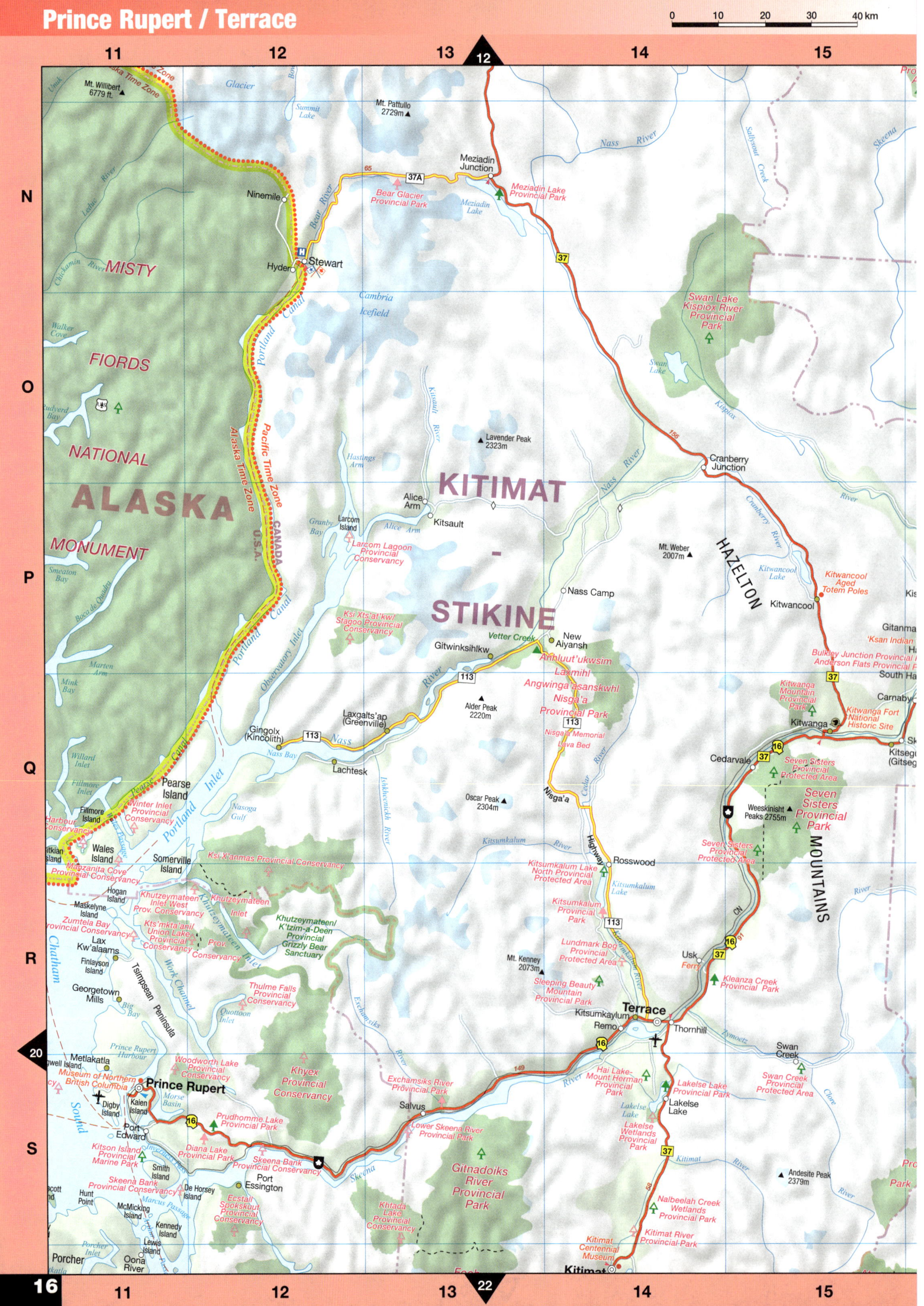
0 10 20 30 40 km
KITIMAT - STIKINE
ALASKA
MISTY FIORDS NATIONAL MONUMENT
HAZELTON MOUNTAINS
Prince Rupert
Terrace
Stewart
Hyder
Kitimat
Meziadin Junction
Cranberry Junction
Kitwanga
Kitwancool
New Aiyansh
Nass Camp
Gitwinksihlkw
Laxgalts'ap (Greenville)
Gingolx (Kincolith)
Lachtesk
Rosswood
Usk
Thornhill
Remo
Kitsumkaylum
Lakelse Lake
Salvus
Port Edward
Port Essington
Lax Kw'alaams
Metlakatla
Cedarvale
Alice Arm
Kitsault
Ninemile
Swan Creek
Porcher
Oona River
Georgetown Mills
Mt. Williburt 6779 ft.
Mt. Pattullo 2729m
Lavender Peak 2323m
Mt. Weber 2007m
Alder Peak 2220m
Oscar Peak 2304m
Mt. Kenney 2073m
Weeskinisht Peaks 2755m
Andesite Peak 2379m
Anhluut'ukwsim Laxmihl Angwinga'asanskwhl Nisga'a Provincial Park
Nisga'a Memorial Lava Bed
Nisga'a Highway
Seven Sisters Provincial Park
Kitwanga Fort National Historic Site
Kitwancool Aged Totem Poles
Swan Lake Kispiox River Provincial Park
Meziadin Lake Provincial Park
Bear Glacier Provincial Park
Khutzeymateen/K'tzim-a-Deen Provincial Grizzly Bear Sanctuary
Khyex Provincial Conservancy
Gitnadoiks River Provincial Park
Kleanza Creek Provincial Park
Lakelse Lake Provincial Park
Kitimat Centennial Museum
Museum of Northern British Columbia
Portland Canal
Portland Inlet
Observatory Inlet
Pacific Time Zone
Alaska Time Zone
CANADA
U.S.A.
Cambria Icefield
Nass River
Skeena River
Chatham Sound
11 12 13 14 15
N O P Q R S
12 20 22

Scale 1:1 000 000 Échelle
BRITISH
COLUMBIA
KITIMAT-
STIKINE
BULKLEY-
NECHAKO
Sustut Provincial Park
Sustut Provincial Protected Area
HOGEM RANGES
CONTINENTAL DIVIDE
BABINE RANGE
Motase Peak 2411m
Shelagyote Peak 2466m
Kisgegas Peak 2347m
Mt. Thoen 2291m
Blunt Mtn. 2286m
Eagle Peak 2093m
Babine River Corridor Provincial Park
Bulkley House
Lovell Landing
Takla Landing
Takla Lake
Takla Lake (West Side) Marine Prov. Park
Takla Lake (White Bluff) Marine Prov. Park
Takla Lake (Sandy Point) Marine Prov. Park
Mt. Blanchet Provincial Park
Nation Lakes Provincial Park
Tsayta Lake
Indata Lake
Tchentlo Lake
Leo Creek
Nilkitkwa Lake Provincial Park
Rainbow Alley Provincial Park
Fort Babine
North Spit Provincial Conservancy
Netalzul Meadows Provincial Park
Kispiox
Sik-e-dahk
Two Mile
Hazelton
Hagwilget
New Hazelton
Ross Lake Provincial Park
Seeley Lake Provincial Park
Boulder Creek Provincial Park
Skeena Crossing
Moricetown
Babine Lake (Smithers Landing) Provincial Marine Park
Smithers Landing
Sanctuary Bay Provincial Conservancy
Babine Mountains Provincial Park
Evelyn
Lake Kathlyn
Hudson Bay Mountain
Smithers
Driftwood Canyon Provincial Park
Call Lake Provincial Park
Tyhee Lake Provincial Park
Telkwa
Bear Island Provincial Conservancy
Granisle
Long Island Provincial Conservancy
Red Bluff Provincial Park
Topley Landing Provincial Park
Topley Landing
Wilkinson-Wright Bay Provincial Conservancy
Port Arthur Provincial Conservancy
Sand Point Provincial Conservancy
Babine Lake
Babine Lake (Sandpoint) Prov. Marine Park
Rubyrock Lake Provincial Park
Middle River
Trembleur Lake
Stuart Lake
Barrett Lake
Knockholt
Perow
Topley
Houston
Old Man Lake Provincial Park
Babine Lake (Pendleton Bay) Prov. Marine Park
Ross Lake
Palling
Ethel F. Wilson Memorial Provincial Park
Sutherland River Provincial Park
Decker Lake
Burns Lake
Woyenne
Tintagel
Sheraton
Burns Lake Provincial Park
Tazdli Wyiez Bin/ Burnie-Shea Provincial Park
Morice River
Buck Creek
16 17 18 19 20
N O P Q R S

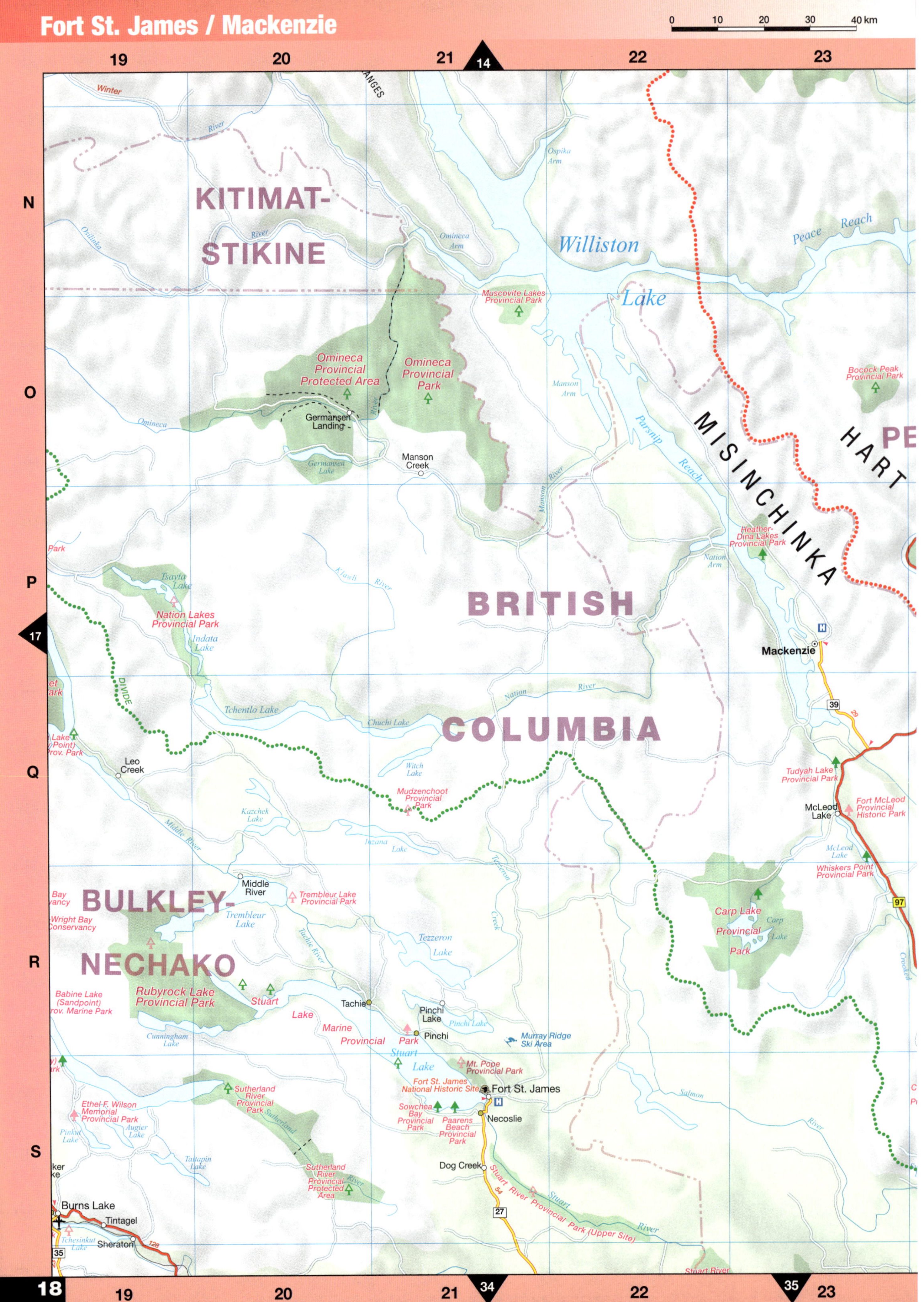

0 10 20 30 40 km
KITIMAT-STIKINE
Williston Lake
Peace Reach
Ospika Arm
Omineca Arm
Muscovite Lakes Provincial Park
Omineca Provincial Protected Area
Omineca Provincial Park
Germansen Landing
Germansen Lake
Manson Creek
Manson Arm
Parsnip Reach
MISINCHINKA
HART
Bocock Peak Provincial Park
Heather-Dina Lakes Provincial Park
Nation Arm
Tsayta Lake
Nation Lakes Provincial Park
Indata Lake
BRITISH COLUMBIA
Mackenzie
Tchentlo Lake
Chuchi Lake
Nation River
DIVIDE
Leo Creek
Witch Lake
Mudzenchoot Provincial Park
Tudyah Lake Provincial Park
McLeod Lake
Fort McLeod Provincial Historic Park
Whiskers Point Provincial Park
Kazchek Lake
Inzana Lake
Middle River
Trembleur Lake Provincial Park
Trembleur Lake
BULKLEY-NECHAKO
Wright Bay Conservancy
Carp Lake Provincial Park
Tezzeron Lake
Rubyrock Lake Provincial Park
Babine Lake (Sandpoint) Prov. Marine Park
Stuart Lake Marine Provincial Park
Tachie
Pinchi Lake
Pinchi
Murray Ridge Ski Area
Cunningham Lake
Mt. Pope Provincial Park
Fort St. James National Historic Site
Fort St. James
Sutherland River Provincial Park
Ethel F. Wilson Memorial Provincial Park
Sowchea Bay Provincial Park
Paarens Beach Provincial Park
Necoslie
Pinkut Lake
Augier Lake
Taltapin Lake
Sutherland River Provincial Protected Area
Dog Creek
Stuart River Provincial Park (Upper Site)
Salmon River
Burns Lake
Tintagel
Tchesinkut Lake
Sheraton
Stuart River

Scale 1:1 000 000 Échelle

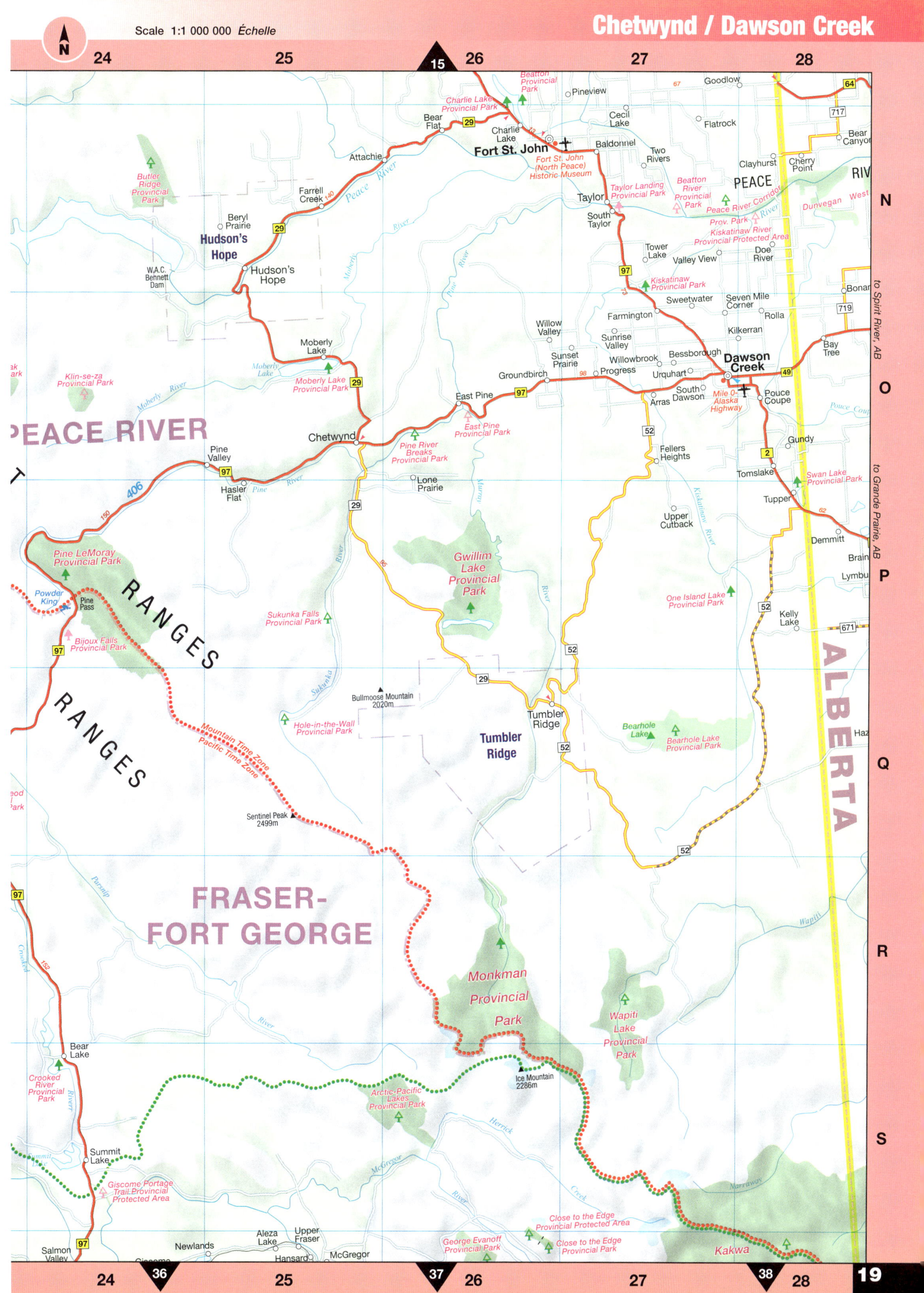

0 10 20 30 40 km
ALASKA
U.S.A.
CANADA
Alaska Time Zone
Pacific Time Zone
Dixon Entrance
SKEENA-QUEEN CHARLOTTE
BRITISH COLUMBIA
HAIDA
GRAHAM ISLAND
PITT ISLAND
BANKS ISLAND
to Ketchican, AK
Prince Rupert
Port Edward
Port Essington
Lax Kw'alaams
Metlakatla
Georgetown Mills
Tsimpsean Peninsula
Lachtesk
Kitkatla
Oona River
Chatham Sound
Brown Passage
Masset
Haida (Old Masset)
Port Clements
Juskatla
Tlell
Lawnhill
Skidegate
Skidegate Landing
Queen Charlotte City
Sandspit
Alliford Bay
Naikoon Provincial Park
Duu Guusd Provincial Conservancy
Nang Xaldangaas Provincial Conservancy
Pure Lake Provincial Park
Agate Beach
Misty Meadows
Rose Point
Rose Spit
Cape Ball
Langara Island
Langara Point
Point Cornwallis
Cape Muzon
Cape Chacon
Cape Fox
Dundas Island
Stephens Island
Porcher Island
McCauley Island
Maude Island
Kumdis Island
Masset Inlet
Virago Sound
Rennell Sound
16
22
101

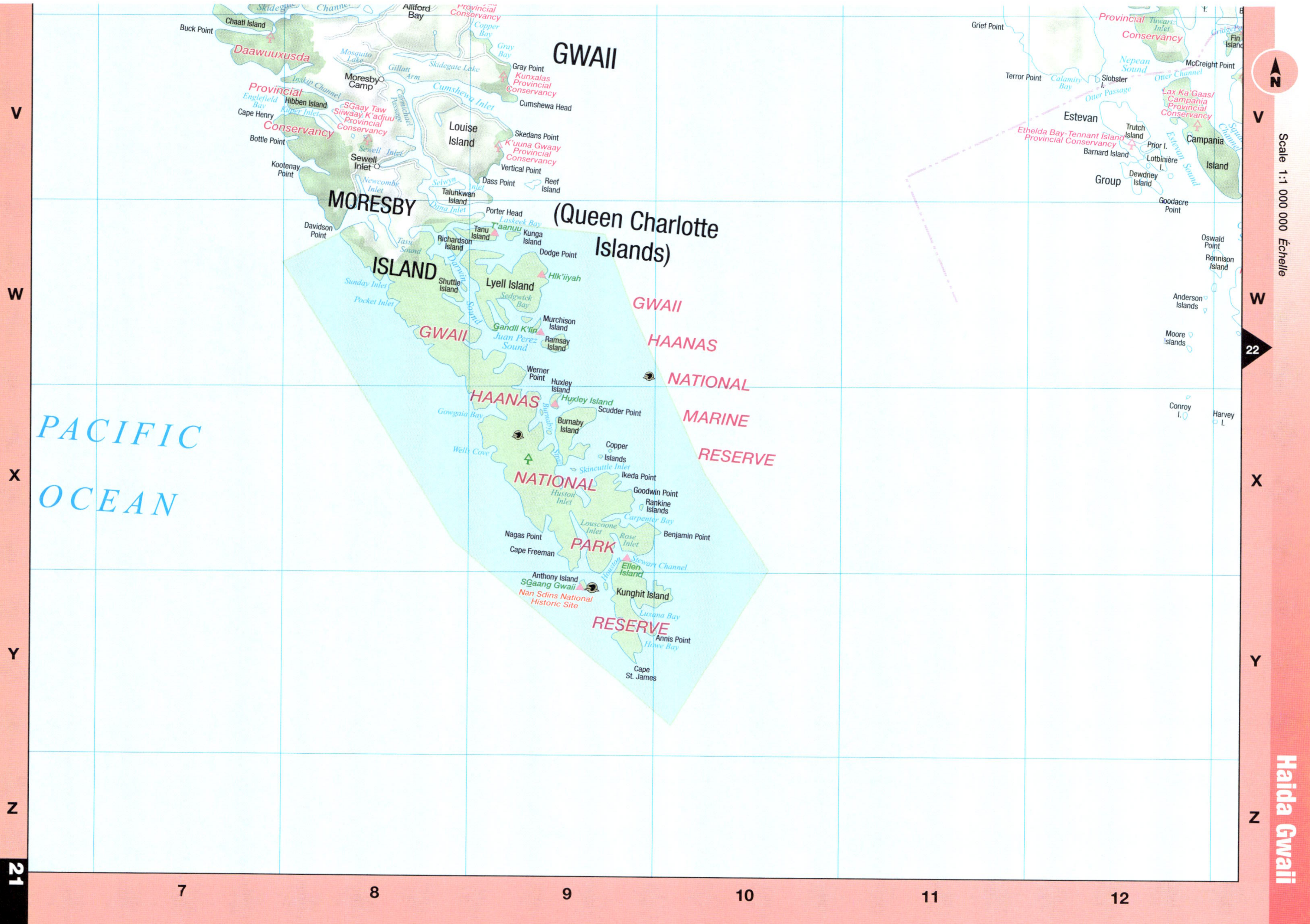
Scale 1:1 000 000 Échelle
N
V
W
X
Y
Z
22
7
8
9
10
11
12
GWAII
MORESBY
ISLAND
(Queen Charlotte
Islands)
GWAII
HAANAS
NATIONAL
MARINE
RESERVE
GWAII
HAANAS
NATIONAL
PARK
RESERVE
PACIFIC
OCEAN
Buck Point
Chaatl Island
Daawuuxusda
Alliford Bay
Provincial Conservancy
Copper Bay
Gray Bay
Gray Point
Kunxalas Provincial Conservancy
Cumshewa Head
Mosquito Lake
Gillatt Arm
Skidegate Lake
Cumshewa Inlet
Moresby Camp
Carmichael Passage
Provincial
Englefield Bay
Hibben Island
Inskip Channel
Kuper Inlet
Cape Henry
Conservancy
Bottle Point
SGaay Taw Siiwaay K'adjuu Provincial Conservancy
Louise Island
Skedans Point
K'uuna Gwaay Provincial Conservancy
Vertical Point
Sewell Inlet
Kootenay Point
Newcombe Inlet
Selwyn Inlet
Dass Point
Reef Island
Talunkwan Island
Dana Inlet
Davidson Point
Porter Head
Laskeek Bay
Taanuu
Tanu Island
Kunga Island
Richardson Island
Tasu Sound
Dodge Point
Hlk'iiyah
Sunday Inlet
Shuttle Island
Darwin Sound
Lyell Island
Sedgwick Bay
Pocket Inlet
Murchison Island
Gandll K'in
Juan Perez Sound
Ramsay Island
Werner Point
Huxley Island
Huxley Island
Scudder Point
Gowgaia Bay
Burnaby Strait
Burnaby Island
Wells Cove
Copper Islands
Skincuttle Inlet
Ikeda Point
Huston Inlet
Goodwin Point
Rankine Islands
Carpenter Bay
Louscoone Inlet
Rose Inlet
Benjamin Point
Nagas Point
Cape Freeman
Houston Stewart Channel
Ellen Island
Anthony Island
SGaang Gwaii
Nan Sdins National Historic Site
Kunghit Island
Luxana Bay
Annis Point
Howe Bay
Cape St. James
Grief Point
Terror Point
Calamity Bay
Slobster I.
Otter Passage
Provincial Conservancy
Tuwartz Inlet
Nepean Sound
Otter Channel
McCreight Point
Fin Island
Lax Ka'Gaas/Campania Provincial Conservancy
Estevan
Etheldra Bay-Tennant Island Provincial Conservancy
Trutch Island
Prior I.
Barnard Island
Lotbinière I.
Estevan Sound
Campania
Island
Squally Channel
Group
Dewdney Island
Goodacre Point
Oswald Point
Rennison Island
Anderson Islands
Moore Islands
Conroy I.
Harvey I.

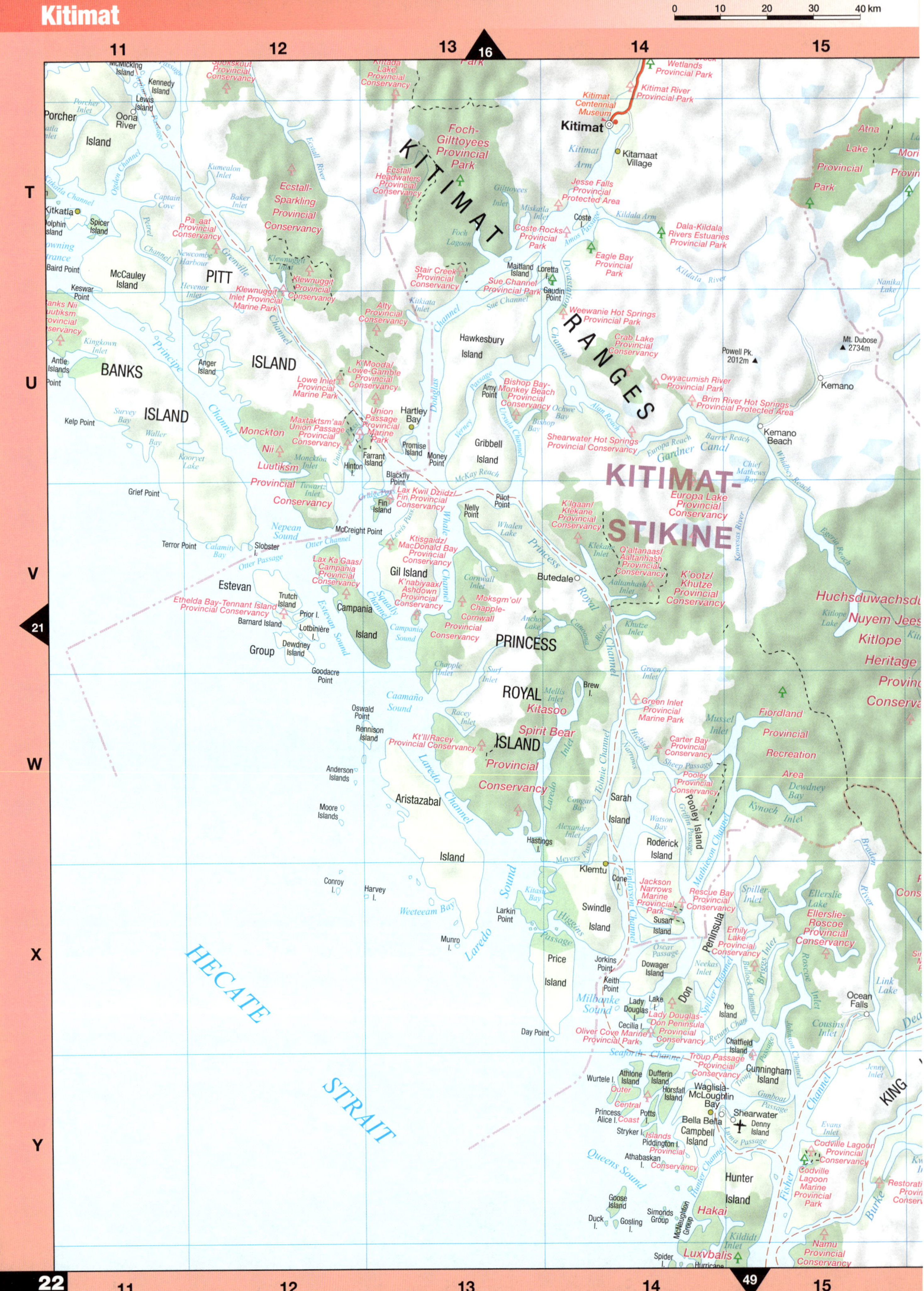
0 10 20 30 40 km
Kitimat
Kitamaat Village
KITIMAT RANGES
KITIMAT-STIKINE
Foch-Gilttoyees Provincial Park
Ecstall-Sparkling Provincial Conservancy
PITT ISLAND
BANKS ISLAND
PRINCESS ROYAL ISLAND
Kitasoo Spirit Bear Provincial Conservancy
Aristazabal Island
Gil Island
Campania Island
Hawkesbury Island
Gribbell Island
Swindle Island
Price Island
Hunter Island
Campbell Island
Bella Bella
Shearwater
Waglisla-McLoughlin Bay
Klemtu
Hartley Bay
Butedale
Kemano
Kemano Beach
Ocean Falls
Estevan Group
HECATE STRAIT
Milbanke Sound
Queens Sound
Gardner Canal
Douglas Channel
Principe Channel
Grenville Channel
Laredo Channel
Laredo Sound
Caamaño Sound
Fiordland Provincial Recreation Area
Hakai Luxvbalis
Huchsduwachsdu Nuyem Jees Kitlope Heritage Provincial Conservancy
Monckton Nii Luutiksm Provincial Conservancy
Mt. Dubose 2734m
Powell Pk. 2012m
Kitkatla
Porcher Island
McCauley Island
Sarah Island
Roderick Island
Pooley Island
Cunningham Island
Don Peninsula
KING

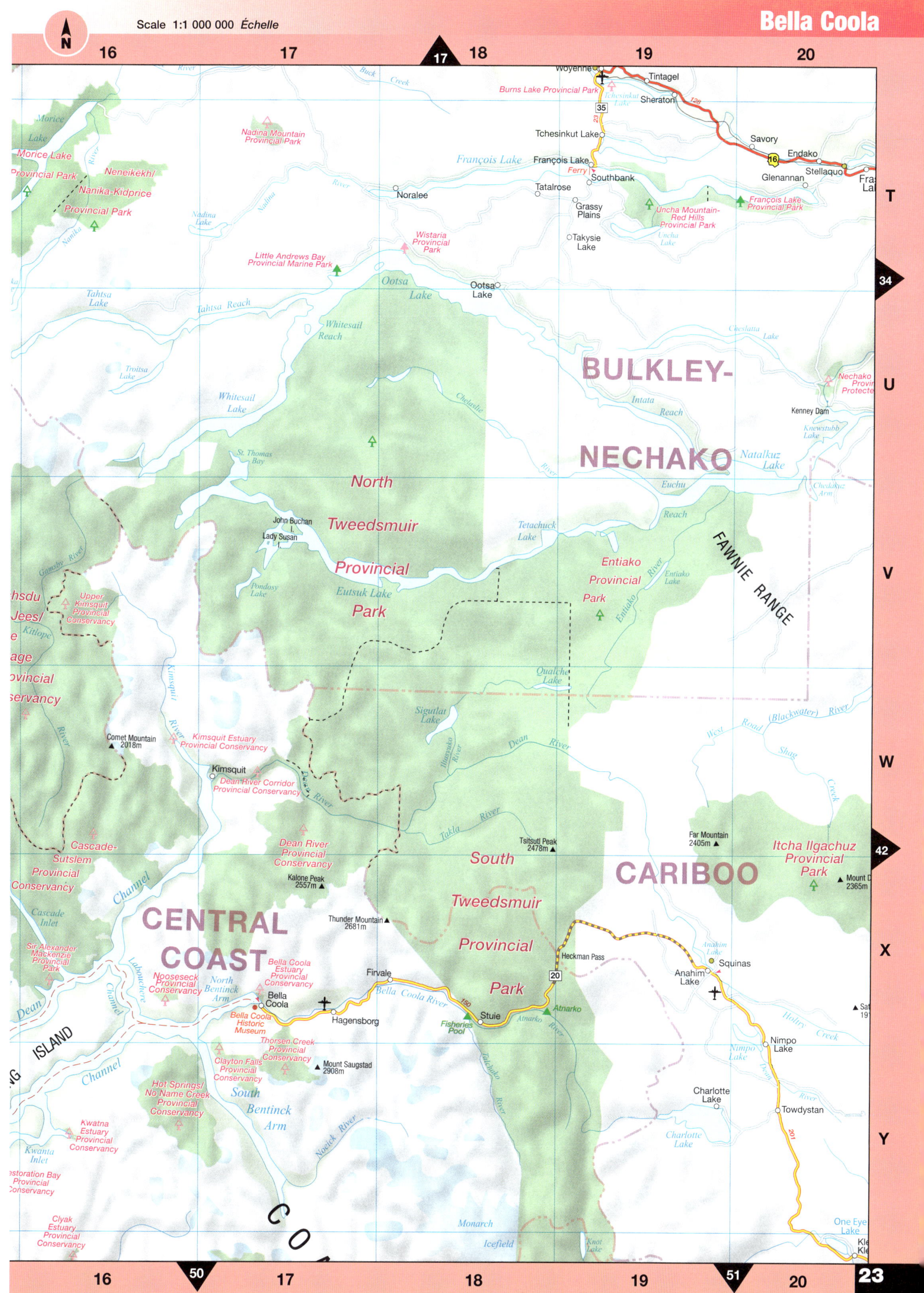
Scale 1:1 000 000 Échelle
BULKLEY-NECHAKO
CENTRAL COAST
CARIBOO
North Tweedsmuir Provincial Park
South Tweedsmuir Provincial Park
Entiako Provincial Park
Itcha Ilgachuz Provincial Park
FAWNIE RANGE
Burns Lake Provincial Park
Nadina Mountain Provincial Park
Morice Lake Provincial Park
Neneikëkh/Nanika-Kidprice Provincial Park
Wistaria Provincial Park
Little Andrews Bay Provincial Marine Park
Uncha Mountain-Red Hills Provincial Park
François Lake Provincial Park
Upper Kimsquit Provincial Conservancy
Kimsquit Estuary Provincial Conservancy
Dean River Corridor Provincial Conservancy
Dean River Provincial Conservancy
Cascade-Sutslem Provincial Conservancy
Sir Alexander Mackenzie Provincial Park
Nooseseck Provincial Conservancy
Bella Coola Estuary Provincial Conservancy
Thorsen Creek Provincial Conservancy
Clayton Falls Provincial Conservancy
Hot Springs/No Name Creek Provincial Conservancy
Kwatna Estuary Provincial Conservancy
Restoration Bay Provincial Conservancy
Clyak Estuary Provincial Conservancy
Bella Coola Historic Museum
Woyenne
Tintagel
Sheraton
Savory
Endako
Stellaquo
Glenannan
Tchesinkut Lake
François Lake
Ferry
Southbank
Tatalrose
Grassy Plains
Takysie Lake
Noralee
Ootsa Lake
Kenney Dam
Kimsquit
Bella Coola
Hagensborg
Firvale
Stuie
Atnarko
Fisheries Pool
Heckman Pass
Anahim Lake
Squinas
Nimpo Lake
Charlotte Lake
Towdystan
Comet Mountain 2018m
Kalone Peak 2557m
Thunder Mountain 2681m
Tsitsutl Peak 2478m
Far Mountain 2405m
Mount Saugstad 2908m
Morice Lake
Nadina Lake
Tahtsa Lake
Tahtsa Reach
Whitesail Reach
Whitesail Lake
Troitsa Lake
St. Thomas Bay
John Buchan I.
Lady Susan I.
Eutsuk Lake
Pondosy Lake
Tetachuck Lake
Intata Reach
Natalkuz Lake
Euchu Reach
Cheslatta Lake
Knewstubb Lake
Chedakuz Arm
Entiako Lake
Qualcho Lake
Sigutlat Lake
Dean River
Takla River
West Road (Blackwater) River
Kimsquit River
Bella Coola River
Atnarko River
Talchako River
Dean Channel
Labouchere Channel
North Bentinck Arm
South Bentinck Arm
Kwatna Inlet
Cascade Inlet
ISLAND
Anahim Lake
Nimpo Lake
Charlotte Lake
One Eye Lake
Monarch Icefield
Knot Lake
16
17
18
19
20
T
U
V
W
X
Y
34
42
50
51
35
16
20
20

0 5 10 15 20 Kilometres kilomètres
Seventh Meridian
Pink Mountain
Boring Ranch
Brady Ranch
Beatton Ranch
McKearney Ranch
Simpson Ranch
Hickethier Ranch
Lexau Ranch
Wagner Ranch
McLean Ranch
Halfway Ranch
Halfway River First Nation
Halfway-Graham
Federal Ranch
Wonowon
PEACE RIVER
Attachie
Farrell Creek
Lynx Creek
Beryl Prairie
Hudson's Hope
Hudson's Hope Museum
W.A.C. Bennett Dam
W.A.C. Bennett Dam (BC Hydro)
Peace Canyon Dam
Peace Canyon Dam (BC Hydro)
Butler Ridge Provincial Park
Williston Lake
ROCKY MOUNTAIN FOOTHILLS
Cameron River
Halfway River
Beatton River
Peace River
TOWNSHIPS
RANGES
HUDSON'S HOPE

Scale 1:500 000 Échelle

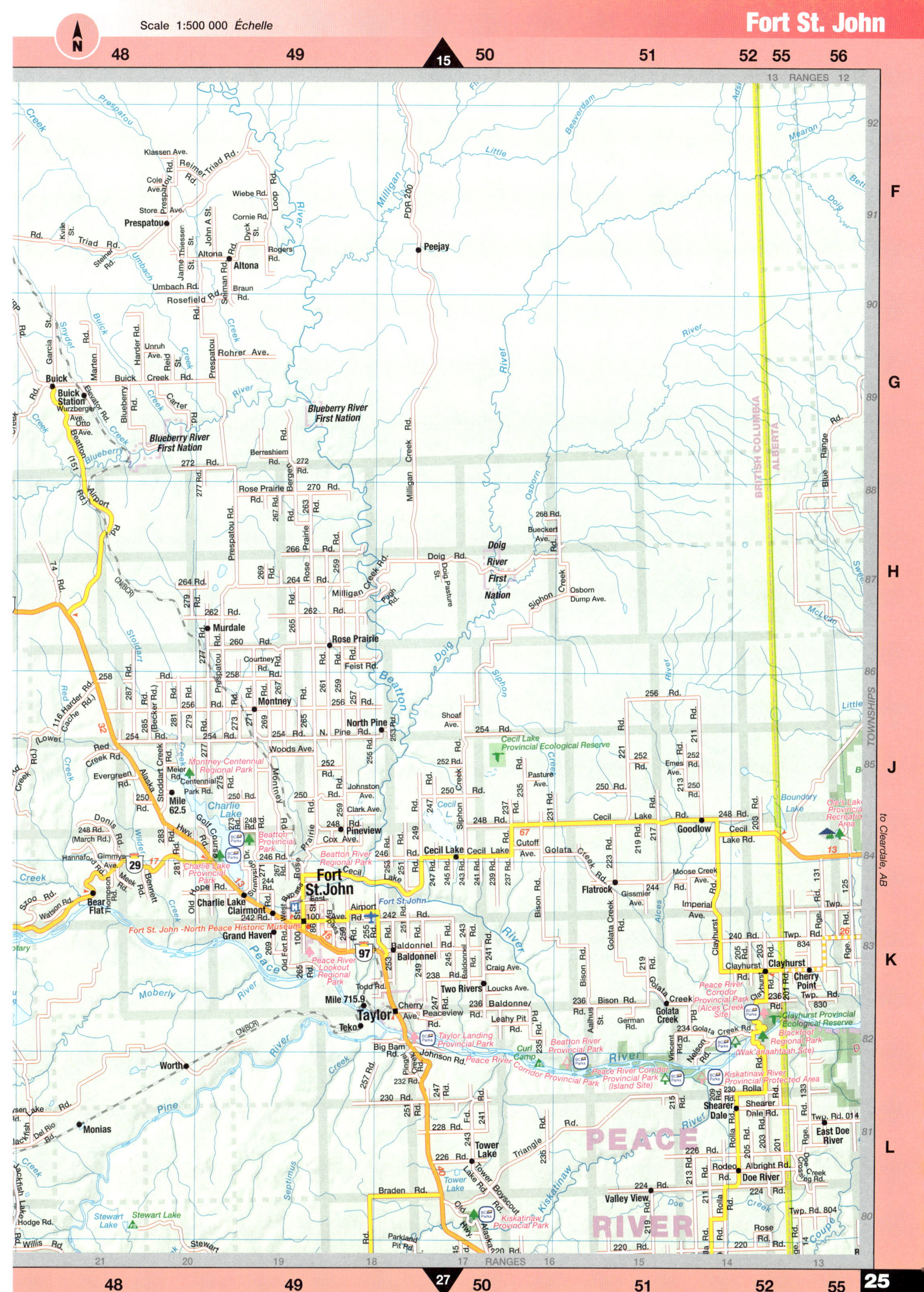

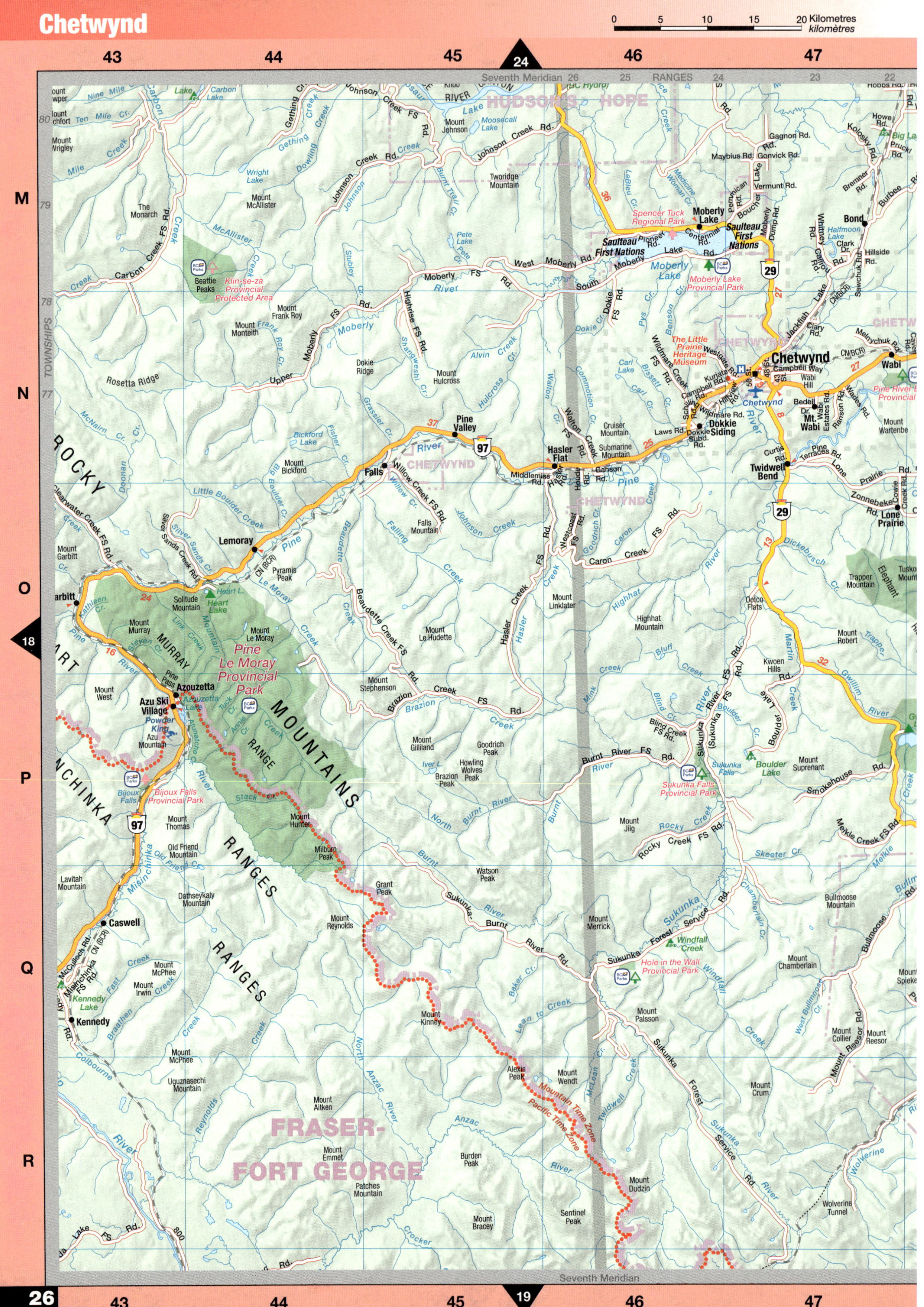
0 5 10 15 20 Kilometres kilomètres
Seventh Meridian
Chetwynd
Moberly Lake
Saulteau First Nations
Spencer Tuck Regional Park
Moberly Lake Provincial Park
The Little Prairie Heritage Museum
Wabi
Pine River Provincial
Dokkie Siding
Twidwell Bend
Lone Prairie
Hasler Flat
Pine Valley
Falls
Lemoray
Azouzetta
Azu Ski Village
Pine Le Moray Provincial Park
Klin-se-za Provincial Protected Area
Bijoux Falls Provincial Park
Sukunka Falls Provincial Park
Hole in the Wall Provincial Park
Boulder Lake
Caswell
Kennedy
ROCKY MOUNTAINS
MURRAY RANGE
HART RANGES
MISINCHINKA RANGES
FRASER-FORT GEORGE
Mountain Time Zone
Pacific Time Zone
HUDSON'S HOPE
Mount Reynolds
Mount Kinney
Mount Aitken
Mount Emmet
Patches Mountain
Burden Peak
Sentinel Peak
Mount Dudzin
Mount Bracey
Wolverine Tunnel
Mount Crum
Mount Wendt
Alexis Peak
Mount Palsson
Mount Merrick
Watson Peak
Grant Peak
Milburn Peak
Mount Hunter
Mount Thomas
Old Friend Mountain
Dathseykaly Mountain
Lavitah Mountain
Mount McPhee
Mount Irwin
Uguznasechi Mountain
Mount Stephenson
Mount Gilliland
Goodrich Peak
Howling Wolves Peak
Brazion Peak
Mount Jilg
Highhat Mountain
Mount Linklater
Falls Mountain
Mount Le Hudette
Pyramis Peak
Solitude Mountain
Mount Murray
Mount Le Moray
Mount West
Azu Mountain
Mount Bickford
Dokie Ridge
Mount Hulcross
Mount Monteith
Mount Frank Roy
Beattie Peaks
Rosetta Ridge
The Monarch
Mount Wrigley
Mount McAllister
Mount Johnson
Twonidge Mountain
Cruiser Mountain
Submarine Mountain
Mount Robert
Trapper Mountain
Mount Suprenant
Bullmoose Mountain
Mount Chamberlain
Mount Collier
Mount Reesor
Mount Wartenbe
Kwoen Hills
Detco Flats
Mount Garbitt
97
29
19
18
24

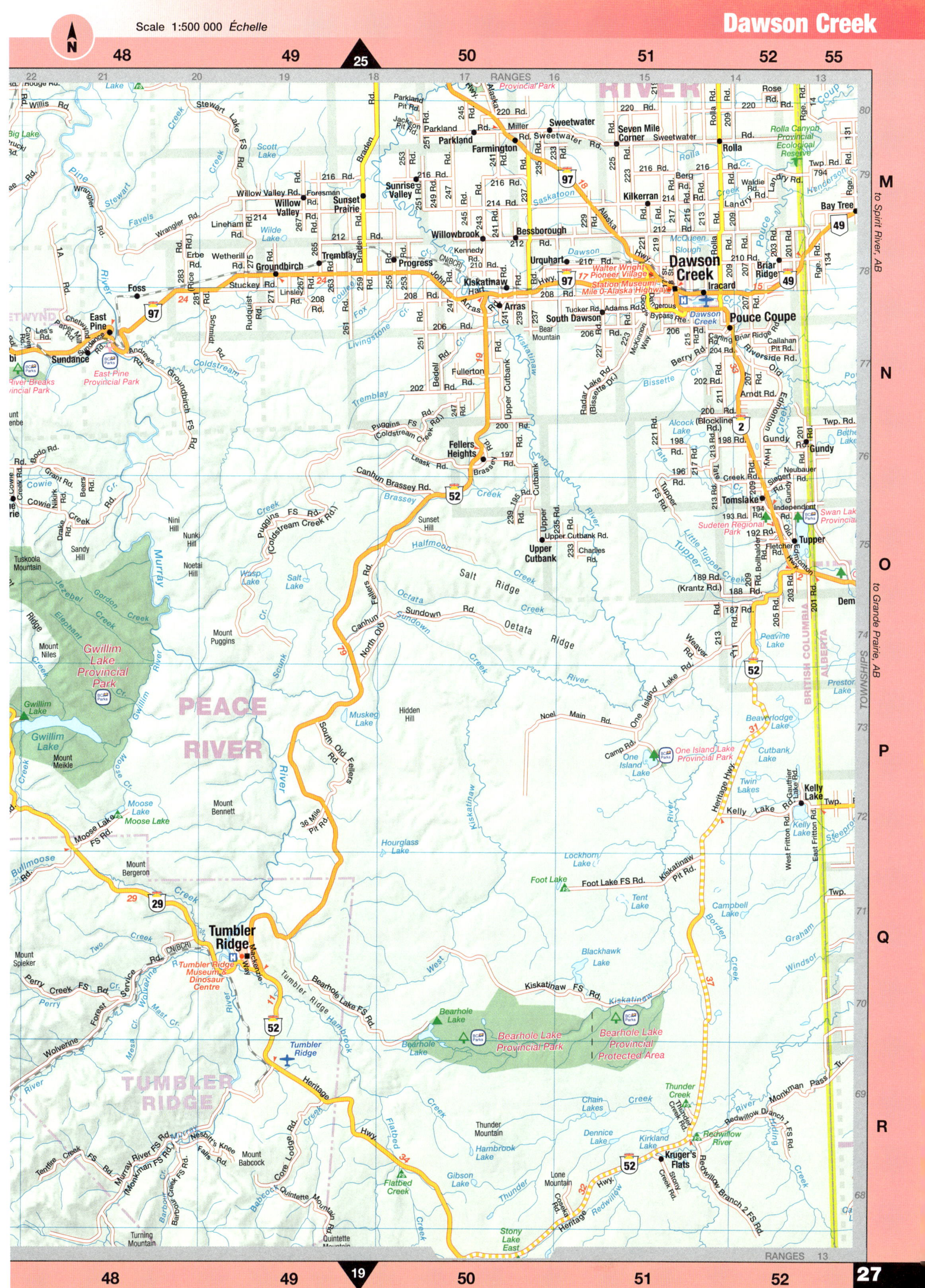
Scale 1:500 000 Échelle
Dawson Creek
Tumbler Ridge
Pouce Coupe
Chetwynd
East Pine
Sundance
Foss
Groundbirch
Progress
Arras
Kiskatinaw
Farmington
Parkland
Sweetwater
Rolla
Kilkerran
Briar Ridge
Bay Tree
Tomslake
Tupper
Gundy
Kelly Lake
Fellers Heights
Upper Cutbank
Kruger's Flats
PEACE RIVER
TUMBLER RIDGE
Gwillim Lake Provincial Park
East Pine Provincial Park
One Island Lake Provincial Park
Bearhole Lake Provincial Park
Bearhole Lake Provincial Protected Area
Sudeten Regional Park
Swan Lake Provincial Park
Rolla Canyon Provincial Ecological Reserve
Tumbler Ridge Museum & Dinosaur Centre
Walter Wright Pioneer Village
Station Museum
Mile 0 Alaska Highway
to Spirit River, AB
to Grande Prairie, AB
BRITISH COLUMBIA
ALBERTA
RANGES

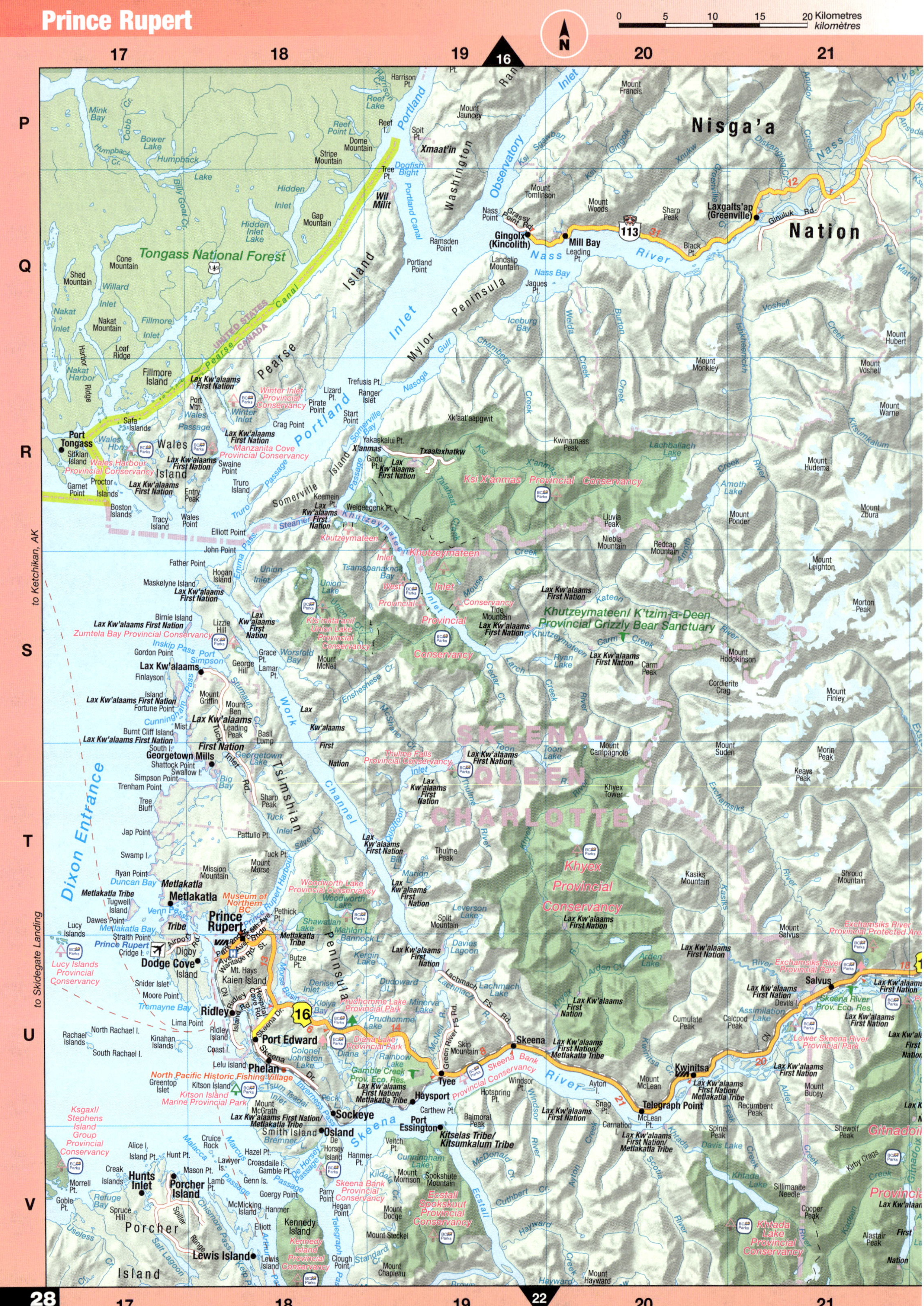
Prince Rupert
Tongass National Forest
Dixon Entrance
Nisga'a Nation
Port Tongass
Prince Rupert
Port Edward
Metlakatla
Skeena River
Portland Inlet
Observatory Inlet
Pearse Island
Wales Island
Porcher Island
to Ketchikan, AK
to Skidegate Landing
Kilometres
kilomètres

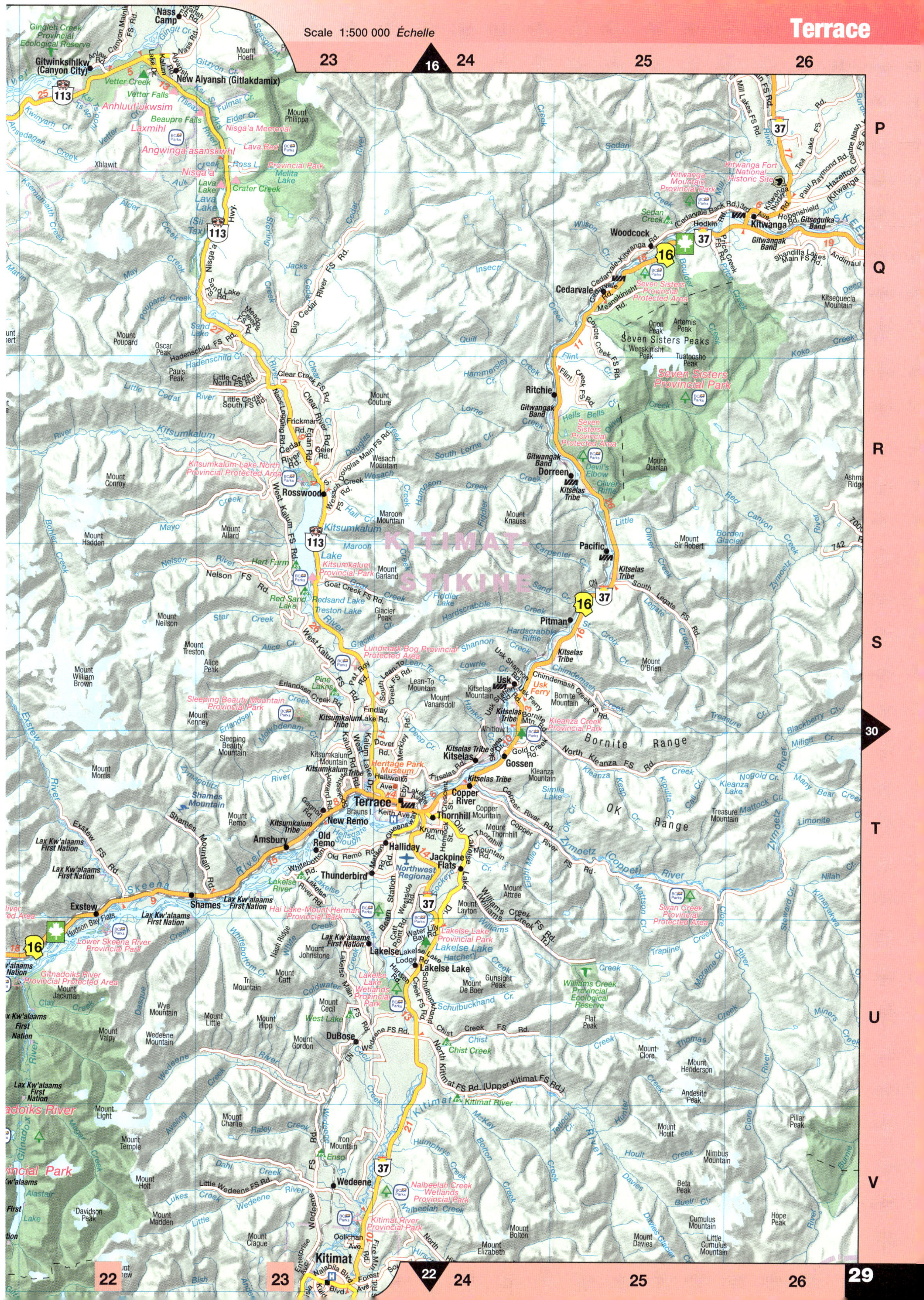
Scale 1:500 000 Échelle
Terrace
Kitimat-Stikine
New Aiyansh (Gitlakdamix)
Gitwinksihlkw (Canyon City)
Kitwanga
Cedarvale
Woodcock
Ritchie
Dorreen
Pacific
Pitman
Usk
Kitselas
Gossen
Copper River
Thornhill
New Remo
Old Remo
Amsbury
Shames
Exstew
Halliday
Jackpine Flats
Thunderbird
Lakelse
Lakelse Lake
DuBose
Wedeene
Kitimat
Rosswood
Seven Sisters Provincial Park
Seven Sisters Peaks
Kitwanga Fort National Historic Site
Nisga'a Memorial Lava Bed Provincial Park
Lakelse Lake Provincial Park
Kleanza Creek Provincial Park
Lower Skeena River Provincial Park
Nalbeelah Creek Wetlands Provincial Park
Kitimat River Provincial Park
Sleeping Beauty Mountain Provincial Park
Kitsumkalum Provincial Park
Heritage Park Museum
Northwest Regional
Bornite Range
OK Range
Skeena
Kitsumkalum Lake

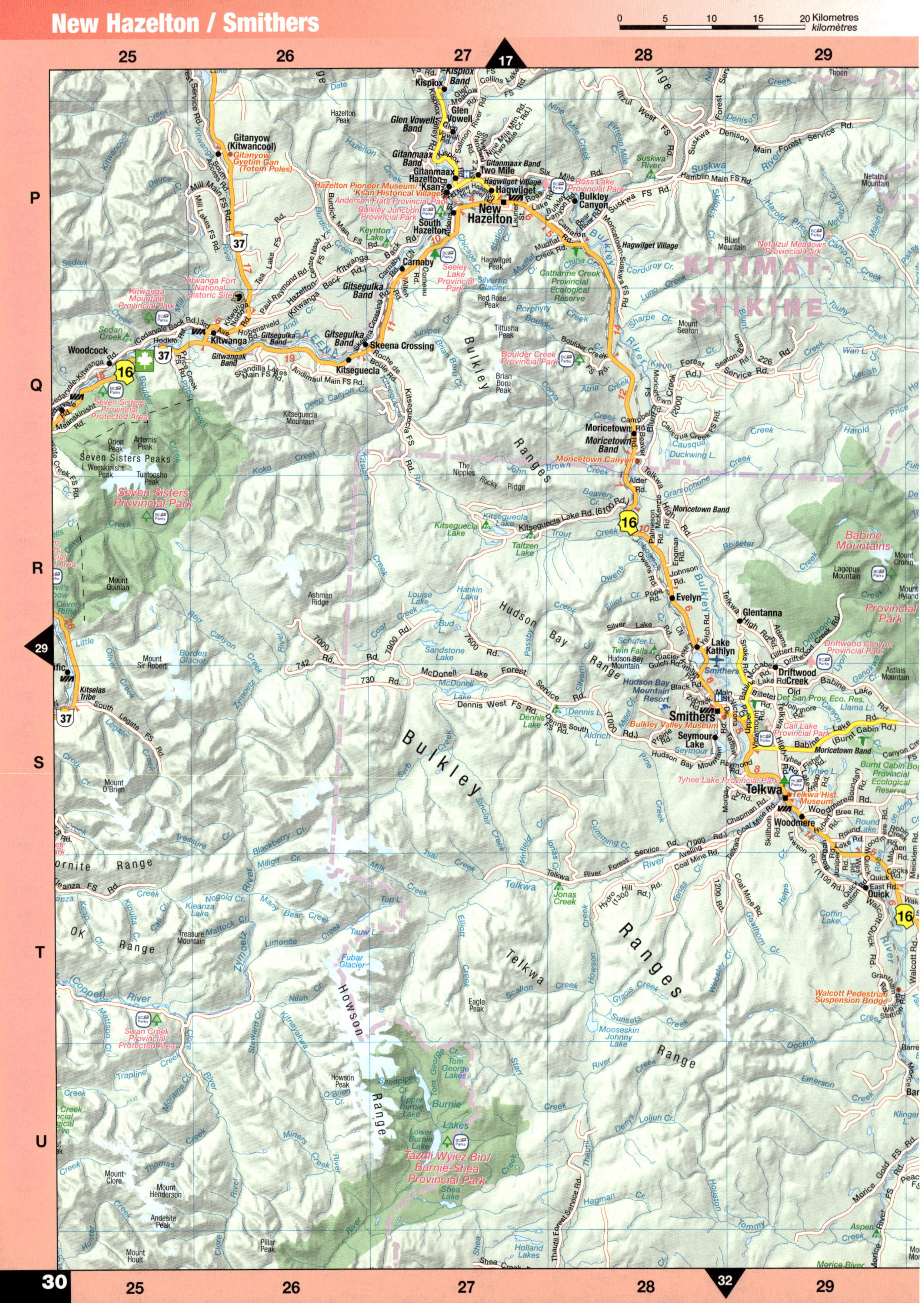
0 5 10 15 20 Kilometres
kilomètres
25
26
27
28
29
17
P
Q
R
S
T
U
29
32
Kispiox
Kispiox Band
Glen Vowell
Glen Vowell Band
Gitanmaax Band
Two Mile
Hagwilget
Hagwilget Village
Gitanmaax
Hazelton
'Ksan
New Hazelton
South Hazelton
Bulkley Canyon
Hazelton Pioneer Museum/
'Ksan Historical Village
Anderson Flats Provincial Park
Bulkley Junction Provincial Park
Ross Lake Provincial Park
Keynton Lake
Carnaby
Seeley Lake Provincial Park
Gitanyow
(Kitwancool)
Gitanyow Gyetim Gan (Totem Poles)
Kitwanga Fort National Historic Site
Kitwanga Mountain Provincial Park
Kitwanga
Gitsegulka Band
Gitsegulka Band
Skeena Crossing
Kitseguecla
Gitwangak Band
Woodcock
Sedan Creek
Seven Sisters Provincial Protected Area
Seven Sisters Peaks
Seven Sisters Provincial Park
Kitseguecla Mountain
Catharine Creek Provincial Ecological Reserve
Boulder Creek Provincial Park
Brian Boru Peak
Tiltusha Peak
Red Rose Peak
Hagwilget Peak
Rocher de Boule Rd.
Bulkley
Ranges
Moricetown
Moricetown Band
Moricetown Canyon
Moricetown Band
Kitseguecla Lake
Taltzen Lake
Kitseguecla Lake Rd.
KITIMAT-STIKINE
Suskwa River
Netalzul Mountain
Netalzul Meadows Provincial Park
Blunt Mountain
Mount Seaton
Hagwilget Village
Babine Mountains
Lagopus Mountain
Mount Cronin
Mount Hyland
Provincial Park
Driftwood Canyon Provincial Park
Astlais Mountain
Glentanna
Evelyn
Lake Kathlyn
Smithers
Driftwood Creek
Hudson Bay Mountain Resort
Twin Falls
Hudson Bay Mountain
Bulkley Valley Museum
Seymour Lake
Call Lake Provincial Park
Babine
Moricetown Band
Burnt Cabin Bog Provincial Ecological Reserve
Tyhee Lake Provincial Park
Telkwa
Telkwa Hist. Museum
Woodmere
Quick
East Rd.
Walcott Pedestrian Suspension Bridge
Hudson Bay Range
McDonell Lake
Dennis Lake
Ashman Ridge
Mount Sir Robert
Borden Glacier
Mount Quinlan
Kitselas Tribe
Mount O'Brien
Bulkley
Telkwa Ranges
Jonas Creek
Treasure Mountain
Howson Range
Fubar Glacier
Eagle Peak
Howson Peak
Swan Creek Provincial Protected Area
Tom George Lakes
Upper Burnie Lake
Lower Burnie Lake
Burnie Lakes
Tazdli Wyiez Bin/
Burnie-Shea Provincial Park
Shea Lake
Mooseskin Johnny Lake
Mount Clore
Mount Henderson
Andesite Peak
Mount Hoult
Pillar Peak
Holland Lakes
Telkwa River
Morice River
16
37

Scale 1:500 000 Échelle

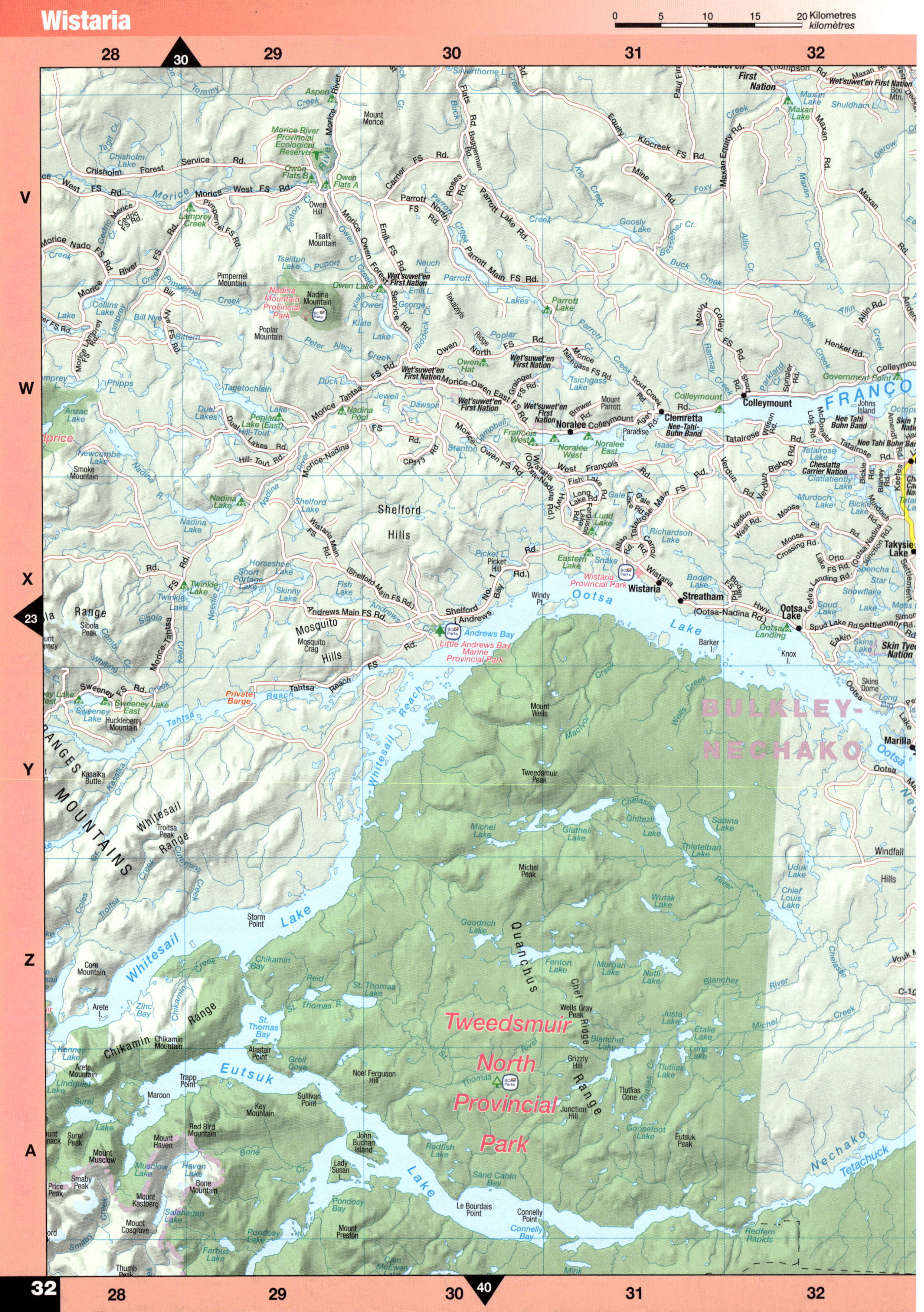
0 5 10 15 20 Kilometres kilomètres
Tweedsmuir North Provincial Park
BULKLEY-NECHAKO
Ootsa Lake
Whitesail Lake
Eutsuk Lake
Shelford Hills
Mosquito Hills
Wistaria
Streatham
Colleymount
Clemretta
Noralee
Ootsa Lake
Marilla
Takysie Lake
Wistaria Provincial Park
Little Andrews Bay Marine Provincial Park
Nadina Mountain Provincial Park
Morice River Provincial Ecological Reserve
Tweedsmuir Peak
Quanchus Range
Chikamin Range
Whitesail Range
Tahtsa Reach
Whitesail Reach
Private Barge
Nechako
Tetachuck

Scale 1:500 000 Échelle
N
Burns Lake
Fraser Lake
Fort Fraser
Endako
François Lake
Entiako Provincial Park
Natalkuz Lake
Knewstubb Lake
Cheslatta Lake
Nechako Range
Fawnie Range

0 5 10 15 20 Kilometres kilomètres
35
36
37
18
38
39
V
W
X
33
Y
Z
A
42
Sutherland River Provincial Protected Area
Marie Lake
Mount Lorenz
Mount Bud
Hannay Lake
Henrietta Lake
Helene L.
Peta Mountain
Pitka Mountain
Angly Lake
Top Lake
Peta Lake
Jean L.
Hanson Lake
Ormond Creek
Oona Lake
Etcho Lake
Ormond Lake
Owl Lake
Tatin Lake
Stern Lake
Simon Bay
Savory
Endako
Stellaquo
Stellat'en First Nation
Fraser Lake
Lejac
Encombe
Peterson's Beach
Nadleh Whut'en First Nation
Fort Fraser
Beaumont Provincial Park
Fraser Lake Museum
Foster Lakes
Fraser Mountain
Drywilliam Lake Provincial Ecological Reserve
Rock Lake
Savory Ridge
Glenannan
François Lake Rd.
Black Point
Sawmill Point
François Lake Provincial Park
Burner Bay
Borel Lake
Nithi Mountain
Anzus Lake
Graham Lake
Holy Cabin Lake
Cabin Lake
Laurie Lake
Smith Creek Rd.
Dorman Lake
Lily Lake
Walton
Tahultzu Lake
Hallett Lake
Holy Cross North FS Rd.
Holy Cross Mountain
Bentzi Lake
Bungalow Lake
Green Creek
Mount Greer
Copley Lake
Holly Cross Lake
Mount Hobson
Crystal Lake
Paddle Lake
Home Lake
Greer Creek Falls
Cutoff Creek
Murray Lake
Bird Lake
Marilla
Nechako Canyon Provincial Protected Area
Rum Cache Lake
Kluskus-Mosquito FS Rd.
Rum Cache (Cicuta) Lake
Fish Lake S.
Fish Lake
Hobson Lake
Knewstubb Lake (Kenney Dam)
Big Bend Arm
Lucas Lake
Johnson Lake
Second Lake
Gluten Lake
Duten Lake
Finger Lake
Willington Lake
Long Lake
Arthur Lake
Yellow Moose Lake
Natalkuz Lake
Entiako Provincial Park
Reservoir
Brewster Lake
Chutanli Lake
Fawnie Dome
Fawnie Nose
Tatelkuz Lake
Tatelkuz Mountain
Suscha Lake
Top Lake
Dog Creek
Kenner Rd.
Stuart River Provincial Park (Upper Site)
Fish Lake N.
Tsan
Barlow Lake Rd.
Braeside
Willowvale
Westar Mill
Engen
Marten Lake
Hasseli
Bearhead Hill
Hidden Mountain Rd.
McCall
Sturgeon Point
Vanderhoof
Vanderhoof Community Museum
Nechako River National Migratory Bird Sanctuary
Geographic Centre of British Columbia
Derksen
Savanovich Rd.
Weneez
Sinkut Falls Rd.
Sinkut River
Saik'uz First Nation
Tachick Lake
Nulki
Nulki Lake
Sinkut Lake
Mapes
Hogsback Lake
McKay Lake
Sinkut Mountain
Welch Lake
Frank Lake
BULKLEY-NECHAKO
Meridian Road/ Vanderhoof Provincial Ecological Reserve
Chilako River Provincial Ecological Reserve
Finger - Tatuk Provincial Park
Tatuk Lake
Tatuk Hills
Mountain Lake
Lavoie Lake
NECHAKO
PLATEAU
Hay Lake
Vance Lake
Turff Lake
Harp Lake
Cory Lake
Badley Lake
Kluskus-Euchiniko FS Rd.
Klunchatistli Lake
Batnuni Lake
Comstock Lake
Snag Lake
Boat Lake
Hanham Lake
Chuniar Lake
Kluskus-Salamander FS Rd.
Swede Creek
Marcel Hills
Titetown Lake
Nechako Range
Kluskus-Ootsa
(Kluskus-Jerryboy FS Rd.)
Heritage Trail

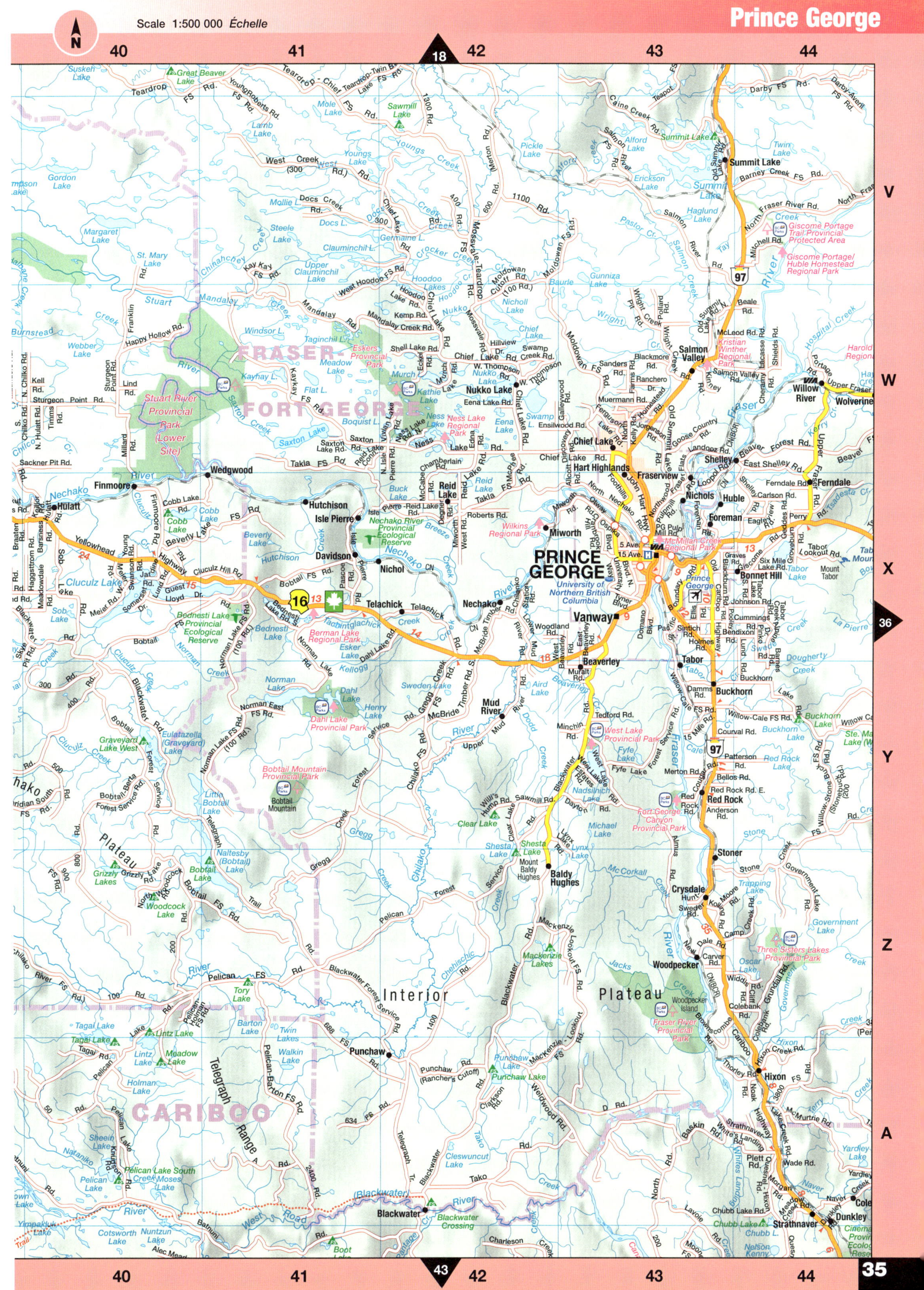
Scale 1:500 000 Échelle
N
40
41
42
43
44
18
36
43
V
W
X
Y
Z
A
PRINCE GEORGE
University of Northern British Columbia
Summit Lake
Salmon Valley
Willow River
Wolverine
Chief Lake
Hart Highlands
Fraserview
Shelley
Ferndale
Nichols
Huble
Foreman
Miworth
Bonnet Hill
Vanway
Nechako
Beaverley
Tabor
Buckhorn
Red Rock
Stoner
Crysdale
Woodpecker
Hixon
Strathnaver
Dunkley
Cole
Baldy Hughes
Mud River
Punchaw
Blackwater
Telachick
Nichol
Davidson
Isle Pierre
Hutchison
Wedgwood
Finmoore
Hulatt
Nukko Lake
Reid Lake
FRASER-FORT GEORGE
CARIBOO
Interior
Plateau
Telegraph Range
Stuart River Provincial Park (Lower Site)
Eskers Provincial Park
Ness Lake Regional Park
Wilkins Regional Park
McMillan Creek Regional Park
Kristian Winther Regional Park
Giscome Portage Trail Provincial Protected Area
Giscome Portage/Huble Homestead Regional Park
Nechako River Provincial Ecological Reserve
Bednesti Lake Provincial Ecological Reserve
Berman Lake Regional Park
Dahl Lake Provincial Park
Bobtail Mountain Provincial Park
West Lake Provincial Park
Fort George Canyon Provincial Park
Fraser River Provincial Park
Three Sisters Lakes Provincial Park
Yellowhead Highway
Nechako River
Fraser River
Blackwater River
97
16

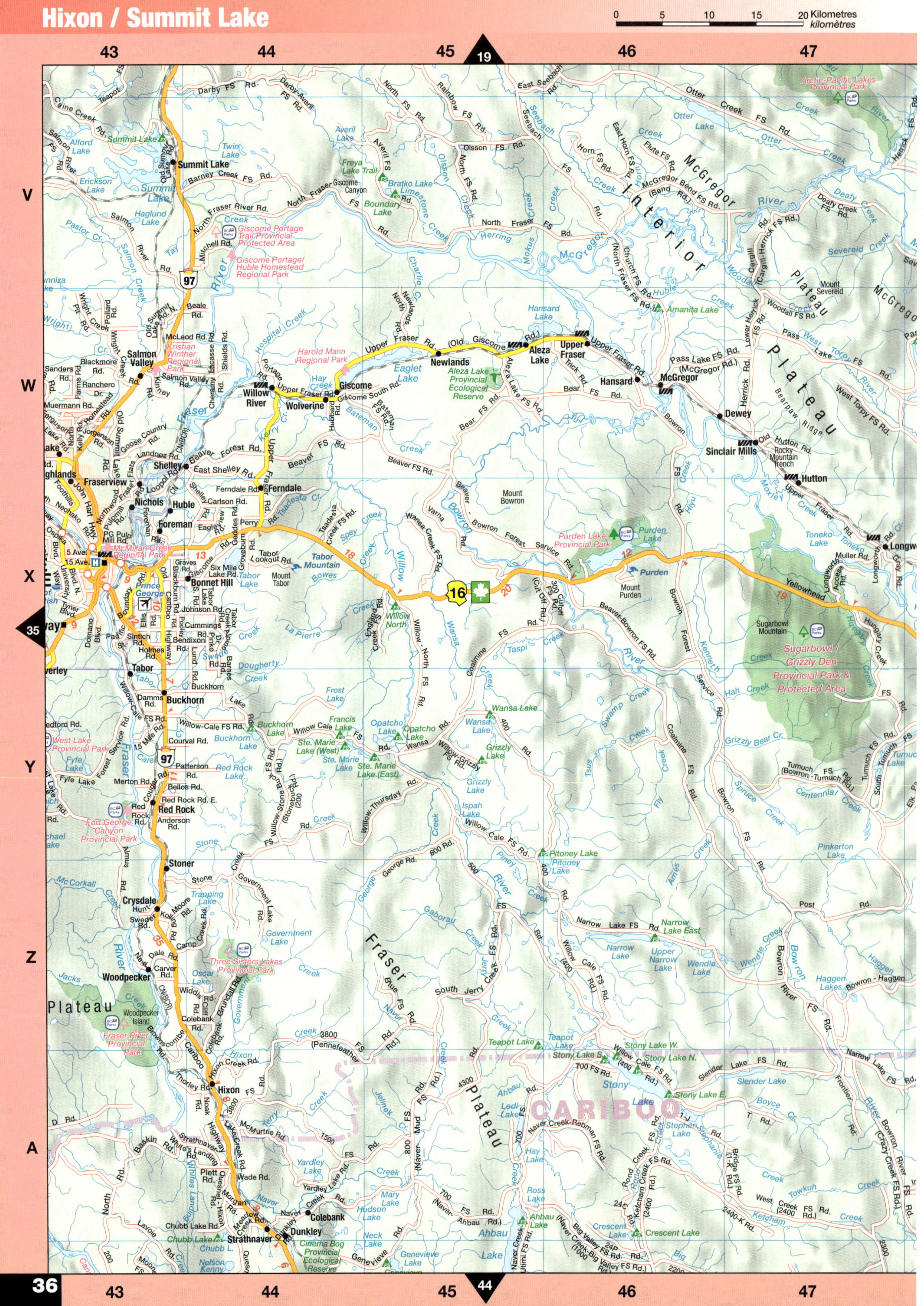
0 5 10 15 20 Kilometres
kilomètres
43
44
45
46
47
19
V
W
X
Y
Z
A
35
44
Summit Lake
Summit Lake
Salmon Valley
Willow River
Wolverine
Giscome
Newlands
Aleza Lake
Upper Fraser
Hansard
McGregor
Dewey
Sinclair Mills
Hutton
Longworth
Shelley
Ferndale
Fraserview
Nichols
Huble
Foreman
Bonnet Hill
Prince George
Tabor
Buckhorn
Red Rock
Stoner
Crysdale
Woodpecker
Hixon
Strathnaver
Colebank
Dunkley
McGregor Interior Plateau
Fraser Plateau
Cariboo
Harold Mann Regional Park
Giscome Portage Trail Provincial Protected Area
Giscome Portage/ Huble Homestead Regional Park
Kristian Winther Regional Park
McMillan Creek Regional Park
Aleza Lake Provincial Ecological Reserve
Purden Lake Provincial Park
Purden Lake
Sugarbowl Mountain
Sugarbowl / Grizzly Den Provincial Park & Protected Area
Arctic Pacific Lakes Provincial Park
West Lake Provincial Park
Fort George Canyon Provincial Park
Three Sisters Lakes Provincial Park
Fraser River Provincial Park
Cinema Bog Provincial Ecological Reserve
Tabor Mountain
Mount Tabor
Mount Purden
Mount Bowron
Mount Severeid
Eaglet Lake
Tabor Lake
Wansa Lake
Grizzly Lake
Pitoney Lake
Stony Lake
Ahbau Lake
Narrow Lake
Teapot Lake
Hansard Lake
Amanita Lake
Bratko Lake
Averil Lake
Freya Lake Trail
Boundary Lake
Twin Lake
Alford Lake
Erickson Lake
Haglund Lake
Otter Lake
Tumuch Lake
Pinkerton Lake
Hoggen Lakes
Slender Lake
Crescent Lake
Chubb Lake
Government Lake
Trapping Lake
Ste. Marie Lake (East)
Ste. Marie Lake (West)
Opatcho Lake
Francis Lake
Frost Lake
Buckhorn Lake
Red Rock Lake
Fyfe Lake
Yardley Lake
Mary Lake
Hudson Lake
Neck Lake
Genevieve Lake
Ross Lake
Hay Lake
Lodi Lake
Stephen Lake
Boyce Lake
Wendle Lake
Upper Narrow Lake
Narrow Lake East
Yellowhead
97
16
Upper Fraser Rd.
Bowron River
Willow River
McGregor River
Fraser River
Salmon River
Naver Creek
Ahbau Creek
Otter Creek FS Rd.
Pass Lake FS Rd.
Beaver Forest Rd.
Beaver FS Rd.
Willow-Cale FS Rd.
Willow North FS Rd.
Coalmine FS Rd.
Hixon Creek Rd.
Strathnaver

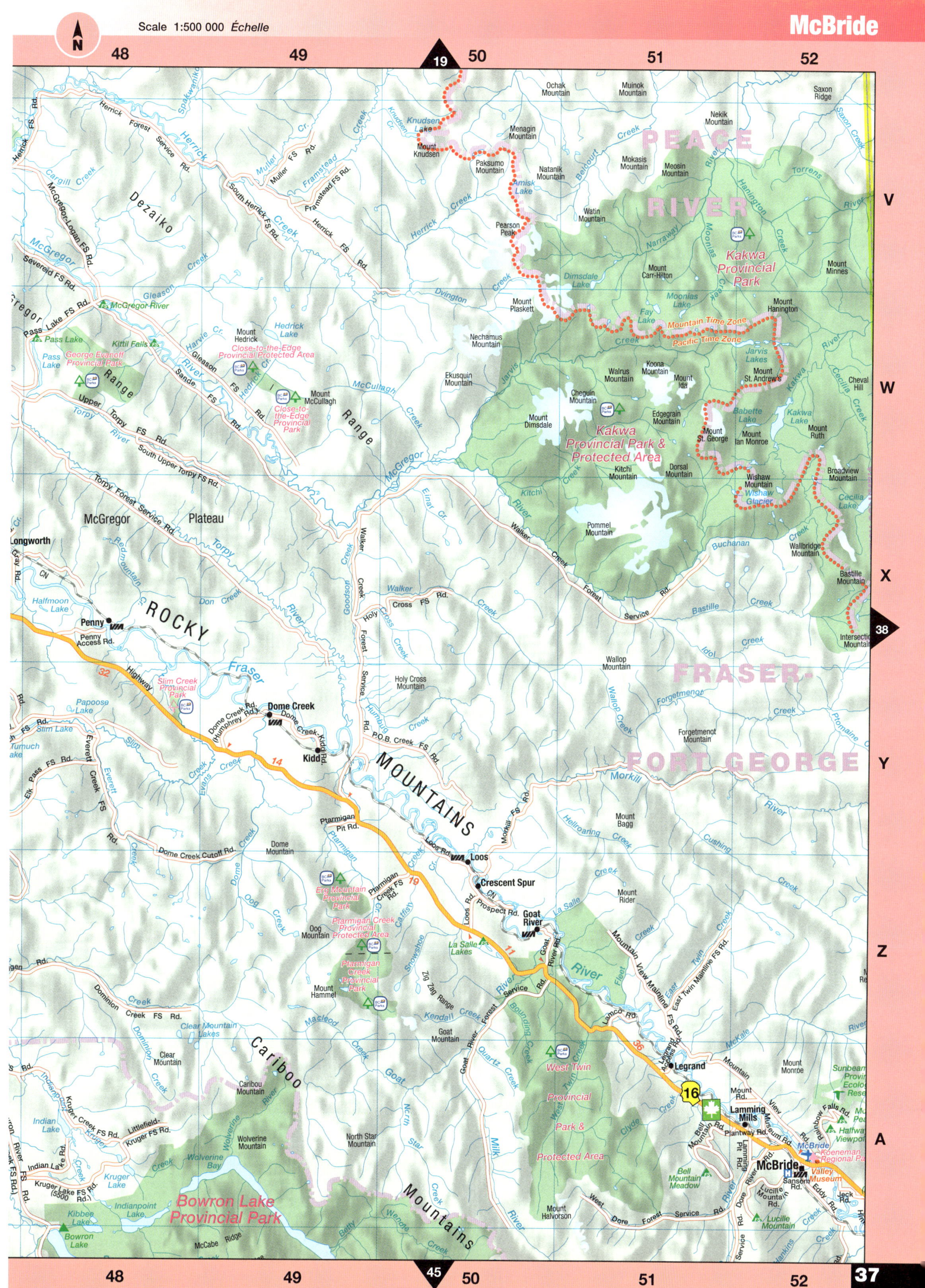
Scale 1:500 000 Échelle
N
48
49
50
51
52
19
38
45
V
W
X
Y
Z
A
PEACE
RIVER
FRASER-
FORT GEORGE
Kakwa Provincial Park
Kakwa Provincial Park & Protected Area
Mountain Time Zone
Pacific Time Zone
Ochak Mountain
Muinok Mountain
Saxon Ridge
Nekik Mountain
Menagin Mountain
Knudsen Lake
Mount Knudsen
Paksumo Mountain
Natanik Mountain
Mokasis Mountain
Meosin Mountain
Amisk Lake
Pearson Peak
Watin Mountain
Dimsdale Lake
Mount Carr-Hilton
Moonias Lake
Mount Minnes
Mount Plaskett
Fay Lake
Mount Hanington
Nechamus Mountain
Jarvis Lakes
Ekusquin Mountain
Walrus Mountain
Koona Mountain
Mount Ida
Mount St. Andrew's
Cheval Hill
Chequin Mountain
Mount Dimsdale
Edgegrain Mountain
Babette Lake
Kakwa Lake
Mount St. George
Mount Ian Monroe
Mount Ruth
Kitchi Mountain
Dorsal Mountain
Wishaw Mountain
Wishaw Glacier
Broadview Mountain
Cecilia Lake
Pommel Mountain
Wallbridge Mountain
Bastille Mountain
Intersection Mountain
Dezaiko
Range
McGregor River
Pass Lake
Kittl Falls
George Evanoff Provincial Park
Mount Hedrick
Hedrick Lake
Close-to-the-Edge Provincial Protected Area
Mount McCullagh
Close-to-the-Edge Provincial Park
Herrick Forest Service Rd.
South Herrick FS Rd.
Muller FS Rd.
Framstead FS Rd.
Herrick FS Rd.
McGregor-Logan FS Rd.
Severeid FS Rd.
Pass Lake FS Rd.
Upper Torpy FS Rd.
South Upper Torpy FS Rd.
Torpy Forest Service Rd.
Walker Creek Forest Service Rd.
McGregor
Plateau
Longworth
Halfmoon Lake
Penny
Penny Access Rd.
ROCKY
MOUNTAINS
Fraser
Slim Creek Provincial Park
Papoose Lake
Slim Lake
Dome Creek
Dome Creek Rd. (Humphrey Rd.)
Dome Creek-Kidd Rd.
Kidd
Holy Cross FS Rd.
Holy Cross Mountain
P.O.B. Creek FS Rd.
Wallop Mountain
Forgetmenot Mountain
Mount Bagg
Dome Creek Cutoff Rd.
Dome Mountain
Ptarmigan Pit Rd.
Loos Rd.
Loos
Crescent Spur
Prospect Rd.
Goat River
Mount Rider
Erg Mountain Provincial Park
Ptarmigan Creek FS Rd.
Ptarmigan Creek Provincial Protected Area
Oog Mountain
Ptarmigan Creek Provincial Park
La Salle Lakes
Mount Hammel
Zig Zag Range
Goat Mountain
Mountain View Mainline FS Rd.
East Twin Mainline FS Rd.
Lamco Rd.
Clear Mountain Lakes
Clear Mountain
Dominion Creek FS Rd.
Cariboo
Mountains
Caribou Mountain
West Twin Provincial Park & Protected Area
Legrand
Lamming Mills
Mount Monroe
McBride
Valley Museum
Koeneman Regional Park
Bell Mountain Meadow
Lucille Mountain
Mount Halvorson
Dore Forest Service Rd.
Kruger Creek FS Rd.
Littlefield-Kruger FS Rd.
Indian Lake
Kruger Lake
Wolverine Mountain
Wolverine Bay
Kibbee Lake
Indianpoint Lake
Bowron Lake
Bowron Lake Provincial Park
North Star Mountain
McCabe Ridge
CN
VIA
14
16
19
11
32
36

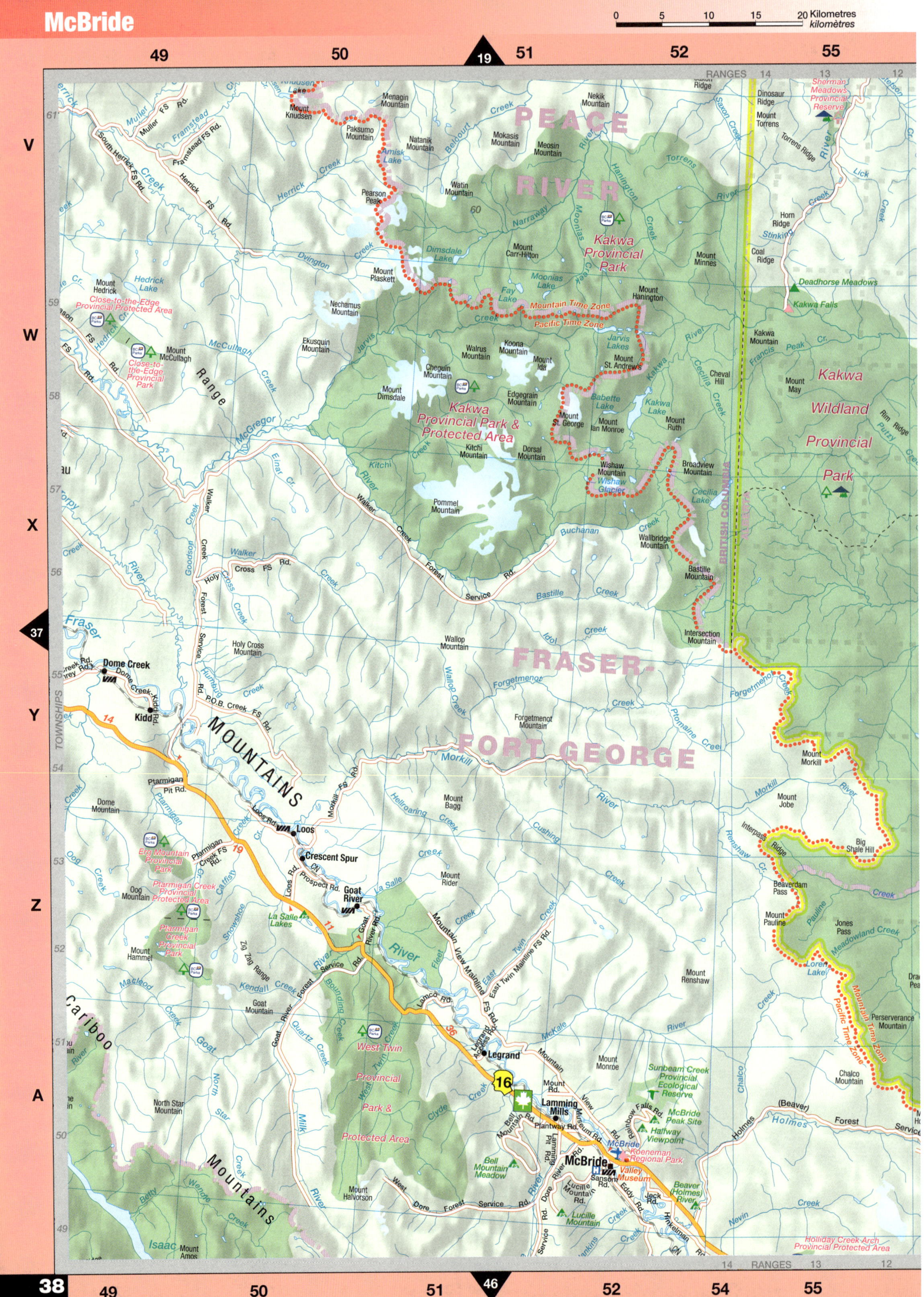
0 5 10 15 20 Kilometres kilomètres
PEACE RIVER
FRASER-FORT GEORGE
Kakwa Provincial Park
Kakwa Provincial Park & Protected Area
Kakwa Wildland Provincial Park
Close-to-the-Edge Provincial Protected Area
Close-to-the-Edge Provincial Park
Erg Mountain Provincial Park
Ptarmigan Creek Provincial Protected Area
Ptarmigan Creek Provincial Park
West Twin Provincial Park & Protected Area
Sunbeam Creek Provincial Ecological Reserve
Holliday Creek Arch Provincial Protected Area
Sherman Meadows Provincial Reserve
Mountain Time Zone
Pacific Time Zone
MOUNTAINS
Cariboo Mountains
McBride
Dome Creek
Kidd
Loos
Crescent Spur
Goat River
Legrand
Lamming Mills
McBride Peak Site
Halfway Viewpoint
Koeneman Regional Park
Valley Museum
Bell Mountain Meadow
Lucille Mountain
Kakwa Falls
Deadhorse Meadows
BRITISH COLUMBIA
ALBERTA
TOWNSHIPS
RANGES
Fraser River
McGregor River
Morkill River
Walker Creek
La Salle Lakes
Mount Knudsen
Mount Torrens
Intersection Mountain
Bastille Mountain
Mount Morkill
Big Shale Hill
Mount Pauline
Jones Pass
Mount Halvorson
North Star Mountain
Goat Mountain
Dome Mountain
Holy Cross Mountain
Wallop Mountain
Forgetmenot Mountain
Mount Bagg
Mount Rider
Mount Renshaw
Mount Monroe
Chalco Mountain
Perserverance Mountain
Isaac
Mount Amos

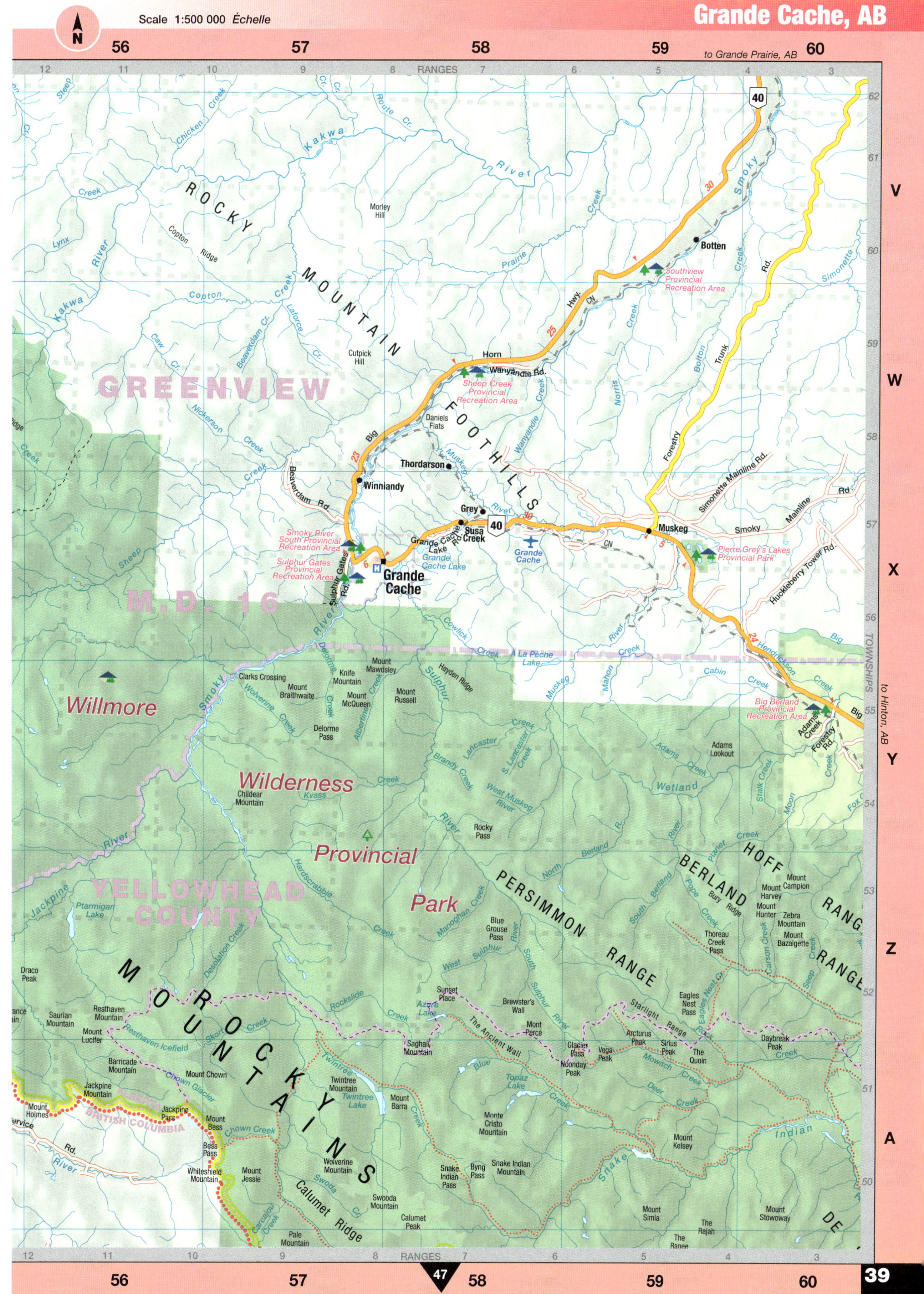

Scale 1:500 000 Échelle
to Grande Prairie, AB
to Hinton, AB
ROCKY MOUNTAIN FOOTHILLS
GREENVIEW
M.D. 16
Willmore Wilderness Provincial Park
YELLOWHEAD COUNTY
ROCKY MOUNTAINS
PERSIMMON RANGE
BERLAND RANGE
HOFF RANGE
Grande Cache
Winniandy
Thordarson
Grey
Susa Creek
Muskeg
Botten
Horn
Southview Provincial Recreation Area
Sheep Creek Provincial Recreation Area
Smoky River South Provincial Recreation Area
Sulphur Gates Provincial Recreation Area
Pierre Grey's Lakes Provincial Park
Big Berland Provincial Recreation Area
Grande Cache Lake
A La Peche Lake
Kakwa River
Smoky River
Sulphur River
Muskeg River
Simonette Mainline Rd.
Huckleberry Tower Rd.
Wanyandie Rd.
Beaverdam Rd.
Forestry Trunk Rd.
Mount Russell
Mount Mawdsley
Mount Braithwaite
Mount McQueen
Knife Mountain
Delorme Pass
Clarks Crossing
Childear Mountain
Rocky Pass
Blue Grouse Pass
Brewster's Wall
Sunset Place
Azure Lake
Saghali Mountain
Mount Chown
Twintree Lake
Mount Barra
Monte Cristo Mountain
Snake Indian Mountain
Byng Pass
Wolverine Mountain
Swoda Mountain
Calumet Peak
Calumet Ridge
Pale Mountain
Mount Jessie
Whiteshield Mountain
Bess Pass
Mount Bess
Jackpine Pass
Jackpine Mountain
Mount Holmes
BRITISH COLUMBIA
ALBERTA
Draco Peak
Saurian Mountain
Resthaven Mountain
Mount Lucifer
Barricade Mountain
Resthaven Icefield
Ptarmigan Lake
Adams Lookout
Mount Campion
Mount Harvey
Mount Hunter
Zebra Mountain
Mount Bazalgette
Thoreau Creek Pass
Eagles Nest Pass
Daybreak Peak
Starlight Range
Arcturus Peak
Sirius Peak
The Quoin
Vega Peak
Glacier Pass
Noonday Peak
Mont Perce
The Ancient Wall
Mount Kelsey
Mount Simla
The Rajah
The Ranee
Mount Stowoway
Cutpick Hill
Morley Hill
Daniels Flats
Copton Ridge
RANGES
TOWNSHIPS

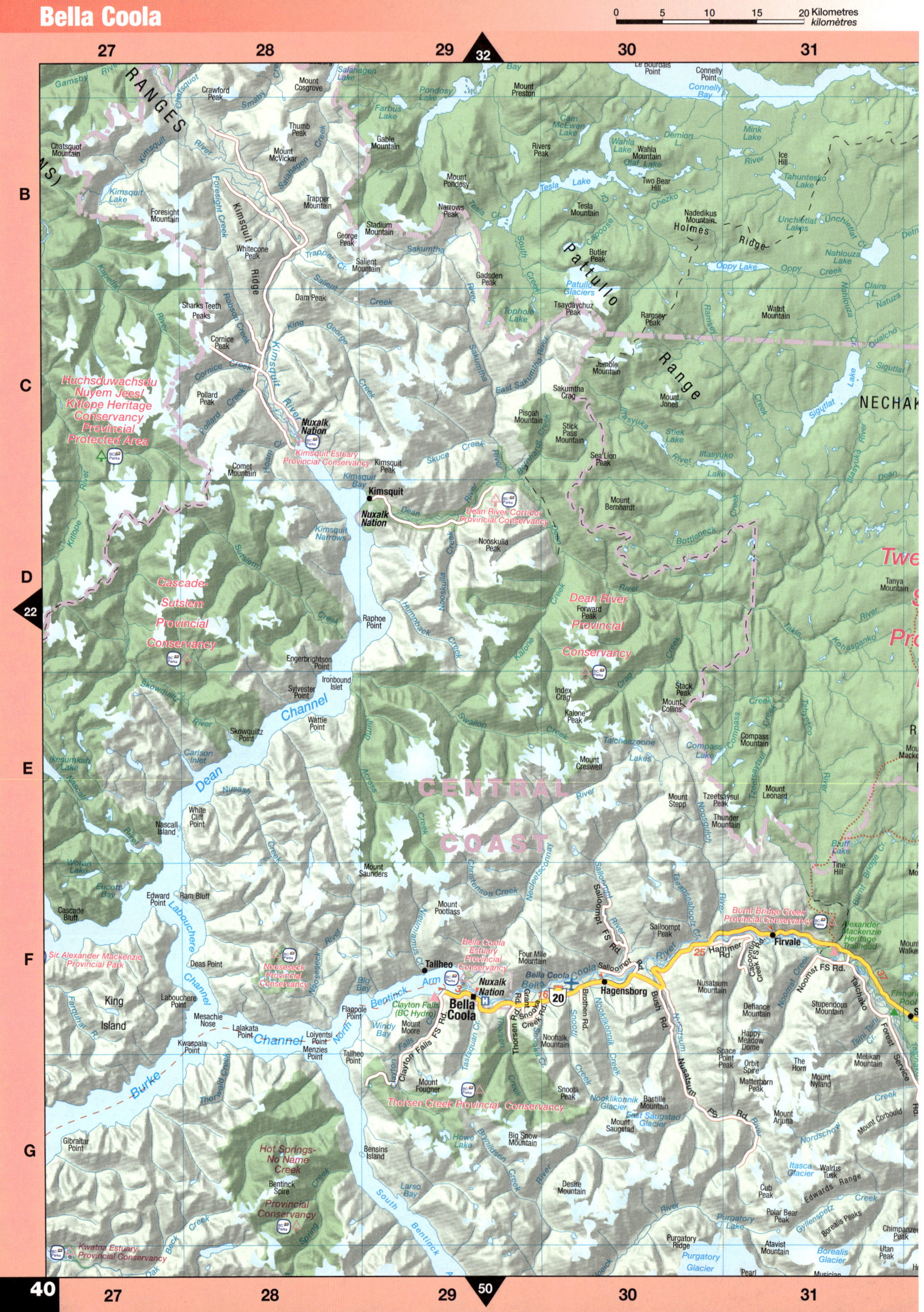
0 5 10 15 20 Kilometres kilomètres
27
28
29
30
31
32
22
50
B
C
D
E
F
G
RANGES
Gamsby River
Chatsquot Mountain
Crawford Peak
Mount Cosgrove
Salahagen Lake
Mount Preston
Le Bourdais Point
Connelly Point
Connelly Bay
Farbus Lake
Pondosy Lake
Cam McEwen Lake
Thumb Peak
Gable Mountain
Mount McVicar
Rivers Peak
Wahla Lake
Wahla Mountain
Olaf Lake
Demion L.
Mink Lake
Ice Hill
Kimsquit Lake
Foresight Mountain
Foresight Creek
Kimsquit Ridge
Trapper Mountain
Mount Pondosy
Tesla Lake
Two Bear Hill
Tahuntesko Lake
Narrows Peak
Tesla Mountain
Chezko
Nadedikus Mountain
Holmes Ridge
Unchietlat Lakes
Unchietlat Cr.
George Peak
Stadium Mountain
Sakumtha
Whitecone Peak
Salient Mountain
Pattullo Range
Butler Peak
Oppy Lake
Oppy Creek
Nahlouza Lake
Dam Peak
Gadsden Peak
Patullo Glaciers
Claire L.
Sharks Teeth Peaks
Tsaydaychuz Peak
Ramsey Peak
Walut Mountain
Tophole Lake
Cornice Peak
Jumble Mountain
Sigutlat Lake
NECHAK
Huchsduwachsdu Nuyem Jees/ Kitlope Heritage Conservancy Provincial Protected Area
Pollard Peak
Sakumtha Crag
Mount Jones
Pisgah Mountain
Stick Pass Mountain
Stick Lake
Nuxalk Nation
Kimsquit Estuary Provincial Conservancy
Kimsquit Peak
Sea Lion Peak
Iltasyuko Lake
Comet Mountain
Kimsquit Bay
Kimsquit
Dean River Corridor Provincial Conservancy
Mount Bernhardt
Kimsquit Narrows
Nooskulla Peak
Bottleneck
Twe
Tanya Mountain
Cascade-Sutslem Provincial Conservancy
Raphoe Point
Dean River Forward Peak Provincial Conservancy
Engerbrighton Point
Ironbound Islet
Sylvester Point
Dean Channel
Wattle Point
Index Crag
Stack Peak
Mount Collins
Kalone Peak
Skowquiltz Point
Carlson Inlet
Tacheeazoone Lakes
Compass Lake
Compass Mountain
Ikesumkah Lake
Mount Creswell
CENTRAL COAST
Mount Leonard
White Cliff Point
Nascall Island
Mount Stepp
Tzeetsaysul Peak
Thunder Mountain
Mount Saunders
Tote Hill
Christenson Creek
Necleetsconnay
Cascade Bluff
Edward Point
Ram Bluff
Mount Pootlass
Burnt Bridge Creek Provincial Conservancy
Alexander Mackenzie Heritage Trailhead
Salloompt Peak
Firvale
Salloompt FS Rd.
Sir Alexander Mackenzie Provincial Park
Deas Point
Nooseseck Provincial Conservancy
Tallheo
Bella Coola Estuary Provincial Conservancy
Four Mile Mountain
Hammer Rd.
Noomst FS Rd.
Nusatsum Mountain
King Island
Labouchere Point
Labouchere Channel
Mesachie Nose
Lalakata Point
Burke Channel
Flagpole Point
Clayton Falls (BC Hydro)
Bella Coola
Nuxalk Nation
Hagensborg
Stupendous Mountain
Defiance Mountain
Windy Bay
Mount Moore
Kwaspala Point
Loiyentsi Point
Menzies Point
North Bentinck Arm
Tallheo Point
Clayton Falls FS Rd.
Noohalk Mountain
Happy Meadow Dome
Space Point Peak
Orbit Spire
Matterhorn Peak
The Horn
Mount Nyland
Melikan Mountain
Mount Fougner
Thorsen Creek Provincial Conservancy
Snootli Peak
Nooklikonnik Glacier
Bastille Mountain
East Saugstad Glacier
Mount Saugstad
Mount Arjuna
Gibraltar Point
Hot Springs-No Name Creek Bentinck Spire Provincial Conservancy
Big Snow Mountain
Howe Lake
Bensins Island
Larso Bay
South Bentinck Arm
Desire Mountain
Itasca Glacier
Walrus Tusk
Cub Peak
Polar Bear Peak
Purgatory Lake
Purgatory Ridge
Purgatory Glacier
Atavist Mountain
Borealis Glacier
Utan Peak
Chimpanzee Peak
Kwatna Estuary Provincial Conservancy
20
25

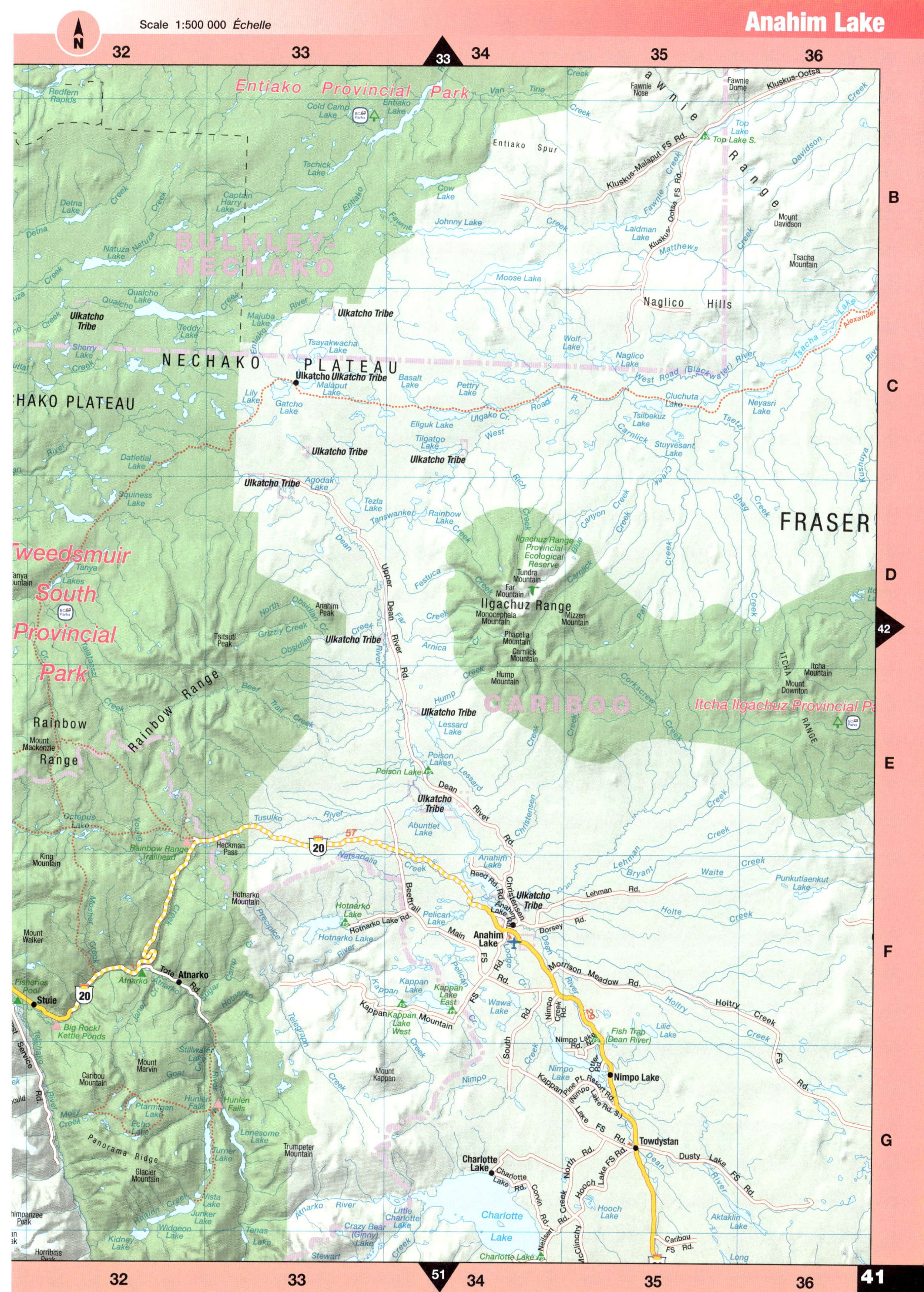
Scale 1:500 000 Échelle
N
32
33
34
35
36
B
C
D
E
F
G
42
51
Entiako Provincial Park
Cold Camp Lake
Entiako Lake
Tschick Lake
Captain Harry Lake
Detna Lake
Natuza Lake
Qualcho Lake
Majuba Lake
Teddy Lake
Sherry Lake
Redfern Rapids
BULKLEY-NECHAKO
Ulkatcho Tribe
NECHAKO PLATEAU
Ulkatcho
Lily Lake
Gatcho Lake
Malaput Lake
Tsayakwacha Lake
Basalt Lake
Pettry Lake
Eliguk Lake
Tilgatgo Lake
Datletlal Lake
Squiness Lake
Agodak Lake
Tezla Lake
Rainbow Lake
Cow Lake
Johnny Lake
Moose Lake
Entiako Spur
Fawnie Nose
Fawnie Dome
Kluskus-Ootsa
Fawnie Range
Top Lake S.
Top Lake
Kluskus-Malaput FS Rd.
Laidman Lake
Mount Davidson
Tsacha Mountain
Naglico Hills
Wolf Lake
Naglico Lake
Cluchuta Lake
West Road (Blackwater) River
Tsilbekuz Lake
Stuyvesant Lake
Neyasri Lake
Ulgako Cr.
FRASER
Tweedsmuir South Provincial Park
Tanya Lakes
Anahim Peak
Tsitsutl Peak
Ilgachuz Range Provincial Ecological Reserve
Tundra Mountain
Far Mountain
Ilgachuz Range
Monocephala Mountain
Mizzen Mountain
Phacelia Mountain
Carnlick Mountain
Hump Mountain
CARIBOO
Itcha Ilgachuz Provincial Park
Itcha Mountain
Mount Downton
ITCHA RANGE
Upper Dean River Rd.
Rainbow Range
Mount Mackenzie
Lessard Lake
Poison Lakes
Poison Lake
Abuntlet Lake
Dean River Rd.
Octopus Lake
Rainbow Range Trailhead
Heckman Pass
King Mountain
Hotnarko Mountain
Hotnarko Lake
Hotnarko Lake Rd.
Pelican Lake
Anahim Lake
Reed Rd.
Christensen Rd.
Lehman Rd.
Punkutlaenkut Lake
Dorsey Rd.
Morrison Meadow Rd.
Holtry Creek FS Rd.
Mount Walker
Atnarko
Tote Rd.
Stuie
Fisheries Pool
Big Rock/ Kettle Ponds
Kappan Lake
Kappan Lake East
Kappan Lake West
Kappan Mountain
Wawa Lake
Nimpo Lake
Nimpo Lake Rd.
Fish Trap (Dean River)
Lilie Lake
Mount Kappan
Mount Marvin
Caribou Mountain
Stillwater Lake
Hunlen Falls
Ptarmigan Lake
Echo Lake
Panorama Ridge
Glacier Mountain
Lonesome Lake
Turner Lake
Trumpeter Mountain
Kappan Lake FS Rd.
Pine Pt. Resort Rd.
Towdystan
Dusty Lake FS Rd.
Charlotte Lake
Charlotte Lake Rd.
Hooch Lake
Aktaklin Lake
Little Charlotte Lake
Crazy Bear (Ginny) Lake
Charlotte Lake
Vista Lake
Junker Lake
Widgeon Lake
Kidney Lake
Tenas Lake
Chimpanzee Peak
Horribitis Peak
Caribou FS Rd.
20
57

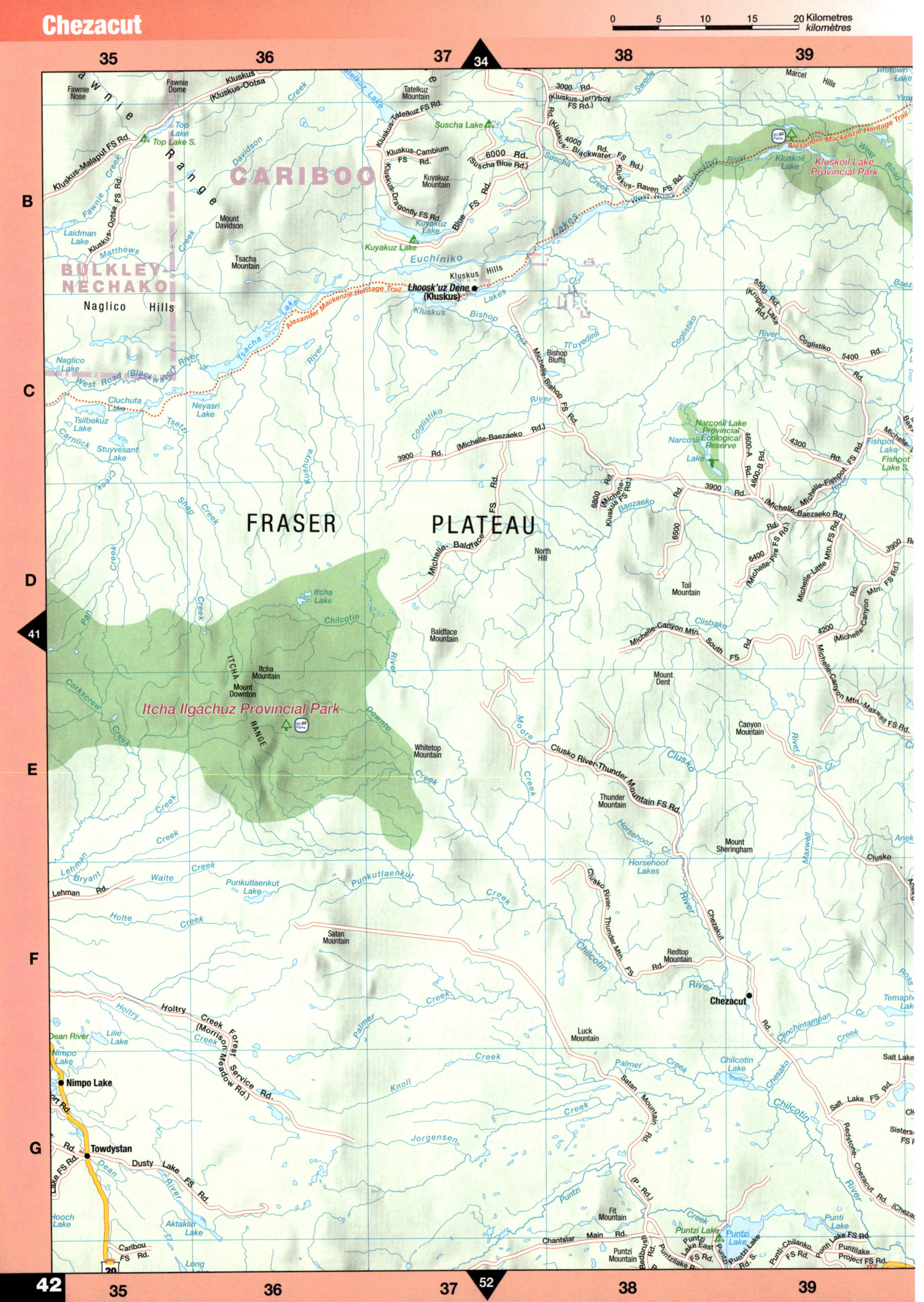

0 5 10 15 20 Kilometres kilomètres
FRASER PLATEAU
CARIBOO
BULKLEY-NECHAKO
Itcha Ilgachuz Provincial Park
Kluskoil Lake Provincial Park
Narcosli Lake Provincial Ecological Reserve
Alexander Mackenzie Heritage Trail
Lhoosk'uz Dene (Kluskus)
Chezacut
Nimpo Lake
Towdystan
Naglico Hills
Kluskus Hills
Fawnie Range
Itcha Range
Fawnie Nose
Fawnie Dome
Mount Davidson
Tsacha Mountain
Tatelkuz Mountain
Kuyakuz Mountain
Itcha Mountain
Mount Downton
Whitetop Mountain
Baldface Mountain
North Hill
Toil Mountain
Mount Dent
Canyon Mountain
Thunder Mountain
Mount Sheringham
Redtop Mountain
Satan Mountain
Luck Mountain
Fit Mountain
Puntzi Mountain
Bishop Bluffs
Top Lake
Top Lake S.
Suscha Lake
Kuyakuz Lake
Laidman Lake
Naglico Lake
Cluchuta Lake
Tsilbekuz Lake
Stuyvesant Lake
Neyasri Lake
Itcha Lake
Narcosli Lake
Kluskoil Lake
Fishpot Lake
Fishpot Lake S.
Punkutlaenkut Lake
Horsehoof Lakes
Chilcotin Lake
Puntzi Lake
Punti Lake
Salt Lake
Nimpo Lake
Lilie Lake
Aktaklin Lake
Hooch Lake
Euchiniko Lakes
Tsacha Lake
Kluskus Lakes
Blackwater River
Chilcotin River
Clusko River
Dean River
Kushuya River
Coglistiko River
Baezaeko River
Kluskus-Ootsa FS Rd.
Kluskus-Malaput FS Rd.
Kluskus-Tatelkuz FS Rd.
Kluskus-Cambium FS Rd.
Kluskus-Dragonfly FS Rd.
Blue FS Rd.
6000 Rd. (Suscha Blue Rd.)
3000 Rd. (Kluskus-Jerryboy FS Rd.)
4000 Rd. (Kluskus-Blackwater FS Rd.)
Kluskus-Raven FS Rd.
West Road (Blackwater) River
Michelle-Bishop FS Rd.
3900 Rd. (Michelle-Baezaeko Rd.)
Michelle-Baldface FS Rd.
6800 Rd. (Michelle-Kluskus FS Rd.)
5500 Rd. (Kruger Lake Rd.)
Coglistiko 5400 Rd.
4300 Rd.
Michelle-Fishpot FS Rd.
4600-A Rd.
4600-B Rd.
6400 Rd. (Michelle-Fire FS Rd.)
Michelle-Little Mtn. FS Rd.
Michelle-Canyon Mtn. South FS Rd.
4200 Rd. (Michelle-Canyon Mtn.)
Michelle-Canyon Mtn.-Maxwell FS Rd.
Clusko River-Thunder Mountain FS Rd.
Clusko River-Thunder Mtn. FS Rd.
Chezakut Rd.
Satan Mountain Rd. (P-Rd.)
Holtry Creek Forest Service Rd. (Morrison Meadow Rd.)
Dusty Lake FS Rd.
Caribou FS Rd.
Chantslar Main Rd.
Redstone-Chezacut Rd.
Salt Lake FS Rd.
Puntzi Lake East FS Rd.
Punti-Chilanko FS Rd.
Puntilake Project FS Rd.
Lehman Rd.
20
35 36 37 38 39
B C D E F G
34 41 52

Scale 1:500 000 Échelle

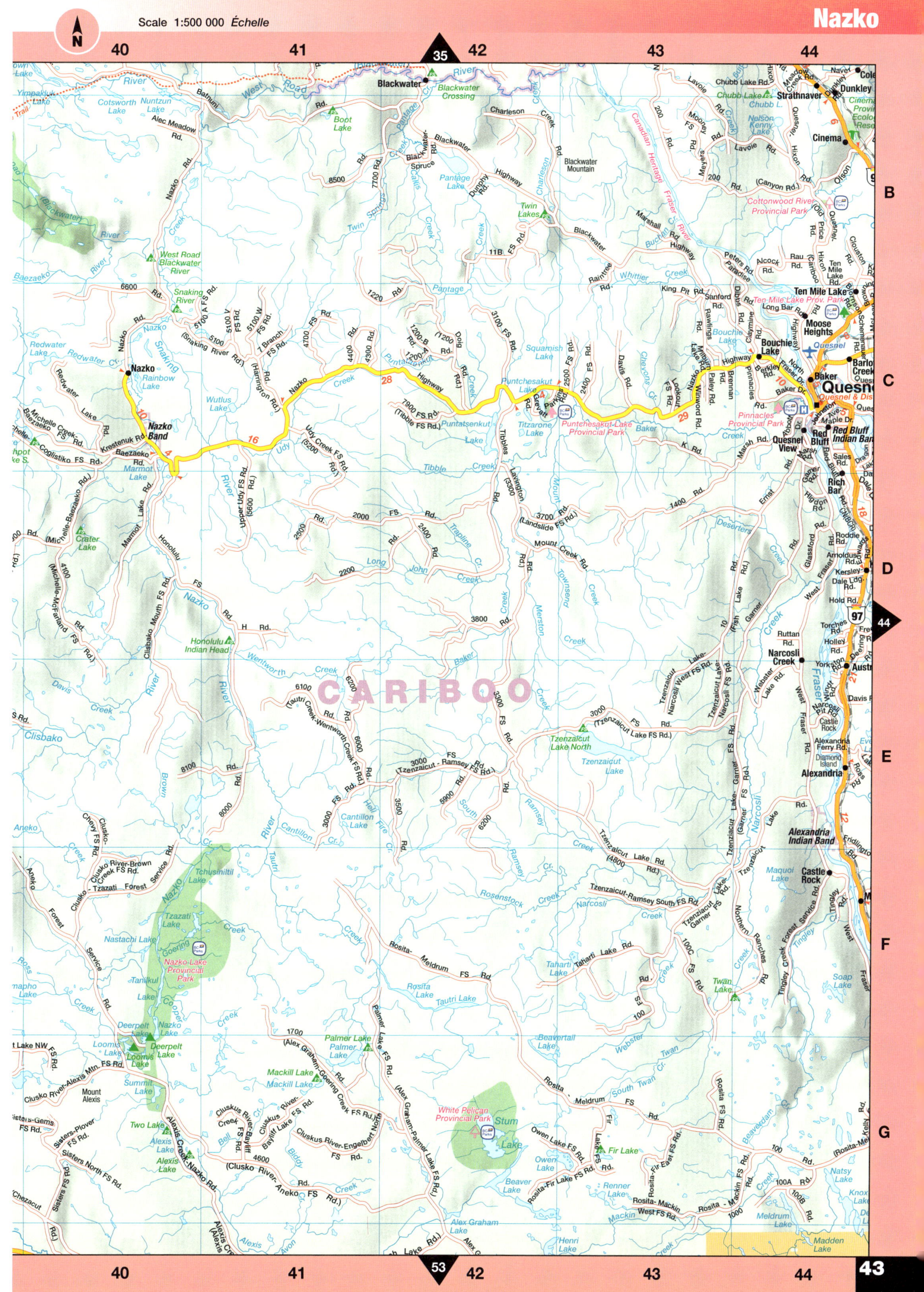

0 5 10 15 20 Kilometres kilomètres
43
44
45
46
47
36
54
B
C
D
E
F
G
Colebank
Dunkley
Strathnaver
Cinema
Cinema Bog Provincial Ecological Reserve
Greening
Cottonwood River Provincial Park
Genevieve Lake
Ahbau Lake
Crescent Lake
Two Sisters Mountain
Hardscrabble Mountain
DISTRICT MUN. OF WELLS
Wells
Wells Historic Museum
Barkerville
Barkerville Provincial Park
Jack of Clubs Lake
Richfield
Richfield Mountain
Island Mountain
Dragon Mountain
Troll Mountain
Pinegrove Mountain
Beaver Pass
Pinegrove
Wingdam
Stanley
Van Winkle
Grub Mountain
Elk Mountain
Bald Mountain
Sovereign Mountain
Bellos
Ten Mile Lake
Ten Mile Lake Prov. Park
Cotwood
Moose Heights
Bouchie Lake
Barlow
Barlow Creek
Cottonwood
Cottonwood House Historic Site
Coldspring House
Lightning Creek
Quesnel
Baker
Quesnel & District Museum
Pinnacles Provincial Park
Quesnel View
Red Bluff
Red Bluff Indian Band
Dragon Lake
Rich Bar
Dragon Mountain
Fraser Plateau
Benson Lake
Robertson Lake
Gravelle Ferry
Kersley
Sundberg Lake
Cariboo Mountain
Keithley Creek Mountain
Duck Creek Mountain
Meridian Mountain
Nyland Lake
Maud Lake
Kangaroo Mountain
Le Bourdais Lake
Beavermouth
Narcosli Creek
Australian
Alexandria
Alexandria Indian Band
Slide Mountain
Quesnel Forks
Quesnel Forks Ghost Town
Forks Mountain
Likely
Cedar Point Provincial Park
Jackpine Lake
Little Lake
Morehead Lake
Bootjack Lake
Jacobie Lake
Polley Lake
Wolverine L.
Castle Rock
Marguerite
Granite Mountain
Macalister
McLeese Lake
UBC Alex Fraser Research Forest (Gavin Lake Block)
Gavin Lake
Big Lake Ranch
Soda Creek
Xat'sull First Nation
Hargreaves
Potato Mountain
Miocene
Ochiltree
Pine Valley
Williams Lake
Comer
Madden Lake
Fir Lake
Twan Lake
Spokin Lake
Dugan Lake
Dewar Lake

Scale 1:500 000 Échelle

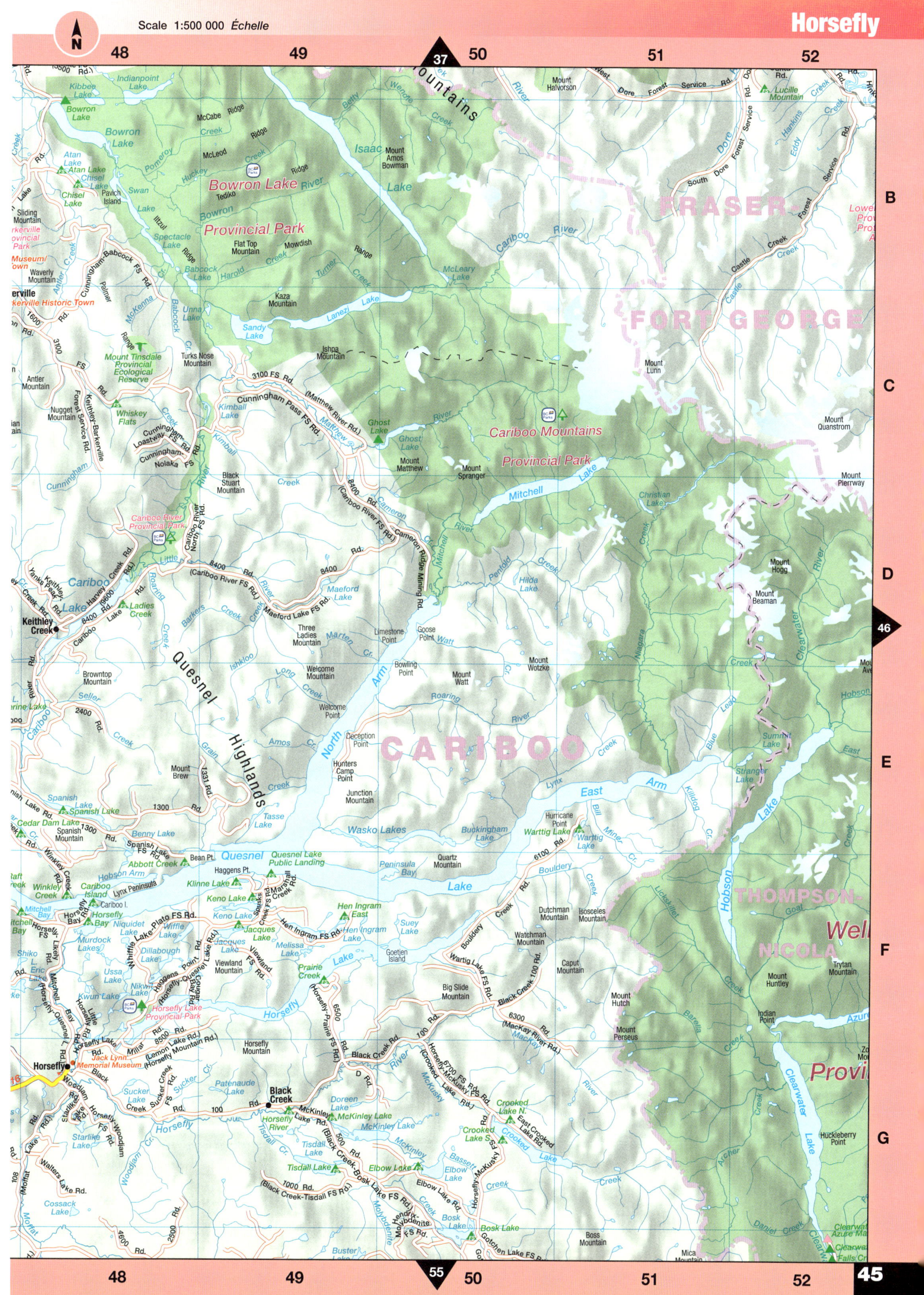

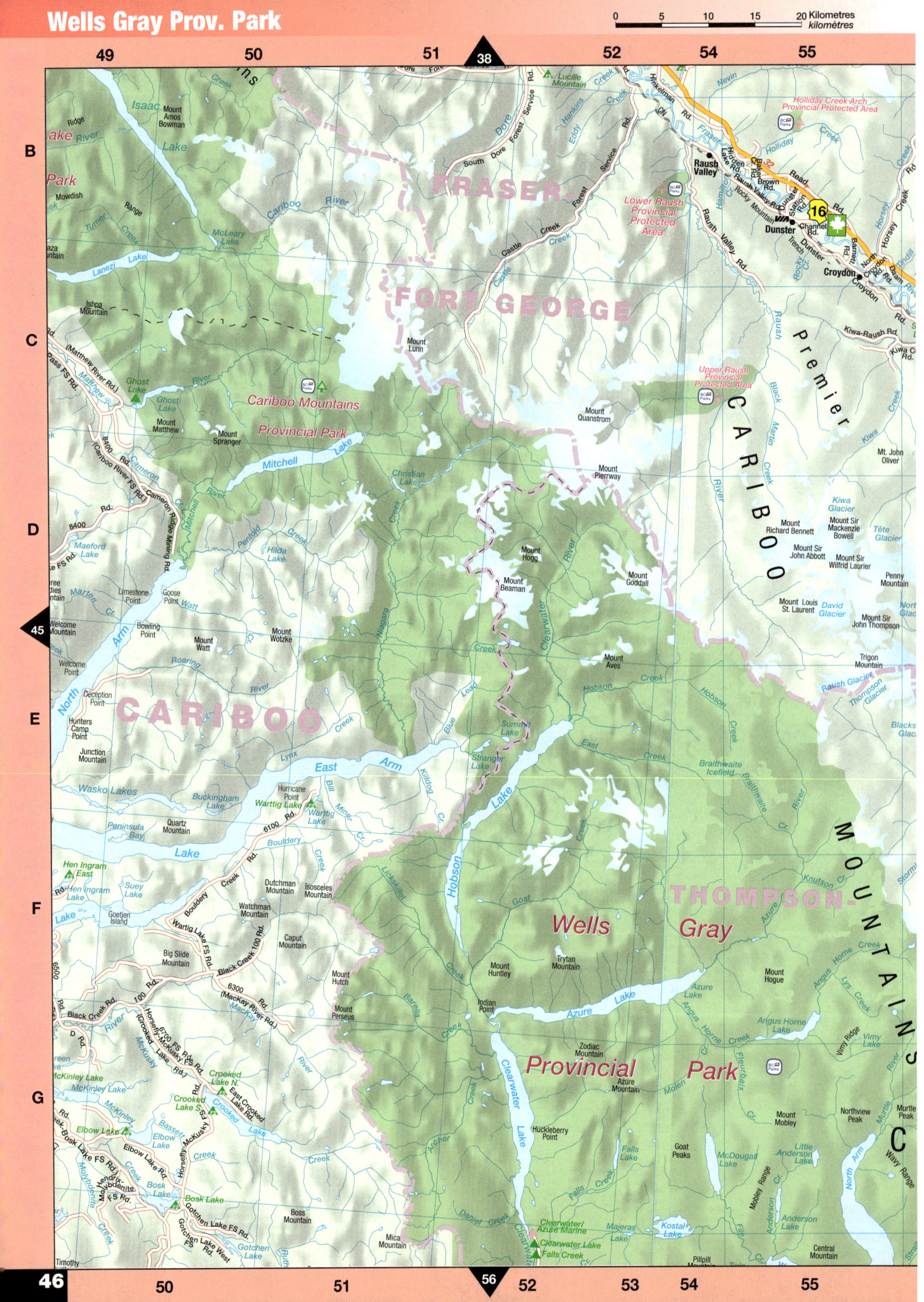

Kilometres kilomètres
0 5 10 15 20
Fraser-Fort George
Cariboo Mountains Provincial Park
Cariboo
Wells Gray Provincial Park
Thompson-Nicola
Premier
Cariboo Mountains
Mitchell Lake
Isaac Lake
Lanezi Lake
Quesnel Lake
East Arm
North Arm
Azure Lake
Clearwater Lake
Hobson Lake
Murtle Lake
Dunster
Croydon
Raush Valley
Lower Raush Provincial Protected Area
Upper Raush Provincial Protected Area
Holliday Creek Arch Provincial Protected Area
Mount Pierrway
Mount Quanstrom
Mount Lunn
Mount Hogg
Mount Beaman
Mount Goddall
Mount Aves
Mount Sprange
Mount Matthew
Mount Watt
Mount Wotzke
Trytan Mountain
Zodiac Mountain
Azure Mountain
Mount Huntley
Mount Hogue
Mount Mobley
Northview Peak
Murtle Peak
Mount Sir Wilfrid Laurier
Mount Sir John Abbott
Mount Sir John Thompson
Mount Sir Mackenzie Bowell
Mount Richard Bennett
Mount Louis St. Laurent
Penny Mountain
Trigon Mountain
Mt. John Oliver
Clearwater/Azure Marine
Clearwater Lake
Falls Creek
Hobson Creek
Braithwaite Icefield
Kiwa Glacier
David Glacier
Raush Glacier
Thompson Glacier
Mica Mountain
Boss Mountain
Caput Mountain
Dutchman Mountain
Isosceles Mountain
Watchman Mountain
Big Slide Mountain
Quartz Mountain
Wasko Lakes
Wartig Lake
Hen Ingram East
Crooked Lake
Elbow Lake
Bosk Lake
McKinley Lake
Ghost Lake

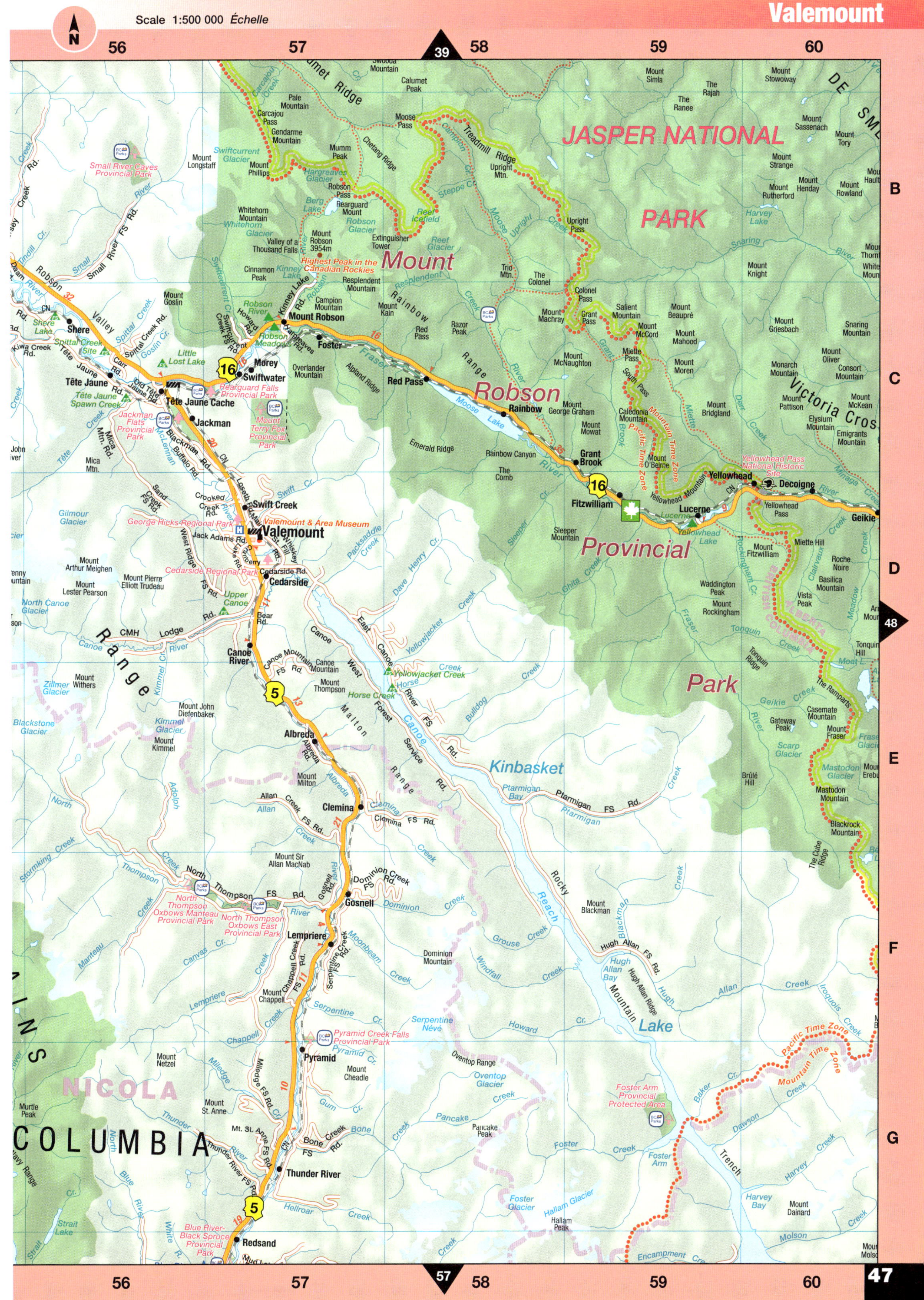
JASPER NATIONAL PARK
Mount Robson Provincial Park
Kinbasket Lake
Valemount
Valemount & Area Museum
Tête Jaune Cache
Tête Jaune
Jackman
Swift Creek
Cedarside
Canoe River
Albreda
Clemina
Gosnell
Lempriere
Pyramid
Thunder River
Redsand
Mount Robson
Highest Peak in the Canadian Rockies
Mount Robson 3954m
Swiftwater
Morey
Foster
Red Pass
Rainbow
Grant Brook
Fitzwilliam
Lucerne
Yellowhead
Decoigne
Geikie
Yellowhead Pass National Historic Site
Yellowhead Lake
Moose Lake
Shere
Small River Caves Provincial Park
Jackman Flats Provincial Park
Rearguard Falls Provincial Park
Mount Terry Fox Provincial Park
George Hicks Regional Park
Cedarside Regional Park
Yellowjacket Creek
Horse Creek
North Thompson Oxbows Manteau Provincial Park
North Thompson Oxbows East Provincial Park
Pyramid Creek Falls Provincial Park
Blue River-Black Spruce Provincial Park
Foster Arm Provincial Protected Area
Pacific Time Zone
Mountain Time Zone
Canoe Range
Malton Range
Overtop Range
Victoria Cross
NICOLA
COLUMBIA
Rocky Mountain Trench

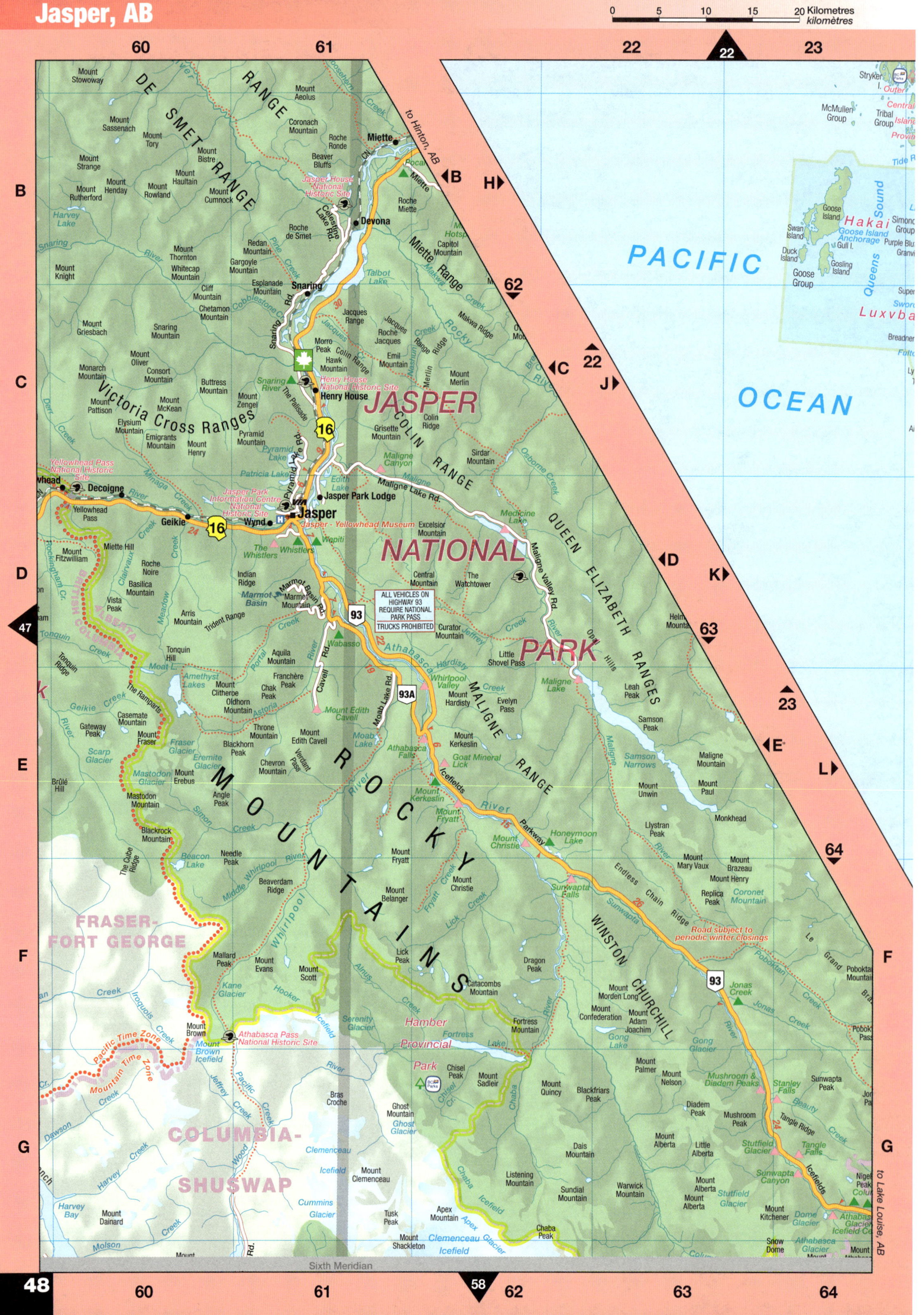
0 5 10 15 20 Kilometres kilomètres
PACIFIC
OCEAN
JASPER
NATIONAL
PARK
ROCKY MOUNTAINS
Jasper
Jasper Park Lodge
Jasper - Yellowhead Museum
Jasper Park Information Centre National Historic Site
Jasper House National Historic Site
Henry House National Historic Site
Henry House
Yellowhead Pass National Historic Site
Athabasca Pass National Historic Site
Miette
Devona
Snaring
Decoigne
Geikie
Wynd
to Hinton, AB
to Lake Louise, AB
ALL VEHICLES ON HIGHWAY 93 REQUIRE NATIONAL PARK PASS
TRUCKS PROHIBITED
Road subject to periodic winter closings
Icefields Parkway
Maligne Lake Rd.
Maligne Lake
Medicine Lake
Pyramid Lake
Patricia Lake
Edith Lake
Talbot Lake
Moab Lake
Beauvert Lake
DE SMET RANGE
Victoria Cross Ranges
COLIN RANGE
QUEEN ELIZABETH RANGES
MALIGNE RANGE
WINSTON CHURCHILL RANGE
Miette Range
Jacques Range
Trident Range
Endless Chain Ridge
Mount Edith Cavell
Athabasca Falls
Sunwapta Falls
Goat Mineral Lick
Honeymoon Lake
Whistlers
Wabasso
Wapiti
Malign Canyon
Hamber Provincial Park
FRASER-FORT GEORGE
COLUMBIA-SHUSWAP
BRITISH COLUMBIA
ALBERTA
Pacific Time Zone
Mountain Time Zone
Sixth Meridian
Hakai
Goose Island
Goose Group
McMullen Group
Tribal Group
Stryker I.
Queens Sound
Luxvbalis
16
93
93A
A B C D E F G
60 61 62 63 64
22 23
47
58

Scale 1:500 000 Échelle
N
24
25
26
27
28
22
61
50
H
J
K
L
M
N
CAMPBELL ISLAND
DENNY ISLAND
KING ISLAND
HUNTER ISLAND
CALVERT ISLAND
CENTRAL COAST
QUEEN CHARLOTTE SOUND
MOUNT WADDINGTON
Namu
Brunswick
Dawsons Landing
Good Hope
Wadhams
Rivers Inlet
Kilbella Bay
Duncanby Landing
Goose Bay
Boswell
Margaret Bay
Nalos Landing
Warner Bay
Kwatna Inlet
Kwatna River
Kwatna Estuary Provincial Conservancy
Codville Lagoon Marine Provincial Park
Codville Lagoon Conservancy
Restoration Bay Provincial Conservancy
Namu Provincial Conservancy
Koeye Provincial Conservancy
Clyak Estuary Provincial Conservancy
Kilbella Estuary Provincial Conservancy
Lockhart-Gordon Provincial Conservancy
Calvert Island Provincial Conservancy
Penrose Island Marine Provincial Park
Ripon Provincial Conservancy
Goose Bay Provincial Conservancy
Cranstown Point Provincial Conservancy
Nekite Estuary Provincial Conservancy
Ugwiwey/Cape Caution-Blunden Bay Provincial Conservancy
Allison Harbour Marine Provincial Park
Fitz Hugh Sound
Fisher Channel
Burke Channel
Hakai Pass
Kwakshua Channel
North Passage
Smith Sound
Smith Inlet
Belize Inlet
Seymour Inlet
Nugent Sound
Moses Inlet
Hardy Inlet
Darby Channel
Draney Inlet
Owikeno Lake
Wannock River
Cape Caution
Egg Island
Table Island
Storm Islands
Southgate
Cape Calvert
Safety Cove
Pruth Bay
Hecate Island
Kelpie Pt.
Koeye Pt.
Ontario Pt.
Kiwash Cove
Warrior Cove
Fougner Bay
Doc Cr.
Gilderssleve Lake
Chuckwalla
Kilbella River
Nelson Narrows
Shotbolt Bay
McPhee Bay
Lewis Range
Mount Robinson
Wilkie Point
Burnett Bay
Bramham Island
Allison Hbr.
Strachan Mainline Rd.
Burnt Island Harbour Mainline Rd.
Wyclees Mainline Rd.
Oner Nallis Mainline Rd.
Smokehouse
Walkum Bay
Mount Annesley
Schwartzenberg Lagoon
Tottenham Range
Mount Manzo Nagano

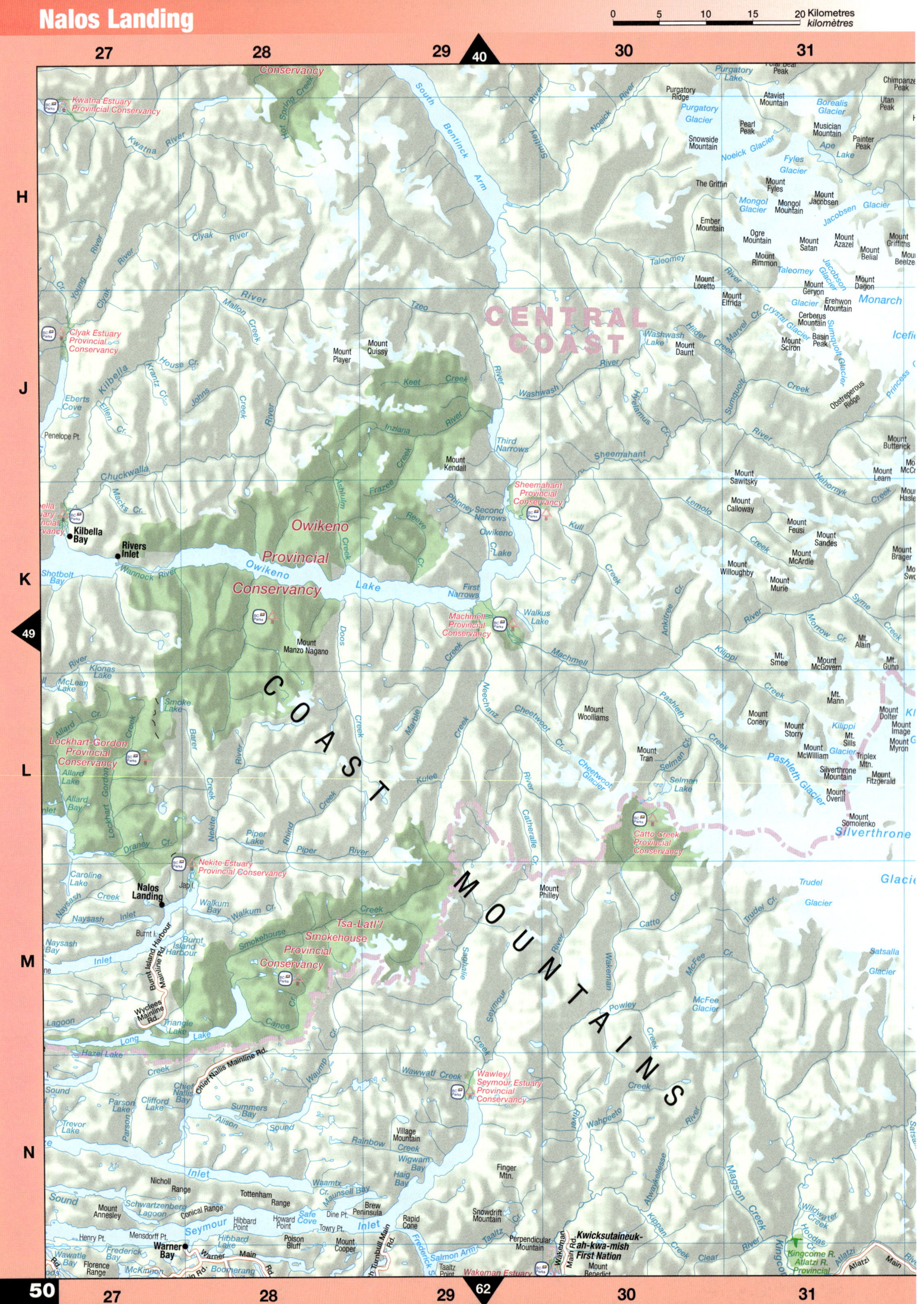
0 5 10 15 20 Kilometres kilomètres
CENTRAL COAST
COAST MOUNTAINS
Owikeno Provincial Conservancy
Owikeno Lake
Rivers Inlet
Kilbella Bay
Nalos Landing
Warner Bay
Lockhart-Gordon Provincial Conservancy
Tsa-Latl'/ Smokehouse Provincial Conservancy
Wawley/ Seymour Estuary Provincial Conservancy
Catto Creek Provincial Conservancy
Machmell Provincial Conservancy
Sheemahant Provincial Conservancy
Nekite Estuary Provincial Conservancy
Clyak Estuary Provincial Conservancy
Kwatna Estuary Provincial Conservancy
Kwicksutaineuk-ah-kwa-mish First Nation
Kingcome R. Atlatzi R. Provincial
Silverthrone Glacier
Monarch Icefield
South Bentinck Arm
Mount Manzo Nagano
Mount Kendall
Mount Player
Mount Quissy
Mount Woolliams
Mount Philley
Finger Mtn.
Snowdrift Mountain
Village Mountain
Purgatory Glacier
Noeick Glacier
Mongol Glacier
Jacobsen Glacier
Fyles Glacier
Borealis Glacier
Pashleth Glacier
Trudel Glacier
Satsalla Glacier
McFee Glacier
Cheetwoot Glacier
Kilippi Glacier
Schwartzenberg Lagoon
Seymour Inlet
Mauneell Bay
Wakeman Estuary
Hot Spring Creek
Conservancy
Penelope Pt.
Shotbolt Bay
Eberts Cove
Naysash Bay
Naysash Inlet
Allard Lake
Allard Bay
Caroline Lake
Piper Lake
Smoke Lake
Klonas Lake
McLean Lake
Hazel Lake
Long Lake
Triangle Lake
Parson Lake
Clifford Lake
Trevor Lake
Chief Nollis Bay
Summers Bay
Wigwam Bay
Haig Bay
Walkum Bay
Burnt Island Harbour
Wyclees Mainline Rd.
Burnt Island Mainline Rd.
Chief Nallis Mainline Rd.
Turnbull Main Rd.
Second Narrows
Third Narrows
First Narrows
Walkus Lake
Washwash Lake
Selman Lake
Purgatory Lake
Mount Annesley
Henry Pt.
Mensdorff Pt.
Florence Range
Nicholl Range
Tottenham Range
Conical Range
Hibbard Point
Howard Point
Poison Bluff
Mount Cooper
Dine Pt.
Towry Pt.
Rapid Cone
Brew Peninsula
Salmon Arm
Perpendicular Mountain
Mount Benedict
Taaltz Point
Mount Sawitsky
Mount Calloway
Mount Willoughby
Mount Murie
Mount Feusi
Mount Sandes
Mount McArdle
Mount Conery
Mount Storry
Mount McWilliam
Mount Tran
Silverthrone Mountain
Mount Overill
Mount Somolenko
Mount Fitzgerald
Triplex Mtn.
Mt. Sills
Mt. Mann
Mt. Smee
Mount McGovern
Mt. Alain
Mt. Gunn
Mount Dolter
Mount Image
Mount Myron
Mount Brager
Mount Learn
Mount Butterick
Obstreperous Ridge
Mount Loretto
Mount Elfrida
Mount Daunt
Mount Sciron
Basin Peak
Cerberus Mountain
Erehwon Mountain
Mount Geryon
Mount Dagon
Mount Belial
Mount Azazel
Mount Satan
Mount Griffiths
Mount Rimmon
Ogre Mountain
Ember Mountain
The Griffin
Mount Fyles
Mongol Mountain
Mount Jacobsen
Snowside Mountain
Pearl Peak
Atavist Mountain
Purgatory Ridge
Musician Mountain
Ape Lake
Painter Peak
Utan Peak
Chimpanzee Peak
Polar Bear Peak

Scale 1:500 000 Échelle

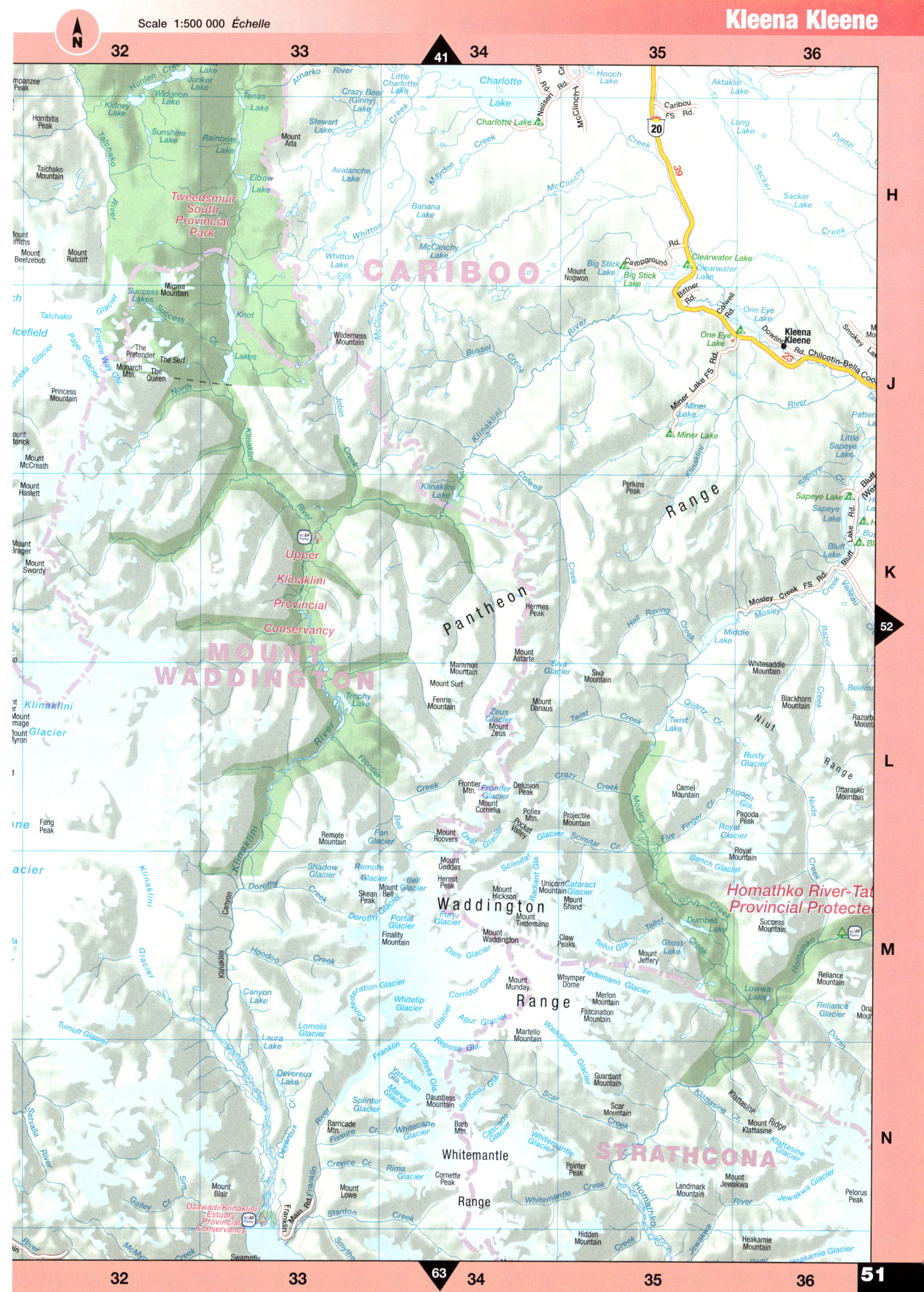

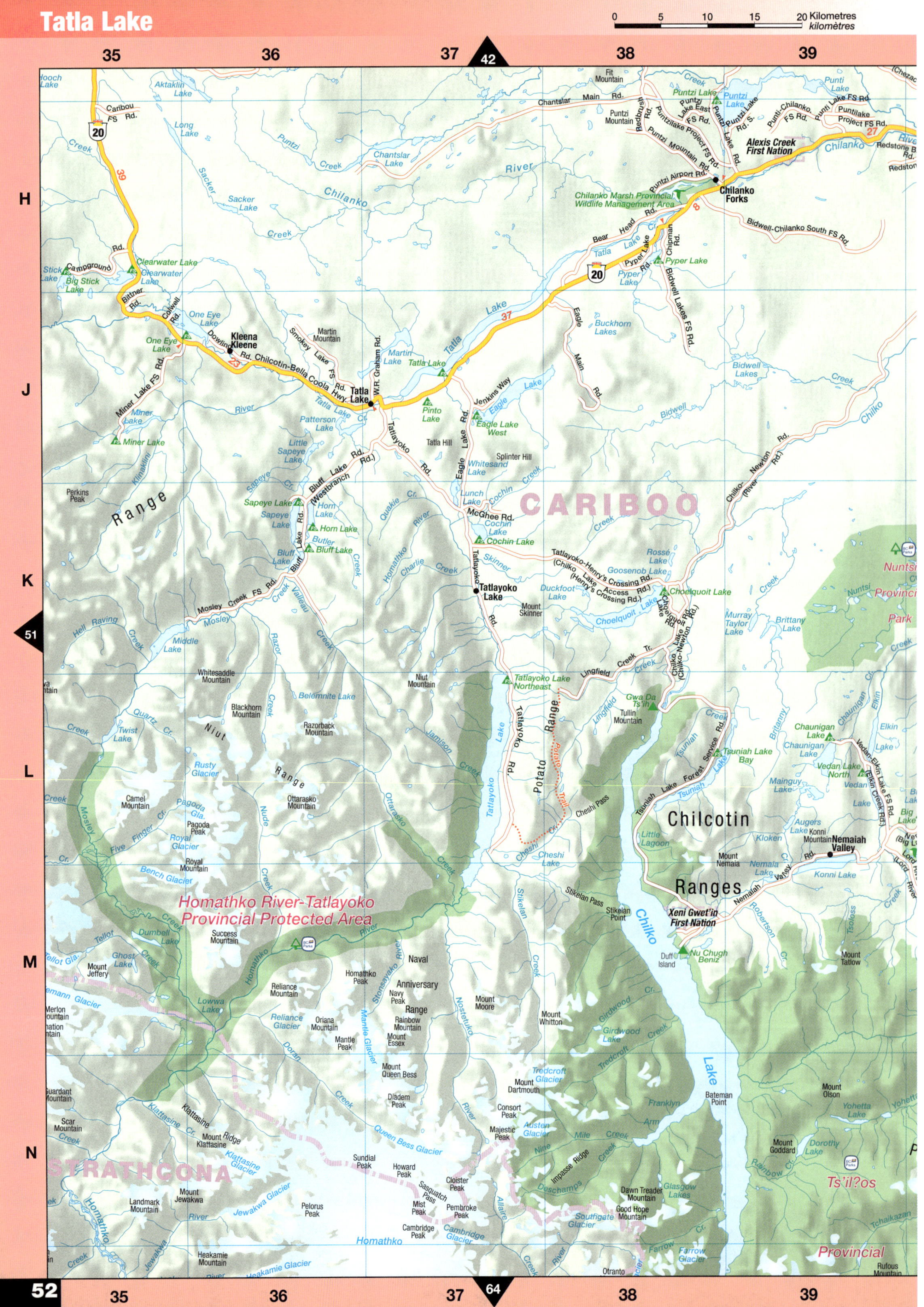
0 5 10 15 20 Kilometres kilomètres
35
36
37
38
39
42
64
51
H
J
K
L
M
N
Tatla Lake
Kleena Kleene
Tatlayoko Lake
Chilanko Forks
Alexis Creek First Nation
Nemaiah Valley
Xeni Gwet'in First Nation
CARIBOO
Chilcotin
Ranges
Niut
Range
Potato Range
Homathko River-Tatlayoko Provincial Protected Area
Chilanko Marsh Provincial Wildlife Management Area
Nuntsi Provincial Park
STRATHCONA
Ts'il?os Provincial
Chilko Lake
Tatlayoko Lake
Tatla Lake
Chilcotin-Bella Coola Hwy.
Puntzi Lake
Eagle Lake
Choelquoit Lake
Konni Lake
Sapeye Lake
Horn Lake
Bluff Lake
Cochin Lake
Pyper Lake
Clearwater Lake
One Eye Lake
Big Stick Lake
Miner Lake
Martin Lake
Patterson Lake
Mount Skinner
Tullin Mountain
Niut Mountain
Whitesaddle Mountain
Mount Nemaia
Mount Tatlow
Mount Moore
Mount Whitton
Mount Dartmouth
Consort Peak
Majestic Peak
Mount Queen Bess
Diadem Peak
Sundial Peak
Howard Peak
Cloister Peak
Sasquatch Pass
Mist Peak
Pembroke Peak
Cambridge Peak
Homathko Peak
Naval
Anniversary
Navy Peak
Range
Rainbow Mountain
Mount Essex
Mantle Peak
Oriana Mountain
Reliance Mountain
Success Mountain
Mount Jeffery
Royal Mountain
Pagoda Peak
Camel Mountain
Ottarasko Mountain
Razorback Mountain
Blackhorn Mountain
Perkins Peak
Mount Ridge Klattasine
Landmark Mountain
Mount Jewakwa
Pelorus Peak
Heakamie Mountain
Otranto
Dawn Treader Mountain
Good Hope Mountain
Mount Goddard
Mount Olson
Bateman Point
Duff Island
Nu Chugh Beniz
Stikelan Pass
Stikelan Point
Cheshi Pass
Cheshi Lake
Gwa Da Ts'ih
Tatlayoko Lake Northeast
Tsuniah Lake Bay
Vedan Lake North
Chaunigan Lake
Queen Bess Glacier
Homathko
Puntzi Airport Rd.
Bidwell-Chilanko South FS Rd.
Tatlayoko-Henry's Crossing Rd.
Mosley Creek FS Rd.
Miner Lake FS Rd.
Tsuniah Lake Forest Service Rd.
Nemaiah Valley Rd.
Chilko-Newton Rd.
Eagle Lake Rd.
Tatlayoko Rd.
McGhee Rd.
Lingfield Creek Tr.
Potato Trail
20
37
23
8
27
39
52

Scale 1:500 000 Échelle

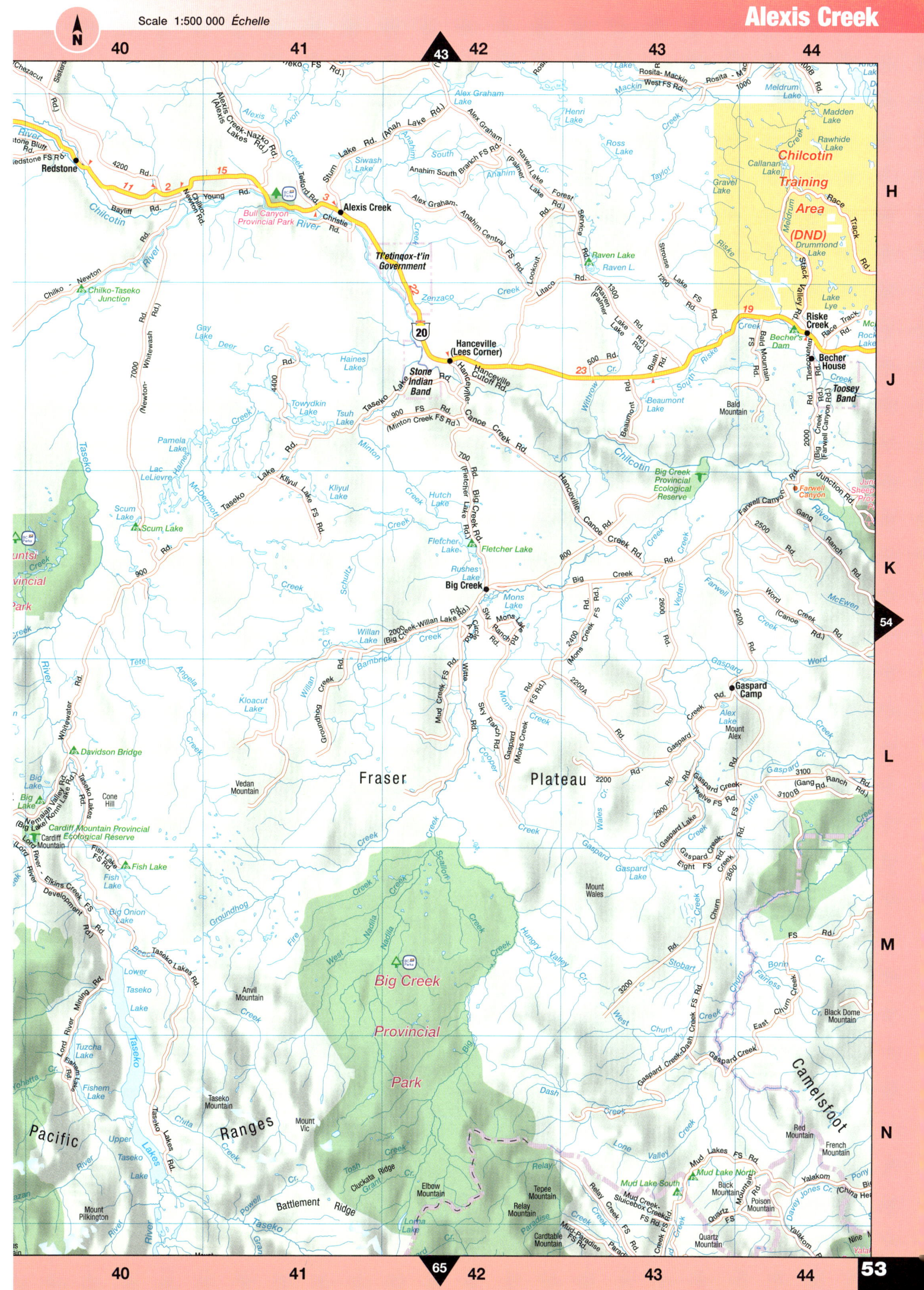

0 5 10 15 20 Kilometres kilomètres
Williams Lake
Chilcotin Training Area (DND)
Riske Creek
Becher House
Toosey Band
McIntyre Lake
Meldrum Creek
South Williams Lake
150 Mile House
Sugarcane
Williams Lake Indian Band
St. Joseph
Mission
141 Mile House
Johnson
Enterprise
Springhouse
127 Mile House
Wright
122 Mile House
Canama
Alkali Lake
Esketemc Band
CARIBOO
Gaspard Camp
Gang Ranch
Dog Creek
Canoe Creek Band
Churn Creek Provincial Protected Area
THOMPSON-NICOLA
Jesmond
Big Bar Creek
Marble Range Provincial Park
Clinton
High Bar First Nation
Camelsfoot Ran
Fraser River
Canadian Heritage Fraser River
Junction Sheep Range Provincial Park
Big Creek Provincial Ecological Reserve
Moose Valley Provincial Park
Lac la Hache Provincial Park
Cariboo Nature Provincial Park
Big Bar Lake Provincial Park
French Bar Creek Provincial Park
UBC Alex Fraser Research Forest (Knife Creek Block)
Museum of the Cariboo Chilcotin
Xat'sull Heritage Village
One Hundred Mile House & Mirage Rock
South Cariboo Historical Museum
Big Bar Reaction Ferry
43 44 45 46 47
H J K L M N
20 97 18 19 15 5 16 14 24 9

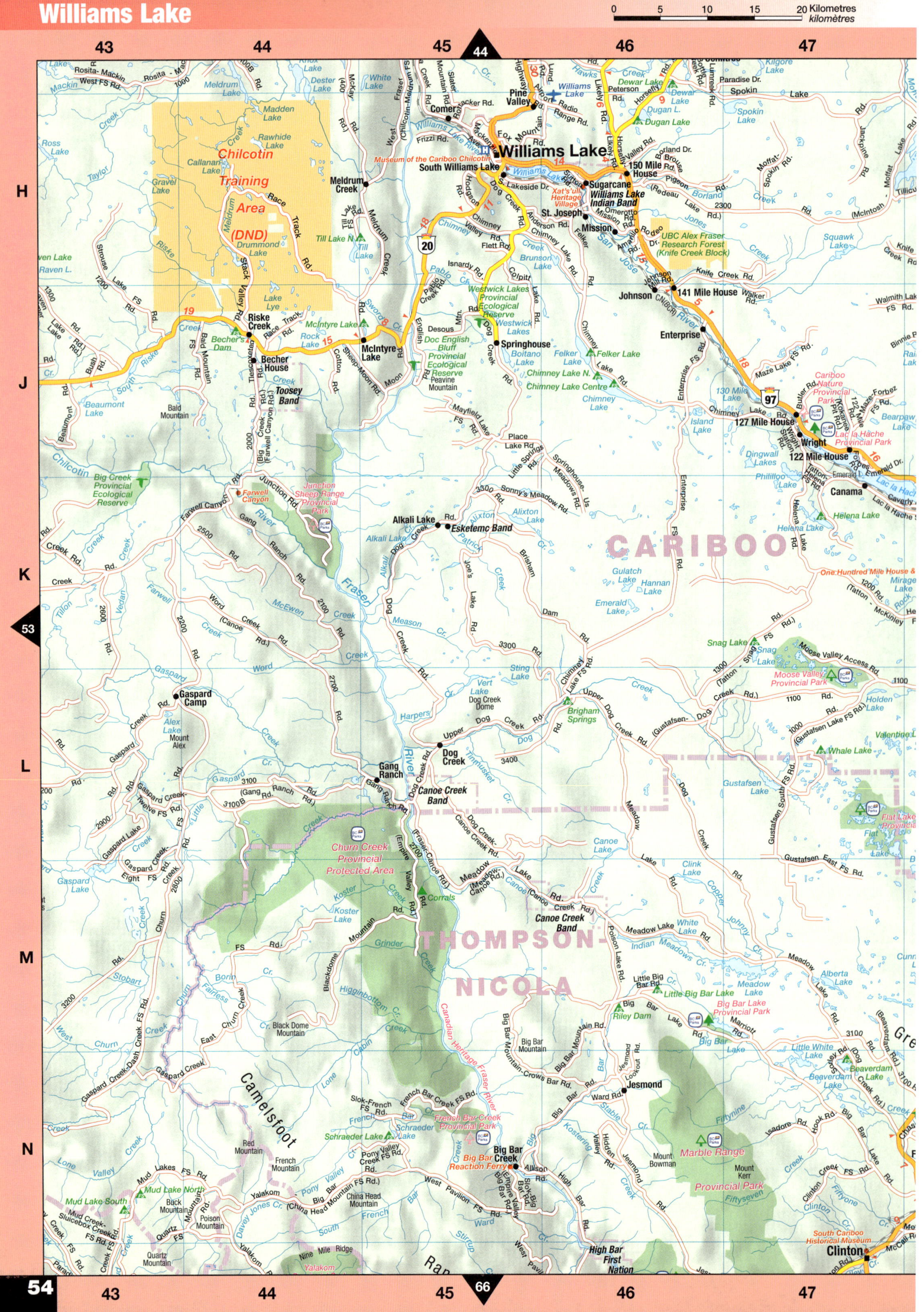

44
53
66

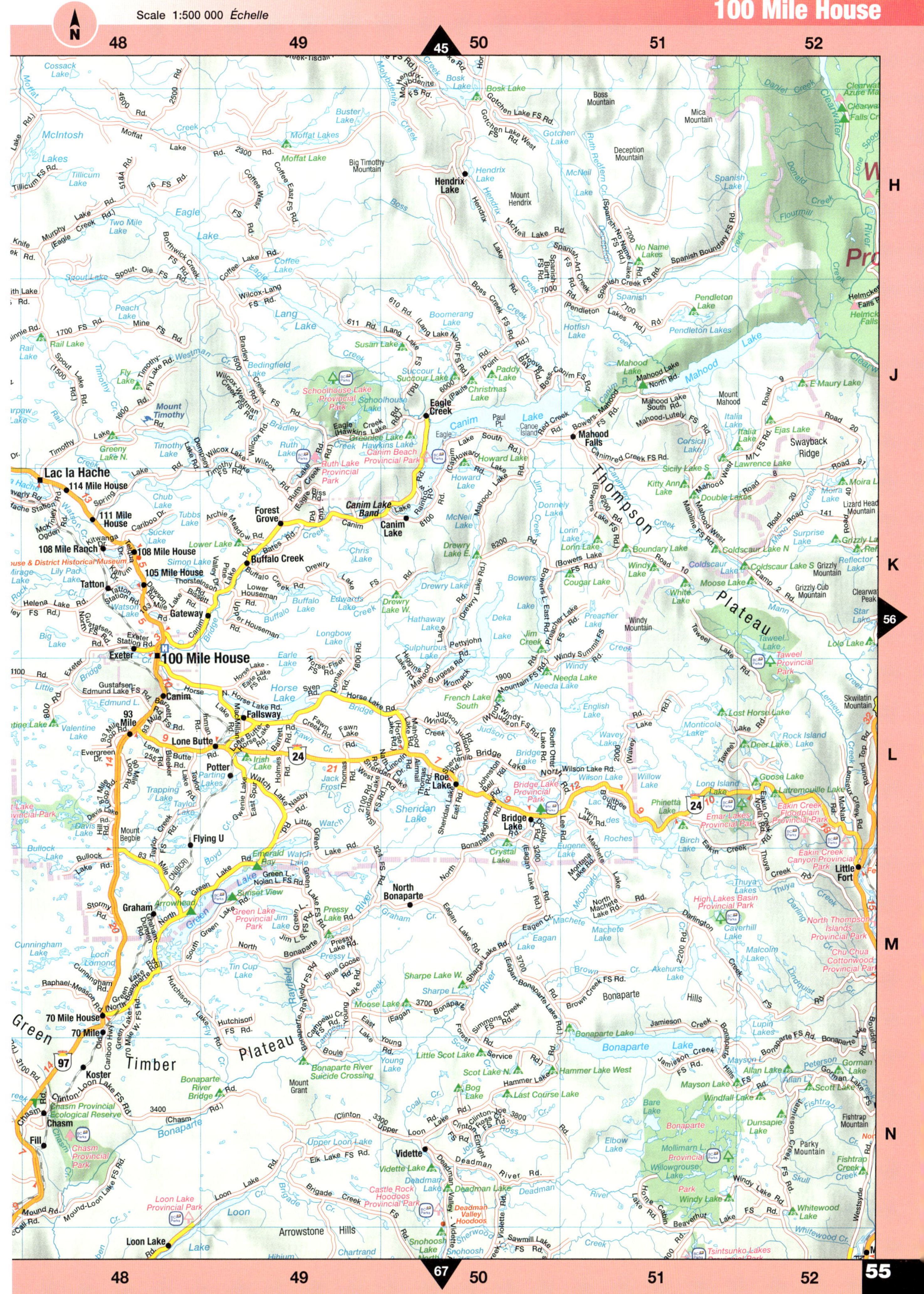

N
Scale 1:500 000 Échelle
48
49
45
50
51
52
H
J
K
56
L
M
N
67
Lac la Hache
114 Mile House
111 Mile House
108 Mile Ranch
108 Mile House
105 Mile House
Tatton
Gateway
Exeter
100 Mile House
Canim
93 Mile
Lone Butte
Potter
Fallsway
Forest Grove
Buffalo Creek
Canim Lake Band
Canim Lake
Eagle Creek
Hendrix Lake
Mahood Falls
Roe Lake
Bridge Lake
Flying U
Graham
North Bonaparte
70 Mile House
70 Mile
Koster
Chasm
Fill
Vidette
Loon Lake
Little Fort
Horse Lake
Sheridan Lake
Canim Lake
Mahood Lake
Bonaparte Lake
Green Lake
Lang Lake
Eagle Lake
Thompson Plateau
Green Timber Plateau
Schoolhouse Lake Provincial Park
Canim Beach Provincial Park
Ruth Lake Provincial Park
Taweel Provincial Park
Bridge Lake Provincial Park
Green Lake Provincial Park
Emar Lakes Provincial Park
Eakin Creek Floodplain Provincial Park
Eakin Creek Canyon Provincial Park
High Lakes Basin Provincial Park
North Thompson Islands Provincial Park
Chasm Provincial Park
Chasm Provincial Ecological Reserve
Loon Lake Provincial Park
Castle Rock Hoodoos Provincial Park
Deadman Valley Hoodoos
Bonaparte Provincial Park
Tsintsunko Lakes Provincial Park
Mount Timothy
Swayback Ridge
Boss Mountain
Mica Mountain
Deception Mountain
Mount Hendrix
Big Timothy Mountain
Mount Begbie
Mount Grant
Windy Mountain
Grizzly Cub Mountain
Skwilatin Mountain
Fishtrap Mountain
Parky Mountain
Arrowstone Hills
Bonaparte Hills
Bonaparte River Suicide Crossing
Bonaparte River Bridge
Big Bar Lake Cariboo Museum
House & District Historical Museum
24
97
5

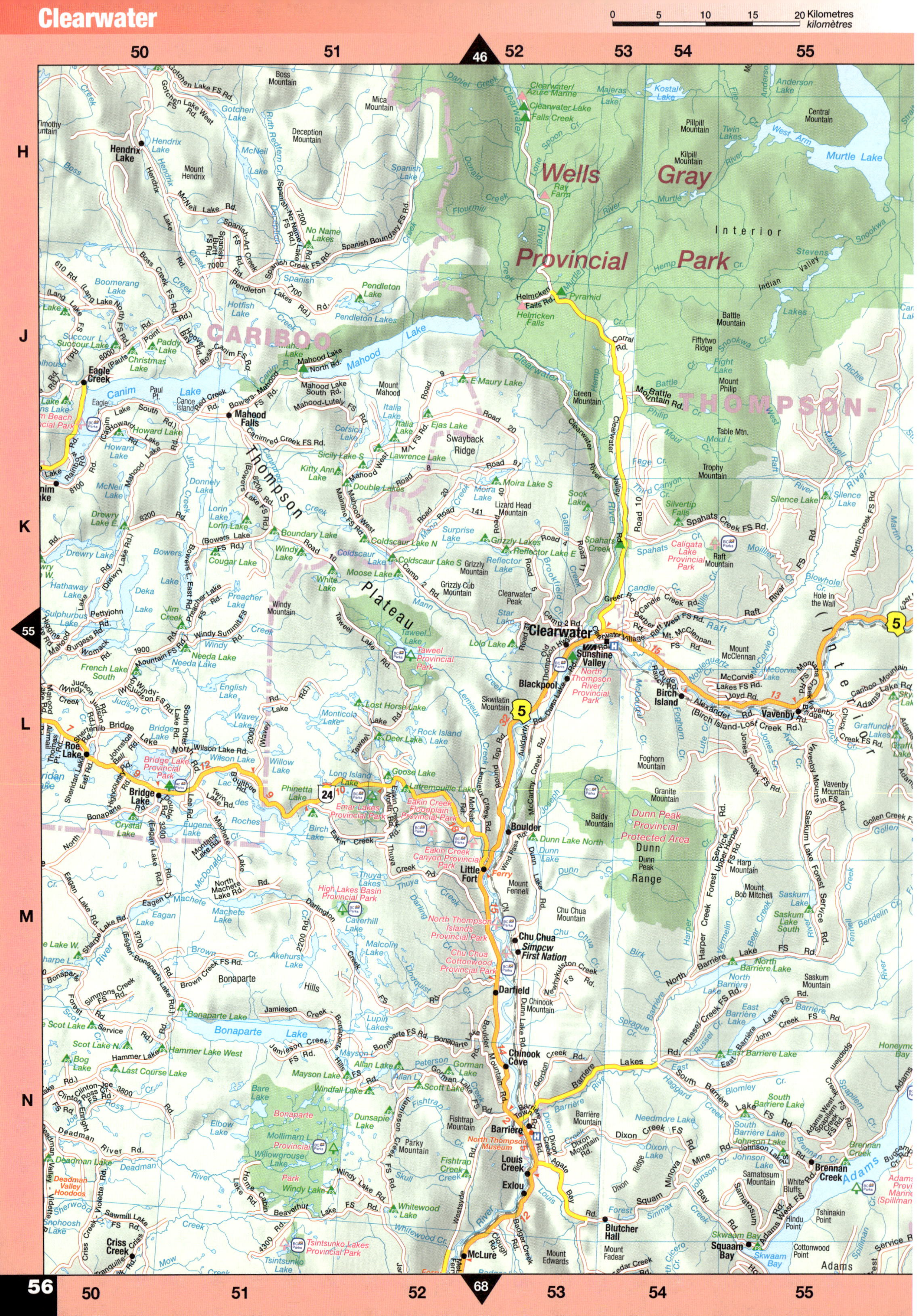
0 5 10 15 20 Kilometres
kilomètres
50
51
46
52
53
54
55
H
J
K
L
M
N
55
5
Wells Gray
Provincial Park
Interior
CARIBOO
THOMPSON-
Thompson Plateau
Clearwater
Hendrix Lake
Eagle Creek
Mahood Falls
Canim Lake
Mahood Lake
Murtle Lake
Helmcken Falls
Sunshine Valley
Blackpool
Birch Island
Vavenby
Roe Lake
Bridge Lake
Little Fort
Boulder
Chu Chua
Simpcw First Nation
Darfield
Chinook Cove
Barriere
Louis Creek
Exlou
McLure
Blutcher Hall
Squaam Bay
Brennan Creek
Crisis Creek
Bonaparte Lake
Dunn Peak Provincial Protected Area
Taweel Provincial Park
North Thompson River Provincial Park
Eakin Creek Floodplain Provincial Park
Eakin Creek Canyon Provincial Park
Emar Lakes Provincial Park
Bridge Lake Provincial Park
High Lakes Basin Provincial Park
North Thompson Islands Provincial Park
Chu Chua Cottonwood Provincial Park
Bonaparte Provincial Park
Tsintsunko Lakes Provincial Park
Caligata Lake Provincial Park
North Thompson Museum
Adams
24
5
68

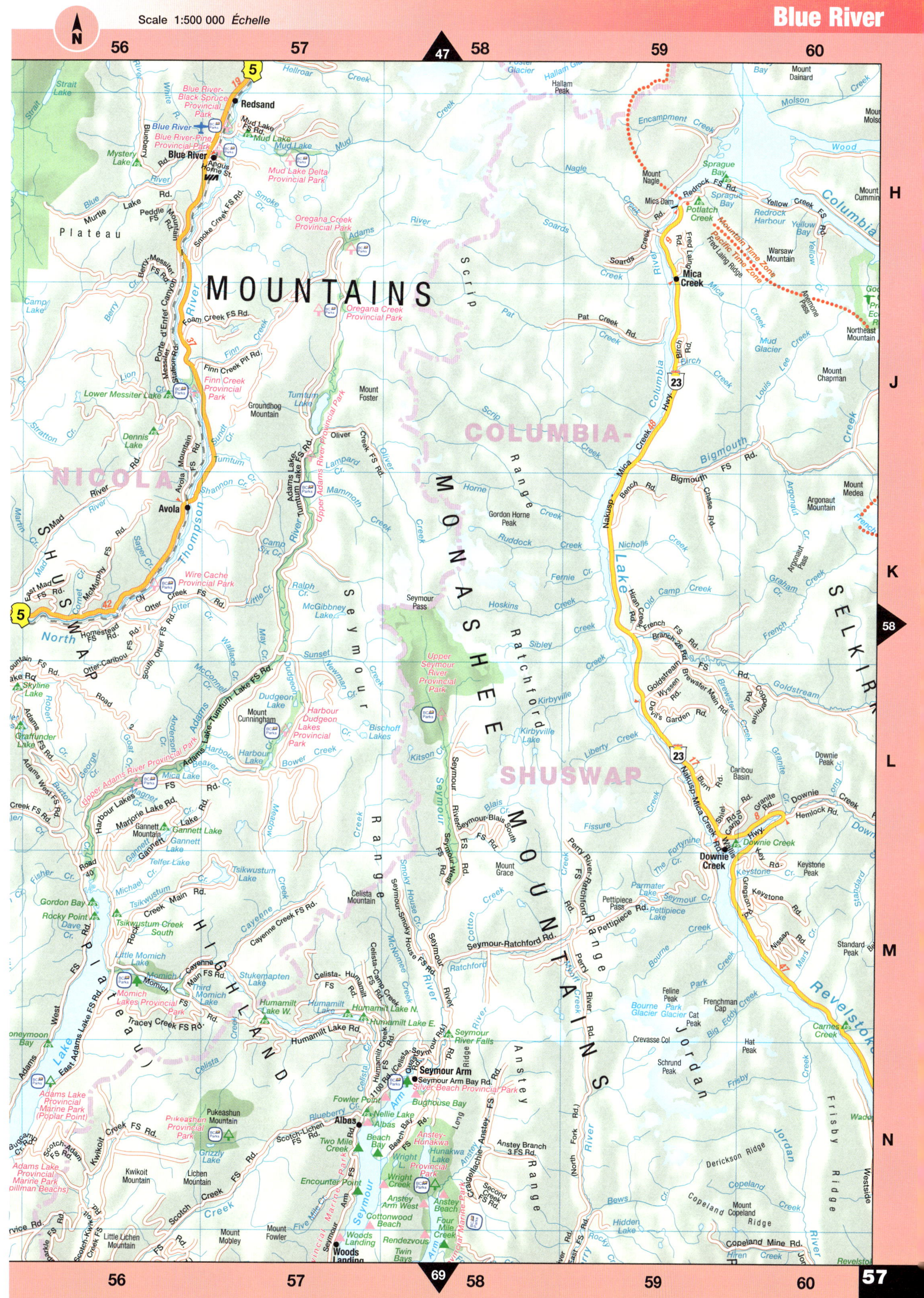

Scale 1:500 000 Échelle
N
56
57
47
58
59
60
H
J
K
L
M
N
58
69
Redsand
Blue River
Blue River-Black Spruce Provincial Park
Blue River-Pine Provincial Park
Mud Lake
Mud Lake Delta Provincial Park
Mystery Lake
Plateau
MOUNTAINS
Oregana Creek Provincial Park
Smoke Creek FS Rd.
Porte d'Enfer Canyon
Foam Creek FS Rd.
Finn Creek Pit Rd.
Finn Creek Provincial Park
Lower Messiter Lake
Groundhog Mountain
Tumtum Lake
Mount Foster
Dennis Lake
NICOLA
Avola
Thompson
Wire Cache Provincial Park
Upper Adams River Provincial Park
Adams Lake-Tumtum Lake Rd.
Oliver
Seymour Pass
Upper Seymour River Provincial Park
McGibbney Lake
Dudgeon Lake
Mount Cunningham
Harbour Dudgeon Lakes Provincial Park
Harbour Lake
Bischoff Lakes
Kitson Cr.
SHUSWAP
HIGHLAND
Plateau
Skyline Lake
Grafunder Lake
Mica Lake
Harbour Lakes
Marjorie Lake Rd.
Gannett Mountain
Gannett Lake
Telfer Lake
Tsikwustum Lake
Gordon Bay
Rocky Point
Tsikwustum Creek South
Little Momich Lake
Momich
Momich Lakes Provincial Park
Third Momich Lake
Stukemapten Lake
Humamilt Lake W.
Humamilt Lake N.
Humamilt Lake E.
Humamilt Lake Rd.
Tracey Creek FS Rd.
Cayenne Creek FS Rd.
Celista Mountain
Seymour-Smoky House FS Rd.
Celista-Humamilt Rd.
Seymour Arm
Seymour Arm Bay Rd.
Silver Beach Provincial Park
Seymour River Falls
Bughouse Bay
Fowler Point
Nellie Lake
Albas
Beach Bay
Two Mile Creek
Anstey-Hunakwa Provincial Park
Hunakwa Lake
Wright Creek
Anstey Arm West
Anstey Beach
Four Mile Creek
Cottonwood Beach
Rendezvous
Twin Bays
Woods Landing
Encounter Point
Mount Fowler
Mount Mobley
Little Lichen Mountain
Lichen Mountain
Kwikoit Mountain
Pukeashun Mountain
Pukeashun Provincial Park
Grizzly Lake
Adams Lake Provincial Marine Park (Poplar Point)
Adams Lake Provincial Marine Park (Spillman Beach)
Honeymoon Bay
East Adams Lake FS Rd.
Scotch-Lichen FS Rd.
Anstey Branch 3 FS Rd.
Second Creek FS Rd.
Anstey Range
MONASHEE
MOUNTAINS
Scrip Range
Ratchford Range
Seymour Range
COLUMBIA-
SHUSWAP
Gordon Horne Peak
Kirbyville Lake
Mount Grace
Seymour-Blais FS Rd.
Seymour-Ratchford Rd.
Perry River-Ratchford Rd.
Pettipiece Pass
Pettipiece Rd.
Pettipiece Lake
Parmater Lake
Feline Peak
Bourne Glacier
Park Glacier
Cat Peak
Frenchman Cap
Crevasse Col
Schrund Peak
Jordan Range
Derickson Ridge
Copeland Ridge
Mount Copeland
Copeland Mine Rd.
Hidden Lake
Frisby Ridge
Westside
Hallam Peak
Hallam Glacier
Foster Glacier
Encampment Creek
Mount Nagle
Mica Dam
Redrock FS Rd.
Sprague Bay
Potlatch Creek
Redrock Harbour
Yellow Creek FS Rd.
Yellow Bay
Warsaw Mountain
Mountain Time Zone
Pacific Time Zone
Fred Laing Ridge
Soards Creek Rd.
Mica Creek
Pat Creek Rd.
Birch Rd.
Mud Glacier
Mount Chapman
Northeast Mountain
Anemone Pass
Mount Dainard
Mount Cummins
Columbia
Mica Creek Hwy.
Nakusp Bench Rd.
Bigmouth
Bigmouth FS Rd.
Chase Rd.
Mount Medea
Argonaut Mountain
Argonaut Pass
Nicholls Creek
Lake
Hiram Creek Rd.
French Branch 26 Rd.
Goldstream
Brewster Main Rd.
Wysen Rd.
Devil's Garden Rd.
Coppermine
Caribou Basin
Downie Peak
Nakusp-Mica Creek Hwy.
Downie Creek
Granite Rd.
Hemlock Rd.
Keystone Peak
Keystone Rd.
Gregson Rd.
Nissan Rd.
Standard Peak
Revelstoke
Carnes Creek
Hat Peak
SELKIRK
23
5

0 5 10 15 20 Kilometres
kilomètres
Sixth Meridian
48
70
57
59
60
61
62
63
H
J
K
L
M
N
Mount Molson
Molson
Encampment Creek
Wood
Wood River FS Rd.
Arm
Mount Shackleton
Clemenceau Icefield
Shackleton Glacier
Chaba Peak
Mount King Edward
Mount Columbia
Columbia Glacier
Columbia Icefield
Snow Dome
Stanley Glacier
Mount Somervell
Tsar Mountain
Cummins Lake Provincial Park
Mount Nagle
Sprague Bay
Mica Dam
Redrock FS Rd.
Potlatch Creek
Yellow Creek FS Rd.
Redrock Harbour
Mount Cummins
Columbia
Yellow Bay
Cummins Arm
Mountain Time Zone
Pacific Time Zone
Fred Laing Ridge
Warsaw Mountain
Mica Creek
Goosegrass Creek Provincial Ecological Reserve
Northeast Mountain
Kinbasket Mountain
Kinbasket Arm
Sullivan River Rd.
Mount Bryce
Mud Glacier
Mount Chapman
Sullivan Arm
Sullivan River Rd.
Hoffa
Main
Vertebrae
Stovepipe Mountain
Lid Mountain
Sophist Mountain
Solitude Mountain
Ladylove Mountain
Goat Peak
Stegosaur Ridge
Windy Arm
Mist Glacier
Neptune Peak
Escarpment Glacier
Kinbasket
Reach
Caribou Creek
Chatter
Ridge
Bigmouth
Mount Medea
Argonaut Mountain
Mermaid Mountain
Mount Ed Falls
Doubletop Mountain
Adamant
Columbia
Tabernacle Mountain
Sullivan FS Rd.
Bush Arm
Goodfellow
Privateer Mountain
Mount Onderdonk
OK Glacier
Whiteface Tower
Adamant Mtn.
Range
Mount Stockmer
Succour Arm
Esplanade Bay
Giant Cedars
Chaperon Mountain
Blackwater
Blackwater Mountain
Felucca Mtn.
Range
Nicholls
Lake
Graham Cr.
SELKIRK
Remillard Glacier
Wart Peak
Craw Peak
Redan Mountain
Austerity Glacier
Azimuth Mountain
Palmer
Gold Arm
COLUMBIA
Hitchhiker Peak
Mount Sir Sandford
Palmer Glacier
Mount Palmer
Range
Sentry Mountain
Esplanade Range
Goldstream Mountain
Goldstream Névé
Sir Sandford Pass
Sir Sandford
Shaw Peak
Gold River
Big
Moberly Pass
Sonata Névé
Sonata Mountain
Centurion Glacier
Centurion Mountain
Argentine Glacier
Pyrite Glacier
Argentine Mountain
Bachelor Pass
Cupola Mountain
Jeb Lake
Susan Lake
Cherub Mountain
Batchelor Creek FS Rd.
Beavermouth
Ventego Mountain
Rogers
Columbia
Downie Peak
Caribou Basin
Downie Creek
SHUSWAP
Bend
Mount Crab
Sorcerer Mtn.
Sorcerer Glacier
Iconoclast Mountain
Ventego Lake
Mount Pearce
Heather Mountain
Mount McNicoll
East Gate
Prairie Hills
Keystone Peak
MOUNTAINS
Tangier Pass
Mystic Mtn.
Nordic Mountain
Road subject to periodic winter closings
Mount Holway
Standard Peak
Belcher Ridge
Mount Sissons
Mount Ansley
Downie Lake
Mount Roger
Bear Creek Falls
Bridgland Peak
Phogg Glacier
Ranges
GLACIER
Feline Peak
Frenchman Cap
Carnes Glacier
Mount Moloch
Mount Graham
Rogers Pass
Rogers Pass National Historic Site
Beaver / Copperstain Valley
Bourne Glacier
Park Glacier
Cat Peak
Roseberry Mountain
Bridgland Pass
Dismal Glacier
Ursus Major Mountain
Rogers Pass
Mount Macdonald
Rogers Pass Centre
Crevasse Col
Revelstoke
Carnes Creek
Fang Glacier
Cheops Mtn.
Avalanche Glacier
Hat Peak
Fang Rock
Hermit
Glacier
Loop Creek
Schrund Peak
Jordan
Glacier
Mount Durrand
Corbin Peak
Hemlock Grove
Mount McGill
Illecillewaet / Asulkan Valleys
Mount Sir Donald
Illecillewaet
Fidelity Mountain
NATIONAL PARK
Mount La Forme
Lookout Mtn.
Wadey
Illecillewaet Névé
Frisby Ridge
Derickson Ridge
Mount Bonney
Mount Smart
Clarke Glacier
Mount Macoun
Deville Glacier
Mount Cotterell
Corbin Pass
Martha Creek Provincial Park
Copeland
Mount Copeland
Ridge
Mount St. Cyr
West Woolsey Cr.
Clachnacudainn Range
Tangier River FS Rd.
Slick Mtn.
Donkin Glacier
Fortitude Mtn.
Patience Mountain
Dawson
Mount Dawson
Mount Topham
The Bishop Range
Black Glacier
Deville Névé
Beaver Overlook
Mount Klotz
Giant Cedars
Albert Canyon (Canyon Hot Springs)
MOUNT REVELSTOKE
Purity Glacier
Purity Range
Copeland Mine Rd.
Hidden Lake
Westside
Nakusp-Mica
Inverness

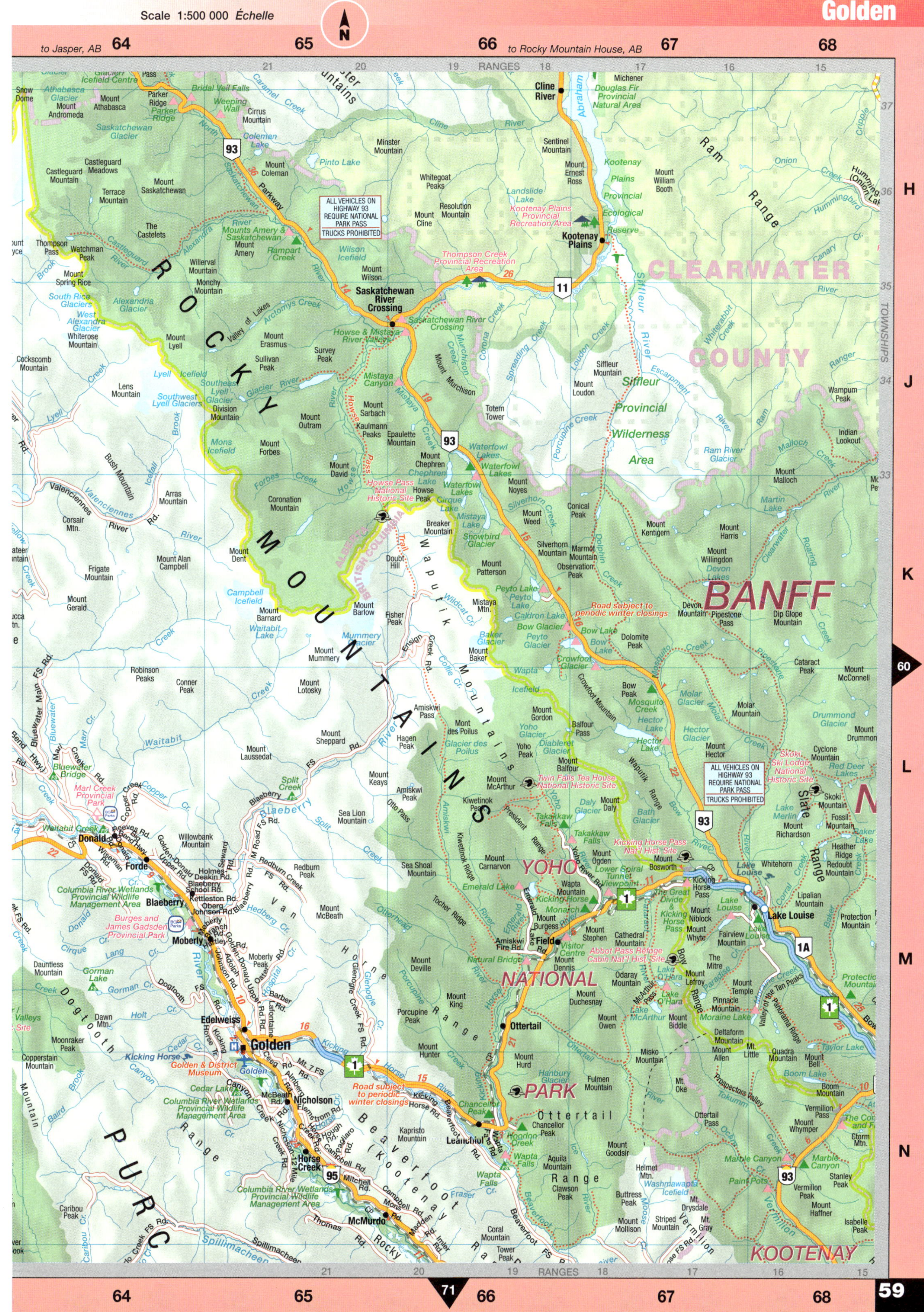

Scale 1:500 000 Échelle
N
to Jasper, AB
to Rocky Mountain House, AB
ROCKY MOUNTAINS
CLEARWATER COUNTY
BANFF
YOHO NATIONAL PARK
KOOTENAY
PURC
Golden
Saskatchewan River Crossing
Kootenay Plains
Cline River
Field
Lake Louise
Donald
Forde
Blaeberry
Moberly
Nicholson
Horse Creek
McMurdo
Edelweiss
Ottertail
Leanchoil
Siffleur Provincial Wilderness Area
Waputik Mountains
ALL VEHICLES ON HIGHWAY 93 REQUIRE NATIONAL PARK PASS TRUCKS PROHIBITED
Road subject to periodic winter closings
Howse Pass National Historic Site
Twin Falls Tea House National Historic Site
Kicking Horse Pass Nat'l Hist. Site
Abbot Pass Refuge Cabin Nat'l Hist. Site
Skoki Ski Lodge National Historic Site
Columbia River Wetlands Provincial Wildlife Management Area
Burges and James Gadsden Provincial Park
Marl Creek Provincial Park
Kootenay Plains Provincial Recreation Area
Thompson Creek Provincial Recreation Area
Douglas Fir Provincial Natural Area
Kootenay Plains Provincial Ecological Reserve
Golden & District Museum
RANGES
TOWNSHIPS

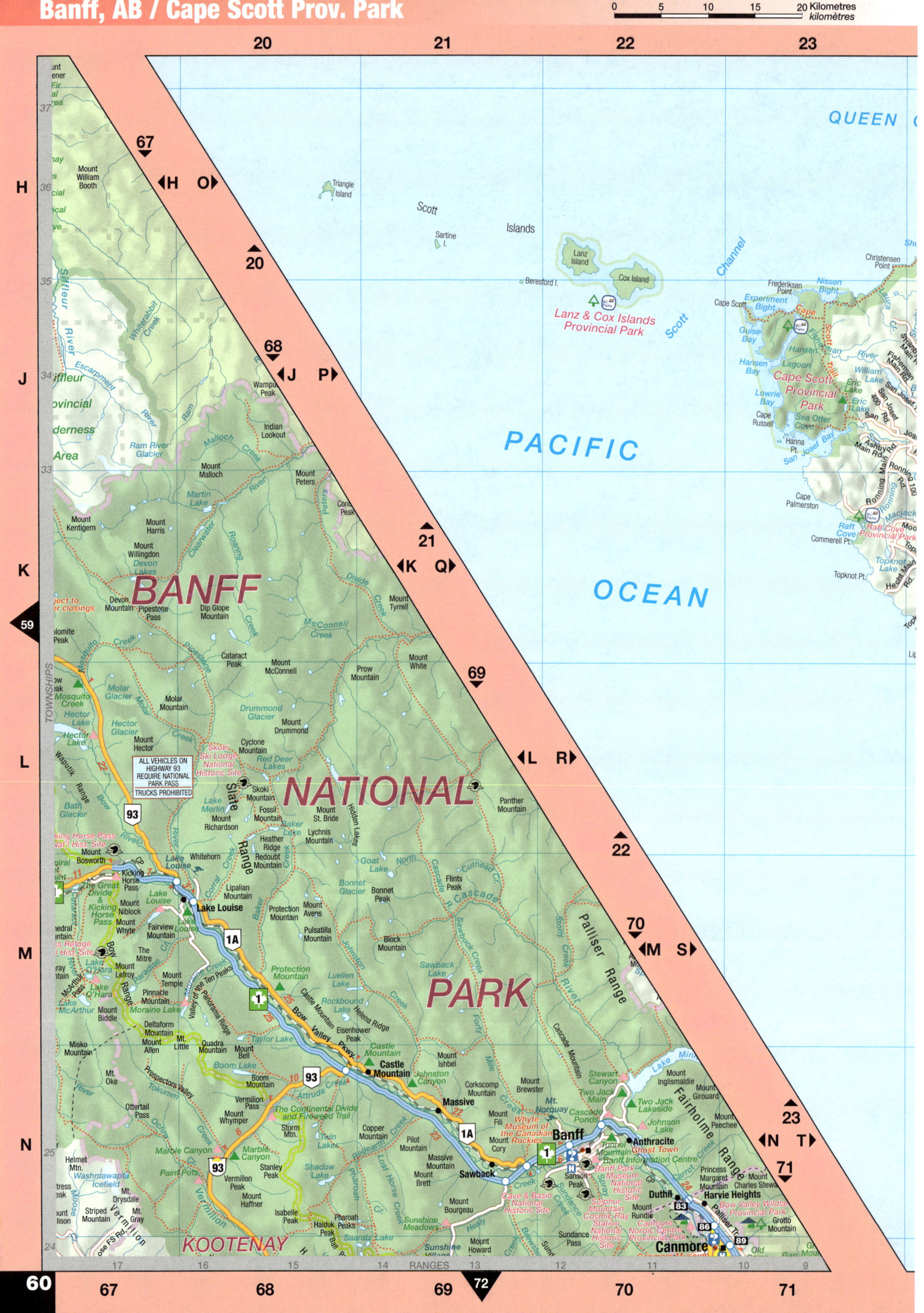
0 5 10 15 20 Kilometres kilomètres
BANFF NATIONAL PARK
PACIFIC OCEAN
QUEEN
Scott Islands
Triangle Island
Sartine I.
Lanz Island
Cox Island
Beresford I.
Lanz & Cox Islands Provincial Park
Scott Channel
Cape Scott Provincial Park
Cape Scott
Hansen Lagoon
Raft Cove Provincial Park
ALL VEHICLES ON HIGHWAY 93 REQUIRE NATIONAL PARK PASS TRUCKS PROHIBITED
Lake Louise
Castle Mountain
Massive
Sawback
Banff
Anthracite
Canmore
Harvie Heights
Duthil
Lake Minnewanka
Fairholme Range
Palliser Range
Sawback Range
Slate Range
Bow Valley Pkwy
Cave & Basin National Historic Site
Bow Valley Wildland Provincial Park
KOOTENAY
TOWNSHIPS
RANGES

Scale 1:500 000 Échelle

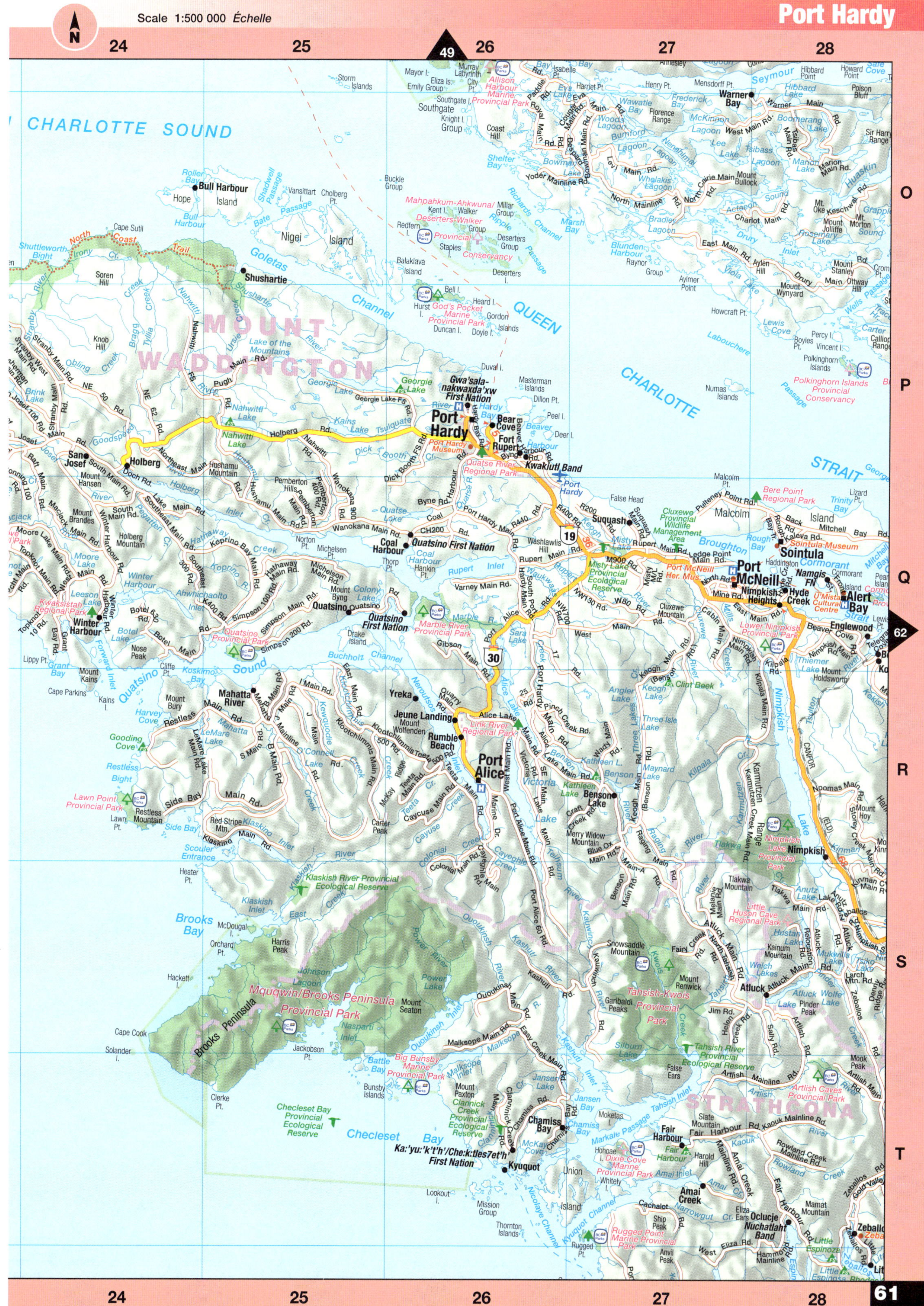

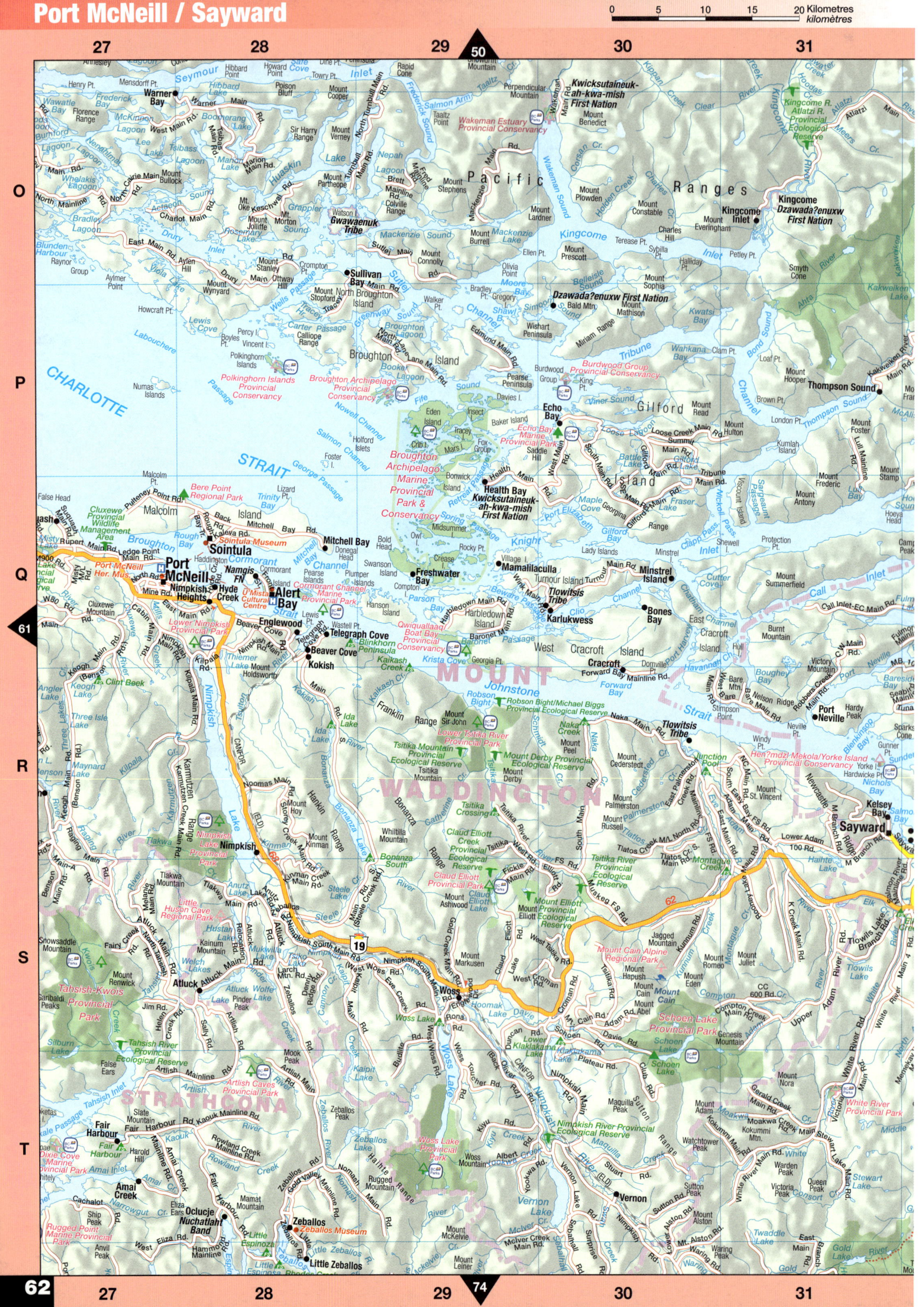
0 5 10 15 20 Kilometres kilomètres
Port McNeill
Sointula
Alert Bay
Sayward
Woss
Zeballos
Little Zeballos
Nimpkish
Atluck
Fair Harbour
Amai Creek
Vernon
Port Neville
Kelsey Bay
Telegraph Cove
Beaver Cove
Kokish
Englewood
Echo Bay
Health Bay
Mamalilaculla
Freshwater Bay
Mitchell Bay
Sullivan Bay
Warner Bay
Kingcome Inlet
Thompson Sound
Minstrel Island
Karlukwess
Bones Bay
Cracroft
Charlotte Strait
Johnstone Strait
Broughton Island
Gilford Island
West Cracroft Island
Pacific Ranges
Mount Waddington
Strathcona
Broughton Archipelago Marine Provincial Park & Conservancy
Schoen Lake Provincial Park
Woss Lake Provincial Park
Tahsish-Kwois Provincial Park
Nimpkish Lake Provincial Park
19
62
50
61
74

Scale 1:500 000 Échelle

0 5 10 15 20 Kilometres
kilomètres
35
36
37
38
39
52
63
76
O
P
Q
R
S
T
Homathko
Icefield
Plateau Peak
Cambridge Peak
Cambridge Glacier
Southgate Glacier
Mountain
Heakamie Mountain
Heakamie River
Heakamie Glacier
Jewakwa
Teaquahan Mountain
Teaquahan
Janus Peak
Gallery Glacier
Gargoyle Cr.
Gargoyle Glacier
Galleon Peak
Bute Glacier
Mount Bute
Mount Grenville
Gunsight Peak
Cumsack Mountain
Cumsack
Homathko Estuary Provincial Park
Potato Pt.
Waddington Harbour
Southgate Peak
Hamilton Pt.
House Mountain
Bear
River
Ward Pt.
Pigeon Valley
Southgate River
Elliot
Creek
Mount Rodney
Littleton Point
Mount Smith
Bear Bay
Purcell Point
Superb Mountain
Mount Sir Francis Drake
Mellersh Point
Mellersh Cr.
Granite Peak
Boyd Pt.
Needle Peaks
STRATHCONA
Paradise
Inlet
Hovel Bay
Orford
Alpha Bluff
Orford Bay
Dupont
Algard
Creek
Cosmos Heights
Clipper Pt.
Amor Pt.
Clipper Cr.
Hillis
Bute
Leask Lake
Mount Eliza
Mount Powell
Mount Doogie Dowler
Ramsay Arm
Downie Range
Quatam
Quatam Bay
Frances Bay
George Head
Mount Hayes
Gastineau
Face Mountain
Brem Bay
Brem River
Brem
Tzela Cr.
Snout Pt.
Toba Inlet
Hat Mtn.
Range
Larson
Raza Passage
Raza Island
Tibbs Point
Pryce Channel
Elizabeth Island
Connis Point
Double
Channel
Brettell Point
Mount Grazebrooke
Mount Whieldon
Attwood Bay
Homfray
Homfray Lake
Hepburn Pt.
Gloucester Pt.
Walsh Cove Provincial Park
Homfray Creek
Derwent Lake
Mount Aiken
Mount Denman
Foster Point
Deer Passage
Redonda Bay
Baile Lake
Dean Pt.
Mount Bunsen
East Redonda Island
Redonda Bay
West Redonda Island
Doctor Bay
Shirley Pt.
Bullock Bluff
REDONDA ISLANDS
Mount Addenbroke
East Redonda Island Provincial Ecological Reserve
Waddington Channel
Pendrell Sound
Ellis Lake
Allies I.
Forbes Bay
Bohn Point
Forbes Cr.
Lewis Channel
Teakerne Arm Provincial Park
Teakerne Arm
Talbot Cove
Roscoe Bay Provincial Park
Price Pt.
Lloyd Pt.
Lloyd Cr.
Dudley Cone
Mount Crawshay
Unwin
Penn Islands
Ha'thayim (Von Donop) Marine Provincial Park
Refuge Lagoon
Refuge Cove
Melville
Otter I.
Unwin Lake
Desolation Sound
Desolation Sound Marine Provincial Park
Klahoose First Nation
Squirrel Cove
Whaletown
CORTES ISLAND
Martin Islands
Kinghorn
Mink I.
Seaford
Mansons Landing
Cortes Island Museum
Kw'as Reg. Park
Cortes Bay
Gifford Peninsula
Malaspina Provincial Park
Bliss Landing
Theodosia Arm
Theodosia Main Rd.
Powell Islets
Townley Islands
Twin Islands
Copeland Islands
Copeland Islands Marine Prov. Park
Okeover Arm Provincial Park
Hidalgo Point
Sutil Pt.
Baker Passage
Smelt Bay Provincial Park
Bunster Range
Heather Main Rd.
Chippewa Main Rd.
Clover Main Rd.
Clover Lake
Frogpond Lake
GOAT ISLAND
Powell Lake
Rainbow Main Rd.
Theodosia Main Rd.
Spur 6
Spur 4
Dagleish Creek
Olsen Lake Rd.
Olsen Cr.
Kulakula Peak
Nanitch Peak
Tolo Mountain
Asymptote Glacier
Mamook Peak
Tahumming Glacier
Tahumming Mountain
Tahumming
Headwall Creek
Icewall Lake
Icewall Creek
Tavistock Mountain
Tavistock Glacier
Mount Filer
Filer
Kite River
Klahoose FN
Boyle Cr.
Julian Peak
Little Toba
POWELL RIVER
Alpine Cr.
Daniels Mainline
Daniels
Powell Lake Mainline Rd.
South Powell Main Rd.
Powell River
Raindrop Lake
Powell Lake Mainline Rd.
Powell Lake Mainline East Rd.
Bradburn Creek
Jim Brown Main Rd.
Brown Creek
Eldred River
D Branch
High Falls Lake
Emma Lake Cabin
Emma Lake
Beartooth Mountain
Goat Mountain
Goat Lake
Overlook Mountain
Goat Lake Rd. 2
Goat Lake Road 1
Toms Thumb
Windsor Lake
Pacific
Skwim Mountain
Mount Sisyphus
Mount Raleigh
Raleigh Cr.
Raleigh Glacier
Mount Eurydice
Styx Glacier
Mount Gilbert
Gilbert Glacier
Falcon Mountain
Compton Névé
Xwitaoz Mountain
Compton Mountain
Compton Glacier
Southgate
Bishop River
Canopus Glacier
Otranto Mountain
Goddard Glacier
Craddock Glacier
Durham Cr.
Norrington Glacier
Farrow Cr.
Farrow Glacier
Chilko Mountain
Provincial Park
Altruist Mountain
Rufous Mountain
Friendly Glacier
Rim Glacier
Edmond
Tchaikazan Glacier
Monmouth Glacier
Monmouth Mountain
Npigwa Glacier
Bishop River Provincial Park
Mount Sawt
Stanley Smith
Donar Glacier
Mount Fulgora
Mount Daphnis
Mount Magaera
Bishop Glacier
Ring Glacier
Mount Tisiphone
Lillooet Mountain
Lillooet Glacier
Dalgleish Cr.
Dalgleish Glacier
Mount Argyll
Montrose
Creek
East Toba River
Sirenia Mountain
Toba
Elaho Range
Albino Glacier
Plateau Icefield
Wave Glacier
Elaho Mountain
Clendinning Range
Clendinning
Beach Mountain
Lunar Creek
Frontline Mountain
Windigger Mountain
Pivotal Mountain
Mount Perkins
Toba River
Mount Tinniswood
Creek
Skwawka River
Mount Alexander
Barkshack Cr.
Barkshack Lake
Mount Victoria
Hunaechin
Mount Albert
Princess Louisa Marine Provincial Park
Princess Louisa Inlet
Macdonald Island
Mount Alfred
Lausmann
Queens Reach
Malibu
Mount Alice
Slane
SUNSHINE COAST
McCannel Lake
Mount Arthur
Jervis Inlet
Patrick Point
Mount Frederick William
Britain
Osgood Cr.
Seshal
Mount Cambridge
Royal Reach

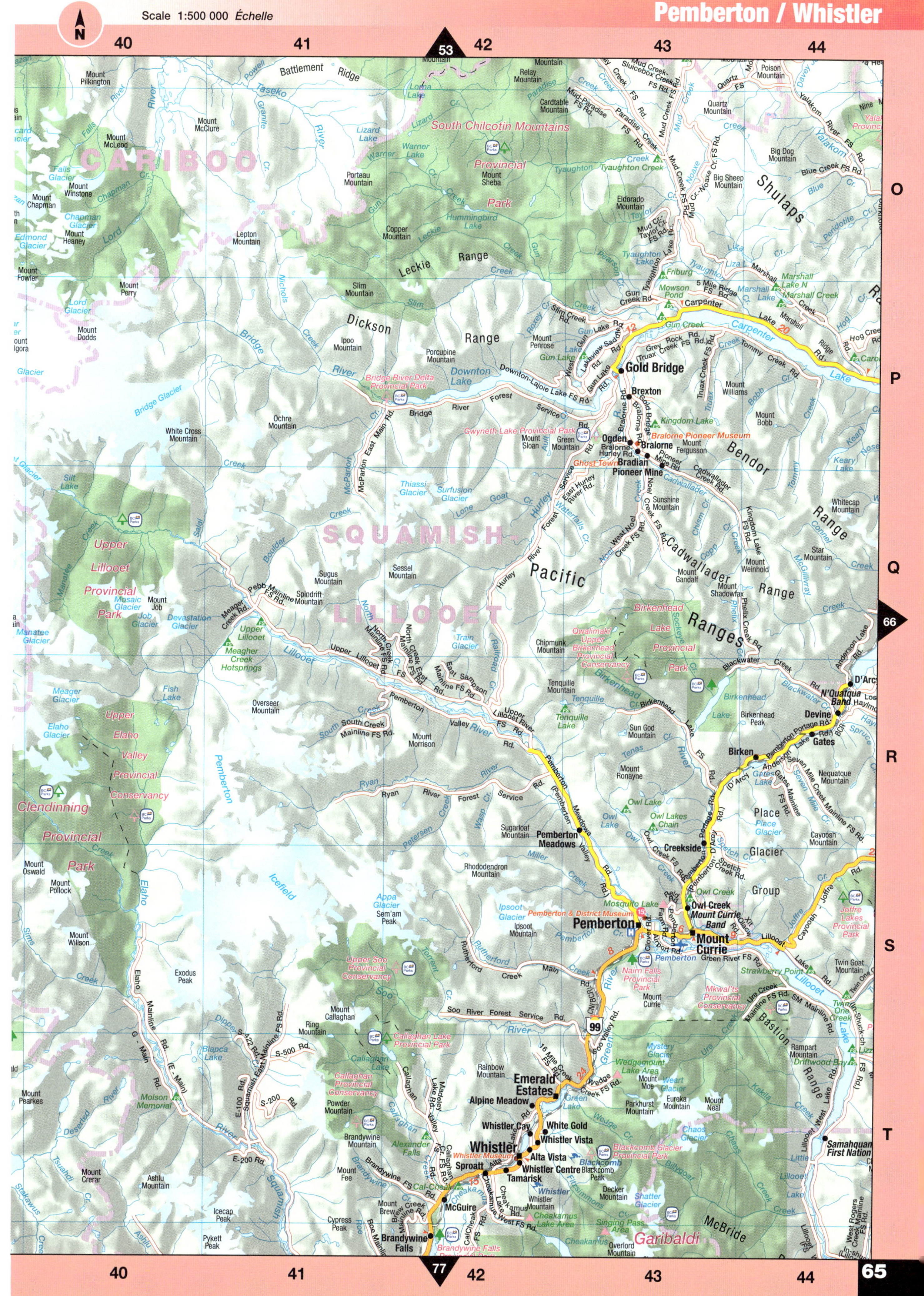

Scale 1:500 000 Échelle
South Chilcotin Mountains Provincial Park
Gold Bridge
Bralorne
Pemberton
Mount Currie
Whistler
Squamish-Lillooet
Cariboo
Pacific Ranges
Upper Lillooet Provincial Park
Clendinning Provincial Park
Birkenhead Lake Provincial Park
Garibaldi

0 5 10 15 20 Kilometres
kilomètres
43
44
45
54
46
47
O
P
Q
65
R
S
T
Clinton
South Cariboo Historical Museum
Edge Hills Provincial Park
High Bar First Nation
Kelly Lake
Lime
Downing Provincial Park
Mount Soues
Pavilion Mountain
Marble Range
Moran Station
Ts'kw'aylaxw First Nation
Pavilion
Marble Canyon Provincial Park
Fountain
Xaxli'p First Nation
Chipuin Mountain
Mount Martley
Upper Hat Creek
Clear Range
Lillooet
Tit'q'et
Lillooet Museum / Miyazaki Heritage House
Seton Lake Reservoir (BC Hydro)
Cayoose Creek Band
Naxwit (BC Hydro)
Kwotlenemo (Fountain) Lake
Blustry Mountain
Texas Creek
Mount Brew
Cottonwood
Cinnamon Cr.
Moha
Fred Antoine Provincial Park
Bridge River Indian Band
Mission Dam
Carpenter Lake
Seton Lake Band
Bridge River (BC Hydro)
Mission Ridge
Shalalth
South Shalalth
Seton Portage
Seton Portage Historic Provincial Park
Seton Lake
Anderson Lake
D'Arcy
N'Quatqua Band
Devine
Gates
Birken
Birkenhead Lake Provincial Park
Birkenhead Peak
Cadwallader Range
Bendor Range
Gold Bridge
Brexton
Bralorne
Bralorne Pioneer Museum
Bradian
Pioneer Mine
Kingdom Lake
Carpenter Lake
Gun Creek
Mowson Pond
Marshall Lake
Yalakom Provincial Park
Shulaps Range
Big Dog Mountain
Big Sheep Mountain
Eldorado Mountain
Quartz Mountain
Poison Mountain
Yalakom Mountain
Beaverdam Creek
Lake La Mare
Hogback Mountain
Leon Creek
Camoo Range
Watson Bar Cr.
Nine Mile Ridge
Squamish-Lillooet
Duffey Lake Provincial Park
Duffey Lake
Cayoosh Mountain
Place Glacier
Glacier Group
Creekside
Owl Creek
Owl Lakes Chain
Owl Lake
Owl Creek Mount Currie Band
Mount Currie
Pemberton
Museum
Nairn Falls Provincial Park
Mkwal'ts Provincial Conservancy
Joffre Lakes Provincial Park
Nlhaxten/Cerise Creek Provincial Conservancy
Mount Caspar
Mount Duke
Twin Goat Mountain
Snowspider Mountain
K'Zuzalt/Twin Two Provincial Conservancy
Lillooet Lake
Strawberry Point
Lizzie Bay
Driftwood Bay
Rampart Mountain
Bastion Range
Brimstone Mountain
Meditation Mountain
Tundra Lake
Stein Lake
Elton Lake
Stein Valley Nlaka'pamux Heritage Provincial Park
Lillooet Range
Petlushkwohap Mountain
Skihist Mountain
Antimony Mountain
Akasik Mountain
Mount Roach
Klowa Mountain
Mount Nielsen
Chochiwa Lake
Chochiwa Glacier
Kwoiek Glacier
Longstog Mountain
Pyramid Mountain
Kwoiek Range
Lytton
Lytton Museum
Lytton Ferry
Lytton First Nation
Winch
Kanaka
Keefers
Botanie Mountain
Botanie Lake
Skwaha Lake Provincial Ecological Reserve
Siwhe Mountain
Evenglow Mountain
Stein Mountain
Askom Mountain
Devils Lake
Samahquam First Nation
Cloudraker Mountain
Arrowhead Mountain
Upper Rogers/kolii7 Provincial Conservancy
Mount Skook Jim
Diversion Peak
Fraser Valley
Mehatl Creek Provincial Park
Garibaldi
McBride Range
Blackcomb Glacier Provincial Park
Chaos Glacier
Shatter Glacier
Decker Mountain
Overlord Mountain
Wedgemount Lake Area
Mystery Glacier
Weart Glacier
Eureka Mountain
Mount Neal
Parkhurst Mountain
Mount Currie
Sun God Mountain
Mount Ronayne
Nequatque Mountain
Whitecap Mountain
Star Mountain
Mount Weinhold
Mount Shadowfax
Mount Gandalf
Sunshine Mountain
Mount Williams
Mount Bobb
Mount Fergusson
Nosebag Mountain
Harry Lake Provincial Park
Blue Earth Lake Provincial Park
Bedard Aspen Provincial Park
Cinquefoil Lake
Sallus Lake
Tiffin Lake
Enterprise Cr.
Cayoosh Cr.
Fraser River
Lillooet River
99
12
1
43
44
45
78
46
47

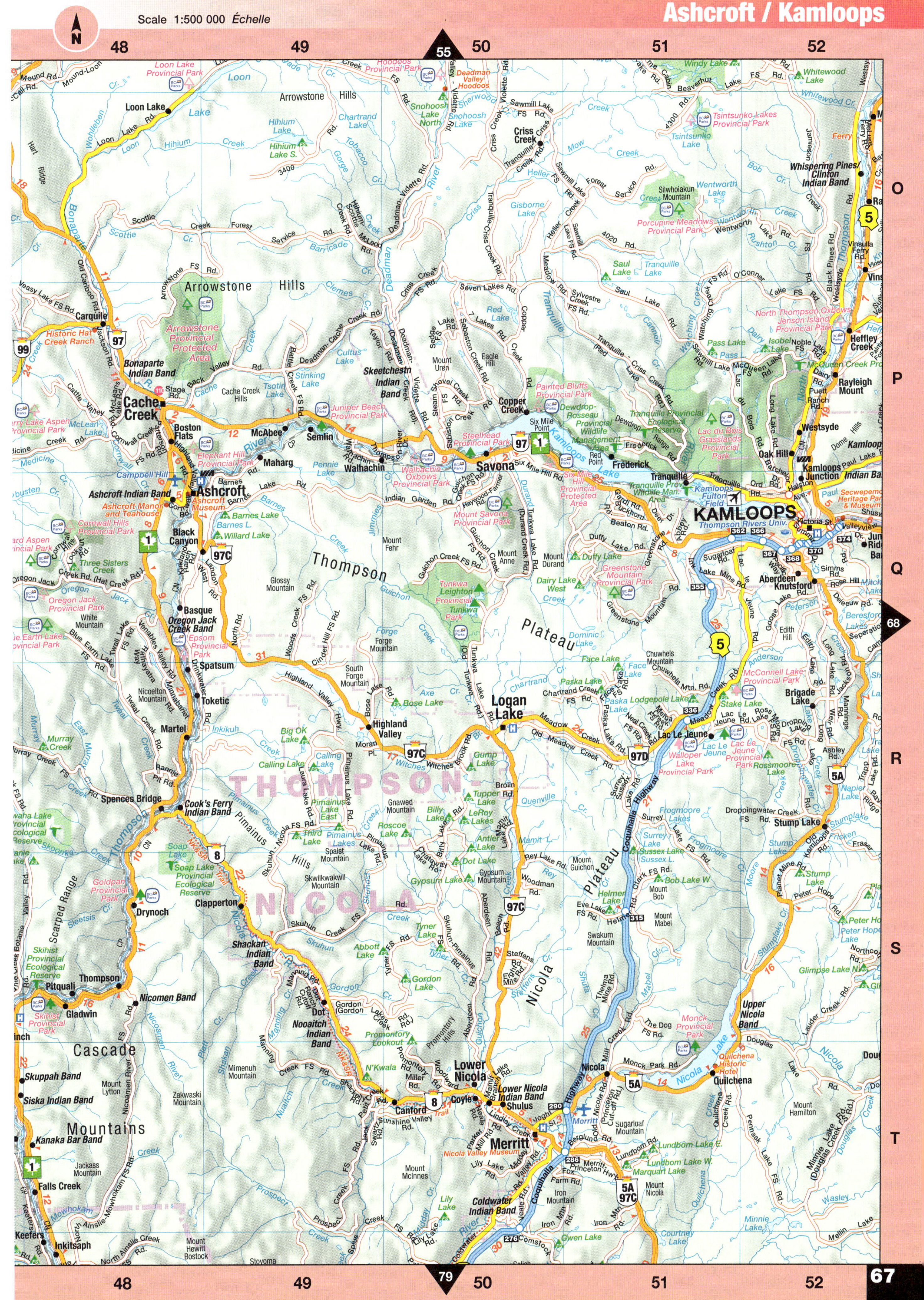

Ashcroft / Kamloops
Scale 1:500 000 Échelle
N
48
49
50
51
52
55
79
68
O
P
Q
R
S
T
Loon Lake Provincial Park
Loon Lake
Arrowstone Hills
Hihium Lake
Chartrand Lake
Deadman Valley Hoodoos
Snohoosh Lake North
Snohoosh Lake
Criss Creek
Tsintsunko Lakes Provincial Park
Tsintsunko Lake
Whitewood Lake
Windy Lake
Whispering Pines/Clinton Indian Band
Gisborne Lake
Silwhoiakun Mountain
Wentworth Lake
Porcupine Meadows Provincial Park
Saul Lake
Tranquille Lake
Arrowstone Hills
Arrowstone Provincial Protected Area
Carquille
Historic Hat Creek Ranch
Bonaparte Indian Band
Cache Creek
Cache Creek Hills
Cultus Lake
Skeetchestn Indian Band
Red Lake
Eagle Hill
Mount Uren
Copper Creek
Painted Bluffs Provincial Park
Dewdrop-Rosseau Provincial Wildlife Management Area
Tranquille Provincial Ecological Reserve
Lac du Bois Grasslands Provincial Park
North Thompson Oxbows Jenson Island Provincial Park
Heffley Creek
McQueen Creek
Rayleigh Mount
Westsyde
Oak Hill
Kamloops Junction
Boston Flats
McAbee
Semlin
Juniper Beach Provincial Park
Steelhead Provincial Park
Six Mile Point
Elephant Hill Provincial Park
Maharg
Walhachin
Walhachin Oxbows Provincial Park
Savona
Kamloops Lake
Six Mile Hill Provincial Protected Area
Red Point
Frederick
Tranquille
Tranquille Prov. Wildlife Man. Area
Kamloops Fulton Field
KAMLOOPS
Thompson Rivers Univ.
Secwepemc Heritage Park & Museum
Valleyview
Ashcroft Indian Band
Ashcroft
Ashcroft Museum
Ashcroft Manor and Teahouse
Barnes Lake
Cornwall Hills Provincial Park
Willard Lake
Black Canyon
Mount Savona Provincial Park
Mount Fehr
Mount Anne
Mount Durand
Duffy Lake
Greenstone Mountain Provincial Park
Aberdeen
Knutsford
Three Sisters Creek
Oregon Jack Provincial Park
Thompson
Glossy Mountain
Tunkwa Leighton Provincial Park
Tunkwa Lake
Dairy Lake West
Plateau
Basque
Oregon Jack Creek Band
White Mountain
Epsom Provincial Park
Spatsum
Forge Mountain
Dominic Lake
Chuwhels Mountain
Edith Hill
Face Lake
Toketic
Nicoelton Mountain
South Forge Mountain
Bose Lake
Logan Lake
Chartrand Creek
Paska Lake
Lodgepole Lake
Stake Lake
McConnell Lake Provincial Park
Brigade Lake
Martel
Inkikuh
Big OK Lake
Highland Valley
Calling Lake
Gump Lake
Lac Le Jeune
Walloper Lake
Lac Le Jeune Provincial Park
Rossmoore Lake
Murray Creek
Spences Bridge
Cook's Ferry Indian Band
THOMPSON-NICOLA
Pimainus Lakes East
Gnawed Mountain
Billy Lake
Tupper Lake
LeRoy Lakes
Brolin
Quenville
Roscoe Lake
Third Lake
Antler Lake
Spaist Mountain
Dot Lake
Gypsum Lake
Gypsum Mountain
Mount Guichon
Frogmoore Lakes
Surrey Lake
Sussex Lake
Bob Lake W
Droppingwater Creek
Stump Lake
Soap Lake Provincial Ecological Reserve
Goldpan Provincial Park
Drynoch
Skwilkwakwil Mountain
Clapperton
Helmer Lake
Mount Bob
Mount Mabel
Swakum Mountain
Peter Hope Lake
Scarped Range
Skihist Provincial Ecological Reserve
Shackan Indian Band
Tyner Lake
Abbott Lake
Steffens
Glimpse Lake
Thompson
Pitquali
Gladwin
Nicomen Band
Skihist Provincial Park
Gordon Lake
Dot
Nooaitch Indian Band
Promontory Lookout
Promontory Hills
Monck Provincial Park
Upper Nicola Band
Nicola Lake
Quilchena Historic Hotel
Quilchena
Cascade
Skuppah Band
Siska Indian Band
Mount Lytton
Zakwaski Mountain
Mimenuh Mountain
N'Kwala
Lower Nicola
Lower Nicola Indian Band
Shulus
Canford
Coyle
Nicola
Merritt
Sugarloaf Mountain
Mount Hamilton
Mountains
Kanaka Bar Band
Jackass Mountain
Nicola Valley Museum
Lundbom Lake E.
Lundbom Lake W.
Marquart Lake
Mount McInnes
Iron Mountain
Mount Nicola
Falls Creek
Coldwater Indian Band
Lily Lake
Gwen Lake
Courtney Lake
Minnie Lake
Keefers
Inkitsaph
Mount Hewitt Bostock
Stoyoma
Comstock
67

0 5 10 15 20 Kilometres
kilomètres
50
51
52
53
54
55
56
O
P
Q
R
S
T
67
80
KAMLOOPS
Chase
Falkland
Westwold
Monte Lake
Monte Creek
Dallas
Barnhartvale
Juniper Ridge
Aberdeen
Knutsford
Westsyde
Rayleigh Mount
Heffley Creek
Vinsulla
McLure
Ramage
Tranquille
Frederick
Savona
Copper Creek
Criss Creek
Lac Le Jeune
Stump Lake
Brigade Lake
Upper Nicola Band
Quilchena
Nicola
Merritt
Douglas Lake
Killiney Beach
Ewing
Fintry
Nahun
Caesars
Wilson Landing
Squilax
Shuswap
Pritchard
Martin Prairie
Holmwood
Campbell Creek
Duck Range
Bestwick
Adams Lake
Squaam Bay
Blutcher Hall
Sun Peaks
Kamloops Lake
Thompson
Okanagan
Plateau
THOMPSON
NICOLA
CENTRAL
OKANAGAN
Aspen

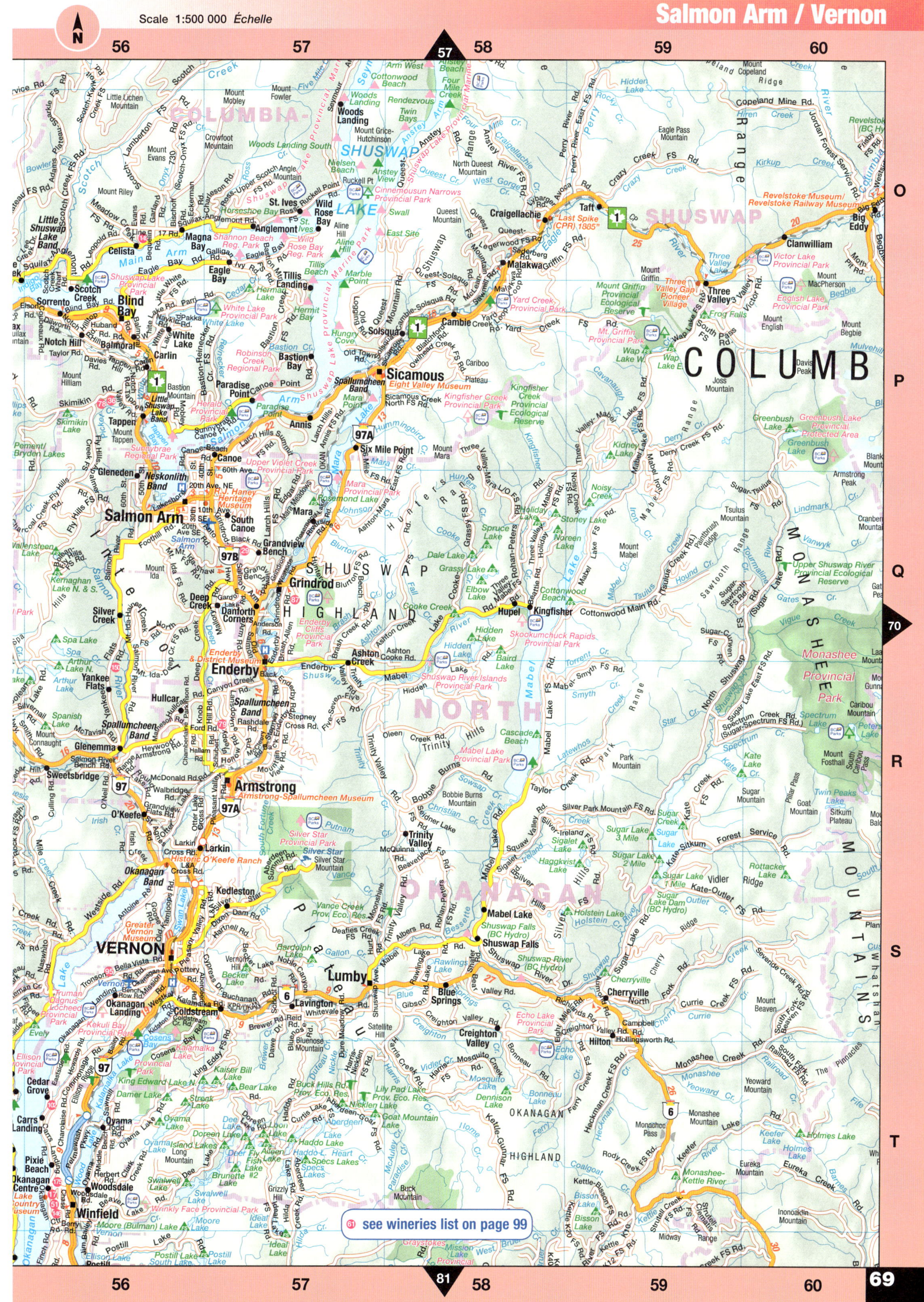
Scale 1:500 000 Échelle
Salmon Arm
Vernon
Sicamous
Enderby
Armstrong
Lumby
Blind Bay
Grindrod
SHUSWAP LAKE
SHUSWAP HIGHLAND
NORTH OKANAGAN
OKANAGAN HIGHLAND
MONASHEE MOUNTAINS
see wineries list on page 99

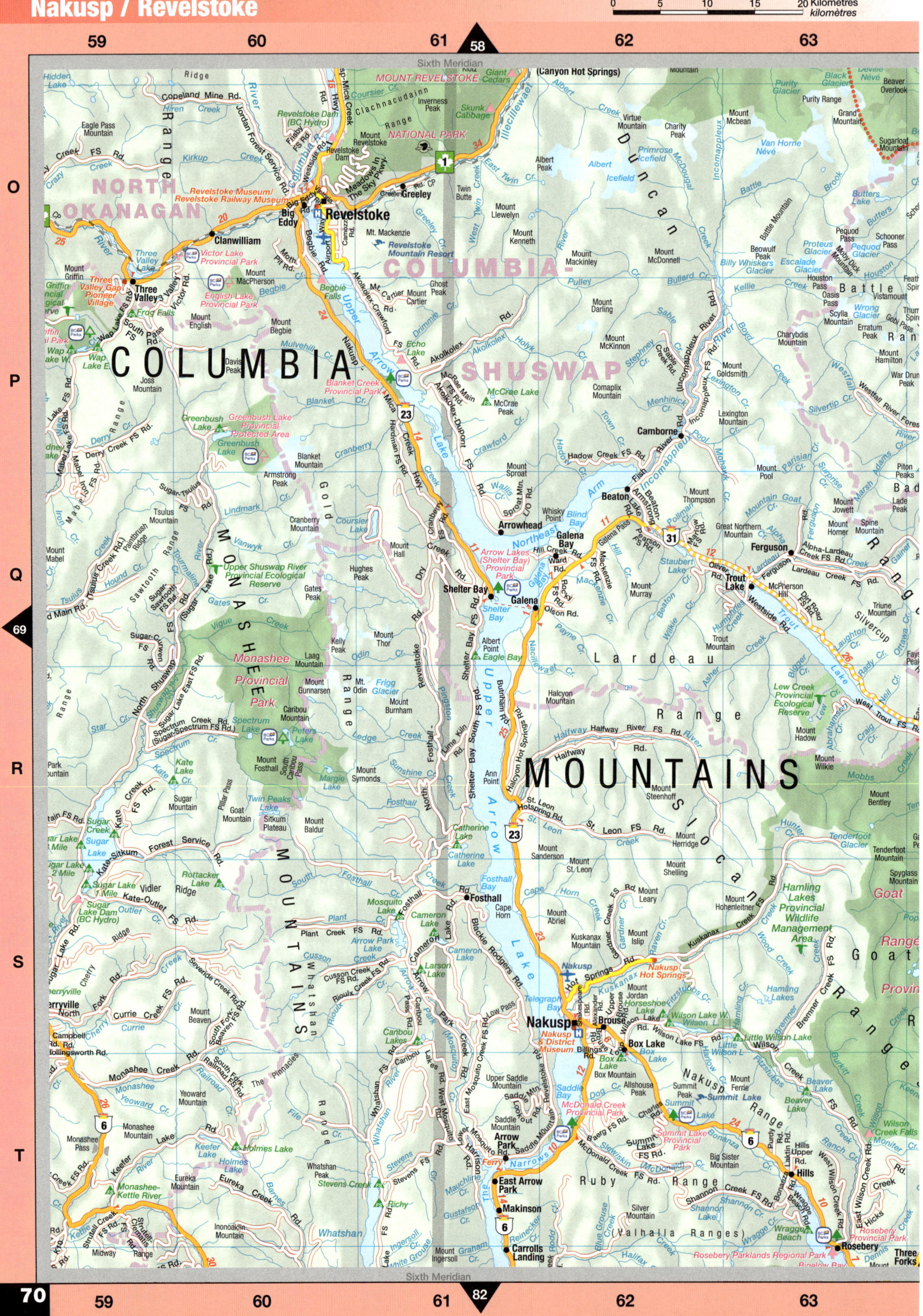

0 5 10 15 20 Kilometres kilomètres
58
Sixth Meridian
59
60
61
62
63
O
P
Q
R
S
T
69
COLUMBIA
MOUNTAINS
MONASHEE
NORTH OKANAGAN
COLUMBIA-SHUSWAP
Revelstoke
Big Eddy
Clanwilliam
Three Valley
Greeley
MOUNT REVELSTOKE NATIONAL PARK
Revelstoke Dam (BC Hydro)
Revelstoke Museum/ Revelstoke Railway Museum
Revelstoke Mountain Resort
Three Valley Gap Pioneer Village
Victor Lake Provincial Park
English Lake Provincial Park
Blanket Creek Provincial Park
Greenbush Lake Provincial Protected Area
Upper Shuswap River Provincial Ecological Reserve
Monashee Provincial Park
Arrow Lakes (Shelter Bay) Provincial Park
Lew Creek Provincial Ecological Reserve
Hamling Lakes Provincial Wildlife Management Area
Nakusp Hot Springs
McDonald Creek Provincial Park
Summit Lake Provincial Park
Rosebery Provincial Park
Rosebery Parklands Regional Park
Monashee-Kettle River
Upper Arrow Lake
Arrowhead
Beaton
Camborne
Galena Bay
Shelter Bay
Galena
Trout Lake
Ferguson
Fosthall
Nakusp
Nakusp & District Museum
Brouse
Box Lake
Arrow Park
East Arrow Park
Makinson
Carrolls Landing
Hills
Rosebery
Three Forks
Ferry
Lardeau Range
Slocan Range
Goat Range
Nakusp Range
Whatshan Range
Ruby Range
(Valhalla Ranges)
Gold Range
Duncan Range
Battle Range
Halfway River
St. Leon Hotspring Rd.
Camp Creek
Mt. Mackenzie
Mount Begbie
Mount Thor
Mount Odin
Mount Symonds
Mount Sanderson
Mount Abriel
Kuskanax Mountain
23
6
31
1

82

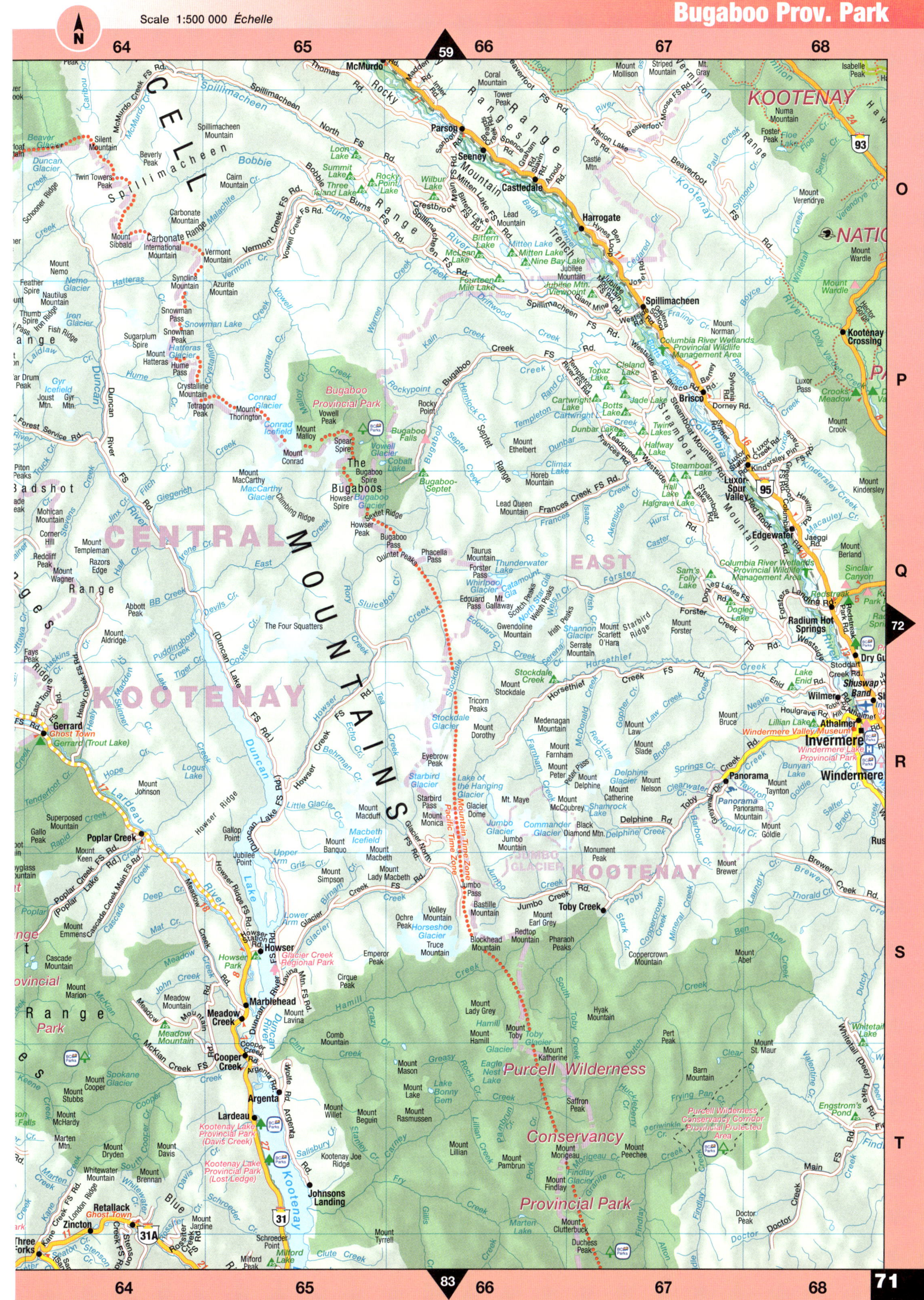
N
Scale 1:500 000 Échelle
64
65
66
67
68
59
72
83
O
P
Q
R
S
T
KOOTENAY
CENTRAL
MOUNTAINS
EAST
KOOTENAY
KOOTENAY
Bugaboo Provincial Park
Purcell Wilderness Conservancy Provincial Park
Purcell Wilderness Conservancy Corridor Provincial Protected Area
Columbia River Wetlands Provincial Wildlife Management Area
Windermere Lake Provincial Park
Kootenay Lake Provincial Park (Davis Creek)
Kootenay Lake Provincial Park (Lost Ledge)
Glacier Creek Regional Park
Windermere Valley Museum
McMurdo
Parson
Seeney
Castledale
Harrogate
Spillimacheen
Brisco
Luxor
Spur Valley
Edgewater
Radium Hot Springs
Dry Gulch
Stoddart Creek
Wilmer
Shuswap Band
Athalmer
Invermere
Windermere
Panorama
Toby Creek
Kootenay Crossing
Gerrard
Ghost Town
Gerrard (Trout Lake)
Poplar Creek
Howser
Marblehead
Meadow Creek
Cooper Creek
Argenta
Lardeau
Johnsons Landing
Retallack
Ghost Town
Zincton
Three Forks
Bugaboos
Mount Conrad
Howser Spire
Bugaboo Spire
Vowell Peak
Mount Malloy
The Four Squatters
Tricorn Peaks
Mount Dorothy
Eyebrow Peak
Starbird Pass
Mount Monica
Glacier Dome
Commander Glacier
Jumbo Glacier
Jumbo Pass
Bastille Mountain
Blockhead Mountain
Redtop Mountain
Pharaoh Peaks
Mount Earl Grey
Coppercrown Mountain
Mount Abel
Hyak Mountain
Pert Peak
Mount St. Maur
Barn Mountain
Saffron Peak
Mount Peechee
Mount Findlay
Mount Clutterbuck
Duchess Peak
Doctor Peak
Mount Toby
Mount Katherine
Eagle Nest Lake
Lake Bonny Gem
Mount Lillian
Mount Pambrun
Mount Morigeau
Mount Lady Grey
Mount Hamill
Comb Mountain
Mount Lavina
Cirque Peak
Emperor Peak
Volley Mountain
Truce Mountain
Horseshoe Glacier
Ochre Peak
Mount Simpson
Mount Lady Macbeth
Mount Macbeth
Mount Banquo
Mount Macduff
Macbeth Icefield
Lake of the Hanging Glacier
Mount Farnham
Mount Peter
Mount Delphine
Mount Catherine
Mount McCoubrey
Delphine Glacier
Mount Nelson
Panorama Mountain
Mount Taynton
Mount Goldie
Mount Brewer
Taurus Mountain
Forster Pass
Whirlpool Glacier
Thunderwater Lake
Catamount Glacier
Mt. Galloway
Scotch Peaks
Welsh Peaks
Irish Peaks
Shannon Glacier
Mount Scarlett O'Hara
Starbird Ridge
Serrate Mountain
Gwendoline Mountain
Mount Stockdale
Stockdale Glacier
Medenagan Mountain
Mount Law
Mount Slade
Mount Bruce
Mount Forster
Mount Ethelbert
Horeb Mountain
Lead Queen Mountain
Septet Ridge
Quintet Peaks
Phacella Pass
Bugaboo Pass
Rockypoint Lake
Bugaboo Falls
Cobalt Lake
Vowell Glacier
Bugaboo-Septet
Silent Mountain
Beverly Peak
Twin Towers Peak
Spillimacheen Mountain
Cairn Mountain
Carbonate Mountain
Mount Sibbald
Carbonate International Mountain
Vermont Mountain
Syncline Mountain
Azurite Mountain
Snowman Pass
Snowman Peak
Snowman Lake
Hatteras Glacier
Mount Hatteras
Hume Pass
Sugarplum Spire
Crystalline Mountain
Tetragon Peak
Mount Thorington
Conrad Glacier
Conrad Icefield
Mount MacCarthy
MacCarthy Glacier
Climbing Ridge
Mount Templeman
Razors Edge
Mount Wagner
Abbott Peak
Mount Aldridge
Mount Johnson
Superposed Mountain
Gallo Peak
Mount Keen
Mount Emmens
Cascade Mountain
Mount Marion
Meadow Mountain
Mount Cooper
Spokane Glacier
Mount Stubbs
Mount McHardy
Marten Mtn.
Mount Dryden
Mount Davis
Mount Brennan
Whitewater Mountain
Mount Jardine
Schroeder Point
Milford Peak
Milford Lake
Kootenay Joe Ridge
Mount Willet
Mount Beguin
Mount Rasmussen
Mount Mason
Mount Tyrrell
Jubilee Point
Gallop Point
Howser Ridge
Duncan Lake
Lardeau
Kootenay Lake
Coral Mountain
Tower Peak
Mount Mollison
Striped Mountain
Mt. Gray
Numa Mountain
Foster Peak
Castle Mtn.
Mount Verendrye
Mount Wardle
Isabelle Peak
Luxor Pass
Mount Crook
Mount Kindersley
Mount Berland
Sinclair Canyon
Lead Mountain
Jubilee Mountain
Mitten Lake
Nine Bay Lake
Fourteen Mile Lake
Loon Lake
Summit Lake
Three Island Lake
Rocky Point Lake
Wilbur Lake
Bittern Lake
Cartwright Lake
Botts Lake
Jade Lake
Twin Lakes
Halfway Lake
Steamboat Lake
Hall Lake
Halgrave Lake
Sam's Folly Lake
Dogleg Lake
Lake Enid
Lillian Lake
Bunyan Lake
Cleland Lake
Topaz Lake
Dunbar Lake
Climax Lake
Whitetail Lake
Engstrom's Pond
Mount Norman
Mount Nemo
Nemo Glacier
Feather Spire
Nautilus Mountain
Thumb Spire
Iron Ridge
Fish Ridge
Iron Glacier
Gyr Icefield
Joust Mtn.
Gyr Mtn.
Star Drum Peak
Forest Service Rd.
Piton Peaks
Badshot
Mohican Mountain
Corner Hill
Redcliff Peak
Range
Fays Peak
Schooner Ridge
Spillimacheen
Bobbie Burns Range
Rocky Range
Mountain Trench
Steamboat Mountain
Beaverfoot Range
Purcell Mountain Time Zone
Pacific Time Zone
Columbia
Kootenay
Duncan
Spillimacheen
Bugaboo
Howser
Lardeau
Toby
Horsethief
Forster
Jumbo
Hamill
Findlay
93
95
31
31A
NATIO

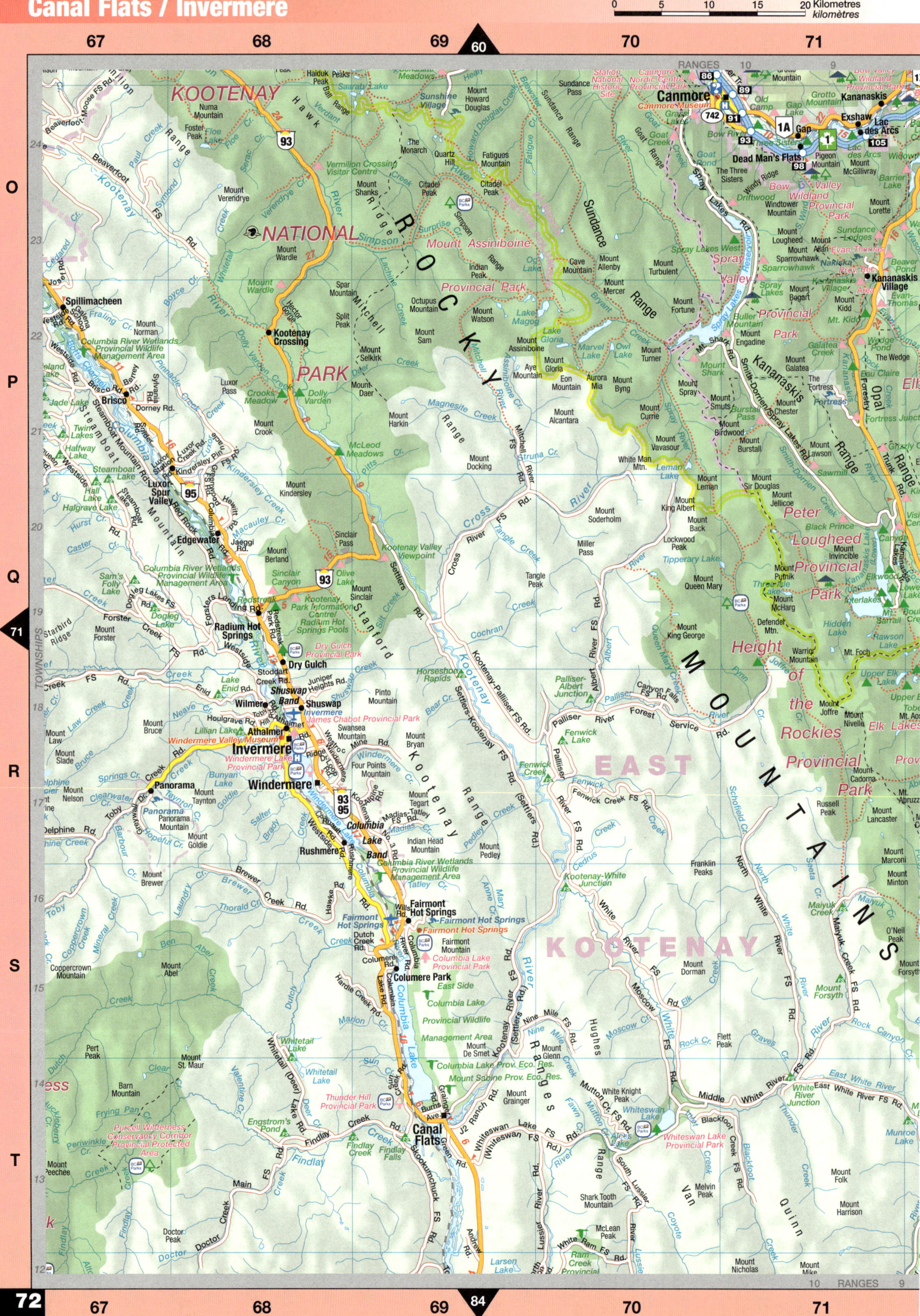

0 5 10 15 20 Kilometres kilomètres
67
68
69
70
71
60
84
O
P
Q
R
S
T
71
TOWNSHIPS
RANGES
KOOTENAY
NATIONAL
PARK
ROCKY
MOUNTAINS
EAST
KOOTENAY
Canmore
Canmore Museum
Canmore Nordic Centre Provincial Park
Dead Man's Flats
Exshaw
Lac des Arcs
Kananaskis Village
Bow Valley Wildland Provincial Park
Spray Valley Provincial Park
Peter Lougheed Provincial Park
Height of the Rockies Provincial Park
Elk Lakes
Mount Assiniboine Provincial Park
Spillimacheen
Brisco
Columbia River Wetlands Provincial Wildlife Management Area
Luxor
Spur Valley
Edgewater
Radium Hot Springs
Dry Gulch
Dry Gulch Provincial Park
Kootenay Crossing
Vermilion Crossing Visitor Centre
Sinclair Pass
Kootenay Valley Viewpoint
Redstreak
Kootenay Park Information Centre
Radium Hot Springs Pools
Wilmer
Shuswap Band
Invermere
Athalmer
James Chabot Provincial Park
Windermere Valley Museum
Windermere Lake Provincial Park
Windermere
Panorama
Columbia Lake Band
Rushmere
Fairmont Hot Springs
Columere Park
Columbia Lake Provincial Park
East Side Columbia Lake Provincial Wildlife Management Area
Columbia Lake Prov. Eco. Res.
Mount Sabine Prov. Eco. Res.
Thunder Hill Provincial Park
Canal Flats
Whiteswan Lake Provincial Park
Purcell Wilderness Conservancy Corridor Provincial Protected Area
Findlay Falls
Palliser-Albert Junction
Kootenay-White Junction
White River Junction
Mitchell Ridge
Stanford Range
Kootenay Range
Van Nostrand Range
Hughes Range
Sundance Range
Kananaskis Range
Opal Range
Mount Kindersley
Mount Assiniboine
Mount Joffre
Mount Harkin
Mount Docking
Mount Bruce
Mount Nelson
Mount Brewer
Mount Abel
Pert Peak
Barn Mountain
Mount St. Maur
Doctor Peak
Mount Peechee
Coppercrown Mountain
Kootenay River
Columbia River
Cross River
Palliser River
Albert River
White River
Findlay Creek
Kootenay-Palliser FS Rd.
Settlers Rd.
Westside Rd.
Toby Creek
Horsethief Creek
Dutch Creek
Lussier River
Larsen Lake

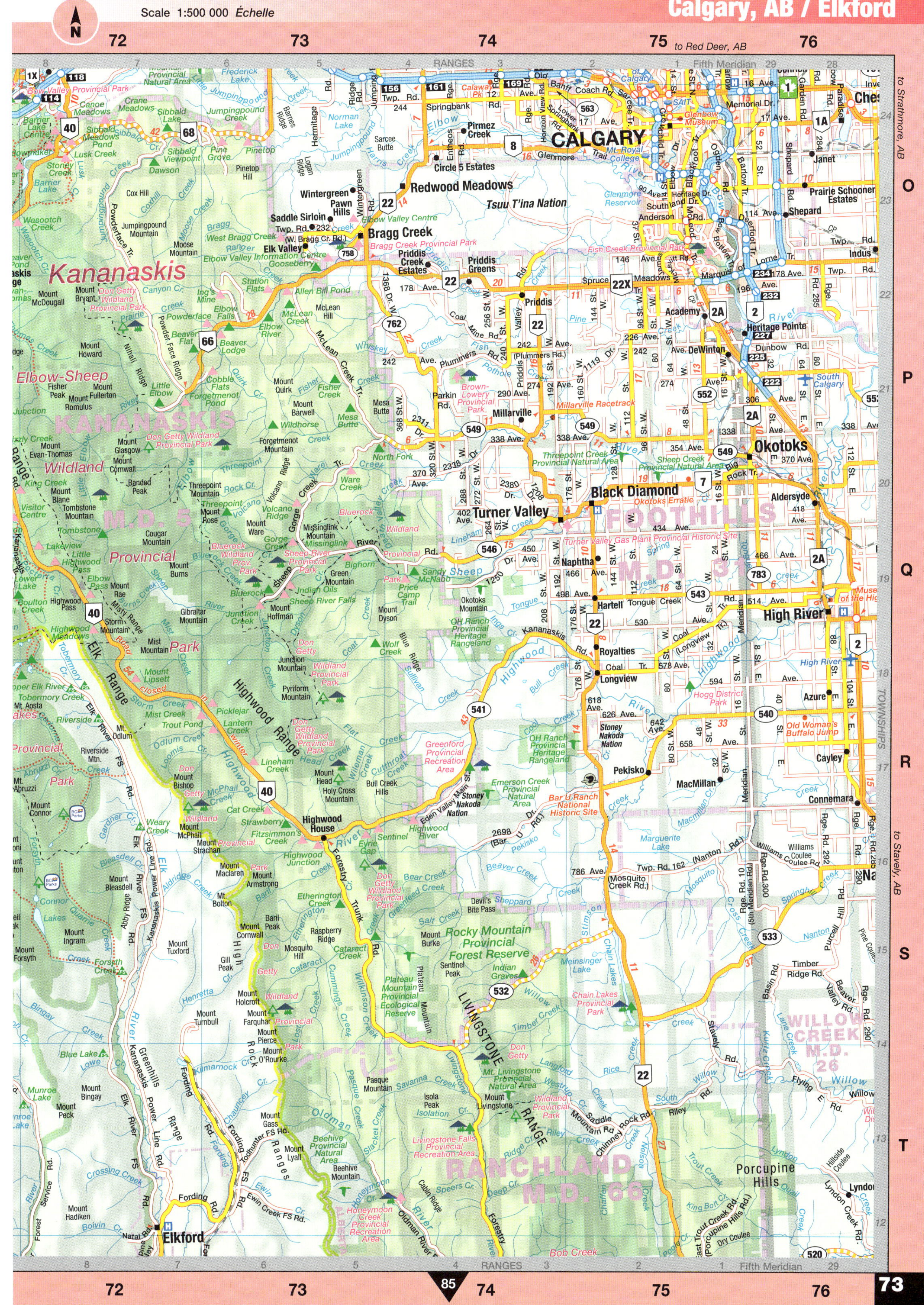
Scale 1:500 000 Échelle
N
to Red Deer, AB
to Strathmore, AB
to Stavely, AB
CALGARY
Bragg Creek
Redwood Meadows
Tsuu T'ina Nation
Kananaskis
Elbow-Sheep Wildland Provincial Park
Okotoks
Black Diamond
Turner Valley
High River
Longview
Highwood House
Elkford
Porcupine Hills
FOOTHILLS M.D. 31
WILLOW CREEK M.D. 26
RANCHLAND M.D. 66
Livingstone Range
Rocky Mountain Provincial Forest Reserve
Fifth Meridian
RANGES
TOWNSHIPS

0 5 10 15 20 Kilometres
kilomètres
27
28
29
62
30
31
U
V
W
X
Y
Z
Zeballos
Zeballos Museum
Little Zeballos
Nuchatlaht Band
Rugged Point Marine Provincial Park
Little Espinoza
Rhodes Creek
Tahsis
Tahsis Museum
Leiner River
Weymer Creek Provincial Park
Mount McKelvie
Mount Leiner
McIver Creek Main Rd.
Mount Alston
Mt. Alston Rd.
Waring Peak
Twaddle Lake
Horseshoe Mountain
Mount Judson
Ehattesaht First Nation
Esperanza
Ceepeecee
Hecate
Blowhole
Catala Island Marine Provincial Park
Nuchatlitz Provincial Park
Nuchatlitz Inlet
Mount Grattan
Mount Alava
Malaspina Peak
Stevens Peak
Conuma Mainline Rd.
Leighton Peak
Muchalat Lake
Gold Muchalat Provincial Park
Upana Caves
Conuma Peak
Tahsis Mountain
Santiago Mountain
Quadra Saddle
Big Baldy Mountain
Gold River
White Ridge Provincial Park
Nootka Sound Historical Museum
Star Lake
Ucona Mountain
Cougar Creek
STRATHCONA
NOOTKA ISLAND
Mowachaht/ Muchalaht First Nation
Bligh Island
Nootka
Yuquot
Friendly Cove Historic Site
Santa Gertrudis-Boca del Infierno Marine Provincial Park
Bligh Island Marine Provincial Park
Resolution Cove Historic Site (Cook Landing [1778])
Mount Serjeant
Mount Rufus
Mount Albemarle
Mount Bauke
Nootka Sound
Muchalat Inlet
Matchlee Mountain
Splendor Mountain
Escalante Point
Escalante Island
Hesquiat Lake Provincial Park
Sydney Cone
Sydney Inlet Provincial Park
Cougar Annie's Garden
Pretty Girl Lake
Megin Lake
Boat Basin
Split Cape
Barcester Bay
Hesquiat Peninsula Provincial Park
HESQUIAT PENINSULA
Hesquiat First Nation
Hesquiat
Estevan Point
Perez Rocks
Stewardson Inlet
Megin River Provincial Ecological Reserve
Lone Wolf Mountain
Sulphur Passage Provincial Park
MacGregor Range
Hot Springs Cove
Maquinna Marine Provincial Park
Sharp Point
FLORES ISLAND
Flores Island Provincial Park
Mount Flores
Ahousat
Ahousaht First Nation (Marktosis)
Gibson Marine Provincial Park
Chetarpe
VARGAS ISLAND
Ahousaht FN
Vargas Island Provincial Park
Cleland Island
Epper Pass Provincial
Tla-o-qui-aht First Nation
Tofino
Tofino Botanical Gardens
Cox Pt.
PACIFIC
OCEAN
Wickaninnish
27
28
29
30
31

Scale 1:500 000 Échelle
CAMPBELL RIVER
COURTENAY
Comox
Cumberland
Union Bay
PORT ALBERNI
Ucluelet
Tofino
Strathcona Provincial Park
VANCOUVER ISLAND
STRAIT OF GEORGIA
COMOX VALLEY
ALBERNI
CLAYOQUOT
Qualicum Beach
Bowser
Fanny Bay
Buckley Bay
Royston
Merville
Black Creek
Oyster River
Saratoga Beach
Beaver Creek
Cherry Creek
Sproat Lake
Great Central
Kleecoot
Port Albion
Bamfield
Kildonan
Ecoole
Savary Island
Lund
Southview
Sliammon
Quinsam
Bliss Landing
Yaculta

0 5 10 15 20 Kilometres kilomètres
35
36
37
38
39
64
U
V
W
X
Y
Z
75
86
87
STRAIT OF GEORGIA
MALASPINA STRAIT
SALISH SEA
POWELL RIVER
NANAIMO
COWICHAN VALLEY
Pacific Ranges
Powell River
Powell River Historical Museum
Sliammon
Sliammon First Nation
Lund
Bliss Landing
Savary Island
Wildwood
Cranberry
Westview
Paradise Valley
Myrtle Point
Pebble Beach
Brew Bay
Lang Bay
Stillwater
Saltery Bay
Saltery Bay Prov. Park
Powell Lake
Haslam Lake
Texada Island
Vananda
Gillies Bay
Blubber Bay
Lasqueti Island
False Bay
Jervis Inlet
Nelson Island
Egmont
Earls Cove
Irvines Landing
Pender Harbour
Garden Bay
Madeira Park
Kleindale
Sechelt Peninsula
Secret Cove
Halfmoon Bay
Sechelt
Porpoise Bay
Welcome Beach
West Sechelt
Selma Park
Wilson Creek
Comox
Comox Air Force Museum
CFB Comox
Little River
Lazo
Royston
Cumberland
Union Bay
Fanny Bay
Buckley Bay
Denman Island
Hornby Island
Bowser
Qualicum Bay
Dunsmuir
Qualicum Beach
Dashwood
French Creek
Parksville
Errington
Coombs
Hilliers
Whiskey Creek
Nanoose Bay
Lantzville
Wellington
East Wellington
Departure Bay
NANAIMO
Nanaimo District Museum
Snuneymuxw First Nation
Gabriola
Gabriola Museum
Duke Point
Harmac
Cedar
South Wellington
Extension
Cassidy
Chemainus First Nation
Ladysmith
Saltair
PORT ALBERNI
Alberni
Tseshaht FN
Beaver Creek
Cherry Creek
Sproat Lake
Kleecoot
Arrowview Heights
Nahmint
Kildonan
Green Cove
Franklin Camp
Nitinat
CF Maritime Test Range (Nanoose Bay Testing Area)
Mt. Arrowsmith Massif Regional Park
Englishman River Falls Provincial Park
Little Qualicum Falls Provincial Park
Rathtrevor Beach Provincial Park
Helliwell Provincial Park
Tribune Bay Provincial Park
Fillongley Provincial Park
Haley Lake Provincial Ecological Reserve
101
19
19A
4

Scale 1:500 000 Échelle
N
40
41
42
43
44
65
U
V
W
X
Y
Z
78
87
Garibaldi
Provincial
Park
McBride
Range
SUNSHINE
COAST
SQUAMISH-
LILLOOET
FRASER
VALLEY
METRO
VANCOUVER
Squamish
Squamish Nation
Brackendale
Garibaldi Estates
Dentville
Darrell Bay
Britannia Beach
Minaty Bay
Porteau
Woodfibre
Lions Bay
Horseshoe Bay
Gibsons
Sechelt
Roberts Creek
Langdale
Granthams Landing
Hopkins Landing
Williamsons Landing
Port Mellon
Seaside Park
New Brighton
Gambier Harbour
Eastbourne
Snug Cove
Seymour Landing
Gower Point
Brandywine Falls
McGuire
Garibaldi
Cheakamus
Paradise Valley
Alvin
Granite Falls
Buntzen Bay
Brighton Beach
Woodlands
Belcarra
Anmore
Deep Cove
Dollarton
Lynn Valley
Seymour Heights
WEST VANCOUVER
NORTH VANCOUVER
VANCOUVER
BURNABY
PORT MOODY
COQUITLAM
PORT COQUITLAM
Pitt Meadows
MAPLE RIDGE
NEW WESTMINSTER
RICHMOND
DELTA
SURREY
LANGLEY
Cloverdale
Fort Langley
White Rock
Blaine
Point Roberts
Tsawwassen
Ladner
Steveston
Boundary Bay
Crescent Beach
Aldergrove
Whalley
Guildford
Port Hammond
Albion
Gulf Islands National Park Reserve
STRAIT OF GEORGIA
GULF ISLANDS
North Galiano
Thetis Island
Kuper Island
Chemainus
BRITISH COLUMBIA
WASHINGTON
U.S.A.
CANADA
Southern Strait of Georgia
see wineries list on page 99
to Bellingham, WA

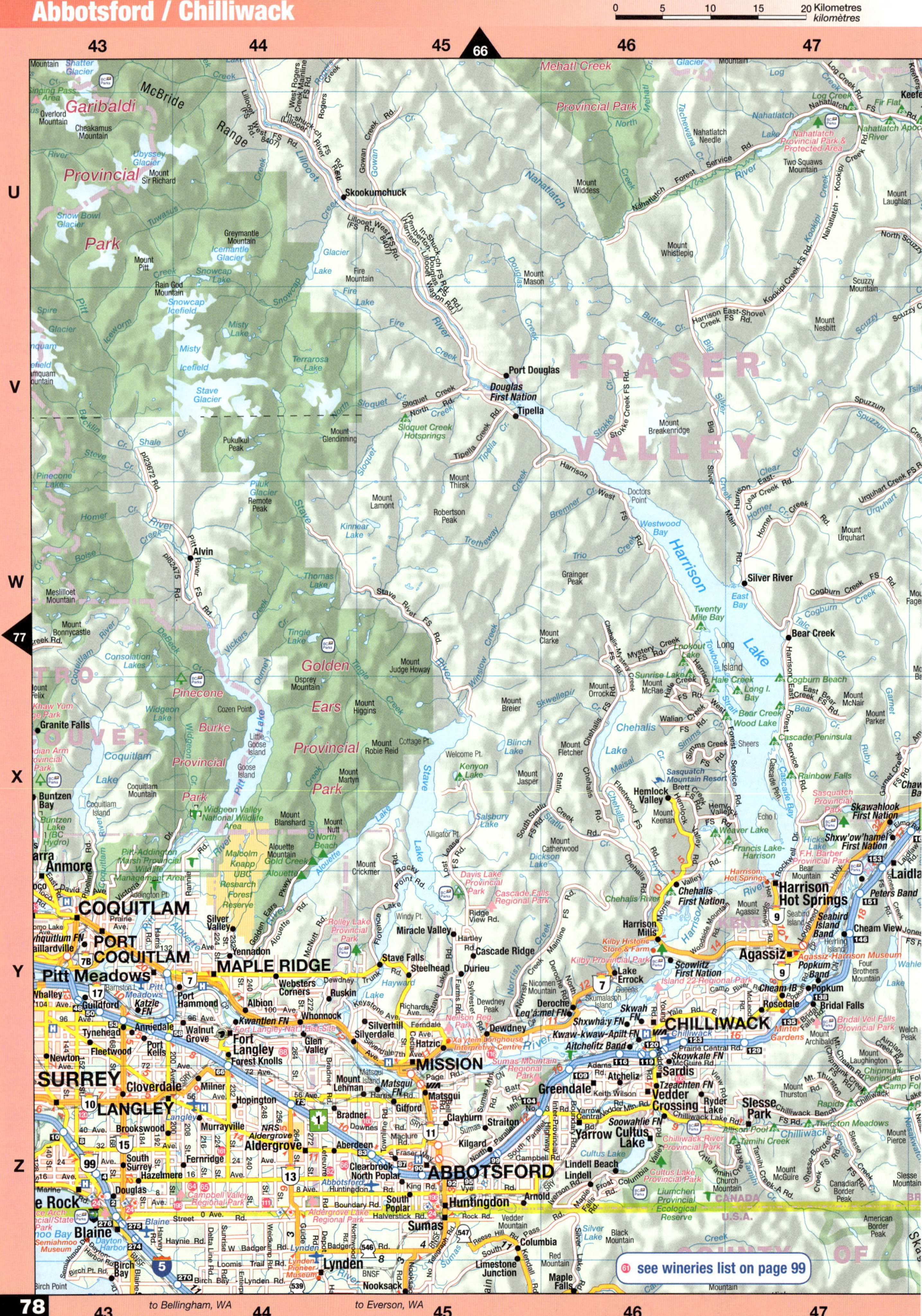
0 5 10 15 20 Kilometres kilomètres
43
44
45
46
47
66
77
U
V
W
X
Y
Z
Garibaldi Provincial Park
McBride Range
Mehatl Creek Provincial Park
Nahatlatch Provincial Park & Protected Area
Skookumchuck
Port Douglas
Douglas First Nation
Tipella
Sloquet Creek Hotsprings
FRASER VALLEY
Harrison Lake
Silver River
Bear Creek
Golden Ears Provincial Park
Pinecone Burke Provincial Park
Widgeon Valley National Wildlife Area
Alouette Lake
Stave Lake
Hemlock Valley
Sasquatch Provincial Park
Harrison Hot Springs
Agassiz
Seabird Island Band
Cheam View
Popkum
Bridal Falls
Bridal Veil Falls Provincial Park
COQUITLAM
PORT COQUITLAM
Pitt Meadows
MAPLE RIDGE
Port Hammond
Albion
Whonnock
Ruskin
Stave Falls
Steelhead
Miracle Valley
Cascade Ridge
Dewdney
Deroche
Lake Errock
Harrison Mills
Kilby Provincial Park
Fort Langley
Walnut Grove
Glen Valley
MISSION
Hatzic
SURREY
Cloverdale
LANGLEY
Aldergrove
Murrayville
Brookswood
Fernridge
Hazelmere
Douglas
Blaine
Lynden
Nooksack
Sumas
Huntingdon
Clearbrook
ABBOTSFORD
Matsqui
Mount Lehman
Bradner
Clayburn
Straiton
Kilgard
Greendale
Yarrow
Cultus Lake
Lindell Beach
Vedder Crossing
Sardis
CHILLIWACK
Rosedale
Ryder Lake
Slesse Park
Columbia Valley
Sumas Mountain Regional Park
Cultus Lake Provincial Park
Chilliwack River Provincial Park
Aldergrove Lake Regional Park
Campbell Valley Regional Park
Cheam Lake
Laidlaw
Peters Band
CANADA
U.S.A.
to Bellingham, WA
to Everson, WA
see wineries list on page 99

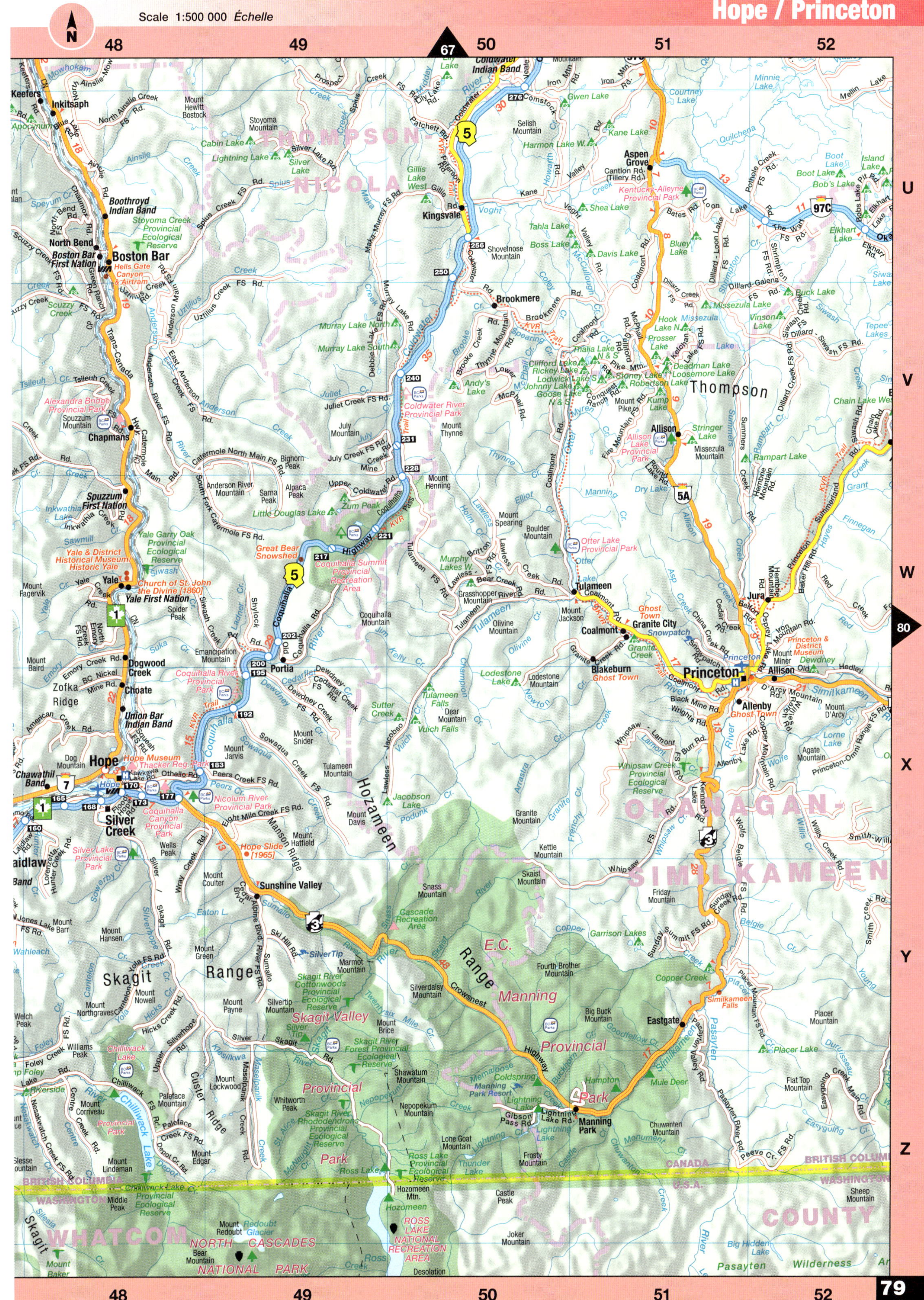
Scale 1:500 000 Échelle
N
48
49
50
51
52
67
80
U
V
W
X
Y
Z
THOMPSON-NICOLA
OKANAGAN-SIMILKAMEEN
WHATCOM
COUNTY
BRITISH COLUMBIA
WASHINGTON
CANADA
U.S.A.
Keefers
Inkitsaph
Boothroyd Indian Band
North Bend
Boston Bar
Boston Bar First Nation
Hells Gate Canyon Airtram
Stoyoma Creek Provincial Ecological Reserve
Alexandra Bridge Provincial Park
Spuzzum Mountain
Chapmans
Spuzzum First Nation
Yale Garry Oak Provincial Ecological Reserve
Yale & District Historical Museum/ Historic Yale
Church of St. John the Divine [1860]
Yale
Yale First Nation
Mount Fagervik
Dogwood Creek
Choate
Zofka Ridge
Union Bar Indian Band
Hope
Hope Museum
Thacker Reg. Park
Dog Mountain
Chawathil Band
Silver Creek
Laidlaw
Silver Lake Provincial Park
Coquihalla Canyon Provincial Park
Nicolum River Provincial Park
Hope Slide [1965]
Sunshine Valley
Coquihalla River Provincial Park
Portia
Emancipation Mountain
Great Bear Snowshed
Coquihalla Summit Provincial Recreation Area
Coquihalla Mountain
Zum Peak
Little Douglas Lake
Mount Henning
Murray Lake North
Murray Lake South
Coldwater River Provincial Park
Kingsvale
Coldwater Indian Band
Shovelnose Mountain
Brookmere
Tahla Lake
Boss Lake
Davis Lake
Shea Lake
Aspen Grove
Kentucky-Alleyne Provincial Park
Thompson
Allison
Allison Lake Provincial Park
Dry Lake
Otter Lake Provincial Park
Tulameen
Coalmont
Granite City
Blakeburn Ghost Town
Princeton
Princeton & District Museum
Allenby Ghost Town
Hedley
Jura
Tulameen Falls
Vuich Falls
Lodestone Mountain
Hozameen
Jacobson Lake
Whipsaw Creek Provincial Ecological Reserve
Granite Mountain
Kettle Mountain
Skaist Mountain
Snass Mountain
Cascade Recreation Area
E.C. Manning Provincial Park
Fourth Brother Mountain
Garrison Lakes
Copper Creek
Similkameen Falls
Eastgate
Big Buck Mountain
Mule Deer
Hampton
Manning Park
Manning Park Resort
Lightning Lake
Gibson Pass Rd.
Frosty Mountain
Chuwanten Mountain
Castle Peak
Hozomeen Mtn.
Hozomeen
Ross Lake Provincial Ecological Reserve
Ross Lake
ROSS LAKE NATIONAL RECREATION AREA
NORTH CASCADES NATIONAL PARK
Desolation
Joker Mountain
Skagit Valley Provincial Park
Skagit River Cottonwoods Provincial Ecological Reserve
Skagit River Forest Provincial Ecological Reserve
Skagit River Rhododendrons Provincial Ecological Reserve
Silver Tip
SilverTip
Skagit
Range
Crowsnest Highway
Chilliwack Lake Provincial Park
Chilliwack Lake
Chilliwack Lake Provincial Ecological Reserve
Mount Lindeman
Middle Peak
Mount Redoubt
Redoubt Glacier
Bear Mountain
Mount Baker
Sheep Mountain
Pasayten Wilderness
Big Hidden Lake
Trans-Canada Hwy.
Coquihalla Highway
Coldwater
KVR Trail
1
3
5
5A
7
97C

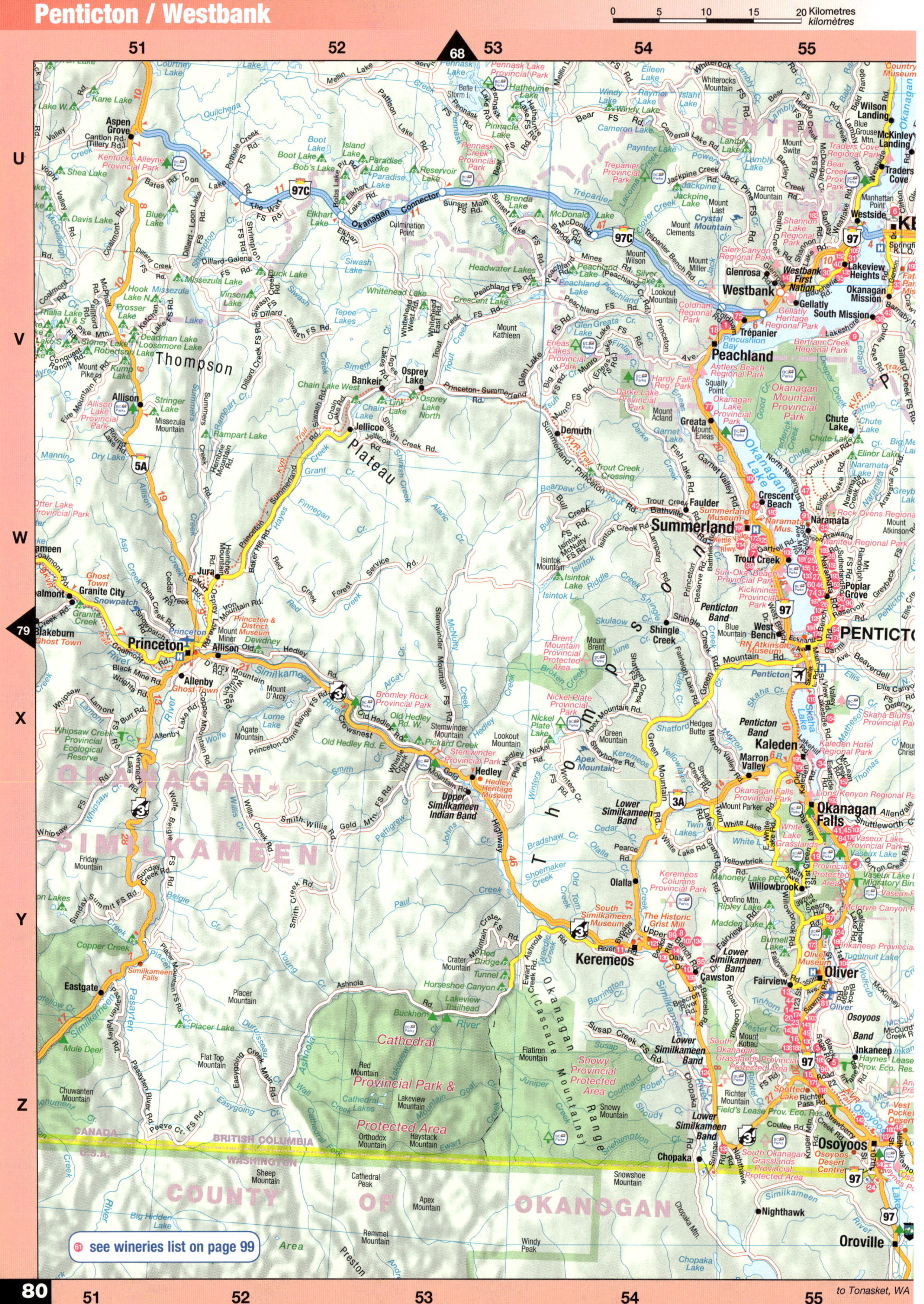
0 5 10 15 20 Kilometres kilomètres
51
52
53
54
55
U
V
W
X
Y
Z
68
79
Aspen Grove
Kentucky-Alleyne Provincial Park
Okanagan Connector
97C
Thompson
Plateau
Allison
Princeton
Princeton & District Museum
Granite City
Blakeburn Ghost Town
Allenby
Jura
Jellicoe
Bankeir
Osprey Lake
Demuth
Hedley
Upper Similkameen Indian Band
Keremeos
South Similkameen Museum
The Historic Grist Mill
Cathedral Provincial Park & Protected Area
Eastgate
Okanagan-Similkameen
Westbank
Westbank First Nation
Gellatly
Trépanier
Peachland
Okanagan Mountain Provincial Park
Summerland
Trout Creek
Penticton
Penticton Band
Kaleden
Okanagan Falls
Oliver
Osoyoos
Chopaka
Nighthawk
Oroville
Kelowna
Okanagan Lake
Skaha Lake
British Columbia
Washington
Canada
U.S.A.
County of Okanogan
Okanagan (Cascade Mountains) Range
Similkameen
97
97C
3
3A
5A
see wineries list on page 99
to Tonasket, WA

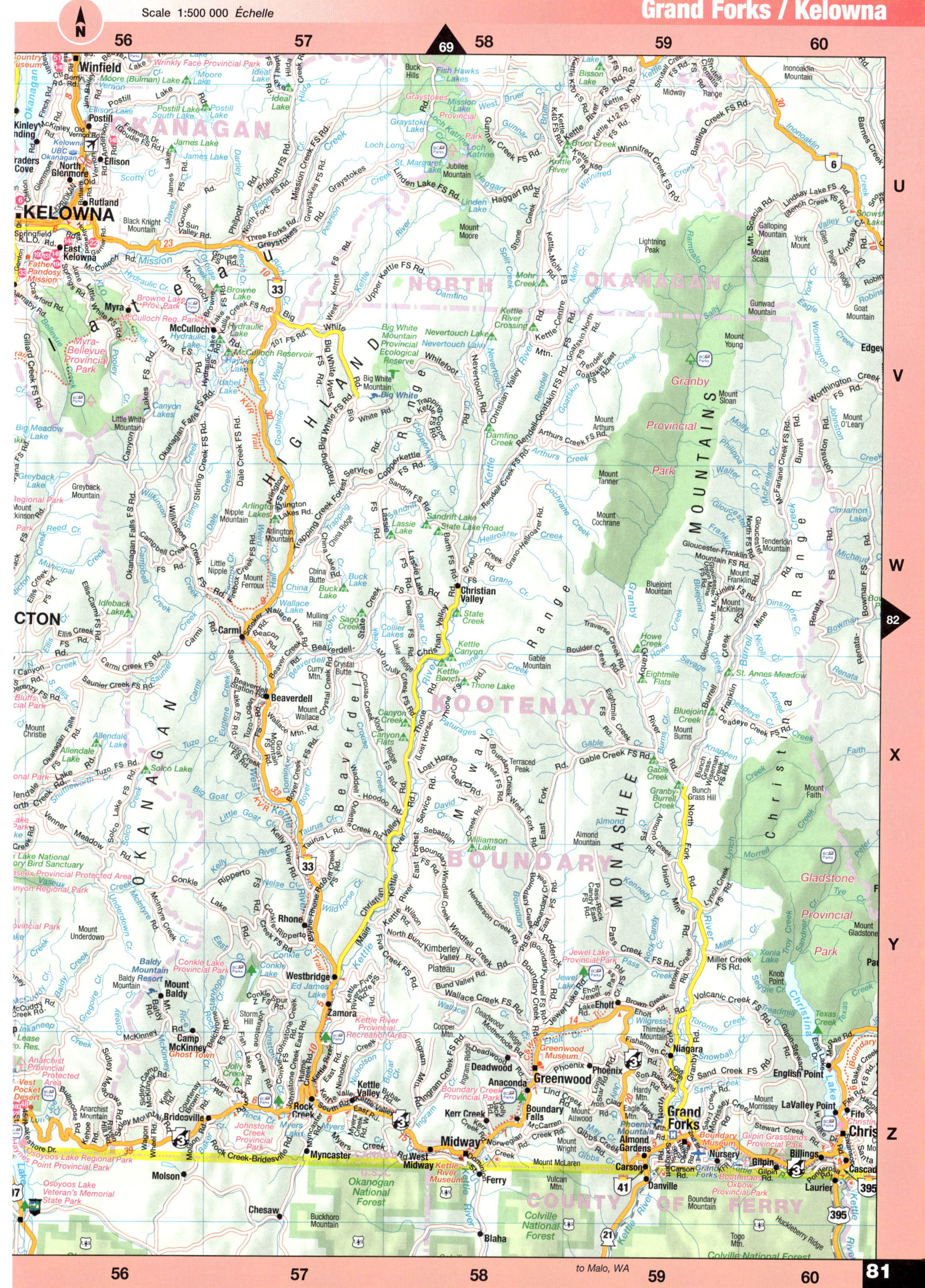
Scale 1:500 000 Échelle
N
56
57
69
58
59
60
U
V
W
X
Y
Z
82
Winfield
Kelowna
East Kelowna
Rutland
Ellison
Glenmore
North Glenmore
Postill
Myra
McCulloch
Carmi
Beaverdell
Westbridge
Rhone
Zamora
Rock Creek
Kettle Valley
Bridesville
Molson
Myncaster
Chesaw
Midway
Greenwood
Anaconda
Boundary Falls
Phoenix
Eholt
Grand Forks
Niagara
Nursery
Gilpin
Billings
Carson
Danville
Christian Valley
Boulder Creek
English Point
LaValley Point
Fife
Laurier
Cascade
Ferry
Blaha
Mount Baldy
Camp McKinney
OKANAGAN
NORTH OKANAGAN
KOOTENAY BOUNDARY
HIGHLAND
MONASHEE
MOUNTAINS
Granby Provincial Park
Gladstone Provincial Park
Myra-Bellevue Provincial Park
Jewel Lake Provincial Park
Boundary Creek Provincial Park
Johnstone Creek Provincial Park
Conkle Lake Provincial Park
Kettle River Provincial Recreation Area
Big White Mountain Provincial Ecological Reserve
Okanogan National Forest
Colville National Forest
COUNTY OF FERRY
Christina Lake
Christina Range
to Malo, WA

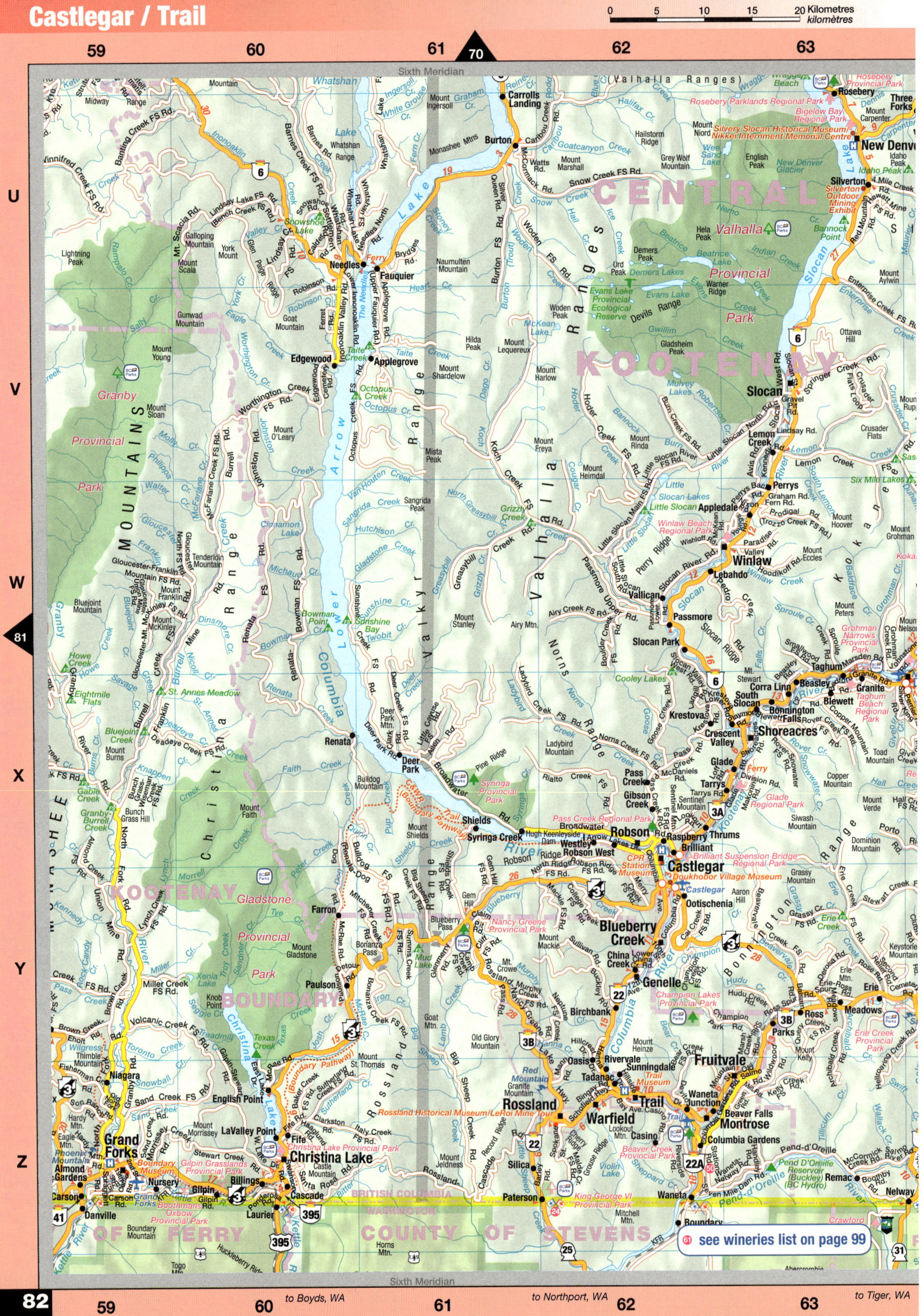
0 5 10 15 20 Kilometres kilomètres
59
60
61
62
63
70
U
V
W
X
Y
Z
81
Sixth Meridian
Carrolls Landing
Burton
Needles
Fauquier
Edgewood
Applegrove
Renata
Deer Park
Shields
Syringa Creek
Robson
Robson West
Castlegar
Brilliant
Thrums
Raspberry
Ootischenia
Blueberry Creek
Genelle
China Creek
Birchbank
Oasis
Rivervale
Tadanac
Sunningdale
Trail
Warfield
Rossland
Fruitvale
Waneta Junction
Beaver Falls
Montrose
Columbia Gardens
Casino
Waneta
Paterson
Silica
Salmo
Ross Spur
Meadows
Erie
Remac
Nelway
Boundary
Christina Lake
Fife
Cascade
Laurier
Gilpin
Billings
Nursery
Grand Forks
Almond Gardens
Carson
Danville
Niagara
English Point
LaValley Point
Paulson
Farron
Slocan
Lemon Creek
Perrys
Appledale
Winlaw
Lebahdo
Vallican
Passmore
Slocan Park
Crescent Valley
Krestova
South Slocan
Shoreacres
Bonnington Falls
Glade
Tarrys
Pass Creek
Gibson Creek
Taghum
Beasley
Blewett
Granite
Corra Linn
New Denver
Silverton
Rosebery
Three Forks
Valhalla Provincial Park
Granby Provincial Park
Gladstone Provincial Park
Syringa Provincial Park
Nancy Greene Provincial Park
Champion Lakes Provincial Park
Erie Creek Provincial Park
Beaver Creek Provincial Park
King George VI Provincial Park
Christina Lake Provincial Park
Gilpin Grasslands Provincial Park
Boothman's Oxbow Provincial Park
Rosebery Parklands Regional Park
Bigelow Bay Regional Park
Silvery Slocan Historical Museum / Nikkei Internment Memorial Centre
Silverton Outdoor Mining Exhibit
Grohman Narrows Provincial Park
Taghum Beach Regional Park
Glade Regional Park
Pass Creek Regional Park
Winlaw Beach Regional Park
Evans Lake Provincial Ecological Reserve
Boundary Museum
Rossland Historical Museum/LeRoi Mine Tour
Trail Museum
CPR Station Museum
Doukhobor Village Museum
Brilliant Suspension Bridge Regional Park
Pend D'Oreille Reservoir (Buckley) (BC Hydro)
Arrow Lake
Lower Arrow Lake
Columbia River
Kootenay River
Slocan River
Slocan Lake
Pend-d'Oreille River
CENTRAL KOOTENAY
KOOTENAY BOUNDARY
Valhalla Ranges
Valkyr Range
Norns Range
Christina Range
Rossland Range
Bonnington Range
Granby Provincial Park
MONASHEE MOUNTAINS
BRITISH COLUMBIA
WASHINGTON
COUNTY OF FERRY
COUNTY OF STEVENS
see wineries list on page 99
to Boyds, WA
to Northport, WA
to Tiger, WA

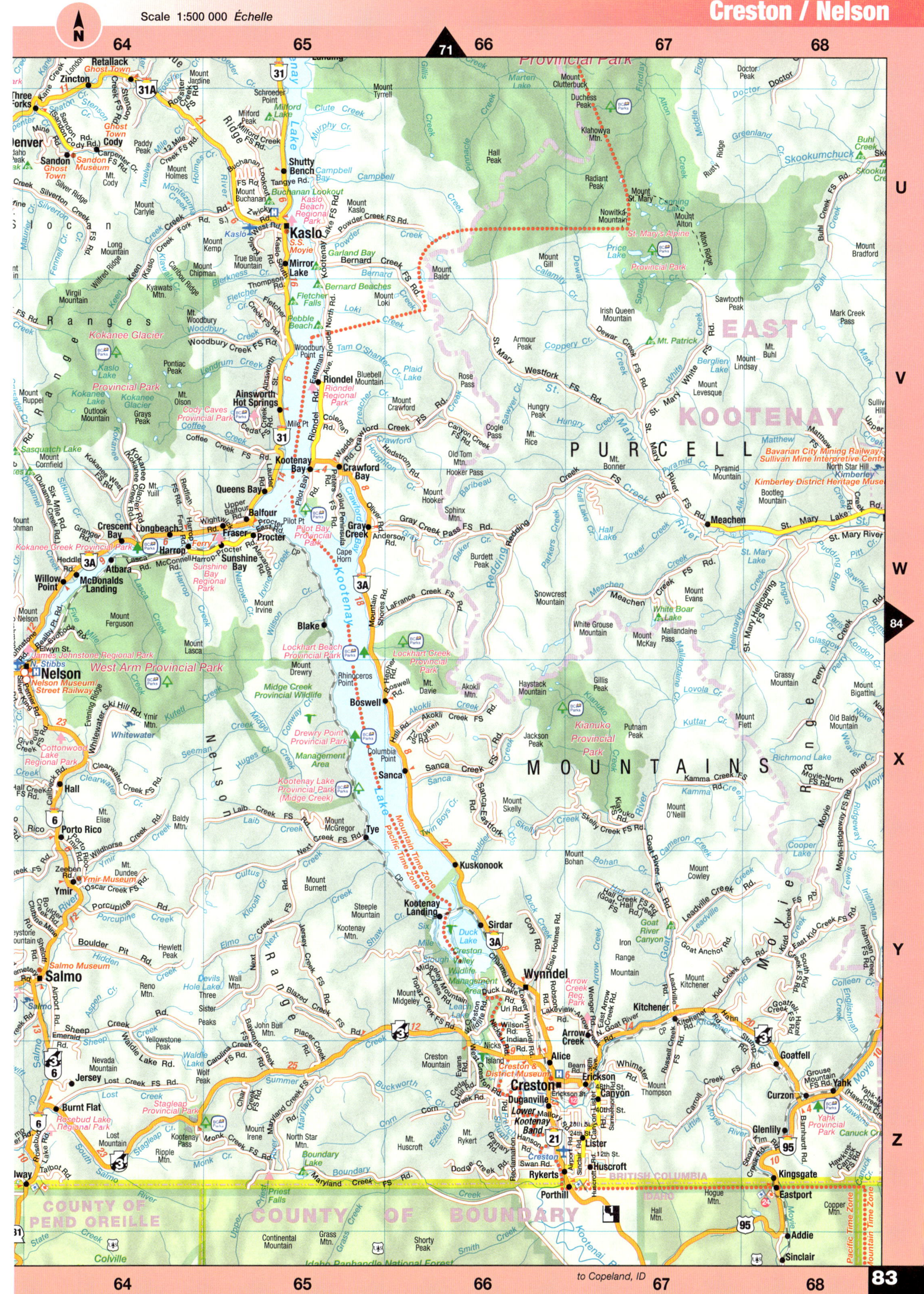

Scale 1:500 000 Échelle
N
64
65
66
67
68
71
84
U
V
W
X
Y
Z
Retallack
Ghost Town
Zincton
Three Forks
Denver
Sandon
Ghost Town
Sandon Museum
Cody
Mount Jardine
Schroeder Point
Milford Lake
Mount Tyrrell
Clute Creek
Murphy Cr.
Shutty Bench
Campbell Bay
Buchanan Lookout
Kaslo Beach Regional Park
Mount Kaslo
Kaslo
S.S. Moyie
Garland Bay
Mirror Lake
Bernard
Bernard Beaches
Mount Loki
Fletcher Falls
Pebble Beach
Woodbury Point
Riondel
Riondel Regional Park
Bluebell Mountain
Plaid Lake
Ainsworth Hot Springs
Cody Caves Provincial Park
Mile Pt
Kootenay Bay
Crawford Bay
Queens Bay
Balfour
Pilot Bay Provincial Park
Gray Creek
Cape Horn
Procter
Harrop
Sunshine Bay
Sunshine Bay Regional Park
Longbeach
Crescent Bay
Fraser
Kokanee Creek Provincial Park
Kokanee Glacier
Kokanee Glacier Provincial Park
Kaslo Lake
Sasquatch Lake
Willow Point
McDonalds Landing
Atbara
Nelson
Nelson Museum
Street Railway
James Johnstone Regional Park
West Arm Provincial Park
Whitewater
Cottonwood Lake Regional Park
Hall
Porto Rico
Ymir
Ymir Museum
Salmo
Salmo Museum
Jersey
Burnt Flat
Rosebud Lake Regional Park
Stagleap Provincial Park
Blake
Lockhart Beach Provincial Park
Lockhart Creek Provincial Park
Midge Creek Provincial Wildlife
Rhinoceros Point
Boswell
Drewry Point Provincial Park
Management Area
Columbia Point
Sanca
Kootenay Lake Provincial Park (Midge Creek)
Tye
Mountain Time Zone
Pacific Time Zone
Kuskonook
Kootenay Landing
Sirdar
Duck Lake
Creston Valley Wildlife Management Area
Wynndel
Arrow Creek Reg. Park
Creston Mountain
Creston & District Museum
Alice Siding
Creston
Erickson
Canyon
Lister
Huscroft
Rykerts
Porthill
Duganville
Lower Kootenay Band
Arrow Creek
Kitchener
Goatfell
Curzon
Yahk
Yahk Provincial Park
Glenlily
Kingsgate
Eastport
Addie
Sinclair
Meachen
St. Mary's Alpine Provincial Park
EAST KOOTENAY
PURCELL MOUNTAINS
Kianuko Provincial Park
White Boar Lake
Bavarian City Mining Railway / Sullivan Mine Interpretive Centre
Kimberley District Heritage Museum
Moyie Range
Nelson Range
Ranges
BRITISH COLUMBIA
IDAHO
COUNTY OF PEND OREILLE
COUNTY OF BOUNDARY
Idaho Panhandle National Forest
Colville
to Copeland, ID
Pacific Time Zone
Mountain Time Zone
Kootenay Lake
Kootenay River

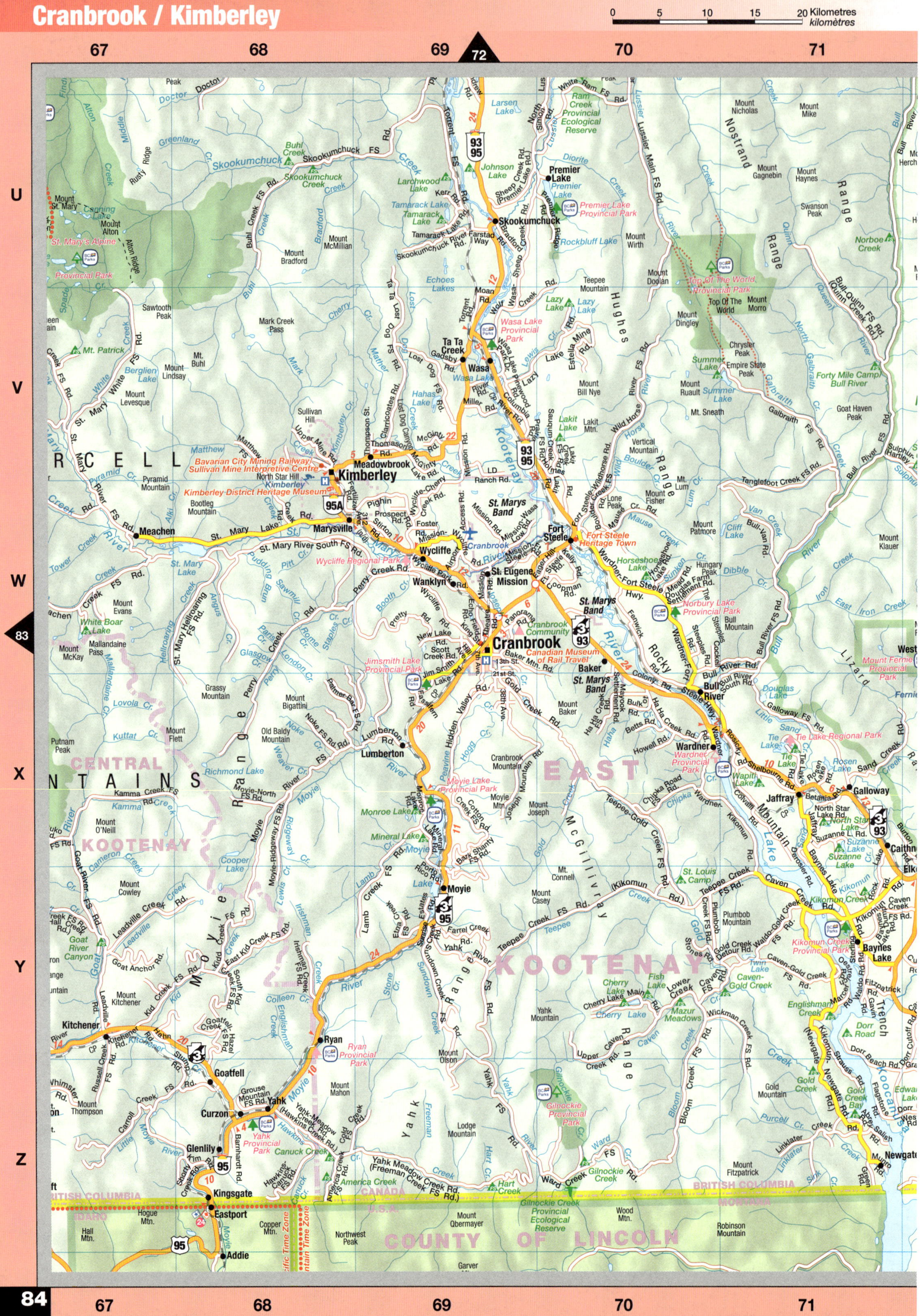

0 5 10 15 20 Kilometres kilomètres
67
68
69
70
71
72
83
U
V
W
X
Y
Z
Kimberley
Cranbrook
Marysville
Meadowbrook
Wycliffe
Wanklyn
St. Eugene Mission
Fort Steele
Fort Steele Heritage Town
Skookumchuck
Ta Ta Creek
Wasa
Wasa Lake Provincial Park
Premier Lake
Premier Lake Provincial Park
Top Of The World Provincial Park
St. Mary's Alpine Provincial Park
Meachen
Bavarian City Mining Railway/ Sullivan Mine Interpretive Centre
Kimberley District Heritage Museum
Wycliffe Regional Park
Cranbrook Community
Canadian Museum of Rail Travel
Jimsmith Lake Provincial Park
Norbury Lake Provincial Park
Mount Fernie Provincial Park
Tie Lake Regional Park
Wardner Provincial Park
Wardner
Bull River
Jaffray
Galloway
Baynes Lake
Kikomun Creek Provincial Park
Lumberton
Moyie Lake Provincial Park
Moyie
Kitchener
Goatfell
Yahk
Yahk Provincial Park
Ryan Provincial Park
Curzon
Glenlily
Kingsgate
Eastport
Addie
Newgate
Gilnockie Provincial Park
Gilnockie Creek Provincial Ecological Reserve
Ram Creek Provincial Ecological Reserve
CENTRAL
KOOTENAY
EAST
KOOTENAY
PURCELL
MOUNTAINS
BRITISH COLUMBIA
CANADA
U.S.A.
IDAHO
MONTANA
COUNTY OF LINCOLN
Moyie Range
Hughes Range
Rocky Range
Nostrand Range
Quinn Range
Mcgillivray Range
Yahk Range
Lizard Range
Trench

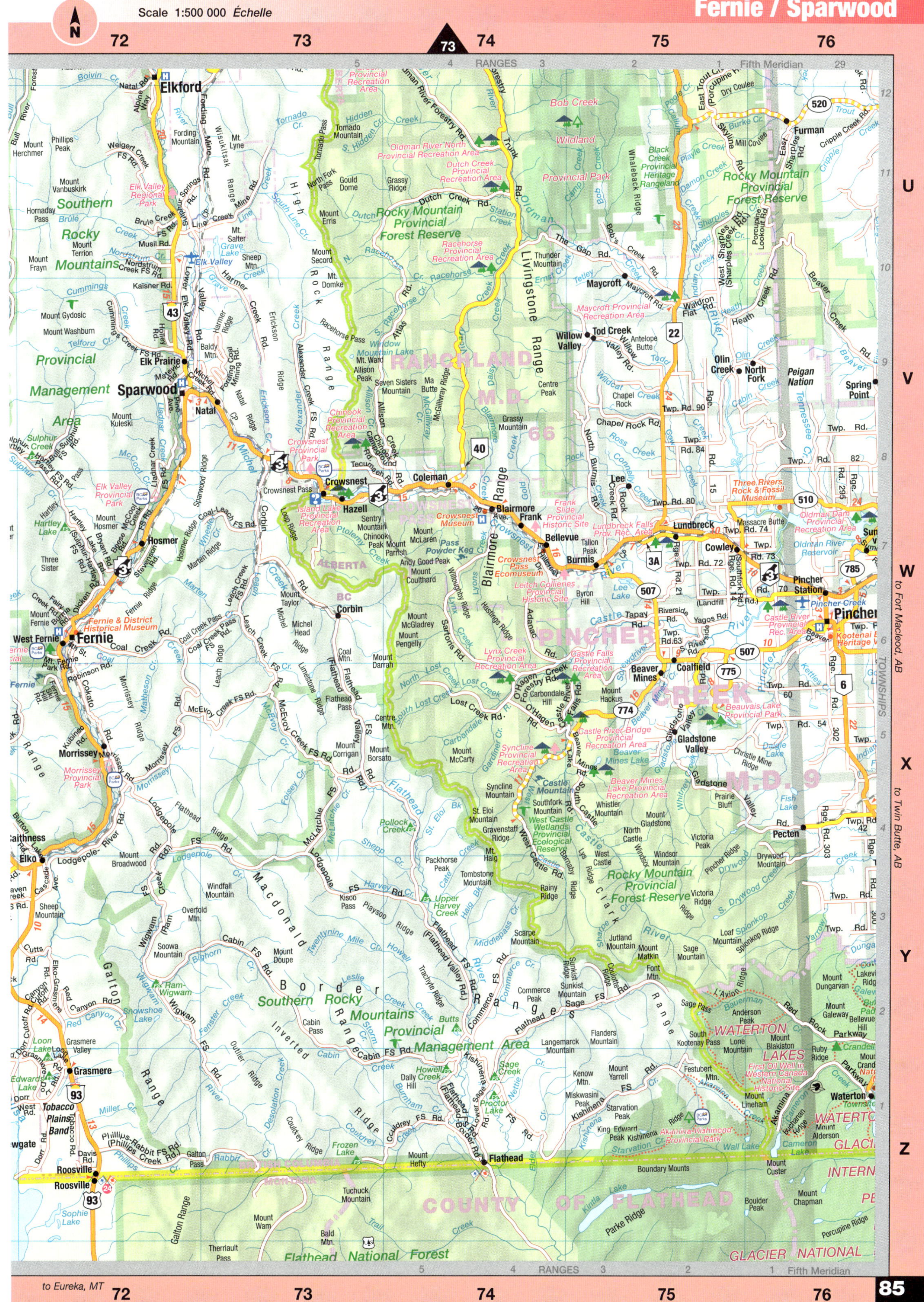
Scale 1:500 000 Échelle
N
72
73
74
75
76
RANGES
Fifth Meridian
TOWNSHIPS
U
V
W
X
Y
Z
to Fort Macleod, AB
to Twin Butte, AB
to Eureka, MT
Elkford
Sparwood
Natal
Fernie
West Fernie
Hosmer
Morrissey
Elko
Grasmere
Roosville
Crowsnest
Hazell
Coleman
Blairmore
Frank
Bellevue
Burmis
Lundbreck
Cowley
Pincher Station
Pincher
Beaver Mines
Coalfield
Gladstone Valley
Pecten
Maycroft
Tod Creek
Willow Valley
Olin Creek
North Fork
Peigan Nation
Spring Point
Furman
Corbin
Flathead
Waterton
Elk Prairie
Southern Rocky Mountains Provincial Management Area
Southern Rocky Mountains Provincial Management Area
Rocky Mountain Provincial Forest Reserve
Rocky Mountain Provincial Forest Reserve
Rocky Mountain Provincial Forest Reserve
RANCHLAND M.D. 66
PINCHER CREEK M.D. 9
COUNTY OF FLATHEAD
Flathead National Forest
WATERTON LAKES
GLACIER NATIONAL
Livingstone Range
High Rock Range
Border Range
Galton Range
Wigwam Range
Clark Range
Fernie & District Historical Museum
Crowsnest Museum
Frank Slide Historic Site
Leitch Collieries Provincial Historic Site
Three Rivers Rock & Fossil Museum
First Oil Well in Western Canada National Historic Site
Tobacco Plains Band

0 5 10 15 20 Kilometres kilomètres
33
34
75
35
36
76
37
Z
A
B
C
D
E
PACIFIC
OCEAN
JUAN DE FUCA STRAIT
RANGES
COWICHAN
ALBERNI-CLAYOQUOT
Nahmint
Kildonan
Green Cove
Ecoole
Franklin Camp
Nitinat
Caycuse
Honeymoon
Gordon River
Sarita
Bamfield
Huu-ay-aht First Nation
Ditidaht First Nation
Whyac
Clo-oose
Pacheedaht First Nation
Port Renfrew
Toquaht First Nation
Uchucklesaht Tribe
Yuutu?it?ath First Nation
Port Albion
Cowichan
Nitinat Lake
Barkley Sound
Effingham Inlet
Alberni Inlet
Imperial Eagle Channel
Trevor Channel
PACIFIC RIM NATIONAL PARK RESERVE
(Broken Group Islands Unit)
(West Coast Trail Unit)
West Coast Trail
Carmanah Walbran Provincial Park
Hitchie Creek Provincial Park
Nitinat River Provincial Park
Nitinat Lake Provincial Ecological Reserve
Klanawa River Prov. Eco. Res.
Thunderbird's Nest/ T'iitsk'in Paawats Provincial Protected Area
Haley Lake Provincial Ecological Reserve
San Juan River Estuary Provincial Ecological Reserve
Avatar Grove Ancient Forest
Pachena Pt.
Valencia Bluffs
Tsusiat Pt.
Tsuquanah Pt.
Carmanah Pt.
Bonilla Pt.
Owen Pt.
San Juan Pt.
Sombrio Pt.
Cape Beale
Tatoosh I.
Cape Flattery
Neah Bay
Makah Cultural Center
Makah Nation
Watch Point
Flattery Rocks National Wildlife Refuge
Point of the Arches
OLYMPIC NATIONAL PARK
Ozette FS
Ozette Lake
Cape Alava
Sand Pt.
Bodelteh Islands
Hoko
Sekiu
Clallam Bay
Sappho
Beaver
112
20
12
to Forks, WA

Scale 1:500 000 Échelle
NANAIMO
Ladysmith
Chemainus
NORTH COWICHAN
Lake Cowichan
Duncan
Cowichan Bay
Shawnigan Lake
Mill Bay
Sidney
North Saanich
Central Saanich
Langford
Sooke
Colwood
Esquimalt
SAANICH
Oak Bay
VICTORIA
Metchosin
Ganges
Gulf Islands National Park Reserve
JUAN DE FUCA STRAIT
Port Angeles
Sequim
Clallam Bay
see wineries list on page 99
to Seattle, WA

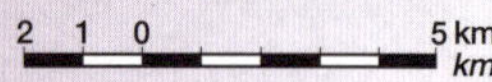

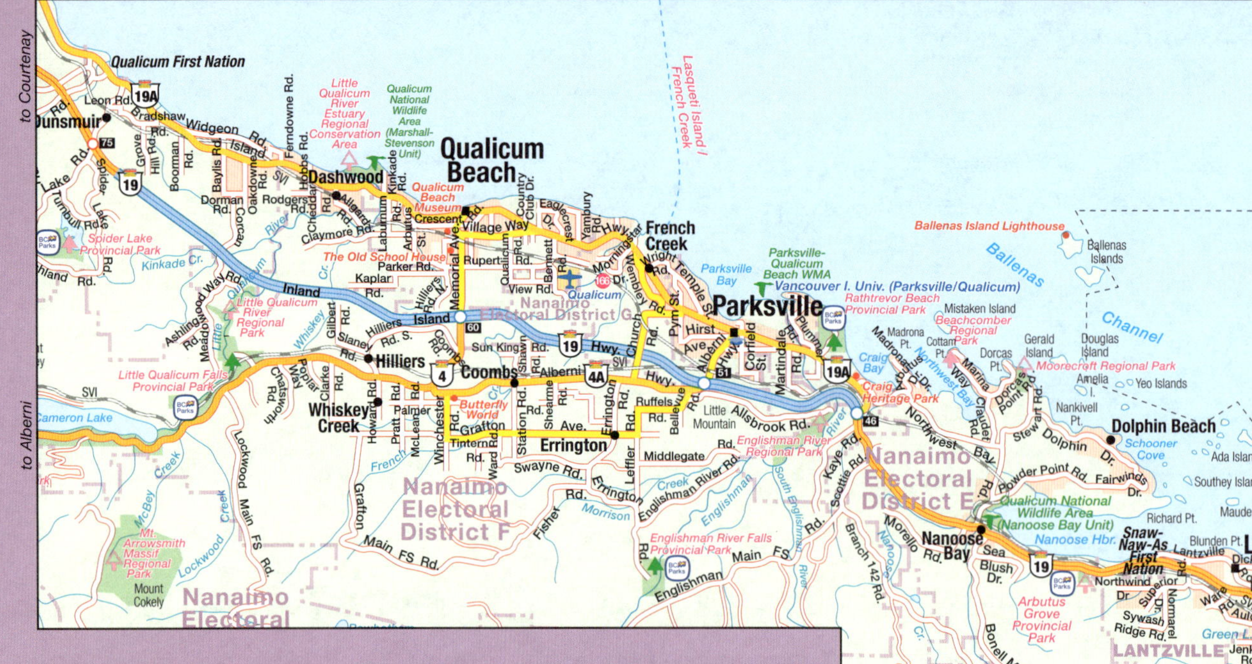

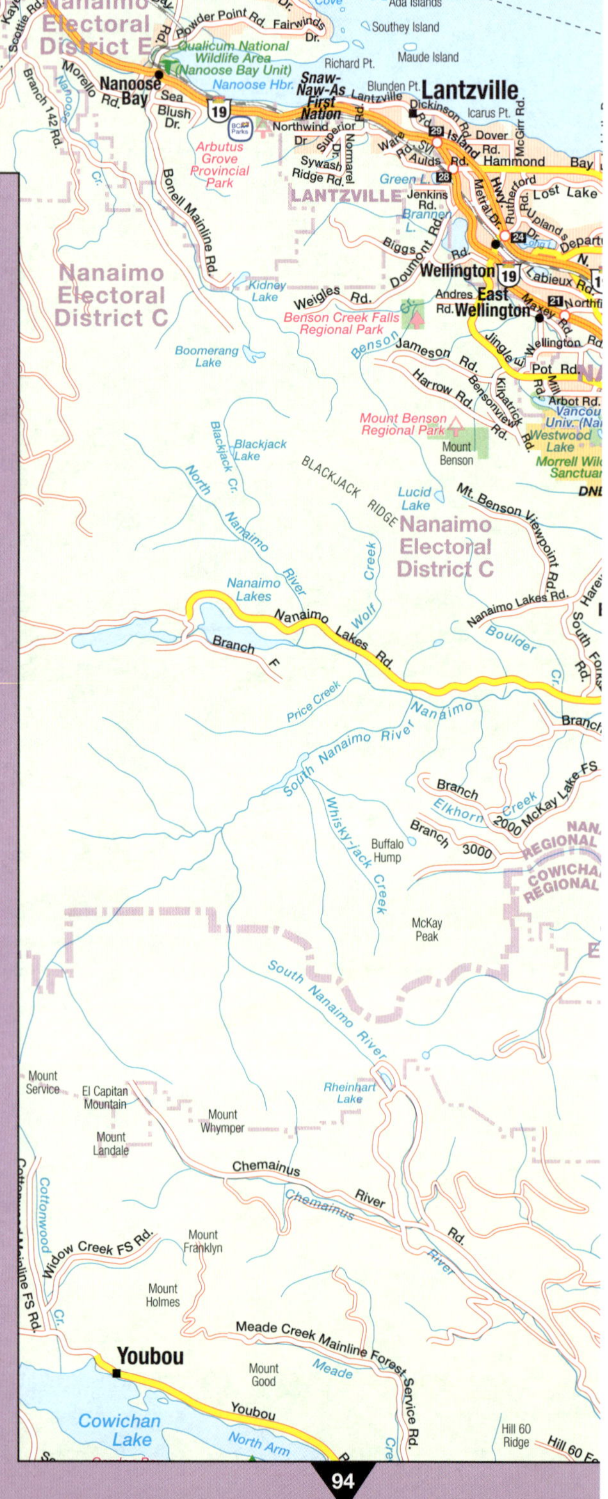

Airports

Abbotsford	**78** Z44-45	Golden	**59** N65	Powell River	**76** V37
Anahim Lake	**23** X19	Grand Forks	**81** Z59	Prince George	**35** X43
Bella Coola	**23** X17	Hope	**79** X48	Prince Rupert	**20** S11
Blue River	**57** H56-57	Invermere	**72** R68	Princeton	**79** W51-52
Boundary Bay	**77** Z42	Kamloops Fulton Field	**67** Q51	Qualicum Beach	**76** X37
Burns Lake	**17** S19	Kaslo	**83** U65	Quesnel	**44** C44
Campbell Hill	**67** P-Q48	Kelowna	**81** U56	Revelstoke	**70** O60-61
Campbell River	**75** U34	Langley	**77** Z43-44	Salmon Arm	**69** Q56-57
Castlegar	**82** Y62	Lillooet	**66** Q46	Sandspit	**20** U8
Chilliwack	**78** Y46	McBride	**38** A52	Sechelt / Gibsons	**77** X40
Comox Valley Regional	**75** V35-36	Merritt	**67** T51	Shearwater	**22** Y15
Cranbrook	**84** W69	N. Stibbs	**83** W-X64	Smithers	**17** R16
Creston	**83** Y66	Nakusp	**69** S62	Squamish	**77** V41-42
Dawson Creek	**19** O27-28	Nanaimo Collishaw	**76** Z39	Terrace	**16** R14
Duncan	**87** B39-40	Oliver	**80** Y55	Tofino	**75** Z32
Elk Valley	**85** U72-73	Pemberton	**65** S43	Trail	**82** Z62
Fairmont Hot Springs	**72** S68-69	Penticton	**80** W-X55	Vancouver International	**77** Y41-42
Fort Nelson	**11** B19	Pitt Meadows	**77** Y43	Vernon	**69** S56
Fort St. John	**19** N26-27	Port Alberni	**75** Y35	Victoria International	**87** B40-41
Gillies Bay	**76** V36-37	Port Hardy	**61** P-Q26	Williams Lake	**54** H45-46

Skiing

Apex Alpine	**80** X54	Mount Timothy	**55** J48
Baldy Mountain Resort	**81** Y56	Mount Washington	**75** V34
Big White	**81** V57-58	Panorama	**71** R67-68
Blackcomb	**65** T43	Phoenix Mountain	**81** Z59
Crystal Mountain	**80** U54-55	Purden	**36** X46
Cypress Bowl	**77** X41-42	Red Mountain	**82** Z61
Fairmont Hot Springs	**72** S69	Revelstoke Mountain Resort	**70** O61
Fernie	**84** X71 **85** X72	Salmo	**83** Y64
Forbidden Plateau	**75** V34	Sasquatch Mountain Resort	**78** X46
Grouse Mountain	**77** X42	Silver Star	**69** R-S57
Hemlock Valley	**78** X46	Silvertip	**79** Y49
Hudson Bay Mountain	**17** R16	Snowpatch	**79** W51
Kicking Horse	**59** M64	Summit Lake	**70** T62-63
Kimberley	**84** V-W68	Sun Peak	**68** O-P54
Manning Park Resort	**79** Z50	Tabor Mountain	**36** X44
Mount Arrowsmith	**76** Y36-37	Troll Mountain	**44** B-C46
Mount Baldy	**81** Y56	Whistler	**64** T42
Mount Cain	**62** S30	Whitewater	**83** X64
Mount Harper	**68** Q52-53		
Mount Seymour	**77** X42-43		

94

see wineries list on page 99
to Sechelt
to Port Mellon
Gibsons
Granthams Landing
Gower Point
Eastbourne
BOWEN ISLAND
Nanoose Bay
Nuclear Testing Area
STRAIT OF GEORGIA (SALISH SEA)
Departure Bay
NANAIMO
Gabriola
GABRIOLA ISLAND
Silva Bay
Harmac
Cedar
Extension
South Wellington
Cassidy
Nanaimo Electoral District B
Southern Strait of Georgia National Marine Conservation Area (Proposed)
Cowichan Valley Electoral District G
GULF ISLANDS
VALDES ISLAND
THETIS ISLAND
Thetis Island
Kuper Island
PENELAKUT ISLAND
North Galiano
GALIANO ISLAND
Montague Harbour
Ladysmith
Saltair
Chemainus
Crofton
Vesuvius Bay
Cowichan Valley Electoral District H
NORTH COWICHAN
VANCOUVER
Southern Gulf Islands Electoral Area
STUART CHANNEL
TRINCOMALI CHANNEL

90
94
95

2 1 0 5 km
km

to Port Mellon

to Squamish

89

see wineries list on page 99

to Swartz Bay

Golden Ears Provincial Park
Pitt Lake
Metro Vancouver Electoral District A
Indian Arm Provincial Park
Pinecone Burke Provincial Park
COQUITLAM
PORT COQUITLAM
Port Moody
Belcarra
Anmore
Pitt Meadows
MAPLE RIDGE
PITT MEADOWS
Haney
Port Hammond
Walnut Grove
Fort Langley
Whonnock
Ruskin
Stave Falls
Steelhead
MISSION
Silverdale
Silverhill
Surrey
SURREY
Newton
North Delta
Guildford
Fleetwood
Cloverdale
LANGLEY
Murrayville
Brookswood
LANGLEY TOWNSHIP
Aldergrove
Aberdeen
Bradner
ABBOTSFORD
White Rock
Crescent Beach
Blaine
Lynden
BRITISH COLUMBIA
CANADA
WASHINGTON
U.S.A.
Semiahmoo Bay
to Bellingham

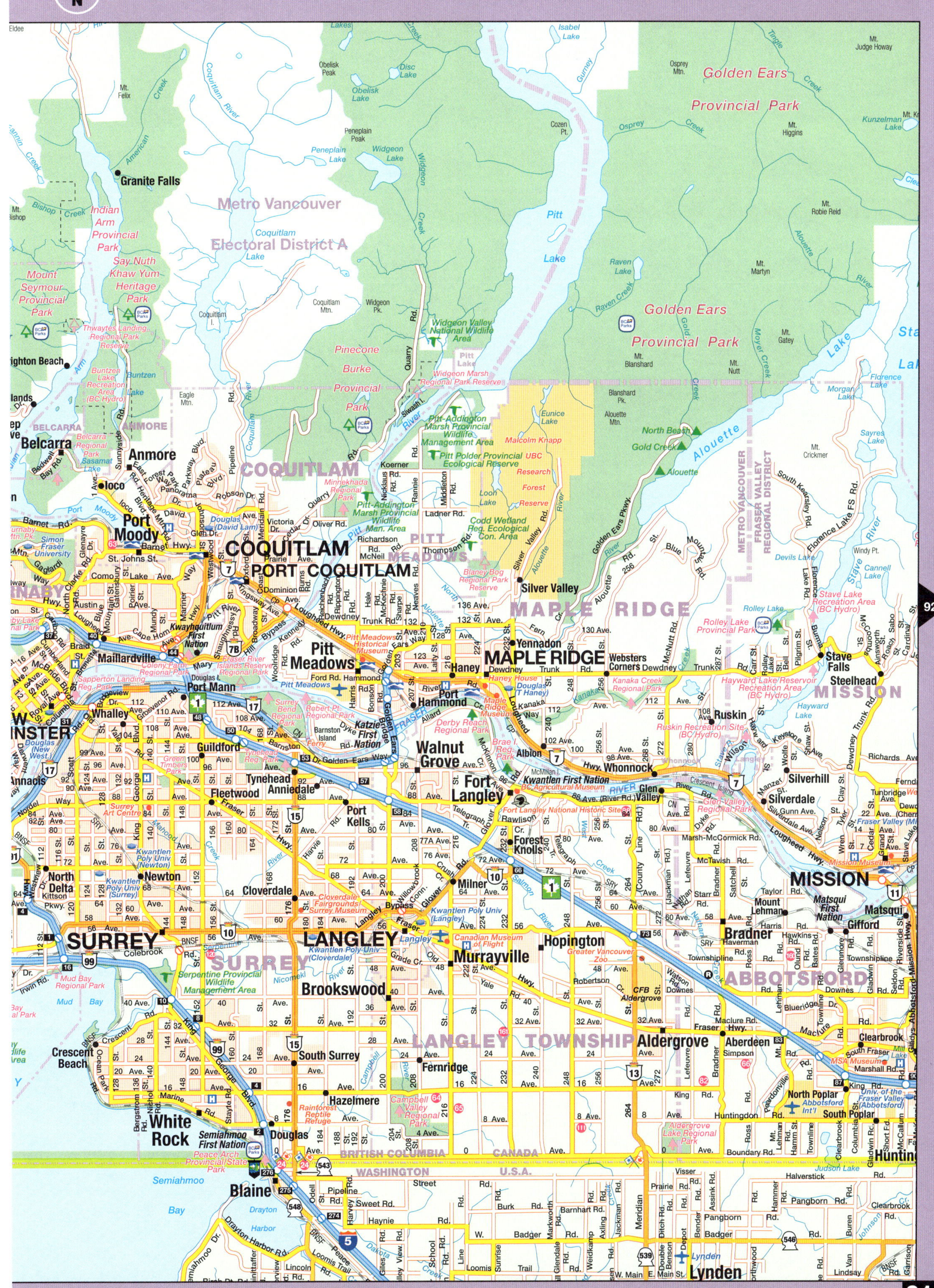

92

2 1 0 5 km

Golden Ears Provincial Park
Pitt Lake
Isabel Lake
Osprey Mtn.
Mt. Judge Howay
Cozen Pt.
Mt. Higgins
Kunzelman Lake
Mt. Kranrod
Clearwater Bay
Mt. Robie Reid
Raven Lake
Mt. Martyn
Mt. Gatey
Mt. Blanshard
Mt. Nutt
Blanshard Pk.
Alouette Mtn.
North Beach
Gold Creek
Alouette Lake
Stave Lake
Kenyon Lake Recreation Area
Welcome Point
Stonerabbit Peak
Mt. Breier
Mt. Orrock
Statlu Lake
Chehalis Lake
Wilson Lake
Blinch Lake
Mt. Fletcher
Mt. Jasper
Mt. Kettley
Mt. Catherwood
Mt. Wardrop
Dickson Lake
Mt. St. Benedict
Statlu Creek Rd.
Fraser Valley Electoral District F
Davis Lake Provincial Park
Cascade Falls Regional Park
Miracle Valley
Stave Lake Recreation Area (BC Hydro)
Rolley Lake Provincial Park
Mt. Crickmer
Devils Lake
Cannell Lake
Windy Pt.
Sayres Lake
Florence Lake
Morgan Lake
METRO VANCOUVER
FRASER VALLEY REGIONAL DISTRICT
Pitt Polder Provincial Ecological Reserve
Malcolm Knapp UBC Research Forest Reserve
Codd Wetland Reg. Ecological Con. Area
Blaney Bog Regional Park Reserve
Silver Valley
MAPLE RIDGE
Haney
Yennadon
Websters Corners
Stave Falls
Steelhead
MISSION
Ruskin
Hayward Lake Reservoir Recreation Area (BC Hydro)
Ruskin Recreation Site (BC Hydro)
Durieu
Cascade Ridge
Scowlitz First Nation
Lake Errock
Deroche
Leq'á:mel First Nation
Fraser Valley Electoral District G
Whonnock
Albion
Port Hammond
Fort Langley
Kwantlen First Nation
Glen Valley
Silverhill
Silverdale
Hatzic
Dewdney
Xá:ytem Longhouse Historic Site
Fraser River Heritage Park
Matsqui Trail Regional Park
FRASER RIVER
Forest Knolls
Milner
Murrayville
Hopington
MISSION
Matsqui First Nation
Matsqui
Gifford
Mount Lehman
Bradner
ABBOTSFORD
Aldergrove
Aberdeen
North Poplar
South Poplar
Huntingdon
Sumas
ABBOTSFORD
Clayburn
Straiton
Kilgard
Sumas First Nation
Sumas Mountain Regional Park
Greendale
Yarrow
Arnold
Lindell
Lindell Beach
Cultus Lake
Fraser Valley Electoral District H
Dewdney Nature Regional Park
Aldergrove Lake Regional Park
LANGLEY TOWNSHIP
CANADA
U.S.A.
BRITISH COLUMBIA
WASHINGTON
Lynden
Columbia
Limestone Junction
Silver Lake Park
Silver Lake
Vedder Mtn.
Black Mtn.
Red Mtn.

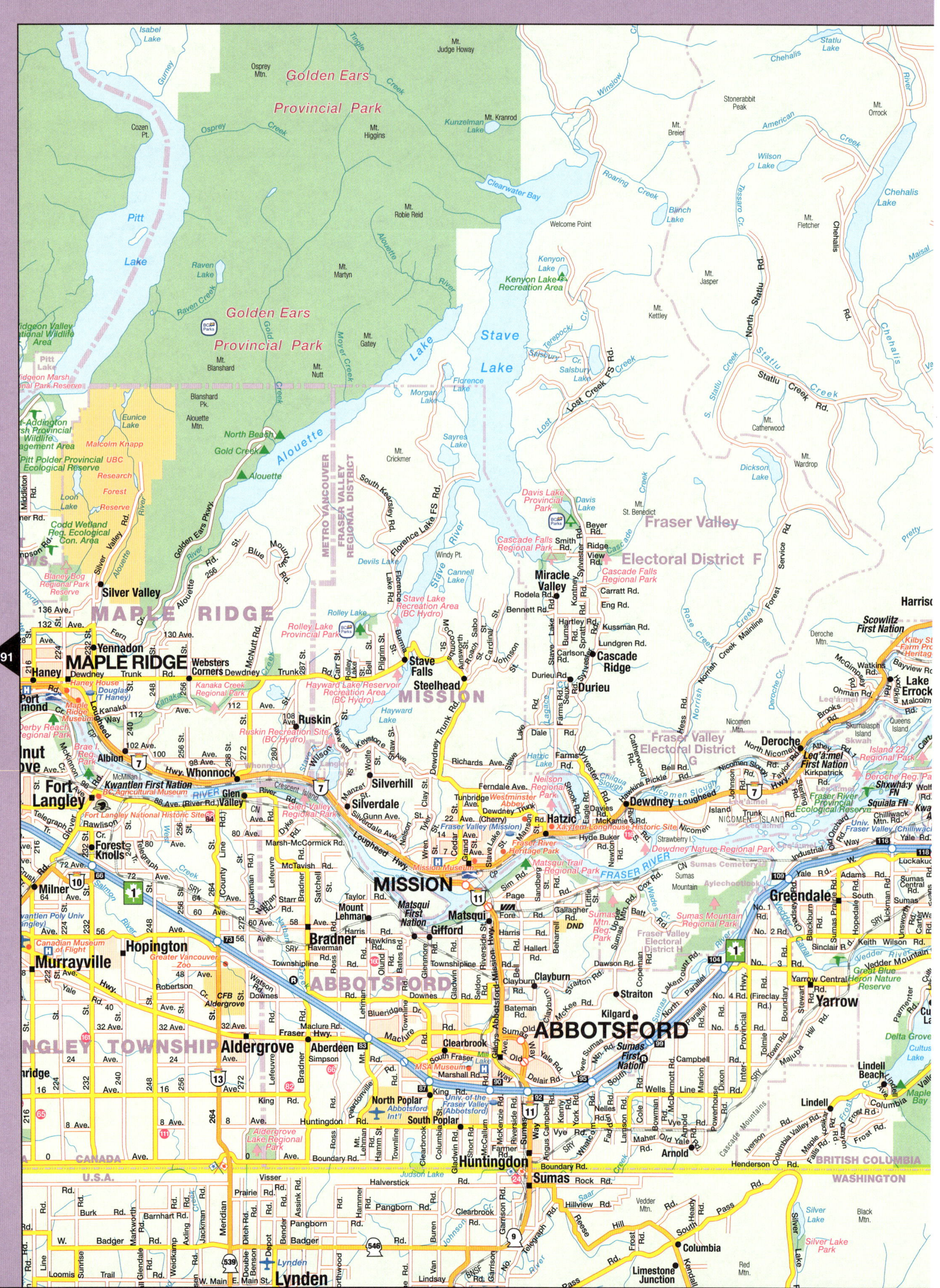

Scale 1:250 000 *Échelle*

B.C. Transit

For information call Translink at 488-8906 or check out the website at www.translink.bc.ca

West Coast Express Stations

Waterfront
Port Moody
Coquitlam Central
Port Coquitlam
Pitt Meadows
Maple Meadows
Port Haney
Mission

B.C. Ministry of Transportation & Highways

Inland Ferry Routes

1-250-387-7788 or on the web at www.th.gov.bc.ca/bchighways/inlandferryschedule/ferryschedule.htm

Adams Lake West	Adams Lake East
Arrow Park	East Arrow Park
Balfour	Kootenay Bay
Barnston Island	Port Kells
Big Bar Creek	West Side of Fraser River
Fauquier	Needles
François Lake	Southbank
Galena Bay	Shelter Bay
Glade	Across Kootenay River to Hwy 3A
Harrop / Proctor	Long Beach
Kootenay Bay	Balfour
Little Fort	East Side of North Thompson River
Longbeach	Harrop / Proctor
Lytton	West Side of Fraser River
McLure	West Side of North Thompson River
Needles	Fauquier
Port Kells	Barnston Island
Shelter Bay	Galena Bay
Southbank	François Lake
Usk (North)	Usk (South)

61 see wineries list on page 99

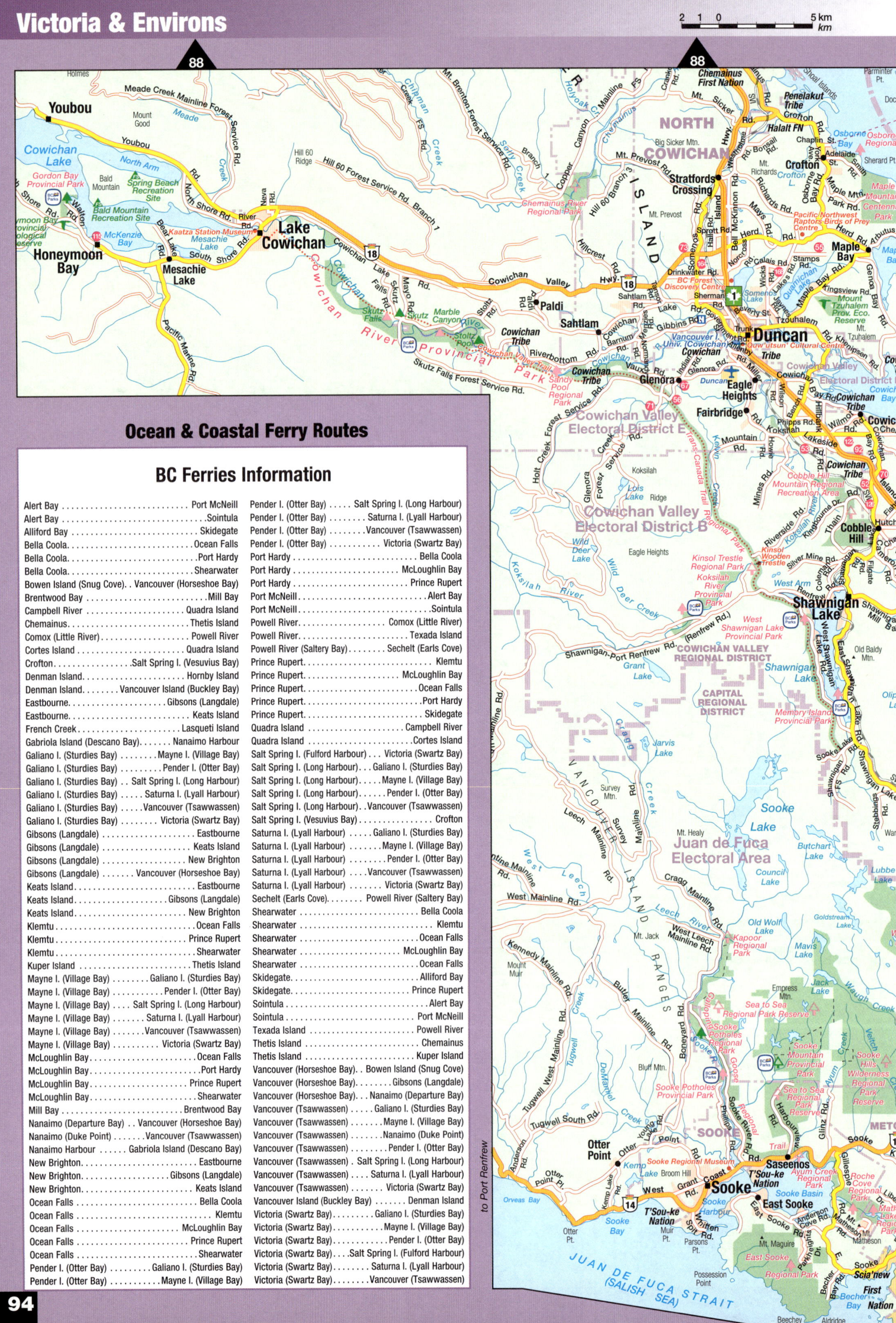

Ocean & Coastal Ferry Routes

BC Ferries Information

From	To
Alert Bay	Port McNeill
Alert Bay	Sointula
Alliford Bay	Skidegate
Bella Coola	Ocean Falls
Bella Coola	Port Hardy
Bella Coola	Shearwater
Bowen Island (Snug Cove)	Vancouver (Horseshoe Bay)
Brentwood Bay	Mill Bay
Campbell River	Quadra Island
Chemainus	Thetis Island
Comox (Little River)	Powell River
Cortes Island	Quadra Island
Crofton	Salt Spring I. (Vesuvius Bay)
Denman Island	Hornby Island
Denman Island	Vancouver Island (Buckley Bay)
Eastbourne	Gibsons (Langdale)
Eastbourne	Keats Island
French Creek	Lasqueti Island
Gabriola Island (Descano Bay)	Nanaimo Harbour
Galiano I. (Sturdies Bay)	Mayne I. (Village Bay)
Galiano I. (Sturdies Bay)	Pender I. (Otter Bay)
Galiano I. (Sturdies Bay)	Salt Spring I. (Long Harbour)
Galiano I. (Sturdies Bay)	Saturna I. (Lyall Harbour)
Galiano I. (Sturdies Bay)	Vancouver (Tsawwassen)
Galiano I. (Sturdies Bay)	Victoria (Swartz Bay)
Gibsons (Langdale)	Eastbourne
Gibsons (Langdale)	Keats Island
Gibsons (Langdale)	New Brighton
Gibsons (Langdale)	Vancouver (Horseshoe Bay)
Keats Island	Eastbourne
Keats Island	Gibsons (Langdale)
Keats Island	New Brighton
Klemtu	Ocean Falls
Klemtu	Prince Rupert
Klemtu	Shearwater
Kuper Island	Thetis Island
Mayne I. (Village Bay)	Galiano I. (Sturdies Bay)
Mayne I. (Village Bay)	Pender I. (Otter Bay)
Mayne I. (Village Bay)	Salt Spring I. (Long Harbour)
Mayne I. (Village Bay)	Saturna I. (Lyall Harbour)
Mayne I. (Village Bay)	Vancouver (Tsawwassen)
Mayne I. (Village Bay)	Victoria (Swartz Bay)
McLoughlin Bay	Ocean Falls
McLoughlin Bay	Port Hardy
McLoughlin Bay	Prince Rupert
McLoughlin Bay	Shearwater
Mill Bay	Brentwood Bay
Nanaimo (Departure Bay)	Vancouver (Horseshoe Bay)
Nanaimo (Duke Point)	Vancouver (Tsawwassen)
Nanaimo Harbour	Gabriola Island (Descano Bay)
New Brighton	Eastbourne
New Brighton	Gibsons (Langdale)
New Brighton	Keats Island
Ocean Falls	Bella Coola
Ocean Falls	Klemtu
Ocean Falls	McLoughlin Bay
Ocean Falls	Prince Rupert
Ocean Falls	Shearwater
Pender I. (Otter Bay)	Galiano I. (Sturdies Bay)
Pender I. (Otter Bay)	Mayne I. (Village Bay)
Pender I. (Otter Bay)	Salt Spring I. (Long Harbour)
Pender I. (Otter Bay)	Saturna I. (Lyall Harbour)
Pender I. (Otter Bay)	Vancouver (Tsawwassen)
Pender I. (Otter Bay)	Victoria (Swartz Bay)
Port Hardy	Bella Coola
Port Hardy	McLoughlin Bay
Port Hardy	Prince Rupert
Port McNeill	Alert Bay
Port McNeill	Sointula
Powell River	Comox (Little River)
Powell River	Texada Island
Powell River (Saltery Bay)	Sechelt (Earls Cove)
Prince Rupert	Klemtu
Prince Rupert	McLoughlin Bay
Prince Rupert	Ocean Falls
Prince Rupert	Port Hardy
Prince Rupert	Skidegate
Quadra Island	Campbell River
Quadra Island	Cortes Island
Salt Spring I. (Fulford Harbour)	Victoria (Swartz Bay)
Salt Spring I. (Long Harbour)	Galiano I. (Sturdies Bay)
Salt Spring I. (Long Harbour)	Mayne I. (Village Bay)
Salt Spring I. (Long Harbour)	Pender I. (Otter Bay)
Salt Spring I. (Long Harbour)	Vancouver (Tsawwassen)
Salt Spring I. (Vesuvius Bay)	Crofton
Saturna I. (Lyall Harbour)	Galiano I. (Sturdies Bay)
Saturna I. (Lyall Harbour)	Mayne I. (Village Bay)
Saturna I. (Lyall Harbour)	Pender I. (Otter Bay)
Saturna I. (Lyall Harbour)	Vancouver (Tsawwassen)
Saturna I. (Lyall Harbour)	Victoria (Swartz Bay)
Sechelt (Earls Cove)	Powell River (Saltery Bay)
Shearwater	Bella Coola
Shearwater	Klemtu
Shearwater	Ocean Falls
Shearwater	McLoughlin Bay
Shearwater	Ocean Falls
Skidegate	Alliford Bay
Skidegate	Prince Rupert
Sointula	Alert Bay
Sointula	Port McNeill
Texada Island	Powell River
Thetis Island	Chemainus
Thetis Island	Kuper Island
Vancouver (Horseshoe Bay)	Bowen Island (Snug Cove)
Vancouver (Horseshoe Bay)	Gibsons (Langdale)
Vancouver (Horseshoe Bay)	Nanaimo (Departure Bay)
Vancouver (Tsawwassen)	Galiano I. (Sturdies Bay)
Vancouver (Tsawwassen)	Mayne I. (Village Bay)
Vancouver (Tsawwassen)	Nanaimo (Duke Point)
Vancouver (Tsawwassen)	Pender I. (Otter Bay)
Vancouver (Tsawwassen)	Salt Spring I. (Long Harbour)
Vancouver (Tsawwassen)	Saturna I. (Lyall Harbour)
Vancouver (Tsawwassen)	Victoria (Swartz Bay)
Vancouver Island (Buckley Bay)	Denman Island
Victoria (Swartz Bay)	Galiano I. (Sturdies Bay)
Victoria (Swartz Bay)	Mayne I. (Village Bay)
Victoria (Swartz Bay)	Pender I. (Otter Bay)
Victoria (Swartz Bay)	Salt Spring I. (Fulford Harbour)
Victoria (Swartz Bay)	Saturna I. (Lyall Harbour)
Victoria (Swartz Bay)	Vancouver (Tsawwassen)

Scale 1:250 000 Échelle

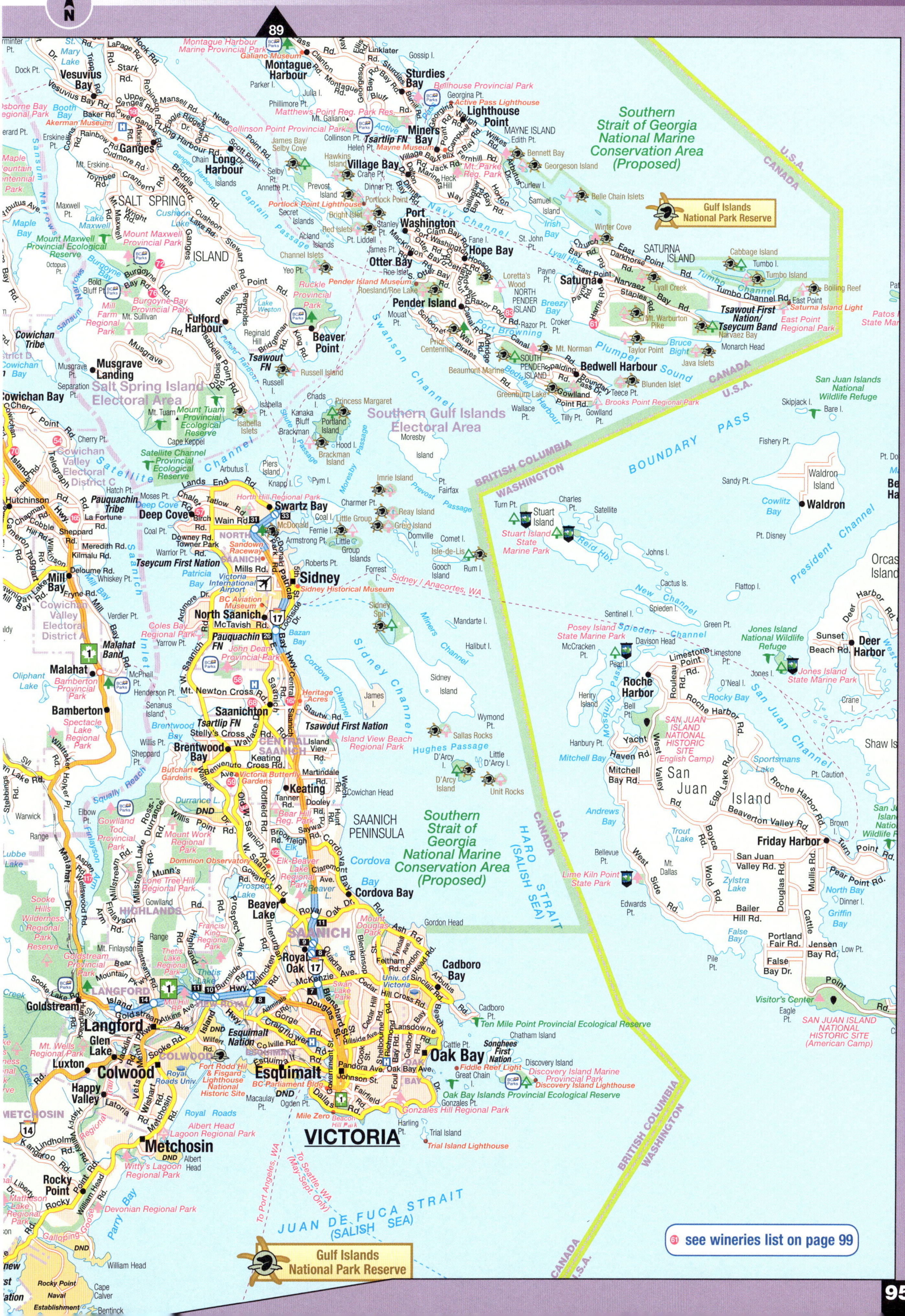
89
Southern Strait of Georgia National Marine Conservation Area (Proposed)
Gulf Islands National Park Reserve
U.S.A.
CANADA
Vesuvius Bay
Montague Harbour
Montague Harbour Marine Provincial Park
Galiano Museum
Sturdies Bay
Bellhouse Provincial Park
Active Pass Lighthouse
Lighthouse Point
Matthews Point Reg. Park Res.
Collinson Point Provincial Park
Tsartlip FN
Miners Bay
Mayne Museum
MAYNE ISLAND
Bennett Bay
Georgeson Island
Ganges
Long Harbour
Village Bay
Mt. Parke Reg. Park
SALT SPRING ISLAND
Mount Maxwell Provincial Park
Mount Maxwell Provincial Ecological Reserve
Portlock Point Lighthouse
Port Washington
Belle Chain Islets
Hope Bay
Otter Bay
SATURNA ISLAND
Saturna
Winter Cove
Tumbo Island
Cabbage Island
Tumbo Channel
Boiling Reef
Saturna Island Light
East Point
East Point Regional Park
Tsawout First Nation/Tseycum Band
Pender Island Museum
Ruckle Provincial Park
Burgoyne Bay Provincial Park
Mill Farm Regional Park
Fulford Harbour
Beaver Point
Pender Island
NORTH PENDER ISLAND
Port Browning
Mt. Warburton Pike
Lyall Creek
Narvaez Bay
Monarch Head
Cowichan Tribe
Musgrave Landing
Salt Spring Island Electoral Area
Tsawout FN
Russell Island
Swanson Channel
SOUTH PENDER ISLAND
Bedwell Harbour
Plumper Sound
Blunden Islet
Brooks Point Regional Park
Cowichan Bay
Mount Tuam Provincial Ecological Reserve
Princess Margaret
Portland Island
Southern Gulf Islands Electoral Area
Moresby Island
San Juan Islands National Wildlife Refuge
Satellite Channel Provincial Ecological Reserve
Cowichan Valley Electoral District C
BRITISH COLUMBIA
WASHINGTON
BOUNDARY PASS
Waldron Island
Waldron
Cowlitz Bay
Pauquachin Tribe
Deep Cove
Swartz Bay
Horth Hill Regional Park
Tsecum First Nation
Sandown Raceway
NORTH SAANICH
Stuart Island
Stuart Island State Marine Park
Reid Hbr.
President Channel
Orcas Island
Mill Bay
Sidney
Sidney Historical Museum
Sidney / Anacortes, WA
Victoria International Airport
BC Aviation Museum
North Saanich
Coles Bay Regional Park
Pauquachin FN
John Dean Provincial Park
Sidney Spit
Miners Channel
Sidney Channel
Sidney Island
James I.
New Channel
Spieden Channel
Posey Island State Marine Park
Jones Island National Wildlife Refuge
Jones Island State Marine Park
Deer Harbor
Roche Harbor
San Juan Channel
Malahat Band
Malahat
Bamberton Provincial Park
Bamberton
Spectacle Lake Regional Park
Saanichton
Tsawout First Nation
Heritage Acres
Tsartlip FN
Brentwood Bay
CENTRAL SAANICH
Island View Beach Regional Park
Sallas Rocks
Hughes Passage
D'Arcy Island
Unit Rocks
SAN JUAN ISLAND NATIONAL HISTORIC SITE (English Camp)
San Juan Island
Friday Harbor
Butchart Gardens
Victoria Butterfly Gardens
Keating
SAANICH PENINSULA
HARO STRAIT (SALISH SEA)
Goldstream Gowland Tod Provincial Park
Mount Work Regional Park
Dominion Observatory
Elk-Beaver Lake Regional Park
Cordova Bay
Mitchell Bay
Lime Kiln Point State Park
Lone Tree Hill Regional Park
HIGHLANDS
Sooke Hills Wilderness Regional Park Reserve
Beaver Lake
SAANICH
Mount Douglas Park
Francis/King Regional Park
Thetis Lake Regional Park
Goldstream Provincial Park
LANGFORD
Royal Oak
Cadboro Bay
Univ. of Victoria
Swan Lake Park
VIEW ROYAL
Langford
Goldstream
Glen Lake
Colwood
COLWOOD
Esquimalt Nation
ESQUIMALT
Esquimalt
Fort Rodd Hill & Fisgard Lighthouse National Historic Site
Royal Roads Univ.
BC Parliament Bldg.
Oak Bay
OAK BAY
Songhees First Nation
Ten Mile Point Provincial Ecological Reserve
Fiddle Reef Light
Discovery Island Marine Provincial Park
Discovery Island Lighthouse
Oak Bay Islands Provincial Ecological Reserve
Gonzales Hill Regional Park
Mile Zero
Beacon Hill Park
VICTORIA
Trial Island Lighthouse
Luxton
Happy Valley
METCHOSIN
Metchosin
Albert Head Lagoon Regional Park
Witty's Lagoon Regional Park
Mt. Wells Regional Park
Rocky Point
Devonian Regional Park
Galloping Goose Regional Trail
To Port Angeles, WA
To Seattle, WA (May–Sept. Only)
JUAN DE FUCA STRAIT (SALISH SEA)
Gulf Islands National Park Reserve
Rocky Point Naval Establishment
SAN JUAN ISLAND NATIONAL HISTORIC SITE (American Camp)
Visitor's Center
see wineries list on page 99

Scale 1:200 000 Échelle

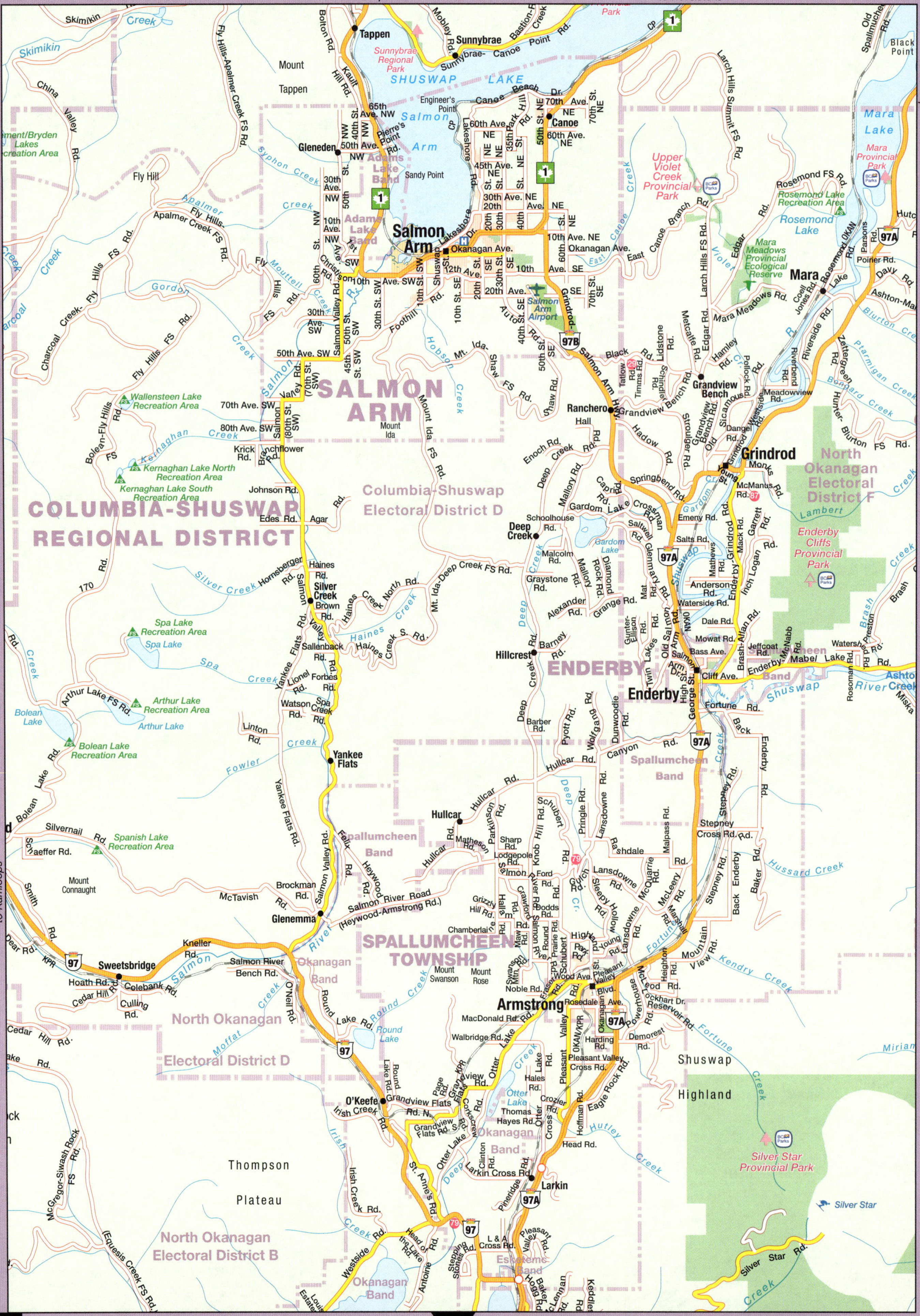

0 2 4 6 km

to Kamloops

to Revelstoke

to Nakusp

SALMON ARM

COLUMBIA-SHUSWAP REGIONAL DISTRICT

Columbia-Shuswap Electoral District D

ENDERBY

North Okanagan Electoral District F

SPALLUMCHEEN TOWNSHIP

North Okanagan Electoral District D

North Okanagan Electoral District B

Thompson Plateau

Shuswap Highland

Salmon Arm

Tappen

Sunnybrae

Canoe

Gleneden

Mara

Grindrod

Grandview Bench

Ranchero

Deep Creek

Silver Creek

Hillcrest

Enderby

Yankee Flats

Hullcar

Glenemma

Sweetsbridge

Armstrong

O'Keefe

Larkin

Shuswap Lake

Mara Lake

Upper Violet Creek Provincial Park

Mara Meadows Provincial Ecological Reserve

Enderby Cliffs Provincial Park

Silver Star Provincial Park

Sunnybrae Regional Park

Salmon Arm Airport

Wallensteen Lake Recreation Area

Kernaghan Lake North Recreation Area

Kernaghan Lake South Recreation Area

Spa Lake Recreation Area

Arthur Lake Recreation Area

Bolean Lake Recreation Area

Spanish Lake Recreation Area

Rosemond Lake Recreation Area

Adams Lake Band

Spallumcheen Band

Okanagan Band

Esketemc Band

to Kamloops

97

0 2 4 6 km
km

Scale 1:200 000 Échelle

96

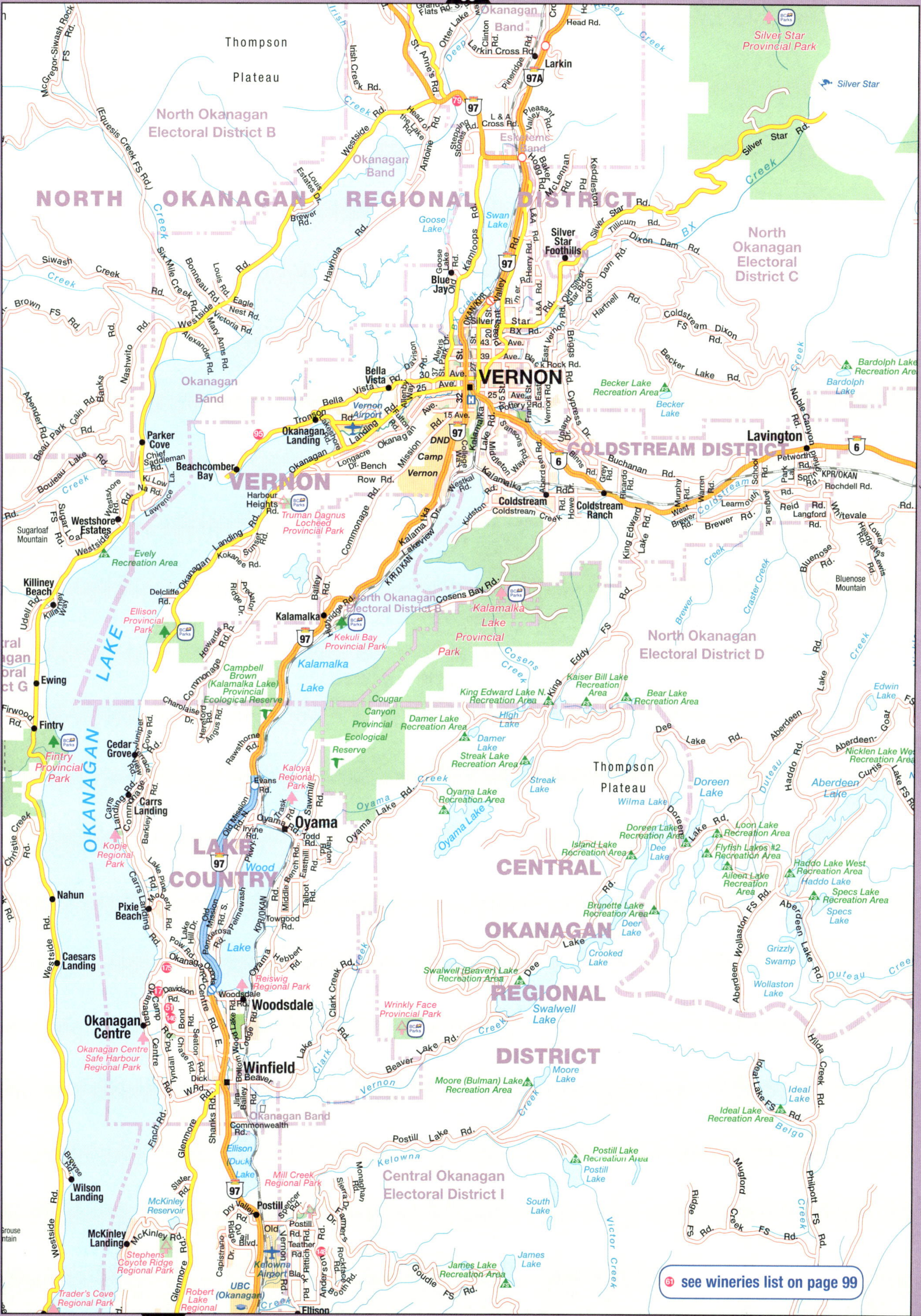
Thompson Plateau
North Okanagan Electoral District B
NORTH OKANAGAN REGIONAL DISTRICT
Okanagan Band
Silver Star Provincial Park
Silver Star
Silver Star Rd.
Larkin
Head Rd.
Larkin Cross Rd.
Otter Lake Rd.
St. Anne's Rd.
Irish Creek Rd.
Westside Rd.
Head of the Lake Rd.
L & A Cross Rd.
Pleasant Valley Rd.
Okanagan Band
Swan Lake
Goose Lake
Silver Star Foothills
Tillicum Rd.
Dixon Dam Rd.
North Okanagan Electoral District C
Blue Jay
Coldstream Dixon Rd.
Becker Lake Rd.
Bardolph Lake Recreation Area
Bardolph Lake
Becker Lake Recreation Area
Becker Lake
Siwash Creek
Brown FS Rd.
Six Mile Creek Rd.
Eagle Nest Rd.
Okanagan Band
Bella Vista
VERNON
Vernon Airport
Okanagan Landing
Parker Cove
Beachcomber Bay
Chief Saddleman Rd.
Longacre Dr.
Bench Row Rd.
Mission Rd.
DND Camp Vernon
Lavington
COLDSTREAM DISTRICT
Coldstream
Coldstream Ranch
Buchanan Rd.
KPR/OKAN
Rochdell Rd.
Whitevale
Lumby
to Lumby
VERNON
Harbour Heights
Truman Dagnus Locheed Provincial Park
Westshore Estates
Sugarloaf Mountain
Evely Recreation Area
Killiney Beach
Ellison Provincial Park
Kalamalka
North Okanagan Electoral District B
Kalamalka Lake Provincial Park
Kekuli Bay Provincial Park
Cosens Bay Rd.
Kalamalka Lake
Bluenose Mountain
Bluenose Rd.
North Okanagan Electoral District D
Ewing
Campbell Brown (Kalamalka Lake) Provincial Ecological Reserve
King Edward Lake N. Recreation Area
Kaiser Bill Lake Recreation Area
Bear Lake Recreation Area
Edwin Lake
Fintry
Fintry Provincial Park
Cedar Grove
Cougar Canyon Provincial Ecological Reserve
Damer Lake Recreation Area
High Lake
Damer Lake
Streak Lake Recreation Area
Streak Lake
Thompson Plateau
Doreen Lake
Wilma Lake
Aberdeen Lake
Nicklen Lake West Recreation Area
Carrs Landing
Kaloya Regional Park
Oyama
Oyama Lake Recreation Area
Oyama Lake
OKANAGAN LAKE
Kopje Regional Park
LAKE COUNTRY
Wood Lake
Island Lake Recreation Area
Doreen Lake Recreation Area
Dee Lake
Loon Lake Recreation Area
Flyfish Lakes #2 Recreation Area
Aileen Lake Recreation Area
Haddo Lake West Recreation Area
Haddo Lake
Specs Lake Recreation Area
Specs Lake
CENTRAL OKANAGAN REGIONAL DISTRICT
Nahun
Pixie Beach
Brunette Lake Recreation Area
Deer Lake
Crooked Lake
Grizzly Swamp
Wollaston Lake
Caesars Landing
Reiswig Regional Park
Woodsdale
Swalwell (Beaver) Lake Recreation Area
Swalwell Lake
Okanagan Centre
Okanagan Centre Safe Harbour Regional Park
Wrinkly Face Provincial Park
Winfield
Beaver Lake Rd.
Moore (Bulman) Lake Recreation Area
Moore Lake
Ideal Lake
Ideal Lake Recreation Area
Okanagan Band
Postill Lake Rd.
Postill Lake Recreation Area
Postill Lake
Ellison (Duck) Lake
Mill Creek Regional Park
Central Okanagan Electoral District I
South Lake
Wilson Landing
McKinley Reservoir
Postill
McKinley Landing
Stephens Coyote Ridge Regional Park
Kelowna Airport
James Lake Recreation Area
James Lake
Trader's Cove Regional Park
Robert Lake Regional
UBC (Okanagan)
Ellison

see wineries list on page 99

98

Scale 1:200 000 *Échelle*

see wineries list on page 99

to Okanagan Falls

British Columbia Wineries - see red bullets on the map

No.	Winery	Map ref.
1	Working Horse	80 V55
2	Stonehill Estate	80 W55
3	Black Hills Estate	80 Y55
4	Blue Mountain	80 X-Y55
5	Burrowing Owl	80 Z55
6	Calona	80 U55
7	Thornhaven Estates	80 W55
8	Clos du Soleil	80 Y55
9	CedarCreek Estate	80 V55
10	Crowsnest	80 Y54
11	Sage Bush	80 Y55
12	Elephant Island	80 W55
13	Fairview Cellars	80 Y55
14	Gehringer Brothers Estate	80 Y55
15	Castoro de Oro Estate	80 Z55
16	Road 13 Vineyards	80 Y55
17	Gray Monk Estate	69 T56
18	Deep Creek / Hainle Vineyards	80 V54-55
19	SeeYa Later Ranch	80 Y55
20	Hester Creek Estate	80 Y55
21	Hillside Winery	80 W55
22	House of Rose	81 U56
23	Inniskillen Okanagan	80 Y55
24	Jackson Triggs	80 Y55
25	Kettle Valley	80 W55
26	La Frenz	80 W55
27	Lake Breeze	80 W55
28	Lang	80 W55
29	Larch Hills	69 Q57
30	Mission Hill Family	80 U55
31	Mount Boucherie Estate	80 U55
32	Nichol	80 W55
33	Tantalus	80 U-V55
34	Blasted Church	80 X55
35	Quails' Gate	80 U55
36	Recline Ridge	69 P56
37	Red Rooster	80 W55
38	Saint Hubertus Estate & Oak Bay Estate	80 V55
39	Dirty Laundry	80 W55
40	Little Straw Vineyards	80 U55
41	Stag's Hollow	80 X55
42	Sumac Ridge Estate	80 W55
43	Summerhill Pyramid	80 V55
44	Tinhorn Creek	80 Y55
45	Wild Goose	80 X55
46	Poplar Grove	80 W55
47	Paradise Ranch	80 W55
48	NK'mip Cellars	80 Z55
49	Silver Sage	80 Y55
50	Columbia Gardens	82 Z62
51	Arrowleaf Cellars	69 T56
52	Glenterra	87 B40
53	Blue Grouse	87 B40
54	Cherry Point	87 B40
55	Alderlea	87 A40
56	Godfrey-Brownell	87 B39
57	Muse	87 B40-41
58	Damali	87 B41
59	Church & State	87 C41
60	Marichel Vineyards	80 W55
61	Saturna Island	87 B42
62	Blossom	77 Y42
63	Andres	77 Y43
64	Township 7	77 Z44 & 80 W55
65	Domaine de Chaberton Estate	77 Z44
66	Pepin Brook Estates	77 Z44
67	Vigneti Zanatta	87 B39
68	De Vine	87 C41
69	Chase & Warren Estate	75 Y35
70	Divino Estate	87 B40
71	Blue Moon	87 B39
72	Salt Spring Vineyards	87 A40
73	Averill Creek	87 A39
74	D'Angelo Estate	80 W55
75	First Estate	80 V55
76	Garry Oaks	87 A40
77	Greata Ranch	80 V54
78	Granite Creek	69 P56
79	Edge of the Earth	69 S56
80	Laughing Stock	80 W55
81	Le Vieux Pin	80 Y55
82	Lotusland Vineyards	78 Z44
83	40 Knots	87 A41
84	Noble Ridge	80 X55
85	Orofino	80 Y54
86	Sonoran Estate	80 W55
87	Baccata Ridge	69 Q57
88	Fort Wine	78 Y44
89	Therapy Vineyards	80 W55
90	3 Mile Estate	81 Z56
91	Van Westen Vineyards	80 W55
92	Venturi-Schulze Vineyards	87 B40
93	Wellbrook	77 Z42
94	Domaine Rochette	87 C41
95	The Rise	69 S56
96	Desert Hills	80 Z55
97	Covert Farms	80 Y55
98	Lulu Island	77 Y42
99	Herder	80 Y54
100	Bonitas	80 W55
101	Isabella	77 Y42
102	50th Parallel Estate	80 W55
103	Oliver Twist	80 Y55
104	Quinta Ferreira	80 Y55
105	Rollingdale	80 U55
106	St. Urban	78 Z46
107	Rustic Roots	80 Y54
108	8th Generation	80 W55
109	Tangled Vines Estate	80 Y55
110	Bonaparte Bend	67 P48
111	Blackwood Lane	78 Z44
112	Carbrea	76 W36
113	Millstone Estate	76 Y39
114	Saxon	80 W55
115	Honeymoon Bay	87 A38
116	Kermode	78 Y45
117	Dragonfly Hill	87 C40
118	Orchard Hill Estate	80 Z55
119	Pentâge	80 X55
120	River's Bend	77 Z43
121	Robin Ridge	80 Y54
122	Rocky Creek	87 B40
123	Sanduz Estate	77 Y42
124	Seven Stones	80 Z54
125	Silkscarf	80 W55
126	Silverside Farm	87 B40
127	Skimmerhorn	83 Z67
128	Spiller Estate	80 W55
129	Starling Lane	87 C41
130	Stoneboat	80 Z55
131	Westham Island Estate	77 Z42
132	Forbidden Fruit	80 Z55
133	Howling Bluff	80 W55
134	Cerelia Vineyards	80 Y54
135	Beaumont Family Estate	80 U55
136	St. Laszlo	80 Y54
137	Adega on 45th Estate	80 Y55
139	Clean Slate	80 Y55
140	Young & Wyse	80 Z55
141	Cassini Cellars	80 Y55
142	La Stella	80 Z55
143	Culmina Family Estate	80 Y55
144	Camelot Vineyards	81 U56
145	Celista Estate	69 O56
146	Ex Nihilo	80 V54
147	Kalala Vineyards	80 U55
148	Ancient Hill	81 U56
149	The Vibrant Wine	81 U56
150	Ovino	69 R56
151	SpierHead	81 U56
152	Volcanic Hills Estate	80 U55
153	Black Widow	80 W55
154	Painted Rock Estate	80 X55
155	Bench 1775	80 W55
156	Kraze Legz	80 X55
157	Meyer Family Vineyards	80 X55
158	Foxtrot	80 X55
159	EauVivre	80 Y54
160	Mount Lehman	78 Z45
161	Backyard Vineyards	78 Z44
162	Beuafort	75 V35
163	Coastal Black	75 V34
164	Deol Family Estate	87 A39
165	Enrico	87 B40
166	MooBerry	76 X37
167	Mount St Michael	87 B40
168	22 Oaks	87 A40
169	Mistaken Identity	87 A40
170	South End Farm	63 T34
171	Gold Hill	80 Z55
172	Heaven's Gate Estate	80 W55
173	Hidden Chapel	80 Y55
174	Intersection Estate	80 Y55
175	Intrigue	69 T56
176	Liquidity	80 X55
177	Upper Bench Estate	80 W55
178	Misconduct	80 W55
179	Monster	80 W55
180	Moon Curser	80 Z55
181	Moraine Estate	80 W55
182	Niche	80 U55
183	Okanagan Crushed Pad	80 W55
184	Perseus	80 W55
185	Platinum Bench Estate	80 Z55
186	River Stone Estate	80 Y55
187	Ruby Blues	80 W55
188	Rustico Farm	80 Y55
189	Serendipity	80 W55
190	Sperling	81 U56
191	Summergate	80 W55
192	Synchromesh	80 X55
193	Terravista	80 W55
194	The View	81 U56
195	Top Shelf	80 X55
196	Mann Farms Estate	78 Z45
197	Pacific Breeze	77 Y42
198	Vista d'oro	77 Z44
199	Domaine Jasmin	77 Z40
200	Hornby Island	76 W36
201	Little Tribune	76 W36
202	Emerald Coast	76 Y36
203	Merridale	87 B40
204	Symphony	87 C41
205	Highland House Farm	87 B41
206	Unsworth	87 B40

Most of the wineries offer tours & tastings

0 .25 .5 .75 1 Kilometre
kilomètre

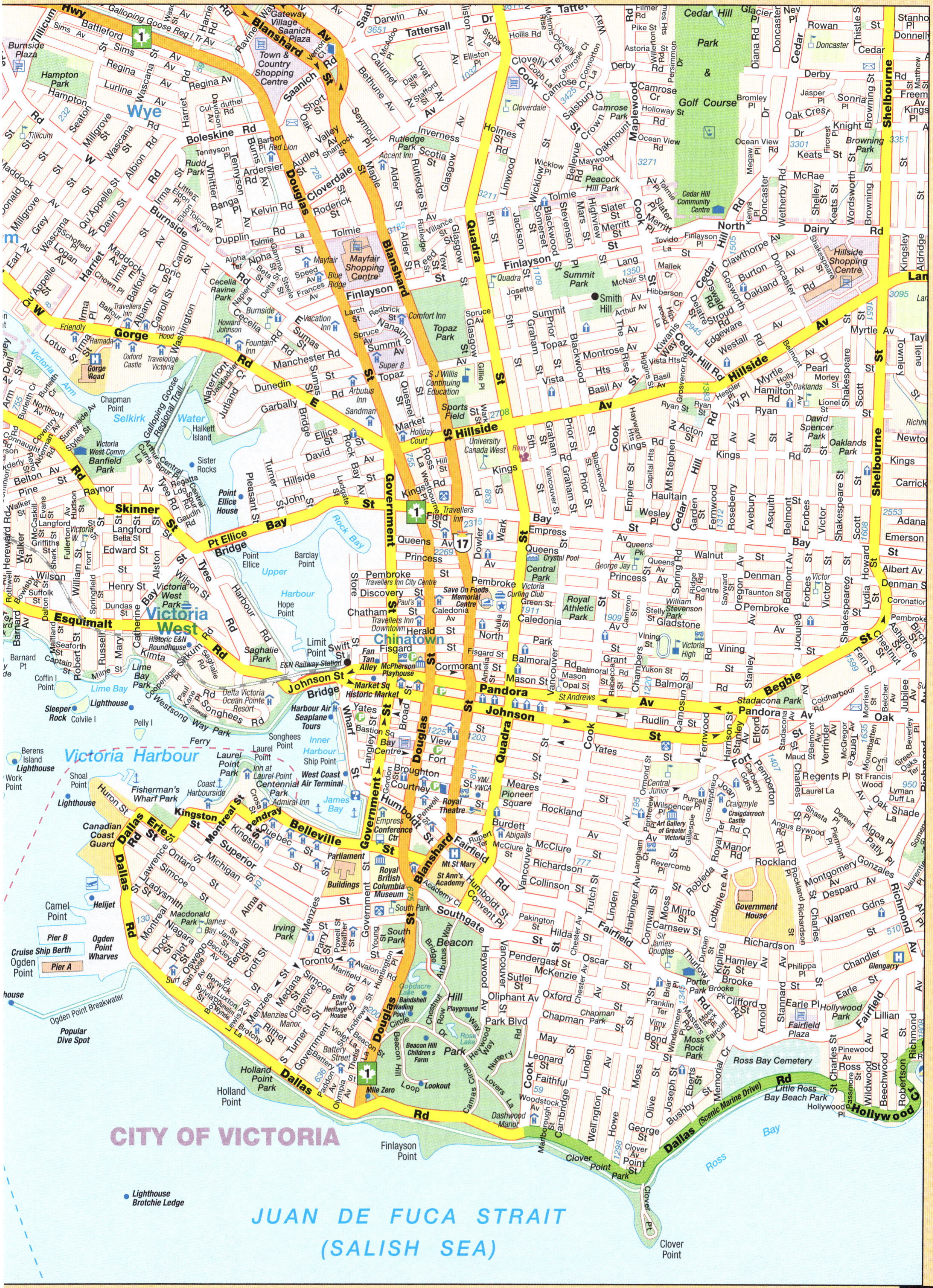

Scale 1:25 000 *Échelle*

CITY OF VICTORIA

JUAN DE FUCA STRAIT
(SALISH SEA)

Victoria Harbour

Victoria West

Chinatown

Wye

Scale 1:25 000 Échelle

0 .125 .25 .375 .5 Kilometre *kilomètre*

Scale 1:13 000 *Échelle*

1 Old Bridge Walk
2 Old Bridge Ct
3 Hemlock Ct
4 Fountain Way Ct

0
.25
.5
.75
1 Kilometre
kilomètre
First Narrows
Lions Gate Bridge Rd
Prospect Point
Squamish Nation
Lower Capilano
DISTRICT OF NORTH VANCOUVER
Siwash Rock
Third Beach
Stanley Park
Pauline Johnson Memorial
The Ferguson Point Tea House
Stanley Park National Historic Site
Beaver Lake
Pipeline Rd
Miniature Railway
Lumberman's Arch
Zoo
Vancouver Aquarium
Malkin Bowl
Rose Garden
Brockton Oval
Totem Poles
SS Empress of Japan Figurehead
Brockton Point
9 O'Clock Gun
Lost Lagoon
Stanley Park Pool
Second Beach
Pitch & Putt
Vancouver Rowing Club
Royal Vancouver Yacht Club
Deadman Island
HMCS Discovery Naval Training Station
Devonian Harbour Park
Harbour Cruises
Coal Harbour
Cardero Park
Coal Harbour Quay
Vancouver Convention & Exhibition Centre (West)
Canada Place
Starboard Theatres
CN Imax Theatre
Sea Bus Terminal
Heliport
Waterfront
Gastown Steam Clock
West End
Roedde House Museum
Barclay Manor
English Bay Beach
English Bay Park
Alexandra Park
English Bay
Nelson Park
St Paul's Hospital
Vancouver Art Gallery
Robson Square
Downtown
Van City Ctr
The Centre
Queen Elizabeth Theatre
Stadium-Chinatown
Rogers Arena
BC Place Stadium
BC Sports Hall of Fame & Museum
Edgewater Casino
Science World
Sunset Beach
Hadden Park
Vancouver Maritime Museum & "St. Roch"
Pacific Space Centre (HR MacMillan Planetarium)
Vancouver Museum
Kitsilano Point
Kitsilano Beach Park
Kitsilano Beach
Vanier Park
Vancouver Aquatic Centre
Burrard Bridge
Granville Bridge
Granville Island Public Market
Granville Island
Emily Carr University
Art Club Theatre
False Creek Yacht Club
Yaletown-Roundhouse
Roundhouse Park
David Lam Park
George Wainborn Park
False Creek
Cambie Bridge
Olympic Vlg
Fairview
Kitsilano
Cornwall
Pt Grey Rd
Broadway
Broadway-City Hall
Vancouver General Hospital
Mount Pleasant
Centre culturel francophone de Vancouver
Vancouver Schoolboard Administration Office
Connaught Park
Kitsilano Community Centre

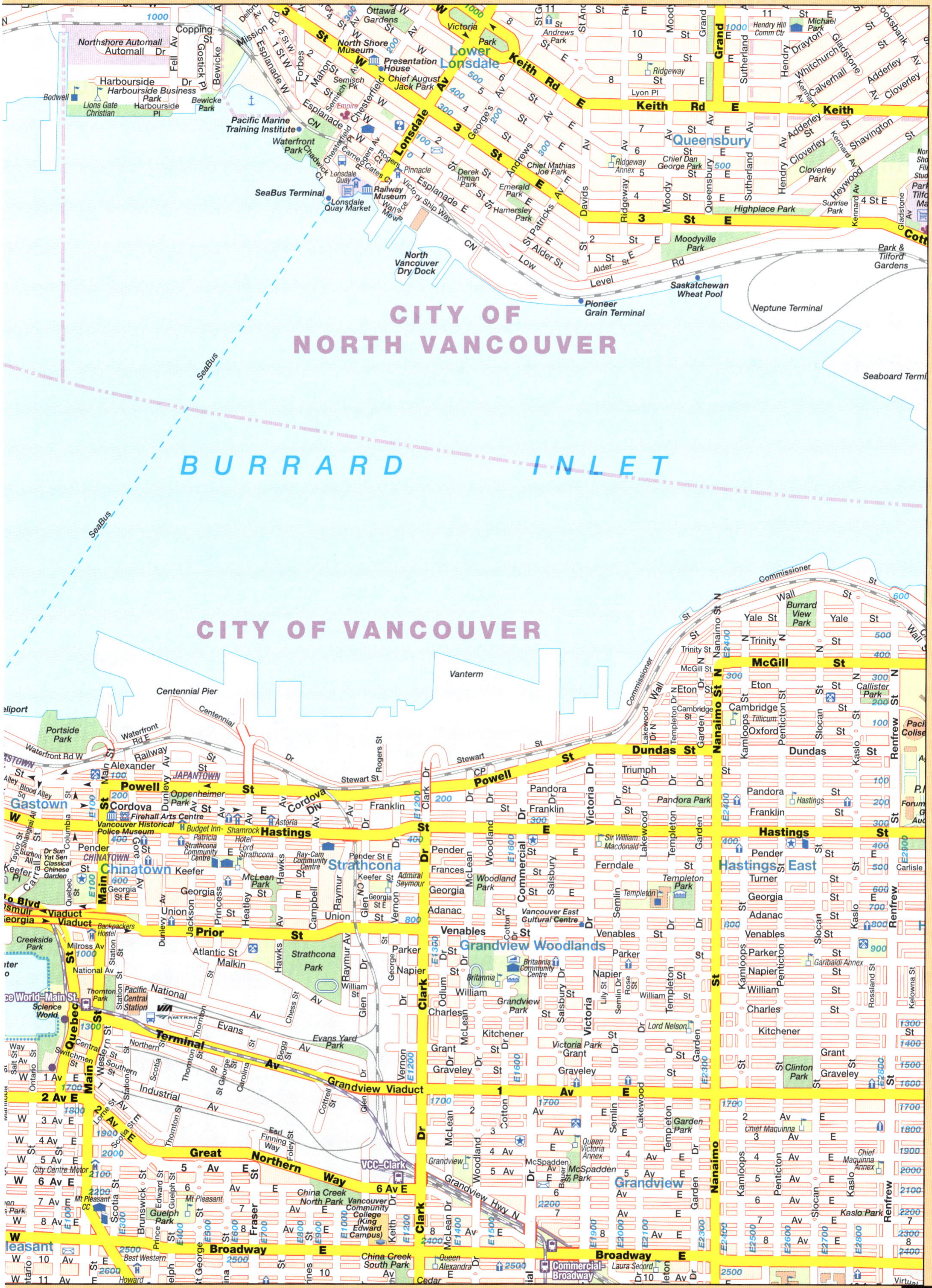

Scale 1:25 000 *Échelle*

Scale 1:25 000 Échelle

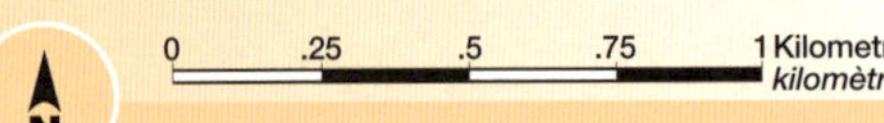

RESORT MUNICIPALITY OF WHISTLER

North Estates
Meadow Park & Sports Centre
Nicklaus North Golf Course
Golden Dreams Conservation Area
Riverside Campground
Lost Lake Park
Chateau Whistler Golf Course
Emerald Forest Conservation Area
Nesters Pond
Nesters
Nesters Market
Nesters Hill Park
Balsam Park
Spruce Grove Park
Spruce Grove
White Gold
Lost Lake
Whistler Cay
Whistler Nature Reserve
Rainbow Falls
Rainbow Park
Snowflake Park
Village North
Upper Village
Whistler Village
Rebagliati Park
Blackcomb Base
Blackcomb Benchlands
Windsurfer Launch
Alta Lake
Blueberry Hill
Blueberry Beach Park
Whistler Golf Course
Whistler Base
Alta Vista
Lakeside Park
Brio
The Whistler Sliding Centre
Alta Lake Park
Wayside Park
Stonebridge
Nordic Estates
Whistler Highlands
Nita Lake
Taluswood
Alpha Lake Park
Gondola Village
Big Timber Park
Bear Creek Estates
Bayshores
Ski Lifts
Whistler Mountain

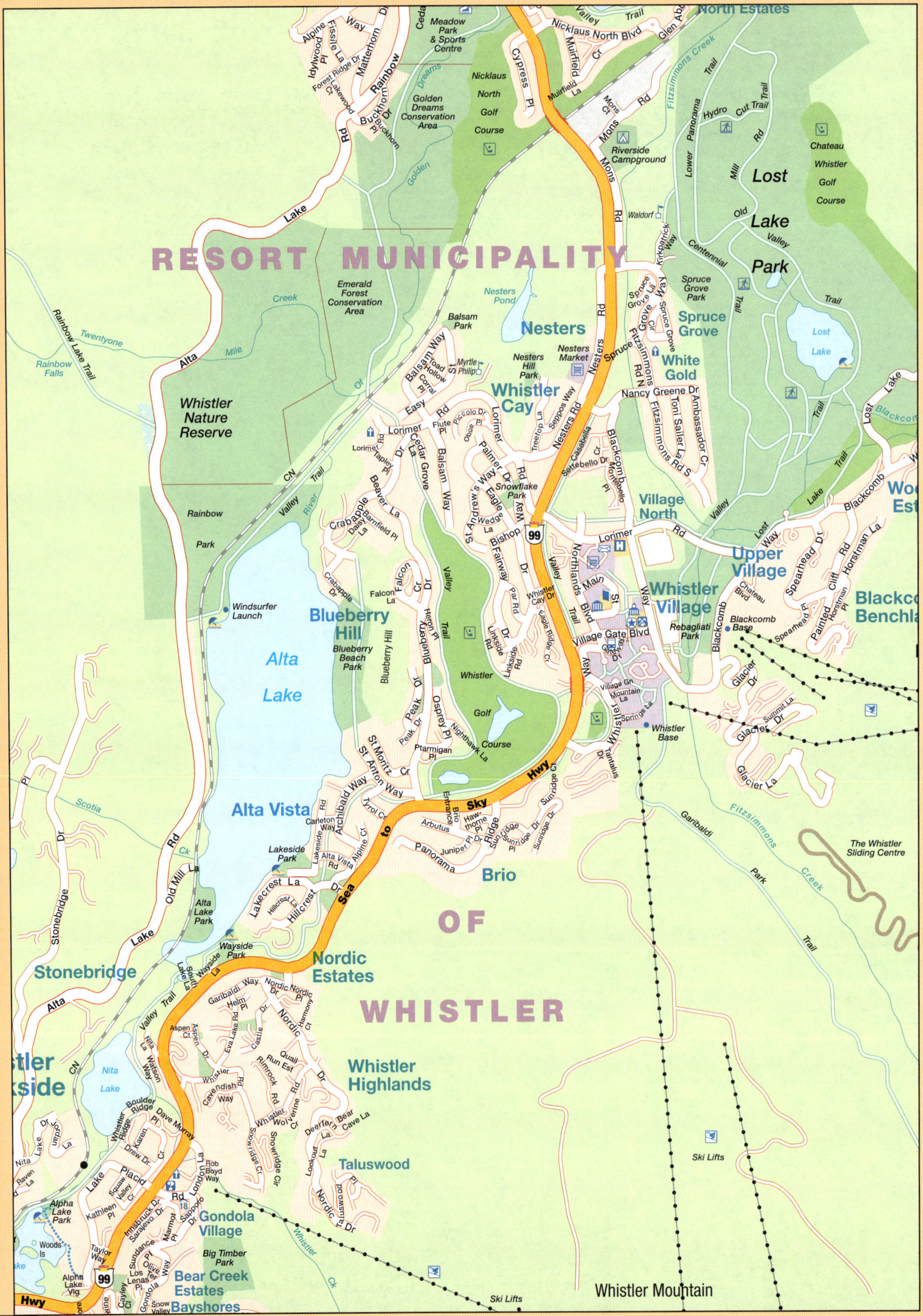

0 .25 .5 .75 1 Kilometre kilomètre

Scale 1:25 000 Échelle

Tk'emlúps te Secwepmc

CITY OF KAMLOOPS

North Shore

West End

City Centre

Upper Sahali

Lower Sahali

Southgate

Mount Paul Industrial Park

THOMPSON RIVER

SOUTH THOMPSON

Paul Peak

Mount Paul Golf Course

Mount Paul Centre

Exhibition Grounds

Horse Race Track

Indian Point Park

Riverside Park

Overlander Park

Pioneer Park

Peterson Creek Park

Peterson Creek Bridge

Royal Inland Hospital

Sahali Centre Mall

Hillside Cemetery

Pleasant Cemetery

6 Avenue Cemetery

Chinese Cemetery

Yellowhead Hwy

Overlander Bridge

Red Bridge

Yellowhead Bridge

Swing Bridge

Victoria St W

Columbia St

Battle St

Summit Dr

Tranquille Rd

Fortune Dr

Princeton-Kamloops Hwy

Scale 1:25 000 Échelle

0 .25 .5 .75 1 Kilometre kilomètre

South Glenmore
Kathleen Lake
North End
Manhattan Point
Sutherland Park
Lake City Casinos
British Columbia Orchard Industry Museum
Grand Okanagan Resort
Kelowna Yacht Club
Kelowna Memorial Arena
Kelowna Museum/Kelowna Art Gallery/Kelowna National Exhibition Centre
Kasugai Gardens
The Fintry Queen Paddlewheeler Cruises
Royal Anne
Veendam Gardens
The Children's Water Park
City Park
William R Bennett Bridge
Prospera Place
Clement Av
Bernard Av
Harvey Av
Springfield Rd
Cadder Av
Pandosy St
Richter St
Ethel St
Gordon Dr
Abbott St
Water St
Ellis St
Burtch Rd
Lakeshore Rd
KLO Rd
South Central
Capri Centre
Coast Capri
Accent Inn
Kelowna Motor Inn
Central/Dehart
St Joseph
Immaculata
Millbridge Park
AS Matheson
Kelowna General
Strathcona Park
Maude Roxby Wetland
Kinsmen Park
Cameron Park
Guisachan Village Mall
Guisachan Heritage Park
Osprey Park
West Av Park
Sewage Treatment
Okanagan University College KLO Campus
Mission Park Shopping Centre
Siesta
KLO Sportfield
Boyce-Gyro Park
Apple Bowl Stadium
Parkinson Recreation Centre
Springfield Centre
Lombardy Park
J Robertson Mem Park
Coronation Park
Calona Vineyards
Kelowna Curling Club
Recreation Av Sports Com
Recreation Av Park
Munson Pond
Central Okanagan Regional District Office
Immaculata Regional
97
OKANAGAN LAKE
South Pandosy
CITY OF KELOWNA

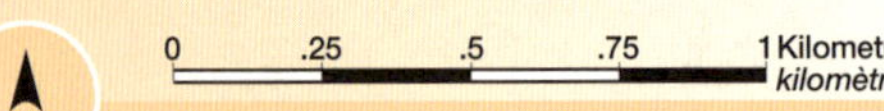

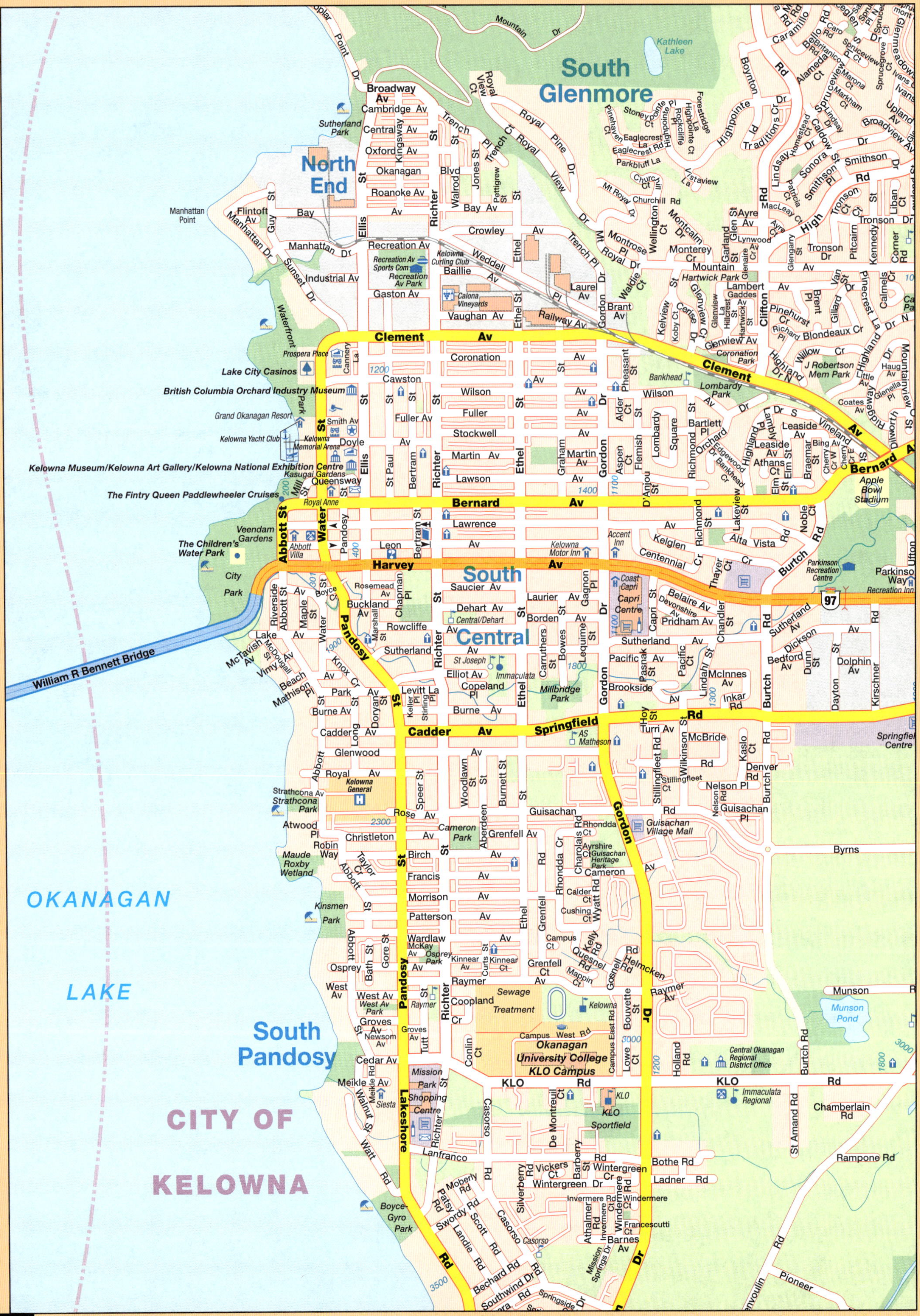

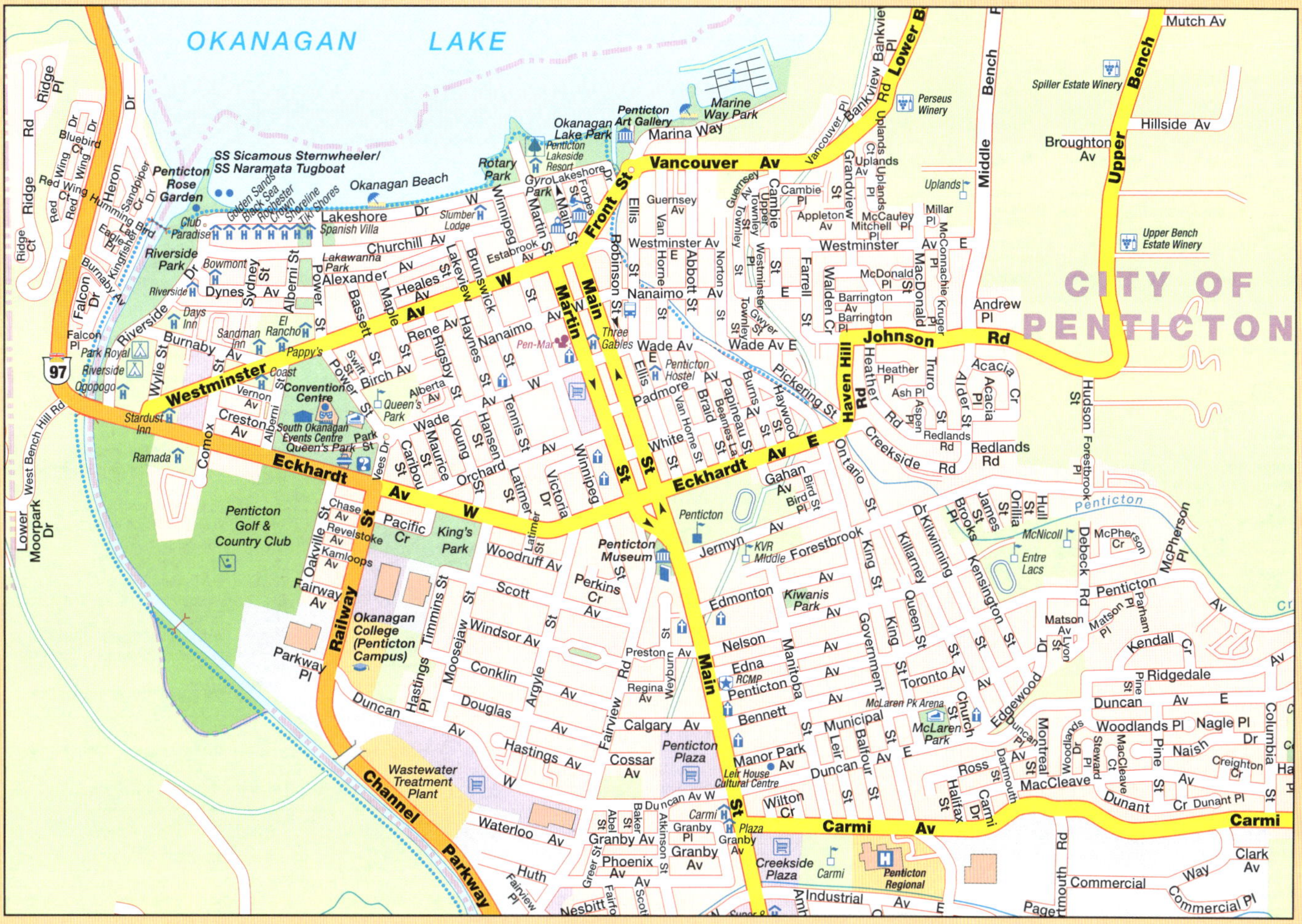

OKANAGAN LAKE

CITY OF PENTICTON

SS Sicamous Sternwheeler/ SS Naramata Tugboat

Penticton Rose Garden

Okanagan Beach

Okanagan Lake Park

Penticton Art Gallery

Marine Way Park

Rotary Park

Gyro Park

Riverside Park

Perseus Winery

Spiller Estate Winery

Upper Bench Estate Winery

Uplands

Convention Centre

South Okanagan Events Centre

Queen's Park

Penticton Golf & Country Club

King's Park

Penticton Museum

Okanagan College (Penticton Campus)

Wastewater Treatment Plant

Penticton Plaza

Leir House Cultural Centre

Creekside Plaza

Penticton Regional

Kiwanis Park

McLaren Park

Entre Lacs

Channel Parkway

CITY OF PRINCE GEORGE

Nechako River

McMillan Creek Regional Park

Cut Banks Park

Parkhill Centre

North Nechako

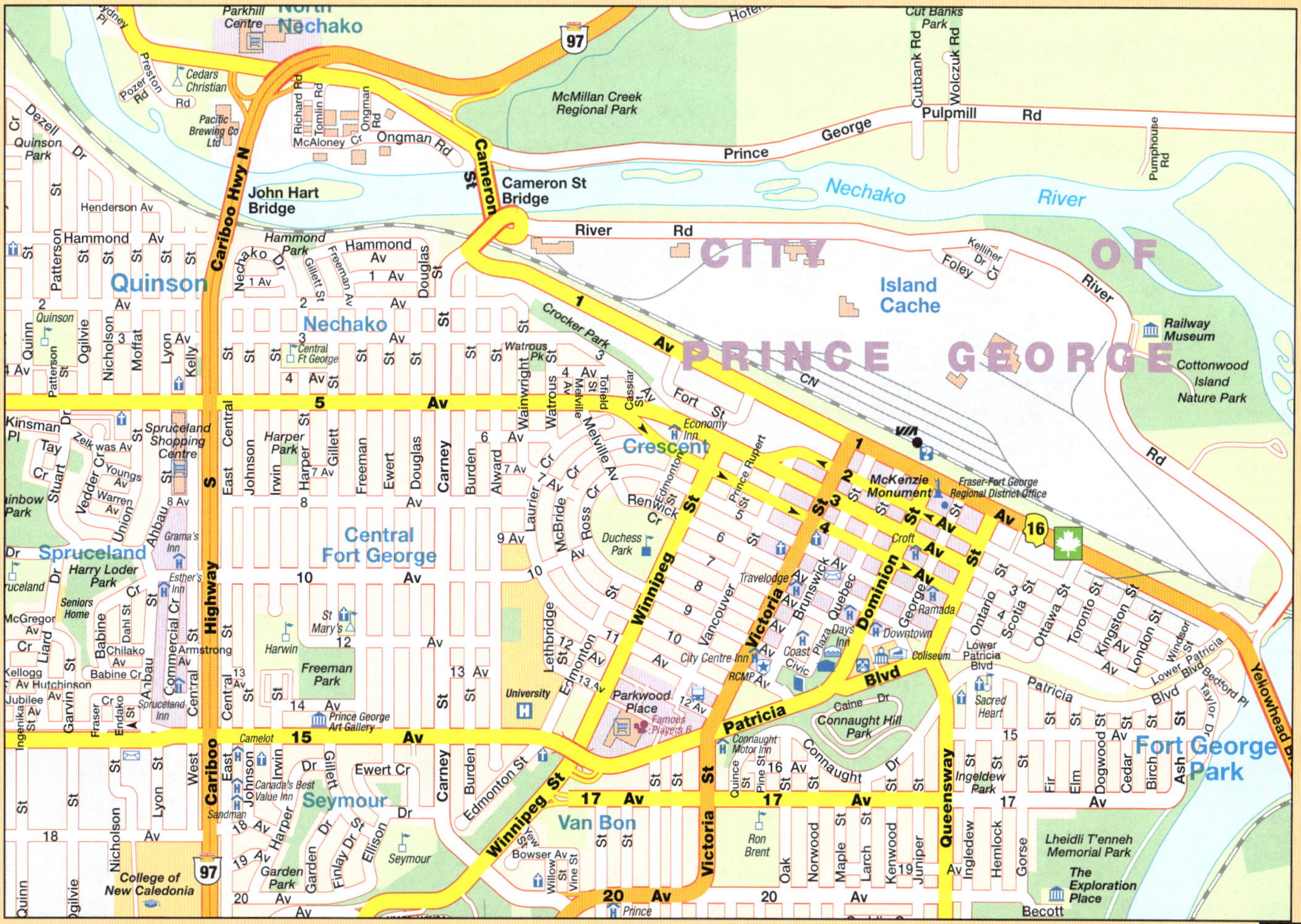

Cedars Christian

Pacific Brewing Co Ltd

John Hart Bridge

Cameron St Bridge

Quinson Park

Quinson

Nechako

Island Cache

Railway Museum

Cottonwood Island Nature Park

Spruceland Shopping Centre

Spruceland

Harry Loder Park

Central Fort George

Crescent

McKenzie Monument

Fraser-Fort George Regional District Office

Duchess Park

Freeman Park

Parkwood Place

Connaught Hill Park

Prince George Art Gallery

Seymour

Van Bon

Fort George Park

Lheidli T'enneh Memorial Park

The Exploration Place

College of New Caledonia

Garden Park

Ron Brent

Ingeldew Park

Sacred Heart

Cariboo Hwy N

Cariboo Highway S

Yellowhead Hwy

Museums

Agassiz-Harrison 78 Y47
Alberni Valley 67 Y36
Armstrong-Spallumcheen 69 R57
Ashcroft 67 Q48-49
Atkinson (R. N.) 80 W55
Boundary 81 Z59
Bralorne Pioneer 65 P43
British Columbia Orchard 80 U55 81 U56
Bulkley Valley 30 S28
Campbell River & District 75 U34
Canadian Museum of Rail Travel 84 W69
Castlegar & District Heritage 82 Y62
Central Interior Railway & Forest Industry 37 X43-44
Chase & District 68 P55
Chemainus Valley Historical 87 A39
Comox Air Force 75 V35-36
Cortes Island 63 T35
Courtenay & District 75 V35-36
Creston & District 83 Z66
Cumberland 75 W34-35
Denman Island 75 W35-36
District 69 Historical 67 X37-38
Doukhobor Village 82 X-Y62
Eight Valley 69 P57-58
Enderby & District 69 Q57
Fernie & District Historical 65 W72
Fort Nelson Heritage 10 F23
Fort St. John (North Peace) Historical 25 K48-49
Fraser-Fort George Historical Museum & Stockade 37 X43
Fraser Lake 34 W36
Gabriola 67 Y39
Golden & District 59 N65
Granisle 31 R31-32
Greater Vernon 69 S56
Greenwood 81 Z58-59
Haney (R. J.) Heritage 69 Q57
Hazelton Pioneer 30 P26-27
Hedley Heritage 80 X53
Hope 79 X48
Jack Lynn Memorial 45 G48
Kaatza Historical 87 A38
Kelowna 80 U55 81 U56
Kettle River 81 Z58
Kimberley District Heritage 84 W68-69
Kitimat Centennial 22 T14
Lake Country 68 T55 69 T56
Lillooet 66 Q46
Lions Bay Historical 77 X41-42
Lytton 66 S47
Museum of Northern British Columbia 28 T18
Museum of the Cariboo Chilcotin 54 H45-46
Nakusp & District 70 S62
Nanaimo District 67 Y38-39
Naramata 80 W55
Nelson 83 X64
Nicola Valley 67 T50
Nootka Sound Historical 74 V31
North Thompson 56 N52-53
Oliver 80 Y55
One Hundred Mile House & District Historical 55 K48
Pemberton & District 65 S43
Port Hardy 61 P26
Port McNeill Heritage 61 Q27
Powell River Historical 67 U36
Princeton & District 80 X52
Qualicum Beach Historical 67 X36-37
Quesnel & District 44 C44
Revelstoke 70 O60
Revelstoke Railway 70 O60
Rossland Historical 82 Z61-62
Salmo 83 Y64
Salt Spring Island 87 A40
Sandon 83 U64
Secwepemc Heritage Park & Museum 68 Q52
Shawnigan Lake Historical 87 B40
Silvery Slocan Historical 82 U63
Sointula 62 Q28
Sooke Regional 87 D39-40
South Cariboo Historical 54 N47 66 O47
South Similkameen 80 Y54
Station 27 M51
Summerland 80 W54-55
Sunshine Coast Maritime 77 X40
Tahsis 74 U28-29
tems swiya 67 X39
Telkwa Historical 30 S29
The Little Prairie Heritage 26 N46-47
Trail 82 Z62
Tumbler Ridge Museum & Dinosaur Centre 27 Q48-49
Ucluelet & Area Historical 75 Z32-33
Valemount & Area 47 D57
Valley 38 A52
Vancouver Island Children's 67 Z39
Vanderhoof Community 34 W39
Whale 74 Y31 75 Y32
Whistler 65 T42
Windermere Valley 72 R68
Yale & District Historical 79 W48
Zeballos 62 T28

Points of Interest

'Ksan Historical Village 30 P26-27
Alex Fraser Research Forest (UBC)
Gavin Lake Block 44 F47
Knife Creek Block 54 H46
Alexander Mackenzie Heritage Trail 42 B37-39 C35-36
Ashcroft Manor and Teahouse 67 Q48
Ayjoomixw Journeys (Wildlife & Cultural Tours) 67 U36-37
Barkerville Historic Town 44 C47 45 C48
Bavarian City Mining Railway 84 V68
Big Bar Reaction Ferry 54 N45
Black Nugget (1881) 67 Z39
Brackendale Art Gallery 77 V42
British Columbia Forest Discovery Centre 87 A39
British Columbia Museum of Mining 77 W41-42
Butchart Gardens 87 C40-41
Capilano Suspension Bridge & Park 77 X42
Chilcotin Training Area (DND) 54 H44
Church of St. John the Divine (1860) 79 W48
Columbia & Western Rail Trail (Boundary Pathway) 81 Y59 Z58-59 82 X60-62 Y60 Z60
Cottonwood House Historic Site 44 C45
Deadman Valley Hoodoos 67 O50
Fairmont Hot Springs 72 S69
Father Pandosy Mission 81 U-V56
Filberg Lodge (1929) 75 V35-36
Fort McLeod Historic Site 18 Q23
Fort Steele Heritage Town 84 W70
Friendly Cove Historic Site 74 W29
Geographic Centre of British Columbia 34 X38-39
Grouse Mountain Skyride 77 X42
Gitanyow Gyetim Gan (Totem Poles) 30 P26
Haig-Brown House 63 T34
Harrison Hot Springs 78 X-Y47
Hells Gate Canyon & Airtram 79 U48
Heritage Park Museum 29 T24
Historic Hat Creek Ranch 67 P48
Historic O'Keefe Ranch 69 S56-57
Historic Yale 79 W48
Hope Slide (1965) 79 X49
Howse Pass Trail 58 J65 K65-66
Huble Homestead Historic Site 36 V44
Hudson's Hope Museum 24 L46
Kamloops Wildlife Park 68 Q52-53
Kettle Valley Steam Railway 80 W55
Kettle Valley Rail Trail 67 T50 79 U50 V50-51 W49-51 X48-49 80 V52-55 W52-55 X52-53 X55 Y55 Z55 81 V57 W57 X57 Y57 Z57-58
Kilby Historic Store & Farm 78 Y46
Kitwancool Aged Totem Poles 16 P15
Last Spike (CPR [1885]) 69 O58-59
LeRoi Mine Tour 82 Z61-62
Malcolm Knapp UBC Research Forest Reserve 78 X-Y44
Marine Ecology Station 87 B40
Maritime Centre 87 B40
McLean Mill Historic Site 75 X35
Mile "O" Alaska Highway 27 N51
Minter Gardens 78 Y47
Miyazaki Heritage House 66 Q46
Murals of Chemainus 87 A40
Moricetown Canyon 30 Q28
Nakusp Hot Springs 70 S62
Nanoose Bay Nuclear Testing Area 67 X-Y39
Nelson Street Railway 83 X64
Nicola Kamloops & Similkameen Rail Trail 67 R48-49 S49 T49-51
Nikkei Internment Memorial Centre 82 U63
North Pacific Historic Fishing Village 28 U17-18
Osoyoos Desert Centre 80 Z55
Peace Canyon Dam 24 L45
Quilchena Historic Hotel 65 T43
Rainforest Interpretive Centre 75 Z32-33
Resolution Cove Historic Site (Cook Landing [1778]) 74 V-W29
Roberts Bank Superport 77 Z41-42
Robson Bight / Michael Biggs Prov. Ecological Res. 62 R29-30
S. S. Moyle 83 U65
Silverton Outdoor Mining Exhibit 82 U63
Similkameen Falls 79 Y51
Spotted Lake 80 Z55
Stanley Park 77 Y42
Sullivan Mine Interpretive Centre 84 V68
The Historic Grist Mill 80 Y54
Three Valley Gap Pioneer Village 69 O-P59
Tofino Botanical Gardens 74 Y31
Twin Falls 30 R28
U'Mista Cultural Centre 62 Q28
University of British Columbia 77 Y41
University of Northern British Columbia 37 X43
University of Victoria 87 C41
Vancouver Island Butterfly World & Gardens 67 Y37
Vest Pocket Desert 80 Z55
W.A.C. Bennett Dam 24 L45
Walcott Pedestrial Suspension Bridge 30 T29
Walton Wright Pioneer Village 27 M51
Wells Historic Museum / Historic Town 44 B47
West Coast Railway Heritage Park 77 V41-42
White Pass & Yukon Railway 6 B6
Xa'ytem Longhouse Interpretive Centre 78 Y45
Xats'ull Heritage Village 54 H46

BC Hydro Recreation Areas & Sites

Bridge River 66 Q54-55
Buntzen Lake 77 X43
Clayton Falls 40 F29
Naxwit 66 Q46
Peace Canyon Dam 24 L45-46
Pend D'Oreille Reservoir 82 Z63
Puntledge River 75 V-W34
Revelstoke Dam 70 O60
Seton Lake Reservoir 66 Q46
Shuswap Falls 69 S58
Shuswap River 69 S58-59
Strathcona Dam 75 U32-33
Sugar Lake Dam 69 S59
W.A.C. Bennett Dam 24 L45

Forest Recreation Sites

Abbott Creek 45 F48
Abbott Lake 67 S49-50
Agate Point 33 W33-34
Ahbou Lake 36 A45-46
Aileen Lake 69 T57
Alder Grove / Sitka Spruce Beach 63 S32-33
Alexander Falls 65 T42
Alexis Lake 43 G40
Allan Lake 56 N52
Allendale Lake 81 X56
Allison Pool 78 Z47
Amanita Lake 36 W46
America Creek 84 Z68
Amor Lake 63 T33
Andy's Lake 79 V50
Angly Lake 34 V36-37
Antler Lake 67 R50
Anzus Lake 33 X35
Apple Point 63 T33
Appleton Creek 76 U36
Apocynum 79 U48
Arden Creek 75 Y35
Arlington Lakes 81 W57
Armor Lake 63 T33
Arthur Lake 34 Z37-38
Arthur Lake North 69 Q-R56
Aspen 30 U29
Atan Lake 45 B48
Augier Lake 31 U34
Badger Lake 68 O53
Baird Lake 69 Q-R58
Bald Mountain 87 A38
Bannock Point 82 U63
Bardolph Lake 69 S57
Barnes Lake 67 Q49
Batnuni Lake East 34 A39
Batnuni Lake West 34 A38-39
Bear Creek (Chilliwack) 78 X47
Bear Lake 69 T57
Beaver (Holmes) River 38 A54
Beaver Lake 70 T63
Beaver North 76 U37-38
Beaver South 76 U38
Beaverdam Creek 66 O44-45
Beaverdam Lake 54 N47 55 N48
Beavermouth 44 D-E45
Becher's Dam 54 J44
Becker Lake 69 S57
Bell Mountain Meadow 37 A51
Bernard Beaches 83 V65-66
Big Bay 63 T33
Big Lake 26 M47 27 M48
Big OK Lake 67 R49
Big Stick Lake 51 H35
Billy Lake 67 R50
Binta Lake 33 X33-34
Binta Lake South 33 X34
Bisson Lake 69 T59
Bittern Lake 71 O66
Blackie's Beach 75 Y35
Blackwater Crossing 35 A42
Blackwell Lake 68 R53
Bleeker Lake 68 R53
Blinkhorn Peninsula 62 Q28-29
Blue Lake 73 T72
Blue Lake (Quesnel) 44 G45
Bluejoint Creek 81 X59
Bluewater Bridge 59 L64
Bluey Lake 79 U51
Bluff Lake 52 K36
Boat Lake West 34 A39
Bob Lake West 67 S51
Bob's Lake (Merritt) 80 U52
Bob's Lake (Sunshine Coast) 76 W37-38
Bobtail Lake 35 Z40-41
Boer Mountain 33 V33
Bog West 55 N50
Bolean Lake 68 R55
Bonanza South 62 R-S29
Bonaparte Lake 55 M50-51
Bonaparte River Bridge 55 N48-49
Bonaparte River Suicide Crossing 55 N49
Boot Lake (Quesnel) 43 B41
Boot Lake (Campbell River) 63 T33
Boot Lake (Westbank) 80 U52
Bootjack Lake 44 E47
Borel Lake 33 X35
Bose Lake 67 R50
Bosk Lake 45 G50
Boss Lake 79 U50-51
Botanie Lake 66 R-S47
Botts Lake 71 P67
Boulder Lake 26 P47
Bouleau Lake 68 S55
Boundary Lake (Arrow & Kootenay Lake) 83 Z65
Boundary Lake (Clearwater) 55 K51
Boundary Lake (Prince George) 36 V44-45
Bowman Point 82 W60
Box Lake 70 T62
Brenda Lake 80 U53
Brennan Creek 56 N55
Brewster Camp 63 T32-33
Brewster Lake (Campbell River) 63 T33
Brewster Lake (Vanderhoof) 34 A37
Brigham Springs 54 L46
Brittany Bay 63 T33
Browne Lake 81 V57
Bruer Creek 81 U58-59
Brunette Lake 69 T57
Buchanan Lookout 83 U65
Buck Lake (Boundary) 81 W57
Buck Lake (Merritt) 80 V52
Buckhorn Lake 36 Y44
Bugaboo-Septet 71 P-Q66
Buhl Creek 84 U68
Burner Bay 33 X35-36
Burnell Lake 80 Y55
Bush Arm 58 K63
Butts 85 Y74
Cabin Lake 79 U49
Cal-Cheak 65 T42
Calling Lake 67 R49
Cameron Lake 70 S61
Camp 5 63 T33
Camp Foley 78 Z47-48
Campbell Lake 63 T33
Campbell Lake (Kamloops) 68 Q52-53
Canuck Creek 84 Z68
Canyon Creek 81 X57-58
Canyon Flats 81 X57-58
Carbon Lake 24 L43-44
Cariboo Island 45 F48
Caribou Creek 58 J62
Caribou Lakes 70 S61
Carnes Creek 58 M60
Carol Lake 66 P44
Carpenter Lake 66 P45
Cartwright Lake 71 P66-67
Cascade Beach 69 R58
Cascade Peninsula 78 X46-47
Cat Lake 77 V42
Catherine Lake 70 R61
Caven-Gold Creek 84 Y71
Cedar Dam Lake 45 E48
Cedar Lake (Campbell River) 63 S33
Cedar Lake (Columbia) 59 N64-65
Chain Lake West 80 V52
Chapman Lake 31 R30
Charcoal Creek 68 Q55
Charlotte Lake 51 H34
Chaunigan Lake 52 L39
Chehalis River 78 Y46
Cherry Lake 84 Y70
Cherryville 69 S59
Chilko-Taseko Junction 53 J40
Chimney Lake Centre 54 J45-46
Chimney Lake North 54 J45-46
Chipmunk Peninsula (Fraser Valley) 78 Z47
Chisel Lake 45 B48
Chist Creek 29 U24
Choelquoit Lake 52 K38
Christmas Lake 55 J50
Chubb Lake 35 A43-44
Chutanli Lake 34 A37
Chute Lake 80 V55
Cinnamon 66 Q45
Clayoquot Arm Beach 75 Z33
Clear Lake 35 Y42
Clearwater Lake 51 H35-36
Cleland Lake 71 P67
Clifford Lake 79 V50-51
Clint Beek 61 R27
Co-op Lake 33 V34
Cobb Lake 35 X40
Cochin Lake 52 K37
Cogburn Beach 78 W-X47
Coldscaur Lake North 56 K51-52
Coldscaur Lake South 56 K52
Colleymount 32 W31
Community Lake SW 68 O53
Cooke Creek 69 Q58
Cooley Lakes 82 W-X62
Copper Creek 79 Y51
Cottonwood 66 Q46
Cottonwood Beach 69 Q58-59
Cougar Creek 74 V29-30
Cougar Lake 55 K50-51
Crescent Lake (Penticton) 80 V53
Crescent Lake (Quesnel) 36 A46
Crooked Lake North 45 G50
Crooked Lake South 45 G50
Crystal Lake (100 Mile House) 55 L50
Curl Camp 25 L50
Cutoff Creek 34 Y36
Dairy Lake West 67 Q50-51
Dakota Ridge 77 W40
Dale Lake 69 Q58
Damer Lake 69 T56
Damfino Creek 81 V58
Dardanelles Lake 68 R53
Davidson Bridge 53 L40
Davis Lake 79 U51
Deadman Lake 55 N50
Deadman Lake (Vernon) 79 V51
Deer Lake 56 L52
Dennis Lake 30 S27-28
Dennison Lake 69 T58
Dewar Lake 44 G46
Dewdney 80 W-X52
Dinner Rock 76 U36
Division Lake 31 U33
Dodd Lake 76 U37-38
Dogleg Lake 71 Q67-68
Dogwood Bay 63 T33
Doreen Lake 69 T56-57
Doris Lake 31 R30
Dorr Road 84 Y71
Dorsey Lake 44 F47
Dot Lake 67 R-S50
Double Lakes 55 K51-52
Downie Creek 58 L60
Drewry Lake East 55 K50
Drewry Lake West 55 K50
Driftwood Bay 66 T44
Duffy Lake 67 Q51
Dugan Lake 54 H46
Dunbar Lake 71 P67
Dunn Lake North 56 L52-53
Dunsapie Lake 55 N52
Eagle Bay 70 Q61
Eagle Creek 33 V33
Eagle Lake West 52 J37
East Barriere Lake 56 N54-55
East Lake 76 V37
East Maury Lake 56 J52
Eastern Lake 32 X31
Edwards Lake 85 Z72
Eightmile Flats 81 X59
Ejas Lake 56 J52
Elbow Lake (Horsefly) 45 G49-50
Elbow Lake (Salmon Arm) 69 Q58
Elinor Lake 80 V55
Elk Bay 63 S33
Elk Creek 63 S32
Elk (Island) Lake 44 F46
Elkhart Lake 80 U52
Emma Lake Cabin 64 T38
Englishman Creek 84 Y71
Engstrom's Pond 72 T68
Enso 29 V23
Erie Creek 82 Y63
Esplanade Bay 58 K62-63
Etcho Lake 34 V37
Evely 69 S-56
Face Lake 67 Q-R51
Fair Harbour 61 T27
Fairy Lake 86 C37
Felker Lake 54 J46
Fenwick Creek 72 R70
Fenwick Lake 72 R70
Findlay Creek 72 T68-69
Findlay Falls 72 T69
Fir Flat 78 U47
Fir Grove 63 T33
Fir Lake 43 G43
Fish Lake (Chilcotin) 53 M40
Fish Lake (Cranbrook) 84 Y70
Fish Lake North 34 V38-39
Fish Lake South 34 Z36
Fish Trap (Dean River) 41 F35
Fishpot Lake South 42 C39 43 C40
Fishtrap Creek 56 N52
Flatbed Creek 27 R50
Fletcher Falls 82 V65
Fletcher Lake 53 K42
Flora Lake 86 A35-36
Fly Fish Lake #2 69 T57
Fly Lake 55 J48
Foot Lake 27 Q50-51
Forest Lake 44 G45-46
Forsyth Creek 73 S72
Forty Mile Camp / Bull River 84 V71
Fourteen Mile Lake 71 O-P66
Francis Lake 36 Y44
Francis Lake-Harrison 78 X47
Francois West 32 W30
Frank Lake 34 Y38-39
French Lake South 55 L50
Freya Lake Trail 36 V44-45
Friburg 65 O43
Frog Falls 69 P59
Frozen Lake 85 Z73
Fry Trestle 63 T32-33
Father & Son Lake 75 Y-Z36
Gable Creek 81 X59
Gannett Lake 57 L56-57
Garland Bay 83 U-V65
Garrison Lakes 79 Y51
Gavin Lake 44 F47
Genevieve Lake 44 B44-45
Georgie Lake 61 P26
Giant Cedars 58 K63
Gillis Lake West 79 U50
Gilnockie Creek 84 Z70
Glimpse Lake North 68 S52
Glimpse Lake SW 68 S52-53
Gluten Lake 34 Z38
Goat Mountain Lake 69 T57-58
Goat River Canyon 83 Y67
Gold Creek Bay 84 Z71
Gooding Cove 61 R24
Goose Lake 56 L52
Goose Lake North & South 79 V50-51
Gordon Bay 57 M56
Gordon Lake 67 S50
Gorman Lake 57 N52
Gosling Bay 63 T33
Gosling Lake 63 T33
Gott Creek 66 R45
Government Point 32 W32
Graffunder Lake 57 L56
Granby-Burrell Creek 81 X59
Granite Creek 79 W51
Grassy Lake 69 Q58
Graveyard Lake West 35 Y40
Gray Lake 63 T33
Great Beaver Lake 35 U40
Greenbush Lake 69 P60
Greenlee Lake 55 J49-50
Greeny Lake North 55 J48

Greer Beaver Lake 35 U40
Greer Creek 34 Y37
Greer Creek Falls 34 Y37-38
Grizzly Creek 82 W61
Grizzly Lake (Prince George) 36 Y45
Grizzly Lake (Vanderhoof) . 35 Z40
Grizzly Lakes 56 K52
Gump Lake 67 R50
Gun Creek 65 P43
Gun Lake 65 P42-43
Guyishton Lake 33 V33
Gwen Lake 67 T50-51
Gypsum Lake 67 S50
Haddo Lake 69 T57
Haggkvist Lake 69 S58-59
Hale Creek 78 X46
Halfway-Graham. 24 H-J45
Halfway Lake 71 P67
Halfway Viewpoint 34 Z38
Halgrave Lake 71 Q67
Hall Lake 71 Q67
Hallett Lake 34 X36
Hammer Lake West . . . 55 N50-51
Hanham Lake 34 A39
Harmon Lake West . . . 79 U50-51
Harper Lake 68 P55
Hart Creek 84 Z69
Hart Farm 29 S23
Hartley Lake 85 W72
Hathueume Lake 80 U53
Headwater Lakes 80 U-V53
Heffley Lake 68 P53
Helen Lake 31 T-U30
Helena Lake 54 K47
Helmer Lake 67 S51
Hen Ingram Lake 45 F49-50
Herman Lake 69 P57
Hidden Lake 69 Q58
Hihium Lake South 67 O49
Hobson Lake 34 Z36-37
Hogsback Lake 34 X39
Holiday Lake 69 Q58
Holmes Lake 70 T60
Holstein Lake 69 S58-59
Home Lake 34 Y37-38
Honeymoon Bay 56 M-N55
Honolulu Indian Head . 43 D40-41
Hook Lake North 79 V51
Horn Lake 52 K36
Horse Creek 47 E57-58
Horsefly Bay 45 F48
Horsefly River 45 G49
Horseshoe Canyon 80 Y53
Horseshoe Lake 84 W70
Horseshoe Lake (Nakusp) 70 S62
Horseshoe Lake (Powell River). 69 S59
Horseshoe Rapids 72 Q-R69
Hotnarko Lake 41 F33
Howard Lake 55 J50
Howe Creek 81 W59
Howell Creek 85 Z74
Howes Lake 44 F45
Howser Park 71 S65
Humamilt Lake East . . 57 M57-58
Humamilt Lake North . 57 M57-58
Humamilt Lake West . . . 57 M57
Hyas Lake 68 P54
Hydraulic Lake 81 V57
Ida Lake 62 R28
Idaho Peak 82 U63
Ideal Lake 81 U57
Idleback Lake 81 W56
Indian Bay 33 W33
Ireland Lake 76 U37
Irish Lake 55 L49
Isintok Lake 80 W54
Island Lake 80 U52
Island Lakes 69 T56-57
Isobel Lake 68 P52
Italia Lake 56 J51-52
Jackpine Lake 80 U54
Jacksons Hole 44 F45
Jacobie Lake 44 E46-47
Jacobson Lake 79 X49-50
Jacques Lake 45 F49
Jade Lake 71 P67
James Lake 81 U56
Jeb Lake 58 L63
Jim Creek 55 K50
Jimmy Lake 68 S54-55
Johnny Lake 79 V50-51
Johnson Lake 84 U69
Johnson Lake (Clearwater) 56 N55
Jolly Creek 81 Z56-57
Jonas Creek 30 T28
Joyce Lake 68 Q55
Jubilee Mountain Viewpoint 71 P66-67
Junction Pool 62 R30-31
Kager Lake 33 V33
Kaiser Bill Lake 69 T57
Kane Lake 79 U51
Kappan Lake East. 41 F34
Kappan Lake West 41 F34
Kate Lake 69 R59-60
Kathleen Lake 61 R26-27
Keno Lake 45 F49
Kennedy Lake 26 Q43
Kenny Dam (Knewstubb Lake) 34 Z35-36
Kenyon Lake 78 X45
Kernaghan Lake North & South 69 Q56
Kettle Bench 81 X58
Kettle Canyon 81 W-X58
Kettle River 81 U58-59
Kettle River Crossing 81 V58
Keynton Lake 30 P26-27
Khartoum Lake 76 U38
Kidney Lake 69 P59
Kikomun Creek 84 Y71
King Edward Lake North . . 69 T56
Kingdom Lake 65 P43
Kitimat River 29 U24
Kitseguecla Lake 30 R27
Kittil Falls 37 W48
Kitty Ann Lake 55 K51
Klein Lake 76 V39
Klinne Lake 45 F48-49
Knob Point 86 A36
Kootenay-White Junction . 72 S70
Kump Lake 79 V51
Kuyakuz Lake 42 B37
Kwotlenemo (Fountain) Lake 66 Q47
La Salle Lakes 37 Z50
Labour Day Lake 76 Z37
Ladies Creek 45 D48
Lake Enid 72 R68
Lake La Mare 66 O44-45
Lakit Lake 84 V70
Lakelse River 29 T23
Lambly Lake 80 U54-55
Lamprey Creek 32 V28-29
Larchwood Lake 84 U69
Larson Lake 70 S61
Lassie Lake 81 X58
Last Course Lake 55 N50-51
Latremoille Lake 56 L52
Laurie Lake 34 X36
Lavoie Lake 34 Z38
Lawrence Lake 55 J51
Lazy Lake 84 V70
Leiner River 74 U29
Leon Creek 66 O46
LeRoy Lakes 67 R50
Lewis Lake 76 U37
Lightning Creek 44 C45-46
Lightning Lake 79 U49
Lillian Lake 72 R68
Lily Lake 67 T50
Link Lake 80 V52-53
Lintz Lake 35 Z40
Little Bear Bay 43 S33
Little Big Bar Lake 54 M46-47
Little Bouleau Lake 68 S55
Little Douglas Lake 79 W49
Little Espinosa 62 T28 74 U28
Little Horseshoe Creek 76 U37-38
Little Horseshoe North 76 U37-38
Little Lost Lake 47 C56
Little McGillivray Lake 68 P54
Little Scot Lake 55 N50
Little Slocan 82 W62
Little Wilson Lake 70 S62-63
Lizard Lake 87 B38
Lizzie Bay 66 T44
Lodestone Lake 79 X50
Lodgepole Lake 67 R51
Lodwick Lake South 79 V51
Log Creek 78 U47
Lois Lake 76 V37-38
Loispoint 76 V38
Lolo Lake 56 K52
Long Island Bay 78 X46-47
Long Point 43 T33
Lookout Lake 78 W46
Loon Bay 43 T33
Loon Lake (Cranbrook) . 85 Y-Z72
Loon Lake (Vernon) 69 T57
Loon Lake (Invermere) . . . . 71)65
Loosemore Lake 79 V51
Lorin Lake 55 K51
Lost Horse Lake 56 L51-52
Lower Beaver Lake . . . 76 U37-38
Lower Klaklakama Lake 62 S29-30 T29-30
Lower Lake 55 K48-49
Lower Messiter Lake 57 J56
Lowry Lake 75 X34
Lucille Mountain 38 A52
Lund Lake 32 X31
Lundbom Lake East 67 T51
Lundbom Lake West 67 T51
Mackenzie Lakes 35 Z42-43
Mackill Lake 43 G41
Madden Lake 80 Y55
Maiyuk Creek 72 S71
Malaspina Lake 74 U29
Maple Grove 86 A37
Marquart Lake 67 T51
Marshall Creek . . . 65 P43 66 P44
Marshall Lake North . . . 66 O-P44
Mary Lake 63 T33
Maud Lake 44 D46
Maxan Lake 32 V32
Mayson Lake 55 N51-52
Mazur Meadows 84 Y70
McBride Creek Site 38 A52
McCrae Lake 70 P61
McCreight Lake 63 S32-33
McCulloch Reservoir 81 V57
McDonald Lake 80 U54
McGillivray Lake 68 P54-55
McGregor River 37 W48
McIntyre Lake 54 J44-45
McKinley Lake 45 G49-50
McLean Lake 71 O66
McNair Lake 62 S33
Meadow Lake 35 A40
Meadow Mountain 71 S64
Meagher Creek Hotsprings 65 Q-R41
Merrill Lake East 63 T33
Meuoon Lake 33 X35
Middle Point 76 U37
Milford Lake 82 U65
Miller Creek 75 U33
Miner Lake 51 J35
Mineral Lake 84 X69
Missezula Lake North . 79 V51-52
Mission Dam 66 P45
Mr. Canoehead 63 T33
Mitchell Bay 44 F47
Mitten Lake 71 O66
Moffat Lake 55 H49
Mohr Creek 81 V58
Mohun Lake 63 T33
Moira Lake South 56 K52
Mollice Lake 33 W33
Molson Memorial 62 T40
Monashee-Kettle River . . . 69 T59
Monroe Lake 84 X69
Montague Creek 62 S30-31
Moore (Bulman) Lake 69 T56
Moose Lake 33 X-Y34
Moose Lake (100 Mile House) 55 M49-50
Moose Lake (Clearwater) 55 K51-52
Moose Lake (Tumbler Ridge) 27 P48
Morin Lake 31 R30
Morrissey Lake 68 P54-55
Mosquito Lake 70 S61
Mount Forsyth 72 S71
Mount Patrick 83 V67
Mowson Pond 65 P43 66 P44
Muchalat Lake 74 U31
Mud Lake (Blue River) 57 H57
Mud Lake (Rossland) 82 Y61
Mud Lake North 53 N43-44
Mud Lake South 53 N43
Munroe Lake 72 T71
Murphy Lakes West 79 W50
Murray Creek 67 R48
Murray Lake North . . . 79 V49-50
Murray Lake South . . . 79 V49-50
Mystery Lake 57 H56
N'Kwala 67 T49-50
Nadina Lake 32 X29
Nadina Pool 32 W29-30
Nahatlatch River 78 U47
Naka Creek 62 R30
Nanton-Ireland North 76 U37
Nanton Lake 76 U37
Narrow Creek 36 Z46
Nahwitti Lake 61 P25
Needa Lake 55 L50-51
Nellie Lake 57 N57-58
Nevertouch Lake 81 V58
Nicklen Lake 69 T57-58
Nine Bay Lake 71 O66-67
Nitinat Lake 86 A36
Nixon Creek 86 A37
No Name Lakes 55 H51
Noisy Creek 69 Q59
Noralee East 32 W31
Noralee West 32 W31
Norboe Creek 84 U71
Noreen Lake 69 Q58-59
North Barrière Lake 56 M55
North Dodd Lake 76 U37-38
North Star Lake 84 X71
Nyland Lake 44 D46
Octopus Creek 82 V60-61
Old Fort 31 R31
Old Hedley Road East . 80 X52-53
Old Hedley Road West . 80 X52-53
One Eye Lake 51 J35-36
Oona Lake. 34 V36
Ootsa Landing. 32 X32
Opatcho Lake 36 Y45
Orchard Meadow 63 T33
Ormond Lake 34 V-W37
Osprey Lake North 80 V53
Owen Flats A 32 V29
Owen Flats B 32 V29
Owen Hat 32 W30
Owen Lake 32 W29-30
Owl Creek 65 S43
Owl Lake 65 S43
Owl Lakes Chain 65 S43
Oyama Lake 69 T56
Paddy Lake 55 J50
Palliser-Albert Junction . . . 72 R70
Palmer Bar Lake 84 X68-69
Palmer Lake 43 G41-42
Paradise Lake 80 U52
Parrott Lake 32 W31
Paska Lake 67 R50-51
Pass Lake (Kamloops) 67 P51
Pass Lake (Prince George) 37 W48
Paul Lake. 31 S31
Peachland Lake 80 U54
Pearson Pond 65 P43
Pebble Beach 82 V65
Pelican Lake South 35 A40
Pement & Bryden Lakes 68 P55 69 P56
Pendleton Lake 55 J51
Peta Lake 34 V36
Peterhope Lake North 68 S52
Peterson's Beach 34 W36-37
Petite Gosling 63 T33
Phinetta Lake 55 L51
Pickard Creek 80 X53
Pimainus Lake East 67 R49
Pinaus Lake East 68 R55
Pinaus Lake West 68 R55
Pine Lakes 29 S23
Pine Point 87 A38
Pine Tree Lake 31 R30-31
Pinkut Lake 31 U33
Pinnacle Lake 80 U53
Pinto Lake 52 J37
Pitoney Lake 36 Y45-46
Placer Lake 80 Y-Z52
Plateau Lake 68 S52
Poison Lake 41 E33-34
Polley Lake 44 F47
Pollock Creek 85 X73-74
Poplar Lake (East) 32 W29
Postill Lake 81 U56
Potlatch Creek 57 H59
Prairie Creek 45 F49
Pratt Lake 68 R53
Pressy Lake 55 M49
Proctor Lake 85 Z74
Promontory Lookout 67 S49-50 T49-50
Prosser Lake 79 V51
Punchaw Lake 35 A42
Puntzi Lake 42 G38 42 H38
Pye Bay 63 S33
Pye Beach 63 S33
Pye Lake 63 S33
Pye Point 63 S33
Pyper Lake 42 H38
Quesnel Forks 44 E47
Quesnel Lake Public Landing 45 F49
Raft Creek 44 F47
Rail Lake 55 J48
Rainbow Alley 31 P30-31
Rainbow Falls 78 X47
Ram-Wigwam 85 Y72
Rampart Lake 79 V51-52
Rapids 78 Z47
Raven Lake 53 H43
Red Bridge 80 Y53
Red Sand Lake 29 S23
Redwillow River 27 R51
Reflector Lake East . . . 56 K52-53
Reservoir Lake 80 U52-53
Resolution Park (Rhodes) . 74 U28
Rhodes Creek 74 U28
Richmond Lake 33 V-W35
Richy 70 T61
Rickey Lake 79 V50-51
Riley Dam 54 M46
Ripley Lake 80 Y55
Riverside (Elkford) 73 R72
Riverside (Hope) 79 Z48
Roberts Lake (Big Lake Ranch) 44 F47
Roberts Lake (Elk Bay) . . . 63 S33
Robertson Lake 79 V51
Rocky Point 57 M56
Rocky Point Lake 71 O65-66
Rogers Creek 66 R45
Roscoe Lake 67 R49-50
Rosemond Lake 69 Q57
Rossmoore Lake 67 R51-52
Rotary 24 K47-48
Rottacker Lake 69 S60
Rum Cache Lake 33 Z35
Sage Creek 85 Z74
Sago Creek 81 W57
St. Annes Meadow 81 X59-60
St. Louis Camp 84 Y70
Ste. Marie Lake (East) . 36 Y44-45
Ste. Marie Lake (West). . . . 36 Y44
Sakeniche Crossing . . . 31 Q33-34
Sam's Folly Lake 71 Q67
San Juan River 87 C38
Sandrift Lake 81 W58
Santiago Creek 74 U29
Sapeye Lake 42 K37
Saskum Lake South 56 M55
Sasquatch Lake 83 V64
Saul Lake 67 O51
Sawmill Lake 35 V42
Sawmill Point 34 W35-36
Schraeder Lake 54 N44-45
Scot Lake North 55 N50
Scott Lake. 56 N52
Scout Beach Site 75 X34
Scum Lake 53 K40
Scuzzy Creek 79 V48
Sedan Creek 29 Q25
Seymour River Falls . . 57 M-N58
Sharpe Lake West 55 M50
Shea Lake 79 U51
Shere Lake 47 C56
Shesta Lake 35 Y-Z42
Shingle Beach 76 W37
Sicily Lake South 55 K51-52
Sigalet Lake 69 R58-59
Silence Lake 56 K55
Silver Lake (Westbank) . 80 U-V54
Silver Lake (Vernon) 79 U49
Silvertip Falls 56 K54-55
Six Mile Lakes 83 V-W64
Skimikin Lake 69 P56
Skmana Lake 68 P55
Skookumchuck Creek 84 U68
Skwaam Bay 56 N55
Skyline Lake 57 L56
Sloquet Creek Hotsprings . 78 V45
Snag Lake (100 Mile House) 54 K46-47
Snag Lake (Quesnel) 34 A39
Snaking River 43 C40
Snohoosh Lake North 67 O50
Snowshoe Lake 82 U60
Sock Lake 56 K53
Solco Lake 81 X56
South Barriere Lake 56 N55
Spa Lake 69 Q56
Spanish Lake (Horsefly) . . . 45 E48
Spanish Lake (Vernon) . . . 69 R56
Specs Lake 69 T57
Spittal Creek Site 47 C56
Split Creek 59 L65
Sprague Bay 57 H59
Spring Beach 87 A38
Spruce Lake 69 Q58
Squamish Riverside 77 U41
Stake Lake 67 R51
Star Lake 74 V31
State Creek 81 W58
State Lake Road 81 W58
Steamboat Lake 71 P-Q67
Stella Bay 63 S33
Stella Beach 63 S33
Stella Lake North 63 S33
Sterling Beach 63 S-T33
Sterling Island 63 T33
Stern Lake 34 W36
Stevens Creek 70 T60-61
Stewart Lake 25 L48
Stockdale Creek 71 R66
Stoney Lake 79 V51
Stony Lake East 36 A46
Stony Lake North 36 A46
Stony Lake South 36 A46
Stony Lake West 36 A46 Z46
Strawberry Point 66 S44
Streak Lake 69 T56-57
Stringer Lake 79 V51
Stuart Island 63 R34-35
Stump Lake 68 S52
Succour Lake 55 J50
Sugar Creek 69 R59
Sugar Lake 1 Mile 69 S59
Sugar Lake 2 Mile 69 S59
Sugar Lake 3 Mile 69 R59
Sullivan Lake West 68 O53
Sulphur Creek 85 V72
Summer Lake 84 V70-71
Summit Lake (Invermere) . 71 O65
Summit Lake (Prince George) 35 V43
Sunrise Lake 78 W-X46
Sunset Lake 31 U31
Sunshine Bay 82 W60-61
Susan Lake 58 L63
Suscha Lake 42 B37
Suskwa River 30 P28
Sussex Lake 67 R-S51
Sutter Creek 79 X49-50
Suzanne Lake 84 X71
Swalwell Lake 69 T56
Sweeney Lake East 32 Y28
Tagai Lake 35 A40
Tahlia Lake North & South 79 V51
Tahtsa Reach 32 Y28
Taltzen Lake 30 R27
Takysie Lake 33 X33
Tamarack Lake 84 U69
Tamihi Creek 78 Z47
Tangiechain Lake 31 R31
Tangier River 58 N61-62
Taite Creek 82 V60-61
Tatla Lake 42 J37
Tatlayoko Lake Northeast 42 L37-38
Teapot Lake 36 Z45-46
Tenquille Lake 65 R42-43
Tête Jaune Spawn Creek . 47 C56
Thalia Lake 79 V50-51
Third Lake 67 R49
Thone Lake 81 X58
Thunder Creek 27 R51
Three Island Lake 71 O65
Three Sisters Creek 67 O48
Thurston Meadows 78 Z47
Tie Lake 84 X71
Till Lake North 54 H44-45
Tisdall Lake 45 G49
Tobermory Creek 73 R72
Tony Lake 76 U37
Top Lake 34 V36
Top Lake South 42 B35-36
Topaz Lake 71 P66-67
Toquart Bay 75 Z33
Tory Lake 35 Z41
Trout Creek Crossing . . 80 V-W54
Trout Lake 33 X35
Tsikwustum Creek South 57 M56
Tsitika Crossing 62 R29
Tsuniah Lake Bay 42 L38-39
Tulameen Falls 79 X50
Tunnel 80 Y53
Tupper Lake 67 R50
Twenty Mile Bay 78 W46
Twin Falls 30 R28
Twin Lake 63 T33
Twin Lakes (Invermere) . . . 71 P67
Twin Lakes (Quesnel) 43 B42
Twin One Creek 66 S44
Twinkle Lake 32 X29
Two Lake 43 G40
Tyaughton Creek 65 O43
Tyee Lake East 44 F45-46
Tyner Lake 67 S50
Tzenzaicut Lake North . 43 E42-43
Uncha Lake 33 X33-34
Upana Caves 74 U30
Upper Canoe 47 D57
Upper Elk River 73 R72
Upper Harvey Creek 85 Y74
Upper Lillooet 65 Q41
Valentine Lake 54 L47 55 L48
Vedan Lake North 52 L39
Vidette Lake 55 N50
Vinson Lake 80 V51-52
Vuich Falls 79 X50
Waitabit Creek 59 L64
Wallensteen Lake 68 Q55 69 Q56
Wansa Lake 36 Y45
Wap Lake East 69 P59
Wap Lake West 69 P59
Wapiti Lake 84 X71
Wapta Falls 59 N66
Warttig Lake 45 E50-51
Weary Creek 73 R72
Weaver Lake 78 X46-47
West Road Blackwater River 43 B40
West Lake 29 U23
Whale Lake 54 L47
Whiskey Flats 45 C48
White Boar Lake 83 W67
White Lake 55 K51
White River Junction 72 T71
Whitehead Lake 80 V53
Whitetail Lake 72 S-T68
Whitewood Lake 56 N52
Wilbur Lake 71 O66
Willard Lake 67 Q49
Williamson Lake 81 X-Y58
Willow North 36 X45
Wilson Lake West 70 S62
Windfall Creek 26 Q46
Windfall Lake 55 N51-52
Windsor Lake 76 U37-38
Windy Lake (Clearwater) . . 55 K51
Windy Lake (Kamloops) . . . 55 N51
Windy Lake (Penticton) . . . 80 U54
Winkley Creek 45 F48
Wolverine Lake . . . 44 E47 45 E48
Wood Lake 78 X47
Woodcock Lake 35 Z40
Woods Lake North 68 R54-55
Woss Lake 62 S29
Wragge Beach 70 T63
Yalakom 66 P45
Yellowjacket Creek . . . 47 E57-58
Zum Peak 79 W49

National Historic Sites

Abbot Pass Refuge Cabin . 59 M67
Athabasca Pass 48 F60-61
Chilkoot Pass 6 B6
Fort Langley 78 Y44
Fort Rodd Hill & Fisgard Lighthouse 87 C41
Fort St. James 18 S21
Gulf of Georgia Cannery 77 Z41-42
Howse Pass 59 K65-66
Kitwanga Fort 30 P-Q26
Log Cabin 6 B6-7
Nan Sdins 21 Y9
Rogers Pass 58 M63
Twin Falls Tea House . . 59 L66-67

National Migratory Bird Sanctuaries

Christie Islet 77 W41-42
George C. Reifel 77 Z41-42
Nechako River 34 W38-39
Shoal Harbour 87 B-C41
Vaseux Lake 80 Y55 81 Y56

National Parks

Glacier 58 M-N63
Gulf Islands Reserve
- Mt. Norman / Beaumont 87 B41-42
- Bennett Bay 87 A41-42
- Brackman Island 87 B41
- Cabbage Island 87 A42
- D'Arcy Island 87 C41
- Georgeson Island 87 A41-42
- Greenburn Lake 87 B41-42
- Isle-de-Lis 87 B41
- James Bay / Selby Cove 87 A41
- McDonald 87 B41
- Mount Norman 87 B41
- Narvaez Bay 87 A-B42
- Portlock Point 87 A41
- Prior Centennial 87 B41
- Princess Margaret 87 B41
- Roesland / Roe Lake 87 A41
- Russell Island 87 B41
- Sidney Spit 87 B41
- Taylor Point 87 B42
- Tumbo Island 87 A42
- Winter Cove 87 A42

Gwaii Haanas Marine Reserve 21 W-X10
Gwaii Haanas Reserve 21 W-Y9
Kootenay 72 O-Q68
Mount Revelstoke 70 O61
Pacific Rim Reserve
- Broken Group Islands Unit 86 A33-34
- Long Beach Unit 74 Z31 75 Z32
- West Coast Trail Unit 86 B34-36

Yoho 59 M-N66

National Wildlife Areas

Alaksen 77 Z41-42
Qualicum
- Marshall-Stevenson Unit 76 X37
- Nanoose Bay Unit 76 Y38
- Rosewall Creek Unit 75 X35-36

Widgeon Valley 78 X44

Others

Creston Valley Wildlife Management Area 83 Y66
Khutzeymateen/K'tzim-a-Deen Provincial Grizzly Bear Sanctuary 28 S19-20
Morice River Provincial Ecological Reserve 32 V29
Muskwa-Kechika Management Area 14 D18
Parksville-Qualicum Beach Wildlife Management Area 76 X37-38
Race Rocks Marine Protected Area 87 D40
Southern Rocky Mountains Provincial Management Area 84 W-X71 85 U72 X-Y73 Z73 Y-Z75
Williams Creek Provincial Ecological Reserve 29 U25

Provincial Marine Parks

Adams Lake
- Poplar Point 57 N56
- Spillman Beach 56 N55 57 N56

Babine Lake
- Hook Bay 31 T33
- Pendleton Bay 31 T-U33
- Pierre Creek 31 T33
- Sandpoint 31 S32-33
- Smithers Landing 31 Q30-31

Big Bunsby 61 T26
Broughton Archipelago 62 P-Q29
Catala Island 74 U27
Codville Lagoon 49 H25
Copeland Islands 75 U35-36
Cormorant Channel 62 Q28
Desolation Sound 64 T36
Discovery Island 87 D41-42
Dixie Cove 61 T27
Echo Bay 62 P30
Garden Bay 76 W39
Gibson 74 Y31
God's Pocket 61 P26
Green Inlet 22 W14
Ha'thayim (Von Donop) 63 T35
Harmony Islands 76 U38-39
Jackson Narrows 22 X14
Jedediah Island 76 W-X38
Kitson Island 20 S11
Klewnuggit Inlet 20 T-U12
Langara Island 20 R7
Little Andrews Bay 32 X30
Lowe Inlet 20 U12
Maquinna 74 X30
Montague Harbour 87 A40-41
Musket Island 76 V37-38
Newcastle Island 76 Y39
Octopus Islands 63 S34
Oliver Cove 22 X14
Penrose Island 49 L25
Pirates Cove 87 Z40
Plumper Cove 77 X40-41
Princess Louisa 64 S-T39
Rebecca Spit 63 T34-35
Rock Bay 63 S33
Rugged Point 61 T27
Sandy Island 75 W35-36
Sechelt Inlets 76 V39 W39 77 V40
Shuswap Lake 69 O-P57 O57 O58
Small Inlet 63 S34
Smuggler Cove 76 W38-39
Stuart Lake 18 R20-21
Takla Lake
- Sandy Point 31 Q33-34
- West Side 17 P18
- White Bluff 17 P18-19

Thurston Bay 63 R-S34
Union Passage 20 U12
Wallace Island 87 A40
Whaleboat Island 77 Z40

Provincial Conservancies

Alty 22 U12-13
Banks Nii Luutiksm 20 U11
Bear Island 31 R31
Bella Coola 40 F29
Bishop Bay 22 U13-14
Broughton Archipelago 62 P28-29 Q29
Burdwood Group 62 P30
Burnt Bridge Creek 40 F31
Callaghan 65 T41
Calvert Island 49 L24-25
Carter Bay 22 W14
Cascade-Sutslem 23 W-X16 40 D27-28
Catto Creek 50 L30
Cetan-Thurston Bay 63 R-S34
Clyak Estuary 49 J27
Codville Lagoon 49 H25-26
Crab Lake 22 U14
Cranstown Point 49 L-M25
Dean River 40 D29-30
Dean River Corridor 40 D30
Dzawadi / Klinaklini Estuary 51 K32-33
Ecstall Headwaters 22 T13
Ecstall Sparkling 22 T12
Ecstall Spokskuut 28 V20
Ellerslie-Roscoe 22 X15
Emily Lake 22 X14-15
Este-Tiwihl / Sigurd Creek 77 U41
Ethelda Bay-Tennant Island 22 V11-12
Europa Lake 22 V14-15
Forward Harbour 63 R32
Gitxaala Nii Luutiksm / Kitkatla 20 S10-11 T10-11
Golden Gate / Xáat Yádi Aani 7 A7
Goose Bay 49 L25-26
Hen?mdzl Mekola / Yorke Islands 62 R31
Hot Springs-No Name Creek 40 G28
Huchsduwachsdu Nuyem Jees / Kitlope Heritage 22 V15-16 W15-16 32 A27 40 C27
Hunwadi / Ahnuati-Bald 63 O32 P32-33
Indian Lake-Hitchcock Creek / Át Ch'îni Shà 7 A8
Kennedy Island 20 S-T11 28 V18
Khtada Lake 28 V21
Khutzeymateen Inlet 28 R-S19
Khutzeymateen Inlet West 28 R18-19 S19
Khyex 28 T19-20
Kilbella Estuary 49 K27
Kimsquit Estuary 40 C28-29
Kitasoo Spirit Bear 22 W13-14
K'lgaan / Klekane 22 V14
Klewnuggit 22 T-U12
K'Mooda / Lowe-Gamble 22 U12-13
K'nabiyaax / Ashdown 22 V13
Koeye 49 J25-26
K'ootz / Khutze 22 V14
Ksgax / Stephens Island Group 20 S10-11 28 U-V17
Ksi X'anmas 28 R19-20
Ktisgaidz / McDonald Bay 22 V13
Kt'll / Racey 22 W13
Kts'mkta'ani / Union Lake 28 S18-19
Kwatna Estuary 40 G27 50 H27
K'Zuzalt / Twin Two 66 S44-45
Lady Douglas-Don Peninsula 22 X14
Lax Ka'Gaas / Campania 22 V12
Lax kul / Nii Luutiksm / Bonilla 20 U10-11
Lax kwax / Dundas-Melville 20 R10
Lax kwil / Dziidz / Fin 22 V13
Lockhart Gordon 49 L27
Long Island 31 R32-33
Lucy Islands 28 U17
Machmell 50 K29
Mahpahkum-Ahkwuna / Deserters-Walkers 61 O26
Manzanita Cove 28 R18
Maxtaktsm'aa / Union Passage 22 U12
Moksgm'ol / Chapple-Cornwall 22 V13
Monarch Mtn. / Xéegi Deiyi 7 A8
Monckton Nii Luutiksm 22 U-V12
Mt. Minto / K'iyán 7 A7-8
Nakina-Inklin Rivers / Yáwu Yaa 7 B8-9
Namu 49 J25-26
Nekite Estuary 50 L-M28
Nlhaxten / Cerise Creek 66 S44-45
Nooseseck 40 F28
Outer Central Coast Islands 22 Y14 48 H23 49 H24
Owienko 50 K28
Pa_aat 22 T11-12
Palemin / Estero Basin 63 R34-35
Penrose-Ripon 49 L25-26
Phillips Estuary / ?Nacinuxw 63 Q34
Polkinghorn Islands 62 P28
Pooley 22 W14
Port Arthur 31 S32
Q'altanaas / Aaltanash 22 V14
Qudes / Gillard-Jimmy Judd Islands 63 R34-35
Qwalimak / Upper Birkenhead 65 Q-R43
Qwiquallaaq / Boat Bay 62 Q29
Rescue Bay 22 X14-15
Restoration Bay 49 H26
Sanctuary Bay 31 Q31-32
Shearwater Hot Springs 22 U14
Sheemahant 50 K29-30
Skeena Bank 28 V18 U19
Stafford Estuary 63 P33-34 Q33-34
Stair Creek 22 T13
Taku River / T'akú Téix' 7 B8
Thorsen Creek 40 G29-30
Thulme Falls 28 T19
Thurston Bay 63 R-S34
Troup Passage 22 Y14-15
Tsa-Latl' / Smokehouse 50 M28-29
Tutshi Lake / T'ooch' Áayi 7 A7
Ugwiwey / Cape Caution 49 M-N25 N26
Ugwiwey / Cape Caution-Blunden Bay 49 M-N25
Upper Elaho Valley 65 R40
Upper Gladys River / Watsix Deiyi 7 A9
Upper Kimsquit 23 V16
Upper Klinaklini 51 K33
Upper Rogers / kolii7 66 T45
Upper Soo 65 T41-42
Washkash Point 63 O33
Wakeman Estuary 62 O29-30
Wales Harbour 28 R17
Wawley / Seymour Estuary 50 N29
Wilkinson-Wright Bay 31 R32-33 S32-33
Willison Creek-Nelson Lake / Sit' Héeni 7 A7
Winter Inlet 28 R18
Woodworth Lake 28 T18-19
Zumtela Bay 28 S17-18

Provincial Ecological Reserves

Aleza Lake 36 W45
Ambrose Lake 76 V38
Baynes Island 77 V41-42
Bednesti Lake 35 X40-41
Big Creek 53 J-K43
Big White Mountain 81 V57-58
Bowser 76 X36-37
Buck Hills Road 69 T57
Burnt Cabin Bog 30 S29-30
Cardiff Mountain 53 L40
Catherine Creek 30 P-Q28
Cecil Lake 25 J50-51
Chasm 55 N48
Checleset Bay 61 T25
Chilako River 34 Z39
Chilliwack River 79 Z48
Cinema Bog 44 B44
Clanninick Creek 61 T26
Claud Elliott Creek 62 R-S29
Clayhurst 25 K52-55
Columbia Lake 72 T69-70
Comox Lake Bluffs 75 W34
Det San 30 S29
Doc English Bluff 54 J45
Drywilliam Lake 34 W36-37
East Redonda Island 64 S-T36
Evans Lake 82 U-V62
Field's Lease 80 Z55
Galiano Island 77 Z40-41
Gamble Creek 28 U18-19
Gilnockie Creek 84 Z69-70
Gingietl Creek 29 P22
Grayling River Hot Springs 58 H-J60
Haley Lake 76 Z37
Haynes' Lease 80 Z55-56
Honeymoon Bay 87 A37-38
Ilgachuz Range 41 D34-35
Kingcome River / Atlatzi River 62 O31
Kingfisher Creek 69 P58
Klanawa River 86 A-B35
Klaskish River 61 S25
Lasqueti Island 76 X37-38
Lew Creek 70 R63
Lily Pad Lake 69 T57-58
Liumchem 78 Z46
Mahoney Lake 80 Y54-55
McQueen Creek 67 P52
Megin River 74 X31
Meridian Road (Vanderhoof) 34 Y38-39
Misty Lake 61 Q27
Morice River 32 V29
Mount Derby 62 R29-30
Mount Elliott 62 S29-30
Mount Griffin 69 P59
Mount Sabine 72 T69-70
Mount Tinsdale 45 C48
Narcosli Lake 42 C38-39
Nechako River 35 X41-42
Nimpkish River 62 T30
Nitinat Lake 86 B36
Ram Creek 84 T-U70
Robson Bight (Michael Bigg) 62 R29-30
Rolla Canyon 27 M52-55
Ross Lake 79 Z50
San Juan Ridge 87 C38
San Juan River Estuary 86 C37
Skagit River Cottonwoods 79 Y49
Skagit River Forest 79 Y49-50 Z49-50
Skagit River Rhododendrons 79 Z49
Skeena River 28 U21
Skihist 67 S48
Skwaha Lake 67 R47-48
Soap Lake 67 S48-49
Stoyoma Creek 79 U48
Sunbeam Creek 38 A52
Sutton Pass 75 Y33-34
Tahsish River 61 S-T27
Takla Lake 31 P33
Torkelsen Lake 31 Q30
Tranquille 67 P51
Tsitika Mountain 62 R29
Tsitika River 62 R-S30
Upper Shuswap River 70 Q60
Vance Creek 69 S57
Westwick Lake 54 J45
Whipsaw Creek 79 X51
Williams Creek 29 U25
Yale Garry Oak 79 W48

Provincial Parks

Adams Lake 68 O55
Akamina-Kishinena 85 Z75
Alexandra Bridge 79 V48
Alice Lake 77 V42
Allison Lake 79 V51
Anderson Bay 76 W38
Anderson Flats 30 P27
Andy Bailey 11 G24
Anhluut'ukwsim Laxmihl Angwinga'asanskwhl Nisga'a 29 P22-23
Anstey - Hunakwa 57 N58
Apodaca 77 X41
Arbutus Grove 76 Y38
Arctic Pacific Lakes 19 S25-26
Arrow Lakes (Shelter Bay) 70 Q61
Artlish Caves 62 T28
Atlin / Téix'gi Aan Tlein 7 A7-8
Atna Lake 22 T15
Babine Meadows 17 Q17
Babine Mountains 30 R29 31 R30
Babine River Corridor 17 P16-17
Bamberton 87 B-C40
Banana Island 68 P-Q55
Barkerville 44 B47
Bear Creek 80 U55
Bear Glacier 16 N13
Bearhole Lake 27 Q-R50
Beatton 25 J49
Beatton River 25 J-K49
Beaumont 34 W37
Beaver Creek 82 Z62
Bedard Aspen 66 Q47 67 Q48
Bellhouse 87 A41
Big Bar Lake 54 M46-47
Big Creek 54 M-N42
Bijoux Falls 26 P43-44
Birkenhead Lake 65 Q-R43
Bishop River 64 P38-39
Blackcomb Glacier 65 T42-43
Blanket Creek 70 P60-61
Bligh Island 74 V-W29
Blue Earth Lake 67 Q48
Blue River-Black Spruce 57 H56-57
Blue River-Pine 57 H56-57
Bobtail Mountain 35 Y41
Bocock Peak 18 O23
Bodega Ridge 77 Z40-41
Bonaparte 55 N51
Boothmans Oxbow 89 Z59-60
Border Lake 12 M11
Boulder Creek 30 Q27-28
Boundary Creek 81 Z58
Bowron Lake 45 B49
Boya Lake 8 A12 9 A13
Boyle Point 76 X36
Brackendale Eagles 77 V41-42
Brandywine Falls 77 U42
Bridal Veil Falls 78 Y47
Bridge River Delta 65 P41-42
Bromley Rock 80 X52-53
Browne Lake 81 V56
Buccaneer Bay 76 X38-39
Buckinghorse River Wayside 14 K23 15 K24
Bugaboo 71 P65
Bulkley Junction 30 P26-27
Bull Canyon 54 H41
Burges and James Gadsden 59 M64
Burgoyne Bay 87 A40
Burns Lake 33 V33
Butler Ridge 24 K44-45
Caligata Lake 56 K55
Call Lake 30 Q26
Callaghan Lake 65 S-T42
Canim Beach 55 J49-50
Cape Scott 60 P23
Cariboo Mountains 45 C50-51
Cariboo Nature 54 J47
Cariboo River 45 D48
Carmanah Walbran 86 B36
Carp Lake 18 R22-23
Castle Rock Hoodoos 55 N50
Cathedral 80 Y-Z53
Cedar Point 44 E47
Champion Lakes 82 Y62
Charlie Lake 25 K48-49
Chase 14 M20
Chasm 55 N48
Chilliwack Lake 79 Y-Z48
Chilliwack River 78 Z46
Choquette Hot Springs 104
Christina Lake 82 Z60
Chu Chua Cottonwood 56 M52-53
Cinnemousun Narrows 69 O57-58
Claud Elliott 62 S29
Clayoquot Arm 75 Y33
Clayoquot Plateau 75 Y33
Clendinning 65 R-S40
Close-to-the-Edge 37 W49
Cody Caves 83 V64-65
Coldwater River 79 V50
Collinson Point 87 A41
Columbia Lake 72 S69
Conkle Lake 81 Y56-57
Coquihalla Canyon 79 X48
Coquihalla River 79 X48-49
Cornwall Hills 67 Q48
Coste Rocks 22 T13-14
Cottonwood River 44 B44
Cowichan River 87 A-B39
Crooked River 19 S24
Crowsnest 85 V-W73
Cummins Lake 58 H61
Cultus Lake 78 Z46
Cypress 77 X41-42
Dahl Lake 27 Y41
Dala-Kildala Rivers Estuaries 22 T14-15
Dall River Old Growth 9 F16
Darke Lake 80 V54
Davis Lake 78 Y45
Dawley Passage 75 Y32
Denetiah 9 F16-17 G16-17
Diana Lake 28 U18-19
Dionisio Point 77 Z40
Downing 66 O47
Drewry Point 83 X65
Driftwood Canyon 30 R29
Drumbeg 77 Z40
Dry Gulch 72 Q68
Duck Lake 76 U37
Duffey Lake 66 R45
Dune Za Keyih 9 G17-18
E. C. Manning 79 Y50-51
Eagle Bay 22 T14
Eakin Creek Canyon 56 L-M52
Eakin Creek Floodplain 56 L52
East Pine 27 N48
Echo Lake 69 S-T58
Ed Bird-Estella Lakes 14 L20
Edge Hills 66 O46
Elephant Hill 67 P48-49
Elk Falls 63 T33-34
Elk Lakes 72 R71 73 R72
Elk Valley 85 W72
Ellison 68 T55 69 T56
Emar Lakes 55 L51-52
Eneas Lakes 80 V54
English Lake 69 P60
Englishman River Falls 76 Y37
Entiako 33 A33-34
Epper Passage 74 Y31 75 Y32
Epsom 67 Q48-49
Erg Mountain 37 Z49
Erie Creek 82 Y63
Eskers 35 W41-42
Ethel F. Wilson Memorial 31 U33
Exchamsiks River 28 U21
F. H. Barber 78 X47
Fillongley 76 W36
Finger-Tatuk 34 Z38
Finlay-Russel 13 J18
Finn Creek 57 J56-57
Fintry 69 T56
Flat Lake 54 L47 55 L48
Flores Island 74 X30
Foch-Gilttoyees 22 T13
Fort George Canyon 35 Y43
Fossli 75 Y35
Foster Arm 70 Q63
Francis Point 76 W38
François Lake 33 X35
Fraser River 35 Z43
Fred-Antoine 66 P45-46
French Beach 87 D38-39
Gabriola Sands 76 Y39
Garibaldi 77 U43
George Evanoff 37 W48
Gilnockie 84 Z70
Gilpin Grasslands 82 Z60
Giscome Portage Trail 36 V44
Gitnadoiks River 28 V21 29 V22
Gladstone 82 Y60
Goat Range 70 S63 71 S64
Gold Muchalat 74 U31
Golden Ears 78 W-X44
Goldpan 67 S48
Goldstream 87 C40
Gordon Bay 86 A37 87 A38
Gowlland Tod 87 C40
Graham Laurier 14 M22
Granby 81 V-W59
Graystokes 81 U58
Great Glacier 104
Green Lake 55 M49
Greenstone Mountain 67 Q51
Grohman Narrows 82 W63
Gwillam Lake 27 O-P40
Gwyneth Lake 65 P42-43
Hai Lake-Mount Herman 29 T-U23
Halkett Bay 77 X41
Hamber 48 F61-62
Harbour Dudgeon Lakes 57 L57
Harry Lake Aspen 66 P47 67 P48
Haynes Point 80 Z55 81 Z56
Heather-Dina Lakes 18 P23
Height of the Rockies 72 Q-R71
Helliwell 76 W36-37
Hemer 76 Z39
Herald 69 P56-57
Hesquiat Lake 74 W29-30
Hesquiat Peninsula 74 W-X29
High Lakes Basin 55 M51-52
Hitchie Creek 86 A35-36
Hole-in-the-Wall 26 Q46
Homathko Estuary 64 O36
Horneline Creek 9 E16-17
Horne Lake 76 X36
Horsefly Lake 45 F48-49
Huihil Creek 68 O-P55
Hyland River 9 C16
Indian Arm 77 X43
Inkaneep 79 Y55
Inland Lake 76 U37
Iskut River Hot Springs 12 K12
Itcha Ilgachuz 42 E35-36
Jackman Flats 47 C56
Jackpine Remnant 10 E22
James Chabot 72 R68
Jewel Lake 81 Y59
Jimsmith Lake 84 X69
Joffre Lakes 66 S44
John Dean 87 B41
Johnstone Creek 81 Z57
Juan de Fuca 86 C37 87 C38
Junction Sheep Range 54 K44
Juniper Beach 67 P49-50
Kakwa 38 V51-52 X51
Kalamalka Lake 69 T56
Kekuli Bay 69 S-T56
Kennedy Lake 75 Z33
Kennedy River Bog 75 Z32-33
Kentucky-Alleyne 79 U51
Keremeos Columns 80 Y54
Khutzeymateen 20 R12
Kianuko 83 X67
Kickininee 80 W55
Kikomun Creek 84 Y71
Kilby 78 Y46
Kin Beach 75 V35
Kinaskan Lake 12 J12-13
King George VI 82 Z62
Kingfisher Creek 69 P58
Kiskatinaw 25 L50
Kitimat River 29 V23-24
Kitson Island 28 U17-18
Kitsumkalum 29 S23
Kitty Coleman 75 V35
Kitwanga Mountain 29 P-Q25
Kleanza Creek 29 S24-25

Kledo Creek 10 F22
Klin-se-za 19 O24
Kluskoil Lake 42 B39
Kokanee Creek 83 W64
Kokanee Glacier 83 V64
Koksilah River 87 B39
Kootenay Lake
Davis Creek 71 T65
Lost Ledge 71 T65
Midge Creek 83 X65
Kotcho Lake Village 11 E25-26
Kwadacha Wilderness 14 H-J20
Lac du Bois Grasslands 67 P51
Lac la Hache 54 J47
Lac Le Jeune 67 R51 68 R52
Lakelse Lake 29 U23-24
Lakelse Lake Wetlands 29 U23-24
Lava Forks 12 M11
Lawn Point 61 R24
Laz & Cox Islands 60 O-P21
Liard River Corridor 10 D-E20
Liard River Hotsprings 9 D18
Little Qualicum Falls 76 X-Y36
Lockhart Beach 83 W65
Lockhart Creek 83 W-X66
Loon Lake 55 N48
Loveland Bay 63 T33
Lower Nimpkish 61 Q27-28
Lower Skeena River 28 U21 29 U22
Lower Tsitika River 62 R29
Mabel Lake 69 R58
MacMillan 76 Y36
Main Lake 63 S-T34
Malaspina 64 T36
Malbeelah Creek Wetlands 29 V24
Mansons Landing 63 T35
Mara 69 Q57
Marble Canyon 66 P47
Marble Range 54 N46-47
Marble River 61 Q26
Marl Creek 59 L64
Martha Creek 58 N60-61
Maxhamish Lake 10 C22-23
McConnell Lake 67 R51 68 R52
McDonald Creek 70 T62
Mehatl Creek 78 U46
Memory Island 87 B39-40
Meziadin Lake 16 N13-14
Milligan Hills 15 J27
Miracle Beach 75 U34-35
Mitlenatch Island Nature 75 U35
Moberly Lake 26 M46-47
Momich Lake 57 M56
Monashee 70 Q-R60
Monck 67 S-T51
Monkman 19 R26
Monte Creek 68 Q54
Monte Lake 68 R54-55
Moose Valley 54 L47
Morden Colliery 76 Z39
Morice Lake 22-23 T15-16 32 W27-28
Morrissey 85 X72
Morton Lake 63 T33
Mount Assiniboine 72 O-P69
Mount Blanchet 31 P33
Mount Edziza 12 H11-12 J11-12
Mount Elphinstone 77 X40
Mount Fernie 84 W-X71 85 W-X72
Mount Geoffrey Escarpment 76 W36-37
Mount Griffin 69 P59
Mount Maxwell 87 A40
Mount Pope 23 V19
Mount Richardson 76 W39 77 W40
Mount Robson 47 B-C58 D-E59
Mount Savona 67 Q50
Mount Seymour 77 X42-43
Mount Terry Fox 47 C57
Moyie Lake 84 X69
Mud Lake Delta 57 H57
Mudzenchoot 18 Q21
Muncho Lake 9 E-F19
Muqqiwn/Brooks Peninsula 61 S25
Murrin 77 W41-42
Muscovite Lakes 18 N-O21
Myra - Bellevue 81 V56
Nadina Mountain 32 W29
Nahatlatch 78 U47
Naikoon 20 T8-9
Nairn Falls 65 S43
Nalbeelah Creek Wetlands 16 S14-15
Nancy Greene 82 Y61
Nation Lakes 18 P19-20
Nazko Lake 43 F40-41
Neneikěkh/Nanika-Kidprice 23 T16
Netalzul Meadows 30 P29
Nickel Plate 80 X54
Nicolum River 79 X48-49
Nilkitkwa Lake 17 P17-18
Nimpkish Lake 62 R-S28
Ningunsaw 12 L12
Nisga'a Memorial Lava Bed 29 P-Q23
Niskonlith Lake 68 P54-55
Nitinat River 86 A36
Norbury Lake 84 W70-71
North Thompson Islands 56 M52
North Thompson Oxbows East 47 F57
North Thompson Oxbows Jenson Island 68 P52
North Thompson Oxbows Manteau 47 F56-57
North Thompson River 56 K-L52
North Tweedsmuir 23 U-V17
Northern Rocky Mountains 10 G21 14 H21
Nuntsi 52 K39 53 K40
Nutchatlitz 74 U28
Okanagan Falls 80 X54-55
Okanagan Lake 80 V54-55
Okanagan Mountain 80 V55
Okeover Arm 76 U36
Old Man Lake 31 U31
Omineca 18 O20
One Island Lake 27 P51
Oregon Jack 67 Q48
Otter Lake 79 W50-51
Owyacumish River 22 U14-15
Paarens Beach 18 S21
Painted Bluffs 67 P50-51
Paul Lake 68 P53
Peace Arch 77 Z43
Peace River Corridor
Island Site 25 L51
Wak'anaahtaah Site 25 K51-52
Pennask Creek 80 U53
Pennask Lake 68 T53
Petroglyph 76 Y39
Pillar 68 Q55 69 Q56
Pilot Bay 83 W65
Pine LeMoray 26 O-P44
Pine River Breaks 26 N47 27 N48
Pinecone Burke 78 X44
Pink Mountain 14 L23
Pinnacles 44 C44
Porcupine Meadows 67 O51
Porpoise Bay 77 W-X40
Porteau Cove 77 W41-42
Premier Lake 84 U70
Prior Centennial 87 B41
Pritchard 68 Q54-55
Prophet River Hotsprings 14 H23
Prophet River Wayside 15 C19
Prudhomme Lake 28 U18-19
Ptarmigan Creek 37 Z49-50
Pukeashun 57 N56-57
Puntchesakut Lake 43 C43
Purcell Wilderness Conservancy 71 T66-67
Purden Lake 36 X46
Pure Lake 20 T8
Pyramid Creek Falls 47 F-G57
Quatsino 61 Q25
Rainbow Alley 17 P17-18
Raft Cove 60 Q23
Rathtrevor Beach 76 X37-38
Read Island 63 T34
Rearguard Falls 47 C56-57
Red Bluff 31 R31-32
Redfern-Keily Creek 14 K22
Rendezvous Island South 63 S35
Roberts Creek 77 X39-40
Roberts Memorial 76 Z39
Roche Lake 68 R53
Roderick Haig-Brown 68 O55
Rolley Lake 78 Y44-45
Rocsoe Bay 64 T36
Roseberry 82 U63
Rosewall Creek 75 X35-36
Ross Lake 30 P28
Rubyrock Lake 17 R19-20
Ruckle 87 A-B41
Ruth Lake 55 J-K49
Ryan 84 Y-Z68
Sabine Channel 76 W38
St. Mary's Alpine 83 U67
Saltery Bay 76 V38
Sandwell 76 Y39 77 Y40
Santa-Boca 74 V-W29
Sargeant Bay 76 W-X39
Sasquatch 78 X47
Scatter River Old Growth 10 D20-21
Schoen Lake 62 S30
Schoolhouse Lake 55 J49
Seeley Lake 30 P-Q27
Seton Portage Historic 66 Q45
Seven Sisters 29 R25
Shannon Falls 77 V-W42
Shuswap Lake 69 P56
Shuswap River Islands 69 Q-R58
Sikanni Old Growth 11 G25
Silver Beach 57 N58
Silver Lake 79 X-Y48
Silver Star 69 R57
Simson 76 X39
Sir Alexander Mackenzie 23 X16
Skaha Bluffs 80 X55-56
Skagit Valley 79 Y-Z49
Skihist 67 S48
Skookumchuck Narrows 76 V39
Skookumchuck Rapids 69 Q58-59
Sleeping Beauty Mountain 29 S22-23
Slim Creek 37 Y48
Small River Caves 47 B56
Smelt Bay 63 T35
Smith River Falls / Fort Halkett 9 D18
Sooke Mountain 87 C40
Sooke Potholes 87 C39-40
South Chilcotin Mountains 65 O42
South Texada Island 76 W38
South Tweedsmuir 23 W-X18
Sowchea Bay 18 S21
Spatsizi Headwaters 12 K-L14
Spatsizi Plateau Wilderness 12 J15
Spider Lake 76 X36
Spipiyus 76 W39
Sproat Lake 75 X-Y35
Squitty Bay 76 X38
Stagleap 83 Z64
Stamp River 75 X35
Stawamus Chief 77 V42
Steelhead 67 P-Q50
Stein Valley Nlaka'pamux Heritage 66 S-T46
Stemwinder 80 X53
Stikine River 12 H12-13
Stone Mountain 10 F20
Strathcona 75 U-W32
Strathcona Westmin 75 W32-33
Stuart Lake 18 R20-21
Stuart River
Lower Site 35 W40
Upper Site 34 V38-39
Sue Channel 22 T-U13
Sugarbowl / Grizzly Den 36 X-Y47
Sukunka Falls 26 P46
Sulphur Passage 74 X30-31
Summit Lake 70 Q62
Sun-Oka Beach 80 W55
Sunnybrae 69 P56
Surge Narrows 63 S34
Sustut 17 N17
Sutherland River 18 S20
Swan Lake 27 O52
Swan Lake Kispiox River 16 O14-15
Sydney Inlet 74 W30
Syringa 82 X61
Tahsish-Kwois 61 S27
Tantalus 77 V41
Tatlatui 13 L16
Tatshenshini-Alsek 6 B-C3
Taweel 56 K-L52
Taylor Arm 75 X-Y35
Taylor Landing 25 K50
Tazdli Wyiez Bin / Burnie-Shea 30 U27
Ten Mile Lake 44 C44
Tetrahedron 77 W40
Tetsa River 10 F21-22
Three Sisters Lakes 34 Z44
Thunder Hill 72 T68-69
Toad River Hotsprings 10 F20
Todagin South Slope 12 J12-13
Top of the World 84 U-V71
Topley 31 S32
Tranquil Creek 75 X32-33
Trembleur Lake 18 R20
Trepanier 80 U54
Tribune Bay 76 W36-37
Truman Dagnus Locheed 69 S56
Ts'il?os 52 N39
Tsintsunko Lakes 67 O51-52
Tudyah Lake 18 Q23
Tunkwa 67 Q50
Tuya Mountains 8 D12
Tweedsmuir North 32 Z30-31 A30-31
Tweedsmuir South 41 D-E32
Tyhee Lake 30 S28-29
Uncha Mountain Red Hills 33 W33-34
Upper Adams River 57 J-K57 L56
Upper Lillooet 65 Q40
Upper Seymour River 57 K-L58
Upper Violet Creek 69 Q57-58
Valhalla 82 U-V63
Vargas Island 74 Y31
Vaseux Lake 80 X55
Victor Lake 70 O60
Wakes Cove 77 Z40
Walhachin Oxbows 67 P-Q50
Walloper Lake 67 R51
Walsh Cove 64 S36
Wapiti Lake 19 R-S27
Wardner 84 X70
Wasa Lake 84 V69
Weewanie Hot Springs 22 U14
Wells Gray 46 G52-55 56 H54-55
West Arm 83 X64-65
West Lake 35 Y43
West Shawnigan Lake 87 B39-40
West Twin 37 A50-51
Weymer Creek 74 U29
Whiskers Point 18 Q-R23
White Lake 69 P56-57
White Pelican 43 G42
White Ridge 74 V31
White River 62 T31
Whiteswan Lake 72 T70
Windermere Lake 72 R68
Wire Cache 57 K56-57
Wistaria 32 X31
Woss Lake 62 T29
Wrinkly Face 69 T56-57
Yahk 84 Z68
Yalakom 66 O44
Yard Creek 69 P58

Provincial Protected Areas

Anarchist 81 Z56
Arrowstone 67 P48-49
Bearhole Lake 27 Q-R51
Bennett Bay 87 A41-42
Brent 80 W54
Brim River Hot Springs 22 U14-15
Buse Lake 68 Q53
Chinchaga Lakes 15 K27
Chuckachida River 13 J16-17
Churn Creek 54 L44-45
Close-to-the-Edge 37 W49
Craig Headwaters 104
Damdochax 12 M15 13 M16
Denison - Bonneau 69 T58
Dune Za Keyih 10 B16
Dunn Peak 56 L54
Ekwan Lake 11 F26-27
Enderby Cliffs 69 Q57
Exchamsiks River 28 T-U21 29 T-U22
Foster Arm 47 G59
Goguka Creek 11 G24
Greenbush Lake 70 P60
Gitnadoiks River 29 U22
Hakai Luxvbalis Prov. Conservancy Area 48 H-J23 49 J-K24
Hay River 11 F27
Holliday Creek Arch 46 B55
Homathko River - Tatlayoko 52 M36-37
Huchsduwachsdu Nuyem Jees 40 C27
Jesse Falls 22 T14
Kiskatinaw River 25 L51
Klin-Se-Za 26 M44
Klua Lakes 11 H24
Kitsumkalum Lake North 29 R22-23
Lower Raush 46 B52
Lundmark Bog 29 S23-24
Maxhamish Lake 10 C22-23
Nechako Canyon 33 Y35-36
Omineca 18 O20
Pitman River 13 H16
Portage Brule Rapids 9 D17
Prevost Island 87 A41
Ptarmigan Creek 37 Z49-50
Purcell Wilderness Conservancy Corridor 71 T67
Russell Island 87 B41
Seven Sisters 29 Q-R25
Sikanni Canyon 15 J24-25 K24-25
Sikanni Chief Falls 14 K23
Six Mile Point 65 P50
Snowy 80 Z54
South Okanagan Grasslands 80 Y-Z55 Z55
South Otter Bay 87 A-B41
Sustut 13 M17
Sutherland River 34 V36
Swan Creek 29 T-U25
Thinahtea North 11 C27
Thinahtea South 11 C-D27
Tumbo Island 87 A42
Upper Raush 46 C54-55
Vaseux 80 Y55 81 Y56
White Lake Grasslands 80 X-Y55

Provincial Recreation Areas

Atlin 6 A8
Coquihalla Summit 79 W49
Fiordland 22 W15
Kettle River 81 Y-Z57
Mount Edziza 12 C11
Paul Lake 68 P52-53
Tweedsmuir North 23 U-V16
Tweedsmuir South 23 W-X19

Provincial Wildlife Management Areas

Boundary Bay 77 Z42
Chilanko Marsh 52 H38
Cluxewe 61 Q27
Dewdrop-Rosseau 67 P50-51
Lazo Marsh / North East Comox 73 V35
Pitt-Addington Marsh 77 X-Y43
Sturgeon Bank 77 Y41
Tatshenshini-Alsek 6 A4-5
Tofino Mudflats 74 Y31 75 Y32
Tranquille 67 Q51

Regional Parks

Albert Head Lagoon 87 D40-41
Anarchist 81 Z56
Antlers Beach 80 V54
Arrow Creek 83 Y67
Beachcomber 76 X-Y38
Benson Creek Falls 76 Y38
Bere Point 62 Q28
Berman Lake 35 X41
Bertram Creek 80 U55
Blackfoot 25 K52
Brilliant Suspension Bridge 82 X62-62
Brooks Point 87 B41-42
Broughton Strait 61 Q27
Burns-Farstad 83 Z67
Campbell Valley 78 Z44
Cascade Falls 78 Y45
Cedarside 47 D56-57
Chemainus River 87 A39
Coldham 80 V54
Coles Bay 87 B40
Cottonwood Lake 83 X64
Craig Road 76 U36
Descanso Bay 76 Y39 77 Y40
Devonian 87 D40
Dan Bosch 76 V38-39
East Point 87 A-B42
East Sooke 87 D40
Egmont 76 V39
Elk-Beaver Lake 87 C41
Elk Valley 85 U72
Englishman River 76 Y37
Gellatly Heritage 80 V55
George Hicks 47 D57
Glacier Creek 71 S65
Glade 82 X63
Glen Canyon 80 U55
Goose Spit 75 V-W35
Griscome Portage / Huble Homestead 36 V44
Hardy Falls 80 V54
Harold Mann 36 W44
Haywire Bay 76 U37
Heart / Stocking Lake 87 Z-A39
Horne Lake 76 X36
Horth Hill 87 B40-41
Iona Island 77 Y41
Island 22 78 Y46-47
Island View Beach 87 C41
James Johnstone 83 W64
John Daly 76 W39
Kaleden Hotel 80 X55
Kapoor 87 C40
Kaslo Beach 83 U65
Katherine Lake 76 W38
Kenyon 80 Y54-55
Kinsol Trestle 87 B39-40
Koeneman 38 A52
Kristian Winther 36 W43-44
Kwaksistah 61 Q24
Link River 61 R26
Lions 80 X54-55
Little Huson Cave 62 S28
Little Qualicum River 76 X36
Little Qualicum River Estuary 76 X36-37
Lynn Headwaters 77 X42
Manitou 80 W55
Matheson Lake 87 D40
Matthews Point 87 A41-42
McCulloch 81 V56
McIntyre Canyon 80 Y55 81 Y56
McMillan Creek 35 X43
Mill Farm 87 A-B40
Montney Centennial 25 J48-49
Moorecroft 76 Y38
Morning Beach 78 W36
Mount Arrowsmith Massif 76 Y36-37
Mount Cain Alpine 62 S30
Mount Geoffrey 76 W36
Mount Parke 87 A41
Mount Work 87 C40
Myrtle Rocks 76 V37
Neilson 78 Y45
Ness Lake 35 W42
Nymph Falls 75 V-X34
Osborne Bay 87 A40
Osoyoos Lake 81 Z56
Pacific Spirit 77 Y41
Palm Beach 76 V37
Pass Creek 82 X62
Peace River Lookout 25 K49
Quatse River 61 P26
Riondel 83 V65
Robinson Creek 69 P57
Roche Cove 87 D40
Rock Ovens 80 W55 81 W56
Rosebery Parklands 82 U62-63
Rosebud Lake 83 Z64
Sandy Pool 87 B39
Seal Bay 75 V35
Shannon Beach 69 O57
Shannon Lake 80 U55
Shelter Point 76 W36-37
Spencer Tuck 26 M46
Spectacle Lake 87 C40
Spragge 76 V36-37
Storie Creek 75 U34-35
Sudeten 19 P27-28
Sumas Mountain 78 Y-Z45
Sunshine Bay 83 W64-65
Thacker Mountain 79 X48-49
Thetis Lake 87 C40
Tie Lake 84 X71
Traders Cove 80 U55
Wild Rose Bay 69 O57
Wilkins 35 X42
Winlaw Beach 82 W62
Witty's Lagoon 87 D40-41
Wycliffe 84 W68-69

Place Name Index

How to use this index

To find a place, search through the alphabetically arranged columns. Note the page number and reference square to the right of the place name. For example, to find the location of Caycuse:

Caycuse 86 A37

Place name — Page number — Reference Square

70 Mile ... 55 M-N48
70 Mile House ... 55 M48
93 Mile ... 55 L48
100 Mile House ... 55 K48-49
105 Mile House ... 55 K48-49
108 Mile House ... 55 K48
108 Mile Ranch ... 55 K48
111 Mile House ... 55 K48
114 Mile House ... 55 K48
122 Mile House ... 54 J47 55 J48
127 Mile House ... 54 J47
141 Mile House ... 54 J46-47
150 Mile House ... 54 H46

Abbotsford ... 78 Z45-46
Aberdeen (Kamloops) ... 67 Q51 68 Q52
Aberdeen (Metro Vancouver) ... 78 Z44-45
Adams Lake ... 68 O55
Adams Lake Band ... 68 O-P55
Agassiz ... 78 Y47
Ahousaht First Nation ... 74 Y31
Ahousaht First Nation(Marktosis) ... 74 X-Y31
Ahousat ... 74 X31
Ainsworth Hot Springs ... 83 V65
Aitchelitz Band ... 78 Y46
Albas ... 57 N57
Alberni ... 76 Y36
Albert Canyon ... 58 N62
Albion ... 78 Y44
Albreda ... 47 E57
Aldergrove ... 78 Z44
Alert Bay ... 62 Q28
Alexandria ... 44 E44
Alexandria Indian Band ... 44 E44
Alexis Creek ... 53 H41-42
Alexis Creek First Nation ... 52 H39
Aleza Lake ... 19 S25
Aleza Lake ... 36 W45-46
Alice ... 83 Z66-67
Alice Arm ... 16 P13
Alkali Lake ... 54 K45
Allenby ... 79 X51 80 X52
Alliford Bay ... 20 U8 21 V8
Allison ... 79 V51
Allison ... 80 X52
Almond Gardens ... 81 Z59
Alpine Meadow ... 65 T42
Alta Vista ... 65 T42-43
Altona ... 15 D21
Altona ... 25 F49
Alvin ... 78 W44
Amai Creek ... 61 T27
Amsbury ... 29 T23
Anaconda ... 81 Z58
Anahim Lake ... 23 X19
Anahim Lake ... 41 F34
Anglemont ... 69 O57
Anmore ... 77 X-Y43
Annacis ... 77 Y42-43
Anniedale ... 77 Y43
Annis ... 69 P57
Appledale ... 82 W63
Applegrove ... 82 V61
Argenta ... 71 T65
Armstrong ... 69 R57
Arnold ... 78 Z45-46
Arras ... 19 O27
Arras ... 27 N50
Arrow Creek ... 83 Y-Z67
Arrow Park ... 70 T61
Arrowhead ... 70 Q61-62
Arrowview Heights ... 76 Y36
Ashcroft ... 67 Q48-49
Ashcroft Indian Band ... 67 Q48
Ashton Creek ... 69 Q-R57
Aspen Grove ... 79 U51
Atbara ... 83 W64
Atcheliz ... 78 Z46
Athalmer ... 72 R68
Atlin ... 7 A8
Atluck ... 61 S27 62 S28
Atnarko ... 41 F32-33
Attachie ... 19 N25
Attachie ... 24 K47
Australian ... 44 D-E44
Avola ... 57 K56
Azouzetta ... 26 P43-44
Azu Ski Village ... 26 P43

Baker (Cariboo) ... 44 C44
Baker (East Kootenay) ... 84 W70
Baldonnel ... 15 D21
Baldonnel ... 19 N27
Baldonnel ... 25 K50
Baldy Hughes ... 35 Z42-43
Balfour ... 83 W65
Balmoral ... 69 P56
Bamberton ... 87 C40
Bamfield ... 86 A34
Bankeir ... 80 V52
Barkerville ... 44 C47 45 C48
Barlow ... 44 C44
Barlow Creek ... 44 C44
Barnhartvale ... 68 Q52
Barrett ... 31 U30
Barrett Lake ... 17 S17
Barrett Lake ... 31 U30
Barrière ... 56 N53
Basque ... 67 Q48-49
Bastion Bay ... 69 P57
Bates Beach ... 75 V35
Baynes Lake ... 84 Y71
Beachcomber ... 76 Y38
Bear Cove ... 61 P26
Bear Creek ... 78 W47
Bear Flat ... 19 N26
Bear Flat ... 25 K48
Bear Lake ... 19 S24
Beasley ... 82 X63
Beaton ... 70 Q62
Beatton Ranch ... 24 G44
Beatton River ... 15 C20
Beaver Cove ... 62 Q28
Beaver Creek ... 75 X35
Beaver Falls ... 82 Z63
Beaver Lake ... 87 C41
Beaver Pass ... 44 C46
Beaver Point ... 87 B41
Beaverdell ... 81 X57
Beaverley ... 35 X-Y43
Beavermouth ... 58 L63
Becher House ... 54 J44
Bedwell Harbour ... 87 B41-42
Belcarra ... 77 X43
Bell II ... 12 D12
Bella Bella ... 22 Y14
Bella Coola ... 23 X17
Bella Coola ... 40 F29
Bellos ... 44 B44-45
Benson Lake ... 61 R27
Beryl Prairie ... 19 N25
Beryl Prairie ... 24 L45
Bessborough ... 27 M50
Bestwick ... 68 Q53
Bevan ... 75 V-W34
Big Bar Creek ... 54 N45
Big Bay ... 63 R34-35
Big Creek ... 53 K42
Big Eddy ... 70 O60
Big Lake Ranch ... 44 F46
Billings ... 82 Z60
Billings Bay ... 76 V38
Birch Island ... 56 L54
Birchbank ... 82 Y62
Birken ... 65 R43 66 R44
Black Canyon ... 67 Q48
Black Creek (Cariboo) ... 45 G49
Black Creek (Comox-Strathcona) ... 75 U-V34
Blackpool ... 56 L53
Blackwater ... 35 A41-42
Blaeberry ... 59 M64
Blake ... 83 W65
Blakeburn ... 79 W51
Blewett ... 82 X63
Blind Bay ... 69 P56
Blind Channel ... 63 R33
Bliss Landing ... 64 T36
Bloedel ... 63 T34
Blowhole ... 74 U28-29
Blubber Bay ... 76 V36
Blue River ... 57 H56
Blue Springs ... 69 S58
Blueberry Creek ... 82 Y62
Blueberry River FN ... 25 G48-49
Blutcher Hall ... 56 N54 68 O54
Boat Basin ... 74 W29-30
Bob Quinn Lake ... 12 C-D11
Bold Point ... 63 T34
Bonaparte Indian Band ... 67 P48
Bond ... 26 M47
Bones Bay ... 62 Q30
Bonnet Hill ... 36 X44
Bonnington Falls ... 82 X63
Boothroyd Indian Band ... 79 U48
Boring Ranch ... 24 F43
Boston Bar ... 79 U48
Boston Bar First Nation ... 79 U48
Boston Flats ... 67 P48
Boswell (Central Coast) ... 49 M26
Boswell (Central Kootenay) ... 83 X65-66
Bouchie Lake ... 44 C44
Boulder ... 56 L52
Boundary Bay ... 77 Z42
Boundary Falls ... 81 Z58
Bowser ... 76 X36
Box Lake ... 70 S62
Brackendale ... 77 V42
Bradian ... 65 P-Q43
Bradner ... 78 Z44-45
Brady Ranch ... 24 G43
Braeside ... 34 W38
Bralorne ... 65 P43
Brandywine Falls ... 77 U41-42
Brem River ... 64 R36
Brennan Creek ... 56 N55
Brentwood Bay ... 87 C40
Brew Bay ... 76 V37
Brexton ... 65 P43
Briar Ridge ... 27 M52
Bridal Falls ... 78 Y47
Bridesville ... 81 Z56-57
Bridge Lake ... 55 L50
Bridge River Indian Band ... 66 P45-46
Brigade Lake ... 68 R52
Brighton Beach ... 77 X42-43
Brilliant ... 82 X62
Brisco ... 71 P67
Britannia Beach ... 77 W41
Brookmere ... 79 V50
Brookswood ... 77 Z43
Brouse ... 70 S62
Brunswick ... 49 K26
Buccaneer Bay ... 76 W-X39
Buckhorn ... 35 Y43 36 Y44
Buckinghorse River ... 14 C18 15 C19
Buckley Bay ... 75 W35
Buffalo Creek ... 55 K49
Buick ... 15 D20
Buick ... 25 G48
Buick Station ... 25 G48
Bulkley Canyon ... 30 P28
Bulkley House ... 17 O18
Bull Harbour ... 61 O24-25
Bull River ... 84 X70-71
Buntzen Bay ... 77 X43
Burnaby ... 77 Y42-43
Burns Lake ... 17 S19
Burns Lake ... 33 V33
Burns Lake Tribe ... 33 V33-34
Burnt Flat ... 83 Z64
Burton ... 82 U61-62
Butedale ... 22 V13-14

Cache Creek ... 67 P48
Caesars ... 68 T55
Caithness ... 84 X71 85 X72
Cambie ... 69 P58
Camborne ... 70 P62
Camp McKinney ... 81 Z56-57
Campbell Creek ... 68 Q53
Campbell River ... 63 T34 75 U34
Canal Flats ... 72 T69
Canama ... 54 K47
Canford ... 67 T50
Canim ... 55 L48
Canim Lake ... 55 K49-50
Canim Lake Band ... 55 K49-50
Canoe ... 69 P-Q57
Canoe Creek Band ... 54 L45 M45-46
Canoe River ... 47 D57
Canyon ... 83 Z67
Canyon City (Gitwinksihlkw) ... 29 P22
Canyon Hot Springs ... 58 N62
Capilano ... 77 X-Y42
Carlin ... 69 P56
Carmi ... 81 W57
Carnaby ... 16 Q15 17 Q16
Carnaby ... 30 P27
Carquile ... 67 P48
Carr's Landing ... 68 T55 69 T56
Carrolls Landing ... 70 T61 82 U61-62
Carson ... 81 Z59
Cascade ... 82 Z60
Cascade Ridge ... 78 Y45
Casino ... 82 Z62
Cassidy ... 76 Z39
Castle Rock ... 44 F44
Castledale ... 71 O66-67
Castlegar ... 82 X-Y62
Caswell ... 26 O43
Cawston ... 80 Y54-55
Caycuse ... 86 A37
Cayoose Creek Band ... 66 Q46
Cecil Lake ... 15 D21
Cecil Lake ... 19 N27
Cecil Lake ... 25 J50
Cedar ... 76 Z39
Cedar Grove ... 69 T56
Cedarside ... 47 D57
Cedarvale ... 16 Q15
Cedarvale ... 29 Q25
Ceepeecee ... 74 U29
Celista ... 69 O56
Central Saanich ... 87 C41
Chamiss Bay ... 61 T26
Chapmans ... 79 V48
Charlie Lake ... 15 D20-21
Charlie Lake ... 19 N26
Charlie Lake ... 25 K49
Charlotte Lake ... 23 Y19
Charlotte Lake ... 41 G34
Chase ... 68 P55
Chasm ... 55 N48
Chawathil Band ... 78 X47 79 X48
Cheakamus ... 77 V41-42
Cheam Indian Band ... 78 Y47
Cheam View ... 78 Y47
Chehalis First Nation ... 78 Y46
Chemainus ... 87 A39-40
Chemainus First Nation ... 76 Z39
Cherry Creek ... 76 Y36
Cherry Point ... 87 B40
Cherryville ... 69 S59
Cheslatta ... 33 X33
Cheslatta Carrier Nation ... 32 W32 X32 33 W33-34 X33-35 Y33-35
Chetarpe ... 74 Y31
Chetwynd ... 19 O25
Chetwynd ... 26 N47
Chezacut ... 42 F38-39
Chilanko Forks ... 52 H38-39
Chilliwack ... 78 Y46-47
China Creek ... 82 Y62
Chinook Cove ... 56 N52-53
Choate ... 79 X48
Chopaka ... 80 Z54
Christian Valley ... 81 W58
Christina Lake ... 82 Z60-61
Chu Chua ... 56 M52-53
Chute Lake ... 80 V55
Cinema ... 44 B44
Clairmont ... 25 K49
Clanwilliam ... 70 O60
Clapperton ... 67 S48-49
Clayburn ... 78 Z45
Clayhurst ... 15 D21
Clayhurst ... 19 N27-28
Clayhurst ... 25 K51-52
Clearbrook ... 78 Z44-45
Clearwater ... 56 K52-53
Clemina ... 47 E57
Clemretta ... 32 W31
Clinton ... 66 O47
Clo-oose ... 86 B35-36
Cloverdale ... 77 Z43 78 Z44
Coal Harbour ... 61 Q25-26
Coal River ... 9 A15
Coalmont ... 79 W51
Cobble Hill ... 87 B40
Cody ... 83 U64
Coldspring House ... 44 C45
Coldstream ... 69 S56-57
Coldwater Indian Band ... 67 T50
Colebank ... 36 A44
Colleymount ... 32 W32
Columbia Gardens ... 82 Z62-63
Columbia Lake Band ... 72 R68-69 S69
Columere Park ... 72 S69
Colwood ... 87 C40-41
Comer ... 54 H45
Comox ... 75 V35
Contact Creek ... 9 A14
Cook's Ferry Indian Band ... 67 R48-49
Coombs ... 76 Y37
Cooper Creek ... 71 T65
Copper Creek ... 67 P50
Copper River ... 29 T24
Coquitlam ... 77 Y43 78 Y44
Corbin ... 85 W73
Cordova Bay ... 87 C41
Corra Linn ... 82 X63
Cortes Bay ... 63 T35
Cottonwood ... 44 C45
Cotwood ... 44 C44-45
Courtenay ... 75 V34-35
Cowichan ... 87 B39-40
Cowichan Bay ... 87 B40
Cowichan Tribe ... 87 A-B40 B39
Coyle ... 67 T50
Cracroft ... 62 Q-R30
Craigellachie ... 69 O58
Cranberry ... 76 U37
Cranberry Junction ... 16 O14-15
Cranbrook ... 84 W69-70
Crawford Bay ... 83 V65
Creekside ... 65 R-S43
Creighton Valley ... 69 S-T58
Crescent Bay ... 83 W64
Crescent Beach (Metro Vancouver) ... 77 Z43
Crescent Beach (Okanagan-Similkameen) ... 80 W55
Crescent Spur ... 37 Z50
Crescent Valley ... 82 X62-63
Creston ... 83 Z66
Criss Creek ... 67 O50
Crofton ... 87 A40
Crowsnest ... 85 W73
Croydon ... 46 B55
Crysdale ... 35 Z43 36 Z44
Cultus Lake ... 78 Z46
Cumberland ... 75 W34-35
Curzon ... 84 Z68

D'Arcy ... 66 R44
Dallas ... 68 Q52-53
Danforth Corners ... 69 Q57
Danskin ... 33 W33
Darfield ... 56 M52
Darrell Bay ... 77 W42
Dashwood ... 76 X36-37
Davidson ... 35 X41
Dawson Creek ... 19 O27-28
Dawson Creek ... 27 M51
Dawsons Landing ... 49 K26
Deadwood ... 81 Z58
Dease Lake ... 8 B11-12
Decker Lake ... 17 S19
Decker Lake ... 33 V33
Deep Cove (Cowichan Valley) ... 87 B40
Deep Cove (Metro Vancouver) ... 77 X42-43
Deep Creek ... 69 Q56-57
Deer Park ... 82 X61
Delta ... 77 Z42
Demuth ... 80 V54
Dentville ... 77 V42
Departure Bay ... 76 Y39
Deroche ... 78 Y45-46
Devine ... 66 R44
Dewdney ... 78 Y45
Dewey ... 36 W46-47
Ditidaht First Nation ... 86 A36
Dodge Cove ... 28 U17-18
Doe River ... 15 D21-22
Doe River ... 19 N28
Doe River ... 25 L52
Dog Creek (Bulkley-Nechako) ... 34 V38
Dog Creek (Cariboo) ... 54 L45
Dogwood Creek ... 79 W-X48
Doig River First Nation ... 25 H50
Dokkie Siding ... 26 N46-47
Dollarton ... 77 Y42-43
Dolphin Beach ... 76 Y38
Dome Creek ... 37 Y49
Donald ... 59 L64
Donald Landing ... 31 U33
Dorreen ... 29 R24-25
Dot ... 67 S49
Douglas ... 77 Z43
Douglas First Nation ... 78 V45
Douglas Lake ... 68 T52
Downie Creek ... 57 L-M59
Driftwood Creek ... 30 S29
Dry Gulch ... 72 Q-R68
Drynoch ... 67 S48
DuBose ... 29 U23
Duck Range ... 68 Q54
Duganville ... 83 Z66
Duke Point ... 76 Y39
Duncan ... 87 A-B40
Duncan Bay ... 63 T34
Duncanby Landing ... 49 L26
Dunkley ... 36 A44 44 B44
Dunsmuir ... 76 X36
Dunster ... 46 B55
Durieu ... 78 Y45
Dzawada?enuxw First Nation ... 62 O31 P30

Eagle Bay ... 69 O-P57
Eagle Creek ... 55 J50
Eagle Heights ... 87 B39-40
Earls Cove ... 76 V38
East Arrow Park ... 70 T61-62
East Gate ... 58 M63
East Kelowna ... 81 U56
East Pine ... 19 O26
East Pine ... 27 N48
East Sooke ... 87 D40
East Wellington ... 76 Y38
Eastbourne ... 77 X41
Eastgate ... 79 Y51
Echo Bay ... 62 P30
Ecoole ... 75 Z34
Edelweiss ... 59 M65
Edgewater ... 72 Q68
Edgewood ... 82 V60
Egmont ... 76 V39
Ehattesaht First Nation ... 74 U28
Eholt ... 81 Y59
Ekins Point ... 77 W41
Elk Bay ... 63 S33
Elk Prairie ... 85 V72
Elkford ... 73 T72-73
Elko ... 85 X-Y72
Ellison ... 81 U56
Emerald Estates ... 78 Z46
Encombe ... 33 W36 34 W37
Endako ... 33 W35-36
Enderby ... 69 Q-R57
Engen ... 34 W38
Englewood ... 62 Q28
English Point ... 82 Z60
Enterprise ... 54 J46
Erickson ... 83 Z67
Erie ... 82 Y63
Errington ... 76 Y37
Esketemc Band ... 54 K45
Esperanza ... 74 U28
Esquimalt ... 87 D41
Estevan Point ... 74 X29
Evelyn ... 17 Q16
Evelyn ... 30 R28
Ewing ... 68 T55
Exeter ... 55 K-L48
Exlou ... 56 N53
Exstew ... 29 T22
Extension ... 76 Z38-39

Fair Harbour ... 61 T27
Fairbridge ... 87 B39-40
Fairmont Hot Springs ... 72 S69
Fairview ... 80 Y55
Falkland ... 68 R55
Falls ... 26 N45
Falls Creek ... 67 T48
Fallsway ... 55 L49
False Bay ... 76 W-X37
Fanny Bay ... 75 W35
Farmington ... 19 O27
Farmington ... 27 M50
Farrell Creek ... 19 N25
Farrell Creek ... 24 L46
Farron ... 82 Y60
Faulder ... 80 W54
Fauquier ... 82 U61
Federal Ranch ... 24 J44
Fellers Heights ... 19 O27
Fellers Heights ... 27 N-O50
Ferguson ... 70 Q63
Ferndale ... 36 X44
Fernie ... 85 W72
Fernridge ... 78 Z44
Field ... 59 M66
Fife ... 82 Z60
Fill ... 55 N48
Finmoore ... 35 X40
Fintry ... 68 T55
Fireside ... 9 A14
Firvale ... 23 X17-18
Firvale ... 40 F31
Fitzwilliam ... 47 D59
Five Mile ... 7 A8
Flathead ... 85 Z74
Flatrock ... 19 N27
Flatrock ... 25 K51
Fleetwood ... 77 Y43
Flying U ... 55 L48-49
Forde ... 59 M64
Foreman ... 35 X43 36 X44
Forest Grove ... 55 K49
Forest Knolls ... 78 Y-Z44
Forestdale ... 31 U31-32
Fort Babine ... 17 P17
Fort Babine ... 31 P30-31
Fort Fraser ... 34 W37
Fort Langley ... 78 Y44
Fort Nelson ... 11 B19
Fort Rupert ... 61 P26
Fort Saint James ... 18 S21-22
Fort Saint John ... 15 D20-21
Fort Saint John ... 19 N26
Fort Saint John ... 25 K49
Fort Steele ... 84 W70
Fort Ware ... 14 C16
Forty Mile Flats ... 12 C11
Foss ... 27 M-N48

Foster 47 C57
Fosthall 70 S61
Fountain 66 P-Q46
François Lake 23 T18-19
François Lake 33 W33
Franklin Camp . . 75 Z35 76 Z36
Fraser 6 A6 7 A7
Fraser 83 W65
Fraser Lake 33 W36
Fraser Lake 33 W36
Fraserview 35 X43
Frederick 67 P51
French Creek 76 X37
Freshwater Bay 62 Q29
Fruitvale 82 Z62-63
Fulford Harbour 87 B40-41

Gabriola 76 Y39
Galena 70 Q62
Galena Bay 70 Q62
Galloway 84 X71
Gambier Harbour 77 X41
Gang Ranch 54 L45
Ganges 87 A40
Garbitt 26 O43
Garden Bay 76 W38-39
Garibaldi 77 U42
Garibaldi Estates . . . 77 V41-42
Gaspard Camp . . 53 L43 54 L44
Gates 66 R44
Gateway 55 K48-49
Gellatly 80 V55
Genelle 82 Y62
George River 63 Q33
Georgetown Mills 16 R11
Georgetown Mills . . . 28 T17-18
Germansen Landing . . . 18 O20
Gerrard 71 R64
Gibson Creek 82 X62
Gibsons 77 X40
Gifford 78 Z45
Gillies Bay 76 V37
Gilpin 82 Z60
Gingolx 16 Q12
Gingolx (Kincolith) 28 Q19
Giscome 36 W44-45
Gitanmaax 16 P15 17 P16
Gitanmaax 30 P27
Gitanmaax Band 30 P27
Gitanyow (Kitwancool) . . 30 P26
Gitlakdamix (New Aiyansh) 29 P22-23
Gitsegulka Band 30 P26-27 Q26
Gitwangak Band 29 R24-25 30 Q26
Gitwinksihlkw 16 P13
Gitwinksihlkw (Canyon City) 29 P22
Glacier 58 N63
Glade 82 X62-63
Gladwin 67 S48
Glen Lake 87 C40
Glen Valley 78 Y44
Glen Vowell 30 P27
Glen Vowell Band 30 P27
Glenannan 33 W35
Glendale Cove 63 Q32
Gleneden 69 Q56
Glenemma 69 R56
Glenlily 84 Z68
Glenora 12 C10
Glenora 87 B39
Glenrosa 80 U-V55
Glentanna 30 R29
Goat River 37 Z50
Goatfell 84 Z68
Golata Creek 25 K51
Gold Bridge 65 P43
Gold River 74 V31
Golden 59 M-N65
Good Hope 49 L26
Good Hope Lake 8 A12
Goodlow 15 D21
Goodlow 25 J51
Goose Bay 49 L-M26
Gordon River 86 A-B37
Gosnell 47 F57
Gossen 29 T24
Gower Point 77 X40
Graham 55 M48
Grand Forks 81 Z59
Grand Haven 25 K49
Grandbirch 27 M49
Grandview Bench 69 Q57
Granisle 17 Q-R18
Granisle 31 R31-32
Granite 82 X63
Granite Bay 63 S34
Granite City 79 W-X51
Granite Falls 77 X43
Grant Brook 47 C59
Grantham 75 V35
Granthams Landing . 77 X40-41
Grasmere 85 Z72
Grassy Plains 23 T19
Grassy Plains 33 W33
Gravelle Ferry 44 D45
Gray Creek 83 W65-66
Great Central 75 X35
Greata 80 V54
Greeley 70 Q61
Green Cove 75 Z35
Greendale 78 Z45-46
Greening 44 B44
Greenville 16 Q12-13
Greenville (Laxgaltsap) 28 Q20-21
Greenwood 81 Z58-59
Grindrod 69 Q57
Groundbirch 19 O26
Groundbirch 27 M49
Guildford 77 Y43
Gundy 19 O28
Gundy 27 N52
Gwa'sala-nakwaxda'xw First Nation 61 P26
Gwawaenuk Tribe . . . 62 O28-29

Hagensborg 23 X17
Hagensborg 40 F30
Hagwilget 17 P16
Hagwilget 30 P27
Hagwilget Village . . . 30 P27-28
Haida (Old Masset) 20 S8
Halalt First Nation 87 A40
Halfmoon Bay 76 W39
Halfway Ranch 24 H46
Halfway River FN 24 J46
Hall 83 X64
Halliday 29 T24
Hanceville (Lees Corner) 53 J42
Hansard 36 W46
Happy Valley 87 C-D40
Hardwicke Island 63 R32
Hargreaves 44 G45
Harmac 76 Z39
Harrison Hot Springs . . 78 Y47
Harrison Mills 78 Y46
Harrogate 71 O67
Harrop 83 W64
Hartley Bay 22 U13
Hasler Flat 19 P25
Hasler Flat 26 N46
Hatzic 78 Y45
Haysport 28 U19
Hazelmere 77 Z43 78 Z44
Hazelton 17 P16
Hazelton 30 P27
Headquarters 75 V34
Health Bay 62 P-Q29
Hecate 74 U28
Hedley 80 X53
Heffley Creek 68 P52
Hemlock Valley 78 X46
Hendrix Lake 55 H50
Heriot Bay 63 T34
Hesquiaht First Nation 74 X29-30
Hesquiat 74 X29-30
Heydon Bay 63 Q33
Hickethier Ranch 24 H45
High Bar First Nation . . . 66 O46
Highland Valley . . . 67 R49-50
Highlands 87 C40
Hilliers 76 X37
Hills 70 T63
Hilton 69 S-T59
Hixon 36 A44
Hkusam 63 R32
Holberg 61 P24
Holmwood 68 Q54
Homalco Band 75 U34
Homfray Creek 64 S36
Honeymoon Bay . 86 A37 87 A38
Hope 79 X48
Hope Bay 87 A41
Hopington 78 Z44
Hopkins Landing 77 X40
Horse Creek 59 N65
Horsefly 45 G48
Horseshoe Bay 77 X41-42
Hosmer 85 W72
Hot Springs Cove 74 X30
Houston 17 S17
Houston 31 U30
Howser 71 S65
Huble 35 X43 36 X44
Hudson's Hope 15 D20
Hudson's Hope 19 N24-25
Hudson's Hope 24 L46
Hulatt 35 X40
Hullcar 69 R56
Huntingdon 78 Z45
Hunts Inlet 28 V17
Hupel 69 Q58
Huscroft 83 Z67
Hutchison 35 X41
Hutton 36 W-X47
Huu-ay-aht First Nation 86 A34-35
Hyde Creek 62 Q28

Inkaneep 80 Z55
Inkitsaph 79 U48
Invermere 72 R68
Ioco 77 Y43
Iracard 27 M-N51
Irvines Landing 76 W38
Iskut 12 C12
Isle Pierre 35 X41-42

Jackman 47 C56-57
Jackpine Flats 29 T24
Jackson Bay 63 R32
Jade City 8 A12
Jaffray 84 X71
Jellicoe 80 V52
Jersey 83 Z64
Jesmond 54 N46
Jeune Landing 61 R26
Johnson 54 J46
Johnsons Landing 71 T65
Jordan River 87 C-D38
Jumbo Glacier 71 R-S66
Juniper Ridge 68 Q52
Jura 79 W51 80 W52
Juskatla 20 T8

K'ómoks First Nation . 63 R32
K'ómoks First Nation 75 V-W35
Ka:'yu:'k't'h' Che:k:tles7e't'h First Nation 61 T26
Kaleden 80 X55
Kamloops 67 Q51 68 Q52
Kamloops Indian Band 68 P-Q52
Kamloops Junction . . 68 P-Q52
Kanaka 66 T47
Kanaka Bar Band 67 T48
Karlukwess 62 Q30
Kaslo 83 U65
Katzie First Nation 77 Y43
Keating 87 C41
Kedleston 69 S57
Keefers 78 U47 79 U48
Keithley Creek 45 D48
Kelly Lake 19 P28
Kelly Lake (Peace River) 27 P52
Kelly Lake (Thompson-Nicola) 66 O47
Kelowna 80 U55 81 U56
Kelsey Bay 62 R31
Kemano 22 U15
Kemano Beach 22 U15
Kennedy 26 Q43
Keremeos 80 Y54
Kerr Creek 81 Z58
Kersley 44 D44
Kettle Valley 81 Z57
Kidd 37 Y49
Kilbella Bay 49 K27
Kilbella Bay 49 K27
Kildonan 75 Z35
Kilgard 78 Z45
Kilkerran 27 M51
Killiney Beach 68 T55
Kimberley . . . 84 V68-69 W68-69
Kimsquit 23 W17
Kimsquit 40 D29
Kincolith 16 Q12
Kincolith (Gingolx) 28 Q19
Kingcome 62 O31
Kingcome Inlet 62 O31
Kingfisher 69 Q58-59
Kingsgate 83 Z67 84 Z68
Kingsvale 79 U50
Kiskatinaw 27 M-N50
Kispiox 16 P15 17 P16
Kispiox 30 P27
Kitamaat Village 22 T14
Kitchener 83 Y67
Kitimat 22 T14
Kitimat 29 V23
Kitkatla 22 T11
Kitsault 16 P13
Kitseguecla 30 Q26-27
Kitseguecla (Gitsegulka) 16 Q15 17 Q16
Kitselas 29 T24
Kitselas Tribe 28 V19 29 R25 S24-25 T24
Kitsumkalum Tribe 28 V19 29 S23 T23
Kitsumkaylum 16 R14
Kitwancool 16 P15
Kitwancool (Gitanyow) . 30 P26
Kitwanga 16 Q15
Kitwanga 30 Q26
Klahoose First Nation 63 T35 64 R37
Kleecoot 75 Y35
Kleena Kleene 52 J36
Kleindale 76 W39
Klemtu 22 X14
Kluskus 42 B-C37
Knockholt 17 S17
Knockholt 31 U30-31
Knutsford 68 Q52
Kokish 62 Q-R28
Kootenay Bay 83 V-W65
Kootenay Crossing 72 P68
Kootenay Landing 83 Y66
Koster 55 N48
Krestova 82 X62
Kruger's Flats 27 R51
Kuper Island 77 Z40
Kuskonook 83 Y66
Kwakiutl Band 61 P26-27
Kwantlen First Nation . . 78 Y44
Kwaw-kwaw-Apilt First Nation 78 Y46
Kwayhquitlum First Nation 77 Y43
Kwicksutaineuk-ah-kwa-mish Band 62 Q29-30
Kwicksutaineuk-ah-kwak-ah-mish First Nation 50 N30 62 O30
Kwinitsa 28 U20
Kyuquot 61 T26

Lac la Hache 55 J-K48
Lac Le Jeune 67 R51
Lachtesk 16 Q12-13
Ladner 77 Z42
Ladysmith 76 Z39
Lafarge 77 Y42
Laidlaw 78 X47 79 X48
Lake Babine Nation . . . . . 31 P30-31 Q30-31 R31 T33 U33 . . . . . 33 V33
Lake Cowichan 87 A38-39
Lake Cowichan First Nation 87 A38
Lake Errock 78 Y46
Lake Kathlyn 17 R16
Lake Kathlyn 30 R28-29
Lakelse 29 U23-24
Lakelse Lake 16 S14
Lakelse Lake 29 U24
Lakeview Heights 80 U55
Lamming Mills 38 A52
Lang Bay 76 V37
Langdale 77 X40
Langford 87 C40
Langley 77 Z43
Lantzville 76 Y38
Lardeau 71 T65
Larkin 69 R-S57
LaValley Point 82 Z60
Lavington 69 S57
Lawnhill 20 U8
Lax Kwalaams 16 R11
Lax Kwalaams 28 S17-18
Lax Kwalaams FN . . 28 R17-18 . . . . . S17-20 T17-21 U19-21 V21 . . . . . 29 T22-23 U22-23 V22
Lax Kwalaams FN Metlakatla Tribe 28 U18-21 V18-20
Laxgalts'ap 16 Q12-13
Laxgaltsap (Greenville) 28 Q20-21
Lazo 75 V35
Leanchoil 59 N66
Lebahdo 82 W62-63
Lee Creek 68 O-P55
Legrand 37 A51
Lejac 33 W36
Lemon Creek 82 V63
Lemoray 26 O44
Lempriere 47 F57
Leo Creek 17 Q19
Leq'á:mel First Nation 78 Y45-46
Lewis Island 28 V18
Lexau Ranch 24 H45
Lhoosk'uz Dene 42 B37
Liard River 9 A15
Lighthouse Point 87 A41
Likely 44 E47
Lillooet 66 Q46
Lime 66 O47
Lindell 78 Z46
Lindell Beach 78 Z46
Lions Bay 77 X41-42
Lister 83 Z67
Little Fort 56 M52
Little River 75 V35
Little Shuswap Lake Band 68 O55 P55 69 O56 P56
Little Zeballos 74 U28-29
Logan Lake 67 R50-51
Lone Butte 55 L48-49
Lone Prairie 19 O-P26
Lone Prairie 26 O47
Long Harbour 87 A41
Longbeach 83 W64
Longworth 36 X47
Loon Lake 67 O48
Loos 37 Z50
Louis Creek 56 N52-53
Lovell Landing 17 P18
Lower Kootenay Band . . . 83 Z66
Lower Nicola 67 T50
Lower Nicola Indian Band 67 T50
Lower Post 9 A13
Lower Similkameen Band 80 X54 Y55 Y-Z54 Z55
Lucerne 47 D59
Lumberton 84 X69
Lumby 69 S57
Lund 76 U36
Luxor-Spur Valley 72 P68
Luxton 87 C40
Lyackson First Nation . . . 77 Z40
Lynn Valley 77 X42
Lynx Creek 24 L46
Lytton 66 S47
Lytton First Nation 66 T47

Mabel Lake 69 S58
Macalister 44 F44-45
Mackenzie 18 P23
Madeira Park 76 W39
Magna Bay 69 O56-57
Maharg 67 P49
Mahatta River 61 R25
Mahood Falls 55 J51
Maillardville 77 Y43
Makinson 70 T61-62
Malahat 87 C40
Malahat First Nation . . . 43 B40
Malahat Indian Band . . . 87 B40
Malakwa 69 O58
Malibu 64 T39
Mamalilaculla 62 Q29-30
Manning Park 79 Z51
Manson Creek 18 O21
Mansons Landing 63 T35
Mapes 34 X39
Maple Bay 87 A40
Maple Ridge 78 Y44
Mara 69 Q57
Marblehead 71 S65
Margaret Bay 49 M26
Marguerite 44 F44
Marilla 32 Y32 33 Y33
Marron Valley 80 X55
Martel 67 R48
Marten Lake 34 W37
Martin Prairie 68 Q54-55
Marysville 84 W68-69
Masset 20 S8
Matsqui 78 Z45
Matsqui First Nation . . . 78 Z45
Mayne 87 A41
McAbee 67 P49
McBride 38 A52
McCall 34 W38
McCulloch 81 V56-57
McDonalds Landing . . . 83 W64
McGregor 36 W46
McGuire 65 T42
McIntyre Lake 54 J45
Mckearney Ranch 24 H44
McKinley Landing 81 U56
McLean Ranch 24 H45
McLeese Lake 44 F45
McLeod Lake 18 Q23
McLure 68 O52
McMurdo 59 N65
McNab Creek 77 W41
Meachen 83 W67 84 W68
Meadow Creek 71 S65
Meadowbrook (Comox-Strathcona) 75 V35
Meadowbrook (East Kootenay) 84 V69
Meadows 82 Y63
Meldrum Creek 54 H44-45
Merritt 67 T50
Merville 75 V35
Mesachie Lake 87 A38
Metchosin 87 D40-41
Metlakatla 16 S11
Metlakatla 28 T17-18
Metlakatla Tribe . 28 T17-18 U18
Meziadin Junction 12 D12
Meziadin Junction 16 N13
Mica Creek 57 H-J59
Middle River 18 R20
Midway 81 Z58
Mile 62.5 . . . . . 25 J48
Mile 715.9 . . . . . 25 K49
Mill Bay 28 Q20
Mill Bay 87 B40
Milner 78 Z44
Milnes Landing 87 D40
Minaty Bay 77 W41-42
Minstrel Island 62 Q30
Miocene 44 G47
Miracle Valley 78 Y45
Mirror Lake 83 U-V65
Mission (Cariboo) 54 H46
Mission (Fraser Valley) 78 Y-Z45
Mitchell Bay 62 Q28-29
Miworth 35 X42-43
Moberly 59 M64-65
Moberly Lake 19 O25
Moberly Lake 26 M46
Moha 66 P45
Monias 25 L48
Montague Harbour 87 A41
Monte Creek 68 Q54
Monte Lake 68 R54
Montney 15 D20-21
Montney 25 J49
Montrose 82 Z62-63
Moose Heights 44 C44
Moran Station 66 O-P46
Moresby Camp 21 V8
Morey 47 C57
Moricetown 17 Q16
Moricetown 30 Q28
Moricetown Band 30 Q28 R28 S29
Morrissey 85 X72
Mount Baldy 81 Y56
Mount Currie 65 S43
Mount Currie Band 65 S43 66 S44
Mount Lehman 78 Z44-45
Mount Robson 47 C57
Mount Wabi 26 N47
MowachahtFirst Nation 74 V30-31
Moyie 84 Y69
Mud River 35 Y42
Muncho Lake . . . 9 B15 10 B16
Murdale 25 H49
Murrayville 78 Z44
Musgrave Landing 87 B40
Musqueam Indian Band 77 Y41
Myncaster 81 Z57
Myra 81 V56
Myrtle Point 76 V37

N'Quatqua Band 66 R44
Nadleh Whut'en First Nation 34 W37
Nahmint 75 Z35 76 Z36
Nahun 68 T55
Nakusp 70 S61-62
Nalos Landing 49 M27
Namu 49 J25
Namu 49 J25
Nanaimo 76 Y38-39
Nanoose Bay 76 Y38
Naramata 80 W55
Narcosli Creek 44 D-E44
Nass Camp 16 P14
Nass Camp 29 P22
Natal 85 V72-73
Nation 28 Q21
Nazko 43 C40
Nazko Band 43 C40
Nechako 35 X42
Necoslie 18 S21
Nee Tahi Buhn Band 32 W31-32 33 W33
Needles 82 U60-61
Nelson 83 X64
Nelson Forks 10 A18
Nelway 82 Z63 83 Z64
Nemaiah Valley 52 L39
Neskonlith Band . 68 P55 69 Q56
New Aiyansh 16 P14
New Aiyansh (Gitlakdamix) 29 P22-23
New Brighton 77 X41
New Denver . . . 82 U63 83 U64
New Hazelton 17 P-Q16
New Hazelton 30 P27
New Remo 29 T23
New Westminster . . . 77 Y42-43
Newgate 84 Z71
Newlands 36 W45
Newton 77 Y43
Niagara 81 Z59
Nichol 35 X41-42
Nichols 35 X43
Nicholson 59 N65
Nicola 67 T51
Nicomen Band 67 S48
Nimpkish 62 R28
Nimpkish Heights 61 Q27 62 Q28
Nimpo Lake 41 G35
Nisgaa 28 P20-21
Nitinat 86 A37
Nooaitch Indian Band 67 S-T49
Nootka 74 V29
Noralee 23 T18
Noralee 32 W31
North Bend 79 U48
North Bonaparte 55 M50
North Bulkley 31 T-U31
North Campbell River . . 63 T34
North Cowichan 87 A39-40
North Delta 77 Y-Z43
North Galiano 77 Z40
North Glenmore 81 U56
North Pine 15 D21
North Pine 25 J49-50
North Poplar 78 Z44-45
North Saanich 87 B41
North Vancouver 77 Y42
Notch Hill 69 P56
Nuchatlaht Band . 61 T27 62 T28
Nukko Lake 35 W42-43
Nulki 34 X38
Nursery 81 Z59
Nuxalk Nation . . 40 C28 D29 F29

O'Keefe 69 R56
Oak Bay 87 C-D41
Oak Hill 68 P52
Oasis 82 Y62
Ocean Falls 22 X15
Ochiltree 44 G46
Oclucje 62 T28
Ogden 65 P43
Okanagan Band 69 S56
Okanagan Centre 68 T55 69 T56
Okanagan Falls 80 X55
Okanagan Landing 69 S56
Okanagan Mission . . . 80 U-V55
Olalla 80 Y54
Old Fort 31 Q-R31
Old Fort Nelson 11 B19
Old Remo 29 T23
Oliver 80 Y55
Oona River 22 T11
Ootischenia 82 Y62-63
Ootsa Lake 23 T-U18
Ootsa Lake 32 X32
Oregon Jack Creek Band 67 Q48-49
Osland 28 U-V18
Osoyoos 80 Z55
Osoyoos Band 80 Y55
Osprey Lake 80 V53
Otter Bay 87 A41
Otter Point 87 D39
Ottertail 59 M66
Owen Bay 63 S34
Owl Creek 65 S43
Oyama 69 T56
Oyster River 75 U34-35

Pacheedaht First Nation 86 B36
Pacific 29 R-S25
Paldi 87 A39
Palling 17 S18-19
Palling 31 U33
Palling Station 31 U32
Panorama 71 R67 72 R68
Paradise Point 69 P57
Paradise Valley (Powell River) 76 V37
Paradise Valley (Squamish Lillooet) 77 V41-42
Parkland 27 M50
Parks 82 Y63
Parksville 76 X37-38 Y37-38

Parson 71 O66
Pass Creek 82 X62
Passmore 82 W62
Paterson 82 Z61
Paulson 82 Y60
Pauquachin First Nation 87 B41
Pavilion 66 P46-47
Peachland 80 V54-55
Pebble Beach 76 V36-37
Peejay 25 F50
Pemberton 65 S43
Pemberton Meadows 65 R42-43
Pender Harbour 76 W38
Pender Island 87 A-B41
Pendleton Bay 31 T33
Penelakut Tribe 87 A40
Penny 37 X48
Penticton 80 W55 81 W56
Penticton Band 80 W54-55 X55
Perow 17 R18
Perow 31 T31
Perrys 82 W63
Peters Band 78 Y47 79 Y48
Phelan 28 U18
Phillips Arm 63 R34
Phoenix 81 Z58-59
Pinchi 18 R21
Pinchi Lake 18 R21
Pine Valley 19 O25
Pine Valley 26 N45
Pine Valley 44 G45-46 54 H45-46
Pinegrove 44 C46
Pineview (Fraser-Fort George) 35 X43
Pineview (Peace River) 25 J49-50
Pink Mountain 15 C19
Pink Mountain 24 F44
Pioneer Mine 65 P43
Pitman 29 S24-25
Pitquali 67 S48
Pitt Meadows 77 Y43
Pixie Beach 69 T56
Pleasant Camp 6 A5
Popkum 78 Y47
Popkum Band 78 Y47
Poplar Creek 71 R64
Poplar Grove 80 W55
Porcher Island 28 V17-18
Porpoise Bay 76 W-X39
Port Alberni 76 Y36
Port Albion 75 Z33
Port Alice 61 R26
Port Clements 20 T8
Port Coquitlam 77 Y43 78 Y44
Port Douglas 78 V45-46
Port Edward 16 S11
Port Edward 28 U18
Port Essington 16 S12
Port Essington 28 U-V19
Port Hammond 77 Y43 78 Y44
Port Hardy 61 P26
Port Kells 77 Y43
Port McNeill 61 Q27 62 Q28
Port Mellon 77 W40
Port Moody 77 Y42-43
Port Neville 62 R31
Port Renfrew 86 C37
Port Washington 87 A41
Porteau 77 W41-42
Portia 79 W-X49
Porto Rico 83 X64
Postill 81 U56
Potter 55 L49
Pouce Coupe 19 O28
Pouce Coupe 27 N51-52
Powell River 76 U36-37 V36-37
Premier Lake 84 U70
Prespatou 15 C20-21
Prespatou 25 F48
Priestly 33 W34-35
Prince George 35 X42-43
Prince Rupert 16 S11-12
Prince Rupert 28 T18
Princeton 79 X51
Pritchard 68 O54-55
Procter 83 W65
Progress 19 O27
Progress 27 M50
Prophet River 11 B19
Punchaw 35 A41-42
Puntledge 75 V34-35
Pyramid 47 G57

Qualicum 76 X36
Qualicum Beach 76 X37
Qualicum First Nation 76 X36
Quathiaski Cove 63 T34
Quatsino 61 Q25
Quatsino First Nation 61 Q25-26 Q26
Queen Charlotte City 20 U8
Queens Bay 83 W65
Quesnel 44 C44
Quesnel Forks 44 E47
Quesnel View 44 C44
Quick 30 T29
Quilchena 67 T51 68 T52
Quinsam 75 U33

Radium Hot Springs 72 Q68
Rainbow 47 C58
Ramage 68 O52
Raspberry 82 X62
Raush Valley 46 B54
Rayleigh Mount 68 P52
Read Island 63 T34-35
Red Bluff 44 C44
Red Bluff Indian Band 44 C44
Red Pass 47 C58
Red Rock 35 Y43
Redonda Bay 63 S35
Redsand 57 H57
Redstone 53 H40
Refuge Cove 64 T36
Reid Lake 35 X42
Remac 82 Z63
Remo 16 R14
Renata 82 X60
Retallack 71 T64
Revelstoke 70 O60-61
Rhone 81 Y57
Rich Bar 44 D44
Richfield 44 C47
Richmond 77 Y41-42
Ridley 28 U18
Riondel 83 V65
Riske Creek 54 J44
Ritchie 29 R24
River Jordan 87 C-D38
Rivers Inlet 49 K27
Rivers Inlet 49 K27
Rivervale 82 Y-Z62
Roberts Creek 77 X40
Robson 82 X62
Robson West 82 X62
Rock Creek 81 Z57
Rocky Point 87 D40
Roe Lake 55 L50
Rogers 58 L63
Rogers Pass 58 M63
Rolla 19 O28
Rolla 27 M51-52
Roosville 85 Z72
Rose Lake 31 U32
Rose Prairie 15 D21
Rose Prairie 25 H49
Rosebery 70 T63 82 U63
Rosedale 78 Y47
Ross 82 Y63
Ross Lake 17 S18
Rossland 82 Z61-62
Rosswood 16 Q-R14
Rosswood 29 R23
Roy 63 R33
Royston 75 W35
Rumble Beach 61 R26
Rushmere 72 R68
Ruskin 78 Y44
Rutland 81 U56
Ryan 84 Y68
Ryder Lake 78 Z46-47
Rykerts 83 Z66

Saanich 87 C41
Saanichton 87 B40-41 C41
Sahtlam 87 A-B39
Saik'uz First Nation 34 X38-39
St. Eugene Mission 84 W69
St. Ives 69 O57
St. Joseph 54 H46
St. Marys Band 84 W69 X70
Salmo 83 Y64
Salmon Arm 69 Q56
Salmon Valley 35 W43
Saltair 87 A39
Saltery Bay 76 V38
Salvus 16 S13
Salvus 28 U21
Samahquam First Nation 66 T44
San Josef 61 P24
Sanca 83 X65-66
Sandon 83 U64
Sandspit 20 U8-9
Saratoga Beach 75 U34-35
Sardis 78 Z46
Sarita 86 A34-35
Saturna 87 A42
Saulteau FN 26 M46-47
Savary Island 75 U35 76 U36
Savona 67 P50
Savory 33 W35
Savory 33 W35
Sayward 62 R31
Scia'new First Nation 87 D40
Scotch Creek 69 O-P56
Scowlitz First Nation 78 Y46
Seabird Island Band 78 Y47
Seacrest 76 Y38
Seaford 63 T35
Seaside Park 77 W40-41
Sechelt 76 X39
Sechelt Indian Band 76 X39 77 X40
Secret Cove 76 W39
Seeney 71 O66
Selma Park 76 X39
Semlin 67 P49
Seton Lake Band 66 P-Q45
Seton Portage 66 Q45
Seven Mile Corner 27 M51
Sewell Inlet 21 V8
Seymour Arm 57 N58
Seymour Heights 77 X42
Seymour Lake 30 S28
Seymour Landing 77 X41
Shackan Indian Band 67 S49
Shalalth 66 Q45
Shames 29 T22-23
Shawnigan Lake 87 B40
Shearer Dale 25 L51-52
Shearwater 22 Y15
Shelley 36 W44
Shelter Bay 70 Q61
Shelter Point 75 U34
Sheraton 17 S19 23 T19
Sheraton 33 V34
Shere 47 C56
Shields 82 X61
Shingle Creek 80 W54
Shirley 87 D39
Shoreacres 82 X63
Shulus 67 T50
Shushartie 61 O25
Shuswap 68 P55
Shuswap Band 72 R68
Shuswap Falls 69 S58
Shutty Bench 83 U65
Shxw'ow'hamel First Nation 78 X47
Shxwhá:y First Nation 78 Y46
Sicamous 69 P58
Sidney 87 B41
Sik-e-dahk 17 P16
Sikanni Chief 15 C19
Silica 82 Z61-62
Silver Creek (Columbia-Shuswap) 69 Q56
Silver Creek (Fraser Valley) 79 X48
Silver River 78 W47
Silver Valley 78 Y44
Silverdale 78 Y44-45
Silverhill 78 Y45
Silverton 82 U63
Simpcw First Nation 56 M52-53
Simpson Ranch 24 H44
Sinclair Mills 36 W47
Sinkut River 34 X39
Sirdar 83 Y66
Siska Indian Band 66 T47 67 T48
Six Mile Point 69 P57-58
Skawahlook First Nation 78 X47
Skeena 28 U19
Skeena Crossing 17 Q16
Skeena Crossing 30 Q27
Skeetchestn Indian Band 67 P49-50
Skidegate 20 U8
Skidegate Landing 20 U8
Skin Tyee Nation 32 W32 X32 33 W33 X33
Skookumchuck (East Kootenay) 84 U69-70
Skookumchuck (Fraser Valley) 78 U44-45
Skowkale First Nation 78 Y46
Skuppah Band 67 T48
Skwah First Nation 78 Y46
Slesse Park 78 Z47
Sliammon 76 U36
Sliammon First Nation 76 U36-37
Slocan 82 V63
Slocan Park 82 W62
Smith River 9 A15
Smithers 17 R16
Smithers 30 S28
Smithers Landing 17 Q18
Smithers Landing 31 Q31
Snaw-Naw-As First Nation 76 Y38
Snug Cove 77 X41
Snuneymuxw First Nation 76 Y39
Sockeye 28 U18-19
Soda Creek 44 G44-45
Sointula 62 Q28
Solsqua 69 P57-58
Songhees Nation 87 C41
Sooke 87 D39
Soowahlie First Nation 78 Z46
Sorrento 69 P56
South Canoe 69 Q57
South Dawson 27 N50-51
South Hazelton 16 P15 Q15 17 Q16
South Hazelton 30 P27
South Mission 80 V55
South Poplar 78 Z44-45
South Shalalth 66 Q45
South Slocan 82 X63
South Surrey 77 Z43
South Taylor 19 N27
South Wellington 76 Z38-39
South Williams Lake 54 H45-46
Southbank 23 T19
Southbank 33 W33
Southview 76 U36
Spallumcheen Band 69 P57 R56-57
Sparwood 85 V72
Spatsum 67 R48-49
Spences Bridge 67 R48
Spillimacheen 71 P67
Springhouse 54 J45-46
Sproat Lake 75 Y35
Sproatt 65 T42
Spuzzum First Nation 79 W48
Squaam Bay 68 O54-55
Squamish 77 V41-42
Squamish Nation 77 V41-42 W41-42
Squilax 68 P55
Squinas 23 X19
Squirrel Cove 63 T35
Stanley 44 C46-47
Stave Falls 78 Y45
Steelhead 78 Y45
Stellaquo 33 W36
Stellaquo 33 W36
Stellat'en FN 33 W36 X34
Steveston 77 Y41-42 Z41
Stewardson Inlet 74 X30
Stewart 16 N12
Stikine 12 D10
Stillwater 76 V37-38
Stone Indian Band 53 J42
Stoner 35 Z43 36 Z44
Strachan Creek 77 X41-42
Straiton 78 Z45
Stratfords Crossing 87 A40
Strathnaver 36 A44
Streatham 32 X31
Stuart Island 63 S34
Stuie 23 X18
Stuie 41 F32
Stump Lake 68 R52
Sturdies Bay 87 A41
Sugarcane 54 H46
Sullivan Bay 62 O28-29
Summerland 80 W54-55
Summit Lake 19 S24
Summit Lake 35 V43
Sun Peaks 68 O-P54
Sundance 27 N48
Sunningdale 82 Z62
Sunrise Valley 19 O27
Sunrise Valley 27 M50
Sunset Beach 77 X41
Sunset Prairie 19 O26-27
Sunset Prairie 27 M49-50
Sunshine Bay 83 W65
Sunshine Valley (Fraser Valley) 79 Y49
Sunshine Valley (Thompson-Nicola) 56 K52-53
Suquash 61 Q27
Surge Narrows 63 S34-35
Surrey 77 Z43
Swan Creek 16 S15
Swartz Bay 87 B41
Sweetsbridge 69 R56
Sweetwater 19 O27
Sweetwater 27 M50-51
Swift Creek 47 D57
Swiftwater 47 C57
Syringa Creek 82 X61

T'it'kit 66 Q46
T'Sou-ke Nation 87 D39
Ta Ta Creek 84 V69
Tabor 35 X-Y43
Tachie 18 R20
Tadanac 82 Z62
Taft 69 O59
Taghum 82 X63
Tahsis 74 U29
Takla Lake First Nation 31 P32-33
Takla Landing 17 P18
Takla Narrows 31 Q33
Takysie Lake 23 T19
Takysie Lake 32 X32 33 X33
Tallheo 40 F29
Tamarisk 65 T42
Tappen 69 P56
Tarrys 82 X62
Tatalrose 23 T18-19
Tatla Lake 52 J36-37
Tatlayoko Lake 52 K37
Tatogga 12 C12
Tatton 55 K48
Taylor 15 D21
Taylor 19 N27
Taylor 25 K49-50
Tchesinkut Lake 23 T18-19
Tchesinkut Lake 33 W33
Teakerne Arm 64 T36
Teko 25 K49
Telachick 35 X42
Telegraph Cove 62 Q28-29
Telegraph Creek 12 C10
Telegraph Point 28 U20
Telkwa 17 R16-17
Telkwa 30 S29
Ten Mile Lake 44 B-C44
Terrace 16 R14
Terrace 29 T23-24
Tête Jaune 47 C56
Tête Jaune Cache 47 C56
Texas Creek 66 R46
Theodosia Arm 64 T36
Thetis Island 77 Z40
Thompson 67 S48
Thompson Sound 62 P31 63 P32
Thornhill 16 R14
Thornhill 29 T24
Three Forks 82 U63 83 U64
Three Valley 69 P59
Thrums 82 X62
Thunder River 47 G57
Thunderbird 29 T23
Thurlow 63 R33-34
Tibbets 33 V34
Tillis Landing 69 O-P57
Tintagel 17 S19
Tintagle 33 V33-34
Tipella 78 V45-46
Tl'etinqox-t'in Government Office 53 H41-42
Tla-o-qui-aht First Nation 74 Y31 75 Y32
Tlatlasikwala Band 62 Q28
Tlell 20 U8
Tlowitsis Tribe 62 Q30
Toad River 10 B16
Toba 64 R38
Tobacco Plains Band 85 Z72
Toby Creek 71 S66-67
Tofino 74 Y31 75 Y32
Toketic 67 R48-49
Tomslake 19 O27-28
Tomslake 27 O51-52
Toosey Band 54 J44
Topley 17 S18
Topley 31 T31
Topley Landing 17 R18
Topley Landing 31 S32
Toquaht First Nation 75 Z33
Towdystan 41 G35
Tower Lake 19 N27
Tower Lake 25 L50
Traders Cove 80 U55 81 U56
Trail 82 Z62
Tranquille 67 Q51
Tremblay 27 M49
Trépanier 80 V55
Trinity Valley 69 R-S58
Trout Creek 80 W55
Trout Lake 70 Q63
Trutch 14 C18 15 C19
Ts'kw'aylaxw First Nation 66 P46
Tsartlip First Nation 87 C40
Tsawout First Nation 87 C41
Tsawwassen 77 Z42
Tsawwassen First Nation 77 Z42
Tseshaht First Nation 75 Y35
Tseycum First Nation 87 B40-41
Tulameen 79 W51
Tulsequah 7 B8
Tumbler Ridge 19 Q26-27
Tumbler Ridge 27 Q48
Tupper 19 P28
Tupper 27 O52
Turtle Valley 68 P55
Tuwanek 76 W39 77 W40
Twidwell Bend 26 N47
Twin Creeks 77 X40
Two Mile 17 P16
Two Mile 30 P27
Two Rivers 19 N27
Two Rivers 25 K50
Txaalaxhatkw 28 R19
Tye 83 X65
Tyee 28 U19
Tynehead 77 Y43
Tzeachten First Nation 78 Z46

Uchucklesaht Tribe 75 Z34-35
Ucluelet 75 Z32-33
Ùksan 30 P27
Ulkatcho 41 C33
Ulkatcho Tribe 41 C32-34 D33 E34 F34
Union Bar Indian Band 79 X48
Union Bay 75 W35 76 W36
Upper Cutbank 27 O50
Upper Fraser 19 S25
Upper Fraser 36 W46
Upper Hat Creek 66 Q47
Upper Nicola Band 67 S51 68 S52
Upper Similkameen Indian Band 80 X53
Urquhart 27 M50-51
Usk 16 R14
Usk 29 S24

Valemount 47 D57
Valley View 25 L51
Valleyview 19 N27
Vallican 82 W62
Van Winkle 44 C47
Vananda 76 V36-37
Vancouver 77 Y41-42
Vanderhoof 34 W39
Vanway 35 X43
Vavenby 56 L55
Vedder Crossing 78 Z46
Vernon (Mount Waddington) 62 T30
Vernon (North Okanagan) 69 S56
Vesuvius Bay 87 A40
Victoria 87 D41
Vidette 55 N50
View Royal 87 C40-41
Village Bay 87 A41
Vinsulla 68 O-P52

Wabi 26 N47
Wadhams 49 L26
Waglisla-McLoughlin Bay 22 Y14-15
Wagner Ranch 24 H45
Walhachin 67 P49
Walnut Grove 78 Y44
Waneta 82 Z62
Waneta Junction 82 Z62
Wanklyn 84 W69
Wardner 84 X70
Warfield 82 Z62
Warner Bay 49 N27 61 O27
Wasa 84 V69
Watson 33 V-W34
Websters Corners 78 Y44
Wedeene 29 V23
Wedgwood 35 W-X41
WeiWaiKai First Nation 75 U34
Welcome Beach 76 X39
Wellington 76 Y38
Wells 44 B47
Weneez 34 X39
West Bench 80 W55
West Fernie 84 W71 85 W72
West Midway 81 Z58
West Sechelt 76 X39
West Vancouver 77 X41-42
Westbank 80 V54-55
Westbank First Nation 80 U-V55
Westbridge 81 Y57
Westley 82 X62
Westside 80 U55
Westsyde 68 P52
Westview 76 V36-37
Westwold 68 R54-55
Wetsuweten FN 31 U31-33 32 V30 W30-31
WeWaiKai First Nation 63 T33-34
WeWaiKum First Nation 63 T34
Whaletown 63 T35
Whalley 77 Y43
Whiskey Creek 76 Y37
Whispering PinesIndian Band 68 O52
Whistler 65 T42
Whistler Cay 65 T42
Whistler Centre 65 T42-43
Whistler Vista 65 T42-43
White Gold 65 T42-43
White Lake 69 P56
White Rock 77 Z43
Whonnock 78 Y44
Whyac 86 B35
Wil Milit 28 Q19
Wild Rose Bay 69 O57
Wildwood 76 U37
Wiley 31 T31
Williams Beach 75 U-V35
Williams Lake 54 H45-46
Williams Lake Indian Band 54 H46
Williamsons Landing 77 X40
Willow Point 83 W64
Willow River 36 W44
Willow Valley 19 O26
Willow Valley 27 M49
Willowbrook 80 Y55
Willowvale 34 W37
Wilmer 72 R68
Wilowbrook 27 M50
Wilson Creek 76 X39 77 X40
Wilson Landing 80 U55
Winch 66 S47 67 S48
Windermere 72 R68
Winfield 69 T56
Wingdam 44 C46
Winlaw 82 W63
Winter Harbour 61 Q24
Wistaria 32 X31
Wolverine 36 W44
Wonowon 15 D19-20
Wonowon 24 G46
Woodcock 29 Q25
Woodfibre 77 W41
Woodlands 77 X43
Woodmere 30 S29
Woodpecker 35 Z43 36 Z44
Woods Landing 69 O57
Woodsdale 69 T56
Woodwards Landing 77 Z42
Worth 25 L48
Woss 62 S29
Woyenne 17 S18-19
Wright 54 J47
Wycliffe 84 W69
Wynndel 83 Y66-67

Xanmas 28 R18-19
Xat'sull First Nation 44 G45
Xaxli'p First Nation 66 O46-47
Xeni Gwet'in First Nation 52 M38
Xmaatin 28 P19

Yaculta 63 T34 75 U34
Yahk 84 Z68
Yale 79 W48
Yale First Nation 79 W48
Yankee Flats 69 R56
Yarrow 78 Z46
Yennadon 78 Y44
Ymir 83 Y64
Youbou 87 A38
Yreka 61 R26
Yuquot 74 W29
Yuutu?it?ath First Nation 75 Z33

Zamora 81 Y57
Zeballos 62 T28
Zincton 71 T64

Road Index

How to use the index

To find a road, search through the alphabetically arranged columns. Note the page number and the reference square to the right of the road.

For example, to find the location of Bush Road:

Bush Rd. **53** J43

Turn to page **53** and locate the squares J43. Scan through the squares to find the road.

0 Ave. . . . **78** Z44
1, HFW-Rd. . . . **24** H45-46
1 Rd., No. . . . **77** Y41-42
1-J Rd. . . . **36** A46
1-K Rd. . . . **36** A46
1A Rd. . . . **27** M-N48
2, Rd. . . . **57** L56
2 Ave. . . . **30** P27
2 Rd., No. . . . **77** Y-Z42
2nd Ave. . . . **28** U18
2nd St. . . . **81** Z59
3 Rd., No. . . . **77** Y-Z42
3 Valley-Victor Rd. . . **69** P59 **70** O60 P60
3rd Ave. (Alberni-Clayoquot) . . . **75** Y35
3rd Ave. (Kitimat-Stikine) . . . **30** Q26
3rd Lake Rd. . . . **76** U38
4, Rd. . . . **56** K52
4, Spur . . . **64** T37
4 Ave. . . . **77** Y41-42
4 Rd., No. . . . **77** Y42
4 Mile Creek Rd. . . . **82** U63 **83** U64
4th St. . . . **85** W72
4th of July Creek FS Rd. . . . **81** X57-58
5, Rd. . . . **56** K52
5 Ave. . . . **35** X43
5 Mile Ridge FS Rd. . . . **65** P43
5th Av. . . . **33** V33
6, Spur . . . **64** T37
6 Rd., No. . . . **77** Y42
6 Mile Creek Rd. . . . **69** R-S56
6th Ave. . . . **28** T18
7 Branch FS Rd. . . . **43** C41
7 Lakes Rd. . . . **67** P50
7th Ave. (East Kootenay) . . . **84** W69
7th Ave. (Fraser Valley) . . . **78** Y45
8, Rd. . . . **56** K52
8 Ave. . . . **77** Z43
8 St. . . . **27** M51
8 Mile Creek Rd. . . . **44** B47
9, Rd. . . . **56** J52
9A Rd. . . . **24** G46
9B Rd. . . . **24** G-H46
10, Rd. (Cariboo) . . . **55** K51
10, Rd. (Thompson-Nicola) . . . **56** K54
10 Rd. (Fish Lake Rd.) . . **43** D43 **44** D44
10th Ave. SE . . . **69** Q56-57
11, Rd. . . . **56** K53
11 St. . . . **77** Y42-43
11B FS Rd. . . . **43** B42
12 Mile Creek FS Rd. . . . **83** U64
12th St. . . . **83** Z67
13 A Rd. . . . **44** C46
13D Rd. . . . **44** C46
13th St. . . . **84** W69
14 Mile Rd. . . . **34** W38
15 Ave. . . . **35** X43
15 Mile Rd. . . . **35** Y43
16 Ave. (Vancouver) . . . **77** Y41-42
16 Ave. (White Rock) . . . **77** Z43 **78** Z44
16 Mile Creek FS Rd. . . . **65** T42-43
17 Rd. . . . **61** Q26-27
17 St. . . . **27** M51
19th St. . . . **81** Z59
20, Rd. . . . **56** J-K52
20th Ave. NE . . . **69** Q56-57
20th Ave. SE . . . **69** Q56
21st St. . . . **84** W-X69
22, Rd. . . . **80** Z55
24 Ave. . . . **77** Z43 **78** Z44
24C Rd. . . . **36** A46
24P Rd. . . . **44** B46
24th St . . . **83** Z67
25 Rd. . . . **61** R26
28th St. . . . **83** Z67
30th St. . . . **69** P-Q56
31, Rd. . . . **56** K52
32 Ave. . . . **77** Z43
33 Ave. . . . **77** Y42
34 St. . . . **77** Z42
36 Mile Pit Rd. . . . **27** P49
36th Ave. . . . **83** Z67
38th Ave. . . . **84** X69
40, Rd. (Adams Lake) . . . **57** M56
40, Rd. (Clearwater) . . . **56** K52
40, Rd. (Squamish-Lillooet) . . **66** P44-46
40 Ave. . . . **77** Z43
40th St. (Creston) . . . **83** Z67
40th St. (Salmon Arm) **69** P56-57 Q56-57
41 Ave. . . . **77** Y42
41B St. . . . **77** Z42
43 St. . . . **26** N47
45th St. . . . **80** Z55 **81** Z56
48 St. (Chetwynd) . . . **26** N47
48th St. (Creston) . . . **83** Z67
49 Ave. . . . **77** Y42
49 Rd. . . . **24** F46
50 Rd. . . . **35** A40
50 Rd., NE . . . **61** P24
50 St. (Chetwynd) . . . **26** N47
50th St. (Salmon Arm) . . . **69** P-Q56
52 St. . . . **77** Z42
56 Ave. . . . **78** Z44
56 St. . . . **77** Z42
60th Ave. . . . **69** P-Q57
60th St. . . . **69** Q56
62 Rd., NE . . . **61** P24
64 Ave. . . . **77** Z43
64 St. . . . **77** Z42
68 St. . . . **77** Z42
72 Ave. . . . **77** Y-Z43 **78** Z44
72 St. . . . **77** Z42
74 Rd. . . . **25** H48
76 FS Rd. . . . **55** H48
82 Rd. . . . **24** G46-47
83 Mile Rd. . . . **55** M48
86 St. . . . **25** K49
87 Mile Loop Rd. . . . **55** L48
90 Mile Loop Rd. . . . **55** L48
91, Rd. . . . **56** J52
93 Mile FS Rd. . . . **55** L48
93 Mile Loop Rd. . . . **55** L48
96 Ave. . . . **77** Y43 **78** Y44
97 Rd. . . . **24** F43
100 Ave. (Fort St. John) . . . **25** K49
100 Ave. (Maple Ridge) . . . **78** Y44
100 Rd. . . . **35** V-W42
100 Rd. (Black Creek) . . . **45** G49
100 Rd. (Meldrum Lake) . . . **44** G44
100 Rd. (Tagai Lake) . . . **35** Z40
100 St. . . . **25** K49
100 A Rd. . . . **44** G44
100 B Rd. . . . **44** G44
100 FS Rd. . . . **43** F43
100C FS Rd. . . . **43** F43
100th St. . . . **82** Y62
103 Mile Lake Rd. . . . **55** K48
104 Ave. . . . **77** Y43
104 St. . . . **43** C41
107th St. . . . **80** Z55
108 Rd. (Moffatt Lake Rd.) . . . **44** G47
116 Ave. . . . **77** Y43
116 Rd. . . . **25** J48
117 Rd. . . . **24** H45-46
120 St. . . . **77** Y-Z43
122 Mile Rd. . . . **54** J47
123 St. . . . **80** Y55
126 Rd. . . . **24** J47 **25** J48
128 St. . . . **77** Z43
12th Ave. . . . **82** Y62
131st St. . . . **80** Y55
132 Ave. . . . **77** Y43 **78** Y44
140 St. . . . **77** Z43
141, Rd. . . . **56** K52
144 St. . . . **77** Y-Z43
152 St. . . . **77** Y-Z43
155 Main Rd. . . . **76** Y37
157 Rd. . . . **24** H47
165 Rd. . . . **24** F44
168 St. . . . **77** Y-Z43
169 Rd. . . . **24** G44
170 Rd. . . . **24** G43
184 St. . . . **77** Z43
186 Rd. . . . **27** O51-52
187 Rd. . . . **24** F43-44 **27** O51-52
188 Rd. . . . **27** O51-52
189 Rd. . . . **27** O51
192 Rd. . . . **24** F43 **27** O52
192 St. . . . **77** Z43
193 Rd. . . . **27** O51-52
194 Rd. . . . **27** O52
196 Rd. . . . **27** N-O51
197 Rd. . . . **27** N50
198 Rd. . . . **27** N51 N51-52
200 Ave. . . . **77** Y-Z43
200 Rd. (Bulkley-Nechako) . . . **35** Z40
200 Rd. (Canyon Rd.) . . . **43** B43 **44** B44
200 Rd. (Peace River) . . . **27** N50 N51-52
200 St. . . . **77** Z43
201 Rd. . . **25** K52 L52 **27** M52 N52 O52-53
202 Rd. . . . **27** N50 N51
203 Rd. . . . **25** J52 K52 L52 **27** M52 O52
204 Rd. . . . **27** N51
205 Rd. . . . **25** K52 L52 **27** O52
206 Rd. . . . **27** N50 N51
207 Rd. . . . **27** M-N52
208 Rd. . . . **27** N48
208 Rd. . . . **27** N49 N50 N50-51
208 St. . . . **78** Z44
209 Rd. . . . **25** L51 L51 **27** M51 M51-52 N-O52 O52
210 Rd. . . . **27** M50 M51 M52
211 Rd. . . . **25** J51 L51 **27** N51 O51-52
212 Rd. . . . **27** M49-50 M51
213 Rd. . . . **25** J51 L51 **27** M51 N-O51 O51
214 Rd. . . . **27** M49 M50
215 Rd. . . . **25** L51 **27** M51 N51
216 Rd. . . . **27** M49 M50 M51 M51-52
216 St. . . . **78** Z44
217 Rd. . . . **25** J51 **27** M51 N51
218 Rd. . . . **27** M51
219 Rd. . . . **25** J51 K51 L51 **27** M51
220 Rd. (Peace River) . . . **25** L52 **27** M50 M51 M52
220 Rd. (Squamish) . . . **77** U41
221 Rd. . . . **25** J51 **27** M51 N51
223 Rd. . . . **25** J-K51 **27** M51 N51
224 Rd. . . . **25** L51 L52
224 St. . . . **78** Y-Z44
225 Rd. . . . **27** M51
226 Rd. (Kitimat-Stikine) . . . **30** Q29
226 Rd. (Peace River) . . . **25** L50 L51
227 Rd. . . . **25** H-J49 **27** N51
228 Rd. . . . **25** L50
229 Rd. . . . **27** M51
230 Rd. (Peace River) . . . **25** L50 L51-52
230 Rd. (Squamish) . . . **77** U41
231 Rd. . . . **25** J50
232 Rd. . . . **25** L50
232 St. . . . **78** Y-Z44
233 Rd. . . . **27** M50-51 O51
234 Rd. . . . **25** K51
235 Rd. . . . **25** J50 K-L50 L50-51 **27** M50 O50-51
235 Rd. . . . **27** O50-51
236 Rd. . . . **25** K50 K51 K52
237 Rd. . . . **25** J50 J-K50 **27** M50 M-N50
238 Rd. . . . **25** K50
239 Rd. . . . **25** J-K50 **27** M-N50 O50
240 Rd. . . . **25** K51-52
240 St. . . . **78** Y-Z44
241 Rd. . . **25** J-K50 K50 L50 **27** M50 M-N50
242 Rd. . . . **25** K49 K50
243 Rd. . . . **25** J-K50 K50 L50 **27** M50
244 Rd. . . . **25** K49
244 Rd. . . . **25** K51
245 Rd. . . . **25** J-K50 K50 **27** M50
246 Rd. . . . **25** J49 J50
246th Ave. . . . **80** Z55
247 Rd. . . . **25** J50 J-K50 K50 L50 **27** M50 M-N50 N50
248 Rd. . . . **25** J48 J49 J50 J51-52
248 St. . . . **78** Z44
249 Rd. . . . **25** J50 K50 **27** M50
250 Rd. . . . **25** J48 J49 J50 J51
251 Rd. . . . **25** J-K50 K50 L50 **27** M50 N50
252 Rd. . . . **25** J49 J50 J51 **27** M-N50
253 Rd. . . **25** J50 J-K50 K50 **27** M50 M-N50
254 Rd. . . . **25** J48 J49 J50
255 Rd. . . . **25** J49 K49-50 **27** M-N50
255 Rd. . . . **55** L48
256 Rd. . . . **25** J48-49 J50 J51
256 St. . . . **78** Z44
257 Rd. . . . **25** H-J49 L49-50
258 Rd. . . . **25** H-J49 J48
259 Rd. . . **25** H49 H-J49 J49 K49 **27** M-N49
260 Rd. . . . **25** H49
261 Rd. . . . **25** H-J49 **27** N49
262 Rd. . . . **25** H49
263 Rd. . . . **25** H49 **27** M-N49
264 Rd. . . . **25** H48-49 K49
264 St. . . . **78** Z44
265 Rd. . . . **25** H49 J49 K49 **27** M49
266 Rd. . . . **25** H49
267 Rd. . **25** H49 H-J49 K49 **27** M49 M-N49
268 Rd. . . . **25** H50-51
269 Rd. . . . **25** H49 J49 K49
270 Rd. . . . **25** H49
271 Rd. . . . **25** J49 J-K49 **27** M-N49
272 Rd. . . . **25** G48-49 G49
272 St. . . . **78** Y-Z44
273 Rd. . . . **25** J49
275 Rd. . . . **25** J49 **27** M49
277 Rd. . . . **25** G-H49 H49 J49
279 Rd. . . . **25** H48-49 J48
281 Rd. . . . **25** J48 J-K48 **27** N48-49
283 Rd. . . . **25** J48 **27** M48
285 Rd. . . . **25** J48
287 Rd. . . . **25** H-J48
300 Rd. . . . **35** V41
300 Rd. (Mapes) . . . **35** Y40
300 Rd. (Nulki) . . . **34** Y38
300 Cutoff FS Rd. . . . **36** X46
300 FS Rd. . . . **44** C45
312 Ave. . . . **84** W69
324 FS Rd. . . . **55** M49-50
350th Ave. . . . **80** Y55
392nd Ave. . . . **80** Y55
396th Ave. . . . **80** Y55
400 Rd. (Bulkley-Nechako) . . . **34** Y39 **35** Y40
400 Rd. (Cariboo) . . . **44** G44 **54** H44
400 Rd. (Pitoney Lake) . . . **36** Y45 Z46
413 Rd. . . . **31** Q30
422 Rd. . . . **31** Q30
424 Rd. . . . **31** Q30
437 Rd. . . . **31** P30
500 Rd. . . . **33** Z34 Z35 Z36
500 Rd. (Black Creek) . . . **45** G49
500 Rd. (Bradley Creek FS Rd.) **55** J49
500 Rd. (Bulkley-Nechako) . . . **35** Y40
500 Rd. (Cottonwood) . . . **44** C45
500 Rd. (Riske Creek) . . . **53** J43
500 FS Rd. . . . **36** Z45
518A Rd. . . . **55** H48
578 Main Rd. . . . **76** U37
600 Rd. (Bulkley-Nechako) . . . **34** Y39
600 Rd. (Cariboo) . . . **44** B45
609 FS Rd. . . . **44** F45
610 Rd. (Lang Lake North FS Rd.) . . . **55** J50
611 Rd. (Lang Lake FS Rd.) . . **55** J49-50
612 FS Rd. . . . **44** F45
634 FS Rd. . . . **35** A41-42
688 FS Rd. . . . **35** A41
700 Rd. (Big Creek) . . . **53** J-K42
700 Rd. (Dunkley) . . . **36** A45
700 FS Rd. . . . **33** W34
730 Rd. (Bulkley-Nechako) . **30** S26-27
730 Rd. (Columbia-Shuswap) . . **69** O56
742 Rd. . . . **30** R-S26
800 Rd. . . . **55** L48
800 Rd. (Bulkley-Nechako) . . **35** Y-Z40
800 Rd. (Cariboo) . . . **53** K42-43
800 Rd. (Fraser-Fort George) . . . **26** R44
900 Rd. (Cariboo) . . . **53** K40
900 FS Rd. . . . **35** Z40
900 FS Rd. . . . **53** J42
1000 Rd. (Ahbau Lake) . . . **36** A46
1000 Rd. (Gustafsen Lake FS Rd.) . . . **54** L47
1000 Rd. (Rosita-Macklin FS Rd.) . . . **43** G43 **44** G44
1000 Rd. (Tisdall Lake) . . . **45** G49
1100 Rd. . . . **35** V42
1100 Rd. (Cariboo) . . . **54** L47
1100 Rd. (Columbia-Shuswap) . . . **57** N57-58
1200 Rd. (Bulkley-Nechako) . . . **30** T28
1200 Rd. (Puntatsenkut Lake) . . **43** C42
1200 Rd. (Strouse Lake FS Rd.) . . . **53** H-J43
1200 Rd. (Tatton-McKinley FS Rd.) . . . **54** K47 **55** K48
1200-A Rd. . . . **43** C42
1200-B Rd. . . . **43** C42
1220 Rd. . . . **43** C41-42
1300 Rd. (Likely) . . . **44** C46 D47 E47 **45** E48 E49
1300 Rd. (Raven Lake Rd.) . . . **53** J43
1300 Rd. (Tatton-Snag FS Rd.) . . . **54** K46-47 L46-47
1331 Rd. . . . **45** E49
1400 Rd. (Fraser-Fort George) . . **35** Z42
1400 Rd. (Narcosli Creek) . . . **43** D43
1400 Rd. (Wolverine-Rollie Rd.) . . . **44** D-E47
1500 Rd. (Sprout Lake Rd.) . . . **55** J48
1500 FS Rd. . . . **36** A44-45
1600 Rd. (Barkerville) . . . **45** C48
1600 Rd. (Gavin Lake Rd.) . . . **44** F47
1600 Rd. (Lac la Hache) . . . **55** J48
1700 Rd. . . . **43** G41
1700 FS Rd. . . . **55** J48
1800 Rd. (100 Mile House) . . . **55** K-L49
1800 Rd. (Blue Lake Rd) . . . **44** G45
1800 FS Rd. . . . **44** D45
1900 Rd. (Windy Mountain FS Rd.) . . . **55** L50
2000 Rd. (Becher House) . . . **54** J44
2000 Rd. (Big Creek) . . . **53** K42
2000 Rd. (Wavey Lake Rd.) . . . **55** L51
2000 FS Rd. . . . **43** D41-42
2100 Rd. . . . **44** B47
2100 Rd. . . . **54** K44
2100 Rd. . . . **55** L49
2200 Rd. (Akehurst Lake) . . . **55** M51
2200 Rd. (Crescent Lake) . . **44** B46-47
2200 Rd. (Gaspard Camp) . . . **53** K43 L43 **54** K44
2200 Rd. (Nazko) . . . **43** D41
2200 A Rd. . . . **53** L43
2300 Rd. (Bowron Lake) . . . **44** B47
2300 Rd. (McIntosh-Moffatt Lake Rd.) . . . **54** H46-47 **55** H48-49
2400 Rd. (Boot Lake) . . . **35** A41 **36** A46
2400 Rd. (Bowron Lake) . **36** A47 **44** B46
2400 Rd. (Likely) . . . **45** E48
2400 Rd. (Long John Creek) . . **43** D42
2400 Rd. (Mons Creek FS Rd.) . **53** K43
2400-K Rd. . . . **36** A46-47
2400 FS Rd. . . . **43** C43
2500 Rd. (Gaspard Camp) . . . **54** K44
2500 Rd. (Horsefly) . . . **45** G48 **55** H48
2500 Rd. (Long John Creek) . . **43** D41
2500 FS Rd. . . . **43** C43
2600 Rd. . . . **53** K43
2700 Rd. (Cravelle Ferry) . . . **44** D45
2700 Rd. (Empire Valley Rd.) **54** L-M45
2700 Rd. (Gang Ranch) . . . **54** L44
2800 Rd. (Curn Creek FS Rd.) . . . **53** M43 **54** M44
2900 Rd. . . . **53** L43
3000 Rd. . . . **34** A38 **42** B38
3000 FS Rd. . . . **43** E41-43
3100 Rd. . . . **54** M47
3100 Rd. (Gang Ranch) . . . **54** L44
3100 B Rd. . . . **54** L44
3100 FS Rd. . . . **43** C42
3100 FS Rd. . . . **45** C48-49
3200 Rd. (Eagan Lake Rd.) . . **55** L-M50
3200 Rd. (Gaspard Camp) . . . **53** M43
3300 Rd. (Alkali Lake) . . . **54** K45
3300 Rd. (Clinton-Upper Loon Lake Rd.) . . . **55** N49-50
3300 Rd. (Lavington Rd.) . . . **43** C-D42
3300 FS Rd. . . . **43** E42
3400 Rd. (Bonaparte River) . **55** N48-49
3400 Rd. (Dog Creek) . . . **54** L45-46
3400 Rd. (Hihium Lake) . . . **67** O49
3500 Rd. (Cantillon Lake) . . . **43** E-F42
3500 Rd. (Norton-Tregillus FS Rd.) . . . **44** B-C46
3600 FS Rd. . . . **44** C45-46
3700 Rd. (Cariboo) . . . **43** D42-43
3700 Rd. (Eagan-Bonaparte FS Rd.) . . . **55** M-N50
3700 Rd. (Eagan-Bonaparte Lake Rd.) . . . **55** M50
3800 Rd. (Baker Creek) . . . **43** D42
3800 Rd. (Vidette) . . . **55** N50-51
3800 FS Rd. . . . **36** A44-45
3900 Rd. . . . **42** C37 D38 **43** D40
4000 Rd. . . . **42** B38
4020 Rd. . . . **67** O51
4100 Rd. (Nazko) . . . **43** D40
4200 Rd. . . . **42** D39
4200 Rd. (Redstone) . . . **53** H40
4300 Rd. (Fraser-Fort George) . . **36** A45
4300 Rd. (Nazko) . . . **42** C39 **43** C41
4300 Rd. (Tsintsunko Lake) . . . **67** O51
4400 Rd. (Cariboo) . . . **53** J41
4400 Rd. (Nazko) . . . **43** C41
4600 Rd. (Alexis Lake) . . . **43** G41
4600 Rd. (Chilcotin DND) . . . **55** H48
4600-A Rd. (Nazko) . . . **42** C39
4600-B Rd. . . . **42** C-D39
4700 FS Rd. . . . **43** C41
4800 Rd. . . . **43** E-F43
4900 FS Rd. . . . **44** D46
5100 Rd. (Snaking River Rd.) **43** C40-41
5100 A FS Rd. . . . **43** C40-41
5100 V FS Rd. . . . **43** C41
5100W FS Rd. . . . **43** C41
5200 Rd. . . . **43** C-D41
5400 Rd. . . . **42** C39
5500 Rd. (Bowron Lake) . . . **37** A48
5500 Rd. (Nazko) . . . **42** B-C39
5600 Rd. . . . **43** D41
5600 Rd. . . . **44** C46
5900 Rd. . . . **43** E42
6000 Rd. (Cantillon Lake) . . . **43** E41
6000 Rd. (Pauls Point Rd.) . . . **55** J50
6100 Rd. (Cantillon Lake) . . . **43** E41
6100 Rd. (Quesnel Lake) **45** E50-51 F50
6100 FS Rd. . . . **34** Z38
6200 Rd. . . . **43** E41
6200 Rd. . . . **43** E42
6300 Rd. . . . **45** F50
6400 Rd. . . . **42** D39
6500 Rd. (Horsefly Lake) . . . **45** F-G49
6500 Rd. (Narcosli Lake) . . . **42** D38
6600 Rd. . . . **43** C40
6700 FS Rd. . . . **45** G50
6800 Rd. . . . **42** C-D38
7000 Rd. . . . **30** R26-27
7000 Rd. (Pendleton Lakes Rd.) . . . **55** J50-51
7000 Rd. (Scum Lake) . . . **53** J40
7100 Rd. (Pendleton Lakes Rd.) **55** J51
7200 Rd. . . . **55** H-J51
7600 Rd. . . . **30** R27
7700 Rd. . . . **43** B41
7900 Rd. . . . **30** R27
7900 FS Rd. . . . **43** C42
8000 Rd. . . . **43** E41
8100 Rd. . . . **43** E40-41
8100 Rd. (Canim Lake South Rd.) . . . **55** J-K50
8200 Rd. (Bowers FS Rd.) . . **55** K50-51
8200 Rd. (Cariboo) . . . **44** G46-47
8300 Rd. . . . **44** F46
8400 Rd. . . . **45** D48 D49
8407, FS Rd. . . . **78** U44-45
8500 Rd. (Cariboo) . . . **43** B41
8500 Rd. (Lemon Lake Rd) . . **45** F-G48
9600 Rd. . . . **45** D48

A Rd. . . . **35** A41
A-1100 Rd. . . . **77** U40
A-600 Rd. . . . **77** U41
A-730 Rd. . . . **77** U41
A Branch Rd. . . . **76** U38
Aalhus St. . . . **25** K51
Abbey Rd. . . . **67** Q51
Abbott Dr. . . . **44** C44
Aberdeen Rd. (Merritt) . . . **67** S50
Aberdeen Rd. (Vernon) . . . **69** S56
Aberdeen-Goat FS Rd. . . . **69** T57
Aberdeen Lake Rd. . . . **69** T57
Aberdeen Summit Rd. . . . **69** S57
Abrey Rd. . . . **84** Z71
Adam Rd. . . . **62** S30
Adam Main Rd. . . . **62** R31
Adamants Rd. . . . **58** L60
Adams Rd. (Bowen Island) . . . **77** X41
Adams Rd. (Bulkley-Nechako) . . **30** R29
Adams Rd. (Chilliwack) . . . **78** Y-Z46
Adams Rd. (Dawson Creek) . . . **27** N51
Adams FS Rd. . . . **57** L56
Adams Lake Rd. . . . **56** L55 **57** L56
Adams Lake-Tumtum Lake FS Rd. . . . **57** J-K57 L56-57
Adams Plateau-Sparkle FS Rd. . . . **57** N56 **69** O56
Adams Plateau FS Rd. . . **68** O55 **69** O56
Adams West-Spapilem Creek FS Rd. . . . **56** N55
Adams West FS Rd. **56** N55 **57** M56 N56
Adolph Johnson Rd. . . . **59** M65
Agate Bay Rd. . . . **56** N53

Ager Rd. 32 W31
Ainslie Rd. 79 U48
Ainsworth St. (Central Kootenay) 83 V65
Airmail Rd. 55 L50
Airplane Creek Rd. 78 Y47
Airport Rd. 28 T17-18 U17-18
Airport Rd. (Creston) 83 Z67
Airport Rd. (Fort Saint John) 25 K49-50
Airport Rd. (Lillooet) 66 Q46
Airport Rd. (Pemberton) 65 S43
Airport Rd. (Port Alberni) 75 X35
Airport Rd. (Salmo) 83 Y64
Airport Rd. (Sparwood) 85 V72
Airport Rd. (Williams Lake) 54 H45-46
Airport Way 70 O60
Airport Access Rd. 84 W69
Airstrip Rd. 63 S32
Airy Creek FS Rd. 82 W62
Aitken Creek Rd. 24 G47 H47 25 G48
Aiyansh Rd. 29 P22
Akokli Creek Rd. 83 X66
Akolkolex Rd. 70 P61
Akolkolex-Crawford FS Rd. 70 P60-61
Akolkolex-Dupont FS Rd. 70 P-Q61
Alaska Hwy. 25 J48 27 M51
Alberni Hwy. 76 Y37
Albers Rd. 69 S58
Albert Rd. 62 T29
Albert River FS Rd. 72 Q-R70
Albreda Rd. 47 E57
Albright Rd. 25 L52
Alcock Rd. 44 B44
Alden Rd. 81 Z57
Alder Rd. 30 R28
Aldous St. 30 P27
Alec Meadow Rd. 43 B40
Alex Graham-Anahim Central FS Rd. 53 H42
Alex Graham-Goering Creek FS Rd. 43 G41
Alex Graham-Raven Lake FS Rd. 53 H42-43
Alexander Rd. (Clearwater) 56 L54-55
Alexander Rd. (Nakusp) 70 S62
Alexander Rd. (Procter) 83 W65
Alexander Creek FS Rd. 85 V73
Alexandria Ferry Rd. 44 E44
Alexis Creek-Nazko Rd. 43 G40-41
Alexis Creek-Nazko Rd. 53 H41
Alexis Lakes Rd. 43 G41 53 H41
Alice Lake Main Rd. 61 R26-27
Allan Rd. 32 X31
Allan Creek FS Rd. 47 E57
Allcott Rd. 35 W-X43
Allen Rd. 82 X61
Allenby Lake Rd. 79 X51 80 X52
Allendale Lake Rd. 80 X55 81 X56
Alligator Mainline Rd. 87 C39
Allin Rd. 32 W32
Allison Rd. 54 N45-46
Almberg Rd. 59 N65
Almond Creek FS Rd. 81 X-Y59
Almus Rd. 35 Y-Z43
Alouette Rd. 78 Y44
Alpha-Lardeau Creek FS Rd. 70 Q63
Alpine Dr. 36 X44
Alpine Rd. (East Kootenay) 72 R69
Alpine Rd. (Fraser Valley) 79 Y49
Alpine Way 85 U72
Alta Lake Rd. 65 T42
Altona Rd. 25 F49
Amai Creek Mainline Rd. 61 T27 62 T28
Amarillo Rd. 54 H46
Amendt Rd. 32 W32
America Creek FS Rd. 84 Z68-69
American Creek Rd. 79 X48
Amiskwi Fire Rd. 59 M66
Amor Lake Rd. 63 T33
Anah Lake Rd. 53 H41-42
Anahim Lake Rd. 41 F34
Anahim South Branch FS Rd. 53 H42
Anders Rd. 32 W32 33 W33
Anderson Rd. (Cariboo) 54 H45-46
Anderson Rd. (Enderby) 69 Q57
Anderson Rd. (Kelowna) 81 U56
Anderson Rd. (Prince George) 35 Y43
Anderson Rd. (Sooke) 87 D39
Anderson-Gray Creek Rd. 83 W65-66
Anderson Bay Rd. 76 W38
Anderson Lake Rd. 66 Q-R44
Anderson Main FS Rd. 79 U-V48
Anderson River FS Rd. 79 V48
Anderton Rd. 75 V35
Andimaul Main FS Rd. 30 Q26
Andrew Rd. 72 T69 84 U69
Andrews Rd. 27 N48
Andrews Bay Rd. 32 X30
Andrews Bay Rd. (Wistaria Main FS Rd.) 32 X30-31
Andrews Main FS Rd. 32 X29-30
Angus Horne St. 57 H57
Anlaw Rd. 29 P22
Anns Rd. 31 S32
Ansley Branch 3 FS Rd. 57 N58
Anstey River FS Rd. 69 O58
Antoine Rd. 69 S56
Antoine Lake Rd. 44 F47 45 F48
Anutz Lake Rd. 62 S28
Apex Mountain Rd. 80 X54
Apple River Main Rd. 63 P-Q34
Applegrove Rd. 82 U-V61
April Point Rd. 63 T34
Arawana Rd. 80 W55
Arawana FS Rd. 80 V-W55
Arbutus St. 77 Y42
Archibald Creek Rd. 82 Y-Z63
Archie Meadow Rd. 55 K49
Argenta Rd. 71 T65
Argonaut Rd. 63 T34
Argonaut Main Rd. 75 U33
Arlington FS Rd. 81 W57
Arlington Lakes Rd. 81 W57
Arndt Rd. 27 N52
Arnold Rd. 71 O66
Arnoldus Rd. 44 D44
Arras Rd. 27 N50
Arrow Lakes Dr 82 X62
Arrow Park Creek Rd. 70 S-T61
Arrowstone FS Rd. 67 O48-49 P48
Arthur Dr. 77 Z42
Arthurs Creek FS Rd. 81 V58-59
Artlish Rd. 62 S28
Artlish Main Rd. 62 T28
Artlish Mainline Rd. 61 T27 62 T28
Ash River Rd. 75 X34-35
Ashby Main Rd. 60 P23
Ashley Rd. 68 R52
Ashlu Main Rd. 77 U40-41
Ashnola Rd. 80 Y52-54
Ashton-Mara East FS Rd. 69 Q57-58
Ashton Cooke Rd. 69 Q57-58
Ashton Creek FS Rd. 69 Q57
Athalmer Rd. 72 R68
Atlatzi Main Rd. 62 O31 63 O32
Atleo Main Rd. 74 X31
Atluck Rd. 62 S28
Atluck Main Rd. 61 S27 62 S28
Atluck Relocation Rd. 62 S28
Atrevida Rd. 76 U36
Augier Rd. 31 U33
Augier Co-op Rd. 33 V34
Augier Ling Rd. 33 V34
Augier Main FS Rd. 33 V34
Auldgirth Rd. 56 L52
Aulds Rd. 76 Y38
Aumond Rd. 69 S59
Auto Rd. 69 Q56-57
Aveling Coal Mine Rd. 30 S-T28
Averil FS Rd. 77 W42
Avis Rd. 82 V63
Avoca Rd. 69 O58-59
Avola Mountain FS Rd. 57 H-J56
B Rd. 58 J-K62 K63
B & K Rd. 77 X40
B Main Rd. 61 R25
Babine Dr. 31 R32
Babine Lake Rd. 31 T-U33 33 V33
Babine Lake Rd. (Burnt Cabin Rd) 30 S29 31 Q-R31 R30
Back Rd. 62 Q28
Back Rd. (Mount Waddington) 62 T29
Back Rd. (Thompson-Nicola) 68 R54-55
Back Enderby Rd. 69 R57
Back Valley Rd. 79 Z48
Badger Creek Rd. 56 N52-53 68 O52-53
Badger Creek FS Rd. 68 O52
Baerg FS Rd. 70 T62
Baezaeko Rd. 43 C40
Baggerman Rd. 32 V30
Baggi Rd. 76 U36
Bailey Rd. 68 P55
Bailey Rd. (North Okanagan) 69 S-T56
Baker Dr. 44 C44
Baker Creek Rd. 46 B55
Baker Creek FS Rd. 82 Z60
Baker Hill Rd. 80 W52
Baker Mountain Rd. 84 W69-70
Bald Hill Rd. 33 V-W33
Bald Mountain FS Rd. 54 J44
Bald Range Creek Rd. 68 T55 80 U55
Baldhill Creek FS Rd. 66 S47
Baldonnel Rd. 25 K50
Balmoral Rd. 69 P56
Balsam Rd. 82 Y63
Bamfield Rd. (Bamfield) 86 A34-36
Bamfield Rd. (Port Alberni) 76 Y-Z36
Banon Creek FS Rd. 87 A39
Banting Creek FS Rd. 81 U59
Barber Rd. 56 K54
Barber Rd. 59 M65
Barbour Creek FS Rd. 27 R48
Barcelo Rd. 80 Y54
Bare Main Rd. 62 R31
Bark Shanty FS Rd. 84 X69
Barkerville Hwy. 44 C45-46
Barkley Rd. 75 Z33
Barkley St. 24 L46
Barley Rd. 82 Z61-62
Barnaby Rd. 80 V55 81 V56
Barnes Rd. 36 X-Y44
Barnes Rd. (Central Kootenay) 82 U60
Barnes Rd. (Thompson-Nicola) 67 P-Q49
Barnes Creek FS Rd. 82 U60
Barnes Lake Rd. 67 Q49
Barnet Rd. 77 Y43
Barnett Rd. (Cariboo) 55 L48
Barnett Rd. (Fraser-Fort George) 46 B55
Barney Creek FS Rd. 36 V44
Barnhartvale Rd. 68 Q53-54
Baronet Main Rd. 62 Q29
Barrett Rd. (Cariboo) 55 L49
Barrett Hat Rd. 31 T-U30
Barrett Station Rd. 31 U30
Barrière Lakes Rd. 56 N52-54
Barriere Town Rd. 56 N52-53
Barsness Rd. 35 X40
Barth FS Rd. 81 W58
Bartholomew Rd. 63 T35
Bartley Rd. 80 U55
Bartley Creek Rd. 80 U55
Basin Mainline Rd. 74 U-V28
Baskin Rd. 35 A43
Bastin Rd. 44 D45
Bastion-Reinecker Creek FS Rd. 69 P56-57
Bastion Creek FS Rd. 69 P57
Bastion Mountain FS Rd. 69 O57
Batchelor Dr. 68 P-Q52
Batchelor Creek FS Rd. 58 L62
Bates Rd. (Aspen Grove) 79 U51
Bates Rd. (Buffalo Creek) 55 K49
Bates Beach Rd. 75 V35
Bathfield Rd. 80 W54
Bathville Rd. 80 W54
Batnuni Rd. 34 A38-39 35 A40-41 43 B41
Batnuni Lake FS Rd. 34 A38-39
Batt Rd. 78 Z45
Battle Creek FS Rd. 67 P49
Battle Mountain Rd. 56 J54
Bave Rd. 34 W39
Bay Ave. 82 Z62
Bay View Rd. 77 X41
Bayliff Rd. 53 H40
Baylis Rd. 76 X36
Baynes Lake Dump Rd. 84 Y71
Bayonne Creek FS Rd. 83 Y-Z65
Bayview Rd. 33 W36 34 W37
BC Nickel Mine Rd. 79 X48
Beach Dr. 87 C-D41
Beach Rd. (Burns Lake) 33 V33
Beach Bay FS Rd. 57 N58
Beach Main FS Rd. 63 S33
Beacon Rd. 81 W57
Bealby Point Rd. 83 W64
Beale Rd. 35 W43
Beam Station Rd. 29 T-U24
Bear Rd. 47 D57
Bear Bight Rd. 63 S33
Bear Creek Rd. 79 W50
Bear Creek Rd. 82 Y-Z62
Bear Creek Mainline Rd. 87 C38
Bear FS Rd. 36 A45-46
Bear FS Rd. 80 U53-55
Bear Head Rd. 52 H38
Bear River Rd. 30 P28
Bear Valley Rd. (Lumby) 69 S58
Beards Creek Rd. 71 O66
Bearhead Rd. 34 W38
Bearhole Lake FS Rd. 27 Q49
Bearn Ave. 83 Z67
Beasley Rd. 82 W-X63
Beaton Rd. (Kamloops) 67 Q51
Beaton-Armstrong Lake Rd. (Beaton) 70 Q62
Beattie Dr. 24 L46
Beattie Rd. 69 Q58
Beatton Airport Rd. 24 F47 F-G47 25 G-H48
Beau Park Rd. 68 S55 69 S56
Beaudette Creek FS Rd. 26 O44-45
Beaumont Rd. 53 J43
Beautiful FS Rd. 68 S54
Beaver Rd. 30 Q28
Beaver-Bowron FS Rd. 36 X45-46
Beaver-Bowron FS Rd. 36 X46
Beaver Cove Rd. 62 Q28
Beaver Creek Rd. (Alberni-Clayoquot) 75 X-Y35
Beaver Creek Rd. (Kootenay Boundary) 81 W-X57
Beaver Forest Rd. 35 W-X43 36 W44
Beaver FS Rd. 36 W44-45
Beaver Harbour Rd. 61 P26
Beaver Lake Rd. 63 T34
Beaver Lake Rd. (Cariboo) 44 F45-46
Beaver Lake Rd. (Central Okanagan) 69 T56
Beaver Lake Mainline Rd. 76 U37-38
Beaver Pass Rd. 44 B46
Beaver Point Rd. 87 A41
Beaverdam Rd. 54 M47 55 N48
Beaverdell Rd. 80 W-X55 81 X56
Beaverdell-State Creek FS Rd. 81 W57-58
Beaverdell Station Rd. 81 X57
Beaverfoot Rd. 59 N66
Beaverfoot-Moose FS Rd. 71 O67
Beaverfoot FS Rd. 59 N66
Beaverhut Lake FS Rd. 55 N51 56 N52
Beaverjack FS Rd. 69 R-S58
Beavermouth Rd. 44 E45
Beavervale Creek FS Rd. 82 Y63
Becker Rd. 25 J48
Becker Rd. 34 W37
Becker Lake Rd. 69 S57
Beckman Rd. 24 L46
Becks Rd. 80 Y54
Beddis Rd. 87 A40-41
Bedell Dr. 26 N47
Bedell Rd. 27 N50
Bedford Rd. 82 X63
Bedingfield Rd. 74 X31
Bednesti Lake Rd. S. 35 X41
Bedore Rd. 31 U32
Beech Rd. 67 S50
Beeftrail Main Rd. 41 F34
Beers Rd. 27 O48
Beese Rd. 85 W72
Begbie Rd. 70 O60
Beggs Rd. 83 W64-65
Belchrome FS Rd. 81 Y-Z57
Belfort Rd. 79 W51 80 W52
Bell Rd. (Cariboo) 55 L50
Bell Rd. (Clayburn) 78 Z45
Bell Rd. (Texada Island) 76 W37-38
Bell Mountain Rd. 37 A51
Bella Vista Rd. 69 S56
Bellos Rd. 35 Y43 36 Y44
Bells Lake Rd. 44 G47
Ben Hynes Loop 71 O67
Bench Rd. 57 K59
Bench Creek FS Rd. 82 U60
Bench Row Rd. 69 S56
Bendixon Rd. 35 X43 36 X44
Bennett Rd. 25 K48
Benson Rd. 61 Q-R27
Benson Main Rd. 61 S27
Bequelin Rd. 69 O56
Berg Rd. 27 M51
Bergen Rd. 25 G-H49
Berglund Rd. 67 T51
Berkley Rd. 44 C44
Bernard Creek FS Rd. 83 U65-66 V66
Berreshiem Rd. 25 G49
Berrey Rd. 71 P67
Berry Rd. 27 N51
Berry Messiter FS Rd. 57 H56
Beryl Prairie Rd. 24 K-L45
Betania Rd. 84 X71
Betts Rd. 84 X70
Bevan Rd. 75 V-W35
Bever Rd. 24 L45
Beveridge Lake FS Rd. 44 G47
Beverly Lake FS Rd. 35 X40-41
Beverly Main Rd. 75 Y34
Bickle Rd. 32 W-X32
Bidwell-Chilanko South FS Rd. 52 H39
Bidwell Lakes FS Rd. 52 H-J38
Big Bam Rd. 25 K-L50
Big Bar Rd. 54 N46
Big Bar Lake Rd. 54 M46 M-N47
Big Bar Mountain Rd. 54 M-N46
Big Bar Mountain-Crows Bar Rd. 54 M45 N45-46
Big Bend Hwy. (Bush River FS Rd.) 58 L63 59 L64
Big Cedar River FS Rd. 29 Q23
Big Creek Rd. 53 K42-43 54 J44
Big Creek-Willan Lake Rd. 53 K42
Big Eddy Rd. 70 O60
Big Fir FS Rd. 80 V54
Big Lake Rd. 44 F46
Big Lake Rd. W. 44 F-G46
Big Lake-Tyee Lake Rd. 44 F46
Big Lake Konni Lake Rd. 52 L39 53 L40
Big Lake FS Rd. 44 G46
Big Loon Rd. 31 R-S32 S33
Big Sheep Creek Rd. 82 X62
Big Sheep Creek FS Rd. 82 Y61
Big Silver Main Rd. 78 V46 W46-47
Big Tree Main South FS Rd. 63 S32
Big Valley FS Rd. 36 A46 44 B46
Big White Rd. 81 V57-58
Big White West FS Rd. 81 V57
Bigmouth FS Rd. 57 J59 K59 58 J60
Bigtree Main North FS Rd. 63 S32
Bill Nye FS Rd. 32 W28
Billeter Rd. 30 S29
Billings Rd. 70 S-T62
Billy Lake Rd. 67 R50
Bingay Rd. 82 Z62
Binnie Rd. 54 J47 55 J48
Binta Rd. 33 X33
Binta Black Point FS Rd. 33 X34
Binta Cheslatta FS Rd. 33 X34
Binta FS Rd. 33 X34 X35
Binta Knapp FS Rd. 33 X34-35
Binta Main FS Rd. 33 X34
Binta Mine Rd. 33 X33
Binta North FS Rd. 33 X34
Binta WO Rd. 33 X34
Birch Rd. 34 W38
Birch Rd. 57 J59
Birch Hill Rd. 44 C44
Birch Island-Lost Creek Rd. 56 L54-55
Birch River-Lost Creek Rd. 56 L55 57 L56
Bird Lake Rd. 33 Y35
Birkenhead Lake FS Rd. 65 R43
Bischoff Rd. 69 O56
Bison Rd. 25 K50 K51
Biss Rd. 55 K49
Bissett Rd. 55 K48-49
Bissette Dr. 27 N51
Bittern Lake FS Rd. 71 O66
Bittner Rd. 51 H-J35
Bjornson Rd. 44 C44
Black Rd. (Bulkley-Nechako) 30 S28
Black Rd. (North Okanagan) 69 Q57
Black Creek Rd. 45 G48
Black Creek-Bosk Lake FS Rd. 45 G49-50
Black Creek-Tisdall FS Rd. 45 G49
Black Creek 100 Rd. 45 F50
Black Mine Rd. 79 X51
Black Pines Rd. 68 O-P52
Black Sage Rd. 80 Y-Z55
Black Tusk Rd. 77 U42
Blackdome Mountain Rd. 54 M44-45
Blackfoot Creek FS Rd. 72 T70-71
Blackie Rodgers Rd. 70 S61
Blackman Rd. 47 C56-57
Blackmore Rd. 35 W43
Blackwater Hwy. 43 B42 B43
Blackwater Rd. (Bulkley-Nechako) 34 X39 35 X40 Y40
Blackwater Rd. (Fraser-Fort George) 35 A42
Blackwater Rd. (Fraser-Fort George) 35 Y43 Z42
Blackwater-Spruce Rd. 43 B42
Blackwater Creek Rd. 65 R43 66 R44
Blackwater FS Rd. 35 Z41-42
Blackwater Lake Rd. 63 S-T33
Blackwater Ridge Rd. 58 L63
Blaeberry Rd. 59 M65
Blaeberry FS Rd. 59 L65
Blaeberry School Rd. 59 M64-65
Blair Creek FS Rd. 68 Q55
Blaney Rd. 32 W-X32
Blatchford Rd. 69 P58
Blazed Creek FS Rd. 83 Y65
Bleeker Rd. 55 L48
Bleeker Lake FS Rd. 68 R53
Blewett Rd. 82 X63
Blind Bay Rd. 69 P56
Blind Creek FS Rd. 26 P46
Blind Creek Mainline Rd. 63 Q32-33
Blockline Rd. 27 N51
Bloom Creek FS Rd. 84 Y-Z70
Blowdown Creek Rd. 66 R-S45
Blowhole Mainline Rd. 74 U28-29
Blubber Bay Rd. 76 V36
Blue Rd. 34 A37 42 B38
Blue Creek FS Rd. 66 O44
Blue Earth Lake FS Rd. 67 Q-R48
Blue FS Rd. (Bulkley-Nechako) 42 B37
Blue FS Rd. (Fraser-Fort George) 36 Z45
Blue Goose Rd. 55 M49
Blue Grave Creek Rd. 24 H43-44
Blue Lake Rd. (Fraser Valley) 79 U48
Blue Lake Rd. (Hargreaves) 44 G45
Blue Lake Rd. (Thompson-Nicola) 67 T48
Blue Lake Main FS Rd. 86 B35
Blue Mountain Rd. 34 W38
Blue Ox Main Rd. 61 R27
Blueberry Rd. (Peace River) 25 G48
Blueberry Rd. (Thompson-Nicola) 57 H56
Bluenose Rd. 69 S-T57
Bluewater Main FS Rd. 59 K-L64
Bluff Lake Rd. 52 J-K36
Blundell Rd. 77 Y42
Blunt Creek FS Rd. 30 Q28-29
Blythe-Rhone Rd. 81 Y57
Bobbie Burns Rd. 69 R58
Bobbie Burns FS Rd. 71 O65-66
Bobs Lake Pit Rd. 80 U52
Bobtail-Berta FS Rd. 35 Y40
Bobtail FS Rd. 35 X40-41 Y40 Z40-41
Boden FS Rd. 32 X32
Bodo Rd. 27 N48
Boer Mountain Rd. 33 V33
Bolean-Fly Hills FS Rd. 69 Q56
Bolean Lake Rd. 68 R55 69 R56
Bollhalder Rd. 27 O52
Bolton Rd. 34 W37-38
Bomberger FS Rd. 33 V-W35
Bonanza Rd. 70 T63
Bonanza Creek FS Rd. 82 Y61
Bonaparte Rd. 55 M49
Bonaparte-Rayfield FS Rd. 55 M-N49
Bonaparte FS Rd. 56 M-N52
Bonaparte Lake Rd. 56 M-N52
Bone Creek FS Rd. 47 G57
Boneyard Rd. 87 C39
Bonneau Rd. 69 T58
Bonney Beef Rd. 34 W38
Boothby Rd. 82 Z63
Bootjack Lake Rd. 44 E-F47
Boring Rd. 24 L45
Borland Dr. 54 H46
Bornite Mountain Rd. 29 S24-25
Borthwick Creek FS Rd. 55 H-J48
Bose Lake Rd. 67 R49
Boss-Canim FS Rd. 55 J50-51
Boss Creek FS Rd. 55 J50
Boswell Rd. 83 X66
Botanical Beach Rd. 86 C37
Botanie Creek Rd. 66 S47
Botanie Valley Rd. 66 S47 67 S48
Botel 630 Rd. 61 Q24
Botel Main Rd. 61 Q24-25
Bottle Creek Rd. 44 G46
Boucher Lake Rd. 26 M47
Boucherie Rd. 80 U-V55
Boulder Creek Rd. (Central Kootenay) 83 Y64
Boulder Creek Rd. (Cowichan Valley) 87 A39
Boulder Creek Rd. (Kootenay Boundary) 81 W-X59
Boulder Creek Rd. (Squamish-Lillooet) 66 R46
Boulder Creek FS Rd. (Central Kootenay) 82 W62
Boulder Creek FS Rd. (East Kootenay) 84 W70
Boulder Creek FS Rd. (Kitimat-Stikine) 30 Q28
Boulder Lake Rd. 26 P47
Boulder Mainline Rd. 63 P-Q34
Boulder Mountain Rd. 56 M-N52
Boulder Pit Rd. 83 Y64
Bouldery Creek Rd. 45 F50
Boule-Young Lake Rd. 55 M-N49
Bouleau Lake Rd. 68 S55
Boultbee Rd. 55 L51
Boundary Rd. 77 X43
Boundary Rd. 78 Z44-46
Boundary Rd. (Bulkley-Nechako) 30 S29
Boundary-Jewel FS Rd. 81 Y58
Boundary Bay Rd. 77 Z42
Boundary Creek Rd. 81 Y-Z58
Boundary Creek East FS Rd. 81 Y58
Boundary Creek FS Rd. 81 Y58
Boundary Creek West FS Rd. 81 X58
Boundary Windfall Creek FS Rd. 81 Y58
Bourgon Rd. 30 S-T29
Bowen Rd. 76 Y39
Bowen Bay Rd. 77 X41
Bowers-Mahood FS Rd. 55 J51
Bowers Lake East Rd. 55 K50
Bowers Lake FS Rd. 55 K51
Bowers Lake FS Rd. (8200 Rd.) 55 K50-51
Bowman Main Rd. 61 O27
Bowron-Haggen Rd. 36 Z47 37 Z48
Bowron-Tumuch Rd. 36 Y47
Bowron FS Rd. 36 X46 Y46-47 Z47
Bowron Lake Rd. 44 B47 45 B48
Bowron River FS Rd. 36 A47
Boyds Rd. 87 D39
Boyscout Rd. 25 L50
Boysen Rd. 24 L47 25 L48
Braaten Rd. 34 X39 35 X40
Braden Rd. (Capital RD) 86 B37
Braden Rd. (Peace River) 25 L49 L50 27 M49 M49
Bradford Rd. 84 U69
Bradley Creek FS Rd. (500 Rd.) 55 J49
Bradner Rd. 78 Y-Z44
Braindead Rd. 58 L61
Bralorne Rd. 65 P43
Bralorne-Hurley Rd. 65 P43
Branch Dr. 44 G47
Branch 103 Rd. 75 X35
Branch 110 Rd. 75 W-X34
Branch 124 Rd. 75 X34
Branch 16 Rd. 58 K62
Branch 26 Rd. 57 K59
Branch 41 Rd. 76 V38
Branch 44 Rd. 76 V38
Branch 8 Rd. 58 J62
Branch 83 Rd. 75 X34-35
Brandywine FS Rd. 65 T41-42
Brash-Allen Rd. 69 Q57
Brash Creek Rd. 69 Q57
Brassey Rd. 27 N50
Braun Rd. 25 F-G49
Braun Rd. 33 X33
Brazion Creek FS Rd. 26 P45

Bree Rd. 30 S29
Bremner Rd. 26 M47
Bremner Creek FS Rd. 70 S63
Brenda Mines Rd. 80 U54
Brennan Rd. 43 C43
Brent Main FS Rd. 63 S34
Brett Creek FS Rd. 78 X46
Brett Mainline Rd. 62 O29
Brew Creek Mainline Rd. 65 T42 77 U42
Brewer Rd. 32 W31
Brewer Rd. 69 S57
Brewer Creek Rd. 72 S68
Brewster Lake Rd. 63 T33
Brewster Main Rd. 57 L59
Briar Ridge Rd. 27 N52
Bridal Falls Rd. 78 Y47
Bridge FS Rd. 36 A47
Bridge Lake North Rd. 55 L50
Bridge River Rd. 66 P46
Bridge River FS Rd. 65 P42-43
Bridges Rd. 75 V35
Brigade Creek FS Rd. 55 N49-50 67 O50
Brisco Rd. 71 P67
Brisham Dam Rd. 54 K45-46
Britannia Creek Rd. 77 W42
Broadwater Rd. 82 X61-62
Brodick Rd. 74 U28
Brolin Rd. 67 R50
Brooke Creek Rd. 79 V50
Brookmere Rd. 79 V50
Brooks Rd. 76 W39
Brophy Rd. 34 X37
Brothen Rd. 40 F30
Brouse Rd. 54 H46
Brouse Loop Rd. 70 S-T62
Brown Rd. 33 W33
Brown Rd. 46 B55
Brown Creek Rd. 81 Y59
Brown Creek-Eholt Rd. 81 Y59
Brown Creek FS Rd. 55 M51
Browne Lake FS Rd. 81 V57
Browning Rd. 44 B-C44
Browns Bay Rd. 63 T33-34
Brownscombe Rd. 35 Z43
Brule Creek FS Rd. 85 U72
Bryant Rd. (East Kootenay) 85 W72
Bryant Pit Rd. 34 W37
Brydges Rd. 82 U61
Bubar Rd. 81 Z57-58
Buchanan Rd. 69 S57
Buchanan Lookout FS Rd. 83 U65
Buck Flats Rd. 31 U30 32 V30
Buckhorn Rd. 67 Q51
Buckhorn Lake Rd. 36 Y44
Buckley Rd. 82 Y62
Buckley Bay Main Rd. 75 W35
Buckskin Rd. 44 G45
Budlite Rd. 62 S-T29
Bueckert Ave. 25 H50
Buffalo Rd. 47 C56
Buffalo Creek Rd. 35 K49
Bugaboo Creek FS Rd. 71 P66-67
Bugaboo Mainline Rd. 86 B37
Bugcamp Creek Rd. 56 N55 57 N56
Buhl Creek FS Rd. 84 U68
Buick Creek Rd. 25 G48
Bulkley Canyon Rd. 30 P28
Bulkley South Rd. 31 U32
Bulkot Rd. 84 X70
Bull-Quinn FS Rd. 84 U-V71
Bull-Sulphur FS Rd. 85 V72
Bull-Van Rd. 84 W71
Bull Creek FS Rd. (Kootenay Boundary) 81 Y57
Bull Creek FS Rd. (Okanagan-Similkameen) 80 W54
Bull Mountain Rd. 44 G45
Bull River Rd. 84 W70-71
Bull River FS Rd. 73 T72 84 U71 V-W71 85 U72
Bull River South Rd. 84 X71
Bulldog FS Rd. 82 X-Y60 Y61
Bullmoose Rd. 26 Q47 27 Q48
Bullmoose Rd. 81 Z56
Bullock Lake Rd. 55 M48
Bunch Grass-Wiseman Creek FS Rd. 81 X59
Bund Valley Rd. 81 Y58
Bunting Lake Rd. 44 G46
Burbee Rd. 26 M47 27 M48
Burdick Main FS Rd. 30 P26-27
Burgess Rd. 55 L50
Burkhardt Rd. 84 Z68
Burkholder FS Rd. 66 O44
Burma Rd. (East Kootenay) 85 W72
Burma Rd. (Powell River) 76 U-V37
Burn Rd. 57 L59
Burn Creek FS Rd. 82 V62
Burns Ave. 72 T69
Burnt Cabin Rd. 30 S29
Burnt Creek FS Rd. (2000 Rd) 30 Q28
Burnt Island Harbour Mainline Rd. 49 M27
Burnt River FS Rd. 26 P46
Burr Rd. 79 X51
Burrard Ave. 34 W39
Burrell Rd. 82 V60
Burrell Creek FS Rd. 81 W59 X59 82 W60
Burton FS Rd. 82 U-V61
Burton Lake Rd. 84 X71 85 X72
Bush Rd. 40 F30
Bush Rd. 53 J43
Bush-Sullivan FS Rd. 58 K62-63
Bush (North) River Rd. 58 H63 J63 59 J64
Bush Creek Rd. 68 O55
Bush River FS Rd. 58 K-L63
Butler Rd. 54 J47
Butler Mainline Rd. 87 C39
Butler Ridge Rd. 24 J44-45
Butnham Rd. 70 R61
Buttle Lake Rd. 75 V33
Buxton Rd. 44 E46
Bye Rd. 31 T31
Byne Rd. 61 Q26
Byng Rd. 61 P26
Bypass Rd. 80 Y54
C-10 Rd. 32 Z32 33 Z33
C-3 Rd. 33 Z33
C-4 Rd. 33 Z33
C-6 Rd. 33 Z33
C-8 Rd. 33 Z33
C Branch Rd. 63 S32 T32
C M H Lodge Rd. 47 D56-57
Cabin FS Rd. 85 Y73 Z73-74
Cabin Main Rd. 61 Q27 62 Q28
Cachalot Rd. 61 T27
Cacoontin Creek FS Rd. 40 F31
Cadwallader Creek Rd. 65 P-Q43
Cahilty Creek FS Rd. 68 O54
Cahilty Main FS Rd. 68 O54-55
Cai Creek FS Rd. 82 Y62
CalCheak FS Rd. 65 T42 77 U42
Calder Rd. 82 U60
Call Inlet-EC Main Rd. 62 Q31
Callaghan Creek Rd. 65 T42
Callaghan Valley FS Rd. 65 T42
Callahan Pit Rd. 27 N51
Callano Rd. 33 W36
Callazon-Clearwater Creek FS Rd. 26 N-O43
Callbeck Rd. 83 X64
Calliou Rd. 26 M47
Cambie St. 77 Y42
Cambie-Solsqua Rd. 69 P58
Cameron Rd. 30 P28
Cameron FS Rd. 24 F-G44
Cameron Lake Rd. (Central Kootenay) 70 S61
Cameron Lake Rd. (Central Okanagan) 80 U54
Cameron Main Rd. 76 Y36
Cameron Ridge Mining Rd. 45 D50
Camozzi Rd. 70 O60
Camp Rd. 27 P51
Camp 2 Rd. 56 K52-53
Camp Creek Rd. 35 Z43 36 Z44
Camp River Rd. 78 Y46-47
Campbell Rd. (Columbia-Shuswap) 59 N65-66
Campbell Rd. (Fraser Valley) 78 Z45-46
Campbell Rd. (Moricetown) 30 Q28
Campbell Rd. (North Okanagan) 69 S59
Campbell Rd. (Peace River) 26 N46
Campbell Rd. (Uncha Lake) 33 X33
Campbell Way 26 N47
Campbell Creek Rd. 68 Q52-53
Campbell Creek FS Rd. 81 W56
Campbell Meadows Rd. 68 Q53
Campbell Range Rd. 68 Q53
Campeau Creek FS Rd. 55 M49
Camper Mainline Rd. 86 B36-37
Campground Rd. 51 H35
Canada St. 77 Y42-43
Canal Rd. 87 B41
Canal Main Rd. 75 Y35
Candle Creek Rd. 56 K54
Canhun Brassey Rd. 27 N49-50 O49-50
Canhun Sundown Rd. 27 O49-50
Canim Lake Rd. 55 K48-50
Canim Lake South Rd. (8100 Rd.) 55 J-K50
Canimred Creek FS Rd. 55 J51
Canoe Rd. 54 K44
Canoe Beach Rd. 69 P56-57
Canoe Creek Rd. 54 M45-46
Canoe Mainline Rd. 76 V37
Canoe Mountain FS Rd. 47 D-E57
Canoe Point Rd. 69 P57
Canoe West FS Rd. 47 D57 E57-58
Cantelon-Yola FS Rd. 79 Y48
Cantlon Rd. 79 U51
Canyon Dr. 24 L45
Canyon Rd. (200 Rd.) 43 B43 44 B44
Canyon Rd. (Kootenay Boundary) 81 Z57
Canyon-Lister Rd. 83 Z67
Canyon Creek Rd. (Columbia-Shuswap) 59 N65
Canyon Creek Rd. (North Okanagan) 69 R57
Canyon Creek FS Rd. 30 S29 31 S30
Canyon Creek FS Rd. 83 V66
Canyon Cutoff Rd. 85 Y72
Canyon Falls FS Rd. 72 R70
Canyon Lakes FS Rd. 81 V56
Canyon Mainline FS Rd. 29 P22
Cape Mudge Rd. 63 T34
Capilano Rd. 77 X42
Carbon Creek FS Rd. 26 M43
Cargill-Herrick FS Rd. 36 V47
Cariboo Dr. 55 K48
Cariboo Hwy. 35 A43 36 A44 44 G45
Cariboo Lake Rd. 45 D48
Cariboo Main Rd. 75 U33-34
Cariboo Mountain FS Rd. 56 L55 57 L56
Cariboo River Rd. 44 E47 45 D48 E48
Cariboo River FS Rd. 45 D48-50
Cariboo River North FS Rd. 45 D48-49
Caribou Rd. 57 L59 58 L60
Caribou Creek Rd. 82 U61-62
Caribou FS Rd. 51 H35
Caribou Lakes Rd. 70 S-T61
Caribou Pass Rd. 70 S61
Carling Rd. 27 N51
Carlson Rd. 36 X44
Carlson Point Rd. 76 W39
Carmanah A Rd. 86 A36
Carmanah Main Rd. 86 A36
Carmen Hill Rd. 34 X39
Carmi Ave. 80 W55
Carmi Rd. 81 W-X56
Carmi Creek FS Rd. 81 X56
Carnaby Rd. 30 P27
Carolina Creek FS Rd. 83 Z65
Caron Creek FS Rd. 26 O46
Carpenter Rd. 33 X33
Carpenter Creek FS Rd. 83 U64
Carpenter Lake Rd. 65 P43 66 P44
Carr Rd. 47 C56
Carr's Landing Rd. 69 T56
Carrier FS Rd. 32 V30
Carrington Bay Rd. 63 T35
Carroll Rd. 32 X31
Carroll Creek FS Rd. 83 Z67 84 Z68
Carson Rd. 81 Z59
Carson Ranch Rd. 66 O-P47
Carter Rd. 25 G48
Carter St. 24 L46
Cascade Ave. 85 Y72
Cascade Creek Main FS Rd. 71 S64
Casino Rd. 82 Z62
Castle Creek FS Rd. 45 B51 46 B52
Catermole Main Rd. 79 V-W48
Catermole North Main FS Rd. 79 V48-49
Catt Point Rd. 29 U24
Cattle Valley Rd. 67 P48
Causqua Creek FS Rd. 30 Q28
Cave Rd. 44 G47
Caven Rd. 27 N48
Caven-Gold Creek FS Rd. 84 Y71
Caven Creek Rd. 84 Y71
Caven Creek FS Rd. 84 Y71 85 Y72
Caven Creek FS Rd. 84 Y71 85 Y72
Caverly Rd. 54 K47
Caycoosh Creek-Highlead FS Rd. 66 R46
Caycuse-Gordon River Hookup 86 A37
Caycuse Main Rd. (Cowichan Valley) 86 A36-37
Caycuse Main Rd. (Mount Waddington) 61 R26
Cayeghle Main Rd. 61 R-S26
Cayenne Creek FS Rd. 57 M57
Cayoosh-Joffre Rd. 66 S44
CC 600 Rd. 62 S31
Cecil Lake Rd. 25 J50-52 K49-50
Cedar Blvd. 79 Y49
Cedar Rd. 76 Z39
Cedar St 78 Y45
Cedar Creek Rd. (Cariboo) 44 E47 45 E48
Cedar Creek Rd. (Comox-Strathcona) 75 U33
Cedar Creek Rd. (Okanagan-Similkameen) 79 W51
Cedar Creek FS Rd. (Central Kootenay) 83 V65
Cedar Creek FS Rd. (Thompson-Nicola) 68 O54
Cedar Creek Mainline Rd. 87 C38-39
Cedar Hill Rd. (Central Kootenay) 83 Z66
Cedar Hill Rd. (Columbia-Shuswap) 68 R55 69 R56
Cedar River Rd. 29 R23
Cedarside Rd. 47 D57
Cedarvale Rd. 29 Q25
Cedarvale-Kitwanga Rd. 29 Q25
Cedarvale Back Rd. 29 Q25 30 Q26
Ceeg Rd. 59 N65
Celista-Camp Creek FS Rd. 57 M57-58
Celista-Humamilt FS Rd. 57 M57
Celista-Seymour Rd. 57 N58
Centennial Rd. 26 M46
Centennial Park Rd. 25 J48-49
Central Rd. 76 W36
Central (High) Rd. 76 V37
Central North Rd. 86 A35
Central South Main Rd. 86 A35
Centre Creek Rd. 79 Z48
Centre Nash Y FS Rd. 30 P26
Cerantes Rd. 86 C37
CH200 Rd. 61 Q26
Chain Lake Rd. 80 V52
Chamberlain Rd. 35 W42
Chamberlaine Rd. 69 R56
Chamiss Rd. 61 T26
Chamiss Bay Rd. 61 T26-27
Champion Creek FS Rd. 82 Y62
Champion Park Rd. 82 Y62-63
Chance Creek FS Rd. 77 U41-42
Channel Rd. (Central Kootenay) 83 Y66
Channel Rd. (Fraser-Fort George) 46 B55
Chantslar Main Rd. 42 G38 52 H38
Chapman Rd. 31 R30-31
Chapman Rd. (Bulkley-Nechako) 30 S29
Chapman FS Rd. 31 R-S30 S-T31
Chappell Creek FS Rd. 47 F57
Char Creek FS Rd. 83 Z65
Charcoal Creek-Fly Hills FS Rd. 68 Q55 69 Q56
Charles Rd. 70 T62
Charleson Rd. 69 O57
Charleson Creek Rd. 43 B42
Charlies Rd. 27 O51
Charlot Main Rd. 61 Q27 62 Q28
Charlotte Lake Rd. 41 G34
Charolaise Rd. 69 T56
Chartrand Creek FS Rd. 67 R50-51
Chase Rd. (Central Okanagan) 69 T56
Chase Rd. (Columbia-Shuswap) 57 K59
Chase-Falkland Rd. 68 P-R55
Chase Bridge Rd. 68 P55
Chase Creek FS Rd. 68 Q55
Chasm Rd. 54 N47 55 N48
Chasm Rd. 55 N48-49
Chataway Lakes Rd. 67 R-S50
Chaumox Rd. 79 U48
Cheakamus Lake Rd. 65 T42
Cheakamus West FS Rd. 65 T42 77 U42
Cheekye River FS Rd. 77 U-V42
Chehalis Rd. 78 X46 Y46
Chehalis-Mystery Creek FS Rd. 78 W-X46
Chehalis FS Rd. 78 W-X46
Chemainus Rd. 76 Z39 77 Z40
Chemainus River Rd. 87 A38-39
Cheramy Rd. 36 W44
Cherry Ave. 25 K50
Cherry Lake Main Rd. 84 Y70
Cherry Point Rd. 87 B40
Cheslaslie Main FS Rd. 33 Z33
Cheslatta Rd. 33 X-Y33
Chetwynd Paper Mill Rd. 27 N48
Chezakut Rd. 42 F38-39 43 G40 53 H40
Chidley Rd. 80 V55
Chief Nallis Mainline Rd. 50 M-N28
Chilako FS Rd. 35 Y42
Chilako River FS Rd. 34 Z39 35 Z40
Chilanko Station Rd. 35 X42
Chilcotin-Bella Coola Hwy. 52 J36
Chilcotin-Meldrum FS Rd. 44 G45 54 H45
Chilhil Reserve Rd. 66 Q47
Chilko-Newton Rd. 52 J-K39 K-L38 53 H-J40
Chilko Lake Rd. 52 K-L38
Chilko Lake Access Rd. 52 K38
Chilliwack Bench FS Rd. 78 Z47
Chilliwack FS Rd. 79 Z48
Chilliwack Lake Rd. 78 Z46-47 79 Z48
Chimdemash Creek FS Rd. 29 S24-25
Chimney Lake Rd. 54 H45-46 J46-47
Chimney Lake FS Rd. 54 K-L46
Chimney Valley Rd. 54 H45
China Creek Rd. 76 Y36
China Creek Rd. 79 W51
China Head Mountain FS Rd. 54 N44-45
China Lake Rd. 81 W57
China Nose Rd. 31 U31
China Valley Rd. 68 Q55 69 P56 Q56
Chip Dump Rd. 44 C45
Chipka Road FS Rd. 84 X70
Chipman Rd. 52 H38
Chipmunk Creek FS Rd. 78 Y-Z47
Chippewa Main Rd. 64 T36-37
Chisholm FS Rd. 32 V28-29
Chist Creek FS Rd. 29 U24
Choelquoit Lake Rd. 52 K38
Chopaka Rd. 80 Z54
Chowsunket Rd. 33 W36
Christensen Rd. (Dean River Rd) 41 F34
Christian Valley Rd. 81 V58 W-Y58
Christie Rd. (Cariboo) 53 H41
Christie Creek Rd. 68 T55
Chubb Lake Rd. 35 A43 36 A44
Chuck Creek FS Rd. 56 L55
Church FS Rd. 36 V-W46
Churn Creek FS Rd. (2800 Rd.) 53 L43 M43 54 L44 M44
Chute Lake Rd. 80 V-W55
Chuwhels Mountain Rd. 67 R51
Cicero Creek FS Rd. 68 O54
Cinder Hill FS Rd. 67 Q-R49
Cinquefoil Creek Rd. 66 Q-R47
Circle A Rd. 53 K42
Claim Pit Rd. 82 Y61
Clanninick Creek Main Rd. 61 T26
Clark Ave. 25 J49-50
Clark Dr. (Peace River) 26 M47
Clark Rd. 82 X61
Clark Rd. (Bulkley-Nechako) 33 Y33
Clark Creek Rd. 69 T56
Clark FS Rd. 67 S51
Clarkson Av 75 U34
Clarkson Rd. 35 A42
Clarkston Rd. 82 Z60
Clarricoates Rd. 84 V69
Clary Rd. 26 N47
Classen Ave. 25 F48
Claud Elliott Lake Rd. 62 S29
Clayhurst Rd. 25 K51 K51-52
Claymine Rd. 44 C44
Clayoquot Arm Rd. 75 Y-Z33
Clayton Falls FS Rd. 40 F-G29
Clear Creek Rd. 78 V-W47
Clear Creek FS Rd. 29 R23
Clear Lake Sawmill Rd. 77 Y42
Clear River Rd. 29 R23
Clearview Dr. 33 V33
Clearwater Creek FS Rd. 83 X64
Clearwater River Rd. 56 J52-53 K53
Clearwater Valley Rd. 56 J-K53
Clearwater Village Rd. 56 K53-54
Clemina FS Rd. 47 E57-58
Cliff Rd. 36 Z44
Cliff FS Rd. 82 Y61
Clifton Rd. 81 U56
Clinton-Enright FS Rd. 55 N49
Clinton-Joe Ross Creek FS Rd. 55 N50
Clinton-Loon Lake FS Rd. 55 N48
Clinton-Upper Loon Lake Rd. (3300 Rd.) 55 N49-50
Clinton Creek FS Rd. 54 N47
Clisbako Mouth FS Rd. 43 D40
Clough Rd. 56 N52 68 O52
Clouston Rd. 44 B44
Clover Rd. 65 S43
Clover Main Rd. 64 T37
Clowhom Lake Rd. 77 V40-41
Club Rd. 62 T30
Clubine Mine Rd. 83 Y64
Cluculz Hill Rd. 35 X40-41
Cluske River-Thunder Mountain FS Rd. 42 E38
Clusko-Aneko FS Rd. 42 E39 F39 43 F40
Clusko-Chevy FS Rd. 43 E-F40
Clusko-Tzazati FS Rd. 43 F40
Clusko River-Alexis Mountain FS Rd. 43 G40
Clusko River-Aneko FS Rd. 43 G41
Clusko River Bayliff Lake FS Rd. 43 G41
Clusko River-Brown Creek FS Rd. 43 F40
Clusko River-Thunder Mountain FS Rd. 42 F38
Cluskus River-Bayliff Creek FS Rd. 43 G41
Cluskus River-Engelbert North FS Rd. 43 G41
Coal-Leach FS Rd. 85 W73
Coal Creek Rd. 85 W72
Coal Creek Pass FS Rd. 85 W72-73
Coal Harbour Rd. 61 P-Q26
Coal Mine Rd. 30 T29
Coalmine FS Rd. 36 X45 Y45-46
Coalmont Rd. 79 V51 V-W50 W-X51
Cobb Lake Rd. 35 X40
Cobble Hill Rd. 87 B40
Cober Rd. 68 Q55
Cochrane Rd. 76 X36
Cockell Rd. 84 W70
Cocks Rd. 30 T29
Coffee Creek FS Rd. 83 V64-65
Coffee East FS Rd. 55 H49
Coffee Lake Rd. 55 H49
Coffee West FS Rd. 55 H49
Cogburn Creek FS Rd. 78 W47
Coglistiko Rd. 42 C39 43 C40
Cokato Rd. 85 X72
Cold Creek Rd. 68 P52
Cold Creek FS Rd. 84 Z68-69
Coldstream Creek Rd. 27 N49-50 O49
Coldstream Creek Rd. 69 S56-57
Coldwater Rd. 67 T50 79 U-V50
Cole Ave. 25 F48
Colebank Rd. 36 Z44
Coleman Rd. (Alberni-Clayoquot) 75 X-Y35
Coleman Rd. (Bates Beach) 75 V35
Coleman Rd. (Central Kootenay) 83 V65
Coleman Rd. (Franklin Camp) 75 Z35 76 Z36
College Creek FS Rd. 82 Y62
Colleymount Rd. 32 W31 W32 33 W33
Colonial Main Rd. 61 R-S26
Colony Rd. 84 W-X70
Colpitt Lake Rd. 54 H-J45
Columbia Ave. 82 X-Y62
Columbia Gdns. 82 Z62-63
Columbia Rd. (Central Kootenay) 82 Y62
Columbia Rd. (East Kootenay) 72 Q68
Columbia Lake Rd. 72 S69
Columbia River Rd. (Fairmont Hot Springs) 72 S69
Columbia River Rd. (Kimberley) 84 V69
Columbia Valley Rd. 78 Z46
Columbia West FS Rd. 58 L63
Columere Rd. 72 S69
Colvalli Rd. 84 X71
Colwell Rd. 51 J35
Comeau Rd. 30 P-Q27
Commerce FS Rd. 85 Y74
Commonage Rd. 69 S-T56
Community Lake FS Rd. 68 O53
Como Rd. 81 Z59
Como Lake Ave. 77 Y43
Comox Rd. 75 V35
Comox Tr. 75 X35
Comox Lake Rd. 75 W34-35
Comox Lake Main Rd. 75 W34
Comox Valley Pkwy. 75 V-W35
Compton Creek Main Rd. 62 S30-31
Comstock Rd. 79 U50
Condensory Rd. 75 V35
Confederation Lake Rd. 76 U37
Conkle-Ripperto Creek FS Rd. 81 Y57
Conkle Johnstone Creek FS Rd. 81 Y-Z57
Conkle Lake Rd. 81 Y56-57
Conkle Spur Z FS Rd. 81 Y57
Conquest Ranch Rd. 79 V51
Conrad Lake Rd. 31 U32
Conroy Creek FS Rd. 77 U42
Consinka Mainline Rd. 86 A35
Conuma Mainline Rd. 74 U30
Cook Cr. Rd. 76 X36
Cook Rd. 34 V38
Cook Creek FS Rd. 75 X35 76 X36
Cooke-Grassy FS Rd. 69 Q58
Cooper Creek Rd. 71 S-T65
Coopman Rd. 84 W70
Copeland Mine Rd. 69 P59 70 P60
Copper Canyon Mainline Rd. 87 A39
Copper Creek Rd. (Columbia-Shuswap) 59 L64
Copper Creek Rd. (Thompson-Nicola) 67 P50
Copper Mountain Rd. 80 X52
Copper Mountain FS Rd. 82 X63
Copper River Rd. 29 T24
Copper River FS Rd. 29 T24-25
Copperkettle FS Rd. 81 V58 W57-58
Coppermine Rd. 58 L60
Coquihalla Hwy. 67 R51 T50-51 79 W49-50
Coquihalla Pass 79 W50
Corbin Rd. 85 W73
Corcan Rd. 76 X36
Cordero Mainline Rd. 63 R33
Cordova Bay Rd. 87 C41
Core Lodge Rd. 27 R49
Corkscrew Rd. 34 X38-39
Corkscrew Creek Rd. 34 X38
Corn Creek Rd. 83 Z66
Cornie St. 25 F49
Cornwall Rd. 67 Q48
Cornwall Creek FS Rd. 67 P48
Cornwall Hills Lookout Rd. 67 Q48
Coral Rd. 56 J53
Corrigan Rd. 76 Z36
Corvin Rd. 41 G34
Cory Rd. 83 Y66
Coseka Rd. 27 R50-51
Cosens Bay Rd. 69 S56-57 T56
Cotton Rd. 54 J44
Cotton Creek FS Rd. 84 X69
Cottonwood Main Rd. (Tsuius Creek Rd.) 69 Q59
Cottonwood Mainline Rd. 86 A37 87 A38
Coubeaux Rd. 69 P56
Cougar Rd. 77 Y43
Cougar Bay Rd. 45 F48
Cougar Creek Rd. 74 V29-30
Cougar Main Rd. 61 O26-27
Couldrey FS Rd. 85 Z74
Coulee Rd. 80 Z55
Coulson Rd. 24 L45
Coulthard Rd. 44 G44
County Ln. 78 Y-Z44

Courtenay Brown Rd. 81 Z56
Courtney Rd. 25 H49
Courval Rd. 35 Y43 36 Y44
Cous Creek Rd. 75 Y35
Cowichan Bay Rd. 87 B40
Cowichan Lake Rd. 87 A39
Cowichan Valley Rd. 87 A38-39
Cowie Creek Rd. 26 047 27 048
Cowley Rd. 75 Y35 76 Y36
Cox Ave. 25 J49
Coyote Creek FS Rd. 29 Q-R25
CP113 Rd. 32 W30
Craft Creek Rd. 61 R27
Cragg Mainline Rd. 87 C39
Craig Ave. 25 K50
Craig Rd. 76 U36
Craigellachie-Ansley FS Rd. 57 N58
Craker Rd. 31 U30-31
Cranberry La. 75 U34
Cranberry St. 76 U37
Cranberry FS Rd. 70 Q61
Cranberry Lake Rd. 47 D57
Cranbrook Hill Rd. 35 X43
Crater Mountain FS Rd. 80 Y53
Crawfish Lake Rd. 74 V28
Crawford Rd. 81 V56
Crawford 1 Rd. 63 R33
Crawford Creek FS Rd. 83 V65-66
Crazy Creek FS Rd. 36 A47
Crazy Creek FS Rd. 69 058
Crazy Lake FS Rd. 44 G46-47
Creighton Valley Rd. 69 S58-59
Crescent St. 29 T24
Crescent Bay Rd. 76 V36
Crescent Lake Rd. 63 T33
Crestbrook Main FS Rd. 71 066
Creston Wildlife Rd. 83 Y66
Cribs Creek FS Rd. 86 B36
Criss Creek-Violette Rd. 55 N50 67 050
Criss Creek FS Rd. 67 0-P50
Crofton Rd. 87 A40
Croman Rd. 62 S30
Cronin Creek FS Rd. 31 R30
Crooked Creek Rd. 47 D56-57
Crooked Lake Rd. 45 G50
Crosley Rd. 76 X36
Cross Creek Rd. 31 T-U33
Cross River FS Rd. 72 Q69
Crouse Creek FS Rd. 81 X57-58
Crowsnest Hwy. 79 Y-Z50 80 X53
Crowston Lake FS Rd. 76 W39
Crowther Rd. 76 U36
Crusader Flats Loop 82 V63
Crystal Creek Rd. 81 X57
Culling Rd. 69 R56
Cumberland Rd. 75 V-W35
Cummings Rd. 35 X43 36 X44
Cummings Creek FS Rd. 85 V72
Cunningham Rd. 55 M48
Cunningham-Babcock FS Rd. 45 B-C48
Cunningham-Leastway FS Rd. 45 C48
Cunningham-Nolaka FS Rd. 45 C48
Cunningham Pass FS Rd. 45 C49
Cupola Creek Rd. 58 L63
Curley 1 Rd. 63 Q33-34
Currie Creek FS Rd. 69 S59 70 S60
Curtis Rd. 26 N47
Curtis Lake FS Rd. 69 T57
Cusson Creek FS Rd. 70 S60-61
Cut Off Rd. 36 X46
Cute Lake Rd. 80 V55
Cutoff Ave. 25 J50
Cutts Rd. 85 Y72
CW Main Rd. 62 R31 63 Q34-35
Cyperss Creek Rd. 24 F44
Cypre East Main Rd. 74 X31 75 X32
Cypre Main Rd. 74 X-Y31
Cypre West Main Rd. 74 X31 75 X32
Cypress Dr. 69 S56-57
Cypress Bowl Rd. 77 X41-42

D Branch 64 T38
D Rd. 45 G49
D'Angio Rd. 76 U36
D'Arcy Mountain Rd. 80 X52
Daam Rd. 46 B55
Dagleish Creek Rd. 64 T37
Dahl Lake Rd. 35 X41-42
Dahlgren Rd. 33 W-X36
Dairy Rd. 68 P52
Dakota Creek Rd. 77 W-X40
Dale Creek FS Rd. 81 V-W57
Dale Lake Rd. 44 D44
Dallas Dr. 68 Q53
Dallas Rd. 87 D41
Dalrymple Creek FS Rd. 63 S32
Daly Dr. 80 Y54
Dam Rd. 34 X38
Damms Rd. 35 Y43
Dangerous Goods Bypass Rte. 27 N51
Daniels Mainline Rd. 64 S37
Danylon Main Rd. 75 Z35
Darby-Averil FS Rd. 36 V44
Darling Mainline Rd. 86 B35
Darlington Creek FS Rd. 55 M51 56 M52
Dart Mainline Rd. 74 U-V29
Datoff Rd. 44 C-D44
Davie Rd. 62 S30
Davie Bay Rd. 76 W37
Davies Rd. (Columbia-Shuswap) 69 P56
Davis Rd. 85 Z72
Davis Rd. (Alexandria) 44 E44
Davis Rd. (Quesnel) 43 C43
Davis Lake Rd. 55 L48
Dawe Dr. 69 S-T57
Dawson Rd. (Cariboo) 55 K48
Day Lake Rd. 31 U31
Dayeezcha FS Rd. 33 X33
Dayton Rd. 35 Y43
Deadeye Creek FS Rd. 81 X59 82 X60
Deadman-Cache Creek Rd. 67 P49
Deadman-Vidette Rd. 67 0-P50
Deadman Creek Rd. 67 P50
Deadman River Rd. 55 N50
Deadman Valley-Vidette Rd. 55 N50 67 050
Deadwood Rd. 81 Z58
Deafies Creek FS Rd. 69 S57
Deafy Creek Rd. 36 V47
Dean River Rd. 41 E34
Dear FS Rd. 81 W-X58
Debbie Lake FS Rd. 79 V49
Deception Lake FS Rd. 31 S30
Decker Rd. (Quesnel) 44 D45
Decker Creek Rd. 31 U33 33 V33
Dee Lake Rd. 69 T56-57
Deeder Rd. 33 W33
Deep Creek Rd. 69 Q56-57 R56
Deepwater Main FS Rd. 63 S-T34
Deer Dr. 67 Q51
Deer Bay Main Rd. 75 Y32-33
Deer Creek FS Rd. 82 X61
Deer Park Rd. 82 X61-62
Deerhorn Rd. 33 Z34
Deering Rd. 44 D44
Deering Rd. 86 C37
Deescius FS Rd. 31 R33
Degner Rd. 35 X42
Del Rio Rd. 25 L48
Del Rio Pit Rd. 24 L47
Deleeuw Rd. 68 Q52
Delphine Rd. 71 R67
Deltaport Way 77 Z42
Dempsey Lake Rd. 55 J48-49
Denison Main FS Rd. 30 P28-29
Denman Rd. 75 W35 76 W36
Dennis South FS Rd. 30 S27-28
Dennis West FS Rd. 30 S27
Denny Ridge Rd. 62 S28
Departure Bay Rd. 76 Y38-39
Depot Cr. Rd. 79 Z48
Derenzy FS Rd. 80 X55 81 X56
Derksen Rd. 34 W39
Derosa Rd. 82 Y63
Derosier Rd. 84 X71
Derry Creek FS Rd. 69 P59
Desous Mountain Rd. 54 J45
Despard Rd. 61 026-27
Devil's Garden Rd. 57 L59
Devito Dr. 82 Z62
Dewar Creek FS Rd. 83 V67
Dewdney-Cedarflat Creek FS Rd. 79 X49
Dewdney Creek FS Rd. 79 X49
Dewdney Trunk Rd. 78 Y44-45
Diamond Head Rd. 77 V42
Dibbs Rd. 43 C43 44 C44
Dick Booth FS Rd. 61 P-Q26
Dicken Rd. 85 W72
Dielman Rd. 31 T30
Dillard-Galena FS Rd. 79 V51 80 V52
Dillard-Loon Lake FS Rd. 79 U-V51
Dillard-Siwash FS Rd. 80 V52
Dillard Creek FS Rd. 79 V51 80 V52
Dilworth Rd. 69 P56
Dirt Road FS Rd. 70 Q63
Discovery Rd. 35 W43
Ditch Rd. 44 E-F47
Division Rd. 82 X63
Division Lake Rd. 31 U33
Dixon Rd. 76 V37
Dixon Creek Rd. 56 N53
Dixon Creek FS Rd. 56 N54
Dixon Dam Rd. 69 S57
Dixon Moutain Rd. 56 N53
Doch Rd. 61 P-Q24
Doctor Creek Main FS Rd. 72 T68
Dodge Creek Rd. 83 Z66
Dog Rd. 82 X-Y60
Dog Creek Rd. 34 W37
Dog Creek Rd. (Bulkley-Nechako) 33 Y33-34
Dog Creek Rd. (Cariboo) 54 H-K45 L45-46 M-N47
Dog Creek-Canoe Creek Rd. 54 L45
Dog FS Rd., The 67 S51
Dog Lake Tr. 34 V37-38
Dog Main Rd. 75 Y35
Dogleg Lakes FS Rd. 71 Q67
Dogtooth FS Rd. 59 M64-65
Dogwood St. 75 U34
Doig Rd. (Cariboo) 43 C42
Doig Rd. (Hendrix Lake) 25 H50
Doig Pasture St. 25 H50
Dokie FS Rd. 26 M-N46
Dokkie Subdivision Rd. 26 N46
Doman Rd. 55 L49
Domano Blvd. 35 X43
Dome Creek Cutoff 37 Z48-49
Dome Creek Rd. 37 Y49
Dome Creek-Kidd Rd. 37 Y49
Dominion St. 81 Z58
Dominion Creek FS Rd. 37 Z48
Dominion Creek FS Rd. 47 F57-58
Donald Rd. 34 W39
Donald Rd. 59 L64
Donald FS Rd. 59 M64
Donald Landing Rd. 31 U33
Donis Rd. 25 J48
Dore River Rd. 38 A52
Doreen Lake Rd. 69 T57
Dorney Rd. 71 P67 72 P68
Dorr Rd. 85 Z72
Dorr Beach Rd. 84 Y-Z71
Dorr Cutoff Rd. 85 Y-Z72
Dorr West Rd. 84 Z71 85 Z72
Dorsey Rd. 41 F34-35
Dot Ranch Cutoff Rd. 67 S49
Double T Rd. 55 L50
Douglas Rd. 24 L47
Douglas Creek FS Rd. 68 T52
Douglas Lake Rd. 68 R54 S52-53 T52-53
Doumont Rd. 76 Y38
Dove Creek Rd. 75 V34-35
Dover Rd. (Kitimat-Stikine) 29 T23-24
Dowling Rd. 52 J36
Downes Rd. 78 Z44-45
Downie Rd. 58 M60-61
Downie Creek FS Rd. 58 L60
Downton-Lajoie Lake FS Rd. 65 P42-43
Downton Creek Rd. 66 Q45
Doyle Rd. 75 U34
Dragon Lake Rd. 44 C44
Drake Rd. 27 048
Drew Rd. 24 L45
Drewry Lake Rd. 55 K50
Drewry Lake FS Rd. 55 K49-50
Driftwood Creek Rd. 30 R29
Drinkwater Rd. 67 R48-49
Dropping Lake FS Rd. 68 R52
Droppingwater Creek FS Rd. 67 R51 68 R52
Drury Main Rd. 62 0-P28
Dry Creek Rd. 70 Q61
Duck Hills FS Rd. 68 Q54
Duck Lake Rd. (Central Kootenay) 83 Y66
Duck Lake Rd. (Powell River) 76 V37
Duck Range Rd. 68 Q54
Dude Ranch Rd. 56 K-L54
Duel Lakes Rd. 32 W29
Duffey Lake Rd. 66 R-S45
Duffy Lake Rd. 67 Q51
Duhamel Creek Rd. 83 W64
Dulce Rd. 77 X41
Dunbar St. 77 Y41-42
Duncan Rd. 62 S29
Duncan St. 76 V37
Duncan Bay Main Rd. 75 U-V34
Duncan Lake FS Rd. 71 R-S65
Duncan River FS Rd. 71 P-Q64 S65
Dunkley Rd. 36 A44
Dunlevy Rd. 24 K44
Dunn Lake Rd. 56 K-L53 M52-53
Dunphy Rd. 43 B42
Dunster-Croydon Rd. 46 B55 C55 47 C56
Dunster Station Rd. 46 B55
Durand Creek Rd. 67 Q50
Dure Meadow Rd. 69 S-T57
Durrell Rd. 44 D44
Dusty Lake FS Rd. 41 G35 42 G36
Dutch Creek Rd. 72 S69
Dutton Creek Rd. 80 Y55 81 Y56
Dyck St. 25 F49
Dyers Main Rd. 63 S32

E-1 Rd. 74 U31
E-100 Rd. 65 T41
E-200 Rd. 65 T41
E Branch Rd. 76 U38
Eagan-Bonaparte FS Rd. (3700 Rd.) 55 L-M50
Eagan-Bonaparte Lake Rd. (3700 Rd.) 55 M50
Eagan Lake Rd. (3200 Rd.) 55 L-M50
Eagen Cr. 55 M50
Eager Hill-Fort Steele Rd. 84 W69-70
Eagle Bay Rd. 69 056-57
Eagle Creek Rd. (Bulkley-Nechako) 33 V33
Eagle Creek Rd. (Cariboo) 55 H48 J-K49
Eagle Main Rd. 52 J38
Eaglecliff Rd. 77 X41
Eakin Rd. 76 X36
Eakin Creek Rd. 55 L51 56 L52
Eakin Settlement Rd. 32 X32 33 X33
East Bypass 25 K49
East Rd. (Anmore) 77 Y43
East Rd. (Comox-Strathcona) 74 U31
East Rd. (Denman Island) 76 W36
East Adams Lake FS Rd. 57 M-N56
East Anderson Creek FS Rd. 79 V48-49
East Arrow Creek Rd. 83 Y67
East Barrière Lake FS Rd. 56 M-N55
East Bear Creek FS Rd. 78 X47
East Beaverley Rd. 35 X-Y43
East Branch Main Rd. 62 T31 74 U31
East Canoe River FS Rd. 47 D57-58 E58
East Crooked Lake Rd. 45 G50
East Fork Rd. 81 X58-59
East Fritton Rd. 27 P-Q52
East Horn FS Rd. 78 V46
East Hurley River Rd. 65 Q42-43
East Kid Creek FS Rd. 84 Y68
East Lake Dr. 82 Y-Z60
East Mad FS Rd. 57 K56
East Main Rd. (Alberni-Clayoquot) 75 Z33
East Main Rd. (Mahatta River) 61 R25
East Main Rd. (Mount Waddington) 62 R31
East Main Rd. (Port McNeill) 61 Q27 62 Q28
East Main Rd. (Warner Bay) 61 Q27
East Mosquito Creek FS Rd. 70 S-T61
East Palmerston Creek Rd. 62 R30
East Point Rd. 87 A42
East Sampson Mainline FS Rd. 65 R42
East Sooke Rd. 87 D40
East Thompson Rd. 35 W42
East Trout FS Rd. 71 R64
East Twin Mainline FS Rd. 37 Z51
East Valley Rd. 31 U30
East White Lake Rd. 80 X55
East White River FS Rd. 72 T71
East Wilson Creek Rd. 70 T63
East Young Lake Rd. 55 M49 N49-50
Eastman Ave. 83 V65
Eastside Rd. (North Okanagan) 69 T56
Eastside Rd. (Okanagan-Similkameen) 80 X55
Easy Creek Main Rd. 61 S-T26
Easygoing Creek Main Rd. 80 Z52
Eby St. 29 T24
Echo Field Rd. (East Kootenay) 84 W69
Echo FS Rd. 33 W34
Eckel Rd. 35 W42
Eckerman Rd. 69 056
Eckhardt Ave. 80 W55
Eddy Rd. 38 A52
Eden Main FS Rd. 75 U33-34
Edgar Rd. 69 Q57
Edgewood Cemetary Rd. 82 V60
Edith Lake Rd. 68 Q-R52
Edmund Main Rd. 62 P29
Edmunds Rd. 44 F44
Edna Rd. 35 W42
Edwards Rd. 34 X38
Edwards Rd. 44 D44
Eena Lake Rd. 35 W42
Egan Rd. 29 R23
Egerton Mainline FS Rd. 63 R34-35
Egmont Rd. 76 V39
Ehattesaht Mainline Rd. 74 U28
Eholt-Jewel Lake Rd. 81 Y59
Eichenberger Rd. 31 U30
Eight Mile Rd. 67 S50
Eight Mile Rd. 69 S58-59
Eight Mile Creek FS Rd. 79 X49
Eightmile Creek FS Rd. 81 X59
Eileen Lake Rd. 68 P54
Elaho Mainline Rd. 65 S-T40
Elbow Lake Rd. 45 G50
Elbow Main Rd. 63 0-P32
Eldred River Rd. 64 S-T38
Eli Rd. 31 U32
Elinor Lake Rd. 80 V-W55
Elk Bay FS Rd. 63 S33
Elk Lake FS Rd. 55 N49
Elk Main Rd. 76 Z36
Elk Pass FS Rd. 73 S74
Elk River FS Rd. 73 R-T72
Elk River Main Rd. 75 U32-34
Elk River Timber Rd. 75 V34
Elkhart Rd. 80 U52
Elkhart Lake Rd. 80 U52
Elkin Creek Rd. 52 L39
Elko-Grasmere Rd. 85 Y72
Elliott Rd. 62 S29-30
Ellis Rd. (Fraser-Fort George) 35 X43
Ellis-Carmi FS Rd. 81 W56
Ellis Canyon FS Rd. 80 W55 81 W56
Ellis Creek FS Rd. 81 W56
Elsie Holmes Rd. 83 Y66
Elson Rd. 68 P55 69 P56
Elwyn St. 83 W64
Emerald Dr. 54 J47
Emerald Rd. 83 Z64
Emerald Lake Rd. 72 Q68
Emes Ave. 25 J51
Emil FS Rd. 32 V30
Emory Creek Rd. 79 W-X48
Empire Valley Rd. (2700 Rd.) 54 L-M45
Empire Valley-Big Bar Rd. 54 N45
Encombe Rd. 33 W36
Endako Mine Rd. 33 W35
Endall Rd. 75 V34
Enderby-Grindrod Rd. 69 Q57
Enderby-Mabel Lake Rd. 69 R57-58
Eneas Lake FS Rd. 80 V54
Engen Rd. 34 W38
England Creek FS Rd. 36 X45
Englewood Dr. 62 S29
English Rd. 54 J45
English Bluff Way 77 Z42
Englishman River Rd. 76 Y37
Engman Rd. 30 R28
Enid Rd. 72 R68
Ensign Creek Rd. 59 K66
Ensilwood Rd. 35 W42-43
Enterprise Ave. 29 V23
Enterprise Creek FS Rd. 82 V63 83 V64
Enterprise FS Rd. 54 J-K46
Equity Mine Rd. 31 U30 32 V31
Erbe Rd. 27 M48-49
Erickson Rd. 75 U34
Erickson St. 83 Z66-67
Erie-Ross Spur Rd. 82 Y63
Erie Creek FS Rd. 82 X-Y63
Erlandsen Creek Rd. 29 S23
Ernst Rd. 44 C-D44
Errington Rd. 76 Y37
Escalante Main Rd. 74 W29-30
Esp-Eli Mainline Rd. 74 U28
Esperon Lake FS Rd. 68 T54-55
Estates Rd. 84 Y69
Estella Mine Rd. 84 V70
Etna Creek FS Rd. 84 Y69
Eureka Creek Rd. 70 T60
Eva Main Rd. 49 N26 61 027
Evans Rd. (Columbia-Shuswap) 69 056
Evans Rd. (East Kootenay) 83 Z66
Eve Creek Rd. 62 S29
Eve Lake FS Rd. 67 S51
Evergreen Dr. 55 L48
Evergreen Rd. 24 G-H47
Ewart Creek Rd. 80 Y54
Ewin Creek FS Rd. 73 T73
Exeter Rd. 55 K-L48
Exeter Station Rd. 55 K-L48
Exstew FS Rd. 29 T22
Extension Rd. 76 Z39
Extravagant Mainline Rd. 74 U29

F Rd. 58 K63
Faber Rd. 75 Y35
Face Lake FS Rd. 67 Q51
Fadear Creek FS Rd. 68 054
Fair Harbour Rd. 61 T27 62 T28
Fairleigh Creek Rd. 80 W-X54
Fairview Rd. 80 Y54-55
Fairy Creek Rd. (Comox-Strathcona) 61 S27
Fairy Creek Rd. (East Kootenay) 85 W72
Falkland Rd. 68 R55
Farmers Dr. 81 U56
Farms Rd. (Fraser-Fort George) 35 W43
Farms Rd. (Fraser Valley) 78 Y45
Farnham Rd. 75 V34
Farrel Creek Rd. 84 Y69
Farrell Creek Rd. 24 K-L46
Farstad Way 84 U69
Farwell Canyon Rd. 54 J44
Fassifern Rd. 84 X69
Fawcett Rd. 34 W37-38
Fawn Creek Rd. 55 L49
Fawn Lake Rd. 55 L49
Feist Rd. 25 H49-50
Felker Rd. 54 H46
Fenwick Rd. 84 W70
Fenwick Creek FS Rd. 72 R70
Ferguson Rd. 70 Q63
Ferguson Lake Rd. 32 X31
Fern Rd. 82 W63
Ferndale Ave. 78 Y45
Ferndale Rd. 36 X44
Fernie Ski Hill Rd. 85 X72
Ferret Rd. 82 V60
Ferry Creek FS Rd. 69 T59
Fertilizer Rd. 84 W68-69
Fickle Main Rd. 62 S29
Field Rd. 77 X40
Fife Rd. 82 Z60
Finch Rd. 81 U56
Findlay Creek Rd. 72 T68-69
Findlay FS Rd. 31 T31
Findlay Lake Rd. 29 S23-24
Finlay Rd. 68 053
Finn Creek Pit Rd. 57 J57
Finney Creek FS Rd. 66 P-Q47
Fir Lake FS Rd. 43 G43
Fire Mountain Rd. 29 V23
Fire Mountain FS Rd. 79 V51
Firebox Creek FS Rd. 81 W57
Fisbee Rd. 68 S55 69 S56
Fish Hatchery Rd. 76 X36
Fish Lake Rd. 32 X31
Fish Lake Rd. 80 V-W54
Fish Lake Rd. 81 Y-Z57
Fish Lake FS Rd. 53 L-M40
Fish River Rd. 70 P-Q62
Fishem Lake Rd. 53 N40
Fisher Rd. 30 S29
Fisheries Rd. (Pinkut Creek Rd) 31 U33
Fisherman Creek Rd. 81 Z59
Fisherman Main Rd. 60 P23 61 P24
Fitzpatrick Rd. 84 Y71
Fiva Creek Rd. 81 Y57-58
Five-Seven-Five FS Rd. 69 R57
Flagstone Rd. 84 Z71
Flathead-Border Rd. 85 Z74
Flathead FS Rd. 85 X73 Y-Z74
Flathead Sage FS Rd. 85 Y74-75
Flathead Valley Rd. 85 X73 Y74
Fleet Mainline Rd. 87 B38
Fleetwood FS Rd. 78 X46
Fleming Rd. 31 S-T33
Flemstrom Rd. 59 N65
Fletcher Rd. 27 052
Fletcher Creek FS Rd. 83 V65
Fletcher Lake Rd. 53 K42
Flett Rd. 54 H45
Flint Creek FS Rd. 29 R25
Flood-Hope Rd. 79 X48
Flora Lake Main Rd. 86 A35-36
Florence Lake Rd. 78 X-Y45
Flute FS Rd. 36 V46
Fly Hills-Apalmer Creek FS Rd. 69 P-Q56
Fly Hills FS Rd. 69 Q56
Foam Creek FS Rd. 57 J56-57
Foley Creek FS Rd. 79 Y-Z48
Foot Lake FS Rd. 27 Q51
Foothill Rd. 69 Q56
Foothills Blvd. N. 35 X43
Forbay Mainline Rd. 87 C38-39
Forbes Rd. 54 J47
Forbidden Plateau Rd. 75 V34
Ford Rd. 69 R56-57
Fording Rd. 73 T72-73
Fording Coal Mining Rd. 85 V73
Fording FS Rd. 73 T73
Fording Mine Rd. 85 U73
Foreman Rd. 35 X43
Foresman Rd. 27 M49
Forest Ave. 29 V23-24
Forest Lake Rd. 44 G46
Forestdale Canyon Rd. 31 U32
Forestry Rd. 68 Q54-55
Forestry Rd. 87 A38
Forestry Point Rd. 31 Q30-31
Forglen Rd. 44 F45
Forster Creek FS Rd. 71 Q67
Forsters Landing Rd. 72 Q68
Fort Babine Rd. 31 P30
Fort Steele-Wildhorse Rd. 84 V-W70
Fortune Main Rd. 75 Y32
Forward Bay Mainline Rd. 62 R30
Foster Rd. 84 W69
Foster Point Rd. 77 Z40
Foul Bay Rd. 87 C-D41
Fountain Creek Rd. 66 Q46 Q-R47
Fox Farm Rd. 67 T50-51
Fox Mountain Rd. 54 H45-46
Framstead FS Rd. 37 V49
Frances Creek FS Rd. 71 Q66-67
Francis Peninsula Rd. 76 W38
François Lake Rd. 33 W33 W35
François Lake Rd. 33 W36
Franklin Rd. 35 V-W40
Franklin Main Rd. 51 N33 63 O33
Franklin Mine Rd. 81 X59 82 W60
Franklin River Rd. 75 Z35 76 Y-Z36 Z36
Fraser Rd. (Comox-Strathcona) 75 W35
Fraser Rd. (Fraser-Fort George) 36 X44
Fraser Rd. (Thompson-Nicola) 68 R52
Fraser Way, S. 78 Z45
Fraser Canoe Rd. 54 L-M45
Fraser Flats Rd. 35 W-X43
Fraser Lake Airport Rd. 33 W36
Fraser South Main Rd. 49 N26
Fred Mainline Rd. 62 Q29
Freddie Main Rd. 74 W29
Frederick Rd. 67 P51
Fredo Lake Mainline Rd. 76 U38
Freeman Rd. 44 D44
Freeman Creek FS Rd. 84 Z69
French Rd. 44 D44-45
French Bar Creek FS Rd. 54 N45
French FS Rd. 44 D45
French FS Rd. 57 K59
Frickman Rd. 29 R23
Fridlington Rd. 44 E-F44
Friessen Rd. 34 X39
Frisby FS Rd. 70 060
Frizzi Rd. 54 H45
Front St. 62 Q28
Frontier Rd. 36 A47
Frost Rd. (Fraser Valley) 78 Z46

Fulford-Ganges Rd. 87 A40
Fullerton Rd. 27 N50
Fulmore Lake Mainline Rd. 62 Q31 63 Q32
Fulton Lake FS Rd. 31 R-S31
Furry Creek Rd. 77 W41-42
Fyfe Lake FS Rd. 35 Y43

G-Main Rd. (Squamish-Lillooet) 65 T40
G Main Rd. (Capital RD) 86 C37 87 C38
Gable Creek FS Rd. 81 X59
Gadsby Rd. 84 V69
Gagnon Rd. (Kitimat-Stikine) 29 T23
Gagnon Rd. (Peace River) 26 M47
Gainsberg Rd. 76 X36
Galbraith FS Rd. 84 V71
Gale Lake Rd. 32 X31
Galena School Rd. 71 P67
Galiano Main Rd. 74 V30
Gallagher Lake Rd. 80 Y55
Galleywood Rd. 35 W42-43
Galligan Rd. 69 O57
Galloway FS Rd. 84 X71
Gang Ranch Rd. 54 K44 L44-45
Gannett Lake Rd. 57 L56-57 M56
Ganson Rd. 26 N-O46
Garcia St. 25 G48
Garden Bay Rd. 76 W38-39
Gardi Rd. 67 Q51
Gardner Creek FS Rd. 70 S62
Gardom Lake Rd. 69 Q57
Garland Rd. 69 O56
Garner Rd. (Cariboo) 44 D-E44
Garner Rd. (Central Okanagan) 81 U56
Garner FS Rd. 44 E44
Garnet Creek FS Rd. 78 X47
Garnet Valley Rd. 80 V54-55 W55
Gartrell Rd. 80 W55
Garvin Rd. 44 D45
Gaspard Rd. 53 L42
Gaspard Creek Rd. 53 L43
Gaspard Creek-Dash Creek FS Rd. 53 M-N43
Gaspard Creek-East Churn Creek FS Rd. 53 N43 54 M-N44
Gaspard Creek-Eight FS Rd. 53 L-M43
Gaspard Creek-Twelve FS Rd., Rd 53 L43
Gaspard Lake Rd. 53 L43
Gates Mainline FS Rd. 66 R44
Gauthier Lake Rd. 27 P52
Gavin Rd. 84 Y71
Gavin Lake Rd. (1600 Rd.) 44 F47
Gavin Lake FS Rd. 44 F46-47
Geddes Rd. 36 X44
Gem Hill FS Rd. 82 X-Y61
Genevieve Rd. 44 B44
Genier Lake Rd. 56 N53
Genoa Bay Rd. 87 A40
George Rd. (600 Rd.) 36 Y-Z45
Georgeson Bay Rd. 87 A41
Georgie Lake FS Rd. 61 P25-26
Gerald Creek Main Rd. 62 T31
German Rd. 25 K51
Getzuni Trail Rd. 33 X34
Giant Mine Rd. 71 P67
Giavanno Mainline Rd. 76 U37
Gibbins Rd. 87 A39
Gibbs Creek Rd. 81 Z59
Gibraltar Mine Rd. 44 F45
Gibson Rd. (North Okanagan) 69 S58
Gibson Main Rd. 61 Q-R26
Gibson Pass Rd. 79 Z50
Giesbrecht Rd. 34 W38
Gilbert Rd. 30 R29
Gilbert Rd. 34 W39
Gilford Main Rd. 62 P-Q30
Gilgan Rd. 33 V33
Gilgan St. 86 A37
Gillard Creek FS Rd. 80 V55 81 V56
Gillies Bay Rd. 76 V36-37
Gillis Rd. 79 U50
Gilpin Rd. (Kootenay Boundary) 82 Z60
Gilpin Rd. (Powell River) 64 T36 76 U36
Gilpin-Stewart Rd. 82 Y-Z60
Gimmys Ave. 25 J-K48
Ginuluk Rd. 28 Q21
Giscome Rd. 36 X44
Giscome South Rd. 36 W44-45
Gissmier Ave. 25 K51
Giveout Creek FS Rd. 82 X63 83 X64
Glacier Creek FS Rd. 71 S65-66
Glacier Gulch Rd. 30 R-S28
Glacier North FS Rd. 71 R-S66
Glad 12 Rd. 86 B36
Glad Lake Mainline Rd. 86 B36
Glade Rd. 82 X63
Glassford Rd. 44 D44
Gleason FS Rd. 37 W48-49
Glen Lake FS Rd. 80 V53-54
Glen Meadow Rd. 30 P27
Glen Vowell Rd. 30 P27
Glenannan Rd. 33 W35
Glendale Rd. 63 Q33
Glenmerry Rd. 82 Y61
Glenmore Rd. 81 U56
Glenogle Creek FS Rd. 59 M65
Glenrosa Rd. 80 U55
Gloucester-Franklin Mountain FS Rd. 81 W59 82 W60
Gloucester-Mount McKinley FS Rd. 81 W59
Gloucester-Union Mine FS Rd. 81 W59
Gloucester North FS Rd. 82 W60
Goat-Hall Creek FS Rd. 83 Y67
Goat Anchor Rd. 83 Y67
Goat Creek FS Rd. 29 S23-24
Goat Lake Rd. 1 64 T38 76 U38
Goat Lake Rd. 2 64 T38
Goat Lake Mainline Rd. 76 U-V37
Goat Mountain FS Rd. 81 X57
Goat River Rd. (Fraser-Fort George) 37 Z50-51
Goat River FS Rd. (East Kootenay) 83 X-Y67
Goat River FS Rd. (Fraser-Fort George) 37 Z50
Goatfell-Hazel Creek FS Rd. 84 Y68
Goatskin North FS Rd. 81 V59
Godfrey Rd. 76 Z39
Golata Creek Rd. 25 J50-51 K51-52
Gold Bridge-Bralorne Rd. 65 P43
Gold Creek Rd. 29 T24
Gold Creek Rd. 84 X69-70
Gold Creek Detour Rd. 84 Y70-71
Gold Creek Main Rd. 62 S29
Gold Mountain Rd. 80 X53
Gold Mountain FS Rd. 80 X52-53
Gold River 7 Rd. 74 U31
Gold River FS Rd. 58 L62
Gold Valley Mainline Rd. 62 T28
Golden-Donald Upper Rd. 59 L-M64 M65
Golden Ears Pkwy. 78 Y44
Goldie Rd. 34 W38
Goldstream FS Rd. 57 L59 58 L60
Golf Course Rd. 25 J49
Gollen Creek FS Rd. 56 L55 57 L56
Gonvick Rd. 26 M47
Goodfare Rd. 68 P55 69 P56
Goose Country Rd. 35 W43
Goose Creek Rd. 82 X62
Goose Lake Rd. (North Okanagan) 69 S56
Goose Lake Rd. (Thompson-Nicola) 68 Q52
Gordon Dr. 80 U55
Gordon Rd. 63 T34
Gordon Creek Rd. (Barriere) 56 N53
Gordon Creek Rd. (Lower Nicola) 67 S49-50
Gordon Lakes Rd. 67 S49-50
Gordon River Main Rd. 86 A37 87 A38
Gordon River Mainline Rd. 86 B37
Gorge Harbour Rd. 63 T35
Gorge Mainline Rd. 86 A35
Gorman Lake FS Rd. 56 N52
Gosnell Rd. 47 F57
Gotchen Lake FS Rd. 55 H50
Gotchen Lake West FS Rd. 55 H50
Gott Creek FS Rd. 66 R45
Goudie Rd. 81 U56-57
Goudie FS Rd. 81 U56
Government Rd. 77 V42
Government Lake Rd. 36 Z44
Gowan Creek Rd. 78 U45
Gower Point Rd. 77 X40
Gowlland Harbour Rd. 63 T34
Grafton Ave. 76 X37
Grafton Rd. 77 X41
Graham Rd. 71 O66
Graham-Dunden Rd. 55 M48
Graham River Rd. 24 J44-45
Grainger Rd. 72 T69
Grainger FS Rd. 32 W30
Granary Rd. 83 Z66
Granby Rd. 81 Y-Z59
Granby River Rd. 81 W-X59
Grand Oro Rd. 80 X-Y55
Grandview Bench Rd. 69 Q57
Grandview Flats Rd. 69 R56
Granger Rd. 83 W64
Granisle Connector 31 R31
Granisle Hwy. 31 S31-32 T31
Granite Rd. (Central Kootenay) 82 X63
Granite Rd. (Columbia-Shuswap) 58 L60
Granite Bay Rd. 63 S-T34
Granite Creek Rd. 79 W50-51
Granite Creek FS Rd. 75 U33
Granite Lake Main Rd. 76 U-V37
Granite Main Rd. 86 A36-37
Grano-Hellroarer Rd. 81 W58
Grano Creek FS Rd. 81 W58
Grant Rd. 40 F29
Grant Rd. (Peace River) 27 N-O48
Grant Bay Rd. 61 Q24
Grantham Rd. 30 T29
Granville St. 77 Y42
Grasmere-Dorr Rd. 85 Z72
Grassy Creek FS Rd. 82 Y63
Grassy Point Rd. 28 Q19
Gravel Creek Rd. 44 G47
Gravel Pit Rd. 82 V63
Graves Rd. 35 X43 36 X44
Gray Rd. 36 X47
Gray-Chapman Crossover Rd. 76 W39 77 W40
Gray Creek Rd. 77 W40
Gray Creek Pass FS Rd. 83 W66
Gray Lake Rd. 63 T33
Graystokes Rd. 81 U57-58
Greasybill Creek Rd. 82 W61
Great Central Lake Rd. 75 X35
Great Central Lake Main Rd. 75 X34
Greeley Rd. 70 O61
Green Rd. (Canal Flats) 72 T69
Green Rd. (East Kootenay) 84 Z71
Green Rd. (Kootenay Boundary) 82 Z63
Green Lake Rd. (Okanagan-Similkameen) 80 X-Y55
Green Lake Rd. (Thompson-Nicola) 55 M48
Green Lake-70 Mile West FS Rd. 55 M-N48
Green Lake-Jim Lake South FS Rd. 55 M49
Green Lake-Nolan Lake FS Rd. 55 M49
Green Lake FS Rd. 55 M49
Green Mountain Rd. 80 W55 X54
Green Ranch Rd. 79 U-V48
Green River FS Rd. 28 U19
Green River FS Rd. 65 S43 66 S44
Greenstone Rd. 67 Q51
Greenstone Mountain Rd. 67 Q51
Greenwood FS Rd. 72 P-Q68
Greer Rd. 56 K53-54
Greer Valley Rd. 34 X38
Gregg Creek FS Rd. 35 Y41-42 Z41
Gregson Rd. 58 M60
Grevatt Rd. 43 C42
Grey Rock Rd. 65 P43
Greyback FS Rd. 80 W55 81 W56
Greystokes FS Rd. 81 U57
Greywall Dr. 71 R67
Grice Bay Rd. 75 Z32
Grierson Mainline Rd. 86 B36-37
Griffin FS Rd. 69 O58-59
Grilse Creek Mainline Rd. 63 T32
Grindrod-Salmon Arm Hwy. 69 Q57
Grindrod Westside Rd. 69 Q57
Grizzly Lake Rd. 35 Z40
Grohman Creek Rd. 82 W63
Groundbirch FS Rd. 27 N48
Groundhog Creek Rd. 53 L41
Grouse Rd. 44 G45
Grouse FS Rd. 81 U57
Grouse Mountain FS Rd. 84 Z68
Groveburn Rd. 36 X44
Grundall Rd. 36 Z44
Grundpark Rd. 34 W39
Grundy Rd. 24 F-G45
Guest Rd. 35 X40
Guichon Creek FS Rd. 67 Q50
Gulliford Rd. 79 V51
Gun Creek Rd. 65 P43
Gun Lake Rd. 65 P43
Gundy Rd. 27 N-O52
Gundy Creek Rd. 24 G45
Gunnar Creek FS Rd. 81 U58
Gunner Main Rd. 75 Y32
Gunpowder Rd. 74 V28-29
Gushwa Rd. 31 U30
Gustafsen-Dog Creek Rd. 54 L46-47
Gustafsen-Edmund Lake FS Rd. 55 L48
Gustafsen-North FS Rd. 55 K48
Gustafsen East FS Rd. 54 L-M47
Gustafsen Lake FS Rd. (1000 Rd.) 54 L47
Gustafsen South FS Rd. 54 L47
Guthrie Rd. 75 V35
Guyishton Lake FS Rd. 33 V33
Gwenie Lake East Spur 55 L49

H Rd. 43 D41
Ha Ha Creek Rd. 84 X70
Ha Ha Creek FS Rd. 84 X70
Haaglund Rd. 82 Z60
Haagsman Rd. 24 K45
Haddo Rd. 69 T57
Hadenschild FS Rd. 29 Q22-23
Hadlow Rd. 68 P-Q54
Hadow Creek FS Rd. 70 P62
Hagan Main FS Rd. 31 Q-R32
Haggart Rd. 81 U58
Haggens Point Rd. 45 F48-49
Haggsttrom Rd. 35 X40
Hahn Rd. 83 Y67
Haisla Blvd. 29 V23
Halcyon Hot Springs Rd. 70 R61
Hale-Vinnie Rd. 68 P-Q53
Hale Creek FS Rd. 78 X46
Halfmoon Carlson FS Rd. 76 W39
Halfway Rd. 70 Q63
Halfway-Graham FS Rd. 24 H43-44
Halfway River FS Rd. 70 R62
Hall Rd. (Kootenay Boundary) 83 X66
Hall Creek FS Rd. 82 X63 83 X64
Hall Creek FS Rd. 83 Y67
Hallam Rd. 69 R56
Halliwell Ave. 29 T23-24
Hallowell FS Rd. 76 V-W39
Halston Ave. 68 Q52
Hamblin Main FS Rd. 30 P28-29
Hamm Rd. 75 U34
Hammer Rd. 40 F30-31
Hammer Lake Rd. 55 N50
Hammond Bay Rd. 76 Y38-39
Hammond Mainline Rd. 62 T28 74 U28
Hamre Rd. 33 W33
Hanceville-Canoe Creek Rd. 53 J42 K42-43
Hanceville Cutoff Rd. 53 J42
Handley Rd. 82 Z63
Hanna Dr. 82 Y62
Hanna Rd. 68 Q54
Hannaford Rd. 25 J-K48
Hannay Rd. 33 V34-35
Hannay Ext. 1 Rd. 33 V35
Hansen Rd. 29 U24
Hanson Rd. 83 Z66
Hanson Lake Rd. 33 V35
Hanson Stake Rd. 33 W35-36
Happy Hollow Rd. 35 W40
Happy Valley Rd. 87 C-D40
Harasymyk Rd. 24 K46
Harbledown Main Rd. 62 Q29
Harbour Hill Mainline Rd. 49 N26
Harbour Lakes FS Rd. 57 L56-57
Harbourview Rd. 87 C-D40
Harder Rd. 25 G48
Hardie Creek Rd. 72 S68-69
Hardman FS Rd. 70 R61
Hardscrabble Rd. 44 B47
Hardwicke BR 100 63 R32
Hardwicke BR 200 63 R32
Hardy Rd. 75 V35
Hardy Bay Rd. 61 P26
Hardy Mountain Rd. 81 Z59
Harewood Mines Rd. 76 Z38-39
Hargreaves Rd. 47 C57
Hargreaves Rd. 76 X39
Harmer Creek Rd. 85 U-V73
Harper Creek FS Rd. 56 L54-55 M54
Harper Lake Rd. 68 P55
Harper Ranch-Pinantan Rd. 68 Q53
Harrington Rd. 43 C41
Harris Rd. (Matsqui) 78 Z45
Harris Rd. (Pitt Meadows) 77 Y43
Harris-Mosquito Creek FS Rd. 69 T58
Harris-Nicklen FS Rd. 69 T57
Harris Creek Rd. (North Okanagan) 69 T58
Harris Creek Main Rd. 86 B37 87 B38
Harrison Rd. 70 T61
Harrison-Lillooet Wagon Rd. (In-Shuck-ch FS Rd.) 78 U-V45
Harrison East-Clear Creek Rd. 78 V-W47
Harrison East-Shovel Creek FS Rd. 78 V46-47
Harrison East FS Rd. 78 W-X47
Harrison Main Rd. 86 A36
Harrison West FS Rd. 78 V-W46 X46-47
Harrop-Procter Rd. 83 W64-65
Harrop Ferry Rd. 83 W64
Hart Rd. 33 W36
Hartley Rd. (Columbia-Shuswap) 59 M65
Hartley Rd. (Fraser Valley) 78 Y45
Hartley Lake Rd. 85 W72
Hartley Pass Rd. 84 V71 85 V72 W72
Hartnell Rd. 69 S57
Harvey Creek Rd. 45 D48
Haslam St. 76 U37
Hasler Rd. 26 N-O46
Hasler Creek FS Rd. 26 O45-46
Hassel Rd. 34 W37-38
Hastings St. 77 Y42
Hat Creek Rd. 66 P-Q47
Hathaway Main Rd. 61 Q25
Hatheume Lake FS Rd. 80 U53
Hatton Mainline Rd. 86 A36-37
Hautete FS Rd. 31 Q32
Hawke Rd. 72 S68
Hawkins-Canuck FS Rd. 84 Z68
Hawkins Creek Rd. 84 Z68
Hawkins Creek FS Rd. 75 U-V33
Hawkins Lake Rd. 55 J49-50
Hawks Creek FS Rd. 44 G46
Haylmore Creek Mainline Rd. 66 R44
Haystack Hill FS Rd. 24 J45
Haywire Bay Rd. 76 U37
Haywood-Farmer Rd. 67 Q50
Hazelton-Kitwanga Back Rd. 30 P26-27 Q26
Head Bay Rd. 74 U29 V30
Heading Creek FS Rd. 31 U30-31
Headquarters Rd. 75 V35
Health Main Rd. 62 P-Q29 Q30
Healy Creek FS Rd. 71 R64
Heather Main Rd. 64 T36-37
Heber Main 30 Rd. 74 U31
Hecht Main Rd. 60 Q23 61 Q24
Heckman Creek FS Rd. 69 T59
Hector Rd. 75 Y35
Heddle Rd. 83 W64
Hedley-Nickel Plate Rd. 80 X53-54
Hedstrom Rd. 83 V-W66
Hefley-Louis Creek Rd. 68 O53
Helen Creek Rd. 61 S27 62 S28
Helena Lake Rd. 54 K47 55 K48
Helene Lake Rd. 33 V35
Helene Lake Rd. Branch/1 33 V35
Heller Creek FS Rd. 67 O50-51
Hellroaring Creek Rd. 82 Y-Z63
Helmcken Rd. 87 C41
Helmcken Falls Rd. 56 J52
Helmer Rd. 67 S51
Hembrie Mountain Rd. 80 V-W52
Hembrie Mountain Rd. 80 W52
Hemlock Rd. 58 L60
Hemlock St. 29 T24
Hemlock Valley Rd. 78 X46
Hemlock Valley FS Rd. 78 X46-47
Hemmingsen Creek Rd. 86 B37
Hen Ingram FS Rd. 45 F49
Henderson Creek Rd. 81 Y58
Henderson Main Rd. 75 Y34 Z34-35
Hendrix-Molybdenite FS Rd. 45 G50 55 H50
Hendrix Lake Rd. 55 H-J50
Henrietta Creek Rd. 33 V35
Henry's Crossing Rd. 52 K38
Henson Hills Rd. 33 Y33
Hepburn Rd. 68 P55
Hepher Rd. 83 X65-66
Herbert Rd. 69 T56
Herbert Main Rd. 74 X31
Herd Rd. 87 A40
Heriot Bay Rd. 63 T34
Heritage Hwy. 27 P51-52 R49 R51
Hern Rd. 63 S32
Herrick Rd. 78 W47
Herrick FS Rd. 36 V47 37 V48-49
Hewatt Mine FS Rd. 82 U63
Hewitt Rd. 72 Q68
Heymyer Rd. 34 X39
Heywood-Armstrong Rd. 69 R56
Hicks Creek Rd. (Central Kootenay) 70 T63
Hicks Creek Rd. (Fraser Valley) 79 Y48
Hicks Hill Rd. 33 W34
Hidden Creek FS Rd. 80 U55
Hidden Lake Rd. (Fraser-Fort George) 46 B55
Hidden Lake Rd. (North Okanagan) 69 Q-R58
Hidden Lake FS Rd. 31 T30
Hidden Mountain Rd. 34 W38
Hidden Valley Rd. 54 N46
Hidden Valley Rd. 84 X69
Hiebert Rd. 33 W-X33
Higdon Rd. 44 D44
Higgins Lake Rd. 55 L50
High Bar Rd. 54 N46
Highcountry Rd. 55 L50
Highland Valley Hwy. 67 R49
Highland Valley Rd. 67 P-Q48
Highline Rd. 66 O44-45
Highrise FS Rd. 26 N45
Hihium-Scottie Creek Rd. 67 O49
Hilda Creek Rd. 69 T57
Hill Ave. 84 W69
Hill Rd. (100 Mile House) 55 L48
Hill Rd. (Alexandria) 44 E-F44
Hill Rd. (Cowichan Valley) 87 B40
Hill-Tout Rd. 32 W29
Hill 60 FS Rd. 87 A39
Hill Creek Rd. 70 Q61-62
Hill Lake Rd. 44 D45
Hillbank Rd. 87 B40
Hillcrest Dr. 82 Y62
Hillcrest Rd. 87 A39
Hilliers Rd. S. 76 X37
Hills Upper Rd. 70 T63
Hillside Dr 82 Z62
Hillside Rd. 26 M47
Hilltop Rd. 69 P56
Hillview Dr. 35 W42
Hillview Rd. 26 N46-47
Hinkelman Rd. 38 A52 46 B52
Hiram Creek Rd. 57 K59
Hisnit 1 Rd. 74 V29
Hixon Creek Rd. (Fraser-Fort George) 36 A44
Hixon Creek Rd. (Vancouver) 77 W43
Hobbs Rd. (Peace River) 24 L47
Hobenshield Rd. 30 Q26
Hodda Lake FS Rd. 26 R43
Hoder Creek FS Rd. 82 V62
Hodge Rd. 25 L48
Hodgson Rd. 54 H45
Hodkin Rd. 29 Q25
Hoeya Main Rd. 63 Q32
Hoffa Main Rd. 58 J62
Hog Creek FS Rd. 66 P44
Holberg Rd. 61 P25
Hold Rd. 44 D44
Holding Rd. 68 O55
Holding-Adams Lake West Rd. 68 O55
Holley Rd. 44 D44
Holley Rd. 85 V72
Hollingsworth Rd. 69 S-T59
Hollywood Rd. 81 U56
Holmes Rd. 35 X43
Holmes Rd. (Cariboo) 55 L49
Holmes Rd. (East Kootenay) 84 V-W70
Holmes-Deakin Rd. 59 L65 M64-65
Holmes (Beaver) FS Rd. 38 A55 39 A56
Holtry Creek FS Rd. 41 F35 42 F36 G36
Holy-Cross Binta FS Rd. 33 X35-36 34 X37
Holy-Cross FS Rd. 33 Y36
Holy Cross-Cabin Lake FS Rd. 33 X35
Holy Cross-Coho FS Rd. 33 Y36
Holy Cross FS Rd. 33 W-X36
Holy Cross FS Rd. 37 X49-50
Holy Cross North FS Rd. 33 X35-36
Home Cabin Lake Rd. 55 N51
Homesite Creek FS Rd. 76 W39
Homestead Rd. 35 W43
Homestead FS Rd. 57 K56
Honolulu FS Rd. 43 D40-41
Hooch Lake FS Rd. 41 G35
Hoodikoff Rd. 82 W63
Hoodoo Lake Rd. 35 V-W42
Hook Rd. 54 N47
Hoover Bay Rd. 55 J50
Horn Rd. 34 W37
Horn FS Rd. 36 V46
Horne Rd. 57 H56-57
Horne Lake Rd. 76 X36
Horne Lake FS Rd. 75 X35 76 X36
Hornet Creek Rd. 78 W47
Horse-Fiset FS Rd. 55 K-L49
Horse Creek Rd. 59 N65
Horse Lake Rd. 55 L48-50
Horse Lake-Earle Lake FS Rd. 55 L49
Horsefly Rd. 44 G46 G47 54 H46
Horsefly-Likely Rd. 54 H46
Horsefly-Likely FS Rd. 44 E-F47 45 F48
Horsefly-McKusky FS Rd. 45 G50
Horsefly-Pairie FS Rd. 45 F-G49
Horsefly-Quesnel Lake Rd. 45 F48-49 G48
Horsefly-Woodjam FS Rd. 45 G48
Horsefly Bay Rd. 45 F48
Horsefly Lake Rd. 45 G48
Horsefly Mountain Rd. 45 G48-49
Horseshoe Creek Rd. 24 H43
Horseshoe Lake Rd. 84 W70
Horsethief Creek FS Rd. 71 R66-67
Horsey Creek Rd. 46 B55 47 B56
Hospital Rd. 33 W33
Hospital Cove Rd. 28 U18
Hossack Rd. 31 U32
Hot Springs Rd. (Alberni-Clayoquot) 74 X30
Hot Springs Rd. (Central Kootenay) 70 S62
Hot Springs Rd. (Fraser Valley) 78 Y47
Hotnarko Lake Rd. 41 F33-34
Houde Rd. 26 N-O46
Hough Rd. 59 N65
Houlgrave Rd. 72 R68
Houston Mainline Rd. 74 W30
Howard Rd. (Comox-Strathcona) 75 V34-35
Howard Rd. (Fraser-Fort George) 47 C57
Howard Rd. (Kitimat-Stikine) 29 T23
Howard Lake Rd. 55 J-K50
Howards Rd. 69 T56
Howe Rd. 26 M47
Howell Rd. 84 X70
Howells Rd. 31 T31
Howser Creek FS Rd. 71 Q-R65
Howser Ridge FS Rd. 71 S65
Howser Station Rd. 71 S65
Hoy Mainline Rd. 49 K25
Huband Rd. 69 P56
Huband Rd. 75 V35
Hubbard Rd. 36 W44
Hubert Rd. 30 S29
Hudson Bay Creek Rd. 68 S-T55
Hudson Bay Mountain Rd. 30 S28
Hudu Creek Rd. 82 Y63
Huff Lake Rd. 68 O52
Hugh Allan FS Rd. 47 F59
Hulatt Rd. 35 X40
Hullcar Rd. 69 R56
Hulme Creek Rd. 81 Z57
Humamilt Creek FS Rd. 57 M58 N57-58
Humamilt Lake Rd. 57 M-N57
Humphrey Rd. 37 Y49
Hungary Creek FS Rd. 36 X-Y47
Hungry Hill Way 31 T30
Hunt-Sweder Rd. 35 Z43

Hunter Ave. 24 K46
Hunter-Blurton FS Rd. 69 Q57
Huntingdon Rd. 78 Z44-45
Hurley-Silver Rd. 66 R45
Hurley River FS Rd. 65 P43 Q42-43
Hurt Rd. 69 S57
Huscroft Rd. 83 Z67
Hush Lake Rd. 44 B44
Hushamu Main Rd. 61 P-Q25
Hutchison FS Rd. 55 M49
Hutchison Lake Rd. 55 M48-49
Hutter Rd. 31 U33
Hyacinthe Bay Rd. 63 T34
Hyas Lake FS Rd. 68 P54
Hyde Creek Rd. 62 Q28
Hydraulic Lake FS Rd. 81 V56-57
Hydro Hill Rd. (1300 Rd) 30 T28

I Main Rd. 61 R25
Ideal Lake FS Rd. 69 T57
Iltzul West FS Rd. 30 P28
Imler Rd. 59 N66 71 O66
Imperial Ave. 25 K51
In-shuck-ch FS Rd. 78 U44-45 V45
Incomappleux FS Rd. 70 P62
Incomappleux River Rd. 70 P62
Independent Rd. 27 O52
Indian Rd. (Central Kootenay) 83 Y-Z66
Indian Rd. (Cowichan Valley) 87 B39
Indian Garden Rd. 67 Q50
Indian Lake Rd. 37 A48
Inga Lake Rd. 24 H46-47
Ingram Creek Rd. 68 R55
Ingram Creek FS Rd. 81 Z58
Ingram Mountain Rd. 81 Z58
Ink Lake Mine Rd. 67 Q51
Inkaneep Rd. 80 Z55
Inkwathia Creek Rd. 79 W48
Inland Island Hwy. 76 X36-37
Inland Lake Rd. 76 U37
Inland Lake FS Rd. 76 U37
Inman Rd. 55 L48-49
Inonoaklin Valley Rd. 82 U-V60
Inter-Provincial Hwy. 78 Z46
Ioco Rd. 77 Y43
Irish Creek Rd. 69 R-S56
Irishman Creek FS Rd. 84 Y68
Iron Clad Rd. 81 Z59
Iron Creek Rd. 24 H45
Iron Mountain Rd. (Okanagan-Similkameen) 80 W52
Iron Mountain Rd. (Thompson-Nicola) 67 T50-51
Iron River Rd. 63 T33-34 75 U34
Irvines Landing Rd. 76 W38
Irwin St. 34 W37
Isabella Point Rd. 87 B40-41
Isadore Rd. 54 N47
Isintok-McNulty FS Rd. 80 W54
Isintok Creek Rd. 80 W54
Island Hwy. 87 B40
Island Lake FS Rd. 33 X34-35
Isle Pierre Rd. 35 X41
Isle Pierre-Reid Lake Rd. 35 X41-42
Isnardy Rd. 54 H45
Itlay Creek FS Rd. 82 Z60-61
Iverson Rd. 78 Z46
Ivy Rd. 69 O57
Izman Creek FS Rd. 66 R-S47

J Branch Rd. 76 U38
J Main Rd. 61 R25
J Main-A Rd. 61 R-S27
J2 Ranch Rd. 72 T69
Jack Adams Rd. 47 D57
Jack Pine FS Rd. 80 U55
Jack Swartz Rd. 67 T49
Jackfish Lake Rd. 24 L47 L47 25 L48 26 M47 M-N47
Jacklah Mainline Rd. 74 W31
Jackpine Rd. 54 H47
Jackpine Alley FS Rd. 34 W38-39
Jackpine Creek Rd. 80 U54
Jackson Rd. (Cache Creek) 67 P48
Jackson Rd. (Kamloops) 68 Q-R52
Jackson Lake Rd. 44 F45-46
Jackson Pit Rd. 27 M50
Jacobson Rd. 44 E-F46
Jaeggi Rd. 72 Q68
Jaffray-Baynes Lake Rd. 84 X-Y71
Jake FS Rd. 33 W34
Jame St. 25 F48
James Lake FS Rd. 81 U56
James Mountain-Alix Creek FS Rd. 44 E44-45
James Mountain FS Rd. 44 E44-45
Jamieson Ave. 24 L46
Jamieson Creek-Bonaparte Hills FS Rd. 55 M51 N51 56 N52
Jamieson Creek FS Rd. 55 N51 56 N52 68 P52
Jardine Rd. 35 X40
Jarman Rd. 31 T31
Jeck Rd. 38 A52
Jellicoe Rd. 80 V52
Jenkins Way 52 J37
Jersey Creek FS Rd. 83 Y65
Jesmond Rd. 54 M-N46 66 O46 O46-47
Jewel Lake Rd. 81 Y58-59
Jim Rd. 61 S27
Jim Bailey Rd. 69 T56 81 U56
Jim Brown Main Rd. 64 S37-38
Jim Smith Lake Rd. 84 W-X69
Jimmy Lake Rd. 68 S54
Jingle Pot Rd. 76 Y38-39
Jinx FS Rd. 31 Q-R32 R32
Joes Lake Rd. 54 K45
John A St. 25 F49
John Creek FS Rd. 56 M55
John Hart Hwy. 27 M-N50 35 X43
Johnny David FS Rd. 31 T31
Johnson Rd. (Babine Lake) 31 S33
Johnson Rd. (Cariboo) 44 C-D44
Johnson Rd. (Evelyn) 30 R28
Johnson Rd. (Fraser-Fort George) 35 X43 36 X44
Johnson Rd. (Peace River) 25 K-L50
Johnson Creek Rd. 26 M44-46
Johnson Creek FS Rd. 24 L44 L45 26 M45
Johnson FS Rd. 24 L44
Johnson Lake FS Rd. 56 N55
Johnson Mill Rd. 54 H-J46
Johnston Ave. (Cariboo) 44 C44
Johnston Ave. (Peace River) 25 J49
Johnston Rd. (Cariboo) 55 L50
Johnston Rd. (Central Kootenay) 82 V-W60
Johnstone Rd. 82 W63 83 W64
Johnstone Creek Rd. 81 Y-Z57
Johnstone Creek East Rd. 81 Z57
Jolly Jack Rd. 81 Z58
Jollymore Rd. 30 S29
Jones Rd. 34 W39
Jones Creek FS Rd. (Thompson-Nicola) 56 L55
Jones Lake FS Rd. 78 Y47 79 Y48
Jordan FS Rd. 70 O60
Jordan Mainline Rd. 87 C39
Jorgenson Rd. 35 W43
Josef Rd. (Central Kootenay) 71 O-P67
Josef Rd. (Peace River) 24 K-L44
Joseph Mountain Rd. 84 X69
Joyce Ave. 76 V37
JR Main-D Rd. 87 C38
Jubilee Pkwy. 75 U34
Jubilee Mountain FS Rd. 71 O-P67
Judson Rd. 55 L50
Juliet Creek FS Rd. 79 V49
July Creek FS Rd. 79 V49
Jumbo Creek Rd. 71 S66-67
Junction Rd. 54 K44
June Springs Rd. 81 U-V56
Juniper Rd. 31 T30
Juniper Heights Rd. 72 R68

K, Branch 76 Z37
K Rd. 43 C43
K. L. O. Rd. 80 U55 81 U56
K Creek Main Rd. 62 S31
K400 Rd. 61 Q25
Kaipit Main Rd. 62 S-T28
Kaisner Rd. 85 V72
Kakweiken River Main Rd. 62 P31 63 P32
Kalamalka Rd. 69 S56-57
Kaleva Rd. 62 Q28
Kallis Creek FS Rd. 81 V57
Kallum Dr. 55 K48
Kalum Lake Dr. (New Aiyansh) 29 P22
Kalum Lake Dr. (Terrace) 29 T23
Kamloops-Shuswap Rd. 68 P55 Q52-54
Kamma Creek FS Rd. 83 X67
Kananaskis Power Line Rd. 73 R-S72 T72
Kane Creek FS Rd. 71 T64 83 U64
Kane Valley Rd. 79 U50-51
Kangaroo Creek FS Rd. 44 D-E47
Kanyon Main Rd. 75 Z35
Kaouk Mainline Rd. 62 T28
Kappan Mountain FS Rd. 41 F33-34
Karjula Rd. 68 Q55
Karmutzen Creek Main Rd. 61 R27 62 R28
Kashutl Rd. 61 S26-27
Kaslo Creek Fork Rd. S, 83 U64-65
Kaslo South Rd. 83 U65
Kaslo West Rd. 83 U65
Kate-Outlet FS Rd. 69 S59 70 S60
Kate-Sitkum FS Rd. 69 R59 S59 70 R60 S60
Kate Creek FS Rd. 69 R59
Kauwinch Rd. 61 S27
Kawkawa Lake Rd. 79 X48
Kay Kay FS Rd. 35 V-W41
Kaye Rd. 76 Y37-38
Keats Rd. 77 X40-41
Keefer Lake Rd. 69 T59 70 T60
Keefers Rd. 67 T48 79 U48
Keefes Landing Rd. 32 W32 X32 33 W33
Keen Creek Rd. 83 U64-65
Keenan Rd. 44 G46
Kehoe Rd. 81 Z56
Keillor Rd. 35 X40
Keith Ave. 29 T24
Keith Rd. 34 W38
Keith Wilson Rd. 78 Z46
Keithley-Barkerville FS Rd. 45 G48
Keithley Creek Rd. 44 D47 E47 45 D48
Kell Rd. 35 W40
Kelly Rd. 44 G44
Kelly Rd. (Bulkley-Nechako) 33 W33
Kelly Rd. (East Kootenay) 84 W70
Kelly Rd. (Okanagan-Similkameen) 81 Z56
Kelly Creek FS Rd. 82 Z63
Kelly Lake Rd. (Peace River) 27 P51-52
Kelly Lake Rd. (Thompson-Nicola) 66 O47
Kelly River Rd. 81 X-Y57
Kemp Rd. 35 W42
Kemp Lake Rd. 87 D39
Kendrick Mainline Rd. 74 V28-29
Kennedy Rd. 26 O43
Kennedy Rd. 27 M50
Kennedy Rd. 82 V63
Kennedy Lake Rd. 79 X51
Kennedy River Rd. 75 Y-Z32
Kenner Rd. 34 V38
Kenney Dam Rd. 33 Y36 34 X38 Y37
Kenquot Main Rd. 75 Y33
Keogh Main Rd. 61 Q-R27
Kerr Rd. 31 T30
Kerr Rd. 84 U69
Kerr Creek Rd. 81 Z58
Kersley-Dale Landing Rd. 44 D44
Keschwal Rd. 62 O28
Ketcham Creek-Willow River FS Rd. 44 B46
Ketcham Creek-Yuzkli Creek FS Rd. 44 B46
Ketcham Creek FS Rd. 36 A46 44 B46 B-C46
Ketchan Lake FS Rd. 79 V51
Kettle-Bisson FS Rd. 69 T59
Kettle-Centre Mountain FS Rd. 81 V58-59
Kettle-Fiva-Riverside FS Rd. 81 Y57
Kettle-Gunnar FS Rd. 69 T58
Kettle-Mohr FS Rd. 81 U-V58
Kettle K10 FS Rd. 69 T59 81 U59
Kettle K12 FS Rd. 81 U59
Kettle K20 FS Rd. 69 T59 81 U59
Kettle K40 FS Rd. 81 U58
Kettle K50 FS Rd. 81 U59
Kettle River East Rd. 81 Z57
Kettle River East FS Rd. 81 X-Y58
Kettle River FS Rd. 69 T59 81 U58-59
Kettle Valley East Rd. 81 Z57-58
Kettle Valley South Rd. 81 Z57
Keuthley-Yanks Peak Rd. 45 D48
Key Rd. 58 L-M60
Keystone Ave. 78 Y44-45
Keystone Rd. 58 M60
Kianuko FS Rd. 83 X67
Kicking Horse Rd. 59 N66
Kicking Horse Tr. 59 M64-65 N65
Kid Creek FS Rd. 83 Y67 84 Y68
Kidston Rd. 69 S56
Kikomun Rd. 84 Y70
Kikomun-Newgate Rd. 84 Y-Z71
Kilpala Rd. 62 Q-R28
Kilpala Main Rd. 62 R28
Kim Rd. 84 Z68
Kindersley-Pinnacle FS Rd. 72 P68
King Rd. (Gulf-Islands) 78 Z45
King St. 84 W69
King Eddy FS Rd. 69 S57 T56-57
King Edward Ave. 77 Y42
King Pit Rd. 43 C43
Kingdom Lake FS Rd. 66 Q44
Kingsway 77 Y42
Kinman Creek Main Rd. 62 S28
Kinney Rd. 35 W43
Kinney Lake Rd. 47 B-C57
Kirby Rd. 44 B44
Kirbys Flat Rd. 66 R47
Kirkland Ranch Rd. 67 Q48
Kishinena FS Rd. 85 Z74-75
Kiskatinaw FS Rd. 27 Q50-51
Kiskatinaw Pit Rd. 27 Q51
Kispiox Rd. 30 P27
Kispiox Valley Rd. 30 P27
Kitchener Rd. 83 Y67
Kite 1200 Rd. 34 Y39
Kitseguecla FS Rd. 30 Q27
Kitseguecla Lake Rd. (6100 Rd) 30 R27-28
Kitselas Rd. 29 T24
Kitsuksis Rd. 75 Y35
Kitt Rd. 24 H47
Kitwancool FS Rd. 30 P26
Kitwanga Dr. 55 K48
Kitwanga Back Rd. 30 P-Q26
Kitwanga North Rd. 30 Q26
Kiwa-Raush Rd. 46 C55
Kiwa Creek Rd. 46 C55 47 C56
Kiyu Rd. 62 T29
Klanawa Rd. 86 A35
Klanawa Main Rd. 86 A35
Klaskino Main Rd. 61 R25
Klassen Ave. 25 F48
Kliyul Lake FS Rd. 53 K41
Klocreek FS Rd. 32 V31
Klootchlimmis 500 Rd. 61 R25-26
Klootchlimmis Main Rd. 61 R25
Kluskus-Blackwater FS Rd. 42 B38
Kluskus-Cambium FS Rd. 42 B37
Kluskus-Chedakuz FS Rd. 33 A35-36
Kluskus-Dragonfly FS Rd. 42 B37
Kluskus-Euchiniko FS Rd. 34 A37-38
Kluskus-Finger North FS Rd. 34 Z38
Kluskus-Hobson FS Rd. 33 Z36 34 Z37
Kluskus-Jerryboy FS Rd. 34 A38 42 B38
Kluskus-Malaput FS Rd. 41 B35
Kluskus-Mosquito FS Rd. 33 Z35
Kluskus-Ootsa FS Rd. 41 B35
Kluskus-Raven FS Rd. 42 B38
Kluskus-Salamander FS Rd. 34 A37-38
Kluskus-Tatelkuz FS Rd. 42 B37
Kluskus FS Rd. 33 A36 34 A37
Kluskus FS Rd. 34 X-Y38 Z37
Knife Creek Rd. 54 H46-47 55 H48
Knight Rd. 75 V35
Knight St. 77 Y42
Knob Hill Rd. 69 R56-57
Knockholt Rd. 31 U30
Knouff Lake Rd. 68 O-P53
Knox Mainline Rd. 63 R33
Knudson Rd. 35 A40
Kobau Lookout FS Rd. 80 Y-Z55
Kobau Mountain Rd. 80 Y-Z55
Kobes Creek FS Rd. 24 J45
Koch Creek FS Rd. 82 V61 W61-62
Kokanee Creek Rd. 83 V-W64
Kokanee Glacier Rd. 83 V-W64
Kokanee Pit Rd. 54 J47
Kokanee West FS Rd. 83 V-W64
Koksilah Rd. 87 B40
Kokummi Main Rd. 62 T30-31
Kolling Rd. 35 Z43
Kolosky Rd. 26 M47
Kookipi Creek FS Rd. 78 V46-47
Kootenay-Palliser FS Rd. 72 Q-R69
Kootenay Lake FS Rd. 83 U-V65
Kootenay No. 3 Rd. 72 R69
Kootenay River FS Rd. (Settlers Rd.) 72 S69
Koprino Bay Main Rd. 61 Q24-25
Krantz Rd. 27 O51
Krestenuk Rd. 43 C40
Krestova Rd. 82 X62
Krestova Lower Rd. 82 X62-63
Kruger Lake Rd. 42 B-C39
Kruger Lake FS Rd. 37 A48
Kruger Mountain Rd. 80 Z55
Krumm Rd. 29 T24
Kubinec Rd. 85 X72
Kuldo Blvd. 29 V23
Kunnum Rd. 62 S30
Kurjata Rd. 26 N46
Kuskanax Creek FS Rd. 70 R63 S62-63
Kvile St. 25 F48
Kwikoit Creek FS Rd. 57 N56
Kwoiek Creek FS Rd. 66 T47
Kwoiek Valley Rd. 66 T47

L&A Rd. 69 S57
L&A Cross Rd. 69 S56
La Rochelle FS Rd. 66 P45
Labour Day Lake Rd. 76 Y36-37
Lac du Bois Rd. 67 P51 68 P52
Lac la Hache Station Rd. 54 K47 55 K48
Lac Le Jeune Rd. 67 Q51 R51 68 Q52 R52
Lacasse Rd. 36 W44
Lachmach FS Rd. 28 U19
Lacon Rd. 76 W36
Ladner Trunk Rd. 77 Z42
Ladybird Creek FS Rd. 82 X61-62
Lafontaine Rd. 59 M65
Lafrance Creek FS Rd. 83 W66
Lagerquist Rd. 44 F44-45
Lahagarte Rd. 24 K46
Laib Creek FS Rd. 83 X65
Laidlaw Rd. 78 X47 79 X48
Lake Rd. 74 U30-31
Lake Bay Rd. 68 P53
Lake Creek Rd. 36 A44
Lake Hislop Rd. 30 S29
Lake Kathlyn Rd. 30 R-S28
Lake Main Rd. 61 Q24
Lakehill Rd. 80 X55
Lakelse Lake Lodge Rd. 29 U24
Lakelse Main FS Rd. 29 U23
Lakelse River Rd. 29 T23
Lakes Rd. 34 X39
Lakes Rd. 87 A40
Lakeshore Dr. 81 Z56
Lakeshore Rd. (Kelowna) 80 U-V55
Lakeshore Rd. (Salmon Arm) 69 P-Q56
Lakeside Rd. 80 X55
Lakeview Rd. (Cariboo) 44 F-G46
Lakeview Rd. (Comox-Strathcona) 63 S33
Lakeview Rd. (Squamish-Lillooet) 65 P43
Lakeview-Arrow Creek Rd. 83 Y66-67 Z67
Lakit Rd. 84 V-W70
Lakit Creek FS Rd. 84 V70
Laktin Rd. 70 T63
Laluwissin Creek FS Rd. 66 R47
Lamb Creek FS Rd. (East Kootenay) 84 X-Y69
Lamb Creek FS Rd. (Kootenay Boundary) 82 Y61
Lambly Creek Rd. 80 U55
Lamco Rd. 37 Z51
Lamming Pit Rd. 38 A52
Lampard Rd. 80 W54
Landaluza Rd. 34 W38
Landon West Rd. 67 Q49
Landooz Rd. 35 W43
Landry Rd. 27 M51-52
Lands End Rd. 87 B40-41
Landslide FS Rd. 43 D42-43
Lane Main Rd. 62 P29
Lang Lake FS Rd. (611 Rd.) 55 J49-50
Lang Lake North FS Rd. (610 Rd.) 55 J50
Langill Rd. 82 X62
Langston Rd. 34 X39
Lansdowne Rd. (North Okanagan) 69 R57
Lantzville Rd. 76 Y38
Larch Hills-Annis FS Rd. 69 P57
Larch Hills FS Rd. 69 Q57
Larch Hills Summit FS Rd. 69 P57
Larch Mountain Rd. 62 S28
Lardeau Creek FS Rd. 70 Q63
Larkin Cross Rd. 69 R-S56
Larson Rd. 34 W39
Larson Landing Rd. 76 U-V37
Lasca Rd. 83 W64
Lassie FS Rd. 81 W57-58
Lassie Lake FS Rd. 81 W58
Lauder Rd. 83 W65
Lauder Creek Rd. 68 S52
Laura Lake Rd. 67 R49
Laurie Main Rd. 86 A36
Laurie Mainline Rd. 74 V28
Laurier St. 30 P27
Lavina Mountain FS Rd. 71 S65
Lavington Rd. (3300 Rd.) 43 C-D42
Lavoie Rd. 35 A43 43 B43 44 B44
Lavoie Gold Rd. 34 Z38
Lawless-Britton FS Rd. 79 W50
Lawless-Jacobson Lake FS Rd. 79 W50 X49-50
Lawless Creek Rd. 79 W50
Lawrenson Rd. 63 S32
Laws Rd. 26 N46
Lawson Rd. (1100 Rd) 30 S-T29
Layton Rd. 34 W38
Lazo Rd. 75 V35
Lazy Lake Rd. 84 V69-70
LD Ranch Rd. 84 V69
Leach Creek FS Rd. 85 W-X73
Leach Creek FS Rd. 85 W73
Leadqueen Frances Rd. 71 P67
Leadville Rd. 83 Y67
Leadville Creek Rd. 83 Y67 84 Y68
Leagh Mainline Rd. 74 U30
Leahy Pit Rd. 25 K50
Leask Rd. 27 N50
Ledge Point Main Rd. 61 Q27
Lee Rd. 55 L50-51
Lee's Rd. 27 N48
Lee Creek Dr. 68 O55 69 O56
Leech Mainline Rd. 87 C39
Lefeuvre Rd. 78 Z44
Legrand Access Rd. 37 A51
Lehman Rd. 41 F35
Lehman Rd. 66 P47
LeMare Lake Main Rd. 61 R24-25
Lemieux Creek Rd. 56 L52
Lemon Creek Rd. 82 V63 83 V64
Lemon Lake Rd. 45 F48-49 G48
Lens Creek Main Rd. 87 B38
Leo Creek FS Rd. 31 Q33
Leo Sakeniche FS Rd. 31 Q33
Leon Creek FS Rd. 66 O46
Leopold Rd. 69 O56
Lerwick Rd. 75 V35
Lesage Rd. 24 L46
Letkiman Ave. 24 G47
Levette Lake FS Rd. 77 V42
Levi Main Rd. 61 Q27
Lewis Lake Camp Rd. 76 U37
Lightning Lake Rd. 79 Z50-51
Likely Rd. 44 E46-47 F-G46 54 H46
Lillian Mainline Rd. 74 W30
Lillooet Lake Rd. (In-Shuch-ch FS Rd.) 66 S-T44
Lillooet River Rd. 78 U44
Lillooet River FS Rd. 65 R42
Lillooet West FS Rd. 66 T44 78 U44 U45
Lily Lake Rd. 67 R49
Lily Lake Rd. (Bulkley-Nechako) 34 W37
Lily Lake Rd. (Thompson-Nicola) 67 T50
Lime Kiln Rd. 70 R61
Lincoln Dr. 55 L50
Lind Rd. 35 W40
Lind Creek Rd. 81 Z58-59
Linden Lake FS Rd. 81 U58
Lindley Creek Rd. 67 T50
Lindsay Rd. 82 V63
Lindsay Creek FS Rd. 82 U60
Lindsay Lake FS Rd. 82 U60
Line 17 Rd. 69 O56
Line Creek Mine Rd. 85 U72-73
Lineham Rd. 27 M49
Lingfield Creek Tr. 52 K-L38
Lingren Rd. 35 X40
Linklater Creek Rd. 84 Z71
Linsley Rd. 27 N49
Linton Rd. 33 X33
Litaco Rd. 53 H42-43
Little Big Bar Rd. 54 M46
Little Cayuse FS Rd. 82 X61
Little Cedar North FS Rd. 29 R23
Little Cedar South FS Rd. 29 R23
Little Green Lake Rd. 55 L-M49
Little Horsefly Rd. 45 F48
Little Lake Rd. 44 E47
Little Shuswap Lake Rd. 68 P55
Little Slocan Main FS Rd. 82 W62
Little Slocan North Rd. 82 V62-63
Little Slocan River FS Rd. 82 V-W62
Little Slocan South Rd. 82 W62
Little Springs Rd. 54 J-K45
Little Swift River FS Rd. 44 C46-47
Little Tamihi Creek Rd. 78 Z46-47
Little Wedeene FS Rd. 29 V23
Little White FS Rd. (Central Okanagan) 81 V56
Little White FS Rd. (Columbia-Shuswap) 69 O-P56
Little Zeballos Rd. 62 T28 74 U28
Littlefield-Kruger FS Rd. 37 A48
Lizzie Creek Main Rd. 66 T44
Lladnar Creek FS Rd. 85 V-W72
Lloyd Dr. 35 X40-41
Lloyd Rd. 56 L55
Loakin Bear Creek Rd. 68 P55
Lochore Creek FS Rd. 66 R47
Lodgepole-River Rd. 85 X-Y72
Lodgepole FS Rd. 85 X72-73 Y73-74
Loff Rd. 82 X62-63
Log Creek Rd. 66 T47 78 U47
Lois FS Rd. 76 U38
Lois Mainline Rd. 76 U-V38
Lone Butte Rd. 55 L48-49
Lone Butte-Horse Lake Rd. 55 L49
Lone Prairie Rd. 26 N-O47
Lone Star Rd. 81 Z59
Long Bar Rd. 44 C44
Long Harbour-Vesuvius Bay Rd. 87 A40
Long Lake Rd. 34 Z37
Long Lake Rd. (Alberni-Clayoquot) 75 W-X34 X34-35
Long Lake Rd. (Brigade Lake) 68 Q-R52
Long Lake Rd. (Thompson-Nicola) 68 Q-R52
Long Lake Main Rd. 63 T33
Longworth Rd. 36 X47
Longworth Access Rd. 36 X47
Lookout Rd. (Central Kootenay) 82 X62
Lookout Rd. (Hanceville) 53 H-J42
Lookout Rd. (Jesmond) 54 M-N46
Lookout FS Rd. 43 C43
Loon Lake Rd. (Aspen Grove) 79 U51 80 U52
Loon Lake Rd. (East Kootenay) 85 Y-Z72
Loon Lake Rd. (Loon Lake) 55 N49 67 O48
Loop Rd. (Bulkley-Nechako) 34 W39
Loop Rd. (Peace River) 25 F49
Loopol Rd. 35 W-X43
Loos Rd. 37 Y-Z50
Loos Rd. 37 Z50
Loose Creek Main Rd. 62 P30
Lord River-Elkins Creek FS Rd. 52 L39 53 L40 M40
Lord River Development Rd. 52 M39 53 M40
Lord River Mining Rd. 53 M39
Lorenzetta-Hunter Creek Rd. 79 X-Y48
Loseth Rd. 47 D57
Lost Rd. 24 H46
Lost Creek FS Rd. 83 Z64
Lost Dog FS Rd. 84 V69
Lost Horse-Thone FS Rd. 81 X58
Lost Horse Creek Rd. 81 X58
Lost Lease FS Rd. 78 X-Y45
Lost Valley FS Rd. 66 R44-45
Loubert Rd. 76 V37

Loucks Ave. 25 K50
Lougheed Hwy. 78 X-Y47
Lowe Dr. 80 Y54
Lower Rd. 77 X40
Lower Adam 100 Rd. 62 R31
Lower Alston Rd. 62 T30 74 U30
Lower Cache Rd. 25 J48
Lower Campbell Lake Rd. 63 T33
Lower Caven Creek FS Rd. 84 Y70
Lower China Creek Rd. 82 Y62
Lower Duck Range Rd. 68 Q54
Lower Elk Valley Rd. 85 U-V72
Lower Herrick FS Rd. 36 W47
Lower Houseman Rd. 55 K49
Lower Innonoaklin Rd. 82 U60-61 V61
Lower McPhail Rd. 79 V50
Lower Mosquito Rd. 70 T61
Lower Mud River Rd. 35 X42
Lower Sage Rd. 85 Z74
Lower Wynndel Rd. 83 Y-Z66
Lowry 10 Rd. 75 X34
Lucille Mountain Rd. 38 A52
Lucky Creek FS Rd. 75 Z33-34
Lull Mainline Rd. 62 P-Q31
Lumberton Rd. 84 X69
Lumreek Rd. 44 G46 54 H46
Lund Rd. 44 G46
Lund Rd. (Finmoore) 35 X40
Lund Rd. (Fraser-Fort George) 36 X-Y44
Lund Rd. (Houston) 31 U30
Lundbom Rd. 67 T51
Lussier Main FS Rd. 84 U70
Luxor Creek Rd. 72 P68
Luxor Station Rd. 71 P-Q67
Lybarger Rd. 69 O58
Lynch Creek FS Rd. 81 Y59
Lynes Rd. 68 R55
Lynes Creek Rd. 44 G45
Lynx Lake Rd. 35 Y42-43
Lyon Lake Rd. 76 W39

M-1000 Rd. 74 U28
M Branch Rd. 62 R-S31
M Road FS Rd. 59 L65
M12 Rd. 33 Y34
M25 Rd. 33 Y34
M32 Rd. 33 Y34
M4 Rd. 86 A37
M900 Rd. 61 Q27
Mabel-Smyth FS Rd. 69 R58-59
Mabel Iron FS Rd. 69 P-Q59
Mabel Lake Rd. 69 R-S58 S57
Mabel Lake FS Rd. 69 P59 Q58-59 R58
Macaulay Rd. 75 U34
Machete Lake Rd. 55 L-M51
Macjack Main Rd. 61 Q24
Mackay River Rd. 45 F-G50
Mackenzie Ave. 54 H45
Mackenzie Way 27 Q49
MacKenzie-Lookout FS Rd. 35 A42-43
Mackenzie FS Rd. 70 Q62
Mackenzie Main Rd. 62 Q29
Mackie FS Rd. 82 Y62
Macktush Main Rd. 75 Y-Z35
Maclure Rd. 78 Z45
MacMillan Rd. 55 L49
Mad River Rd. 57 J-K56
Madden Rd. 59 N66
Madeley Lake Rd. 65 T42
Madias-Tatley FS Rd. 72 R69
Maeford Lake FS Rd. 45 D49
Maggie Lake FS Rd. 75 Z33
Mahatta River Main Rd. 61 Q-R25
Mahood-Lutely FS Rd. 55 J51
Mahood Lake Rd. 55 K-L50
Mahood Lake North Rd. 55 J51
Mahood Lake South Rd. 55 J51
Mahood West Mainline FS Rd. 55 J51 K51 56 J52
Main Rd. 76 W37-38
Main Rd. S. 62 R28 S28-29
Main St. (Fraser-Fort George) 47 D57
Main St. (Kitimat-Stikine) 30 S28
Main St. (Metro Vancouver) 77 Y42
Main St. (Okanagan-Similkameen) 80 W-X55
Main Kettle River Rd. 81 Y57
Mainline FS Rd. 62 R-S30
Maiyuk Creek FS Rd. 72 S71
Maka-Murray FS Rd. 79 U49-50
Makonin Rd. 82 X63
Malahat FS Rd. 87 C40
Malakwa Loop Rd. 69 O-P58
Malaspina Rd. 76 U36
Malaspina FS Rd. 64 T36 76 U36
Malksope Main Rd. 61 S26
Mallory Dr. 75 Y35 76 Y36
Mallory Rd. (Central Kootenay) 83 Z66-67
Mallory Rd. (North Okanagan) 69 Q57
Mamit Lake Rd. 67 R50
Mamit Lake Branch Rd. 67 T50
Mamquam Rd. 77 V42
Mamquam River Rd. 77 V42
Mandalay Creek Rd. 35 W41-42
Mann Rd. 82 Z62
Manning Creek FS Rd. 67 S-T49
Mannings Rd. (Brigade Lake) 68 R52
Mannings Rd. (Dot) 67 S49
Manson Ave. 76 U37
Mapes Rd. 34 X39
Maple Dr. 44 C44
Maple Rd. 76 V39
Maple Bay Rd. 87 A40
Maple Falls Rd. 78 Z46
Marble Bay Rd. 87 A38
Marcer Rd. 84 Y71
March Rd. 25 J48
Marilla Rd. 33 Y33-35
Marine Ave. 76 U-V37
Marine Dr. (Port Alice) 61 R26
Marine Dr. (Vancouver) 77 X42
Marine Dr., NW 77 Y41
Marine Dr., SE 77 Y42
Marine Dr., SW 77 Y41-42
Marine Rd. 77 Z43
Marion Lake FS Rd. 71 O67
Marion Main Rd. (Alberni-Clayoquot) 75 Y34
Marion Main Rd. (Mount Waddington) 62 Q28
Marjorie Lake Rd. 57 L56
Marl Creek Rd. 59 L64
Marlow FS Rd. 70 Q62
Marmot Lake Rd. 43 C-D40
Marriott Rd. 54 M47
Marron Valley Rd. 80 X54-55
Marsden Rd. 82 W63
Marsh Rd. 43 C43 D43 44 C44
Marsh Creek Rd. 82 Y-Z63
Marshall Rd. 43 B43
Marshall Creek Rd. 45 F49
Marshall Creek Rd. 66 O-P44
Marten Rd. 25 G48
Marten Rd. 34 A37
Martin Mountain FS Rd. 68 Q54
Martin Prairie Rd. 68 Q54-55
Marvinus Rd. 74 V29
Maryland Creek FS Rd. 83 Z65
Maselpanik Creek Rd. 79 Z49
Mass Rd. 31 T32-33
Matevic Rd. 85 V72
Matheson Rd. 69 R56
Mathews Rd. 44 C44
Matlset Main Rd. 75 Y32
Matson Rd. 29 T23-24
Matthew Creek FS Rd. 84 V-W68
Matthew River Rd. 45 C49
Maud Lake FS Rd. 44 D-E46
Maunders Rd. 34 W39
Mause Creek Rd. 84 W70
Maxan Rd. 31 U32 32 V32
Maxan-China Nose FS Rd. 31 U31-32
Maxan Creek Rd. 31 U32
Maxan Equity Rd. 32 V31-32
Maybius Rd. 26 M46-47
Mayfield Lake FS Rd. 54 J45
Mayook Settlement Rd. 84 W-X70
Maze-Forbez FS Rd. 54 J47
Maze Lake FS Rd. 54 J47
MB 100 62 Q31 63 Q32
MB BR 70 63 Q-R32
McBeath Rd. 59 N65
McBride St. 28 T-U18
McBride Timber Rd. 35 X42
McBride Timber Rd. S. 35 Y42
McCabe Rd. 30 S29
McCabe Rd. 35 X42
McCall Rd. 34 W38
McCall Rd. 54 N47 55 N48 66 O47
McCarren Creek Rd. 81 Z58-59
McCarthy Creek Rd. 56 L52
McCleery Rd. 69 R57
McClelland Rd. 34 W39
McClinchy Creek North Rd. 41 G35 51 H35
McClure Main Rd. 86 A-B37
McConnell Rd. (Kootenay Boundary) 83 W64
McCool Creek FS Rd. 85 W72
McCormack Rd. 82 U61-62
McCormick Creek Rd. 82 Z63
McCorvie Lakes FS Rd. 56 L54-55
McCoy Lake Rd. 75 Y35
McCuddy Creek Rd. 80 Y55 81 Y56
McCulloch Rd. 26 Q43
McCulloch Rd. 81 U-V56
McCurdy Creek Main Rd. 74 V30-31
McDaniels Rd. 82 X62
McDonald Rd. (Bulkley-Nechako) 34 W-X39
McDonald Rd. (North Okanagan) 69 R56
McDonald Creek Rd. 80 U54
McDonald Creek FS Rd. 70 T62
McDonald Landing Rd. 32 W32
McDonell Lake FS Rd. (7000 Rd) 30 S27-28
McDougall Rd. 44 E45 F45-46
McDougall Creek FS Rd. 80 U55
McEvoy Creek FS Rd. 85 X72-73
McFarlane Creek FS Rd. 82 V-W60
McGeachy Pit Rd. 34 X39
McGhee Rd. 52 K37
McGillivray Creek FS Rd. 66 R47
McGillivray Lake FS Rd. 68 P54
McGinty Rd. 84 V69
McGinty Lake Rd. 84 V69
McGregor Rd. 36 W46-47
McGregor-Logan FS Rd. 37 V48
McGregor-Siwash Rock FS Rd. 68 R-S55
McGregor Bend FS Rd. 36 V46
McGregor Creek FS Rd. 68 S55
McGuire Rd. 78 Y-Z46
McIntosh-Moffatt Lake Rd. (2300 Rd.) 54 H46-47 55 H48-49
McIntyre Creek Rd. 81 Y56
McIver Creek Main Rd. 62 T29-30 74 U29-30
McKay Rd. 44 G44
McKay Rd. 44 G44 54 H44
McKay Lake FS Rd. 76 Z38-39
McKean Rd. 82 W62-63
McKenzie Ave. 87 C41
McKenzie Rd. (Bulkley-Nechako) 30 R28
McKian Creek FS Rd. 71 T64-65
McKilligan Rd. 31 U30
McKilligan FS Rd. 31 U30-31
McKim Rd. 68 Q54
McKinley Rd. 81 U56
McKinley-Ogden Rd. 55 K48
McKinley Lake Rd. 45 G49
McKinney Rd. 80 Y55 81 Y56 Z56
McKinnon Way 27 N51
McLatchie FS Rd. 85 X73
McLean Rd. (Cariboo) 44 C44
McLean-Sawmill Rd. 69 O-P58
McLean Creek Rd. 80 X55
McLeans Lake Rd. 67 P48
McLeod Rd. 35 W43 36 W44
McLeod Rd. 67 O49
McLeod Rd. (Bulkley-Nechako) 34 W39
McLeod Rd. (Fraser Valley) 78 Y47
McLure Ferry Rd. 68 O52
McMurdo Creek FS Rd. 59 N64 71 O64
McMurphy FS Rd. 57 K56
McMurtrie Rd. 36 A44
McNab Rd. 56 L52
McNair Creek Rd. 77 W40
McNeil Lake Rd. 55 H50
McNeill Lake FS Rd. 76 W39 77 W40
McNolty Rd. 34 W38
McNulty Rd. 68 Q54
McNutt Rd. 78 Y44
McParlon East Main Rd. 65 P41-42 Q41
McPhail Rd. 79 V51
McPhee Rd. (Fraser-Fort George) 35 W-X42
McQueen Lake FS Rd. 67 P51 68 P52
McQuinna Rd. 69 R-S58
McRae Rd. 82 Y60 Z60
McRae Main FS Rd. 70 P61
McTavish Rd. (Columbia-Shuswap) 69 R56
Meachen Creek FS Rd. 83 W67
Mead Rd. 84 W70
Meade Creek Mainline Rd. 87 A38
Meadow Rd. 67 O-P50
Meadow Canoe Rd. 54 M45
Meadow Creek Rd. (Cariboo) 36 A44
Meadow Creek Rd. (Central Kootenay) 71 S64-65
Meadow Creek Rd. (Thompson-Nicola) 67 R50-51
Meadow Creek FS Rd. 29 Q23
Meadow Creek FS Rd. 69 O56
Meadow Lake Rd. 54 L-M46 M-N47
Meadow Lake Rd. 54 M45-46
Meadow Mountain Rd. 71 S64-65
Meadowdale Rd. 35 X40
Meadows Rd. 82 Y63
Meadows In The Sky Pkwy. 70 O60-61
Meager Creek Rd. 65 Q41 R40
Meanskinisht Rd. 29 Q25
Meanwhile Rd. 31 U31-32
Medicine Creek Rd. 66 P47 67 P48
Medicine Women FS Rd. 24 L46 26 M46
Meek Rd. 25 K48
Mehatta Mainline Rd. 61 R25
Meicklem Rd. 31 S-T30
Meier Rd. 25 J48
Meier Rd. 35 X40
Meier Rd. W. 35 X40
Meikle Creek FS Rd. 26 P47
Melanie Main Rd. 61 S27
Melba Creek FS Rd. 67 R51
Meldrum Creek Rd. 54 H45
Mellin Creek Rd. 68 T53
Mellin Lake FS Rd. 68 T52-54 80 U52
Melnychuk Rd. 26 N47
Memekay-Salmon 100 Hookup 63 T32
Memekay 30 Rd. 63 T32
Memekay East Mainline Rd. 63 T32
Memekay Mainline Rd. 63 T32-33
Memekay West Main Rd. 63 S-T32
Memorial Ave. 76 X37
Menzie Main FS Rd. 63 S-T33
Menzies Lockout Rd. 63 S33
Menzies Main Rd. 63 T32 T33
Mercs Rd. 75 X34
Meridian South FS Rd. 34 Y39 35 Y40
Merkley Rd. 29 S-T24
Merrill Lake Rd. 63 T33
Merritt-Princeton Hwy 67 T51
Merry Creek FS Rd. 82 Y62
Merton Rd. 35 Y43
Merville Rd. 75 V35
Messiter Station Rd. 57 J56
Metchosin Rd. 87 D40
Meyers Rd. 43 B43
Mica Mountain Rd. 47 C56
Michel Creek Rd. 85 V72-73
Michelle-Baezaeko Rd. 42 C37 D38-39 43 D40
Michelle-Baldface FS Rd. 42 C-D37
Michelle-Bishop FS Rd. 42 C37-38
Michelle-Canyon Mountain-Maxwell FS Rd. 42 D-E39
Michelle-Canyon Mountain FS Rd. 42 D39
Michelle-Canyon Mountain South FS Rd. 42 D38-39
Michelle-Coglistiko FS Rd. 42 C39 43 C40
Michelle-Fire FS Rd. 42 D39
Michelle-Fishpot FS Rd. 42 C-D39
Michelle-Kluskus FS Rd. 42 C-D38
Michelle-Little Mountain FS Rd. 42 D39
Michelle-McFarland FS Rd. 43 D40
Michelmoon Creek FS Rd. 66 P45
Michelson Main Rd. 61 Q25
Michigan Rd. 75 X34
Midday Valley Rd. 67 T50
Middle Bench Rd. 69 T56
Middle White River FS Rd. 72 S71 T70-71
Middlemiss Rd. 26 N45-46
Middlepoint Rd. 76 W39
Midgeley Mountain Access Rd. 83 Y66
Milburn Lake Rd. 43 C43
Milford Creek FS Rd. 83 U65
Mill Rd. 74 V31
Mill Rd. (Kootenay Boundary) 82 Z63
Mill Rd. (Thompson-Nicola) 68 R54
Mill Bay Rd. (Bulkley-Nechako) 31 S32
Mill Bay Rd. (Cowichan Valley) 87 B40
Mill Creek Rd. 67 S-T51
Mill Lakes FS Rd. 30 P26
Mill Main FS Rd. 30 P26
Millar Rd. 24 L46
Millar Rd. 45 F-G48
Millar Main Rd. 74 X31
Millard Rd. 35 W40
Miller Rd. 67 T50
Miller Rd. (Cowichan Valley) 87 B40
Miller Rd. (East Kootenay) 84 V69
Miller Rd. (Metro Vancouver) 77 X41
Miller Rd. (Peace River) 27 M50
Miller Creek FS Rd. 81 Y59 82 Y60
Milligan Rd. 76 Y36
Milligan Creek Rd. 25 G-H50 H49-50
Mills Rd. 87 B41
Minchin Rd. 77 Y42-43
Mine Rd. (Central Kootenay) 83 U64
Mine Rd. (Mount Waddington) 61 Q27
Mine Creek Rd. 79 V49
Mine FS Rd. 55 J48
Miner Lake FS Rd. 51 J35
Mineral Lake Rd. 84 X-Y69
Minger Rd. 33 W34
Minnabariet Rd. 67 R48
Minova Mine Rd. 56 N54
Minto Rd. 75 W35
Minton Creek FS Rd. 53 J42
Minute Creek FS Rd. 86 C37
Miracle Beach Connector 75 U34
Miracle Beach Dr 75 U-V34
Misery Creek East Branch FS Rd. 77 V40
Misery Creek South Branch FS Rd. 77 V40
Misinchinka FS Rd. 26 Q43
Mission Rd. 84 V69
Mission Rd. (Cariboo) 54 H46
Mission Rd. (East Kootenay) 84 W69
Mission Rd. (North Okanagan) 69 S56
Mission-Fort Steele Rd. 84 W69-70
Mission-Wasa Low Rd. 84 W69
Mission-Wycliffe Rd. 84 W69
Mission Creek FS Rd. 81 U57
Mission Mountain Rd. 66 P-Q45
Misty Mainline Rd. 61 Q27
Mitchell Rd. 36 V44
Mitchell Rd. 59 N65
Mitchell Bay Rd. 45 F-G48
Mitchell Bay Rd. 62 Q28
Mitchell Bay FS Rd. 31 S31-32 T30-31 T31 U30
Mitchell River FS Rd. 71 P-Q67
Mitchener Creek FS Rd. 82 Y60-61
Mitten Lake FS Rd. 71 O66
Miworth Rd. 35 X42-43
Miworth West Rd. 35 X42
Moakwa Creek Main Rd. 62 T31
Moan Rd. 84 V69
Moberly Rd. 58 L61
Moberly Branch Rd. 59 M64-65
Moberly Dump Rd. 26 M47
Moberly FS Rd. 26 M45
Mobley Rd. 69 P56
Moffat-Spokin Rd. 54 H47
Moffat Lake Rd. (Alexandria) 44 E44
Moffatt Lake Rd. (108 Rd.) 44 G47
Moffatt Lake Rd. (Eagle Lake) 55 H48-49
Moha Rd. 66 Q46
Mohun Lake East Rd. 63 T33
Mohun Lake West Rd. 63 T33
Moldowan Cutoff Rd. 35 V-W42
Mollice Lake Rd. 33 W33
Molson Rd. 81 Z56-57
Molybdenite Creek Rd. 66 R46
Momich FS Rd. 57 M56-57
Monashee Creek Rd. 69 T59 70 S60 T60
Monck Park Rd. 67 T51
Monk Creek FS Rd. 83 Z64-65
Monkman FS Rd. 27 R48
Monkman Pass Tr. 27 R52
Monroe Lake Rd. 84 X69
Mons Rd. 59 N65-66
Mons Creek FS Rd. (2400 Rd.) 53 K-L43 L42
Mons Lake Rd. 53 K42
Mont Colley FS Rd. 32 W31-32
Montana Creek FS Rd. 56 K-L55
Montana Lake Rd. 55 M51
Monte-Glimpse FS Rd. 68 S53
Monte Creek-George FS Rd. 68 R53-54
Monte Hills FS Rd. 68 R54
Montgomery Rd. 31 T31-32
Montney Rd. 25 J49
Moon Rd. 54 J45
Moon Creek Rd. 66 P-Q45
Mooney FS Rd. 43 B43
Mooney Pit Rd. 34 W38
Moonshine FS Rd. 69 S57
Moore Rd. 35 Z43 36 Z44
Moore-Richardson Rd. 68 Q-R53
Moore Lake Main Rd. 61 Q24
Moose Creek Ave. 25 K51
Moose Crossing Rd. 32 X32
Moose Horn Rd. 33 X33
Moose Lake FS Rd. 27 P48
Moose Pit Rd. 32 X32
Moose Valley Access Rd. 54 K-L47
Mooyah Main Rd. 74 V-W30
Moran Pl 67 R49
Morden Rd. (Bulkley-Nechako) 30 S-T29
Morehead-Beavermouth FS Rd. 44 D45 E45-46
Morgan Rd. 30 S28-29
Morgan Rd. 36 A44
Morice-Nadina FS Rd. 32 W29-30
Morice-Owen East FS Rd. 32 W30
Morice-Tahtsa FS Rd. 32 X28-29
Morice Cedric FS Rd. 32 V28
Morice Gold FS Rd. 30 U29 31 U30
Morice Lamprey FS Rd. 32 W28
Morice Nado FS Rd. 32 V28
Morice Owen FS Rd. 32 V29-30 W30
Morice Peacock FS Rd. 31 U30
Morice River Rd. 31 U30
Morice River FS Rd. 32 V-W28
Morice Tahtsa FS Rd. 32 W29-30
Morice Telkwa FS Rd. 30 U29 31 U30
Morice Tsichgass FS Rd. 32 W31
Morice West FS Rd. 32 V28-29
Moricetown-Suskwa FS Rd. 30 P-Q28
Moricetown FS Rd. 30 Q28
Morkill FS Rd. 37 Y50
Morris Valley Rd. 78 X46-47 Y46
Morrison Main FS Rd. 31 P-Q31
Morrison Mainline FS Rd. 31 Q-R32
Morrison Meadow Rd. 41 F34-35
Morrison Meadow Rd. 42 F-G36
Morrison West FS Rd. 31 Q31
Morrissey Rd. 85 X72
Morrissey Creek Rd. 81 Z59 82 Z60
Morrissey FS Rd. 85 X72
Moscow Rd. 72 S70
Mosley Creek FS Rd. 52 K36
Mossvale Rd. 77 W42
Mossvale-Teardrop FS Rd. 35 V-W42
Moth Pit Rd. 70 O60
Motherlode Rd. 81 Z58
Mouat Bay Rd. 76 W37
Mound Rd. 55 N48
Mound-Loon Lake FS Rd. 55 N48
Mount Rd. 38 A52
Mount 7 FS Rd. 59 N65
Mount Alston Rd. 62 T30 74 U30
Mount Baldy Rd. 81 Y56 Z56-57
Mount Cain Rd. 62 S30
Mount Cartier Rd. 70 P61
Mount Cheam Rd. 78 Y-Z47
Mount Creek Rd. 43 D42-43
Mount Crucil Rd. 77 W40
Mount Davis Way 31 U30
Mount Fernie Park Rd. 85 W-X72
Mount Gardner Rd. 77 X41
Mount Ida-Deep Creek FS Rd. 69 Q-R56
Mount Ida-Haines Creek North FS Rd. 69 Q56
Mount Ida-Shaw FS Rd. 69 Q56-57
Mount Ida FS Rd. 69 Q56
Mount Lolo Rd. 68 P52
Mount Mahoney Rd. 76 U37
Mount McClennan FS Rd. 56 K54
Mount Randolph FS Rd. 80 W55
Mount Reesor Rd. 26 Q-R47
Mount Saint Anne FS Rd. 47 G57
Mount Scacia Rd. 82 U60
Mount Seymour Rd. 77 X42
Mount Sicker Rd. 87 A39-40
Mount Thurston Rd. 78 Z47
Mountain St. 82 Z62-63
Mountain House Rd. 44 G45-46
Mountain Shores Rd. 83 W65
Mountain View Rd. (Fraser-Fort George) 37 A51 38 A52
Mountain View Rd. (North Okanagan) 69 R57
Mountain View Mainline FS Rd. 37 Z51
Mountainview Dr. 31 U30
Mowing Machine FS Rd. 68 S54
Moyie-North FS Rd. 84 X68
Moyie-Ridgeway FS Rd. 84 X68
Moyie River FS Rd. 84 X68
Muchalaht Dr. 74 V31
Muchalat Lake Rd. 74 U30
Mud-Paradise FS Rd. 65 O43
Mud Creek-Noaxe Creek FS Rd. 65 O43
Mud Creek-Sluicebox Creek FS Rd. 53 N43
Mud Creek-Taylor Creek FS Rd. 65 O43
Mud Creek FS Rd. 53 L42 N43 65 O43
Mud Lake FS Rd. 57 H57
Mud Lakes FS Rd. 53 N43 54 N44
Mudflat Creek Rd. 30 P27-28
Muermann Rd. 35 W43
Muir Rd. 33 Y33
Muir Mainline Rd. 87 C-D39
Muirhead-Boxton Creek FS Rd. 44 E46
Muller Rd. 36 X47
Muller FS Rd. 37 V49
Munro Rd. 84 Z71
Munro FS Rd. 80 V54
Munro Lake FS Rd. 80 V54
Muralt Rd. 35 Y43
Murch Lake Rd. 35 W42
Murdoch Rd. 32 X32
Murphy Creek FS Rd. 82 Y61-62
Murphy Lake Rd. 55 H48
Murray Rd. 33 W33
Murray Creek FS Rd. 66 R47 67 R48
Murray Lake Rd. 79 V49-50
Murray River FS Rd. 27 R48
Murtle Lake Rd. 57 H56
Museum Rd. 38 A52
Museum Creek Rd. 76 Z36
Musgrove Ave. 24 J47
Musil Rd. 85 U72
Muskeg FS Rd. 62 S30
Mutton Creek FS Rd. 72 T70
Myers Rd. 24 F43
Myers Creek Rd. W. 81 Z57
Myers Creek East Rd. 81 Z57-58
Myncaster Rd. 81 Z57
Myra FS Rd. 81 V56
Mystery Creek FS Rd. 78 W46

Nadira Main Rd. 76 Z36
Nahatlatch-Kookipi Creek Rd. 78 U47
Nahatlatch FS Rd. 78 U46-47 79 U48
Nahmint Main Rd. 75 Y34 Y-Z35
Nahwitti Rd. 61 P25
Nakusp-Mica Creek Hwy. 57 J-K59 L59 58 L60 N60 70 O-P60 P61
Nalabila Blvd. 29 V23
Nanaimo Lakes Rd. 76 Z37-38
Nanaimo River Rd. 76 Z39
Naramata Rd. 80 W55
Narcosli Pit Rd. 44 E44
Narrow Lake FS Rd. 36 A47 37 A48
Narrow Lake FS Rd. 36 Z46
Narvaez Bay Rd. 87 A42
Nasby Rd. 55 L49
Nass Rd. 29 P22
Nass Logging Rd. 29 R23
Naswhito Rd. 69 S56
Natal Rd. 85 U72
Nath Rd. 55 L49-50
Natowite FS Rd. 31 Q32-33
Natulkuz-500 Rd. 33 Z36
Naubauer Rd. 27 N-O52

Nautley Rd. 34 W37
Naver-Ahbau Rd. 36 A45
Naver-Mud FS Rd. 36 A45
Naver Creek Rd. 36 A44-45
Naver Creek-Big Valley FS Rd. 36 A46 44 B46
Naver Creek-Rebman FS Rd. 36 A45-46
Naver Creek-Utimi FS Rd. 36 A45 44 B45
Nayki Rd. 69 P56
Nazko Hwy. 43 C41-43 44 C44
Nazko Rd. 43 B-C40
NC Main Rd. 62 R31
Neal Creek FS Rd. 67 R51
Neale Rd. 67 T50
Nechako Ave. 34 W39
Nechako Pit Rd. 34 W38
Needles North Rd. 82 U61
Neilsen Rd. 41 G34-35 51 H34
Nelson Rd. (Peace River) 25 K-L51
Nelson FS Rd. 29 S23
Nemaiah Valley Rd. 52 L39 M39 53 L40
Neptune Creek FS Rd. 82 Y62
Nesakwatch Creek FS Rd. 79 Z48
Nesbitt's Knee Falls Rd. 27 R48-49
Nesook Mainline Rd. 74 V30
Ness Lake Rd. N. 35 W42
Neubauer Rd. 27 N-O52
Nevertouch Rd. 81 V58
New Bird Rd. 33 Y34
New Dale Rd. 35 Z43
New Hazelton Hi-Level Rd. 30 P27
New Lake Rd. 84 W69
Newgate Rd. 84 Y-Z71
Newhykulston Creek FS Rd. 56 M53
Newlands North Rd. 36 W45
Newstead Main Rd. 86 A-B35
Newton-Whitewash Rd. 53 J40
Next Creek FS Rd. 83 X-Y65
Nichol Rd. 34 W38
Nicholson-12 Mile Creek Rd. 59 N65
Nicholson Creek Rd. 81 Y-Z57
Nicks Island Rd. 83 Y-Z66
Nicoamen River FS Rd. 67 S-T48
Nielson Rd. 83 W64
Nighthawk Rd. 80 Z55
Nikirk Rd. 27 O48
Nilkitkwa FS Rd. (4000 Rd) 31 P-Q30 Q-R30
Nilkitkwa Lake FS Rd. 31 P30
Nimpkish Rd. 62 T30 74 U30
Nimpkish Main Rd. (Comox-Strathcona) 62 T30
Nimpkish Main Rd. (Mount Waddington) 61 Q27 62 Q28
Nimpkish Main South Rd. 74 U30-31
Nimpkish South Main Rd. 62 S28-29
Nimpo Creek Rd. 41 F34-35
Nimpo Lake Rd. N. 41 F-G35
Nimpo Lake Rd. S. 41 G35
Nine Mile FS Rd. 72 S69-70
Nine Mile Mountain Rd. (Two Mile Creek Rd) 30 P27
Nisgaa Hwy. 29 Q23
Niskonlith Lake Rd. 68 P54-55
Nissan Rd. 58 M60
Nithi Rd. 33 W-X36
Nithi Pit Rd. 33 X36
Nitinat Rd. 86 A36
Nitinat River Rd. 76 Z36-37
Nixon Rd. 82 W63
Noak Rd. 36 A44
Noble Canyon Rd. 69 S57
Noble Lake FS Rd. 68 P52
Noel Creek FS Rd. 65 Q43
Noel Main Rd. 27 P50-51
Noisy Creek FS Rd. 69 Q59
Noke FS Rd. 84 X68
Nomas Main Rd. 62 R28
Nomash Main Rd. 62 T28-29
Noomst FS Rd. 40 F31
Nordstrum Creek FS Rd. 85 U72
Norman East FS Rd. 35 Y41
Norman Lake Rd. 35 X-Y41
Norman Lake FS Rd. 35 X-Y41
Norman Wood Rd. 58 K-L60
Norns Creek FS Rd. 82 X62
Norrish Creek Mainline FS Rd. 78 Y45-46
North Parallel 78 Z45
North Rd. 31 U33 32 W32
North Rd. 32 W32
North Rd. (Cariboo) 35 A43
North Rd. (Mitchell Bay FS Rd) 31 S31-32 T30-31 U30
North Rd. (Mount Waddington) 61 Q27
North Rd. (Nanaimo) 76 Y39
North Rd. (Sunshine Coast) 76 U-V38
North Rd. (Thompson-Nicola) 67 Q49
North-Cairie Main Rd. 61 Q27
North-Lane Main Rd. 62 P29
North Ainslee Creek FS Rd. 79 U48
North Ainslie-Mowhokam FS Rd. 67 T48 79 U48
North Barrière Lake FS Rd. 56 M54-55
North Bend FS Rd. 79 U48
North Bonaparte Rd. 55 L-M49 L-M50 M48-49
North Bund Valley Rd. 81 Y58
North Cache Creek Rd. 24 J47 25 J48
North Chilko Rd. 35 W40
North Cove Rd. 77 Z40
North Creek East Mainline FS Rd. 65 Q-R42
North Creek Mainline FS Rd. 65 Q41-42
North Croydon Rd. 46 B55
North Deroche Rd. 78 Y46
North Downie Rd. 58 L60-61 M61
North Emory Creek FS Rd. 79 W48
North End Rd. 87 A40
North Escalante Rd. 74 W29
North Fork Rd. (Comox-Strathcona) 74 V30
North Fork Rd. (Kootenay Boundary) 81 X-Z59
North Fork Rd. (North Okanagan) 69 S59
North Fork FS Rd. 81 U57
North Fosthall-Revelstoke Rd. 70 Q-R61
North Fraser Dr. 44 C44
North Fraser River Rd. 36 V44
North FS Rd. 36 A45
North FS Rd. 71 P66-67
North Goat River Rd. (East Kootenay) 83 Y67
North Gowlland Harbour Rd. 63 T34
North Green Lake Rd. 55 M48-49
North Hirsch FS Rd. 29 V24
North Horse Lake Rd. 55 L49
North Hulatt Rd. 35 W40
North Isle Pierre Rd. 35 W-X42
North Kitimat FS Rd. 29 U24
North Kleanza FS Rd. 29 T24-25
North Lake FS Rd. 76 V39
North Laluwissin Creek FS Rd. 66 Q-R47
North Lussier River Rd. 72 T70 84 U69-70
North Machete Lake Rd. 55 M51
North Main Rd. 63 T32
North Mainline Rd. (Capital RD) 87 C38
North Mainline Rd. (Heydon Bay) 63 Q33
North Mainline Rd. (Warner Bay) 61 Q27
North Naramata Rd. 80 V-W55
North Nechako Rd. 35 X43
North Old Fellers Rd. 27 O49-50
North Paldi Rd. 87 A39
North Pine Rd. 25 J49
North Ridge FS Rd. 82 Y61-62
North Scuzzy Creek FS Rd. 78 U47 79 U48
North Shore Rd. 86 A37 87 A38
North Shore Rd. (Stella Rd) 33 W36 34 W37
North Shuswap FS Rd. 69 Q59 70 Q60 R60
North Spencer Rd. 66 R-S47
North Star Lake Rd. 84 X71
North Tahsish Rd. 61 S27
North Thompson FS Rd. 47 F56-57
North Turnbull Main Rd. 50 N29 62 Q29
North White River FS Rd. 72 R-S71
North Woodcock Rd. 35 Z40
Northcott Rd. 68 S52
Northeast Main Rd. 61 P24-25
Northern Ranches Rd. 44 F44
Northside Rd. 34 W39
Northwest Bay Rd. 76 Y38
Northwood Pulp Mill Rd. 35 X43
Norton-Tregillus FS Rd. (3500 Rd.) 44 B46 C45-46
Norton Creek Rd. 44 C45
Norwegian Creek Rd. 81 Z58
Nose Bay FS Rd. 31 R32-33
Nosebag Mountain FS Rd. 66 P-Q45
Notch Hill Rd. 69 P56
NR-WS Hookup 75 Y-Z33
Number 3 Rd. 78 Z45-46
Nusatsum FS Rd. 40 G30-31
NW130 Rd. 61 Q27
NW700 Rd. 61 Q26
Nyland Lake-Sundberg Creek FS Rd. 44 D45-46
Nyland Lake FS Rd. 44 C45 D-E46

O'Conner Lake FS Rd. 67 O51 68 O52 P52
O'Neil Rd. 69 R56
Oak Rd. 58 M61
Oak St. 77 Y42
Oberg Johnston Rd. 59 M64-65
Octopus Creek FS Rd. 82 V60-61
Oestreich Rd. 84 Y71
Okanagan Ave. 69 S56
Okanagan Connector 80 U52-53
Okanagan Centre Rd. 69 T56
Okanagan Falls FS Rd. 81 V56-57 W56 X56
Okanagan Landing Rd. 69 S-T56
Oktwanch Main Rd. 74 U30
Old Aiyansh FS Rd. 29 P22-23
Old Alaska Hwy. 25 J48 27 M51
Old Babine Lake Rd. 30 S29
Old Cariboo Hwy. (Cariboo) 44 B44
Old Cariboo Hwy. (Fraser-Fort George) 35 X43
Old Cariboo Hwy. (Thompson-Nicola) 55 M-N48
Old Cariboo Rd. 67 O-P48
Old Coquihalla Rd. 79 W49
Old Edmonton Hwy. 27 N52
Old Edmonton Hwy. 27 O52
Old Fort Rd. 25 K49
Old Hedley Rd. 80 X52 X53
Old Hope Rd. 25 K48-49
Old Hutton Rd. 36 W47
Old Kaleden Rd. 80 X55
Old Kamloops Rd. (Columbia-Shuswap) 69 S56
Old Kamloops Rd. (Thompson-Nicola) 68 R-S52
Old Lakelse Lake Dr. 29 T24
Old Logging Rd. 69 P57
Old Main Rd. 80 W55
Old Meadow Creek Rd. 67 R50-51
Old Nicola Rd. 67 T51
Old North Fork Rd. 81 Z59
Old Remo Rd. 29 T23
Old Salmo Rd. 82 Z63
Old Salmon Arm Rd. 69 Q57
Old Summit Lake Rd. 35 V43
Old Summit Lake Rd. N. 35 W43
Old Tête Jaune Rd. 47 C56
Old Thompson Hwy. 56 K52
Old Town Rd. 69 P57
Old Tunkwa Rd. 67 R50
Old Vernon Rd. 81 U56
Oldfield Rd. 87 C41
Oleen Creek Rd. 69 R58
Oliver Rd. (Central Kootenay) 83 W65
Oliver Rd. (Columbia-Shuswap) 70 Q62-63
Oliver Rd. (Mount Waddington) 62 S-T29
Oliver Creek FS Rd. 57 J57
Olsen Lake Rd. (dfglm) 64 T37
Olson Rd. (Bulkley-Nechako) 33 W33
Olson Rd. (Cariboo) 44 B44
Olson Rd. (Columbia-Shuswap) 70 Q62
Olsson FS Rd. 36 V45
Omerotto Rd. 54 H46
Omineca Way 31 U30
One Island Lake Rd. 27 O-P51
Oolichan Ave. 29 V23
Ootsa-Nadina Rd. 32 X31-32
Ootsa Lake Rd. 32 Y32 33 Y33
Ootsa Lake Rd. E. 33 Y-Z33
Ootsa Main FS Rd. 32 Y32 33 Y33
Ootsa Nadina Junction Rd. 32 X32
Ootsanee FS Rd. 33 X33
Opheim Lake Rd. 44 F46
Ord Rd. 68 Q52
Oregon Jack Creek Rd. 67 Q48
Osatulk Rd. 33 V33
Osborn Dump Ave. 25 H51
Osborne Bay Rd. 87 A40
Oscar Creek FS Rd. 83 Y64
Ospika Blvd. N. 35 X43
Osprey Lake Rd. 80 W52
Oster Rd. 59 M65
Othello Rd. 79 X48
Otter Rd. 41 G35
Otter-Caribou FS Rd. 57 K-L56
Otter Creek FS Rd. 36 V46-47
Otter Creek FS Rd. 57 K56-57
Otter Lake Rd. 69 R56-57
Otter Lake Cross Rd. 69 R56
Otter Point Rd. 87 D39
Otter Valley Rd. 79 U-V51
Otto Ave. 25 G48
Otto Lake FS Rd. 32 X32
Otway Rd. 35 X43
Oullette Creek Rd. 81 X57
Ououkinsh Main Rd. 61 S26
Owen Lake FS Rd. 43 G42-43
Owen North FS Rd. 32 W30-31
Owens Rd. 30 R28
Owl Creek FS Rd. 65 R-S43
Owlhead Creek FS Rd. 69 P58
Oyama Rd. 69 T56
Oyama Lake Rd. 69 T56
Oyster River Main Rd. N. 75 U33-34 V33
Oyster River Main Rd. S. 75 U-V34

P.O.B. Creek Rd. 37 Y49-50
P30 Rd. 74 U27
Pablo Creek Rd. 54 H-J45
Pacific Way 68 Q52
Pacific Marine Rd. 86 B-C37 87 A-B38
Pacific Rim Hwy. 75 X33-34 Y33-34 Z32
Paddle Rd. 49 N26 61 O26
Paddle Hill FS Rd. 33 W-X35
Padgett Rd. 76 V37
Page Rd. 78 Z45
Pakka Rd. 69 P56
Paleface Creek FS Rd. 79 Z48
Paley Rd. 43 C43
Palling Rd. E. 31 U33
Palling Rd. W. 31 U33
Palliser River FS Rd. 72 R70-71
Palmer-Forsyth Rd. 68 P52
Palmer Bar FS Rd. 84 X68-69
Palmer Lake Rd. 53 H42 J43
Palmer Lake FS Rd. 43 F-G42
Palmeson Rd. 30 R28
Panorama Rd. 84 W69
Paradise Dr. 44 G46-47
Paradise Rd. 43 B43 44 C44
Paradise Creek FS Rd. 65 O43
Paradise Valley Rd. (Central Kootenay) 82 W63
Paradise Valley Rd. (Squamish-Lillooet) 77 U-V42
Park Ave. 28 U18
Park Rd. 31 U33
Parker Rd. (Bulkley-Nechako) 34 X38-39
Parker Mill Rd. 67 T50
Parkins Rd. 43 C42-43
Parkinson Rd. (Capital RD) 86 C37
Parkinson Rd. (North Okanagan) 69 R56
Parkland Rd. 27 M50
Parkland Pit Rd. 25 L50 27 M50
Parri Rd. 69 P56-57
Parrott Lake Rd. 32 V30
Parrott Main FS Rd. 32 V30
Partington Rd. 33 W33
Pasayten River Rd. 79 Z51
Pasayten Valley Rd. 79 Y-Z51
Pascoe Rd. 35 X41
Paska Lake Rd. 67 R51
Pass Rd. (Columbia-Shuswap) 58 M60-61
Pass Rd. (Kootenay Boundary) 82 Y61
Pass-Rock Candy East FS Rd. 81 Y59
Pass Creek Rd. 82 X62
Pass Lake FS Rd. 36 W46-47
Pass Main Rd. 76 Y36
Passmore Lower Rd. 82 W62
Passmore Upper Rd. 82 W62
Pasture Ave. 25 J50
Pat Creek Rd. 57 J59
Pat Roy Rd. 29 S23
Patchett Rd. 79 U50
Paterson Lake Rd. 63 T33
Patricia Bay Hwy. 87 B41-42
Patterson Rd. (Fraser-Fort George) 35 Y43 36 Y44
Patterson Rd. (Thompson-Nicola) 67 P48
Pattison Lake Rd. 80 U52-53
Paul Creek FS Rd. 68 P54
Paul Fire Rd. 31 U31
Paul Lake Rd. 68 P52
Paul Raymond Rd. 30 P-Q26
Pauls Point Rd. (6000 Rd.) 55 J50
Paulson Detour Rd. 82 Y60
Pavilion-Clinton Rd. 66 O-P47
Pavilion Mountain Rd. 66 O46-47 P46
Pavilion Mountain Lookout Rd. 66 O47
Paxton Valley Rd. 68 Q54-55 R54
Paxton Valley FS Rd. 68 Q54
PD Rd. 24 F45
PD Rd. O9C 24 G45-46
PDR 200 25 F50
Peace FS Rd. 33 W34
Peaceview Rd. 25 K50
Peachland Creek Rd. 80 U-V54
Peachland FS Rd. 80 U-V53
Peacock West FS Rd. 30 U29 31 U30
Pear Lake Rd. 66 O46-47
Pearce Rd. 80 X54
Pearson Rd. Branch/1 33 V35
Pearson Rd. Branch/2 33 V35
Pearson FS Rd. 70 Q62
Pebb Mainline FS Rd. 65 Q41
Peddle Mountain FS Rd. 57 H56
Pedro Creek Rd. 82 W62-63
Peers Creek FS Rd. 79 X49
Peeve Creek FS Rd. 79 Z51 80 Z52
Pelican-Holman FS Rd. 35 Z40-41
Pelican FS Rd. 35 Y-Z42 Z41
Pelican Lake Rd. 35 A40
Pelican Lake Rd. 35 Z40
Pelmewash Pkwy. 69 T56
Pemberton-D'Arcy Rd. 65 R-S43
Pemberton-Douglas FS Rd. 78 U-V45
Pemberton 400 Rd. 61 Q25
Pemberton Farm Rd. 65 S43
Pemberton Main Rd. 61 Q25
Pemberton Meadows Rd. (Pemberton Valley Rd) 65 R42-43 S43
Pemberton Portage Rd. 65 R-S43
Pemberton Valley Rd. 65 R42
Pemmican Rd. 26 M47
Pend-d'Oreille Rd. 82 Z63
Pendleton Rd. 31 T33
Pendleton Lakes Rd. (7000, 7100 Rd.) 55 J50-51
Peninsula Rd. 75 Z32-33
Pennask FS Rd. 80 U53
Pennask Lake Rd. 80 U53
Pennask Lake FS Rd. 68 T52
Pennefeather Rd. 36 Z44-45
Pennt Access Rd. 37 X48
Perrier Rd. 82 X63
Perry Rd. 36 X44
Perry Creek Rd. 84 W-X68
Perry Creek FS Rd. 27 Q48
Perry River Rd. (North Fork Rd.) 55 M50 69 O58-59
Perry River-Ratchford FS Rd. 57 L-M59
Perry River East FS Rd. 57 N59 69 O59
Perrys Back Rd. 82 W63
Peter Hope Rd. 68 S52
Peters Rd. (Cariboo) 43 B43 44 B44
Peters Rd. (Central Kootenay) 83 W65
Peters Creek FS Rd. 44 C46
Peterson Rd. (Cariboo) 44 G46 54 H46
Peterson Rd. (Thompson-Nicola) 79 U50
Petit Creek Rd. 67 T49
Petkau Rd. 33 Y33
Pettipiece Rd. 57 M59
Pettyjohn Rd. 55 K50
PG Pulp Mill Rd. 35 X43
Phantom Rd. 31 T33
Phelix Creek Rd. 66 Q44
Phillips Creek Rd. 85 Z72-73
Phillips East Main Rd. 63 Q34
Phillips Main Rd. 63 Q34
Phillips Rabbit FS Rd. 85 Z72
Philpott Rd. 81 U57
Philpott FS Rd. 81 U57
Phoenix Rd. 81 Z58-59
Pickell Pit Rd. 24 J47
Pierce Mainline Rd. 49 L25-26
Piercy Rd. 75 V35
Pigeon Rd. 54 H46
Piggott Main Rd. 75 V34
Pighin Rd. 84 W69
Pike Mountain Rd. 79 V51
Pilkey Point Rd. 77 Z40
Pilot Bay Rd. 83 W65
Pilot Peninsula FS Rd. 83 W65
Pimainus Lake Rd. 67 R-S49
Pimpernel FS Rd. 32 V29
Pinatan Cake Rd. 68 P53
Pinaus Lake Rd. 68 R55
Pinch Creek Rd. 61 R26-27
Pine Ave. 85 V72
Pine Point Resort Rd. 41 G35
Pine Terrace Rd. 26 N47
Pine Valley Dr. 55 K49
Pinewood Rd. 84 V69
Pingel Creek Rd. 25 L50
Pink Mountain Rd. 24 F43
Pinko Rd. 36 X44
Pinkut Creek Rd. 31 U32-33
Pinnacles Rd. 44 C44
Pioneer Rd. 26 M46
Pioneer Mine Rd. 65 P43
Pipeline Rd. 77 X-Y43
Pirates Rd. 87 B41
Pit Rd. 33 X33 Y33
Pitka Creek FS Rd. 34 V38
Pitt River FS Rd. 78 W44
pl23672 Rd. 77 V-W43
pl82475 Rd. 77 W43 78 W44
Place Lake Rd. 54 J45
Placer Creek Rd. 83 Y-Z65
Placer Mountain FS Rd. 79 Y51 80 Y52
Planet Mine Rd. 68 S52
Plant Creek FS Rd. 70 S60-61
Plantway Rd. 38 A52
Plateau Rd. 62 T30
Playmor Rd. 82 X63
Pleasant Valley Rd. 69 R57 S56-57
Plett Rd. 36 A44
Ployart Rd. 75 V34
Plumber Mainline Rd. 74 V28-29
Plumbob Creek FS Rd. 84 Y70-71
Plumper Bay Rd. 63 T34
Point Rd. 63 T35
Poison Creek FS Rd. 31 U31
Poison Lake Rd. 54 M46
Pollard Rd. 35 W43
Ponderosa Rd. 82 Z60
Pony Valley Creek FS Rd. 54 N44-45
Pooley Rd. 35 X43
Pope Rd. 30 R28
Popkum Rd. 78 Y47
Poplar Creek FS Rd. 71 S64
Poplar Lake Rd. 71 R-S64
Porcupine Rd. 83 Y64
Porlier Pass Rd. 87 A40-41
Port Albion Rd. 75 Z33
Port Alice Rd. 61 Q26
Port Alice 60 Rd. 61 S26
Port Eliza Mainline Rd. 74 U27
Port Hardy Main Rd. 61 Q-R26
Portage Rd. (D'Arcy-Anderson Lake Rd.) 65 R43 66 R44
Portage Rd. (Fraser-Fort George) 36 W44
Porte d'Enfer Canyon Rd. 57 J56
Porto Rico Rd. (Central Kootenay) 82 X63 83 X64
Porto Rico Rd. (East Kootenay) 84 X69
Porto Rico-Ymir Rd. 83 X-Y64
Post Rd. 36 Z47
Postill Lake Rd. 81 U56
Pothole Creek FS Rd. 79 U51 80 U52
Pottery Rd. 69 S56
Powder Creek FS Rd. 83 U65-66
Powder Point Rd. 76 Y38
Powell Rd. 24 L46
Powell Rd. 68 P-Q53
Powell Lake Mainline Rd. 64 S37-38
Powell Lake Mainline East Rd. 64 S38
Power Line FS Rd. 68 R-S54
Prairie Ave. 77 Y43
Prairie Rd. 84 V69
Prairie Rd. (Bulkley-Nechako) 30 S28
Prairie Central Rd. 78 Y46-47
Preacher Lake FS Rd. 55 K50-51
Premier Lake Rd. 84 U69
Premier Ridge Rd. 84 U70
Prespatou Rd. 25 F48 F48-49 H49 H-J49
Pressy Lake Rd. 55 M49
Pretty Rd. 84 W69
Price Rd. 44 B44
Price Creek FS Rd. 29 Q25 30 Q26
Priestly Hill Rd. 33 W34
Priestly Station Rd. 33 W34
Princeton Ave. 80 V54
Princeton-Omni Range FS Rd. 80 X52
Princeton-Summerland Rd. 80 V53 V-W52
Princeton Cut-off Rd. 67 T51
Princeton Reserve Rd. 80 W54
Pritchard-Pritchard Rd. 68 P-Q54
Procter East Rd. 83 W65
Prodigal Rd. 82 W63
Promontory Rd. (Thompson-Nicola) 67 T50
Prospect Rd. 37 Z50
Prospect Rd. 84 W69
Prospect Creek FS Rd. 67 T49
Prospect Lake Rd. 87 C40-41
Pruckl Rd. 26 M47 27 M48
Pryor Rd. 76 U36
Ptarmigan Creek FS Rd. 79 Z49-50
Ptarmigan FS Rd. 47 E58-59
Ptarmigan Pit Rd. 37 Y49
Puch Rd. 25 H50
Puett Ranch Rd. 68 P52
Puggins FS Rd. 27 N49-50 O49
Pugh Rd. 25 H49-50
Pugh Main Rd. 61 P25
Pulteney Point Rd. 61 Q27 62 Q28
Punchaw Rd. 35 A42
Punti-Chilanko FS Rd. 52 H39
Punti Lake FS Rd. 42 G39 52 H39
Puntzi Airport Rd. 52 H38
Puntzi Lake Rd. 52 H38-39
Puntzi Lake Rd. S. 52 H39
Puntzi Mountain Rd. 52 H38
Puntzilake Project FS Rd. 52 H38 H39
Puntzio Lake East FS Rd. 52 H38
Purdy Rd. 70 T63
Pye Lake East Rd. 63 S33
Pye Lake West Rd. 63 S33
Pyper Lake Rd. 52 H38

Quadra St. 87 C41
Quarry Main Rd. 61 R26
Quartz Creek FS Rd. 58 M63
Quartz Mountain FS Rd. 53 N43 54 N44
Quast Rd. 57 N58
Quatsino Rd. 61 Q25-26
Queensway 29 T24
Queest-Anstey Rd. 69 O58
Queest-Legerwood FS Rd. 69 O58
Queest-Mountain FS Rd. 69 O58
Queest-Solsqua FS Rd. 69 O-P58
Queest Mountain Rd. 69 P57-58
Query Creek FS Rd. 82 Y63
Quesnel-Hixon Rd. (Old Cariboo Hwy.) 36 A44 44 B-C44
Quesnel Canyon Rd. 44 C44-45
Quesnel Forks Rd. 44 E47
Quesnel Hydraulic Rd. 44 C44 D44-45
Quick East Rd. 30 T29
Quick Station Rd. 30 T29
Quick West Rd. 30 T29
Quilchena Creek Rd. 67 T51
Quinn Creek Rd. 84 U-V71
Quinsam Rd. 75 U33-34
Quintette Mountain Rd. 27 R49

R Branch Rd. 76 U38
R200 Rd. 61 Q27
R400 Rd. 61 Q26-27
R440 Rd. 61 Q26
Race Track Rd. 54 H-J44
Race Track Rd. 54 J44

Radar Lake Rd. 27 N51
Radio Range Rd. 54 H46
Raft Main Rd. 61 P-Q24
Raft River FS Rd. 56 K55
Raging Main Rd. 61 R-S27
Rainbow Rd. 55 K50
Rainbow Rd. 87 A40
Rainbow Falls Rd. 38 A52
Rainbow FS Rd. 36 V45
Rainbow Main Rd. 76 U37
Raintree Rd. 43 B-C43
Rainy Day Lake Rd. 76 V38
Rainy River Rd. 77 W40
Ram Creek Rd. 85 X-Y72
Ranch Rd. 24 K46
Ranch Rd. 44 C45
Ranchero Dr. 35 W43
Range Rd. 69 R56
Rannie Rd. 78 X-Y44
Rannie Pit Rd. 67 R48
Ranson Rd. 26 N47
Raphael-Meason Rd. 55 M48
Rashdale Rd. 69 R57
Rathayatra Way 67 Q-R48
Rau Rd. 44 B44
Raush Valley Rd. 46 B54-55
Raven Hill Rd. 81 Z56
Raven Lake Rd. (1300 Rd.) 53 J43
Raven Ridge Rd. 68 R52
Rawlings Rd. 43 C43
Rawlings Lake Rd. 59 S58
Raymond Rd. (Priestly) 33 W34-35
Raymond Rd. (Smithers) . . . 30 S28-29
Read Rd. 46 B55
Reclamation Rd. 83 Z66
Recreation Rd. 75 Z32
Red Rd. 33 Z36
Red Bluff Rd. 44 C-D44
Red Canyon Rd. 85 Y72
Red Creek Rd. 55 J50-51
Red Creek Rd. (Capital RD) 86 C37 87 C38
Red Creek Rd. (Peace River) . . . 25 J48
Red Creek FS Rd. 80 W52-53
Red Lake Rd. (Tranquille-Criss Creek Rd.) 67 P51
Red Mountain Rd. 82 U63
Red Rock Rd. (East Kootenay) . 72 Q68
Red Rock Rd. (Fraser-Fort George) 35 Y43
Red Rock Rd. E. 35 Y43 36 Y44
Redbrush Rd. 52 H38
Redburn Creek FS Rd. 59 L-M65
Redding Creek FS Rd. 83 W66-67
Redeau Lake Rd. 54 H46
Redfish FS Rd. 83 W64
Redrock FS Rd. 57 H59
Redroofs Rd. 76 W-X39
Redstone-Chezacut Rd. 42 G39
Redstone Bluff Rd. 52 H39 53 H40
Redstone FS Rd. 52 H39 53 H40
Redstreak Park Rd. 72 Q68
Reduction Rd. 44 C47 45 C48
Redwater Lake Rd. 43 C40
Redwillow Branch 1 FS Rd. . 27 R51-52
Redwillow Branch 2 FS Rd. . 27 R51-52
Reed Rd. 41 F34
Reed Rd. 77 X40
Reeves Rd. 59 L64
Reid Rd. (North Okanagan) 69 S57
Reid Rd. (Squamish-Lillooet) . . . 65 S43
Reid St. 25 G48
Reid Lake Connector 35 W41-42
Reimer Rd. 25 F48-49
Reinhardt Creek Rd. 87 A38
Relay Creek FS Rd. 53 N43 65 O43
Renata-Bowman FS Rd. 82 W60
Renata-Dog FS Rd. 82 X-Y61
Renata FS Rd. 82 W-X60
Rendell-Goatskin East FS Rd. . . 81 V59
Rendell-Goatskin FS Rd. 81 V58
Rendell Creek FS Rd. 81 V-W58
Renfrew Rd. 43 B40
Reserve Rd. 24 H-J46
Reservoir Rd. 80 W55
Restless Main Rd. 61 R24-25
Rey Lake Rd. 67 S50
Rialto Creek FS Rd. 82 X62
RIC 7 . . . . 63 R33
RIC 9 . . . . 63 R33
RIC Mainline 1 . . . . 63 R33
Rice Rd. 27 M48
Richards Ave. 78 Y45
Richlands Rd. 69 S59
Richmond Frwy. 77 Y42
Richter Pass Rd. 80 Z55
Ridge Dr. 72 R68
Ridge Rd. (Alberni-Clayoquot) . . 76 Z36
Ridge Rd. (Cariboo) 44 F46
Ridge View Rd. 78 Y45
Ridley Island Rd. 28 U18
Rimrock Rd. 44 F45
Riondel Rd. 83 V65
Riondel North Rd. 83 V65
Rioulx Creek FS Rd. 70 S60-61
Ripperto FS Rd. 81 Y57
Ritherdon Rd. 75 Z35
River Rd. (Cowichan Valley) . 87 A39-40
River Rd. (East Kootenay) 84 V69
River Rd. (Fraser-Fort George) . 35 X42
River Rd. (Kitimat-Stikine) 30 P27
River Rd. (Okanagan-Similkameen) 80 Y54
Riverside Rd. 87 B40
Riverside Rd. (Alberni-Clayoquot) 75 Y34-35
Riverside Rd. (Kootenay Boundary) 82 Z62
Riverside Rd. (North Okanagan) 69 Q57
Riverside Rd. (Peace River) . . . 27 N52
Robbers Creek Main Rd. 62 R31
Robbin's Range Rd. 68 Q53
Robbins Rd. 44 D44
Robbins Creek Rd. 68 Q54
Robbins Range Rd. 68 Q54
Roberts Rd. 35 X42
Roberts Rd. 76 V37-38
Roberts Flume FS Rd. 77 X40
Robertson Rd. (Cariboo) 44 F-G45
Robertson Mainline Rd. 87 B38
Robin Creek Rd. 30 S29
Robinson Ave. 80 W55
Robinson Rd. (Central Kootenay) 82 U-V60
Robinson Rd. (East Kootenay) . 85 X72
Robinson Rd. (Peace River) 24 J47
Robson Ridge FS Rd. 82 X-Y62
Roche Lake Rd. 68 R52-53
Rocher de Boule Rd. 30 Q27
Rock Bay FS Rd. 63 S33
Rock Bay North FS Rd. 63 S33
Rock Creek-Bridesville Rd. 81 Z57
Rock Creek Main Rd. 57 M56-57
Rock Lake Rd. 84 X-Y71
Rockwell Dr. 78 X-Y47
Rocky Creek FS Rd. 26 P46
Rocky FS Rd. 70 Q62
Rocky Point Rd. 78 X-Y45
Roddie Rd. 44 D44
Rodeo Dr. 54 H46
Rodeo Rd. 25 L51-52
Roderick Rd. 81 Y58
Rody Creek FS Rd. 69 T59
Roe Mainline FS Rd. 77 U41-42
Roger Creek Rd. 76 Z36
Rogers Rd. 25 F49
Rogers Rd. 58 L-M63
Rogers Creek FS Rd. . 66 T44-45 78 U44
Rohan-Peters Rd. 69 Q58
Rohan-Peters FS Rd. 69 S58
Rohrer Ave. 25 G49
Rolla Rd. . 25 L51 L51-52 L52 27 M51 M51
Rona Rd. 62 S29
Rond Creek FS Rd. 36 A46
Rondeau Rd. 31 T31
Ronning 100 Rd. 60 Q23 61 Q24
Ronning Main Rd. 60 P-Q23
Rooney Lake Main Rd. 62 S31
Rosa Prairie Rd. 25 H49 J-K49
Rosander Mainline Rd. 86 A-B36
Rose Dr. 44 G46-47
Rose Rd. (Central Kootenay) . . . 82 Y63
Rose Rd. (Peace River) 25 L52
Rose Hill Rd. 68 Q52
Rose Lake Cutoff Rd. 31 U32
Rose Prairie Rd. 25 H49 J-K49
Rosebud Lake Rd. 83 Z64
Rosefield Rd. 25 G48-49
Rosemond Lake Rd. 69 Q57
Rosen Lake Rd. 84 X71
Roses Rd. 32 V30
Rosette Lake Rd. 44 E47
Rosewall FS Rd. 75 X35
Rosicky Rd. 84 X71
Rosita-Fir East FS Rd. 43 G43
Rosita-Fir Lake FS Rd. 43 G42-43
Rosita-Mackin FS Rd. (1000 Rd.) 43 G43 44 G44
Rosita-Mackin West FS Rd. . . . 43 G43
Rosita-Meldrum FS Rd. 43 F42 G42-43 44 G44
Rosita FS Rd. 43 G43
Ross Rd. 44 E44
Ross St. 24 L46
Ross-Ruckell Point FS Rd. 69 P57
Ross-Upper Scotch FS Rd. 69 Q57
Ross Lake Rd. 30 P27-28
Ross Moore Lake FS Rd. 68 R52
Ross Spur Rd. 82 Y63
Rossiter Creek FS Rd. . . 71 T64 83 U64
Rossiter Main Rd. 75 V33-34
Rossland-Cascade Rd. 82 Z61
Rossland-Nancy Greene Lake Hwy. 82 Y61-62 Z62
Rottacker Rd. 54 H45
Rough Bay Tr. 62 Q28
Round Lake Rd. (Bulkley-Nechako) 30 S29
Round Lake Rd. (North Okanagan) 69 R56
Round Lake Rd. (Okanagan-Similkameen) 79 V-W51
Round Top Rd. 56 L52
Rover-Snowater FS Rd. 82 X63
Rover Creek FS Rd. 82 X63
Rowland Creek Mainline Rd. . . . 62 T28
Royal Ave. 77 Y43
Royal Main Rd. 61 Q26
Royston Rd. 75 W35
Ruault Rd. 72 R68
Rudquist Rd. 27 N49
Rupert Rd. 76 X37
Rupert Main Rd. 61 Q26-27
Rushmere Rd. 72 R-S68
Russel Creek FS Rd. 56 M54-55
Russell Creek FS Rd. 83 Y-Z67
Ruth Lake Rd. 55 J-K49
Rutherford Rd. 76 Y38-39
Rutherford Creek Main Rd. . 65 S42-43
Rutland Rd. 81 U56
Ruttan Rd. 44 D44
Ryan Rd. 75 V35
Ryan River FS Rd. 65 R41-42
S-200 Rd. 65 T41
S-422 Rd. 65 S-T41
S-500 Rd. 65 T41
S Main Rd. 61 R25
Sabiston Rd. 67 P50
Sable Creek Rd. 70 P62
Sackner Pit Rd. 34 W39 35 W40
Sackville Rd. 75 V35
Saddle Rd. 65 P43
Saddle Mountain-Revelstoke Rd. 70 T61-62
Saddle Mountain Lookout Rd. . . 70 T61
St. Agnes Rd. 69 R56
St. Elmo Rd. 78 X47 79 X48
St. John's Point Rd. 76 W36
St. Leon FS Rd. 70 R62
St. Leon Hotspring Rd. 70 R61-62
St. Mary-Hellroaring Creek FS Rd. 84 W68
St. Mary Lake Rd. 84 W68
St. Mary River FS Rd. 83 V-W67
St. Mary River South FS Rd. 84 W68-69
St. Mary Westfork FS Rd. . . 83 V66-67
St. Mary White FS Rd. 83 V67
St. Marys Pit Rd. 33 Y33
Sales Rd. 44 C44
Salish Rd. 84 Z71
Salloompt Rd. 40 F30
Salloompt FS Rd. 40 F30
Sallus Creek Rd. 66 P46
Sally Rd. 62 S-T28
Salmo River Rd. 82 Z63 83 Z64
Salmon-North Chaperron FS Rd. 68 S54
Salmon Falls FS Rd. 68 S54
Salmon River Rd. 35 V43
Salmon River Rd. (Columbia-Shuswap) 69 Q-R56
Salmon River Rd. (Kitimat-Stikine) 30 P27
Salmon River Bench Rd. 69 R56
Salmon River FS Rd. (Columbia-Shuswap) 68 S54
Salmon River FS Rd. (Fraser-Fort George) 35 V43
Salmon River Mainline Rd. 62 S31 63 S32
Salmon River Mainline Rd. . 63 T32-33
Salmon Valley Rd. (Fraser-Fort George) 35 W43 36 W44
Salt Lake FS Rd. 42 G39
Salt Lake NW FS Rd. . . . 42 G39 43 G40
Samatosum Rd. 56 N55
Samuelson Rd. 83 Z67
San Josef 100 Rd. 60 P23 61 P24
San Josef 400 Rd. 60 P23
San Josef Main Rd. 60 P23 61 P24
Sanborn Rd. 71 Q66
Sanca-Eastfork Rd. 83 X66
Sanca Creek FS Rd. 83 X66
Sand Creek Rd. (East Kootenay) 84 X71
Sand Creek Rd. (Kootenay Boundary) 81 Z59
Sand Creek FS Rd. 47 D56
Sand Creek FS Rd. 81 Z59 82 Z60
Sand Lake FS Rd. 29 Q23
Sand River Rd. 75 Y33
Sande FS Rd. 37 W48-49
Sanders Rd. 35 W43
Sandon Rd. 83 U64
Sandon-Cody Rd. 83 U64
Sandrift FS Rd. 81 W58
Sanford Rd. 43 C43
Sansom Rd. 38 A52
Saratoga Rd. 75 U34
Sardine FS Rd. 44 D45
Saskum Lake FS Rd. 56 L-M55
Satan Mountain Rd. (P-Rd.) . . . 42 G38
Satchie Main Rd. 74 W29 W-X30
Sather FS Rd. 33 X-Y34
Satna Rosa Rd. 82 Z60
Saul Lake Rd. 67 P51
Saunders Main Rd. 74 U31
Saunier Creek FS Rd. 81 X56
Saunier Lake FS Rd. 81 X57
Sauqum Creek FS Rd. 84 V70
Savory Rd. 33 W35
Sawchuk Rd. 26 M47
Sawmill Rd. (Central Okanagan) 69 T56
Sawmill Rd. (Okanagan-Similkameen) 80 Y55
Sawmill Lake Rd. 67 P51
Sawmill Lake FS Rd. 67 O50-51
Saxton Rd. 35 W41
Sayward Rd. (Comox-Strathcona) 62 R31 63 R32 S32
Schemenauer Rd. 44 C44
Schilling Rd. 26 N46
Schmidt Rd. 27 N49
Schoen Rd. 62 S30
Schofield Hwy. 82 Z62
School Rd. (North Okanagan) . . . 69 S57
Schubert Rd. 69 R57
Schulbuckhand Creek FS Rd. . . . 29 U24
Scotch-Adam FS Rd. 57 N56
Scotch-Kwikoit Creek FS Rd. 57 N56 69 O-P56
Scotch-Lamberton FS Rd. 69 O56
Scotch-Lichen FS Rd. 57 N57
Scotch-Onyx FS Rd. 69 O56
Scotch Creek FS Rd. . . 57 N56-57 69 O56
Scotch Creek Wharf Rd. 69 O-P56
Scott Rd. (Thompson-Nicola) . . . 68 Q52
Scott Creek Rd. 84 W69
Scottie Creek FS Rd. 67 O48-49
Scuitto Creek Rd. 68 Q53
Scuzzy Creek FS Rd. 78 V47 79 V48
SE Main Rd. (Cracroft) 62 P-Q30
SE Main Rd. (Port Alice) 61 R26
Seabird Mainline Rd. . . . 62 R31 63 R32
Seacrest Hill Rd. 80 Y55
Seaford Rd. 63 T35
Seaton Basin Rd. 30 Q28-29
Seaview Rd. 75 U34-35 V35
Seawater Rd. 27 M51-52
Sebastian Creek Rd. 81 X58
Sebaston Creek Rd. 67 P50
Sechelt-Chapman FS Rd. 77 W-X40
Sechelt-Crucil FS Rd. . . . 76 X39 77 X40
Sechelt-Dakota FS Rd. 77 W40
Sechelt-Roberts Creek Rd. 77 X40
Sechelt Inlet Rd. 76 W39
Second Creek FS Rd. 57 N58
Second Relief Rd. 82 Y63
Sederberg Rd. 69 O58
Sedge Lake FS Rd. 67 P50
Seebach FS Rd. 36 V45-46
Seidner Lake FS Rd. 69 R57
Seiman Rd. 25 F-G49
Sentinel Mountain FS Rd. 82 X62
Seperation Rd. 68 Q52
Serpentine Creek FS Rd. 47 F57
Service Rd. 68 R54-55
Seton-Retask Rd. 66 Q45
Seton Portage Rd. 66 P-Q45 Q45
Seton Ridge Rd. 66 Q45
Settlement Rd. (Bulkley-Nechako) 32 X32 33 X33
Settlement Rd. (Fort Fraser) . . 34 W37
Settlers Rd. 72 Q69
Settlers-Kootenay FS Rd. 72 R69
Seven Lakes Rd. 67 P50
Seven Mile Creek Mainline FS Rd. 66 R44
Seven Mile Dam Rd. (Central Kootenay) 82 Z62-63
Seven Mile FS Rd. (Bulkley-Nechako) 33 W33-34
Severeid FS Rd. 37 V-W48
Severide Creek Rd. 70 S60
Seward Rd. 59 L-M65
Seymour-Blais South FS Rd. . . 57 L58
Seymour-Ratchford FS Rd. 57 M58
Seymour-Smoky House FS Rd. 57 M58
Seymour Arm Bay Rd. 57 N58
Seymour Arm FS Rd. . . . 57 N57 69 O57
Seymour Mainline FS Rd. 77 X42
Seymour River Rd. 57 M58
Seymour River FS Rd. 57 L-M58
Seymour West FS Rd. 57 L-M58
Shackelly Rd. 67 T49
Shakespeare Rd. 70 S62
Shalalth Rd. 66 Q45
Shames Mountain Rd. 29 T22-23
Shandilla Lakes Main FS Rd. . . . 30 Q26
Shannon Creek FS Rd. 70 T62-63
Shannon Lake Rd. 80 U55
Sharpe Rd. (Bulkley-Nechako) 33 W36
Sharpe Lake Rd. 55 M50
Shatford Creek FS Rd. 80 W-X54
Shaw Creek Main Rd. 76 Z37
Shawnigan-Port Renfrew Rd. 87 B39-40
Shawnigan Lake-Mill Bay Rd. . . 87 B40
Shearer Dale Rd. 25 L52
Sheep-Moon Rd. 54 J44-45
Sheep Creek Rd. (Central Kootenay) 83 Y64
Sheep Creek Rd. (East Kootenay) 84 U69
Sheep Creek Rd. (Okanagan-Similkameen) 80 X54
Shelbourne Rd. 84 X71
Shelford Main FS Rd. 32 X29
Shelford No. 1 Rd. 32 X30
Shell Beach Rd. 76 Z39
Shell Lake Rd. 35 W42
Shelley Rd. 36 X44
Sheloff Rd. 83 Y64
Shelter Bay FS Rd. 70 Q-R61
Shelter Bay South FS Rd. 70 R61
Shelter Point Rd. 76 W37
Sheraton FS Rd. 33 V34-35
Sheridan Lake East Rd. 55 L50
Sheridan Lake FS Rd. 55 L49-50
Sheridan Lake West Rd. . . . 55 L49-50
Sheringham Point Rd. 87 D39
Shertenlib Rd. 55 L50
Shiel Rd. 57 L59
Shields Rd. 36 W44
Shields Creek FS Rd. 82 X-Y61
Shingle Spit 76 W36
Shingle Creek Rd. 80 W54
Shinish Creek Rd. 80 V52-53
Ship Creek Rd. 75 Y35 76 Y36
Shoaf Ave. 25 J50
Shoreacres Rd. 82 X63
Short Rd. 32 W32
Shorty Creek Rd. 84 Z68
Shrimpton FS Rd. 80 U52
Shuswap Ave. 69 S57
Shuswap Rd. 68 P55
Shuswap-Chase Creek Rd. 68 P55
Shuswap River Dr. 69 S58-59
Shuttleworth Creek Rd. (Venner Meadow Rd.) 80 X55 81 X56 Y56
Shylock Rd. 79 W49
Sibola Rd. 32 X28
Sicamous Creek North FS Rd. . 69 P58
Side Bay Main Rd. 61 R24-25
Sidley-Camp McKinney Rd. . . . 81 Z56
Sidley Meadows Rd. 81 Z56
Sidley Mountain Rd. 81 Z56
Siegert Rd. 27 N-O52
Sigalet Rd. 69 S58
Silver-Ireland FS Rd. 69 R58-59
Silver Hills FS Rd. 69 S58-59
Silver King Rd. 82 X63 83 X64
Silver Lake Rd. (Bulkley-Nechako) 30 R28
Silver Lake Rd. (Thompson-Nicola) 79 U49
Silver Main Rd. 75 Z34-35
Silver Park Mountain FS Rd. 69 R58-59
Silver Queen Rd. 82 U61
Silver Sands Creek Rd. . . . 26 O43-44
Silver Skagit Rd. 79 Y48 Y-Z49
Silver Standard Rd. 30 P27
Silver Star Rd. 69 S57
Silver Tip FS Rd. 32 V28
Silverado Mainline Rd. 74 W30
Silverdale Ave. 78 Y45
Silvernail Rd. 68 R55 69 R56
Silverton Creek FS Rd. 83 U64
Simmons Creek FS Rd. 55 M50
Simmo Rd. 60 Q52
Simms Creek FS Rd. 78 X46
Simon Rd. 84 U70
Simonds Rd. 32 X32 33 X33
Simonsen Ave. 24 K46
Simpson 100 Rd. 61 Q25
Simpson Main Rd. 61 Q25
Simpson Pit Rd. 24 H44
Sinclair Rd. 83 Z67
Sinkut Falls Rd. 34 X39
Sinkut Lake Rd. 34 X39
Sinkut Mountain FS Rd. 34 X-Y39
Sintich Rd. 35 X43
Siphon Creek Rd. 25 H50-51 J50
Sisters-Gems FS Rd. 42 G39 43 G40
Sisters-Plover FS Rd. 43 G40
Sisters FS Rd. 43 G40
Sisters North FS Rd. 43 G40
Siwash Rd. 80 V52
Siwash-Brown FS Rd. . . 68 S55 69 S56
Siwash Creek Rd. (Columbia-Shuswap) 68 S55 69 S56
Siwash Creek Rd. (Fraser Valley) 79 W48-49
Siwash Creek Rd. (Thompson-Nicola) 68 P53
Siwash Creek FS Rd. 80 V52
Six Mile Rd. 30 P27-28
Six Mile Rd. (Central Kootenay) 83 W64
Six Mile Creek Rd. 68 Q-R55
Six Mile Hill Rd. 67 P-Q50
Six Mile Lake Rd. (Fraser-Fort George) 36 X44
Six Mile Point FS Rd. 69 P-Q57
SK Rd. 74 U30
Skaha Lake Rd. 80 W-X55
Skeena Dr. (Prince Rupert) 28 U18
Skeena Dr. (Terrace) 29 T24
Skeena Crossing Rd. 30 Q26-27
Skelly Creek FS Rd. 83 X67
Skelton Lake FS Rd. . . . 44 E45 F45-46
Ski Hill Rd. (Fraser Valley) 79 Y49
Skillhorn Rd. 30 S29
Skimikin Rd. 69 P56
Skookumchuck FS Rd. 72 T69 84 U68-69
Skookumchuck River Rd. 84 U69
Skuhun-Nicola FS Rd. 67 R-S49
Skuhun-Pimainus FS Rd. 67 S50
Skuhun Creek FS Rd. 67 S49-50
Skullow Lake FS Rd. 44 G46
Skutz Falls Rd. 87 A39
Sky Ranch Rd. 53 K-L42
Skye Pit Rd. 34 X39 35 X40
Slater Mountain Rd. 44 G45 54 H45
Slavin Rd. 71 O66
Sleepy Hollow Rd. (North Okanagan) 69 R57
Slender Lake FS Rd. 36 A46-47
Slesse-Borden Creek FS Rd. . . 78 Z47
Slesse Creek FS Rd. 78 Z47
Sliammon Lake Rd. 76 U36
Slim Creek Rd. 65 P42-43
Slocan St. 82 V63
Slocan River Rd. 82 V63 W62
Slocan Valley West Rd. 82 W-X62
Slocan West Rd. 82 V63
Slok-Big Bar Rd. 54 N45
Slok-French FS Rd. 54 N44-45
Slok-Leon FS Rd. 66 O46
Slok Creek FS Rd. 66 P46
Sloquet Creek North Rd. 78 V45
Slough Creek FS Rd. 44 B-C47
SM Mainline Rd. 66 S44
Small River FS Rd. 47 B56
Smallwood FS Rd. 82 W63
Smedley Rd. 34 W39
Smith Rd. (Columbia-Shuswap) 68 R55 69 R56
Smith Rd. (Comox-Strathcona) 75 V35
Smith-Willis Rd. 80 X52
Smith Creek Rd. 34 X37
Smith Creek Rd. (Central Okanagan) 80 U55
Smith Creek Rd. (Okanagan-Similkameen) 80 Y52
Smith Lake FS Rd. 68 R52
Smoke Creek FS Rd. 57 H57
Smokehouse Rd. 26 P47
Smoker Rd. 81 W57
Smokey Lake FS Rd. 52 J36
Snake Rd. (Babine Lake) 31 T33
Snake Rd. (Smithers) 30 R-S29
Snaking River Rd. (5100 Rd.) 43 C40-41
Snell Rd. 34 W38-39
Snider Rd. 31 T30
Snider Rd. 71 P67
Snooka Creek Rd. 40 F29-30
Snow Creek FS Rd. 82 U62
Snowden FS Rd. 63 T33
Snowpatch Rd. 79 W51
Snowshoe Rd. 82 U60
Soards Creek Rd. 57 H59
Sob Lake Rd. 35 X40
Sobotka Rd. 66 Q47
Soda Creek Rd. . . 44 F44 G44-45 54 H45
Solco Lake FS Rd. 81 X56
Solomon Lake FS Rd. 44 G46
Solsqua-Sicamous Rd. 69 P57-58
Somenos Rd. 87 A39
Somers Rd. 75 X35
Somerset Dr. 35 X40
Son Ranch Rd. 81 Z59
Sonny's Meadow Rd. 54 K45-46
Soo River FS Rd. 65 S42-43
Soo Valley Rd. 65 S-T43
Sooke Rd. 87 C-D40
Sooke Lake Rd. 87 C40
Sooke River Rd. 87 C-D40
Sorcerer Rd. 58 L60-61
Sorcerer Extension Rd. 58 L-M61
Sorley Rd. 54 M-N47
South Parallel 78 Z45-46
South Rd. (Cariboo) 41 F-G34
South Rd. (Nanaimo) 76 Y39
South Rd. (Powell River) 76 V38
South Access Rd. 30 P26
South Bamfield Rd. 86 A34
South Barrière Lake FS Rd. . 56 N54-55
South Chilko Rd. 34 W39 35 W40
South Creek Mainline FS Rd. 65 R41-42
South Dore FS Rd. 38 A52 45 B51 46 B52
South Douglas Main FS Rd. 29 R23-24
South Easy Bay FS Rd. 62 R31
South Fork-Beaven FS Rd. 70 S60
South Fork-Railroad FS Rd. . . . 70 S61
South Fork Catermole FS Rd. 79 W48-49
South Fraser Rd. 77 Y43
South Green Lake Rd. 55 M48-49
South Herrick FS Rd. 37 V49
South Hirsch FS Rd. 29 V24

South Jerry Creek FS Rd. 36 Z45
South Kid Creek FS Rd. 84 Y68
South Lakeside Dr. 54 H45-46
South Lean-To Creek FS Rd. . . 29 S24
South Legate FS Rd. 29 S25
South Lussier River FS Rd. 72 T70
South Main Rd. (Echo Bay) . . 62 P-Q30
South Main Rd. (Holberg) . . . 61 P-Q24
South Main Rd. (Tlowitsis Tribe) 62 R30
South Mainline Rd. (Comox-Strathcona) 63 Q33
South Mainline Rd. (Cowichan Valley) 87 B38
South Moberly Lake Rd. 26 M46
South Nicola River FS Rd. 68 T54
South Old Fellers Rd. 27 P49
South Otter FS Rd. 57 K-L56
South Otter Lake Rd. 55 L50
South Pass Creek FS Rd. 81 Y59
South Pass FS Rd. 69 P59
South Port Hardy Main Rd. 61 Q26
South Powell Main Rd. 64 S37
South Shore Rd. 86 A37 87 A38
South Statlu FS Rd. 78 X45-46
South Taylor Main Rd. 75 Y34-35
South Tumuch FS Rd. . . . 36 Y47 37 Y48
South Upper Torpy FS Rd. 37 W48 X48-49
South Whiteman Creek FS Rd. 68 S-T55
Southeast 300 Rd. 61 Q24-25
Southeast Main Rd. 61 Q24
Southview Rd. 76 U36
Sowaqua Creek FS Rd. 79 X49
Spahats Creek Forest Rd. . . 56 K54-55
Spanish-Art Creek FS Rd. . . . 55 H-J51
Spanish-Burtt FS Rd. 55 H-J50
Spanish-No Name Creek FS Rd. 55 H51
Spanish Boundary FS Rd. 55 H51
Spanish Creek FS Rd. 55 H-J51
Spanish Lake Rd. 44 E47 45 E48
Spanish Lake FS Rd. 45 E-F48
Spapilem Creek FS Rd. 56 M-N55
Spectrum Creek Rd. 69 R59 70 R60
Spence Rd. 71 O66
Spencer Rd. 66 S-T47
Spencer-C Rd. 86 A35
Spencer Creek Rd. 75 Z35
Spencer Main Rd. 75 Y35
Spetch Creek Rd. 65 S43 66 S44
Spider Lake Rd. 76 X36
Spiller Rd. 34 W37
Spillimacheen FS Rd. 71 O-P66
Spillimacheen North FS Rd. 59 N64-65 71 O65-66 P66-67
Spillman Creek FS Rd. . . 57 N56 68 O55
Spirit Lake Rd. 63 S32
Spittal Creek Rd. 47 C56
Spius Creek FS Rd. 67 T49-50 79 U49-50
Spokane St. 82 Z62
Spokeshute Rd. 29 T23
Spokin Lake Rd. 54 H47
Spout-Oie FS Rd. 55 H-J48
Spout Lake Rd. (1500 Rd.) 55 J48
Spraggett Rd. 81 Z59
Sprigler Rd. 32 W32
Spring Lake Rd. (Cariboo) . . . 55 J-K48
Spring Lake Rd. (Powell River) . 76 U37
Springer Creek Rd. 82 V63
Springfield Rd. 80 U55 81 U56
Springhouse-Us Meadows Rd. 54 J-K46
Sproat Mountain L-O Rd. 70 Q61
Sproule Creek Rd. 82 W63
Spruce Meadows Tr. 73 P75
Spruston Rd. 76 Z39
Spud Lake Rd. 32 X32
Spur 18C Rd. 63 Q34
Spur 20 Rd. 63 P-Q34
Spur 31 Rd. 63 P34
Spusks Creek FS Rd. 45 F49
Spuzzum Creek Rd. 78 V47 79 V48
Squaam Bay Rd. 56 N54-55
Squamish East Mainline FS Rd. 65 S-T41
Squamish Main Rd. 77 U41
Squamish Valley Rd. 77 V41-42
Square Lake Rd. 33 Y33
Squaw Valley Rd. 69 R-S58
Squeah FS Rd. 79 X48
Squilax-Anglemont Rd. 68 O-P55 69 O56-57
Squilax-Turtle Valley Rd. 68 P55
Squirrel Cove Rd. 63 T35
SSJ Mainline Rd. 87 B39
Stack Valley Rd. 54 H-J44
Stafford 1000 Rd. 63 P34
Stafford 200 Rd. 63 P33
Stafford 700 Rd. 63 P33
Stafford 800 Rd. 63 P33-34
Stafford Mainline 2 Rd. 63 P33-34
Stage Rd. 67 P48
Staghorn-Kootowis Creek Dr. . . 75 Z32
Stanchfield Rd. 44 G46-47
Stanley Rd. 44 C47
Starlike Lake Rd. 45 G48
Station Rd. (Kootenay Boundary) 82 Z62
Statlu Creek Rd. 78 X46
Stave Lake Rd. 78 Y45
Stave River FS Rd. 78 W45
Stawamus Indian River Rd. . . . 77 W42
Steam Shovel Creek FS Rd. . . . 67 P50
Steamboat Lake Rd. 71 Q67
Steamboat Mountain Rd. 71 P-Q67 72 Q68
Steele Creek Rd. 62 S28-29
Steeples Rd. 84 W70
Steffens Rd. 67 S50
Steiner Rd. 25 F48
Stella Rd. 33 W36 W36 34 W37
Stella FS Rd. 33 W36 34 W37
Stelling Rd. 76 W36
Stellys Cross Rd. 87 C41
Stemwinder Mountain FS Rd. 80 W-X53
Stenson Creek FS Rd. . . 71 T64 83 U64
Stepney Rd. 69 R57
Stepney Cross Rd. 69 R57
Sterling Rd. 84 Y71
Sterling Arm Main Rd. 75 Y35
Stevens FS Rd. 70 T61
Stevenson Rd. 85 W72
Steveston Hwy. 77 Y-Z42
Stewardson Rd. 74 W-X30
Stewart Creek Rd. 82 Z60
Stewart Creek FS Rd. . . 82 Y63 83 Y64
Stewart Lake FS Rd. 27 M48-49
Stewart Lake Main Rd. 62 T31
Stillwater Mainline Rd. . . 76 U38 V37-38
Stirling Arm Dr. 75 Y35
Stirling Creek FS Rd. . . . 81 V56-57 W56
Stirton Rd. 84 W69
Stoddart Creek Rd. (East Kootenay) 72 R68
Stoddart Creek Rd. (Peace River) 25 J48
Stokke Creek FS Rd. 78 V46
Stone Ave. 25 F48
Stone Creek Rd. (North Okanagan) 81 U58
Stone Creek FS Rd. (Fraser-Fort George) 36 Y-Z44
Stonebuck Rd. (200 Rd.) 36 Y44
Stones Rd. 76 W39
Stones Rd. 84 Y70
Stoney Flats Rd. 68 Q55
Stony Creek Rd. 27 R51
Store Ave. 25 F48
Storey Creek Main Rd. 62 R28
Stormy Rd. 55 M48
Stowe Rd. 24 L45
Strachan Mainline Rd. 49 N26
Strain Rd. 24 K44
Stranby Main Rd. 61 P24
Stranby West Main Rd. . . 60 P23 61 P24
Strathcona Pkwy. 75 V34
Strathcona Rd. 75 U33
Strathnaver-White's Landing Rd. 35 A43 36 A44
Strauss Rd. 84 Y-Z71
Strawberry Creek Rd. 80 Z55
Strayhorse Rd. 80 X54
Striegler Rd. 76 W39
Strouse Lake FS Rd. (1200 Rd.) 53 H-J43
Strutell-Clematis FS Rd. 69 T59
Strutell Creek FS Rd. 69 T59
Stuart Rd. 62 T30
Stuckey Rd. 27 M-N49
Stum Lake Rd. 53 H41
Stump Rd. (Bulkley-Nechako) 34 X39 35 X40
Stump Rd. (East Kootenay) . . 84 Y-Z68
Sturdies Bay Rd. 87 A41
Sturgeon Point Rd. 34 W39
Sucker Creek FS Rd. 45 G48
Sucker Lake FS Rd. 68 S54
Sucwoa Mainline Rd. 74 V29
Sugar-Curwen FS Rd. 69 Q59
Sugar-Sawtooth FS Rd. . 69 Q59 70 Q60
Sugar-Spectrum FS Rd. . 69 R59 70 R60
Sugar-Tsuius FS Rd. . . 69 Q59 70 Q60
Sugar Lake Rd. 69 S59 70 Q60
Sugar Lake East FS Rd. . 69 R59 70 R60
Sugar Lake FS Rd. 68 P54
Sugarloaf Rd. 67 Q51
Sugsaw Main Rd. 86 A34-35
Sukunka-Burnt River Rd. . . . 26 Q45-46
Sukunka FS Rd. 26 Q46
Sukunka River FS Rd. 26 O46-47 P46-47
Sullivan Rd. 82 Y62
Sullivan River Rd. 58 H62 J61-62
Sullivan Valley Rd. 68 P52
Sulphur-Hartley FS Rd. 84 V71 85 V72 W72
Sulphur Springs Rd. 85 U72
Sumac Rd. 80 Z54-55
Sumallo River FS Rd. 79 Y49
Sumas Mountain Rd. 78 Z45
Summerland-Princeton Rd. . . 80 V-W54
Summers Creek Rd. 79 V51 W51 80 W52
Summit Dr. 68 Q52
Summit Rd. 24 H43
Summit Rd. (Franklin Camp) 86 A36
Summit Rd. (Port Alberni) 75 Y35
Summit Lake Rd. 31 T-U30
Summit Lake FS Rd. (Cariboo) . 44 G47
Summit Lake FS Rd. (Central Kootenay) 70 T62
Summit Main Rd. (Alberni-Clayoquot) 76 Y36
Summit Main Rd. (Mount Waddington) 62 P30
Summs Creek FS Rd. 82 Y61
Sun Creek Rd. 72 T69
Sun Mainline 1 Rd. 63 R32-33
Sun Peak Rd. 68 P54
Sun Valley Rd. 81 U56
Sundance Rd. 27 N48
Sunday Creek Rd. 79 Y51
Sunday Summit FS Rd. 79 Y51
Sundown Creek FS Rd. 84 Y69
Sunnybrae-Canoe Point Rd. 69 P56-57
Sunnyside Dr 24 J-K44
Sunrise Creek Rd. 84 Y69
Sunset Dr. 87 A40
Sunset FS Rd. 31 U31
Sunset Lake Rd. 31 T-U31
Sunset Lake FS Rd. 80 U53
Sunset Main FS Rd. 80 U53
Sunshine Creek FS Rd. 82 W-X61
Sunshine Valley Rd. 67 T49-50
Suquash Main Rd. 61 Q27
Surge Narrows Rd. 63 S-T34
Surprise Rd. 62 T30 74 U30
Surrey-Sussex Lake Rd. 67 R51
Surrey Lake FS Rd. 67 R51
Survey Mainline Rd. 87 C39
Susan Lake Rd. 58 L63
Susap Creek FS Rd. 80 Y-Z54
Suskwa FS Rd. 30 P28
Sutherland Rd. 80 W55
Sutherland-Angly FS Rd. 76 V37
Sutherland Creek FS Rd. 82 Z60
Sutherland FS Rd. . . 33 V36 34 V37 W37
Sutherland Trout FS Rd. 33 V-W36
Sutil Point Rd. 63 T35
Sutlej Main Rd. 62 Q29
Sutton Rd. (Cariboo) 54 H46
Sutton Rd. (Mount Waddington) 62 T30
Suzanne Lake Rd. 84 X71
Sven Rd. 55 L49
Swamp Creek Rd. 35 W42
Swan Rd. (Cariboo) 44 F46
Swan Rd. (Central Kootenay) . . . 83 Z66
Swans Lake Rd. 31 U31
Swanson Ave. 24 K46
Swanson Rd. 44 G46-47
Swanson Rd. (Bulkley-Nechako) 35 X40
Swanson Rd. (Kootenay Boundary) 82 Z60
Swede Creek FS Rd. 34 A38-39
Sweeney FS Rd. 32 Y28
Sweetwater Rd. 27 M50-52
Swift Creek FS Rd. 77 U-V42
Swift River-Bendixon Lake FS Rd. 44 C-D46
Swift River-Meridian Mountain.FS Rd. 44 C-D47
Swift River-Porter Creek FS Rd. 44 D47
Swift River-Sovereign Creek FS Rd. 44 C45-46
Swift River FS Rd. 44 C46 D47
Swift River North FS Rd. 44 C-D47
Swiftcurrent Creek FS Rd. 47 C57
Sylvania Rd. 71 P67
Sylvester Rd. 78 Y45
Sylvestre Creek FS Rd. 67 P51
Szoo Rd. 25 K48
T Rd. 36 A47
Ta Ta Lost Dog FS Rd. 84 U-V69
Table. Rd. 24 L44-45
Table Creek FS Rd. 24 L44-45
Tabor Creek Rd. 36 X44
Tabor Lake South Rd. 36 X44
Tabor Lookout Rd. 36 X44
Tachek FS Rd. 31 T31
Tagai Rd. 35 A40
Taharti Lake Rd. 43 F43
Tahtsa Reach FS Rd. 32 X30 Y29
Takla FS Rd. 35 W41
Tako Rd. 35 A42
Takysie Mountain Rd. 33 X33
Takysie Pit Rd. 33 X33
Talbot Rd. 83 Z64
Talbot Cove Rd. 63 T35 64 T36
Talchako FS Rd. 40 F31 G31 41 G32
Taman Rd. 31 U32
Tamarack Lake Rd. 84 U69
Tamihi Creek-A Rd. 78 Z47
Tangier River FS Rd. 58 N62
Tanglefoot Creek FS Rd. 84 V-W71
Tangye Rd. 83 U65
Tann Rd. 44 G46
Tappen-Notch Hill Rd. 69 P56
Tappen Valley Rd. 69 P56
Tarrys Rd. 82 X62-63
Taseko Lake Rd. 53 J42 J-K41
Taseko Mines Rd. 53 L-N40
Tatalrose Rd. 32 W31-32
Tatalrose Main FS Rd. 32 W-X31
Tate Creek Rd. 27 N51-52 O51-52
Tatlayoko Rd. 52 J-K37
Tatlayoko-Henry's Crossing Rd. 52 K37-38
Tatlow Rd. (Bulkley-Nechako) 30 S28-29
Tatton Rd. 55 K48
Tatton-Helena FS Rd. 54 J-K47
Tatton-McKinley FS Rd. (1200 Rd.) 54 K47 55 K48
Tatton-Snag FS Rd. (1300 Rd.) 54 K46-47 L46-47
Tatuk Rd. 34 Z39
Tatuk Lake Rd. 34 Z39
Taurus Lake Rd. 81 X-Y57
Tautri Creek-Wentworth Creek FS Rd. 43 E41
Taweel Lake Rd. 55 K51 L51 56 L52
Taylor Rd. 67 P49-50
Taylor Rd. (Bulkley-Nechako) . . 34 W38
Taylor Rd. (Columbia-Shuswap) 69 P56
Taylor Creek Rd. 69 R58-59
Taylor Creek FS Rd. 55 L-M48
Taylor Lake Rd. 55 L48
Taylor Main Rd. 75 X33
Tchesinkut East Rd. 33 W33-34
Tea Lake FS Rd. 30 P26
Teapot FS Rd. 35 V43
Teardrop Chief FS Rd. 35 V41
Teardrop Jumping FS Rd. 34 V39
Teasdale Rd. 44 F47
Tedford Rd. 77 Y43
Teepee-Gold Creek FS Rd. . . . 84 X-Y70
Teepee Creek FS Rd. 84 Y69-71
Teer Rd. 31 U30
Teeta 500 Rd. 61 R26
Teeta Main Rd. 61 R26
Telegraph Rd. 87 B40
Telegraph Tr. (Fraser-Fort George) 35 A42
Telegraph Cove Rd. (Mount Waddington) 62 Q28
Telegraph Trail Rd. 35 Y-Z41
Telford Rd. 53 H41
Telkwa Coal Mine Rd. 30 S29
Telkwa High Rd. 30 R28-29 S29
Telkwa River FS Rd. (1000 Rd) 30 S-T28
Telqua Dr. 55 K48
Templeton River FS Rd. 71 P66-67
Ten Mile Lake Rd. 44 B44
Tentfire Creek FS Rd. 27 R48
Tepee Lakes Rd. 80 V52
Tercer FS Rd. 33 W34
Terrace Mountain Main FS Rd. 68 T55
Tetachuck FS Rd. 33 A33
Tête Jaune Rd. 47 C56
Texas Creek Rd. 66 Q-R46 R47
Texas Creek-Skimath Creek FS Rd. 66 R46
Texas Creek FS Rd. 66 R46
Thautil FS Rd. 30 U28 32 V28
Theatre Rd. 84 W69
Thelma Mine Rd. 67 S51
Theodosia FS Rd. 64 T36 76 U36
Theodosia FS Rd. 64 T36 76 U36
Theodosia FS Rd. 76 U36
Theodosia FS Rd. 1 . . . . 76 U36
Theodosia Main Rd. 64 T36-37
Thiessen St. 25 F48
Thistle Mine Rd. 76 Y-Z36
Thomas Rd. (Cariboo) 55 L49
Thomas Rd. (Columbia-Shuswap) 59 N65
Thomas Point Rd. 55 L50
Thomason Rd. 84 V69
Thompson Rd. (Bulkley-Nechako) 31 U32
Thompson Rd. (Central Kootenay) 83 U-V65
Thompson Rd. (East Kootenay) 84 V69
Thompson Rd. (Peace River) . . . 25 K48
Thompson St. 84 V69
Thompson River Dr. 67 P49-50
Thone Rd. 81 X58
Thorley Rd. 35 A43 36 A44
Thornhill Mountain Rd. 29 T24
Thorsen Rd. 40 F-G29
Thorstelnson Rd. 55 K48-49
Three Forks Rd. 81 U57
Three Rivers Mainline Rd. 87 C38
Three Valley-Mabel-Holiday FS Rd. 69 Q58
Three Valley-Mabel FS Rd. 69 Q58
Three Valley-Mabel Lake FS Rd. 69 P59
Three Valley-Mara L-O FS Rd. 69 P-Q58
Thunder Creek Rd. 27 R51
Thunder River FS Rd. 47 G57
Thuya Creek Rd. 56 M52
Thynne Mountain Rd. 79 V50
Tibbets Creek Rd. 33 V34
Tibble FS Rd. 43 C42
Tibbles Rd. 43 C-D42
Tibbles FS Rd. 43 C42
Tie Lake Rd. 84 X71
Tiffin Creek FS Rd. 66 P46-47
Till Lake FS Rd. 54 H44
Tillery Rd. 79 U51
Tillicum FS Rd. 54 H47 55 H48
Timms Rd. 35 W40
Timothy-Fly Lake Rd. 55 J48
Timothy Lake Rd. 55 J48
Tin Hat Rd. 76 U37
Tingley Rd. 44 F44
Tingley Creek FS Rd. 44 F44
Tintagle Rd. 33 V33
Tipella Creek Rd. 78 V45
Tlakwa Main Rd. 62 S28
Tlatos Creek Mainline North Rd. 62 R30
Tlatos Creek South Main Rd. . 62 R-S30
Tlexcoxeten Rd. 54 J44
Tlowils Lake Branch Rd. 62 S31
Tlupana River Rd. 74 V30
Tobacco Rd. 85 Z72
Toby Creek Rd. 71 R67
Toby Hill Rd. 72 R68
Tochcha Main FS Rd. 31 R32-33
Tod Mountain Rd. (Sun Peaks Rd.) 68 P52-53
Todd Rd. 69 T56
Todd Rd. (Peace River) 25 K49-50
Todd Rd. (Thompson-Nicola) . . 68 Q52
Todhunter FS Rd. 73 T73
Tofino Main Rd. 75 Y33
Tom Cole Mountain FS Rd. 66 P47
Toma Valley Hwy. 75 W34 X35
Tommy Creek Rd. 66 P44
Tompkins Rd. 24 L45
Topaz Creek FS Rd. 83 Y66
Topaze Creek Rd. 63 Q-R32
Topknot 10 Rd. 60 Q23 61 Q24
Topknot Main Rd. 61 Q24
Topley Landing Rd. 31 R31
Topley Landing Rd. (Granisle Hwy) 31 S31-32 T31
Toquart FS Rd. 75 Z33
Torches Rd. 44 D44
Torpy FS Rd. 37 X48
Torrent Rd. 84 V69
Torrent FS Rd. 84 U69
Tote Rd. 41 F32
Toucher Rd. 62 T29
Tower Lake Rd. 25 L50
Townline Rd. 78 Z45
TR 11 Rd. 86 B37
TR 2 Rd. 86 A37
TR 8 Rd. 86 A37
Tracey Creek FS Rd. 57 M56
Tracey Main Rd. 62 P28-29
Tranquil Main Rd. 75 Y32
Tranquille Rd. 67 Q51 68 Q52
Tranquille-Criss Creek Rd. 67 Q50
Trans-Canada Hwy. 79 V48
Trapp Lake Rd. 68 R52
Trapping-Big White FS Rd. . . 81 V-W57
Trapping-Copper Kettle FS Rd. 81 V58
Trapping Creek FS Rd. 81 W57
Traverse Creek Rd. 81 W-X59
Tree to Sea Dr. 74 U29 V31
Trépanier Bench Rd. 80 U54
Triad Rd. 25 F48-49
Triangle Rd. 25 L50-51
Tribune Main Rd. 62 P-Q30
Trick Rd. 36 W46
Trinity Valley Rd. 69 R57-58 S58
Trip Rd. 55 K49
Tronson Rd. 69 S56
Trout Creek Rd. 32 W31
Trout Creek Rd. 80 W54
Trout Creek FS Rd. 80 V53
Trout Lake Rd. 76 W39
Trozzo Creek FS Rd. 82 W63
Truax Creek FS Rd. 65 P43
Tsadestsa Creek FS Rd. 36 X44
Tsibas Main Rd. 62 Q28
Tsileuh Creek FS Rd. 79 V48
Tsitika Rd. 62 S30
Tsitika River FS Rd. 62 R29 S30
Tsitika West Rd. 62 R-S29
Tsolum Main Rd. 75 V34
Tsolum River Rd. 75 V34-35
Tsowwin Main Rd. 74 V29
Tsuniah Lake FS Rd. 52 L38
Tuck Inlet Rd. 28 S-T18
Tucker Rd. 27 N51
Tugwell West Mainline Rd. 87 C39
Tulameen FS Rd. 79 W50
Tulameen River Rd. 79 W50
Tumbledown Rd. 58 M61
Tumuch Rd. 36 Y47
Tumuch FS Rd. 36 Y47
Tuna Mainline Rd. 62 R31 63 S32
Tungsten FS Rd. 83 X66
Tunkwa Rd. 67 Q50
Tunkwa Lake Rd. 67 Q-R50
Tupper FS Rd. 27 O51
Turn Harbour Main FS Rd. . . . 31 R-S33
Turn Mainline 1 . . . . 63 R-S33
Turnbull Main Rd. 62 Q29
Turnour Main Rd. 62 Q30
Turtle Valley Rd. 68 Q55
Tuzo-Logan FS Rd. 81 X57
Tuzo Creek FS Rd. 81 X57
Tuzo FS Rd. 81 X56
Twaal Creek Rd. 67 R48
Twall Lake FS Rd. 67 Q48
Twelve Mile Rd. 24 L45
Twig Creek FS Rd. 68 R54
Twin Lake Rd. 55 L51
Twin Lakes Rd. 80 X54-55
Twin One Creek Rd. 66 S44
Two Mile Creek Rd. 30 P27
Tyaughton Lake Rd. 65 Q43
Tyee Lake Rd. 44 F45
Tyhee Lake Rd. 30 S29
Tyner Blvd. 35 X43
Tyner FS Rd. 37 S50
Tzartus FS Rd. 86 A34-35
Tzenzaicut-Ramsey FS Rd. 43 E42
Tzenzaicut Lake Rd. 43 E43 F43 44 E44 F44
Tzenzaicut Lake-Garner FS Rd. 43 E43 F43 44 E44
Tzenzaicut Lake-Narcosli FS Rd. 43 D-E43
Tzenzaicut Lake-Narcosli West FS Rd. 43 D-E43
Tzenzaicut Lake-Ramsey South FS Rd. 43 F43
Tzenzaicut Lake FS Rd. 43 E43
Tzouhalem Rd. 87 A-B40
Ubedam Mainline Rd. 74 U29
Ucona Rd. 74 V31
Ucona-29 Rd. 74 V31
Udy Creek FS Rd. 43 C41
Umbach Rd. 25 F48
Umiti Pit Rd. 44 B45
Uncha Lake Rd. 33 W-X33
Uncha Mountain Rd. 33 W33
Uncha South FS Rd. 33 X33
Union Mine Rd. 81 Y59
Union Pacific Rd. 24 J44
University Way 35 X43
Unruh Ave. 25 G48
Upper Adam River Rd. 62 S31
Upper Balfour Rd. 83 W65
Upper Bench Rd. (Keremeos) . . 80 Y54
Upper Bench Rd. (Penticton) . . . 80 W55
Upper Cache Rd. 24 J-K47
Upper Caven Creek Rd. 84 Y-Z70
Upper Coldwater Rd. 79 W49-50
Upper Cutbank Rd. . . 27 N-O50 O50-51
Upper Dean River Rd. . . 41 D33-34 E34
Upper Dog Creek Rd. 54 L45-46
Upper Fauquier Rd. 82 U-V61
Upper Fraser Rd. . . . 36 W44-45 X44 X47
Upper Fulton FS Rd. (3000 Rd) 31 Q-R30
Upper Halfway Rd. 24 H44-46
Upper Harper FS Rd. 56 L-M55
Upper Hitchie Rd. 86 A36
Upper Houseman Rd. 55 K49
Upper Kettle FS Rd. 81 U57-58 V57
Upper Kitimat FS Rd. 29 U24
Upper Level Rd. 24 J-K44
Upper Lillooet FS Rd. . . . 65 Q41 R41-42
Upper Mackay FS Rd. 66 O-P46
Upper Mine Rd. 84 V68
Upper Moberly FS Rd. 26 N44
Upper Mud River Rd. 35 Y42
Upper Silverhope Rd. 79 Y-Z48
Upper Udy FS Rd. 43 D41
Upper Viewmount Rd. 30 S29
Ure Creek Mainline FS Rd. 66 S44
Uri Rd. 83 Y66
Urquhart Creek FS Rd. 78 V47 W47 79 V48
Usk Ferry Rd. 29 S24
Usk Shannon Rd. 29 S24
Usk Station Rd. 29 S24
Uztilius Creek FS Rd. 79 V48-49
Uztilus Creek Rd. 79 V48
V.L.A. Rd. 68 P55
Valdez Rd. 63 T34
Valenciennes River Rd. 59 K64
Valentine Mainline Rd. 87 C39
Vallee Creek Rd. 31 T30
Valley Rd. 54 H46
Valley Rd. (Bulkley-Nechako) . . . 31 U32
Valley View Rd. 80 X55
Valleyview Dr. 68 Q52
Van Horlick Creek Rd. 66 S45
Varna Rd. 36 X45
Varney Main Rd. 61 Q26
Vaughan Mainline Rd. 74 U29

Vaux Rd. 87 B39
Vavenby Bridge Rd. 56 L55
Vavenby Mountain FS Rd. 56 L55
Veale Rd. 67 T50
Veasy Lake FS Rd. 66 P47 67 P48
Vedan-Elkin Lake FS Rd. 52 L39
Vedder Rd. 78 Y-Z46
Vedder Mountain Rd. 78 Z46
Venables Valley Rd. 67 Q-R48
Ventura Mainline Rd. 63 S34
Verdun Rd. 32 W-X32
Verdun Bishop Rd. 32 W-X32
Verdun West Rd. 32 X32
Vermont Creek FS Rd. 71 O65
Vermunt Rd. 26 M47
Vernon Lake Rd. 62 T30
Vessey Rd. 33 V33
Victoria Dr. 77 X-Y43
Victoria Dr. (Bulkley-Nechako) 30 S28-29
Victoria Rd. 70 O60
Victoria St 68 Q52
Victoria Creek Rd. 44 C45
Victoria Lake Main Rd. 61 R-S26
Victoria Main Rd. 62 T31
View Rd. 78 Z46
View Main Rd. 75 Y34
Viewland FS Rd. 45 F49
Village Bay Rd. 63 T34
Vincent Rd. 25 K-L51
Vinsula Ferry Rd. 68 O52
Vinsulla-Knouff Lake Rd. 68 O52-53
Vivian Lake Rd. 35 W42
Voght St. 67 T50
Voght Valley Rd. 79 U50-51
Volcanic Creek FS Rd. 81 Y59 82 Y60
Vouk Main FS Rd. 32 Z32 33 Z33
Vowell Creek FS Rd. 71 O65
Vye Rd. 78 Z45

W.R. Graham Rd. 52 J37
W100-A Rd. 87 C38
W100-C Rd. 87 C38
W80 Rd. 61 Q27
Wabi Estates Rd. 26 N47
Waddell-Hoodoo Rd. 81 X57-58
Wadds Rd. 83 V65
Wade Rd. 36 A44
Wades Rd. 26 N47
Wady Main Rd. 61 R27
Wagon Wheel Rd. 81 Z56
Waiatt Bay Main FS Rd. 63 S34
Wakefield Rd. 30 T29 31 T30
Wakeman Main Rd. 50 N30 62 O30
Walbran Rd. 86 B36-37
Walbridge Rd. 69 R56
Walcan Rd. 63 T34
Walcott Rd. 31 T30
Walcott-Quick Rd. 30 T29
Walcott Station Rd. 30 T29
Waldie Rd. 27 M52
Waldie Lake Rd. 83 Y-Z64
Waldo Rd. 84 Y71
Waldo-Gold Creek Rd. 84 Y71
Walhachin Rd. 67 P49
Walian Creek FS Rd. 78 X46
Walker Rd. 33 W33
Walker Rd. 54 J47
Walker Creek FS Rd. 37 X49-51 Y49
Wall Rd. 33 X33
Wallace Dr. 87 C41
Wallace Rd. 57 L59
Wallace Creek FS Rd. 81 Y58
Wallace Lake Rd. 81 W57
Wallace Mountain Rd. 81 X57
Wallis Rd. 57 L-M59
Walmith FS Rd. 54 J47 55 J48
Walt Lake Rd. 76 U38
Walters Lake Rd. 45 G48
Walton Rd. 34 X37
Walton Rd. 87 A38
Walton Creek FS Rd. 26 N46
Waneta-Nelway Rd. 82 Z62-63
Wanokana 900 Rd. 61 Q25
Wanokana Main Rd. 61 Q25-26
Wansa Rd. 36 Y45
Wansa Creek FS Rd. 36 X45
Wantage Rd. 28 U18
Wap Lake FS Rd. 69 P59
Wapoose FS Rd. 33 X34
Wapta Falls Rd. 59 N66
Ward Rd. 54 N46
Ward Rd. 70 Q62
Ward Creek FS Rd. 84 Z70
Wardner Rd. 84 X70-71
Wardner-Fort Steele Hwy. 84 W70
Wardner-Kikomun Rd. 84 X70-71
Waring Rd. 74 U30
Warner Main Rd. 62 O28
Warren Rd. 68 P-Q54
Wart FS Rd., The 80 U52
Wartig Lake FS Rd. 45 F50
Wasa-Sheep Creek Rd. 84 U-V69
Wasa Lake Park Dr 84 V69
Wash Main Rd. 63 Q34
Watch Lake Rd. 55 L49
Watching Creek FS Rd. 67 O-P51
Water Lily Bay Rd. 29 U24
Watson Rd. (Peace River) 25 K48
Watts Rd. (Central Kootenay) 82 U61-62
Waveland Rd. 75 V35
Wavey Lake Rd. (2000 Rd.) 55 L51
Weaver Rd. 27 O51
Webster Lake Rd. 44 E44
Wedeene FS Rd. 29 U24 V23
Wedge Creek FS Rd. 65 T43
Wegen Rd. 24 L45
Weigert Creek FS Rd. 85 U72
Weir Rd. 68 R52
Weldon Bay Rd. 76 X37
Weldwood Rd. 35 A42-43
Wenger Rd. 83 Y-Z67
Wentworth Lake Rd. 67 O51 68 O52
Wesach Creek FS Rd. 29 R23
West Bypass 25 J-K49
West Rd. (Campbell River) 63 T34
West Rd. (Gold River) 74 U31
West Rd. (Sunshine Coast) 76 V38
West Bare Main Rd. 62 R30-31
West Beaverly Rd. 35 X-Y43
West Bench Dr. 80 W55
West Canton Rd. 74 U29
West Coast Rd. 87 D39
West Creek FS Rd. 36 A47
West Creston Rd. 83 Z66
West Croman Rd. 62 S29-30
West Decker Rd. 31 U32-33 33 V33
West Dore FS Rd. 37 A51
West Eliza Rd. 61 T27 74 U27
West Ewart Mainline Rd. 74 V28
West Fleet Mainline Rd. 87 B38
West Fork Rd. 81 X58
West François Rd. 32 W31
West Fraser Rd. 44 D44 F44 G45 54 H45
West Fritton Rd. 27 P-Q52
West Gun Lake Rd. 65 P43
West Hoodoo FS Rd. 35 V41-42 W41
West Jordan Mainline Rd. 87 B-C39
West Kalum Rd. 29 S-T23
West Kalum FS Rd. 29 R-S23
West Kettle FS Rd. 81 U-V57
West Lake Dr. 82 Z60
West Lake Rd. 35 Y43
West Lake Estates Rd. 35 Y43
West Leech Mainline Rd. 87 C39
West Lillooet Lake Rd. 66 T44
West Main Rd. (Capital RD) 87 C39
West Main Rd. (Echo Bay) 62 P30
West Main Rd. (Port Albion) 75 Z32-33
West Main Rd. (Port Alice) 61 R26
West Main Rd. (Port McNeill) 61 Q27
West Main Rd. (Warner Bay) 61 O27 62 O28
West Main Rd. (Winter Harbour) 61 Q24
West Mainline Rd. (Mount Waddington) 63 S32
West Moberly Rd. 26 M45-46
West Mosquito Rd. 70 T61
West Noel Creek FS Rd. 65 Q43
West Pavilion Rd. (Slok Creek Rd.) 66 O45-46 P46
West Pavilion FS Rd. 54 N45
West Ridge FS Rd. 47 D56-57
West Riverbottom Rd. 87 A-B39
West Rogers Creek Mainline FS Rd. 66 T44 78 U44
West Saanich Rd. 87 B40-41
West Sand River Rd. 75 Y33
West Shawnigan Lake Rd. 87 B40
West Thompson Rd. 35 W42
West Thurlow Mainline Rd. 63 R32-33
West Torpy FS Rd. 36 W47
West Tranquil Main Rd. 75 Y32
West Trout FS Rd. 70 R63 71 R64
West Tsitika Rd. 62 S29-30
West Wilson Creek Rd. 70 T63
West Woss Rd. 62 S28-29
West Woss Main Rd. 62 S-T29
Westcoast Rd. 44 G45
Western Mine Rd. 75 V33
Westfall River FS Rd. 70 P63 71 P64
Westgate Rd. 26 N46-47
Westkal Rd. 69 S56
Westlake Rd. 80 U55
Westman Lake Dr. 33 X33
Westminster Hwy. 77 Y42
Westroc Mine Dr. 72 R68-69
Westside Rd. (Invermere) 71 P-Q67 72 Q-R68 S69
Westside Rd. (Kitimat-Stikine) 29 T24
Westside Rd. (Revelstoke) 58 N60 70 O60
Westside Rd. (Thompson-Nicola) 66 T47
Westside Rd. (Trout Lake) 70 Q63
Westside Rd. (Vernon-Kelowna) 68 S55 T55 69 S56 80 U55
Westsyde Rd. 56 N52 68 O-P52
Westwood Rd. 34 W38
Wet Creek Rd. 24 J44
Wetaskiwin Rd. 68 R55
Wetherill Rd. 27 M49
Whaletown Rd. 63 T35
Whatshan FS Rd. 70 S-T61 82 U61
Whatshan Lake Rd. 82 U60
Whatshan Lake FS Rd. 70 T61 82 U61
Whatshan Settlement Rd. 82 U60
Whiffle Lake-Plato FS Rd. 45 F48
Whimster Rd. 83 Z67
Whipsaw-Lamont FS Rd. 79 X51
Whipsaw FS Rd. 79 X-Y51
Whiskey Fill Rd. 47 D57
Whistle Creek Rd. 80 X53
White Lake Rd. (Columbia-Shuswap) 69 P56
White Lake Rd. (Okanagan Falls) 80 X55
White Ram FS Rd. 72 T70 84 U70
White Rapids Rd. 76 Z39
White River Rd. 62 S31
White River FS Rd. 72 S70
White River Main Rd. 62 T31
White River Main 4 Rd. 62 S31 63 S32
Whitebottom Rd. 29 T23
Whitefoot Rd. 81 V58
Whitehead East Rd. 80 V53
Whitehead West Rd. 80 V53
Whiteman-Bouleau FS Rd. 68 S55
Whiteman-Granite FS Rd. 68 S55
Whiteman Creek Rd. 68 S55 69 S56
Whiteman Creek FS Rd. 68 S54
Whiterock FS Rd. 68 T54-55 80 U55
Whiteswan FS Rd. 72 T69-70
Whiteswan Lake FS Rd. 72 T69-70
Whitetail (Deer) Lake Rd. 72 S-T68
Whitevale Rd. 69 S57
Whitewater Rd. 53 L40
Whitewater Ski Hill Rd. 83 X64
Whitney Rd. 26 M47
Wickman Creek FS Rd. 84 Y70-71
Widdis Rd. 35 Z43 36 Z44
Wiebe Rd. 25 F49
Wiggins Rd. 44 G47
Wightwick Rd. 83 W64-65
Wigwam FS Rd. 85 Y72-73 Z73
Wilcox Rd. 55 J-K49
Wilcox-Lang FS Rd. 55 J49
Wilcox-Westman Creek FS Rd. 55 J49
Wilcox Lake-Timothy Lake FS Rd. 55 J-K49
Wild Horse River FS Rd. 84 V70
Wilde Rd. 76 U36
Wildhorse Creek Rd. 83 X-Y64
Wildmare Rd. 26 N46-47
Wildmare Creek FS Rd. 26 N46
Wildwood Rd. 82 Y-Z63
Wilkinson Rd. 87 C41
Wilkinson Creek FS Rd. 81 W56-57
Willi's Hump Rd. 35 Y42
Williams Beach Rd. 75 V35
Williams Creek Tr. 29 T-U24
Williams Creek FS Rd. 29 T-U24
Williams Lake Cutoff Rd. 44 G45
Willies Ranch Rd. 80 X52
Willis Pt. 87 C40
Willis Rd. 27 M48
Willis Creek Rd. 80 X-Y52
Willow-Cale FS Rd. 35 Y43 36 Y44-45 Z45-46
Willow-Cale FS Rd. 36 A46
Willow-Grizzly FS Rd. 36 Y45
Willow-North FS Rd. 36 X-Y45
Willow-Stone Buck FS Rd. 36 Y44
Willow-Thursday Rd. 36 Y45
Willow Creek FS Rd. 26 N-O45
Willow Valley Rd. 27 M49
Willowbrook Rd. 80 Y55
Willowvale Rd. 34 W37
Wills Rd. 72 S69
Wilson Rd. 32 W32
Wilson Rd. (Central Kootenay) 83 Y66
Wilson Rd. (Kootenay Boundary) 81 Y58
Wilson Rd. (Thompson-Nicola) 68 P52
Wilson Creek Rd. 77 X40
Wilson Creek FS Rd. 70 S-T63
Wilson Lake Rd. (Cariboo) 55 L50-51
Wilson Lake Rd. (Central Kootenay) 70 S62
Wilson Lake FS Rd. 70 S62
Wind Pass Rd. 56 L-M52
Windermere Loop Rd. 72 R68
Windfall Creek Rd. (Kootenay Boundary) 81 Y58
Windfall Creek Rd. (Peace River) 24 J44
Windsor Main Rd. 76 U37-38
Windt Rd. 44 E44
Windy-Judson Creek Rd. 55 L50
Windy-Judson FS Rd. 55 L50
Windy Lake Rd. 56 N52
Windy Mountain FS Rd. (1900 Rd.) 55 L50
Windy Summit FS Rd. 55 K-L51
Wink Main Rd. 62 Q29-30
Winkley Creek Rd. 45 E-F48
Winnifred Creek FS Rd. 81 U59
Winter Harbour Rd. 61 Q24
Winters Creek FS Rd. 80 X54
Winword Rd. 43 C43
Wiseman Rd. 59 L-M64
Wishloff Rd. 82 W62
Wistaria Hwy. 32 X31-32
Wistaria Main FS Rd. 32 X29-30
Witches Brook Rd. 67 R50
Witte Rd. 53 L42
Woden FS Rd. 82 U61-62
Wolf Creek Rd. 84 V69-70
Wolfe Rd. 71 T65
Wolfe Beigie FS Rd. 79 X-Y51
Wolverine-Rollie Rd. (1400 Rd.) 44 D-E47
Wolverine FS Rd. 27 Q48
Womack Rd. 55 L50
Wood River FS Rd. 58 H60-61
Woodall FS Rd. 36 W47
Woodbury Creek FS Rd. 83 V64-65
Woodhaven Rd. 87 D39
Woodjam Rd. 45 G48
Woodland Rd. 34 X39 35 X40 X42-43
Woodland Rd. 68 Q53
Woodman Rd. 67 S50
Woodmere Rd. 30 S29
Woodpecker FS Rd. 33 Z34
Woods Ave. 25 J49
Woods Creek FS Rd. 67 Q49
Woodsdale Rd. 69 T56
Woodside Mountain Rd. 78 Y46
Woodward Rd. 67 T50
Woolsey Creek FS Rd. 58 N61
Word Creek Rd. 54 K44
Worthington Creek FS Rd. 82 V60
Woss Rd. 62 S-T29
Wragge Beach Rd. 70 T63
Wrangler Rd. 27 M48
Wray Creek Rd. 79 X-Y48
Wright Creek Rd. 35 W43
Wright Creek Pit Rd. 35 W43
Wright Station Rd. 54 J47
Wrights Rd. 79 X51
Wurzberger Ave. 25 G48
Wyclees Mainline Rd. 49 M27
Wycliffe Rd. 84 W69
Wycliffe-Cherry Creek Rd. 84 W69
Wye Creek Mainline Rd. 87 C38
Wyssen Rd. 57 L59

Xit Olacw Rd. 65 S43 66 S44

Y Meadows FS Rd. 68 S54
Yahk-Meadow Creek Rd. 84 Z68-69
Yahk FS Rd. 84 Z69
Yahk River FS Rd. 84 Y69
Yalakom Rd. 66 P45
Yalakom-Big Bar Rd. 54 N44-45
Yalakom River Rd. 66 O44-45
Yale Rd. E. 78 Y46
Yale Creek Rd. 79 W48
Yankee Flats Rd. 69 Q-R56
Yard Creek FS Rd. 69 P58-59
Yard Creek Loop Rd. 69 P58
Yardley Lake Rd. 36 A44
Yarrow Central Rd. 78 Z46
Yelch Rd. 30 R28
Yellow Creek FS Rd. 58 H60
Yellow Point Rd. 76 Z39
Yellowbrick Rd. 80 X-Y55
Yellowhead Hwy. 35 X40 36 X47 37 Y48
Yoder Mainline Rd. 61 O26-27
Yoho River Rd. 59 L-M67
Yookwa Rd. 62 T29-30
York Rd. (Bulkley-Nechako) 33 X33
York Rd. (Comox-Strathcona) 75 U34
Yorkston Rd. 44 D-E44
Youbou Rd. 86 A37 87 A38 A38
Young Rd. 35 X40
Young Rd. (Cariboo) 53 H40-41
Young Rd. (Fraser Valley) 78 Y46
Young FS Rd. 35 V41
Youngs Rd. 82 W63

Zeballos Rd. 62 S-T28
Zeeben Rd. 83 Y64
Zelenski Rd. 34 X37
Zillinsky Rd. 76 V37
Zobnick Rd. 30 S28
Zonnebeke Rd. 26 O47
Zschiedrich Rd. 44 D44
Zuciarte Main Rd. 74 V-W29
Zwicky Rd. 83 U65